Essential AWS Certification Books from Sybex

AWS Certified Solutions Architect Study Guide with 900 Practice Test Questions: Associate (SAA-C03) Exam, 4th Edition — ISBN: 978-1-119-98262-3, October 2022

AWS Certified Developer Study Guide: Associate (DVA-C02) Exam, 2nd Edition — ISBN: 978-1-394-27480-2, January 2025

AWS Certified Cloud Practitioner Study Guide: Foundational (CLF-C02) Exam, Second Edition — ISBN: 978-1-394-23563-6, December 2023

AWS Certified Machine Learning Engineer Study Guide: Associate (MLA-C01) Exam — ISBN: 978-1-394-31995-4, June 2025

AWS Certified Security Study Guide: Specialty (SCS-C02) Exam, 2nd Edition — ISBN: 978-1-394-25346-3, August 2025

AWS Certified AI Practitioner Study Guide: Foundational (AIF-C01) Exam — ISBN: 978-1-394-32819-2, October 2025

AWS® Certified CloudOps ENGINEER STUDY GUIDE

ASSOCIATE (SOA-C03) EXAM

AWS®
Certified CloudOps ENGINEER STUDY GUIDE

ASSOCIATE (SOA-C03) EXAM

DARIO CABIANCA with JUSTIN ROBERTS

Published by John Wiley & Sons, Inc., Hoboken, New Jersey.

For general information on our other products and services or for technical support, please contact our Customer Care Department within the United States at (800) 762-2974, outside the United States at (317) 572-3993 or fax (317) 572-4002. For product technical support, you can find answers to frequently asked questions or reach us via live chat at https://sybexsupport.wiley.com.

Wiley also publishes its books in a variety of electronic formats. Some content that appears in print may not be available in electronic formats. For more information about Wiley products, visit our website at www.wiley.com.

Library of Congress Control Number: 2026944255

Paperback ISBN: 9781394419135
ePDF ISBN: 9781394419159
ePub ISBN: 9781394419142

Cover Design: Wiley
Cover Image: © Jeremy Woodhouse/Getty Images

This book would not have been possible without the support and encouragement of my family.

Foreword

Every organization I work with is somewhere on the cloud journey. Some are lifting their first workloads out of on-premises data centers. Others are running thousands of microservices across multiple AWS Regions. What they all have in common is the same fundamental realization: getting to the cloud is only half the challenge. Operating well once you are there is what separates the companies that thrive from the ones that simply survive.

Cloud operations is the discipline that makes that distinction real. It is not a single tool or a single team. It is a continuous practice of deploying with confidence, monitoring with precision, sustaining performance under pressure, securing what matters, and optimizing relentlessly. When done well, it becomes invisible. Applications are available. Teams move fast. Costs stay predictable. Customers never notice the complexity behind the experience. When done poorly, it announces itself through outages, escalations, and budget surprises that nobody planned for.

In my role leading Solutions Architecture for Amazon Web Services, I see this play out every day with some of the largest e-commerce and retail brands in the world. The organizations that invest in operational maturity consistently outpace their peers. They ship faster because their deployment pipelines are repeatable and auditable. They recover faster because they have thought through resilience before the incident, not after. They spend less because they treat cost optimization as a continuous loop rather than as an annual exercise. And they build trust with their customers because reliability is a promise they can actually keep.

This is exactly the ground that Dario and Justin cover in this book. What sets their approach apart is that it is not just exam preparation. It is a working reference for the operational realities that cloud engineers face in production every day. The five-phase CloudOps cycle they introduce in Chapter 1—Deploy, Monitor, Sustain, Secure, and Optimize—provides a mental model that is as useful in a war room as it is in a study session. Their treatment of observability in Chapter 6 goes well beyond CloudWatch configuration. It teaches you how to think about which signals actually matter and how to close the loop between detection and automated remediation. And their coverage of reliability and business continuity in Chapter 7 grounds the concepts of RTO, RPO, and fault isolation in practical architectural patterns that you can apply immediately.

I have had the privilege of working alongside Dario through our partnership with Trace3, where his depth in cloud operations and his ability to translate complex architectures into clear, actionable guidance have been evident time and again. That same clarity runs through every chapter of this book. Whether you are preparing for the SOA-C03 exam or building the operational foundation for a production environment, you will find the structured, practical, and deeply informed perspective that makes the difference between passing an exam and truly understanding the craft.

Cloud operations is not a destination. It is the work you do every single day to earn the trust of the people who depend on your systems. This book will help you do that work well.

Ross Dyer
Head of Solution Architecture, E-commerce
Amazon Web Services

Acknowledgments

In addition to my family, I would like to express my deep appreciation to Annie Melnick and Kenyon Brown, the acquisition editors at Wiley, whose early support and guidance helped set this project in motion. I am equally grateful to Navin Vijayakumar and Pete Gaughan, the managing editors, for their careful review of the figures and visual elements to ensure a clear and engaging reading experience.

I would also like to acknowledge the exceptional work of Adaobi Obi Tulton, the project editor, whose steady coordination and attention to detail guided the book through each stage of production.

My thanks extend to CJ Taylor, the technical editor, for his thorough validation of the material and for ensuring that the exam questions reflect the expectations of the real exam. I am similarly grateful to Kezia Endsley, the copy editor, and Maduramuthu Krishnaraj, the content refinement specialist, for their precise and thoughtful review of the copyedits and proofs.

I would also like to recognize Justin Roberts—former colleague at GE—for his contributions to shaping the book's table of contents and for his work on Chapter 2.

Finally, I wish to honor the memory of Professor Giovanni Degli Antoni, my doctoral advisor, whose mentorship at the University of Milan continues to inspire my scientific curiosity. The Department of Computer Science now carries his name, a fitting recognition of his enduring influence.

About the Authors

Dario Cabianca is a computer scientist (PhD, University of Milan), author, and AWS Practice Director at Trace3—a leading IT consultancy and AWS Advanced Consulting Partner offering AI, data, cloud, and cybersecurity solutions for clients across industries. At Trace3, Dario oversees the practice nationally, serving customers, building partnerships, and evangelizing the company's portfolio of AWS competencies and services. He is the author of the *AWS Certified Machine Learning Engineer Study Guide* (Sybex) and is a co-inventor of the published USPTO patent application "Mainframe Change Data Capture and Streaming Data Tokenization" (US-20240394230-A1). Dario has worked with global consulting firms and enterprises for more than two decades and has earned ten cloud certifications across AWS, Google Cloud, Microsoft Azure, and ISC2.

Justin Roberts has worked in operations-focused roles and other disciplines for over two decades, including systems administration, networking, application development, and information security. He is a graduate of the GE Information Management Leadership Program and previously worked at AWS as a Solutions Architect, at Churchill Downs as a Principal Cloud Architect, and at GE as a Senior Cloud Technologist. He is currently the Director of Engineering—Platform Services for TwinSpires Racing, managing the design and operations of their cloud computing infrastructure. He holds numerous certifications, including 14 from AWS; is a recipient of the AWS Golden Jacket for holding every AWS certification simultaneously; and is an SME for the AWS Certified Data Engineer Associate certification.

About the Technical Editor

CJ Taylor is a principal software engineer at Lifeway Christian Resources, an AWS Certified Golden Jacket recipient for holding all active AWS certifications, and a former Senior Solutions Architect on the AWS Certification team. During nearly four years at AWS, he served as a technical lead and reviewer for certification exams across the program at every level and was the sole technical reviewer for the Generative AI Developer Professional exam through its beta launch. He holds 13 active AWS certifications spanning every level of the program and received the 2023 AWS Legend Award for his contributions to AWS Certification exam quality and development. CJ is an admin of the AWS Certified Golden Jacket Community on LinkedIn and is based in the Louisville, Kentucky area.

Contents at a Glance

Contents

Introduction

Cloud operations—CloudOps—has become the connective tissue of modern cloud engineering. It sits at the intersection of architecture, design, solution delivery, and day-to-day operations, ensuring that every workload deployed to the cloud is reliable, observable, secure, cost-efficient, and continuously improving. In practice, CloudOps touches every domain that matters in contemporary AWS environments: compute, storage, databases, networking, observability, reliability engineering, security, DevOps automation, and increasingly Machine Learning (ML) and Artificial Intelligence (AI). It is the discipline that turns cloud architecture into cloud reality.

This evolution is precisely why AWS rebranded the former AWS SysOps Administrator—Associate (SOA-C02) certification into the AWS CloudOps Engineer—Associate (SOA-C03). The role has outgrown its historical boundaries. Today's CloudOps Engineers are not simply administering systems—they are orchestrating distributed architectures, enforcing governance, optimizing cost and performance, and enabling teams to build and operate resilient cloud-native applications at scale. The new exam reflects this expanded scope, emphasizing operational excellence, automation, multi-service integration, and the ability to manage complex, production-grade AWS environments.

The rise of AI has only accelerated the demand for CloudOps expertise. Modern ML and generative AI workloads require massive, elastic compute capacity—capacity that only hyperscale cloud providers can deliver. But provisioning that infrastructure is just the beginning. These workloads must be deployed, monitored, secured, scaled, patched, and continuously optimized. Whether the operators are humans or increasingly automated systems, CloudOps remains the backbone that keeps AI workloads performant, secure, cost-efficient, and trustworthy. As organizations race to adopt AI, they simultaneously race to hire CloudOps Engineers who can run these systems responsibly and efficiently.

This book was written to prepare you for that reality. Our methodical, structured approach breaks down every SOA-C03 exam objective into clear explanations, scenario-driven examples, and operationally grounded guidance. Combined with Sybex's proven certification framework and the authors' real-world CloudOps experience, this study guide equips you with both the knowledge and the mindset needed to excel on the exam. More importantly, it gives you the foundation to launch—or accelerate—a successful career as an AWS CloudOps Engineer.

The AWS Certified CloudOps Engineer—Associate Exam

The AWS Certified CloudOps Engineer—Associate Exam is intended to validate the candidate's ability to deploy, manage, and operate workloads on AWS. The exam covers a wide array of topics with emphasis on performing operations using the AWS Command Line Interface (AWS CLI) and the AWS Management Console.

Key areas include supporting workloads and implementing architectural requirements with the AWS Well-Architected Framework, monitoring, logging, troubleshooting systems, performing business continuity and disaster recovery procedures, implementing security controls, and applying networking concepts.

The exam consists of 65 questions and has a duration of 130 minutes. Of these, 50 are scored and 15 are unscored pilot questions. It is available in multiple languages, including English, Japanese, Korean, and Simplified Chinese. The exam costs $150 USD, and it can be taken at a Pearson VUE testing center or online as a proctored exam. This certification is valid for three years.

Your exam results are presented as a scaled score ranging from 100 to 1,000. To pass, a minimum score of 720 is required. This score reflects your overall performance on the exam and indicates whether you have successfully passed.

The official exam guide is available at: `https://docs.aws.amazon.com/aws-certification/latest/sysops-administrator-associate-03/sysops-administrator-associate-03.html`.

Exam policies can change from time to time. We highly recommend that you check the AWS site for the most up-to-date information when you begin preparing, when you register, and again a few days before your scheduled exam date.

Why Become AWS CloudOps Engineer Certified

One of the strongest reasons to pursue the AWS CloudOps Engineer certification is the mindset it instills. CloudOps introduces a cultural shift grounded in automation, agility, efficiency, operational excellence, and cost optimization—five areas that define effective cloud operations. Unlike DevOps, which focuses primarily on the software development lifecycle, CloudOps is concerned with running and sustaining the cloud environment itself. It is about ensuring that the infrastructure hosting your workloads is performant, highly available, reliable, secure, and cost-efficient. Adopting this mindset naturally pushes teams toward cloud-native best practices and operational excellence.

As organizations mature in the cloud, CloudOps principles become part of the engineering team's DNA. Infrastructure as Code (IaC) enables rapid, repeatable, and predictable deployments. Immutable infrastructure ensures consistency and portability across platforms. Policy-as-Code (PaC) enforces governance at scale without slowing innovation. Whether you work in a fast-moving startup or a global enterprise, these practices elevate your ability to operate modern cloud environments with confidence and precision.

Preparing for the SOA-C03 exam exposes you to the operational dimensions of nearly every major AWS service—compute, containers, serverless, databases, storage, observability, networking, security, business continuity, disaster recovery, and cost optimization. You learn not only how these services function, but how to run them in production, troubleshoot them under pressure, and optimize them for real-world workloads. This blend of technical depth and operational discipline is exactly what employers seek as cloud adoption accelerates.

Earning this certification signals that you can bring order, efficiency, and resilience to complex AWS environments. It strengthens your career prospects, aligns you with one of the fastest-growing roles in cloud engineering, and positions you to contribute meaningfully in a dynamic, rapidly evolving industry. For many professionals, it becomes the foundation of a long, impactful CloudOps career.

How to Become AWS CloudOps Engineer Certified

Your journey to become AWS CloudOps Engineer certified begins with a structured approach that covers AWS foundational elements, hands-on practice, and thorough exam preparation. This study guide is crafted to mirror that journey.

AWS Foundational Elements Start by acquiring a solid understanding of the AWS building blocks: infrastructure, landing zones, organizations, accounts, and the security constructs that bind them together. Because the SOA-C03 exam is deeply operational, it's not enough to simply know what these components are—you must understand how they are configured, governed, and managed to drive real business outcomes. This is where the concept of *workload* becomes central. In AWS, a workload is more than an application; it is the sum of its architecture—defining how its components and supporting resources interact—its operational requirements, and the business value it delivers.

The AWS Well-Architected Framework is the authoritative guide you will use to shape your decisions about how workloads should be deployed, monitored, operated, secured, and optimized. It provides the lens through which CloudOps Engineers evaluate trade-offs, follow best practices, and ensure that every workload meets expectations for reliability, performance efficiency, cost optimization, operational excellence, security, and sustainability. As you prepare for the exam, this framework becomes your compass—helping you connect the high-level principles of cloud architecture with the day-to-day realities of running production systems at scale.

Hands-on Practice You learn CloudOps by doing. Once you understand the AWS foundational elements, the next step is to apply them in real scenarios. There is no way to truly learn without getting your feet wet—by practicing hands-on and codifying what you study. Deploying resources, configuring services, and troubleshooting issues yourself is what transforms conceptual knowledge into operational skills.

This study guide deliberately emphasizes the AWS CLI. Beyond being required for the SOA-C03 exam, the CLI exposes the underlying control plane APIs in a consistent, unified way across all AWS services. Working through the CLI reinforces automation, repeatability, and the mindset of operating at scale—core principles of modern CloudOps.

Hands-on practice is where CloudOps thinking becomes CloudOps capability. It builds the intuition and confidence needed to run real workloads and prepares you for both the exam and the role itself.

Exam Preparation Effective preparation begins with the AWS official exam guide (at the link previously provided), which outlines every objective you are expected to master.

Use it as your roadmap, then reinforce your understanding through practice exams and scenario-based questions that mirror real CloudOps challenges. This study guide supports that process by breaking down 100% of the exam objectives across 11 chapters, and supplementing your learning with 215 in-chapter questions and explanations, two full practice exams (with 65 questions each), 100 flash cards, and a comprehensive glossary. Regular review, repetition, and targeted practice will help solidify key concepts and close any remaining knowledge gaps. On exam day, manage your time carefully and leverage the knowledge you've acquired to extract the key elements from each question so you can answer accurately and confidently.

Don't just study the questions and answers! The questions on the actual exam will be different from the practice questions included in this book. The exam is designed to test your knowledge of a concept or objective, so use this book to learn the objectives behind the questions.

Who Should Buy This Book

This book is intended for a broad audience of infrastructure, software, database, and cloud engineers or architects with ideally one year of hands-on experience using AWS services. Because the certification has a strong engineering focus, readers should have basic familiarity with shell scripting, and at least one cloud-supported programming language—TypeScript, Go, JavaScript, Python, Java, or C#.

To get the most value from this book, it's highly recommended that you have access to an AWS account.

Study Guide Features

This study guide utilizes a number of common elements to help you acquire and reinforce your knowledge. Each chapter includes:

Summaries The summary section briefly explains the key concepts of the chapter, allowing you to easily remember what you learned.

Exam Essentials The exam essentials section highlights the exam topics and the knowledge you need to have for the exam. These exam topics are directly related to the task statements provided by AWS, which are available in the upcoming exam objectives section.

Review Questions A set of questions helps you assess your knowledge and your exam readiness.

Answers to Review Questions Detailed explanations covering rationales for correct answers and clear guidance on why the remaining options are incorrect help you understand the reasoning behind the questions.

Interactive Online Learning Environment and Test Bank

An online learning environment accompanies this study guide, designed to simplify your learning experience. Whether you're preparing at home or on the go, this platform is here to make studying easier and more convenient for you. The following learning resources are included:

Practice Tests This study guide includes a total of 240 questions. All 215 questions in the guide are available in our proprietary digital test engine, along with 25 questions in the assessment test at the end of this introduction. The digital test engine also provides two full-length practice exams, each with 65 questions.

Electronic Flash Cards One hundred questions in a flash card format (a question followed by a single correct answer) are provided.

Glossary The key terms and AWS services you need to know for the exam are available as a searchable glossary in PDF format along with their definitions.

The online learning environment and the test bank are available at `https://www.wiley.com/go/sybextestprep`.

Like all exams, the CloudOps Engineer certification from AWS is updated periodically and may eventually be retired or replaced. At some point after AWS is no longer offering this exam, the old editions of our books and online tools will be retired. If you have purchased this book after the exam was retired, or are attempting to register in the Sybex online learning environment after the exam was retired, please know that we make no guarantees that this exam's online Sybex tools will be available once the exam is no longer available.

Conventions Used in This Book

This study guide uses certain typographic styles in order to help you quickly identify important information and to avoid confusion over the meaning of words such as onscreen prompts.

In particular, look for the following styles:

- *Italicized text* indicates key terms that are described at length for the first time in a chapter. These words are likely to appear in the searchable online glossary. (Italics are also used for emphasis.)
- A `monospaced font` indicates the contents of a program or configuration files, messages displayed as a text-mode macOS/Linux shell prompt, filenames, text-mode command names, and Internet URLs.

In addition to these text conventions, which can apply to individual words or entire paragraphs, a few conventions highlight segments of text:

A note indicates information that's useful or interesting, but that's somewhat peripheral to the main text. A note might be relevant to a small number of networks, for instance, or it might refer to an outdated feature.

A tip provides information that you should understand for the exam. A tip can save you time or frustration and might not be entirely obvious. A tip might describe how to get around a limitation or how to use a feature to perform an unusual task.

AWS Certified CloudOps Engineer Exam Objectives

This study guide is designed to comprehensively address each exam objective, reflecting the exam weighting outlined in the official guide, as illustrated in the following table:

Domain	Weight Percentage
Domain 1: Monitoring, Logging, Analysis, Remediation, and Performance Optimization	22%
Domain 2: Reliability and Business Continuity	22%
Domain 3: Deployment, Provisioning, and Automation	22%
Domain 4: Security and Compliance	16%
Domain 5: Networking and Content Delivery	18%

Domain 1: Monitoring, Logging, Analysis, Remediation, and Performance Optimization

Task Statement 1.1: Implement Metrics, Alarms, and Filters by Using AWS Monitoring and Logging Services

Knowledge of	Chapter(s)
Skill 1.1.1: Configure AWS monitoring and logging by using AWS services (for example, Amazon CloudWatch, AWS CloudTrail, Amazon Managed Service for Prometheus).	6
Skill 1.1.2: Configure and manage the CloudWatch agent to collect metrics and logs from EC2 instances, Amazon ECS clusters, or Amazon Elastic Kubernetes Service (Amazon EKS) clusters.	6

Knowledge of	Chapter(s)
Skill 1.1.3: Configure, identify, and troubleshoot CloudWatch alarms that can invoke AWS services directly or through Amazon EventBridge (for example, by creating composite alarms and identifying their invokable actions).	6
Skill 1.1.4: Create, implement, and manage customizable and shareable CloudWatch dashboards that display metrics and alarms for AWS resources across multiple accounts and AWS Regions.	6
Skill 1.1.5: Configure AWS services to send notifications to Amazon Simple Notification Service (Amazon SNS) and to invoke alarms that send notifications to Amazon SNS.	6

Task Statement 1.2: Identify and Remediate Issues by Using Monitoring and Availability Metrics

Knowledge of	Chapter(s)
Skill 1.2.1: Analyze performance metrics and automate remediation strategies by using AWS services and functionality (for example, CloudWatch, AWS User Notifications, Lambda, Systems Manager, CloudTrail, auto scaling).	3, 6
Skill 1.2.2: Use EventBridge to route, enrich, and deliver events, and troubleshoot any issues with event bus rules.	6
Skill 1.2.3: Create or run custom and predefined Systems Manager Automation runbooks (for example, by using AWS SDKs or custom scripts) to automate tasks and streamline processes on AWS.	3, 6

Task Statement 1.3: Implement Performance Optimization Strategies for Compute, Storage, and Database Resources

Knowledge of	Chapter(s)
Skill 1.3.1: Optimize compute resources and remediate performance problems by using performance metrics, resource tags, and AWS tools.	2, 3, 6
Skill 1.3.2: Analyze Amazon Elastic Block Store (Amazon EBS) performance metrics, troubleshoot issues, and optimize volume types to improve performance and reduce cost.	5
Skill 1.3.3: Implement and optimize S3 performance strategies (for example, AWS DataSync, S3 Transfer Acceleration, multipart uploads, S3 Lifecycle policies) to enhance data transfer, storage efficiency, and access patterns.	5

(*Continued*)

(Continued)

Knowledge of	Chapter(s)
Skill 1.3.4: Evaluate and select shared storage solutions (for example, Amazon Elastic File System [Amazon EFS], Amazon FSx), and optimize the solutions (for example, EFS lifecycle policies) for specific use cases and requirements.	5
Skill 1.3.5: Monitor Amazon RDS metrics (for example, Amazon RDS Performance Insights, CloudWatch alarms), and modify configurations to increase performance efficiency (for example, Performance Insights proactive recommendations, RDS Proxy).	4
Skill 1.3.6: Implement, monitor, and optimize EC2 instances and their associated storage and networking capabilities (for example, EC2 placement groups).	3, 5, 6

Domain 2: Reliability and Business Continuity

Task Statement 2.1: Implement Scalability and Elasticity

Knowledge of	Chapter(s)
Skill 2.1.1: Configure and manage scaling mechanisms in compute environments.	3, 4, 5
Skill 2.1.2: Implement caching by using AWS services to enhance dynamic scalability (for example, CloudFront, Amazon ElastiCache).	4, 5, 10
Skill 2.1.3: Configure and manage scaling in AWS managed databases (for example, Amazon RDS, DynamoDB).	4

Task Statement 2.2: Implement Highly Available and Resilient Environments

Knowledge of	Chapter(s)
Skill 2.2.1: Configure and troubleshoot Elastic Load Balancing (ELB) and Amazon Route 53 health checks.	7, 10
Skill 2.2.2: Configure fault-tolerant systems (for example, Multi-AZ deployments).	4, 7

Task Statement 2.3: Implement Backup and Restore Strategies

Knowledge of	Chapter(s)
Skill 2.3.1: Automate snapshots and backups for AWS resources (for example, EC2 instances, RDS DB instances, EBS volumes, S3 buckets, DynamoDB tables) by using AWS services (for example, AWS Backup).	3, 4, 5, 7
Skill 2.3.2: Use various methods to restore databases (for example, point-in-time restore) to meet recovery time objective (RTO), recovery point objective (RPO), and cost requirements.	4, 5, 7
Skill 2.3.3: Implement versioning for storage services (for example, Amazon S3, Amazon FSx).	5
Skill 2.3.4: Follow disaster recovery procedures.	7

Domain 3: Deployment, Provisioning, and Automation

Task Statement 3.1: Provision and Maintain Cloud Resources

Knowledge of	Chapter(s)
Skill 3.1.1: Create and manage AMIs and container images (for example, EC2 Image Builder).	3
Skill 3.1.2: Create and manage stacks of resources by using CloudFormation and the AWS Cloud Development Kit (AWS CDK).	8
Skill 3.1.3: Identify and remediate deployment issues (for example, subnet sizing issues, CloudFormation errors, permissions issues).	8
Skill 3.1.4: Provision and share resources across multiple Regions and accounts (for example, AWS Resource Access Manager [AWS RAM], CloudFormation StackSets).	8
Skill 3.1.5: Implement deployment strategies and services.	8
Skill 3.1.6: Use and manage third-party tools to automate resource deployment (for example, Terraform, Git).	8

Task Statement 3.2: Automate the Management of Existing Resources

Knowledge of	Chapter(s)
Skill 3.2.1: Use AWS services to automate operational processes (for example, Systems Manager).	3, 6
Skill 3.2.2: Implement event-driven automation by using AWS services and features (for example, Lambda, S3 Event Notifications).	6, 8

Domain 4: Security and Compliance

Task Statement 4.1: Implement and Manage Security and Compliance Tools and Policies

Knowledge of	Chapter(s)
Skill 4.1.1: Implement AWS Identity and Access Management (IAM) features (for example, password policies, multi-factor authentication [MFA], roles, federated identity, resource policies, policy conditions).	9
Skill 4.1.2: Troubleshoot and audit access issues by using AWS tools (for example, CloudTrail, IAM Access Analyzer, IAM policy simulator).	9
Skill 4.1.3: Implement multi-account strategies securely.	2, 9
Skill 4.1.4: Implement remediation based on the results of AWS Trusted Advisor security checks.	9
Skill 4.1.5: Enforce compliance requirements (for example, region and service selections).	2, 8, 9

Task Statement 4.2: Implement Strategies to Protect Data and Infrastructure

Knowledge of	Chapter(s)
Skill 4.2.1: Implement and enforce a data classification scheme.	9
Skill 4.2.2: Implement, configure, and troubleshoot encryption at rest (for example, AWS Key Management Service [AWS KMS]).	9

Knowledge of	Chapter(s)
Skill 4.2.3: Implement, configure, and troubleshoot encryption in transit (for example, AWS Certificate Manager [ACM]).	9
Skill 4.2.4: Securely store secrets by using AWS services.	9
Skill 4.2.5: Configure reports and remediate findings from AWS services (for example, Security Hub, Amazon GuardDuty, AWS Config, Amazon Inspector).	9

Domain 5: Networking and Content Delivery

Task Statement 5.1: Implement and Optimize Networking Features and Connectivity

Knowledge of	Chapter(s)
Skill 5.1.1: Configure a VPC (for example, subnets, route tables, network ACLs, security groups, NAT gateways, Internet gateway, egress-only Internet gateway).	10
Skill 5.1.2: Configure private networking connectivity.	10
Skill 5.1.3: Audit AWS network protection services (for example, Route 53 Resolver DNS Firewall, AWS WAF, AWS Shield, AWS Network Firewall) in a single account.	10
Skill 5.1.4: Optimize the cost of network architectures	10, 11

Task Statement 5.2: Configure Domains, DNS Services, and Content Delivery

Knowledge of	Chapter(s)
Skill 5.2.1: Configure DNS (for example, Route 53 Resolver).	7, 10
Skill 5.2.2: Implement Route 53 routing policies, configurations, and query logging.	10
Skill 5.2.3: Configure content and service distribution (for example, CloudFront, AWS Global Accelerator).	10

Task Statement 5.3: Troubleshoot Network Connectivity Issues

Knowledge of	Chapter(s)
Skill 5.3.1: Troubleshoot VPC configurations (for example, subnets, route tables, network ACLs, security groups, transit gateways, NAT gateways).	10
Skill 5.3.2: Collect and interpret networking logs to troubleshoot issues (for example, VPC flow logs, ELB access logs, AWS WAF web ACL logs, CloudFront logs, container logs).	10
Skill 5.3.3: Identify and remediate CloudFront caching issues.	10
Skill 5.3.4: Identify and troubleshoot hybrid connectivity issues and private connectivity issues.	10
Skill 5.3.5: Configure and analyze CloudWatch network monitoring services.	10

Assessment Test

1. A CloudOps Engineer needs to receive an alert whenever the average CPU utilization of an Amazon EC2 fleet exceeds 80% for more than five minutes. Which AWS service and feature should be used to achieve this with the least operational overhead?

   A. AWS CloudTrail using insights to detect anomalies

   B. Amazon CloudWatch Alarms monitoring the `CPUUtilization` metric

   C. A custom script on the EC2 instances sending logs to Amazon S3

   D. AWS Config rules to monitor the instance state

2. A CloudOps team is troubleshooting a performance drop in a web application. They need to visualize how a single user request flows through various microservices and identify which service is causing latency. Which service should they use?

   A. Amazon CloudWatch Logs

   B. AWS X-Ray

   C. Amazon Inspector

   D. AWS CloudTrail

3. A CloudOps Engineer notices that an application is frequently running out of memory, but the `MemoryUtilization` metric is missing from the standard CloudWatch EC2 metrics list. What must the engineer do to monitor memory?

   A. Enable Detailed Monitoring in the EC2 console

   B. Use the AWS CLI to describe the instance health

   C. Install the CloudWatch agent on the instance to push memory metrics

   D. Change the instance type to a memory-optimized family

4. A CloudOps team wants to automatically recover an EC2 instance when its `StatusCheckFailed_System` metric triggers an alarm. Which action should they configure in the CloudWatch alarm?

   A. An Amazon SNS notification to the DevOps team

   B. An EC2 Action to recover the instance

   C. An AWS Lambda function to stop and start the instance

   D. An Auto Scaling group lifecycle hook

5. A CloudOps Engineer is tasked with reducing costs for a development environment. They need a way to automatically identify and delete unattached Amazon EBS volumes. Which approach is most efficient?

   A. Manually checking the EBS console once a week

   B. Writing a cron job on a local server to run `aws ec2 delete-volume`

   C. Creating a service request with AWS Support

   D. Using an AWS Config rule with an automated remediation action via AWS Systems Manager

6. A CloudOps team manages an application that requires 99.9% availability. The current architecture uses a single EC2 instance. Which change would most improve the application's reliability?
   A. Upgrading to a larger EC2 instance size
   B. Moving the instance to a private subnet
   C. Deploying the application across multiple Availability Zones using an Auto Scaling group and an ALB
   D. Adding an Elastic IP address to the instance

7. A CloudOps Engineer needs to ensure that an Amazon RDS database can be recovered to a specific point in time within the last 30 days. Which feature should they enable?
   A. Manual snapshots taken every 24 hours
   B. Multi-AZ deployment
   C. Automated backups and set the retention period to 30 days
   D. Enhanced monitoring

8. An application requires highly available file storage that can be accessed by multiple EC2 instances simultaneously within a single region. Which storage solution should a CloudOps Engineer choose?
   A. Amazon Elastic File System (EFS)
   B. Amazon S3 Glacier
   C. Amazon EBS with Multi-Attach enabled
   D. Amazon EC2 Instance Store

9. A CloudOps team needs to test their Disaster Recovery (DR) plan. They want to maintain a scaled-down version of their infrastructure in a second region that can be quickly scaled up if the primary region fails. Which DR strategy is this?
   A. Backup and Restore
   B. Pilot Light
   C. Warm Standby
   D. Multi-site active-active

10. A CloudOps Engineer is configuring an Amazon Route 53 health check. They want to redirect traffic to a static error page on S3 if the primary web server becomes unresponsive. Which routing policy should be used?
   A. Simple routing
   B. Latency routing
   C. Failover routing
   D. Multi-value answer routing

11. A CloudOps Engineer is using AWS CloudFormation to deploy a stack. They need to ensure that if the stack creation fails, the successfully created resources are not deleted so they can troubleshoot. What should they do?

    A. Set Preserve Successfully Provisioned Resources in the Stack Failure Options section of the Configure Stack Options page.

    B. Use a DeletionPolicy of Retain on every resource.

    C. Enable Termination Protection on the stack.

    D. Use a CloudFormation Change Set.

12. A CloudOps team needs to update the application code on a fleet of EC2 instances managed by AWS CodeDeploy. They want to maximize deployment speed while ensuring that at least 70% of instances remain in service during the update. Which deployment configuration should they use?

    A. `CodeDeployDefault.AllAtOnce`

    B. `CodeDeployDefault.OneAtATime`

    C. `CodeDeployDefault.HalfAtATime`

    D. A custom deployment configuration with a minimum healthy hosts requirement of 70%

13. A CloudOps Engineer wants to use the AWS CDK to deploy infrastructure. What does the CDK produce after the `synth` command is run?

    A. A Docker image

    B. A CloudFormation template

    C. An executable binary file

    D. A Terraform state file

14. A CloudOps team needs to run a script on 1,000 EC2 instances to patch a software vulnerability without SSHing into each instance manually. Which AWS Systems Manager (SSM) capability should they use?

    A. SSM Parameter Store

    B. SSM Run Command

    C. SSM Session Manager

    D. SSM Distributor

15. A CloudOps team wants to share a set of private subnets from a central networking account with development accounts so that developers can launch resources into the shared subnets without creating their own VPCs. Which service facilitates this process?

    A. AWS Service Catalog

    B. AWS Config

    C. AWS Resource Access Manager (RAM)

    D. AWS PrivateLink

16. A CloudOps team is required to encrypt all data at rest in their Amazon S3 buckets. Which header must they check for in a bucket policy to ensure that objects are uploaded only if they use server-side encryption with AWS KMS (SSE-KMS)?

   A. x-amz-server-side-encryption: `AES256`

   B. Content-Type: `application/json`

   C. x-amz-storage-class: `GLACIER`

   D. x-amz-server-side-encryption: `aws:kms`

17. A CloudOps Engineer needs to provide temporary security credentials to a developer so that they can access an S3 bucket for one hour. Which service should the engineer use?

   A. IAM Groups

   B. AWS Security Token Service (STS)

   C. AWS Organizations

   D. IAM Users with long-term access keys

18. A CloudOps team wants to identify which IAM users have not used their passwords or access keys in the last 90 days. What is the most efficient way to get this information?

   A. Generating an IAM Credential Report

   B. Reviewing CloudTrail logs for the last 90 days

   C. Using AWS Trusted Advisor

   D. Checking the Last Activity column in the EC2 console

19. A CloudOps Engineer needs to protect a public-facing Application Load Balancer (ALB) from common web exploits like SQL injection and cross-site scripting (XSS). Which service should be deployed?

   A. AWS Shield Standard

   B. AWS WAF

   C. Amazon GuardDuty

   D. Amazon Macie

20. A CloudOps Engineer discovers that an S3 bucket is public because a Block Public Access setting is disabled. Which service can automatically notify the team and provide a compliance status for this?

   A. AWS Config

   B. AWS Artifact

   C. AWS Resource Access Manager

   D. AWS CloudShell

21. A CloudOps team is setting up a VPC. They need to allow instances in a private subnet to download software updates from the Internet while preventing Internet requestors from initiating a connection to those instances. What should they use?

    A. Internet gateway

    B. NAT gateway

    C. Virtual private gateway

    D. VPC peering

22. A CloudOps Engineer needs to connect an on-premises data center to a VPC using a dedicated, private connection that bypasses the public Internet. Which service should they choose?

    A. AWS Site-to-Site VPN

    B. AWS Direct Connect

    C. AWS Transit Gateway

    D. Amazon VPC Endpoint

23. A CloudOps team wants to improve the performance of a global website by caching static content (images and CSS) closer to users. Which service should they implement?

    A. Amazon CloudFront

    B. Amazon ElastiCache

    C. Amazon Route 53

    D. Amazon Global Accelerator

24. A CloudOps Engineer needs to restrict outbound traffic from an EC2 instance to a specific IP address range. The solution must provide instance-level control and stateful filtering. Which feature should they modify?

    A. Route table

    B. Security group

    C. Network ACL

    D. Elastic IP

25. A CloudOps team is configuring an Application Load Balancer (ALB). They want to route traffic to different target groups based on the URL path (e.g., `/images` vs `/api`). Which feature of the ALB should they use?

    A. Host-based routing

    B. Path-based routing

    C. Query-string routing

    D. Source IP routing

Answers to Assessment Test

1. B. CloudWatch Alarms are the native way to monitor standard metrics like `CPUUtilization`. Option A is for security/log anomalies; Option C is too much manual work; Option D is for configuration history, not performance alerting.
2. B. AWS X-Ray is specifically designed for distributed tracing in microservices. Option A is for text logs; Option C is for vulnerability scanning; Option D is for API audit logs.
3. C. EC2 does not send OS-level metrics like RAM to CloudWatch by default. The agent is required. Option A only increases the frequency of default metrics (CPU, Disk, Net); Options B and D do not solve the monitoring gap.
4. B. EC2 recovery actions are specific features of CloudWatch alarms that can reboot or move an instance if the system check fails. Option A only notifies; Option C is more complex than the built-in action; Option D is for scaling events.
5. D. AWS Config can detect noncompliant resources (unattached EBS) and trigger SSM documents for remediation. Option A is manual; Option B is outdated and requires managing a separate server; Option C is for technical support.
6. C. High availability requires eliminating single points of failure by spreading across multiple AZs. Option A increases capacity but not availability; Option B is for security; Option D provides a static IP but no redundancy.
7. C. Automated backups allow Point-in-Time Recovery (PITR) for RDS. Option A does not provide continuous point-in-time recovery; Option B is for high availability; Option D is for performance metrics.
8. A. EFS provides a shared file system that multiple instances can mount. Option B is for archiving; Option C allows multiple instances on a single EBS volume, but they must be `io1` or `io2` provisioned IOPS SSD volumes in the same AZ and usually require a clustered file system; Option D is temporary and local.
9. C. Warm Standby is a scaled-down but functional version of the environment. Option A is the slowest; Option B (Pilot Light) only has data and core pieces like DBs running; Option D is full capacity in both regions.
10. C. Failover routing is designed for active-passive setups. Option A is for a single resource; Option B is for performance; Option D is for returning multiple healthy IPs.
11. A. The Preserve Successfully Provisioned Resources setting stops CloudFormation from deleting resources after an error, allowing the engineer to inspect the state. Option B prevents deletion on success/manual deletion; Option C prevents accidental stack deletion; Option D is for previewing changes.

12. D. Custom configurations are needed for specific percentages like 70%. Option A takes everything down; Options B and C use predefined counts (1 or 50%) that might not meet the 70% requirement.

13. B. The CDK "synthesizes" code (TypeScript, Python, etc.) into CloudFormation templates. Options A, C, and D are related to other tools (Docker, Go, and Terraform, respectively).

14. B. The SSM Run Command allows you to execute scripts across a large fleet of instances simultaneously without SSH. Option A is for secrets/config; Option C is for interactive shells; Option D is for software package distribution.

15. C. AWS Resource Access Manager (RAM) is the primary service used to share AWS resources (like subnets, transit gateways, and Route 53 Resolver rules) across AWS accounts or within an AWS Organization. Option A is used to manage and distribute approved portfolios of IT services; Option B is used for assessing, auditing, and evaluating the configurations of AWS resources; Option D is a technology that provides private connectivity between VPCs, services, and on-premises networks.

16. D. `aws:kms` indicates SSE-KMS encryption. Option A is for SSE-S3; Options B and C are unrelated to the encryption algorithm header.

17. B. STS provides short-term, temporary credentials. Options A and D are for long-term users; Option C is for managing multiple AWS accounts.

18. A. The Credential Report is a downloadable CSV that lists all IAM users and their last login/access key usage. Option B is tedious to search manually; Option C shows general best practices; Option D doesn't exist in the EC2 console for IAM users.

19. B. AWS WAF (Web Application Firewall) filters Layer 7 traffic for SQLi and XSS. Option A is for DDoS; Option C is for threat detection (IDS); Option D is for sensitive data discovery in S3.

20. A. AWS Config monitors resource configurations and marks them as noncompliant if they violate rules (like public S3). Option B is for compliance reports (SOC/ISO); Option C is for sharing resources; Option D is a terminal.

21. B. A NAT gateway allows outbound traffic for updates while blocking inbound initiation. Option A allows two-way traffic; Option C is for VPNs; Option D connects two VPCs.

22. B. Direct Connect is the physical, private link. Option A uses the public Internet via an encrypted tunnel; Option C is a hub for multiple VPCs; Option D is for private service access.

23. A. CloudFront is the AWS Content Delivery Network (CDN) that uses Edge Locations. Option B is for database/application caching; Option C is a highly available and scalable cloud Domain Name System (DNS) web service; Option D optimizes the network path but doesn't cache content.

24. B. Security groups are the standard for instance-level outbound (egress) rules. They are stateful, meaning you don't have to manage return traffic rules manually. Network ACLs (Option C) can also restrict outbound traffic, but they are stateless, requiring you to manage both outbound and inbound (return traffic) rules separately. Option A decides where traffic goes, not whether it is allowed; Option D has nothing to do with filtering traffic. It's just a static public IP.

25. B. Path-based routing allows the ALB to look at the URL path and send traffic to specific target groups. Option A uses the domain name (e.g., `api.example.com` vs `images.example.com`); Option C uses parameters in the query string after a ?; Option D uses the client's address.

Introduction to Cloud Operations on AWS

THE AWS CERTIFIED CLOUDOPS ENGINEER–ASSOCIATE (SOA-C03) EXAM OBJECTIVES COVERED IN THIS CHAPTER MAY INCLUDE, BUT ARE NOT LIMITED TO, THE FOLLOWING:

✓ **Domain 3: Deployment, Provisioning, and Automation**

- 3.1 Provision and maintain cloud resources
- 3.2 Automate the management of existing resources

Cloud computing has become an enabler of any company's digital transformation program. Whether your organization is a startup or a large enterprise, a foundational element of its digital transformation relies on its ability to access scalable, flexible, and cost-effective compute, storage, and network infrastructure to support its business processes and operations. This is exactly what the cloud is intended to deliver. By accelerating cloud adoption, organizations are better positioned to innovate, scale, respond to changes, and go to market faster.

However, cloud adoption doesn't happen overnight. The larger the organization, the more important it is to have a cloud strategy. As a result, a robust and well-articulated cloud strategy is essential for organizations seeking to harness the true potential of the cloud. Without a clear roadmap and a set of best practices to guide architecture, build, deployment, monitoring, and ongoing automation, efforts can quickly become fragmented, leading to inefficiencies, cost overruns, and suboptimal use of resources. A solid cloud strategy not only aligns technical initiatives with business objectives, but also ensures consistent governance, security, scalability, and adaptability to change across the cloud environments. By laying this foundation, organizations empower their teams to make informed decisions, anticipate challenges, and rapidly respond to evolving business needs—ultimately turning cloud adoption from a challenging task into a strategic advantage.

Equally important in this journey is the implementation of effective *cloud operations*, also referred to as *CloudOps*. Serving as a "single pane of glass," cloud operations platforms are intended to provide a unified instrumentation and management for both cloud-native and hybrid workloads. Through consolidated dashboards and automated monitoring, organizations gain comprehensive visibility into their resources, performance metrics, and security posture, regardless of where their workloads operate. This holistic approach streamlines troubleshooting, provides optimization, and enables proactive management, allowing IT teams to maintain agility and reliability as their cloud footprint grows. In the modern enterprise, cloud operations becomes the "brain" that orchestrates complexity, enabling organizations to deliver and support resilient and high-performing digital experiences.

This chapter walks you through the CloudOps basic concepts you need for the exam. You will learn the five stages of the CloudOps cycle, which will help you understand your role and duties as a CloudOps engineer. You will also be introduced to the AWS Well-Architected Framework and the AWS Well-Architected Tool. The former—specifically the Operational Excellence pillar—provides the guidelines you need to embed operational best practices directly into architecture, tooling, and review processes of your workloads. The latter provides a unified interface to assess workloads against the framework. Finally, you'll discover how unified CloudOps also enables IT teams to proactively automate tasks and remediate issues before they impact business operations.

Cloud Operations Cycle

Cloud operations is a continuous cycle of essential tasks that keep cloud-based systems running smoothly, securely, and efficiently. These three adverbs—smoothly, securely, and efficiently—were deliberately chosen to capture the core outcomes that every CloudOps engineer strives to deliver. "Smoothly" reflects the need for uninterrupted service and responsive performance, minimizing friction for users and workloads alike. "Securely" emphasizes the constant vigilance required to protect data, identities, and infrastructure from evolving threats. "Efficiently" speaks to the art of balancing cost, speed, and resource utilization—ensuring that cloud environments scale wisely without waste.

At a high level, this continuous cycle is divided in five operational tasks or phases, as illustrated in Figure 1.1.

Let's delve into each phase.

Deploy This phase focuses on launching cloud infrastructure and services in a controlled, repeatable way. It includes provisioning resources, configuring environments, and using automation tools like AWS CloudFormation or HashiCorp Terraform to ensure consistency across deployments. A successful Deploy phase sets the stage for scalability, resilience, and rapid iteration.

FIGURE 1.1 Cloud operations cycle.

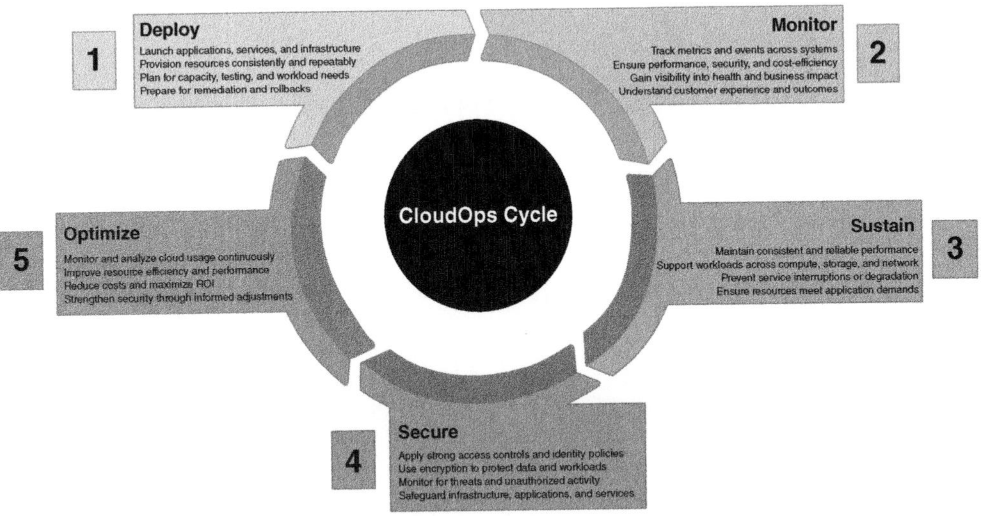

Monitor Once systems are live in a production environment, monitoring ensures visibility into performance, availability, and usage. CloudOps engineers use tools like Amazon CloudWatch, AWS X-Ray, and third-party observability platforms to track metrics, logs, events, and traces. This phase enables early detection of anomalies, supports incident response, and informs optimization decisions.

Sustain Sustaining operations means keeping workloads healthy over time. It involves patching, updating, backing up, and resolving incidents. CloudOps engineers apply runbooks, automate maintenance tasks, and manage support workflows to ensure reliability and minimize downtime. This phase is where operational maturity and team discipline shine.

Secure Security is embedded across all phases, but this dedicated phase focuses on enforcing identity controls, managing vulnerabilities, and ensuring compliance. CloudOps engineers implement IAM (Identity and Access Management) policies, encryption, network segmentation, and threat detection using services like Amazon GuardDuty and AWS Security Hub. The goal is to protect data, workloads, infrastructure, and users without compromising agility.

Optimize Optimization is about refining cloud operations for cost, performance, and resource efficiency. CloudOps engineers analyze usage patterns, right-size instances, tune configurations, and adopt architectural improvements. This phase often leverages AWS Trusted Advisor, AWS Compute Optimizer, and custom dashboards to drive continuous improvement.

Together, the three aforementioned outcomes—smoothly, securely, and efficiently—form the core qualities of any well-architected cloud systems. They are not just aspirational—they are measurable, actionable, and embedded in every phase of the CloudOps cycle: Deploy, Monitor, Sustain, Secure, and Optimize. Each phase contributes to these outcomes in distinct ways, and mastering their interplay is key to becoming a high-impact CloudOps engineer.

Cloud Operations Engineer Roles and Responsibilities

As shown in Figure 1.1, your job starts with *deployment*. Developers write code, build applications, and then hand applications over to the operations team. You—as a CloudOps engineer—are responsible for deploying the necessary infrastructure supporting the application in a live environment (production), provisioning resources consumed by the application at runtime, and getting everything up and running. This process might also include updating code when required. As you'll learn in the upcoming chapters, CloudOps engineers ensure that deployments are version-controlled, repeatable, and auditable.

Once the application is up and running, your journey has just begun! Your next step is to monitor the performance of the overall system—application, infrastructure, identities, and resources provisioned. You will leverage key performance metrics and thresholds to assess whether the system performs as expected, or performs poorly. If you are familiar with TOGAF (The Open Group Architecture Framework), in this step you will be monitoring the *nonfunctional requirements* (NFRs) of your system.

For more information about NFR, visit `https://pubs.opengroup.org/onlinepubs/7699909199/toc.pdf`.

Monitoring your system's performance is a key aspect of this phase, where you are carefully observing the behavior of the system with services like Amazon CloudWatch. The primary objective of the Monitoring phase is to establish comprehensive visibility across applications, underlying infrastructure, and overall operational health, while also connecting technical performance to business outcomes and customer experience. This is achieved by continuously collecting, analyzing, and correlating metrics that reveal how systems behave, how effectively they support business goals, and how changes impact end users.

In the next phase—referred to as Sustain—you will be responsible for building the necessary instrumentation to bring the system back to normal in the event of a failure or underperformance. This last aspect (i.e., the work you do to make the system perform at acceptable levels, even under varying conditions—in alignment with its service level objectives—SLOs) is referred to as *reliability*.

As a pillar of the AWS Well-Architected Framework, Security is another critical responsibility of a CloudOps engineer. AWS manages the security of the cloud, but it is a shared responsibility (Chapter 2 explains in detail the shared responsibility model.) You play a critical role in maintaining the security posture of cloud-based infrastructure by implementing and enforcing robust operational controls. These include defining IAM (Identity and Access Management) policies to ensure least-privilege access, monitoring for anomalous activity using services like AWS CloudTrail and Amazon GuardDuty, and automating compliance checks with tools such as AWS Config, AWS Artifact, and AWS Security Hub. It is important to notice that security applies to all of your responsibilities. You should embed security controls in any operational tasks you own.

Last but not least, you're responsible for Optimization. Just because your system is up and running at acceptable performance levels in AWS, and is proactively being watched by a secure monitoring framework, it doesn't mean you're good to go! Remember, in the cloud, you need to maximize the efficiency, performance, and cost-effectiveness of cloud operations through continuous analysis and refinement. AWS offers services such as AWS Cost Explorer, AWS Compute Optimizer, and AWS Trusted Advisor to identify underutilized resources, right-size instances, and eliminate waste.

Throughout this process, collaboration with cross-functional teams, such as application, infrastructure, data, security, and network engineers, is key to maintaining the overall health and reliability of your cloud environment. Your day-to-day tasks as an AWS CloudOps engineer directly support the six pillars of the AWS Well-Architected Framework—especially Operational Excellence, Security, and Cost Optimization. That's why this framework is the first document listed in the "Recommended AWS knowledge and experience" section of the exam guide. Let's dive in!

AWS Well-Architected Framework

As organizations expand their cloud footprint, the operational surface area grows—more AWS accounts, multi-region deployments, services, and teams introduce greater complexity. Maintaining consistency, visibility, and control becomes a challenge for any IT and business team involved with a workload's lifecycle. AWS CloudOps addresses this challenge by promoting centralized governance, standardized tooling, and automated workflows across environments. But to truly unify operations—across workloads and organizational boundaries—architectural alignment becomes essential. This is where the AWS Well-Architected Framework plays a pivotal role.

The Well-Architected Framework provides a structured methodology for evaluating and improving cloud architectures, grounded in six core pillars:

- Operational Excellence
- Security
- Reliability
- Performance Efficiency
- Cost Optimization
- Sustainability

By embedding operational best practices into architectural reviews and tooling—such as the AWS Well-Architected Tool (introduced in the upcoming sections), AWS Config, and AWS Control Tower—this framework enables centralized oversight of workload health, security posture, and remediation tracking. The Well-Architected Framework helps teams align on shared principles, automate governance, and surface operational gaps early, transforming CloudOps from reactive firefighting into proactive, scalable stewardship.

For you as an AWS CloudOps engineer, this framework will help you as an essential resource to do the following:

- Evaluate existing architectures.
- Plan system improvements.
- Embed best practices in day-to-day operations.
- Align with industry standards and AWS recommendations.

Pillars

Each pillar of the framework is composed of a curated list of design principles and best practices that you should use to architect, build, and operate your solution in AWS. This approach results in stable, efficient, secure, reliable, and cost-effective systems. Every architectural decision for a system operating in AWS should tie back to one (or a collection) of these six pillars.

For the exam our focus is on the Operational Excellence pillar because this pillar concentrates on running and monitoring systems to deliver business value and continuous optimization, which are the main responsibilities of CloudOps engineering. Nonetheless, all six pillars impact cloud operations in different forms. Let's see how.

Operational Excellence

The Operational Excellence pillar is intended to guide you on how to support and operate your applications effectively in AWS and continuously improve processes and procedures to deliver business value.

You may wonder what does "effectively" really mean? The idea is to think of the applications from the customer's standpoint. As a customer, not only you want your applications to run smoothly, with minimal downtime, but you also want quick bug fixes and ideally accelerate delivery of new features in a reliable manner.

Impact on CloudOps Engineering

CloudOps engineers build automation for repetitive tasks, monitor system health, and continuously improve operational procedures. More details will be provided in the upcoming sections.

Security

The Security pillar defines design principles and best practices to help you protect your applications' identities, the infrastructure, the data, and any resource they use in the cloud, on-premises, or both.

Impact on CloudOps Engineering

CloudOps engineers implement guardrails to secure all the aforementioned elements of your system (i.e., identities, infrastructure, data, and any resources consumed by your applications).

For example, you as a CloudOps engineer should enforce IAM policies to "implement a strong identity foundation," which is the first design principle in the Security pillar. If you think about it, this makes complete sense because identities are the first entry point to access a private system. When you implement authentication, authorization, and credential hygiene—which are core best practices derived by this principle—the attack surface of your system is significantly reduced, resulting in a defensible perimeter around your cloud resources.

When it comes to securing data, you should make sure that sensitive data is always encrypted at rest, in use, and in transit, according to the "protect data in transit and at rest" design principle.

To learn more about the Security pillar's design principles, visit `https://docs.aws.amazon.com/wellarchitected/latest/security-pillar/security.html`.

Reliability

The Reliability pillar includes design principles and best practices to help you make sure applications perform their intended functions correctly and consistently. The term "correctly" emphasizes the business functions delivered by the application. You may question whether this is a responsibility of the application team—specifically UAT (User Acceptance Testing)—who work with business users to ensure each function of the application is properly delivered. However, behind the scenes, the application at runtime relies entirely on infrastructure, data, and other assets that you are responsible for. As a result, your duties include making sure all of these assets operate reliably in accordance with the nonfunctional requirements of your applications.

Impact on CloudOps Engineering

CloudOps engineers implement high availability and fault tolerance and have contingency plans in place to make sure systems remain reliable and accessible.

To learn more about the Reliability pillar's design principles, visit `https://docs.aws.amazon.com/wellarchitected/latest/reliability-pillar/design-principles.html`.

Performance Efficiency

The Performance Efficiency pillar covers design principles and best practices to help you use computing resources efficiently in accordance with system requirements and maintain efficiency as demand changes and technologies evolve.

Impact on CloudOps Engineering

CloudOps engineers implement tools to continuously monitor resource utilization, enable auto-scaling and self-healing mechanisms, and optimize workloads to make sure architectures are running efficiently.

To learn more about the Performance Efficiency pillar's design principles, visit `https://docs.aws.amazon.com/wellarchitected/latest/performance-efficiency-pillar/design-principles.html`.

Cost Optimization

The Cost Optimization pillar defines design principles and best practices to guide you on how to operate systems on AWS at the lowest possible cost.

Impact on CloudOps Engineering

CloudOps engineers analyze usage patterns to identify opportunities for cost savings. This analysis facilitates using strategies such as rightsizing resources, using reserved instances, and turning off unused resources.

To learn more about the Cost Optimization pillar's design principles, visit `https://docs.aws.amazon.com/wellarchitected/latest/cost-optimization-pillar/design-principles.html`.

Sustainability

The Sustainability pillar includes design principles and best practices to help you build "frugal architectures." A frugal architecture is intended to minimize resource consumption, while maintaining performance, reliability, and user experience. It prioritizes efficiency across compute, storage, and networking, using just enough to meet demand without excess. Frugal architectures often embrace serverless design patterns, ephemeral infrastructure, and intelligent scaling to reduce idle capacity and environmental impact.

Impact on CloudOps Engineering

CloudOps engineers contribute by implementing energy-efficient practices and optimizing resource utilization.

To learn more about the Sustainability pillar's design principles, visit `https://docs.aws.amazon.com/wellarchitected/latest/high-performance-computing-lens/design-principles-sus.html`.

General Design Principles

In addition to the six pillars, the Well-Architected Framework defines general design principles that help develop the architecture for any cloud-based system. These are the *tenets* you should not only master as an AWS CloudOps engineer, but—most importantly—ensure are clearly traceable in the architecture of your systems running in the cloud. Think of them as the "what," or the high-level imperatives you should aim for when architecting systems in AWS.

These tenets are intended to be general (high-level) by design. As you learn later in the chapter, the framework also provides specialized (low-level) design principles for each pillar.

These tenets are as follows:

Stop guessing your capacity needs. In the cloud, resources (compute, storage, network) can scale in or out (horizontal scaling) or up and down (vertical scaling) based on real-time demands of an application. Horizontal scaling relies on the addition (scaling out) or the removal (scaling in) of resources with the same capacity in response to increasing demand. Vertical scaling relies on the enhancement of an existing resource's capacity—such as upgrading to a larger instance type with more CPU, memory, or storage—to handle increased demand. Since vertical scaling concentrates power in a single resource—with limits to how far it can scale—horizontal scaling is generally the preferred form of scaling in the cloud. By leveraging this cloud "elastic" behavior, you can use as much or as little capacity as you need, and scale in and out automatically.

Test systems at production scale. This general principle promotes the use of ephemeral resources in the cloud. When your system is ready to be stress-tested—to avoid "surprises" upon deployment—this principle encourages you to build a production-scale test environment on demand in the cloud. After testing, you should decommission the test environment resources. Since you only pay for the test environment while it's running, you can simulate a live environment for a significant lower cost than stress-testing on-premises.

For example, your CloudOps team deploys a new version of an application that auto-scales on Amazon ECS, unaware that the Amazon RDS instance's `max_connections` setting is still tuned for the previous, smaller workload. When traffic surges, the scaled-out tasks exhaust the database's connection pool, causing authentication failures and cascading retries—an issue that would have surfaced immediately in a production-scale staging environment.

Automate with architectural experimentation in mind. This general principle ensures that architectural experimentation is a repeatable process. The cloud allows you to provision and dispose of resources programmatically, resulting in quick iterations of architectural changes. By automating version control, change management, and deployment of resources, you help track and roll back changes to cloud infrastructure and applications, thereby enabling repeatability.

Consider evolutionary architectures. This general principle keeps you focused on architecting your solution for extensibility and changes. The former (extensibility) fosters modular design and flexible and loosely coupled architectures that facilitate incremental updates without disrupting the entire system. The latter (change) is unavoidable and allows you to mitigate risks caused by external factors such as evolving customer needs, shifting market conditions, new standards, or emerging technologies. You should leverage cloud services that provide built-in scalability (e.g., serverless), high availability, and fault tolerance to help architectures evolve over time.

Drive architectures by using data. This general principle advocates the use of observability data. This includes performance metrics, usage patterns, cost data, and any other event from cloud resources to help make informed decisions about architecture, resource utilization, and operational costs.

Improve through game days. This general principle promotes the use of *game days* to try and break your system. Given the ease of provision and disposal of resources in the cloud, you should regularly perform game days experiments to simulate different failure scenarios, such as service outages, network disruptions, or resource depletion. The insights gained from these experiments will help you identify areas for improvement and refine incident response procedures, resulting in more resilient and reliable architectures.

Best Practices

AWS develops best practices based on real-world experience running thousands of Internet-scale systems. These practices are primarily shaped by data, and subsequently refined by expert engineers, who work together as a community to validate and share what works.

While design principles are intended as a conceptual framework for architecture decisions (i.e., focusing on the "what to aim for" aspect of the architecture development process), best practices offer specific recommendations on how to implement design principles in your cloud environment. Think of best practices as the "how" to realize those principles in practice. They use concrete actions and implementations, which are ultimately validated by operational outcomes.

Unlike other roles that focus on architecture or development—such as the technical architect (infrastructure) or the solutions architect (software)—the CloudOps engineer is responsible for the day-to-day health, performance, and evolution of the systems running in AWS. As a result, you are not just deploying infrastructure and applications, but you are continuously improving them, responding to events, and automating operations with precision derived from data collected during observability processes. These areas constitute the focus of the Operational Excellence pillar, which is covered in the upcoming sections.

Operational Excellence Pillar

The SOA-C03 exam tests your ability to monitor, troubleshoot, and optimize AWS environments. These tasks are core elements of your day-to-day responsibilities as a CloudOps engineer and are not one-time efforts—they're ongoing operational responsibilities. The Operational Excellence pillar directly addresses these tasks by focusing on continuous improvement, observability, and automated responses. It's the lens through which CloudOps engineers ensure that systems perform efficiently and remain resilient and aligned with business goals.

While other pillars like Security and Reliability are vital, Operational Excellence is the only one that revolves around how you run and maintain your systems in AWS, not just how you build or secure them. It's the core of CloudOps.

Design Principles

The Operational Excellence design principles are outlined in Figure 1.2, which also illustrates how they fit in the overall AWS Well-Architected Framework. The idea is that each pillar drives the development of design principles, which in turn, drive the development of best practices. A pillar's set of best practices is intended to facilitate the decision-making process for the architectural concerns relevant to the pillar.

Figure 1.2 also visualizes the alignment from architectural decisions (at the bottom) all the way up to the Operational Excellence pillar. This bottom-up flow emphasizes how every decision you make—relevant to the Operational Excellence pillar—should trace back to one (or a collection of) design principle(s).

Let's now dive into each Operational Excellence design principle.

Organize teams around business outcomes. This design principle ensures alignment between technical drivers and business drivers. Rather than structuring teams solely by function or technology stack, this principle encourages forming cross-functional groups that own specific outcomes—such as improving customer experience, reducing latency, or increasing deployment velocity. This alignment fosters accountability, accelerates decision-making, and ensures that operational priorities directly support business objectives. By embedding business context into team structure, CloudOps engineers can drive meaningful impact and continuous improvement.

Implement observability for actionable insights. This design principle emphasizes the importance of collecting and analyzing data to understand system behavior and drive informed decisions. Observability goes beyond basic monitoring—it involves capturing metrics, logs,

FIGURE 1.2 Operational Excellence pillar breakdown.

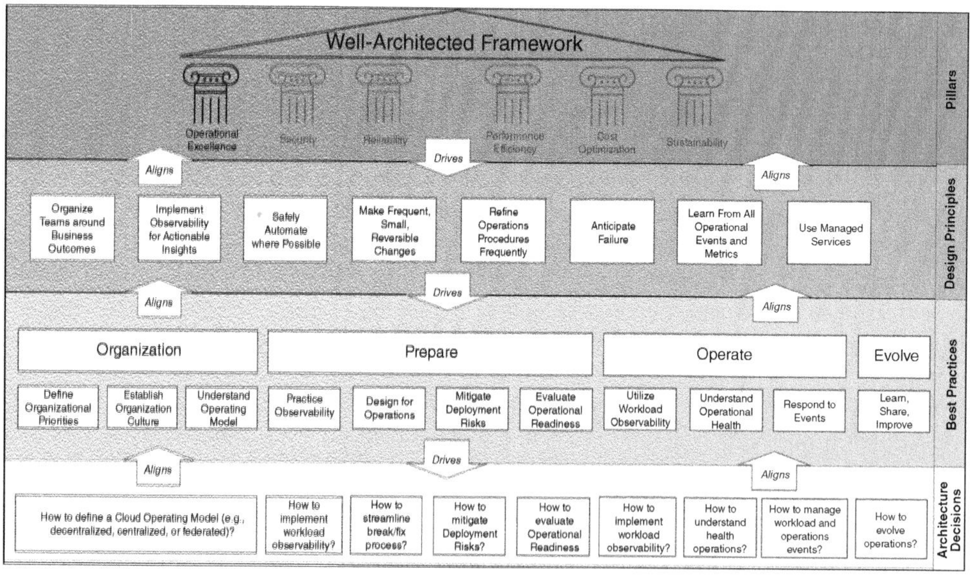

events, and traces that reveal the internal state of workloads. When implemented effectively, observability enables CloudOps engineers to detect anomalies, troubleshoot issues, and optimize performance in real time. The goal is not just visibility, but actionable intelligence that supports continuous improvement and rapid response to operational events.

Safely automate where possible.

> "Good intentions never work, you need good mechanisms to make anything happen."
>
> – *Jeff Bezos*

This design principle encourages CloudOps engineers to reduce manual intervention by implementing automation that is reliable, tested, and validated against production-scale patterns so that deployments, recoveries, and scaling events behave consistently. AWS automation comes in the form of *mechanisms*, which are artifacts responsible for checking adherence to standards and compliance frameworks with rules or processes. Mechanisms help you enhance consistency, streamline operations, and minimize human error—but only when they are designed with safeguards such as version control, rollback capabilities, and clear visibility. Whether you're automating deployments, incident responses, or routine maintenance, the goal is to improve efficiency without compromising control or stability. This principle supports scalable operations while preserving trust in the system's behavior.

To learn more about mechanisms, visit `https://docs.aws.amazon.com/wellarchitected/latest/operational-readiness-reviews/building-mechanisms.html`.

Make frequent, small, reversible changes. This design principle promotes agility and safety in cloud operations by encouraging incremental updates that can be quickly rolled back if needed. Instead of deploying large, risky changes, CloudOps engineers are urged to adopt a continuous delivery mindset—shipping updates in manageable units that reduce blast radius and simplify troubleshooting. This approach not only accelerates innovation but also strengthens system resilience, as each change is easier to test, monitor, and reverse without disrupting the broader workload.

Refine operations procedures frequently. This design principle calls for continuous improvement in how operational tasks are performed. CloudOps engineers should regularly revisit and update runbooks, playbooks, and automation scripts to reflect lessons learned, evolving workloads, and changing business requirements. A key part of this refinement process involves conducting postmortem analyses after operational failures or incidents. These reviews help uncover root causes, identify systemic weaknesses, and generate actionable insights that feed directly into procedural updates. By treating operations as a living discipline and learning from real-world events (successes and failures), teams ensure that their responses remain effective, resilient, and aligned with best practices.

Anticipate failure. This design principle is intended to foster a proactive mindset that recognizes failure as an inevitable aspect of complex distributed systems and prepares for it accordingly. By anticipating failures—whether from infrastructure, application logic, or external dependencies—you can design resilient operations that detect anomalies early, respond automatically, and recover gracefully. This includes implementing monitoring and alerting, defining escalation paths, and conducting chaos engineering experiments to simulate outages. Ultimately, anticipating failure reduces downtime, preserves customer trust, and reinforces a culture of continuous improvement.

Learn from all operational events and metrics. This design principle encourages the use of data to make informed decisions by systematically collecting, analyzing, and responding to operational events and performance metrics. It promotes a culture of continuous improvement where every deployment, incident, and anomaly becomes an opportunity to refine processes and enhance system reliability. By leveraging telemetry, logs, events, and KPIs (Key Performance Indicators), you—as a CloudOps engineer—can identify trends, uncover root causes, and validate the effectiveness of corrective actions. This data-driven approach not only improves operational outcomes but also empowers teams to iterate confidently and evolve their architecture with precision.

Use managed services. This last design principle advocates for leveraging AWS-managed services to reduce operational overhead, improve reliability, and accelerate innovation. By offloading undifferentiated tasks—such as patching, scaling, and infrastructure maintenance—to services like Amazon RDS, AWS Lambda, or Amazon SQS, your team can focus on delivering business value rather than managing servers. Managed services are designed with built-in fault tolerance, monitoring, and security best practices, which help organizations achieve consistent operational outcomes and be adaptive to change. This approach also supports agility by enabling rapid experimentation and streamlined deployment workflows.

Best Practices

Figure 1.2 shows that Operational Excellence best practices fall into four areas: Organize, Prepare, Operate, and Evolve. Each practice area aligns with one (or more) design principle(s). You don't need to study each best practice in detail for the exam, but it's important to grasp the overall idea behind them.

Organize The Organize practice area focuses on defining clear roles, responsibilities, and team structures to support effective cloud operations. It emphasizes assigning ownership for each application, workload, platform, and infrastructure component. Moreover, it requires establishing communication channels and aligning teams with business objectives. When your organization is centered on business functions and outcomes, accountability is well-defined, decision-making is streamlined, and operational tasks are consistently managed and improved over time. This foundation enables teams to respond quickly to change and continuously refine their processes.

Prepare The Prepare practice area is about getting workloads and teams ready for operational success. It involves defining standards, automating processes, and setting up tools that support consistent and repeatable operations. This includes creating runbooks (evaluate operational readiness), implementing change management procedures (design for operations), and configuring monitoring and alerting systems (practice observability). By preparing in advance, your CloudOps team can reduce the risk of failure, respond quickly to issues, and maintain high levels of performance and reliability.

Operate The Operate practice area centers on maintaining workload observability, monitoring operational health, and responding effectively to events. It emphasizes the use of metrics, logs, events, and traces to gain real-time visibility into system behavior, enabling your CloudOps team to detect anomalies and assess performance. Automated responses result in streamlined incident/problem management, reduced downtime, and consistent service delivery. This area fully supports continuous improvement by turning operational insights into actionable refinements across the workload lifecycle.

Evolve The Evolve practice area emphasizes continuous learning, knowledge sharing, and iterative improvement. It encourages teams to reflect on operational experiences, analyze outcomes, and apply lessons learned to refine processes and architectures. When your CloudOps team documents insights, publishes standards and runbooks, and shares them across the organization, it builds a culture of growth and resilience. This ongoing evolution helps workloads adapt to changing requirements, improves operational efficiency, and strengthens long-term reliability.

In the next section you learn how to put the AWS Well-Architected Framework to work with an effective, out-of-the-box tool that measures the architecture of your cloud workloads and generates a list of actionable recommendations.

AWS Well-Architected Tool

The AWS Well-Architected Tool is a free service designed to help cloud architects and engineers evaluate and improve their workloads against the best practices you just learned from the AWS Well-Architected Framework. You can use this tool directly from the AWS Management Console by answering a structured set of questions within each pillar. The tool identifies architectural risks, uncovers improvement opportunities, and prioritizes remediation efforts—all within a guided, repeatable workflow.

You start by defining a *workload* to review. A workload represents a cloud-based application, system, or set of resources that delivers business value. You provide basic metadata—such as the workload name, the review owner, the environment (e.g., production or pre-production), the AWS Regions involved, the architectural design (optional), and so on. This initial step sets the scope for the architectural assessment and ensures that the review is tailored to the workload's context and operational goals.

Once the workload is defined, the tool guides you through a structured set of questions organized under the six pillars of the AWS Well-Architected Framework: Operational Excellence, Security, Reliability, Performance Efficiency, Cost Optimization, and

Sustainability. Since each question is aligned with a pillar, this methodical process helps you uncover risks, trade-offs, and areas of improvement. You can answer these questions collaboratively with your team, document decisions, and flag issues that need remediation.

The tool then generates a prioritized improvement plan, allowing you to track progress and revisit the review as your workload evolves.

The Well-Architected Tool also supports a lens catalog, custom lenses, and milestone tracking. Lenses allow you to tailor the review for specific workload types—like serverless applications or machine learning pipelines—while milestones help you compare architectural decisions over time. This makes the tool not just a one-time checklist, but a living resource for continuous improvement and operational alignment.

Summary

This chapter walked through the foundational concepts of cloud operations in AWS, starting with the five-phase CloudOps Cycle: Deploy, Monitor, Sustain, Secure, and Optimize. It explored how each phase contributes to the health, resilience, and efficiency of cloud workloads, and how they form a continuous loop that supports operational excellence. By framing operations as a cycle rather than a checklist, you can begin to see how cloud systems evolve and adapt over time.

The chapter then examined the roles and responsibilities of a CloudOps engineer, highlighting the blend of technical execution and strategic oversight that defines the role. It looked at how engineers launch infrastructure, monitor performance, sustain uptime, enforce security, and drive cost efficiency. Along the way, the chapter considered the skillsets—like automation, observability, and incident response—that empower engineers to thrive in dynamic, distributed cloud environments.

The AWS Well-Architected Framework was introduced as a structured methodology for evaluating and improving cloud workloads. This chapter explored its six pillars—Operational Excellence, Security, Reliability, Performance Efficiency, Cost Optimization, and Sustainability—and took a deeper dive into the Operational Excellence pillar. Through design principles and best practices, you learned a coherent way to build systems that are not only functional, but also resilient, adaptable, documented, and continuously improving.

Finally, the chapter put theory into practice by introducing the AWS Well-Architected Tool. This tool allows you to define the properties of a workload, analyzes the provided data, and generates a prioritized list of actionable recommendations. You saw how the tool supports milestone tracking, lens customization, and collaborative reviews—making it a powerful resource for aligning architecture with AWS best practices. By the end of the chapter, you should have a good understanding of how CloudOps principles, roles, frameworks, and tools come together to support operational excellence in AWS.

Exam Essentials

Know the tasks of the cloud operations cycle. The CloudOps cycle is comprised of five operational tasks: Deploy, Monitor, Sustain, Secure, and Optimize. Deployment involves provisioning cloud resources and launching workloads using automated, repeatable methods. Monitoring ensures visibility into system health, performance, and usage through metrics, logs, events, and alerts. Sustaining operations means maintaining uptime and reliability through updates, incident response, and support routines. Security focuses on enforcing identity controls, managing vulnerabilities, and applying compliance policies across cloud environments. Optimization involves analyzing usage patterns, tuning configurations, and refining architectures to improve cost-efficiency and performance. Together, these tasks form a continuous loop that supports resilient, scalable, and well-architected cloud systems.

Understand the components of the AWS Well-Architected Framework and how they relate to each other. The framework is built around six core pillars: Operational Excellence, Security, Reliability, Performance Efficiency, Cost Optimization, and Sustainability. Each pillar represents a key dimension of architectural quality, and each provides a lens through which workloads can be evaluated and improved. Beyond the pillars, the framework includes a layered structure of guidance. It begins with general principles that apply across all six pillars—such as "stop guessing your capacity needs" and "consider evolutionary architectures." Each pillar then introduces its own design principles, which translate those general ideas into domain-specific strategies (e.g., "implement observability for actionable insights" in Operational Excellence or "implement a strong identity foundation" in Security). These principles drive best practices, which in turn inform architectural decisions—from how data is encrypted to how workloads are scaled. Understanding this hierarchy is key to adopting the framework effectively.

Know the difference between design principles and best practices. Design principles are high-level, strategic guidelines that shape how you think about building in the cloud. They're conceptual in nature—like "safely automate where possible" (Operational Excellence)—and they help you develop architecture with resilience, agility, and efficiency in mind. Best practices, on the other hand, are the specific, actionable techniques that implement those principles. They translate strategy into execution—for example, using AWS CloudFormation to automate deployments or implementing detailed monitoring with Amazon CloudWatch. While design principles guide your mindset, best practices guide your hands-on decisions. Understanding this distinction helps you connect architectural intent with operational reality.

Understand why the Operational Excellence pillar is relevant to cloud operations. The Operational Excellence pillar is especially relevant to cloud operations because it focuses on how teams run workloads smoothly, securely, and efficiently, respond to events, and continuously improve processes—core responsibilities of any CloudOps engineer. It emphasizes automation, observability, documentation, and iterative improvement, all of which directly support the CloudOps cycle phases like Deploy, Monitor, Sustain, Secure, and Optimize. Design principles such as "make frequent, small, reversible changes," and "anticipate failure" empower teams to build resilient systems that evolve safely and predictably. Best practices derived from these principles guide how engineers manage incidents, conduct postmortem analysis, and refine operational procedures. Put differently, Operational Excellence provides the methodology and mechanisms for delivering reliable, scalable, secure, and adaptive cloud solutions—making it a foundational pillar for anyone operating workloads in AWS.

Know the practice areas of the Operational Excellence pillar. Within the Operational Excellence pillar, this chapter explored four distinct best practices: Organize, Prepare, Operate, and Evolve. *Organize* emphasizes team structure, ownership, accountability, and escalation paths to support the operational requirements of your workloads. *Prepare* focuses on readiness through automation, documentation, and standards. *Operate* ensures workloads run reliably with built-in monitoring, health checks, incident response, and routine execution. *Evolve* drives continuous improvement through analysis, feedback, and refinement. Together, these practice areas form a lifecycle that empowers CloudOps engineers to deliver reliable, scalable, and adaptive cloud solutions, while fostering a culture of excellence.

Understand how the AWS Well-Architected Tool works. You start by defining a workload to review—this includes naming the workload, specifying its environment (e.g., production or pre-production), and identifying its AWS regions and business context. Once the workload is defined, the tool walks you through a structured set of questions aligned with the six pillars of the AWS Well-Architected Framework: Operational Excellence, Security, Reliability, Performance Efficiency, Cost Optimization, and Sustainability. Each question helps uncover risks, trade-offs, and improvement opportunities. As you answer, you can document decisions, flag issues, and collaborate with team members. The tool then generates a prioritized list of actionable recommendations, guiding you toward best practices and architectural alignment. It also supports milestone tracking and custom lenses, making it a dynamic resource for continuous improvement. Understanding this workflow is key to applying the framework effectively and demonstrating operational maturity in AWS.

Review Questions

The following questions are designed to test your understanding of this chapter's material. For more information on how to obtain additional questions, see the Study Guide Features. Answers can be found at the end of this chapter.

1. Which phase of the cloud operations cycle focuses on launching infrastructure and provisioning resources?
   A. Optimize
   B. Secure
   C. Deploy
   D. Sustain

2. What is the primary goal of the Monitor phase in the cloud operations cycle?
   A. Ensure visibility into systems health
   B. Reduce costs
   C. Respond to incidents
   D. Provision resources

3. Which AWS Well-Architected Framework pillar focuses on cost control and resource efficiency?
   A. Reliability
   B. Cost Optimization
   C. Performance Efficiency
   D. Sustainability

4. What is the primary function of the AWS Well-Architected Tool?
   A. Builds architectural patterns
   B. Generates architectures with AI based on a set of requirements
   C. Evaluates workloads against AWS architectural best practices
   D. Monitors billing usage

5. What is the key difference between design principles and best practices in the AWS Well-Architected Framework?
   A. Design principles are strategic guidelines; best practices are actionable techniques
   B. Design principles are optional; best practices are mandatory
   C. Design principles are mandatory; best practices are optional
   D. Design principles are actionable techniques; best practices are strategic guidelines

6. Which practice area of the Operational Excellence pillar focuses on defining team roles and escalation paths?
   - A. Evolve
   - B. Operate
   - C. Prepare
   - D. Organize

7. Which of the following are core responsibilities of a cloud operations engineer? (Select TWO.)
   - A. Architecting workloads
   - B. Developing workloads
   - C. Managing deployments and monitoring workloads
   - D. Ensuring workloads perform reliably

8. Which phase of the cloud operations cycle involves ensuring consistent and reliable performance under varying workloads?
   - A. Deploy
   - B. Optimize
   - C. Sustain
   - D. Monitor

9. What does the Evolve practice area in the Operational Excellence pillar encourage teams to do?
   - A. Launch new workloads
   - B. Encrypt sensitive data
   - C. Monitor system uptime
   - D. Analyze outcomes and improve processes

10. A CloudOps engineer wants to reduce manual intervention during deployment. Which design principle should guide their approach?
    - A. Organize teams around business outcomes
    - B. Safely automate where possible
    - C. Anticipate failure
    - D. Use managed services

11. In what order are the phases of the CloudOps cycle executed?
    - A. Deploy, Monitor, Sustain, Secure, Optimize
    - B. Deploy, Monitor, Secure, Sustain, Optimize
    - C. Deploy, Monitor, Sustain, Optimize, Secure
    - D. Deploy, Monitor, Secure, Optimize, Sustain

12. What is the primary function of a mechanism?
    - A. Enable simplification by removing non-relevant steps in a cloud operations task
    - B. Reduce waste by promoting the use of frugal architectures
    - C. Optimize cost with energy efficient cloud services
    - D. Enable automation by replacing human actions with a scalable and repeatable process

13. Which of the following are general design principles of the AWS Well-Architected Framework? (Select TWO.)
    - A. Automate with architectural experimentation in mind
    - B. Define your system's nonfunctional requirements
    - C. Implement a strong identity foundation
    - D. Consider evolutionary architectures

14. Which of the following are Operational Excellence design principles of the AWS Well-Architected Framework? (Select TWO.)
    - A. Refine operations procedures as needed
    - B. Organize teams around business outcomes
    - C. Make frequent, small, reversible changes
    - D. Avoid failures

15. Which of the following constitute the main focus of the Evolve Operational Excellence practice area? (Select TWO.)
    - A. Failure prevention
    - B. Operational readiness
    - C. Continuous learning
    - D. Iterative improvement

Answers to Review Questions

1. C. The Deploy phase is where the planned architecture is built in the cloud environment. Activities include writing and executing Infrastructure as Code (IaC) templates (like AWS CloudFormation or CDK), configuring resources (servers, storage, networking), migrating data and applications, and performing initial testing to validate that everything is functioning as expected in the new environment. Option A (Optimize) focuses on improving performance and reducing costs after the environment is already live. Option B (Secure) focuses on governance, compliance, and ongoing threat protection rather than initial resource creation. Option D (Sustain) focuses on the day-to-day management, monitoring, and operational health of existing workloads.

2. A. The primary goal of the Monitor phase is to provide real-time visibility and a data-driven understanding of the operational health, availability, and performance of cloud workloads and infrastructure. By continuously collecting and analyzing metrics, logs, and events, organizations can proactively detect and diagnose issues before they impact end users. Other options represent goals of different phases: Option B (Reduce costs) is the central focus of the Optimize phase, which identifies underutilized resources to improve efficiency. Option C (Respond to incidents) is the objective of the Sustain or Operate phase, which uses the data from monitoring to remediate identified problems. Option D (Provision resources) belongs to the Deploy phase, where infrastructure is initially set up and configured.

3. B. The Cost Optimization pillar is specifically designed to help organizations avoid unnecessary expenses and maximize resource efficiency by selecting the most cost-effective resources, right-sizing workloads, and scaling based on demand to achieve business outcomes at the lowest possible price point. In contrast, Option A (Reliability) focuses on the ability of a workload to perform consistently and recover quickly from disruptions rather than financial management. Option C (Performance Efficiency) centers on the efficient use of computing resources to maintain performance as technologies and demands evolve, prioritizing speed and responsiveness over direct cost control. Finally, Option D (Sustainability) focuses on reducing the environmental footprint of cloud workloads by maximizing utilization to decrease energy consumption, which—while often resulting in lower costs—is primarily an ecological rather than a financial objective.

4. C. The primary function of the AWS Well-Architected Tool is to provide a consistent process for measuring and reviewing your cloud architectures against the established design principles and best practices of the AWS Well-Architected Framework. It uses a series of questions across the six pillars to identify high-risk areas and provides an actionable improvement plan to help architects build more secure, resilient, and efficient systems. In contrast, Option A (Builds architectural patterns) is incorrect because the tool is an assessment mechanism for existing or planned designs, not a library for generating pre-built templates or patterns. Option B (Generates architectures with AI based on a set of requirements) is incorrect, as the tool guides humans through a manual or assisted review process to document decisions rather than autonomously generating full architectural diagrams or code from raw requirements. Finally, Option D (Monitors billing usage) is incorrect because financial tracking is the responsibility of services like AWS Billing and Cost Management or AWS Budgets, while the Well-Architected Tool only evaluates the strategy of cost optimization.

5. A. In the AWS Well-Architected Framework, design principles function as high-level, strategic goals—such as "Stop guessing your capacity needs" or "Enable traceability"—that describe the ideal state or mindset for a cloud workload. Best practices are the specific, actionable recommendations or implementation steps (e.g., using Auto Scaling groups or enabling CloudTrail) required to achieve those design goals. Options B (Design principles are optional; best practices are mandatory) and C (Design principles are mandatory; best practices are optional) are both incorrect because the framework is a guide rather than a rigid set of compliance rules; while both are strongly recommended to build a "well-architected" system, they are not strictly "mandatory" in a legal or technical sense unless required by specific organizational policy. Finally, Option D (Design principles are actionable techniques; best practices are strategic guidelines) is incorrect because it reverses the hierarchical definitions provided by AWS.

6. D. The Organize best practice area focuses on how an organization structures its teams and processes to support business outcomes, which specifically includes defining team roles, responsibilities, and clear escalation paths. By ensuring that every team member understands their own role and who to contact when a problem exceeds their authority or capability, an organization can reduce friction and improve the speed of incident response. In contrast, Option A (Evolve) is incorrect because it centers on continuous improvement and learning from operational failures rather than the initial definition of team structures. Option B (Operate) is incorrect, as its primary focus is the day-to-day management and monitoring of live systems to ensure they meet performance and health requirements. Finally, Option C (Prepare) is incorrect because it deals with ensuring that a workload is ready for production, which involves creating runbooks and playbooks and performing operational readiness reviews rather than establishing the high-level team hierarchy.

7. C, D. The correct options are C (Managing deployments and monitoring workloads) and D (Ensuring workloads perform reliably). These roles are considered core responsibilities because cloud operations Engineers are tasked with the "hands-on" day-to-day management of the cloud environment, which involves using automation to deploy resources, maintaining 24/7 visibility into system health through monitoring tools, and troubleshooting incidents to maintain high availability and service quality. In contrast, Option A (Architecting workloads) is incorrect as it is the primary focus of a cloud architect, who designs the high-level strategic blueprints and frameworks rather than managing their daily execution. Similarly, Option B (Developing workloads) is incorrect because it is the responsibility of a cloud developer or software engineer, who focuses on writing application code and building specific software features that run on the cloud infrastructure.

8. C. Maintaining consistent and reliable performance is a key objective of the Sustain phase. Option A (Deploy) focuses on launching resources and building the infrastructure to support a workload in a cloud environment. Option B (Optimize) focuses on reducing costs and maximizing ROI. Option D (Monitor) focuses on tracking metrics and events to gain visibility into health and business impact.

9. D. The correct option is D (Analyze outcomes and improve processes). The Evolve practice area focuses on continuous improvement by encouraging teams to learn from operational events and failures, establishing feedback loops to refine procedures and evolve the workload over time. This approach ensures that lessons learned from post-incident analyses are used to prevent future issues and drive incremental organizational growth. In contrast, Option A (Launch new workloads) is incorrect because it pertains to the Prepare or Deploy phases, which deal with the initial setup and readiness of services. Option B (Encrypt sensitive data) is incorrect as it is a core function of the Security pillar rather than a process improvement area within Operational Excellence. Finally, Option C (Monitor system uptime) is incorrect because it is the primary focus of the Operate practice area, which manages the daily health and visibility of live systems.

10. B. The design principle "Safely automate where possible" is the central guideline for reducing manual intervention in cloud environments. By codifying operational procedures—such as deployments, patching, and resource scaling—teams can eliminate human error, ensure repeatable and consistent results, and allow engineers to focus on higher-value tasks rather than repetitive manual work. In contrast, Option A (Organize teams around business outcomes) is incorrect because it focuses on the structural alignment of personnel

to business goals rather than the technical method of deployment. Option C (Anticipate failure) is incorrect because its primary aim is to build resilient systems that can recover from outages, though automation is often a tool used to achieve that goal. Finally, Option D (Use managed services) is incorrect, as it is a strategy for offloading infrastructure maintenance to a provider, and while it reduces manual effort, it is not the specific design principle that mandates the automation of custom deployment pipelines.

11. A. The correct sequence is "Deploy, Monitor, Sustain, Secure, Optimize," as illustrated in Figure 1.1. The Deploy phase is always the first phase in the cloud operations cycle because it represents the moment when infrastructure, application code, and configurations are introduced into a managed cloud environment. The Optimize phase always takes place after monitoring, sustaining (operating), and securing your workload. This excludes Options C and D from the correct answers. Finally, in the AWS cloud operations model, Sustain/Operate comes before Secure because you cannot meaningfully secure a workload until it is running, observable, and operationally stable. Security is not an abstract layer you bolt on in isolation—it is applied to real systems, with real telemetry, real configuration states, and real operational behaviors. As a result, Option B is incorrect.

12. D. The correct answer is Option D (Enable automation by replacing human actions with a scalable and repeatable process). A mechanism is a "complete process" that ensures consistent results by replacing manual human effort with a systematic, automated, and repeatable virtuous cycle. In contrast, Option A (Enable simplification by removing non-relevant steps ...) is incorrect because simplification is a potential outcome of a process, not the functional definition of the mechanism itself. Option B (Reduce waste by promoting the use of frugal architectures) is incorrect as it describes a specific design goal rather than the underlying structural process. Finally, Option C (Optimize cost with energy efficient cloud services) is incorrect because it identifies a specific objective of the Sustainability pillar rather than the universal definition of a mechanism.

13. A, D. The correct options are A (Automate with architectural experimentation in mind) and D (Consider evolutionary architectures). These are correct because they are two of the six foundational, general design principles meant to guide all cloud architecture by encouraging low-risk testing through automation and building systems that can adapt to future changes. In contrast, Option B (Define your system's nonfunctional requirements) is incorrect because it is a standard engineering task rather than a specific named principle of the framework. Option C (Implement a strong identity foundation) is incorrect because it is a pillar-specific principle belonging to Security rather than a high-level general principle applicable across the entire framework.

14. B, C. The correct options are B (Organize teams around business outcomes) and C (Make frequent, small, reversible changes). These are correct because they are official design principles of the Operational Excellence pillar, focusing on aligning team structures with goals and reducing deployment risk through incremental updates. In contrast, Option A (Refine operations procedures as needed) is incorrect because the official principle mandates refining procedures "frequently" to ensure proactive improvement rather than reactive changes. Option D (Avoid failures) is incorrect because the framework views failures as inevitable; the actual principle is to "anticipate failure" by testing response procedures and learning from events to improve resilience.

15. C, D. The correct options are C (Continuous learning) and D (Iterative improvement), as illustrated in Figure 1.2. These are correct because the Evolve practice area focuses on creating a culture of learning from operational events and dedicating time to incremental, small-scale improvements of systems and procedures. In contrast, Option A (Failure prevention) is incorrect because the framework views failure as inevitable; the goal is to anticipate and learn from failures rather than prevent them entirely. Option B (Operational readiness) is incorrect, as it is the primary focus of the Prepare practice area (also shown in Figure 1.2), which ensures workloads are production-ready before they are launched.

AWS Foundational Elements

THE AWS CERTIFIED CLOUDOPS ENGINEER ASSOCIATE (SOA-C03) EXAM OBJECTIVES COVERED IN THIS CHAPTER MAY INCLUDE, BUT ARE NOT LIMITED TO THE FOLLOWING:

✔ **Domain 2: Reliability and Business Continuity**

- 2.2 Implement highly available and resilient environments

✔ **Domain 3: Deployment, Provisioning, and Automation**

- 3.1 Provision and maintain cloud resources

✔ **Domain 4: Security and Compliance**

- 4.1 Implement and manage security and compliance tools and policies

Amazon Web Services (AWS) offers a vast and resilient cloud ecosystem, and mastering its foundational elements is essential for success in the SOA-C03 certification. This chapter introduces the core building blocks that underpin every AWS environment, starting with the global infrastructure that powers its availability and performance. Understanding Regions, Availability Zones, and AWS Resources is not only critical for designing well-architected solutions—it's also directly tested in the exam's "Reliability and Business Continuity" Domain 2.

Next, we explore landing zones and account structures, which are central to secure Multi-Account governance. The SOA-C03 exam emphasizes best practices for identity boundaries, organizational units (OUs), and service control policies (SCPs), all of which are scaffolded by a well-architected landing zone. Whether you're deploying a single workload or managing enterprise-scale environments, this section equips you with the architectural clarity and governance strategies needed to meet exam objectives.

Security constructs such as IAM roles, IAM policies, service control policies (SCPs), and encryption mechanisms form the backbone of AWS security—and they're heavily featured in SOA-C03's "Security and Compliance" Domain 4. This chapter outlines how to implement least privilege access, defense in depth, protect sensitive data, and align with audit and compliance requirements. These foundational security principles are key exam topics, and a solid understanding of them will help you select the correct answer in several scenario-based exam questions.

Finally, we examine resource hierarchy, tagging strategies, and the AWS Command Line Interface (CLI)—tools that support automation, cost optimization, and operational visibility. The SOA-C03 exam expects candidates to understand how tagging enables governance and how the CLI can be used for deployment, troubleshooting, and scripting. Together, these elements provide the operational fluency needed to navigate real-world AWS environments, and excel in the certification exam.

AWS Global Infrastructure Overview

AWS provides a highly available technology infrastructure platform with multiple locations worldwide. The AWS Cloud is comprised of a large number of data centers distributed in these locations, and grouped in regions and Availability Zones. Each *Region* is a separate geographic area with multiple, distinct locations known as *Availability Zones*.

FIGURE 2.1 AWS Regions and Availability Zones.

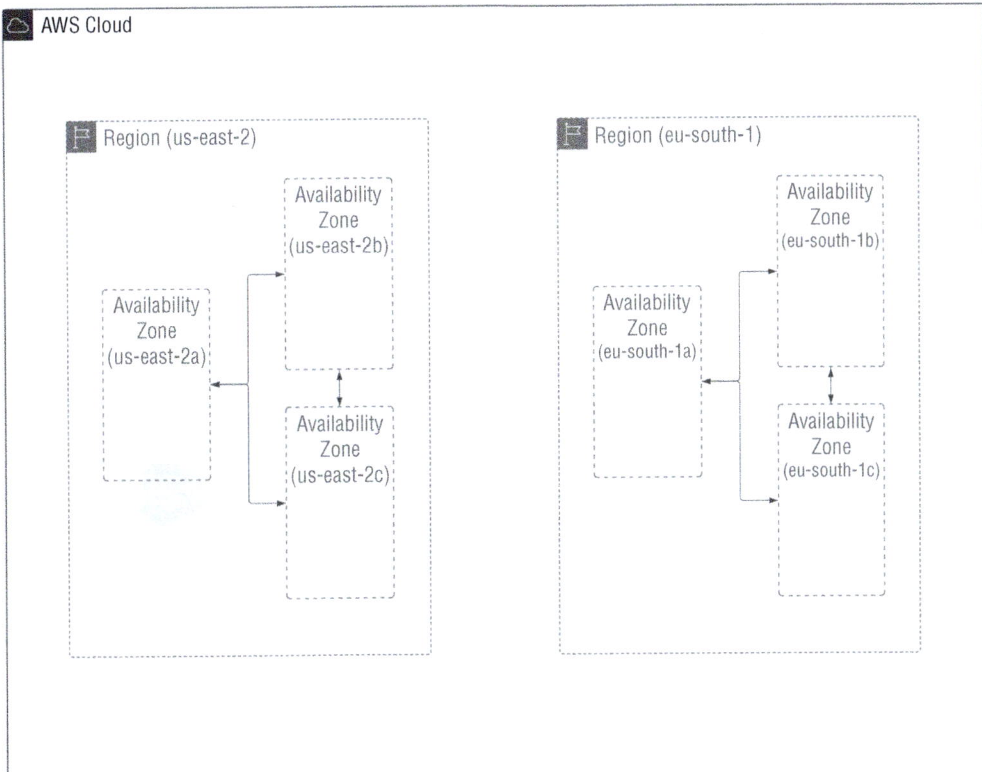

Figure 2.1 illustrates how two regions—`us-east-2` located in USA (Ohio), and `eu-south-1` located in Europe (Milan)—are divided into three Availability Zones each.

As of early-2026, the AWS Cloud spans 120+ Availability Zones within 38+ Geographic Regions. AWS continuously expands its global infrastructure, so check `https://aws.amazon.com/about-aws/global-infrastructure/` for the most current information.

Before diving deeper into AWS Regions and Availability Zones, it's important to understand the concept of an AWS *Resource*. In the context of the SOA-C03 exam, think of a resource as any entity of an AWS service that can be provisioned, configured, and managed to support a workload. With AWS, you can perform the aforementioned operations on a resource manually using the AWS Management Console, or programmatically using tools like the AWS CLI (covered later in the chapter), the AWS SDK (Software Development Kit), or third-party tools like HashiCorp Terraform. Examples of AWS Resources include an Amazon EC2 instance, an IAM user, or an Amazon S3 bucket.

Resources exist to support workloads. A *workload* is a set of interdependent components (code, configurations, and AWS Resources) that together deliver business value. A workload may be a web application, a Machine Learning (ML) pipeline, or a complex enterprise system. The components of a workload typically include compute (e.g., Amazon EC2 instances, AWS Lambda functions), storage (e.g., Amazon S3 buckets, EBS volumes), data (e.g., Amazon RDS databases, DynamoDB tables), and networking (e.g., VPCs, subnets, gateways) resources. For a workload to be resilient and performant, its resources should operate harmoniously across multiple Availability Zones within one or more regions—leveraging the AWS global infrastructure to meet business, compliance, and operational objectives.

The AWS Well-Architected Framework Reliability Pillar recommends deploying all production workloads across at least two Availability Zones. This includes compute (EC2, containers), databases (RDS Multi-AZ), and load balancers. Single-AZ deployments should only be used for non-production environments. To learn more, visit: `https://docs.aws.amazon.com/wellarchitected/latest/framework/rel_fault_isolation_multiaz_region_system.html`

Regions

A Region is a physical geographical area in the world, logically comprised of three or more Availability Zones. Each Region is designed to be completely isolated from all other Regions. This design ensures fault tolerance, data sovereignty, and operational independence—allowing workloads to remain resilient even in the event of a regional disruption. AWS currently operates dozens of Regions across the globe, each offering a consistent set of core services and infrastructure capabilities. When deploying resources, selecting the appropriate Region is a strategic decision that affects latency, compliance, cost, and service availability.

Exam tip: Even though an AWS Region is intentionally isolated from others by design, you can still build Multi-Region architectures by leveraging services like AWS Transit Gateway, VPC Peering, and others. For more details, refer to Chapter 10.

For you—as an AWS CloudOps engineer—understanding the concept of Regions is essential. Many AWS services are Region-specific, meaning their configurations and data do not automatically replicate across regions. This has direct implications for disaster recovery planning, cross-region replication, and global application design. The exam often tests your ability to choose Regions based on business requirements, regulatory constraints, and performance goals.

Availability Zones

An Availability Zone (AZ) is a group of one or more data centers within a Region, each with redundant power, networking, and connectivity. AZs are physically separated (max 100 km/62 miles from each other) to minimize the risk of correlated failures, yet they are close enough to support synchronous replication and low-latency communication. All AZs within a Region are interconnected through high-bandwidth, low-latency networking built on fully redundant, dedicated metro fiber. This AZs interconnectivity provides high-throughput performance and encrypted traffic between zones. Additionally, all AZs within a Region connect to the Internet through two separate transit centers, where AWS peers with multiple Tier-1 ISPs (Internet Service Providers). This architectural design allows AWS customers to build highly available and fault-tolerant applications by distributing resources across multiple AZs. For example, deploying EC2 instances in separate AZs can protect against data center outages, while maintaining seamless service continuity.

Availability Zones play a key role in building reliable, secure, and high-performing systems—all skills that are essential for mastering AWS Cloud operations and passing the SOA-C03 exam. The exam often tests your ability to design resilient architectures using Multi-AZ deployments, especially for services like Amazon RDS, ELB (Elastic Load Balancing), and auto-scaling. You'll need to recognize how AZs contribute to high availability, disaster recovery, and performance optimization. Additionally, knowing which AWS services support AZ-level configuration—and how to leverage that for fault isolation—is essential for passing scenario-based questions and applying these principles in real-world environments.

For a complete list of AZs, visit: `https://docs.aws.amazon.com/global-infrastructure/latest/regions/aws-availability-zones.html`

Resources

Resources were introduced at the beginning of this section as the core entities that make up any AWS workload. These include compute instances, storage buckets, database instances, networking gateways, and many other service-specific entities.

In AWS, each resource is uniquely identified by an *Amazon Resource Name (ARN)*, a standardized string that encodes its partition, service, Region, account, and type.

For example:

- The EC2 instance `MyEC2instance` in the `us-east-1` Region, owned by the AWS account `123456789012` is denoted by the ARN: `arn:aws:ec2:us-east-1:123456789012:instance/MyEC2instance`
- The IAM role `MyRole` owned by the AWS account `123456789012` is denoted by the ARN: `arn:aws:iam::123456789012:role/MyRole`

This format follows the standard ARN structure:

```
arn:partition:service:region:account-id:resource-type/resource-id
```

Let's break down each component:

- `arn`: Fixed prefix identifying this as an Amazon Resource Name
- `partition`: `aws` for commercial AWS Regions, `aws-cn` for AWS China Regions, `aws-us-gov` for AWS GovCloud (US) Regions, and `aws-eusc` for AWS European Sovereign Cloud
- `service`: The AWS service namespace (e.g., `ec2`, `s3`, `iam`)
- `region`: The AWS Region code (e.g., `us-east-1`)—empty for global services
- `account-id`: The 12-digit AWS account ID
- `resource-type/resource-id`: Varies by service; identifies the specific resource

You may have noticed the latter ARN has no Region in its string. This is because the `MyRole` resource is an entity of the AWS IAM service, which is a global service, not regional. The next section explains this notion in detail.

The concept of AWS account will be introduced shortly. For the time being, think of an AWS account as a container of AWS Resources and services, serving as the primary boundary for billing, IAM, and resource ownership.

Control Plane and Data Plane

Each AWS Resource is provisioned and managed through AWS's exposed APIs, which are accessed via the AWS Management Console, the AWS CLI, the AWS SDK, or Infrastructure-as-Code (IaC) tools like AWS CloudFormation, or HashiCorp Terraform. These interactions occur through the *control plane*, which governs the lifecycle of AWS Resources (i.e., how resources are created/read/updated/deleted/listed (CRUDL), configured, tagged, and secured).

Once provisioned, resources operate within the *data plane*, where actual workload execution takes place—such as reading from an S3 bucket, processing data in an EC2 instance, or transmitting packets through a VPC. This separation between control and data planes is foundational to AWS's architecture, and it directly impacts how services behave, scale, and recover.

Fault Isolation Boundaries

In AWS, every resource—whether it's an Amazon EC2 instance, an Amazon S3 bucket, or an AWS Lambda function—is an instantiation of a service, and thus inherits the fault tolerance behavior of that service. This inheritance is critical to understanding how failures propagate (or don't) across the cloud infrastructure.

AWS services are architected with different *fault isolation boundaries*, which define the scope within which a failure is contained (i.e., its blast radius), and beyond which operations remain unaffected. These boundaries are not arbitrary—they reflect deliberate design choices made by AWS that balance performance, cost, and resilience.

Table 2.1 shows how AWS service types are mapped to fault isolation boundaries.

Figure 2.2 illustrates an example of the fault isolation boundaries for the services: AWS IAM, Amazon S3, and Amazon EC2 with respect to the `us-east-2` and `eu-south-1` Regions.

TABLE 2.1 Fault Isolation Boundaries by AWS Service Type

Service Type (Fault Isolation Boundary)	Scope of Fault	Example Services	How You Use for Resilience
Zonal	Single-AZ	Amazon EC2, Amazon EBS	Launch instances across multiple AZs and distribute traffic with an Application Load Balancer (ALB).
Regional	Multiple AZs in a Region	Amazon S3, Amazon DynamoDB, Amazon SQS, Elastic Load Balancing (ELB)	The service automatically handles AZ failure. For Multi-Region resilience, you build your own replication and failover strategy across regions.
Global	Multiple Regions	AWS IAM, Amazon Route 53, Amazon CloudFront	The service is highly resilient and managed by AWS. Design your application to avoid dependencies on a single service control plane.

FIGURE 2.2 AWS service types.

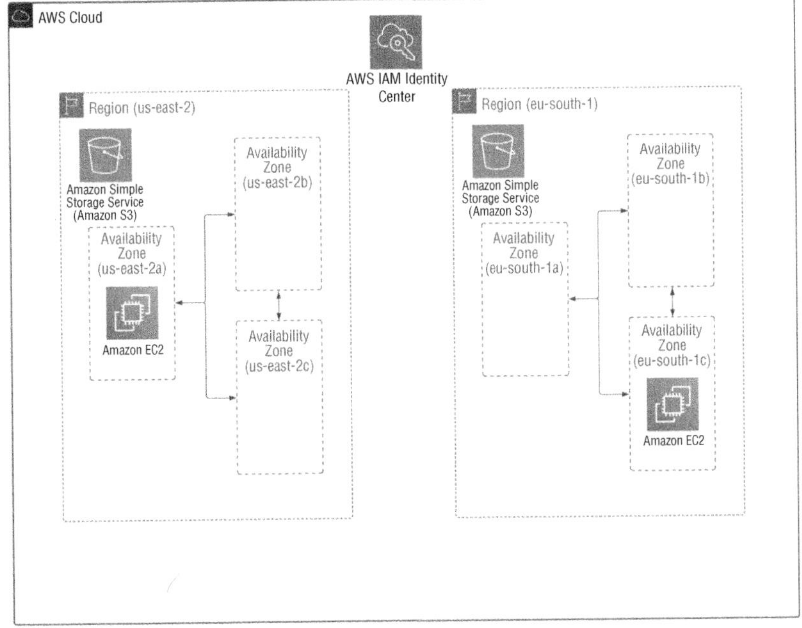

As a CloudOps engineer, understanding how resources inherit these boundaries—and how they interact across the control and data planes—is essential for designing resilient architectures, troubleshooting effectively, and aligning with AWS operational best practices.

For more information, visit: `https://docs.aws.amazon.com/whitepapers/latest/aws-fault-isolation-boundaries/aws-service-types.html`

Landing Zones and Account Structures

Beyond physical infrastructure (Regions, AZs, and Resources), AWS provides logical architecture for access control, ownership, operations, and cost management. This section covers how resources are structured, secured, and managed across organizations—critical topics for SOA-C03.

So far, we've explored how AWS Regions and AZs provide fault isolation boundaries, enabling fault-tolerance, high-availability and resilience. We've seen how resources like Amazon EC2 instances and Amazon S3 buckets are deployed into these AZs, inheriting the durability and latency characteristics of their services. But infrastructure alone doesn't define operational control. To manage resources effectively, AWS introduces a logical isolation boundary: the AWS account.

Accounts

An AWS *account* is the atomic unit of ownership, access control, and billing in AWS. Any resource is created within an account, and that account determines:

- Who can access the resource (via IAM identities and IAM policies).
- Who owns and manages it (via control plane operations).
- Who pays for it (via consolidated billing or per-account charges).

Let's elaborate more the aforementioned concepts:

Ownership. An AWS account is the definitive owner of all resources provisioned within it. Every resource, such as an Amazon S3 bucket or an Amazon EC2 instance, is uniquely identified by its Amazon Resource Name (ARN) that includes the account ID of its owner. The account's root user, associated with the email used to create it, holds ultimate ownership and control.

Access Control. An AWS account serves as a rigid security and access control boundary. By default, no access is allowed between different AWS accounts. Access control is managed through the AWS Identity and Access Management (IAM) service, which is scoped to a Single-Account. To grant access to resources in another account, you must explicitly configure cross-account permissions. This isolation is a cornerstone of the AWS Well-Architected Framework's Security Pillar you learned in Chapter 1, as it limits the blast radius of a potential security breach.

Billing. An AWS account is the primary unit for cost allocation. All charges for resources are attributed to the specific account in which they are used. In a Multi-Account setup with AWS Organizations (discussed shortly), the billing for all member accounts is consolidated under a single management account, but cost data can still be tracked and analyzed on a per-account basis.

Every AWS account has a single *root user* that has full permissions to all AWS Resources in the account by default. As a security best practice, we recommend that you never use the root user except for a few tasks that explicitly require a root user's permissions.

Single-Account vs. Multi-Account

As your organization grows, you might wonder: should we stick with one AWS account, use a few, or set up many? Managing just one account might seem easier for a CloudOps engineer—but that's not the best practice. In fact, AWS recommends using multiple accounts to improve security, organization, and scalability. This practice aligns with the first design principle of the Security pillar: "Implement a strong identity foundation," which essentially advocates separation of duties and the principle of least privilege.

If you think about it, this totally makes sense. Why would you want to delegate so many responsibilities to one Single-Account when you have a large organization to manage in AWS? A single AWS account results in a single point of failure, and won't allow your organization to scale efficiently as new business units are incorporated in your organization—each with different security, financial, and operational requirements.

Managing Multi-Accounts

While an AWS account provides the atomic isolation boundary for ownership, access control, and billing, AWS provides services to manage and govern a collection of accounts centrally. This centralization aspect addresses the significant administrative challenges that arise as organizations scale their cloud footprint from a few accounts to dozens or even hundreds. Instead of managing each account in a silo, central governance services like AWS Organizations and AWS Control Tower create an overarching framework to enforce policies, manage identities, and track costs across the entire enterprise from a single pane of glass. These two services are in scope for the SOA-C03 exam, and a solid understanding of what they do and how they work is required to pass the exam.

Before deep diving into AWS Organizations and AWS Control Tower, we need to introduce the concept of a *landing zone*, which serves as the basic, well-architected starting point for an organization's cloud journey, allowing them to quickly and confidently deploy workloads while maintaining security and compliance.

Landing Zones

According to AWS, a *landing zone* is *a well-architected, Multi-Account AWS environment that is scalable and secure.* Just as an airport's landing zone provides a scalable (multiple aircrafts can land and take off at different times), and secure space for aircrafts (strict security controls are in place to prevent unauthorized access to an aircraft), a cloud landing zone provides a scalable and secure environment for your cloud workloads. Without a landing zone, scaling on the cloud can become chaotic, with inconsistent security, manual processes, limited automation, and elevated risks. A landing zone provides the following benefits:

- **Automated governance:** Guardrails are automatically enforced to prevent or detect non-compliant activities.
- **Standardized security:** All accounts and workloads are subject to a consistent security baseline.
- **Centralized logging:** Logs from all accounts are consolidated into a dedicated, secure logging account for easy auditing and monitoring.
- **Simplified identity management:** User access is managed centrally, often integrated with an organization's existing identity provider (IdP) (e.g., Microsoft Entra ID, Okta, and so on).
- **Streamlined account provisioning:** The process of creating new, pre-configured accounts is also automated, speeding up developer workflows.
- **Cost visibility and control:** A unified billing structure provides clear cost allocation, and policies can prevent costly misconfigurations.

AWS Organizations

AWS Organizations is a managed service intended to help you centrally manage and govern your cloud environment, as your cloud footprint scales. This service allows you to automate the creation of new AWS accounts with a predefined baseline configuration, provision resources, group accounts in alignment with your organization business needs, and enforce policies to (groups of) accounts for governance.

With AWS Organizations you no longer have to manage your accounts on a one-by-one basis. This service enables you to administer accounts as a single unit, referred to as an *Organizational Unit (OU).*

There are two types of accounts in an organization: a *management account* and one or more *member accounts.* Your workloads typically reside in member accounts, with the exception of some centrally managed processes that are owned by either the management account, or other accounts assigned as delegated administrators for specific AWS services.

Management Account The management account serves as the authoritative owner of the organization, holding overarching control over its security, infrastructure, and financial policies. It functions as the payer account, bearing responsibility for all charges incurred by member accounts within the organization.

Member Account A member account refers to any AWS account within an organization that is not the management account. As an organization administrator, you can create new member accounts or invite existing ones to join. You also have the ability to apply policies that govern the behavior and access of these accounts.

A member account can belong to only one organization at a time.

This separation of duties (management account vs. member accounts) enables you to structure your accounts in a meaningful way, in alignment with your organization business, technical, and operational objectives. For example, you can provide tools and access for your security team to holistically manage your organization security needs. You can also consolidate access to shared services (e.g., Directory Services, Domain Name System, and so on) in accounts for the infrastructure team. You can model your OUs based on a workload environment (development, preproduction, production).

Moreover, AWS Organizations provides predefined policies that enable you to enforce security controls to all the OUs of your organization. These policies are covered in the upcoming sections in this chapter.

AWS Control Tower

AWS Control Tower expands on the foundation of AWS Organizations by offering a delivery mechanism to building a landing zone for your organization. Since AWS Control Tower is a fully managed service, you can quickly launch a governed and well-architected AWS Multi-Account environment that includes centralized logging, IAM, and baseline security controls. This process can be executed from the console, or programmatically using IaC (Infrastructure-as-Code).

A key feature of AWS Control Tower is the *Account Factory*, a self-service portal that automates the provisioning of new AWS accounts. Each account is created with standardized configurations, including networking, logging, and security baselines, tailored to your organization needs. This ensures consistency across environments and reduces the operational overhead of manual setup. AWS Control Tower also integrates with AWS Service Catalog, enabling organizations to offer curated resources and templates to their teams.

With reference to the previous example (in the AWS Organizations section), Figure 2.3 illustrates how you can use the Account Factory feature of AWS Control Tower—as a user of the management account—to create five different accounts in your organization:

- Log Archive Account
- Security Tooling Account
- Shared Services Account
- Network Account
- Application Account

FIGURE 2.3 A landing zone provisioned by AWS Control Tower.

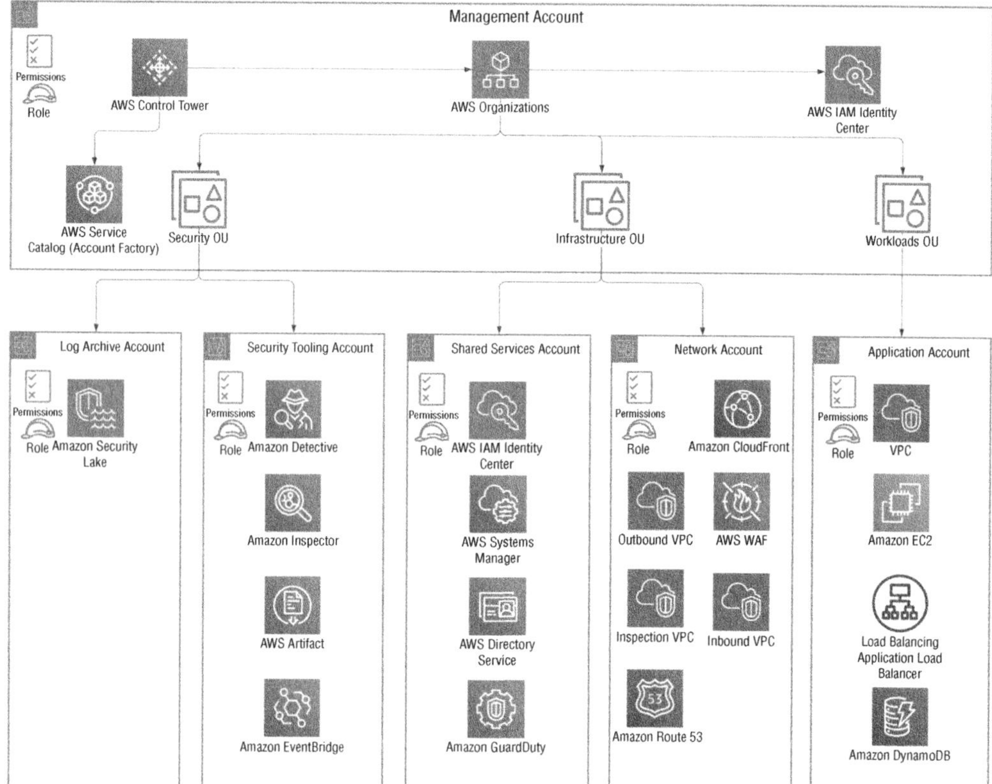

Each account is automatically created with a predefined set of baselines specific to the OU it belongs to. These baselines are comprised of controls—or rules—and can be preventive or detective. Preventive controls are implemented by using service control policies (SCPs, covered in the next section), which are a part of AWS Organizations. Detective controls are implemented by using AWS Config. Examples of AWS Control Tower controls include:

- Disallow creation of access keys for the root user
- Disallow Internet-accessible subnets
- Disallow Internet connection through RDP
- Disallow public write access to Amazon S3 buckets
- Disallow Amazon EBS volumes that are unattached to an Amazon EC2 instance

Figure 2.4 shows the Account Factory page from the AWS Management Console. As you can see on the Network Configuration pane, the current AWS Control Tower setup already includes a few controls, which constrain the VPCs (Virtual Private Cloud networks) of newly created accounts.

When you click the Create Account button, the page shown in Figure 2.5 is displayed.

FIGURE 2.4 Account Factory page.

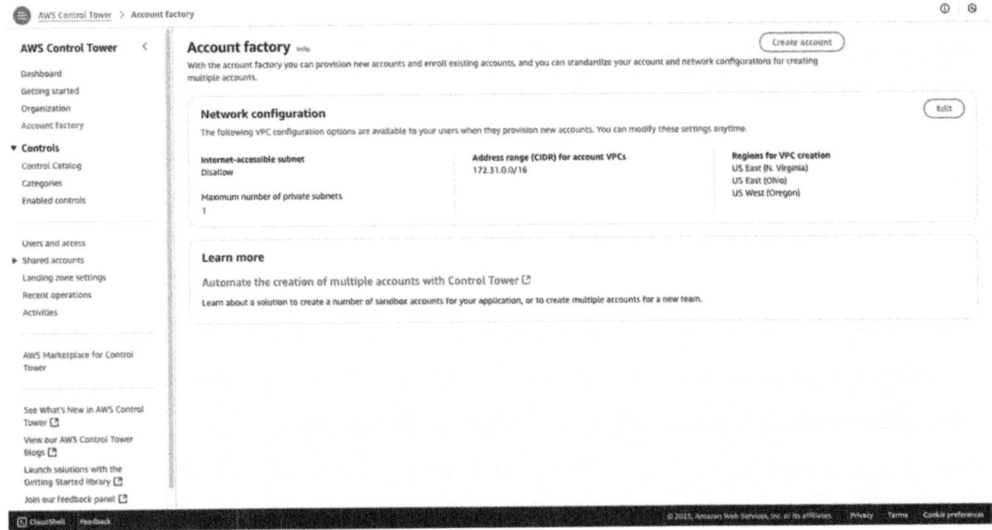

FIGURE 2.5 Account creation page.

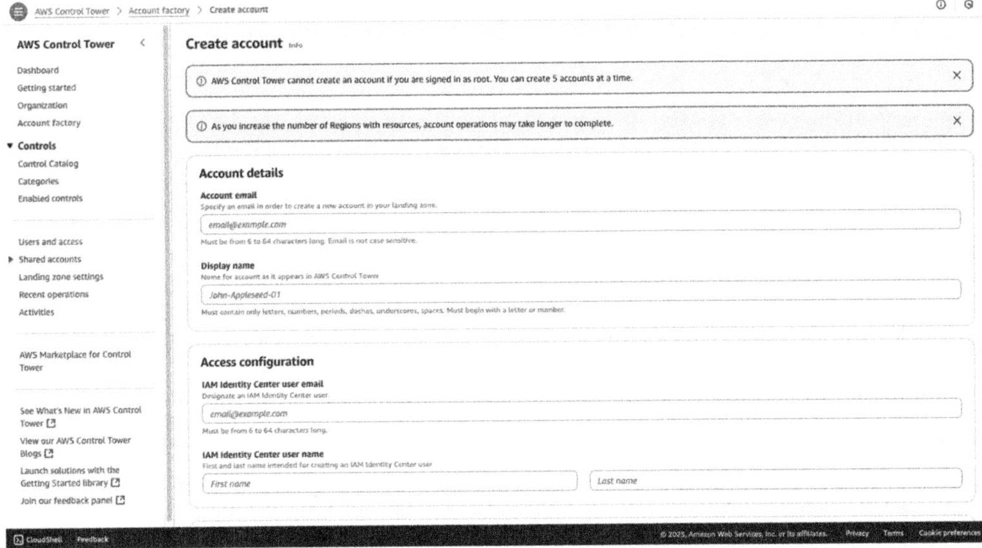

From this page you can specify a few mandatory fields, including (but not limited to): account email, display name, IAM Identity Center user email, IAM Identity Center user first and last name. You will use your IAM Identity Center user email to access your newly created account.

AWS Control Tower is a starting point for a landing zone. It's your job as a CloudOps engineer to determine your organization strategy for networking, access management, and security based on your unique requirements as you build your landing zone.

Foundational Security Constructs

AWS states that "security is our top priority" and as a CloudOps engineer it is your top priority as well. As mentioned in Chapter 1, security is a core pillar of the Well-Architected Framework. There is no single tool or service to fully secure your AWS account and applications. Security should be applied in all layers across your resources and accounts. Understanding how to properly secure workloads, identities, infrastructure, and data on AWS with the appropriate mechanism is a critical task as a CloudOps engineer.

Shared Responsibility Model

Security and compliance in the cloud is a partnership between you and AWS. Security is everyone's responsibility, from security engineers to developers and CloudOps engineers. When running workloads in the cloud, it can be confusing to identify what AWS takes care of for you, and what you are responsible for as a CloudOps engineer. To help understand where these different responsibilities are applied, AWS utilizes a shared responsibility model when it comes to securing workloads in the cloud.

Figure 2.6 illustrates the AWS Shared Responsibility Model. The model is split into two distinct sections separating what AWS is responsible for in securing and administering your workloads on the cloud, and the responsibilities that fall on you. As you can see, AWS is responsible for the security "of the cloud" and you are responsible for security "in the cloud."

Take a look at the bottom half of this model and what security "of the cloud" means. AWS protects the infrastructure, encompassing the hardware, software, networking and facilities that the AWS Cloud runs on. Let's take running a workload in an on-premises managed data center. You would be responsible for patching your network devices, securing access to the facility, replacing failed drives, and physically wiring everything up. In the cloud, these are all things that AWS takes on the responsibility for as a cloud provider.

Looking at the top half of this model, what is security "in the cloud?" AWS provides the services, but it is up to you what services you select and how they are configured and used. For example, look at Amazon Elastic Compute Cloud (EC2). AWS is responsible for the hardware, hypervisor, and providing a means to administer your EC2 instances, but it's your responsibility to secure the instance itself. You are responsible for choosing the operating system and keeping it patched, using necessary encryption for your data, controlling access to and from your instance using AWS provided security group firewalls or controlling who has access to your AWS account and its resources. Understanding this watermark of responsibility is key to securing and managing your workloads on AWS.

FIGURE 2.6 AWS Shared Responsibility Model.

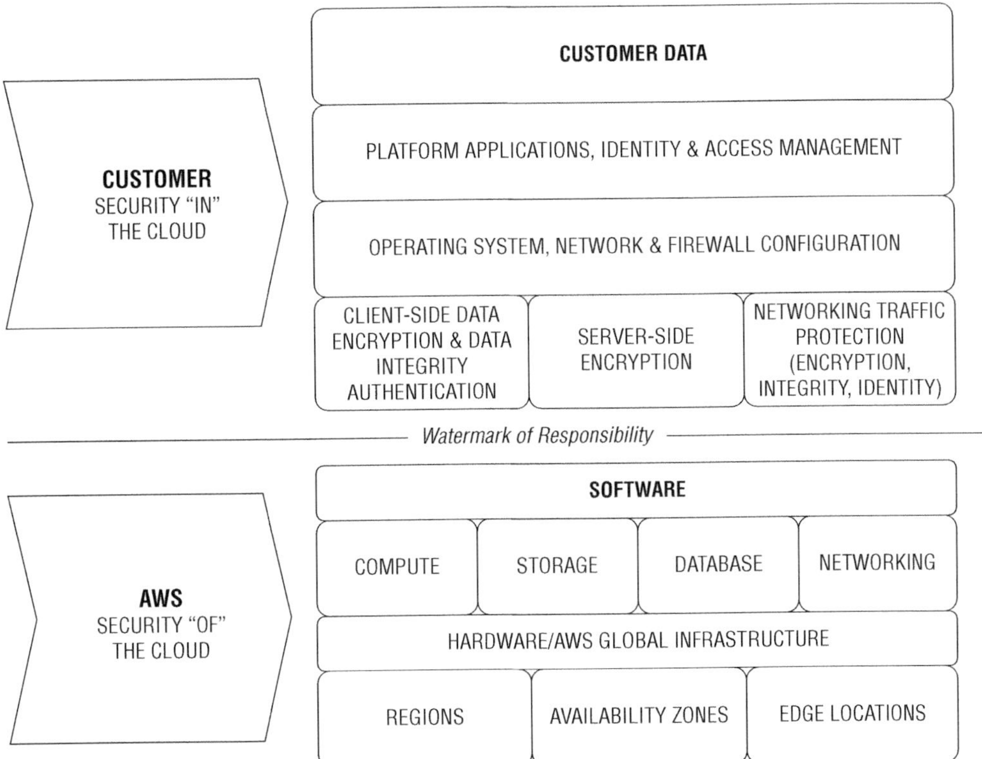

As you move across AWS services, the balance of operational duties shifts: the more managed the service, the more AWS lifts the operational burden. Fully managed offerings like Amazon Relational Database Service (Amazon RDS) push the customer's *watermark of responsibility* higher—as you can see in Figure 2.7—reducing the need to manage underlying infrastructure while still requiring strong governance of identities, permissions, and data access. This natural progression sets the stage for the next section—Identity and Access Management (IAM)—where controlling *who* can do *what* in your AWS environment becomes the core of secure and effective operations.

Identity and Access Management (IAM)

Securing access to your workloads in AWS is a top priority of a CloudOps engineer. AWS Identity and Access Management (IAM) is a foundational service that controls authentication, authorization, and how you centrally manage that access. Through AWS IAM you can create, manage, and control authentication and authorization of all access to your account and underlying resources. AWS IAM is an extremely powerful service to control and secure your landing zone(s) with several tools to administer users, groups,

FIGURE 2.7 Alternate AWS Shared Responsibility Model.

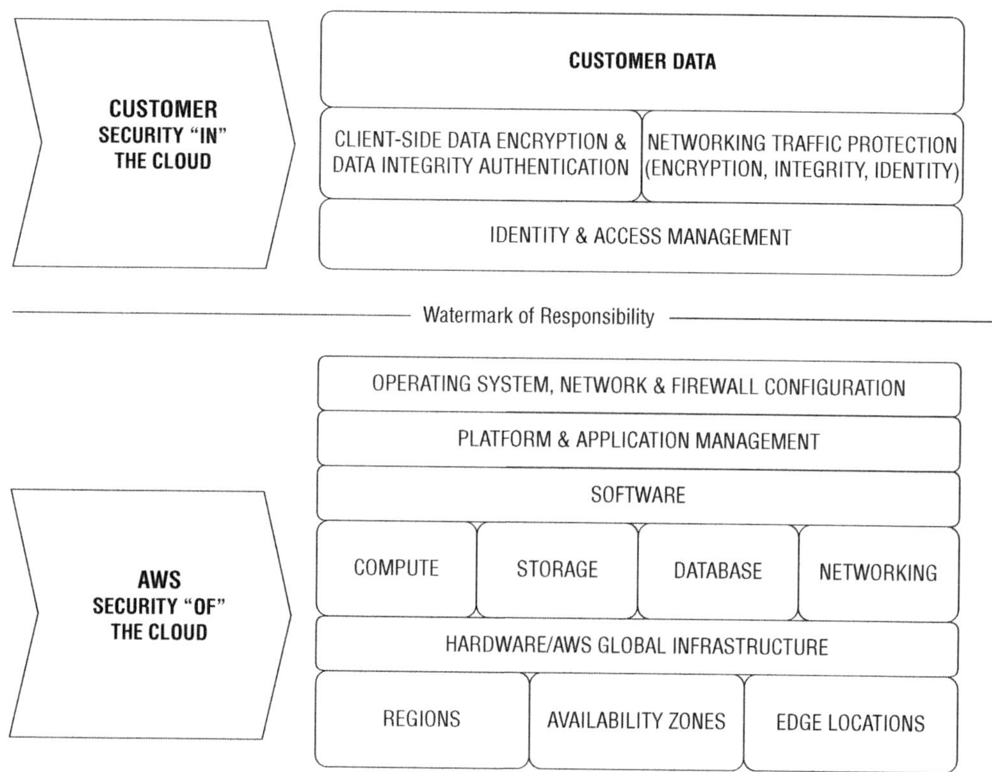

policies, roles, access keys, IdP integrations, Multi-Factor Authentication (MFA) and analysis.

Every AWS account has a *root user* that comes with default credentials for logging in and managing your resources.

The root user for an AWS account is the highest-privilege identity within that account. Do not use the root user for daily management of your AWS accounts!

The root user has full access to your account and should be protected at all costs, using MFA (covered in Chapter 9) and a secure password. Unless you are performing tasks that require root user privileges, you should create other IAM users and roles and use those instead. If using AWS Organizations, you can even remove root user credentials from your member accounts to further protect them. Some tasks, however, do require the use of the root user, such as:

- Closing your AWS account
- Restoring IAM permissions and no other user can be used
- Changing certain account settings restricted to the root user
- Viewing tax invoices and doing some billing tasks

All access to your account and its resources needs to be tightly controlled with a least privileged design philosophy. Any person or service accessing your AWS account should have only the permissions they need and nothing else. AWS IAM allows you to achieve this using several different constructs, we discuss in detail in the following section.

IAM Policies

AWS *IAM policies* are JSON documents that are used to define and manage permissions to IAM resources in AWS. They are the fundamental mechanism for controlling access to your AWS account and resources. Understanding how to read, write, and troubleshoot IAM policies is essential for a CloudOps engineer. An IAM policy is a formal statement of one or more permissions that define *who* can access resources, *what* actions they can perform, *which* resources they can access, and under what *conditions* they can access them. Policies explicitly allow or deny actions to services and resources.

```
{
    "Version": "2012-10-17",
    "Statement": [
        {
            "Effect": "Allow",
            "Action": [
                "s3:*",
                "ec2:Describe*"
            ],
            "Resource": "*"
        }
    ]
}
```

So, what does a policy look like? The previous example shows an IAM policy document. In the policy you define your statement and set an `Effect` of either `Allow` or `Deny`. This is going to be defined if the following actions are being allowed or restricted on the resources defined. From there, you define a list of actions (or verbs) that you want to allow or deny. In this case we are allowing full access to all Amazon S3 service actions with `"s3:*"` and all Amazon EC2 `Describe` operations. As you can see, IAM actions are formatted as `"service:action"`. A full list of services and actions can be found in the AWS documentation. Wild cards are supported as well. Therefore, you can define all actions for a service with `"*"` or a subset of actions as we showed. Next, you define which resources the actions are applied to—in other words, the object(s) the actions use as targets. In the previous example, we allow `"s3:*"` and `"ec2:Describe*"` on all resources with `"*"`.

This example demonstrates IAM policy's syntax. In production environments, always follow the principle of least privilege by specifying only required actions and limiting resources to specific ARNs. For example:

- Instead of `"s3:*"`, use specific actions like `"s3:GetObject"` and `"s3:PutObject"`.
- Instead of `"Resource": "*"`, specify bucket ARNs like `"arn:aws:s3:::my-bucket/*"`.
- Regularly review and refine permissions using IAM Access Analyzer (covered in Chapter 9).

There are a few types of policies. When working with IAM users, groups, and roles, you can apply an *inline policy*. An inline policy is one that is embedded directly into a single user, group, or role.

IAM Users, Groups, and Roles

As discussed in the IAM section, every AWS account comes with a root user by default, which should be heavily protected and used only when strictly necessary. An *IAM user* is a resource construct that allows you to create individual identities that represent a person or an application that interacts with AWS. Every IAM user is a distinct resource with a unique Amazon Resource Name (ARN), its own set of security credentials (like a password or access keys), and specific permissions assigned via policies. Each user has different policies assigned to them for what they need to access, too. You can define if a user should have console access or just API access, create and revoke security credentials for API access, and assign IAM policies. AWS best practices recommend to require Multi-Factor Authentication (MFA) for users, as well as a password rotation policy in line with your organization's security posture. You can easily disable user accounts and their credentials too, and see the time they were used.

Managing many users and their access permission individually is cumbersome. When managing IAM users, you should group users with similar access permissions into *IAM groups*, which are a collection of IAM users that can be managed together consistently. Instead of attaching policies directly to each user, you can group users together and assign policies at the group level. This simplifies permission management because you only assign policies once to a group, and then just add users to the group(s) they need to be in, based on their job function and permission needs.

You cannot nest groups and assign a group to another group, but you can assign an IAM user to multiple groups.

For example, you might establish a Developers group with comprehensive access to development environments while explicitly restricting access to production. By creating an IAM group named "Developers" and attaching a managed IAM policy, you can grant full access to resources specifically tagged as "development." This approach implements a Role-Based Access Control (RBAC) strategy, ensuring that permissions are governed by functional requirements rather than individual user configurations.

IAM users are long-lived constructs that once their access is provisioned, it's in place unless revoked. There is always a threat that their access keys or passwords get exposed, or their account is compromised. Also, most organizations already have an Identity Provider (IdP) in place, such as Microsoft Entra ID for user management. Sometimes you need to let a user from another AWS account access your resources, or you need an AWS service to perform actions in your account on your behalf. This is where IAM roles come in.

An *IAM role* is an identity with specific permissions that can be assumed by trusted entities. Unlike IAM users, roles do not have permanent credentials. Instead, they use temporary security credentials when they are assumed. IAM roles do not have passwords or access keys, and they are defined based on the functions they need to perform on behalf of someone else. A role is a persona that you define, such as Developer, Administrator, Database Administrator, or CloudOps engineer. Each IAM role has specific IAM policies assigned to them based on the access required to perform a specific function or task, following the principle of least privilege.

To set up an IAM role, you need two distinct types of policies:

- **Trust policy:** This defines who is allowed to use the role. The specific entity (like an EC2 instance or a user) that needs to "wear the hat" dictates what goes in this policy.
- **Permission policy:** This defines what that entity is allowed to do once they have assumed the role.

For example, let's say you have an AWS EC2 compute resource that needs to write data to an S3 bucket. Instead of creating an IAM user with long-lived security credentials, you would create an IAM role with a policy that only allows the ability to write to the necessary S3 bucket. You would then assign the following Trust policy:

```
{
    "Version": "2012-10-17",
    "Statement": [
        {
            "Effect": "Allow",
            "Principal": {
                "Service": "ec2.amazonaws.com"
            },
            "Action": "sts:AssumeRole"
        }
    ]
}
```

Before examining the Trust policy, let's understand the *Principal* element. A principal is the entity that is allowed or denied access to a resource. Put simply, a principal is the "who." Principals can be:

- AWS accounts (identified by account ID)
- IAM users or roles (identified by ARN)
- AWS services (identified by service name like `ec2.amazonaws.com`)
- Federated users (from external identity providers)

This Trust policy works like a standard IAM policy, but its job is to define who can "wear the hat" (i.e., who can assume the role). Here, it allows the principal `ec2.amazonaws.com` to perform the `sts:AssumeRole` action. Essentially, you are giving EC2 permission to step into this role and use its permissions. Now that you have this role created with the proper trust relationship, you assign this IAM role to your EC2 instance(s) that need access to that S3 bucket. The EC2 instance then can assume this role and generate temporary credentials to perform the necessary actions on the S3 bucket.

The following snippet shows the Permission policy that you would attach to the IAM role. It defines exactly which actions the IAM role can take on the S3 bucket.

```
{
    "Version": "2012-10-17",
    "Statement": [
        {
            "Sid": "AllowListBucket",
            "Effect": "Allow",
            "Action": "s3:ListBucket",
            "Resource": "arn:aws:s3:::my-example-bucket"
        },
        {
            "Sid": "AllowObjectActions",
            "Effect": "Allow",
            "Action": [
                "s3:GetObject",
                "s3:PutObject"
            ],
            "Resource": "arn:aws:s3:::my-example-bucket/*"
        }
    ]
}
```

There are a few observations that are relevant to the SOA-C03 exam:

- **Resource ARN:** Notice there are two different resource ARNs. You need the bucket ARN (`arn:aws:s3:::my-bucket`) for bucket-level actions like `ListBucket`, and the "slash-star" ARN (`arn:aws:s3:::my-bucket/*`) for object-level actions like `GetObject` or `PutObject`.
- **Identity-based:** Unlike the Trust policy, this policy does not have a `Principal` element because it is attached directly to the principal (the IAM role).

- **Least Privilege:** As mentioned earlier, only the necessary actions (`GetObject`, `PutObject`) are included rather than using `s3:*`, which follows AWS security best practices.

There are several uses for IAM roles other than AWS services like Amazon EC2, AWS Lambda, Amazon RDS, and so on. You can also create trust relationships that allow other AWS accounts the ability to assume an IAM role. For instance, AWS Control Tower requires the ability to assume roles in each enrolled member account to perform governance actions and collect configuration data. AWS Control Tower automatically creates the necessary cross-account roles—such as the `AWSControlTowerExecution` role in each member account—and configures the Trust policy so that the management account (or delegated administrator) can assume these roles. You do not create these roles manually; AWS Control Tower provisions and manages them for you, as part of the landing zone creation.

Put differently, the `AWSControlTowerExecution` role that AWS Control Tower creates inside each enrolled member account has a Trust policy that names the Management Account as the principal allowed to assume it.

```
{
  "Version": "2012-10-17",
  "Statement": [
    {
      "Effect": "Allow",
      "Principal": {
        "AWS": "arn:aws:iam::<management-account-id>:role/AWSControlTowerAdmin"
      },
      "Action": "sts:AssumeRole"
    }
  ]
}
```

AWS Control Tower uses this cross-account access to apply guardrails, collect configuration data, and orchestrate governance actions on each member account enrolled in the organization.

Like most organizations do, let's assume you utilize an IdP like Microsoft Entra ID to manage SSO login across applications in your environment. Instead of creating and managing separate AWS accounts for each employee, you can create IAM roles that match your users' needs and configure your IdP as an identity provider in AWS IAM. Once your IdP is configured, you can then create IAM roles for each employee need, such as developers, administrators, security engineers, and so on. Each role would have a Trust policy that defines a principal of type `Federated` that points to the IdP provider resource.

Service Control Policies (SCPs)

As a cloud engineer you are responsible for your entire AWS environment, not just specific services or resources. As we discussed in the previous section on account management with AWS Organizations, when managing and deploying accounts on AWS you can apply preventive controls on accounts by using *service control policies (SCPs)*. Service control policies are an organizational permission policy you can apply to individual accounts, or organizational units, that allow you to provide guardrails on what permissions can be granted to IAM resources in an account. SCPs themselves do not grant any permissions, but set guardrail restrictions on what permissions can be granted through IAM policies. Put differently, SCPs set limitations on the levels of access that can be granted at different layers of your organization. When evaluating user and role access in AWS, think of service control policies as a filter that all policies are run through.

By default, when you enable service control policies a managed SCP named `FullAWSAccess` is attached at every OU and account, which allows all services and actions. If you remove this policy without replacing it, all actions at that level of the organization will be blocked. There are two strategies in how you can apply SCPs policies.

One method, as shown in Figure 2.8, is an *Explicit Allow* strategy. With this strategy, all actions and resources are prohibited by default, and you have to explicitly allow any permissions. To implement this, you would remove the default `FullAWSAccess` SCP policy applied to the account or organization unit and create new policies with specific allow statements for the actions and resources they apply to. The following example shows an SCP that only allows the creation of EC2 resources in the `us-east-1` Region:

FIGURE 2.8 Explicit Allow flow.

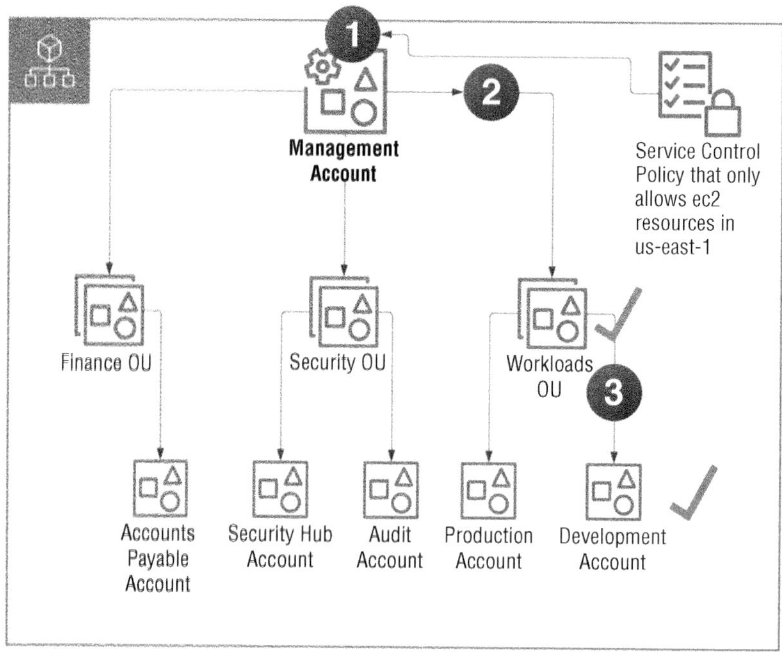

```
{
  "Version": "2012-10-17",
  "Statement": [
    {
      "Sid": "AllowEC2CreationInUsEast1",
      "Effect": "Allow",
      "Action": [
        "ec2:RunInstances",
        "ec2:CreateVolume",
        "ec2:CreateSnapshot",
        "ec2:CreateLaunchTemplate",
        "ec2:CreateLaunchTemplateVersion"
      ],
      "Resource": "*",
      "Condition": {
        "StringEquals": {
          "aws:RequestedRegion": "us-east-1"
        }
      }
    }
  ]
}
```

The other method is the *Explicit Deny* strategy. With this strategy all actions on all resources are allowed by default, and you specifically deny the actions on resources you want to prohibit. To implement this, you leave the default `FullAWSAccess` SCP policy in place and add policies that explicitly deny actions on resources. The following example shows an SCP that limits the ability to create S3 buckets outside the `eu-central-1` Region (Frankfurt, Germany) for data residency needs.

```
{
  "Version": "2012-10-17",
  "Statement": [
    {
      "Sid": "DenyS3BucketCreationOutsideEuCentral1",
      "Effect": "Deny",
      "Action": [
        "s3:CreateBucket"
      ],
      "Resource": "*",
      "Condition": {
        "StringNotEquals": {
          "aws:RequestedRegion": "eu-central-1"
        }
      }
    }
  ]
}
```

Figure 2.9 shows how the flow of this policy strategy works.

FIGURE 2.9 Explicit Deny flow.

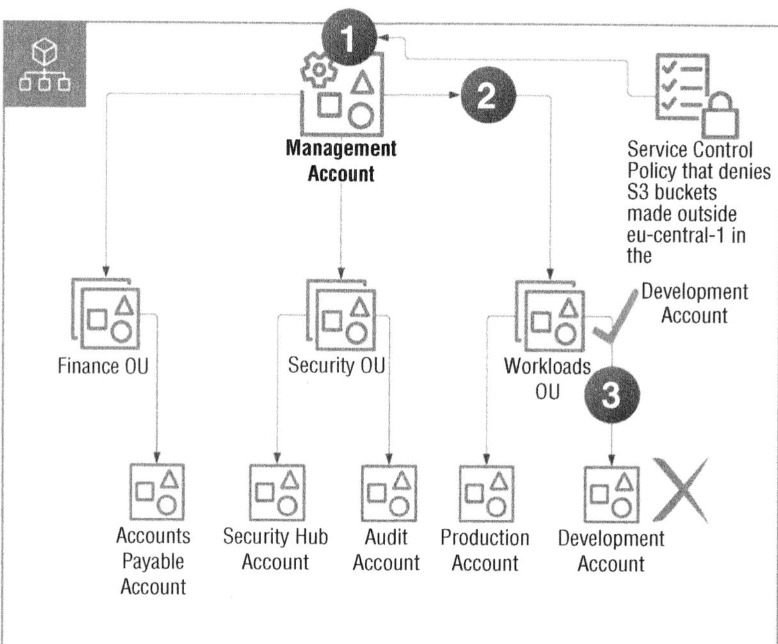

Service control policies are a powerful tool in securing your AWS Organization, but there are some caveats you need to be aware of. SCPs should be used as part of a comprehensive approach to security, and not relied on as the only mechanism to manage access.

- SCPs do not apply to IAM users and roles in the management account.
- SCPs do not apply to service-linked roles used to grant AWS managed services access to operate on your behalf.
- SCPs only apply to member accounts' IAM users and roles. They do not apply to resource-based policies such as S3 bucket policies.
- SCPs affect the root user of member accounts.

For more information, visit: `https://docs.aws.amazon.com/organizations/latest/userguide/orgs_manage_policies_scps.html`

Network Security

There are many layers of security you work with in AWS. We have already covered constructs like IAM policies and SCPs. These constructs focus on controlling authentication and authorization to AWS services, but what about traditional network security controls? In a traditional data center, you might deploy physical network firewalls directly into your network path to inspect and control traffic as it flows between systems. In AWS, however, you do not have access to the physical infrastructure, and your workloads do not run on hardware where you can insert such devices. Instead, you rely on AWS-native networking and security services to provide equivalent inspection and control capabilities. While there are advanced architecture patterns that allow you to implement virtual appliances and complex routing designs, AWS provides built-in network security constructs that you can easily implement in a cloud-native way to manage the flow of traffic in your network.

Before digging into the details of these constructs, you need to understand the difference of stateful and stateless services. A stateful service refers to a service that tracks connections or sessions bi-directionally for both ingress (traffic that initiates from another source and connects to your resource) and egress (traffic that initiates at the resource and connects to an external destination) traffic. Logically, what this means is if you define a rule that allows ingress HTTPS connections from any source to your webserver, the state of that connection is tracked and there is no need to also define an egress rule that allows the return traffic back to the source. The single rule allows for any necessary return traffic for an established connection.

In the case of a stateless rule, the opposite is true. Using the same example of allowing inbound HTTPS connections to your webserver, that rule *only* authorizes the ingress traffic that is destined to your webserver, and session state is not tracked. A second outbound rule that allows the return traffic to the requesting client would also be required for bi-directional network flow to function. The security constructs that AWS provides to apply these rules are Security Groups and Network Access Control Lists (NACLs).

Security Groups

AWS *security groups* act as a virtual stateful firewall for your resources for controlling inbound and outbound network traffic. Security Groups are applied to resources in your AWS VPC such as an EC2 Instance to control network traffic flow. Every AWS Resource in your VPC contains a network interface (known as Elastic Network Interfaces or ENI) that allows it access to your VPC and has a security group. This consists of EC2 servers, VPC-enabled Lambda functions, Application Load Balancers, or any resource that contains an ENI. Every VPC at creation has a default security group that is applied to resources.

As best practice, create a new security group for each resource type instead of using the default VPC security group. When you create a security group, you can define both inbound and outbound rules. Since security groups are stateful, we only need to create an inbound rule to allow HTTPS traffic, and the outbound return traffic will be allowed automatically. Each rule consists of the following information:

- Protocol
- Ports
- Source
- Destination
- Description (optional)

As a CloudOps engineer, controlling access to your AWS Resources in a fine grained, least privileged way is a top priority. For example, look at Figure 2.10. Here you see two EC2 instances, one in a publicly accessible subnet, and one in a private subnet, each with a security group around it. These security groups act as firewalls to manage access to the EC2 resource. Let's say that we want to allow SSH remote access to our public facing server from your businesses office IP address. This will act as an entry point into our network. Looking at Figure 2.10, you can see that before traffic is allowed to reach the EC2 instance, the IP address of your office (3.4.5.6), port (22), and protocol (TCP) is evaluated against the inbound rules of our security group. If a matching rule exists, it will allow traffic to reach the EC2 instance, otherwise the rule will reject traffic, and access will be prevented from ever reaching your resource.

Now that you're logged into your public bastion host, you now want to SSH into your server that's in the same VPC but not publicly accessible.

The same process as before is applied and the traffic from your bastion server is evaluated by the security group around the other server. This is where we can showcase one of the

FIGURE 2.10 Security group example.

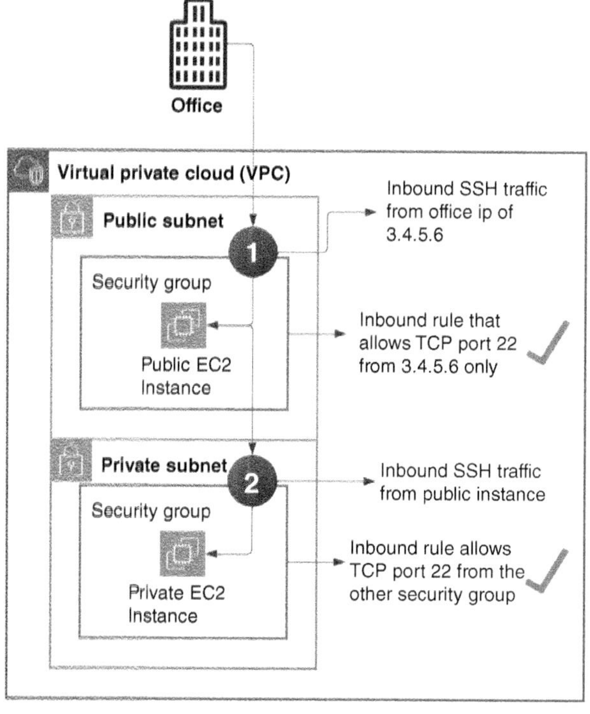

most powerful aspects of using security groups. Instead of creating a rule like before and use the IP address of the bastion server, you can reference the security group assigned to the bastion server as your source by using the security group ID. This has the benefit of not needing to hardcode an IP address in your rules. The IP address of your bastion host can change, and the rules still allow SSH traffic from it. This is a powerful feature that allows traffic from elastic resources that may scale in and out and have different IP address like an Application Load Balancer, or allow access to a group of instances that are all attached to the same security group. As you see in Figure 2.10, the rule is evaluated and confirmed to be from the other security group on port 22. That traffic is allowed, and now you can SSH into your EC2 instance in the private subnet.

Each security group can have 120 combined inbound and outbound rules. By default, a security group has no inbound rules (so all inbound traffic is implicitly denied) and one outbound rule that allows all outbound traffic. Each ENI can have up to five security groups attached by default. This lets you layer your security controls by assigning multiple security groups with distinct purposes—for example, one security group dedicated to allowing SSH access from a bastion host—so that any resource needing that specific access can simply inherit the appropriate security group.

Network Access Control Lists

Another network security construct AWS provides is the use of *Network Access Control Lists* (NACLs). As a CloudOps engineer, it is important to not rely on any single security mechanism and apply a layered security approach. NACLs act as a stateless network firewall that is applied and evaluated at the subnet layer. Each subnet you define in your AWS VPC network has a NACL ruleset applied to it. These rulesets are a list of allow and deny rules for accessing any resource in the subnet they are attached to. The default NACL rules that are created for your AWS VPC will have an allow rule for all traffic for inbound and outbound traffic. Each NACL rule consists of the following components.

- Rule Number
- Protocol
- Port Range
- Source CIDR
- Destination CIDR
- Action

Unlike security groups, the order of the NACL rules matter. Rules are evaluated in ascending order based on their rule numbers. The first rule that matches the port, source IP address, and destination IP address will be acted on and no other rules will be processed. This is an important aspect of building your NACL rulesets.

Because of this, you need to be specific in how you structure your rulesets. When structuring your rulesets, consider these best practices:

- **Space out your rule numbers** (100, 110, 120, etc.) and don't use consecutive numbers (1, 2, 3, 4, etc.). This leaves you room to insert more rules in the future where they need to be for evaluation.
- **Create a default deny rule** and put it at the bottom of your list. This creates a default deny posture for traffic evaluation.
- **Create specific allow rules** for the traffic you want to allow that will be evaluated for allowed traffic before the blanket deny policy is acted on.
- **Put specific rules at the top** of your ruleset, specifically any DENY statements. This allows for your specific rules to trigger before a broader ALLOW or DENY rule from triggering first.
- **Don't forget to match outbound rules.** NACLs are stateless, so unlike security groups, you need rules to account for both inbound and outbound traffic.

The use of both security groups (ENI-level) and NACLs (subnet-level) fully aligns with the AWS Well-Architected Framework Security Pillar principle of "apply security at all layers" through defense in depth. For more information, visit: `https://docs.aws.amazon.com/whitepapers/latest/security-overview-amazon-api-gateway/security-design-principles.html`

Table 2.2 summarizes the key differences between these two essential network security constructs that are heavily tested in the SOA-C03 exam. We revisit them in Chapter 10, to focus more on their operational aspects.

TABLE 2.2 Security Groups vs. NACLs Comparison

Feature	Security Groups (Stateful)	NACL (Stateless)
Applied at	Instance/ENI level	Subnet level
Rule evaluation	All rules evaluated	Rules evaluated in order (lowest → highest). First match wins
Return traffic	Automatic allowed	Must be explicitly allowed
Default behavior	Deny all inbound, Allow all outbound	Allow all inbound and outbound
Support for Deny rules	No (only Allow)	Yes (Allow and Deny)
Rule limit	60 inbound + 60 outbound	20 inbound + 20 outbound (default)

Resource Hierarchies and Tagging

When working with AWS Resources for various workloads, you need a way to organize them based on information such as their purpose, business owner, cost center, or any other relevant information you identify as needed to properly administer them. AWS provides the ability to do this for the majority of resource types through the use of tags.

Tagging

Tags are key-value pairs assigned to an AWS Resource that contains metadata about the resource. Tags consist of a required *tag key* and an optional *tag value*. Tag keys act as a way to search and filter for specific resource values you are looking for. Tag values are optional data you can assign to the key to identify resource-specific information about that key. For example, you may want to assign environment identification information about your resource, so you can easily identify and filter out production resources. If you charge back the cost of running specific resources to different cost centers in your business, you may want to identify the cost center number or business unit responsible for the resource. Table 2.3 shows how this might be laid out for EC2 instances.

You may notice that some resources already have tags applied at creation time by AWS. A number of AWS services such as CloudFormation stacks and Auto Scaling Groups automatically assign tags to resources they create. These tags normally begin with `aws:` in their tag key. For example, when a resource is created by an AWS CloudFormation stack, AWS automatically applies a system tag. This includes the key `aws:cloudformation:stack-name`, whose value is the name of the stack that created the resource. System-created tags cannot be deleted or edited.

Tags follow a basic format with requirements that must be followed.

- There is a limit of 50 user-created tags per resource.
- Tags are unencrypted, so do not store sensitive information in tags.
- Each tag key must be unique for that resource and contain only one value.
- Tag keys and values must be Unicode characters in UTF-8.
- Keys must be between 1 and 128 characters.
- Values must be between 0 and 256 characters.
- Keys and values are case sensitive, so be consistent.
- Resources may vary on allowed character but generally allow letters, numbers, spaces in UTF-8, and the characters _.:/=+@.

TABLE 2.3 Resource Tagging Example

Instance ID	Tag Key	Tag Value
i-1234567890abcdefa	Environment	Development
	CostCenter	34567
	BU	Finance

Resource Groups

Your workloads on AWS will consist of multiple resources. It is useful to be able to view and manage your workload and all the resources that it consists of as a group. The AWS console organizes the AWS services available, but you can also create a custom console that displays a consolidated list of resources that pertain to a set of criteria. AWS provides the construct of a *resource group*, which is a collection of AWS Resources in the same Region. With resource groups, you have a single pane of glass to manage a specific set of resources, instead of having to jump between resource lists to find the resources that are part of a specific workload. Resource groups are a type of resource themselves and have their own ARN format of:

```
arn:aws:resource-groups:region:account:group/group-name
```

When creating a resource group, you can use two types of queries to identify the resources that are part of the group. The first type is a tag-based resource group that identifies resources based on a list of resource types and their tag keys and values. The other method is by the AWS CloudFormation stack that created the resources. You can only base query on a single CloudFormation stack.

Not all resources support the use of Resource Groups Tagging API. For a list of supported resources, visit: `https://docs.aws.amazon.com/resourcegroupstagging/latest/APIReference/supported-services.html`

For more information about resource groups and strategies, visit:

`https://docs.aws.amazon.com/ARG/latest/userguide/resource-groups.html`

Tagging Usage Strategies

Using tags to organize your AWS Resources is recommended. There are a number of ways that tags are useful and can be applied to your overall management strategy.

Tags allow you to filter and manage resources using the AWS API, CLI, SDKs, and Console. In the AWS Management Console, you can display, search, and filter resources based on their tags. When working programmatically—such as through the AWS CLI—you can use tag filters to target only the resources you intend to modify, helping ensure that your commands affect the correct set of resources and reduce the risk of unintended changes.

Tags can also be used with IAM policies to restrict actions to resources with specific tag keys and values. You may want to limit the resources a user can take on allowed actions. For example, your developers may need to be able to create, delete, and modify EC2 instances while doing development work. You can limit the EC2 instances they are allowed to take these actions on to those not tagged as production, or only those that pertain to their business unit or team.

Tags are commonly used for cost allocation. Say you have assigned tags for your resources with a cost center and business unit. You can use tags in the AWS Cost Explorer and billing reports to filter and determine the spend on AWS Resources for a specific cost center or business unit. You can also apply a tag that identifies the application stack, allowing you to attribute and analyze the cost of a specific workload.

For more information, visit: `https://docs.aws.amazon.com/tag-editor/latest/userguide/best-practices-and-strats.html`

AWS CLI

When managing your AWS landing zones, there are a number of ways to create, view, edit, delete, and interact with AWS Resources. As a CloudOps engineer, you will need to be fluent in all of them. Your first time using AWS is usually through the AWS Management Console—a GUI-based web interface you log in to. This is a great way to familiarize yourself with AWS services and visualize your resources, but when working with lots of different resources, you need a quick and programmatic way to administer your environment. AWS provides other ways such as APIs specific to each service, SDKs for several programming languages such as the popular boto3 library for Python, and a command line interface (CLI). While APIs, and SDKs are powerful, they introduce language-specific abstractions that can obscure what's actually happening under the hood. The AWS CLI strikes the right balance for CloudOps engineers by exposing the real API calls in a clear, repeatable, and exam-aligned way—making it the most effective tool for enabling the programmatic access needed for efficient operations at scale.

CLI Structure

```
aws <command> <subcommand> [options and parameters]
```

The structure of the AWS CLI can be seen in the previous example. To enact the CLI, you start with the aws command. After that, you provide a top-level command (the AWS service) and a subcommand (the action to perform on that service). For example, if you wanted to interact with Amazon S3 and list all your buckets, you would use the command `aws s3 ls`. You can also provide available options and parameters to your command as needed. For example, if you wanted to create an S3 bucket you could use this command:

```
aws s3api create-bucket \
  --bucket cloudops-unique-bucket-123 \
  --region us-east-1
```

This will create a new bucket using the S3 API with the name `cloudops-unique-bucket-123` in the `us-east-1` Region. Notice the use of the backslash "\" symbol to break lines and properly indent the command.

Configuring Your CLI

Before you can utilize the AWS CLI, there are some steps you need to take. To communicate to your AWS account, you need to provide credentials for it to use. As discussed, this is through the use of IAM users and roles. By using IAM to authenticate and authorize your interactions through AWS CLI you can control the actions allowed to be performed through IAM policies as discussed previously. This is done through the use of IAM to access keys and secret keys that are created and assigned to an IAM user. These credentials can be revoked and rotated for security purposes.

When configuring your CLI, you can also provide other settings, such as the default Region you want to take actions in. This can be overridden by providing the `--region <region-name>` parameter to your command, as you saw in the previous example when we created an S3 bucket. You can also set the output format you want. The default output format is JSON, but you can also set it to any of these formats.

- json
- yaml
- yaml-stream
- text
- table

Running the `aws configure` command will result in it asking for each value and looks like this:

```
➜ aws configure
AWS Access Key ID [****************SYHU]:
AWS Secret Access Key [****************dzDk]:
Default region name [us-east-2]:
Default output format [json]:
```

Upon completing this, a configuration file and credentials file are created in your home directory for future use. The configuration file will contain your default Region, output format, and any other CLI configuration values you set. Your credentials file will contain your access key, secret key, and session token if you're using temporary credentials generated through your identity provider and the AWS STS service. By default, the files are located at:

- UNIX/Linux-based systems
  - `~/.aws/config`
  - `~/.aws/credentials`
- Windows-based systems
  - `C:\Users\YOUR_USERNAME\.aws\config`
  - `C:\Users\YOUR_USERNAME\.aws\credentials`

In practice, you will often work across multiple AWS accounts—and may assume different personas depending on the task. To manage credentials for these environments, the AWS CLI allows you to create named profiles. Each profile stores a separate set of configuration and credential details, created with a command such as `aws configure --profile <profile-name>`. This creates an additional CLI profile alongside the default one.

To use a non-default profile, simply include the `--profile` parameter in your command. For example, to list Amazon S3 buckets using the development profile, you would run `aws s3 ls --profile development`.

A complete example of a multi-profile configuration file is shown in the following snippet.

```
cat ~/.aws/config
[default]
region = us-east-2
output = json
[development]
region = us-east-1
output = json
```

The corresponding credentials file will look like this:

```
              cat ~/.aws/credentials
              [default]
aws_access_key_id = AKIAIOSFODNN7EXAMPLE
aws_secret_access_key = wJalrXUtnFEMI/K7MDENG/bPxRfiCYEXAMPLEKEY
[development]
aws_access_key_id = ASIAWWR5DP7NWEXAMPLE
aws_secret_access_key = N7xNDpIHS4DqawX2y3Lhz/4IZYIXABEXAMPLEKEY
```

You can also provide the necessary credentials using environment variables or provide a non-standard config file location with an environment variable. Table 2.4 shows a list of some of the available environment variables that you can set.

A full list of available values and their uses can be found at `https://docs.aws.amazon.com/cli/latest/userguide/cli-configure-envvars.html`.

TABLE 2.4 AWS CLI Environment Variables

Environment Variable	Example Value
AWS_ACCESS_KEY_ID	ASIAWWR5DP7NWEXAMPLE
AWS_SECRET_ACCESS_KEY	N7xNDpIHS4DqawX2y3Lhz/4IZYIXABE XAMPLEKEY
AWS_REGION	us-west-2
AWS_DEFAULT_OUTPUT	json
AWS_CLI_AUTO_PROMPT	on
AWS_CONFIG_FILE	/awsconfigs/justin/config

Using the CLI

Now that you know how to configure your CLI, let's look at how to utilize it to administer your AWS environment. As you've seen, the structure of the using the CLI starts with `aws <command>`. So, let's walk through utilizing the CLI to pull a list of all EC2 instances in an AWS account. The command options map to AWS services. In this case, we will be interacting with the EC2 service so we will start with `aws ec2`. From here we need to determine the sub-command we want to use. Each subcommand for a service map to an operation we want to perform on that service. You can see all available actions by running `aws <command> help`, or in this case `aws ec2 help`. A snippet of this output is shown in Figure 2.11.

In this case we want to generate a list of all EC2 instances in running in the `us-west-2` Region in our AWS account. The sub-command we want to use is `describe-instances`. The command we should run is `aws ec2 describe instances`. We specifically want the list for instances in `us-west-2`. The CLI will default to the Region you configured when you set up your CLI. However, to be safe let's call out that we want `us-west-2`. We can do this by adding the `--region us-west-2` argument to our command. This will explicitly specify the Region we want. The resulting command will look like this:

```
aws ec2 describe-instances \
  --region us-west-2
```

Now that we have our command let's run it. In this case we just want a list of instance IDs, but the output will be a list of nested JSON objects with all kinds of information about each instance.

We only want instance IDs though. One of the most powerful advantages of using the CLI is filtering. AWS CLI supports both server-side and client-side filtering. With server-side

FIGURE 2.11 AWS EC2 help output.

```
EC2()                                                          EC2()

NAME
       ec2 -

DESCRIPTION
       You can access the features of Amazon Elastic Compute Cloud (Amazon
       EC2) programmatically. For more information, see the Amazon EC2
       Developer Guide .

AVAILABLE COMMANDS

       o accept-address-transfer

       o accept-capacity-reservation-billing-ownership

       o accept-reserved-instances-exchange-quote

       o accept-transit-gateway-multicast-domain-associations

       o accept-transit-gateway-peering-attachment

       o accept-transit-gateway-vpc-attachment

       o accept-vpc-endpoint-connections

       o accept-vpc-peering-connection

       o advertise-byoip-cidr

       o allocate-address

       o allocate-hosts
```

filtering, you can filter what information is sent to the client. This allows you to optimize the amount of data that is returned to only the resources you want. Client-side filtering is applied once the output has been received on your client and you can further filter out the specific values that are output. In this case, we will use both. First, let's say we only want instances that are tagged for production. We covered previously how you can use tags to organize and identify specific resources, and this is one way you can leverage that. In our case the new command will look like this:

```
aws ec2 describe-instances \
  --region us-west-2 \
  --filters "Name=tag:environment,Values=production"
```

Now we only have output returned from AWS that contain that tag key and value. We used server-side filtering with the `--filters` flag to limit the list of instances returned from the AWS API, ensuring we only receive data for the specific resources that match our criteria.

The output still has lots of information about each instance though. We only want the instance ID. Now we can use client-side filtering to only output the values we care about using the `--query` flag. To use this flag, we need to look at the JSON output and tell it to only return the values we want. This will look like `--query "Reservations[*].Instances[*].InstanceId"`. You will notice the use of wild cards to signify you want

FIGURE 2.12 AWS EC2 output.


```
[
    [
        "i-1234567890abcdef0"
    ],
    [
        "i-0a1b2c3d4e5f67890"
    ],
    [
        "i-abcdef1234567890a"
    ]

]
```


to filter through all values in a JSON array and target a specific value. Our command now looks like this:

```
aws ec2 describe-instances \
  --region us-west-2 \
  --filters "Name=tag:environment,Values=production" \
  --query "Reservations[*].Instances[*].InstanceId"
```

The output is shown in Figure 2.12. Notice that the output is still in JSON format. If you want to make this a text list, you can also add an output flag `--output text` to produce a pure text list.

For more information about the different CLI commands, visit the official documentation at: `https://docs.aws.amazon.com/cli/latest/reference/`.

Summary

In this chapter, we explored the foundational elements required to operate workloads effectively on AWS. We began by defining what constitutes an AWS Resource, then examined the AWS Global Infrastructure and its core components. This included a detailed look at Regions and Availability Zones, how they relate to one another, and how they provide resilience, redundancy, and connectivity. We also introduced the concept of fault isolation boundaries and compared the differences between zonal, regional, and global scopes.

From there, we shifted to account management. We clarified what an AWS account represents and why a multi-account strategy is a best practice for both governance and operational isolation. We discussed AWS landing zones as a well-architected approach for deploying and managing multi-account environments, which naturally led into AWS Organizations and its role in providing centralized governance. We then introduced

AWS Control Tower and explained how it automates the creation of a governed, secure, multi-account environment with integrated logging, IAM, and security controls.

Next, we examined foundational security constructs in AWS, beginning with the shared responsibility model and the division of responsibilities between AWS and the customer. We introduced service control policies (SCPs) and demonstrated how they can be used at the organization level to establish guardrails across AWS accounts and organizational units (OUs).

We then covered resource tagging and how assigning key–value pairs to resources enables better identification, organization, and management. This included an overview of resource groups and how they can be used to visually group tagged resources in the console, followed by guidance on developing effective tagging strategies.

Finally, we concluded the chapter with an introduction to the AWS Command Line Interface (CLI). We walked through configuring the CLI, explaining its command structure and using it to manage AWS Resources programmatically. We also demonstrated how to refine CLI output using filters and queries to support more efficient workflows.

Exam Essentials

Know how the AWS global infrastructure works. The AWS global infrastructure consists of multiple locations worldwide. This consists of a large number of data centers distributed globally and grouped together into geographical locations called Regions. A Region is a physical geographic area in the world that is comprised of three or more Availability Zones. Each Region is designed to be completely isolated from all other Regions, ensuring fault tolerance, data sovereignty, and operational independence. Many AWS services are Region-specific, meaning that they are configured and managed within the confines of a specific Region, and no data is replicated across regions without your consent. An Availability Zone is a group of one or more data centers within a Region, each with redundant power, networking and connectivity no more than 100 km/62 miles from each other.

Understand how fault isolation boundaries drive resilience in AWS. AWS leverages fault isolation boundaries to limit the scope of potential failures and prevent cascading issues across a footprint. Zonal boundaries utilize Availability Zones (AZs) to isolate power or cooling failures, with services like Amazon EC2 and EBS operating within these specific scopes. Regional boundaries isolate issues to a single geographic area, where services like Amazon S3 and DynamoDB automatically replicate data across multiple AZs to survive a single-zone outage. Finally, global boundaries apply to control planes that span the entire AWS network, such as AWS IAM or Amazon Route 53, where a failure could potentially impact all Regions, requiring specialized architectural care for critical configurations.

Understand AWS Account structure and Multi-Account management. An AWS account is an atomic unit of ownership, access control, and billing in AWS. Each account maintains its own resources and is managed separately from others for access control and ownership.

A best practice is to split your AWS environment across multiple accounts to improve security, organization, and scalability. This aligns with the first design principle of the Security pillar of the Well-Architected Framework by enabling separation of duties between operations, security, and workload environments for access control. Landing zones are well-architected, secure, Multi-Account AWS environments designed to enable your organization to scale. Scalability is achieved by using AWS Organizations to centrally deploy, organize, and manage multiple accounts through a unified management experience. By grouping accounts into Organizational Units (OUs), you can apply consistent governance, streamline operations, and scale your environment with clear administrative boundaries. An AWS Organization is composed of a management account, which serves as the parent, and the member accounts it governs. AWS best practices recommend using dedicated accounts for distinct operational domains—such as infrastructure, observability, security, shared services, and workload-specific functions—to improve governance, reduce blast radius, and simplify lifecycle management. AWS Control Tower expands on this foundation and provides a fully managed service you can launch to build landing zones, enforce guardrails, and automate accounts creation.

Understand the Shared Responsibility Model. The AWS Shared Responsibility Model explains the partnership between you and AWS. The model (as shown in Figure 2.6) illustrates a distinct split in responsibilities of securing and running workloads in the cloud. AWS is responsible for the security "of the cloud" while you, as a CloudOps engineer, are responsible for security "in the cloud." AWS takes care of things like power, network connectivity, physical security, and hardware maintenance. As a CloudOps engineer, you take on the security and responsibility of what you put in the cloud. You are responsible for the operating systems of EC2 instances you build, the encryption of the data you store at rest, securing the resources you build in your AWS account, and access management of who can access your account and resources.

Understand how to secure access to your AWS environment with IAM. As a CloudOps engineer, you should understand how AWS Identity and Access Management (IAM) is central to controlling access to your AWS account and Resources. You need to know the key IAM responsibilities, such as creating and managing IAM users for your account, and—most importantly—securing the root IAM user created by default. Understand that the root user has full control of your AWS account and should be locked down, and only used for operations that can be done by the root user. Know that you can manage IAM users more effectively with IAM groups and manage access policies at a group level instead at the individual user level. You should be able to write, read, and apply IAM policies in a least privileged way and utilize managed policies and apply them to other IAM resources for more central management of permissions. You need to be able to comprehend using IAM roles instead of IAM users to take advantage of temporary security credentials through federated logins and cross-account access. You should understand how to use IAM roles to grant AWS services and resources permission to access other AWS services. This is done by allowing those services to assume a role and operate with temporary credentials.

Understand the role of service control policies in Multi-Account governance. In Multi-Account governance, SCPs act as the ultimate guardrails, defining the maximum available permissions for IAM users and roles within an organization. By default, AWS attaches the managed FullAWSAccess policy to every OU and account to ensure no existing workflows are disrupted when SCPs are first enabled. Because SCPs function as a filter that requires an explicit allow at every level of the hierarchy, the presence of FullAWSAccess is what allows services to function; removing it without a replacement policy results in an implicit deny, effectively blocking all actions for those accounts.

Comprehend Core Network Security Constructs in AWS. When securing your resources in AWS at a network layer, you should understand the difference in stateless and stateful network controls concepts. Remember that stateless firewalls need to have both inbound and outbound rules defined for your traffic, while stateful firewalls remember the network sessions and automatically allow return traffic. You need to know that NACLs are stateless network firewalls that are applied at the subnet layer in AWS and that their rules are evaluated in order. Be able to articulate the different parts of a NACL rule and best practices for structuring your rules. You need to know that security groups are stateful firewall applied at the resource level and be proficient in using security groups to secure communication between those resources.

Be able to create and utilize tagging for resource management. When managing your AWS accounts and Resources, you need to know how resource tags are structured. Being able to identify common related resources by department, billing code, workload or other meaningful metadata streamline management. Know the different ways to utilize tagging strategies with your resources to filter API/CLI output and generate custom billing reports. You should understand how resource groups can help group related resources together by workload and be able to view those different related resources at once instead of having to navigate between different services to find them.

Be comfortable configuring and using the AWS CLI. Successfully administrating your AWS environment will require being comfortable with the AWS CLI. The AWS CLI provides programmatic easy access to your AWS Resource through a system interface to interact with the AWS APIs. You should know how to configure your AWS CLI to access your account resources and work with them instead of using the web console. The CLI can be used to script and automate routine actions in managing your AWS Resources. When gathering information about your resources through the CLI you can control the output into different formats and utilize filters and queries to manipulate the output to be exactly what you need. Knowing how to use the CLI to programmatically do operations tasks across a number of resources will enhance your efficiency in operating in AWS.

Review Questions

1. Why is a Region designed to be completely isolated from all other Regions in the AWS Cloud?
   - A. To protect workloads from cyberattacks
   - B. To reduce operational costs
   - C. To prevent sensitive data exfiltration
   - D. To ensure fault tolerance, data sovereignty, and operational independence
2. What's the minimum number of Availability Zones (AZs) in a Region?
   - A. 2
   - B. 1
   - C. 3
   - D. 5
3. What are the primary reasons that all AZs in a Region are redundantly connected to each other? (Select TWO.)
   - A. To increase the resilience and reliability of distributed workloads within the Region
   - B. To support high availability, fault tolerance, and low-latency communication across distributed workloads within the Region
   - C. To promote interoperability across distributed workloads within the Region
   - D. To decentralize cloud operations
   - E. To improve the security posture of distributed workloads within the Region
4. What are the primary reasons that Regions are NOT connected to each other by default? (Select TWO.)
   - A. To support the shared responsibility model
   - B. To limit capital expenditure incurred by investing in network infrastructure
   - C. To maximize fault isolation, meet data sovereignty requirements, and achieve operational independence
   - D. To optimize performance for regional customers
   - E. To limit inter-Region egress cost
5. Which of the following statements are correct? (Select TWO.)
   - A. An AWS Resource is an entity of an AWS service that can be provisioned, configured, and managed to support a workload.
   - B. An AWS Resource is a workload running in AWS.
   - C. An Amazon RDS database instance is an AWS Resource.
   - D. Amazon EC2 is an AWS Resource.
   - E. A SQL Server Database hosted on an Amazon EC2 instance is an AWS Resource.

6. What is the primary function of a control plane in AWS?
   A. To start an EC2 instance
   B. To read and write data from/to an Amazon S3 bucket
   C. To govern the lifecycle of AWS Resources
   D. To perform operations on an existing AWS Resource
7. What are the types of an AWS service's fault isolation boundary? (Select THREE.)
   A. Regional
   B. Multi-Regional
   C. Global
   D. Zonal
   E. Hybrid
   F. Local
8. What are the levels of isolation provided by an AWS account? (Select THREE.)
   A. IAM (access control)
   B. Ownership
   C. Line of Business
   D. Billing
   E. Data Sovereignty
   F. Organization Unit
9. What are the main benefits of using AWS Organizations? (Select TWO.)
   A. Automated account creation with Account Factory
   B. Building landing zones
   C. Centralized management
   D. Governance of multiple accounts at scale
   E. Acceleration of the go-to-market strategy
10. What are the main benefit of using AWS Control Tower? (Select TWO.)
   A. Automated account creation with Account Factory
   B. Building landing zones
   C. Centralized management
   D. Governance of multiple accounts at scale
   E. Acceleration of the go-to-market strategy

11. What IAM resource do you use to grant access to your account from another account?
    A. IAM User
    B. IAM Role
    C. IAM Access Keys
    D. Active Directory
12. In the AWS Shared Responsibility Model, what is NOT something AWS is responsible for?
    A. Network connectivity
    B. Compute hardware
    C. Operating systems
    D. Virtualization hypervisor
13. Security groups are stateless firewalls.
    A. True
    B. False
14. What AWS Resources are NACLs applied to?
    A. EC2 Instances
    B. Security Groups
    C. VPC
    D. Subnets
15. What is a service control policy for?
    A. Granting access to users
    B. Managing access guardrails
    C. Controlling access to organization management account
    D. Defining IAM permissions
16. When creating a NACL rule, what should you NOT do?
    A. Place most specific rules at the top
    B. Create both inbound and outbound rules
    C. Create a default deny rule
    D. Use consecutive numbers for rule numbers
17. How many combined (inbound and outbound) rules are allowed in a security group?
    A. 50
    B. 120
    C. 5
    D. 10

18. When configuring the AWS CLI, what values are required for authentication? (Select TWO.)
   - A. AWS_ACCESS_KEY_ID
   - B. AWS_REGION
   - C. AWS_SECRET_ACCESS_KEY
   - D. AWS_DEFAULT_OUTPUT
   - E. AWS_SESSION_TOKEN

19. What is NOT a benefit of tagging AWS Resources?
   - A. Filter the output of AWS CLI commands
   - B. Restrict resource access in IAM policies
   - C. Cost allocation of resources used for an application
   - D. Override AWS default values

20. What is an advantage of using an IAM role over IAM users?
   - A. Lower cost
   - B. They do not have permanent credentials
   - C. Can be assigned to IAM groups
   - D. Span across AWS accounts

Answers to Review Questions

1. D. AWS designs each Region as a fully isolated fault domain so that failures, outages, or disruptions in one Region cannot cascade into another. This isolation also supports data sovereignty, allowing customers to keep data within specific geographic or regulatory boundaries, and ensures operational independence, meaning each Region can operate, scale, and recover without relying on any other. This architectural choice is what enables AWS to deliver strong resilience, predictable fault tolerance, and compliance guarantees across its global footprint.

2. C. Each AWS Region has at least three AZs. This minimum of three zones allows for application workloads to be distributed so that if one zone is compromised, the remaining two can maintain availability and fault tolerance within the Region.

3. A, B. The redundant high-bandwidth, low-latency networking connections between all AZs within a Single-Region are key to cloud infrastructure design, primarily serving to enhance distributed workload capabilities. Redundant connections support high availability and fault tolerance, which result in higher resilience and reliability for distributed workloads in a Single-Region.

4. C, D. By default, Regions are isolated from each other. This separation is key to fault tolerance; a catastrophic event affecting one Region will not automatically impact another. This isolation also ensures that data stays within specific geographic boundaries to comply

with local data sovereignty laws (e.g., GDPR), and allows for independent operations and updates without cross-region dependencies. Moreover, keeping Regions isolated means that customer data and application resources are physically closer to the end users in that specific geographic area. This proximity reduces network latency, providing faster response times and improved overall application performance for the local customer base.

5. A, C. An AWS Resource is a fundamental component of the AWS environment. Option A correctly defines this concept as a specific entity of an AWS service that is provisioned, configured, and managed by a user to run their applications or support a workload. Option C provides a concrete and correct example: a single RDS database instance is a specific "resource" that belongs to the broader Amazon RDS "service." While an Amazon EC2 instance itself is an AWS Resource, a SQL Server Database installed on it is considered customer content or data, not an AWS Resource.

6. C. In AWS architecture, the control plane refers to the administrative machinery and APIs used to manage the lifecycle of resources—specifically the creation, reading/describing, updating, deleting, and listing (CRUDL) of resources. It acts as the orchestration layer that translates user requests into complex workflows, such as finding a physical host for an EC2 instance, allocating network interfaces, and configuring security groups. Options A and D are specific examples of control plane actions, but Option C provides the most comprehensive and primary definition of its function: governing the entire lifecycle. Option B is a data plane activity. The data plane is responsible for the primary function of the service—actually moving, storing, or processing data—rather than managing the configuration of the service itself.

7. A, C, D. AWS categorizes its services based on their fault isolation boundaries to help customers design resilient workloads. These boundaries define the scope of impact if a service or component within it experiences a failure. Zonal services (Option D) operate within a single Availability Zone (AZ) and are isolated to that specific zone (e.g., an individual EC2 instance or an EBS volume). A failure in one AZ would not impact resources in other AZs. Regional services (Option A) are built across multiple Availability Zones within a Single-Region and present a Single-Regional endpoint to the customer (e.g., Amazon S3, Amazon DynamoDB). They are designed to automatically recover from an AZ failure. Global services (Option C) have control planes and data planes that span across multiple Regions, or whose control plane is hosted in a Single-Region but whose data plane is distributed globally across edge locations (e.g., IAM, Amazon Route 53, Amazon CloudFront). Option B is incorrect. While customers can build Multi-Region architectures for increased resilience and disaster recovery, "Multi-Region" is a design pattern or architectural choice made by the customer, not a standard, predefined service-level fault isolation boundary provided by AWS by default. The standard boundaries are zonal, regional, and global.

8. A, B, D. An AWS account is considered a "hard boundary" that provides several critical layers of isolation to help organizations manage security, costs, and resources. These layers include: IAM (Option A), Ownership (Option B), Billing (Option D). An AWS account acts as an identity and access management isolation boundary. By default, no access is allowed between accounts; permissions must be explicitly granted via cross-account roles or resource-based policies. Resources created within an account are owned by that specific account, regardless of which IAM user or role performed the action. This ensures a clear legal and administrative boundary for all data and infrastructure contained within the account.

The AWS account is the primary unit for financial isolation. It allows organizations to isolate and distinguish 100% of costs and usage for specific workloads. Line of Business (Option C) is incorrect because it describes an organizational strategy rather than a technical level of isolation provided by the account itself.

9. C, D. AWS Organizations is specifically designed to help customers manage and govern multiple AWS accounts from a single, centralized location. Centralized management (Option C) is the core purpose of the service. It allows you to link multiple accounts together for unified billing (consolidated billing), resource sharing (using AWS RAM), and centralized auditing (using organizational CloudTrail). As for governance at scale (Option D), AWS Organizations enables governance across many accounts simultaneously through service control policies (SCPs). You can group accounts into Organizational Units (OUs) and apply policies to the entire group, ensuring consistent security and compliance guardrails without having to configure each account individually. Option B is incorrect because AWS Control Tower is the primary service used to build and set up a landing zone. Option A is incorrect because Account Factory is a feature of AWS Control Tower, not AWS Organizations. Option E is incorrect because it is a business-level outcome typically associated with the AWS Partner Network (APN) or the AWS Marketplace, rather than a direct technical feature of account management.

10. A, B. AWS Control Tower is a service designed to simplify the setup and governance of a secure, compliant, and Multi-Account AWS environment, known as a landing zone. Option B is the primary value proposition of AWS Control Tower. It provides a standardized, automated way to set up a well-architected landing zone based on AWS best practices, incorporating core accounts (like management, log archive, and audit) and foundational guardrails. As for Option A, AWS Control Tower provides a built-in feature called Account Factory. This interface allows users to provision new, pre-configured accounts in a consistent, standardized manner, ensuring every new account adheres to the established landing zone's governance rules automatically. Options C and D are incorrect because they are AWS Organizations' core responsibilities, not AWS Control Tower. Option E is incorrect because it is a business-level outcome typically associated with the AWS Partner Network (APN) or the AWS Marketplace, rather than a direct technical feature of account management.

11. B. An IAM role is the primary resource used to delegate access across different AWS accounts. Unlike an IAM user, which represents a specific person or application with long-term credentials, a role does not have its own permanent password or access keys. Instead, it uses a Trust policy to define which external entities (such as another AWS account ID) are allowed to "assume" it. When a user from another account assumes the role, AWS Security Token Service (STS) provides temporary security credentials that grant the permissions defined by the role's attached policies for a limited time.

12. C. In the AWS Shared Responsibility Model, AWS is responsible for the security "of" the cloud (the underlying infrastructure), while customers are responsible for security "in" the cloud (the resources they deploy). For infrastructure services like Amazon EC2, the customer is responsible for the management and security of the guest operating system (Option C). This includes installing security patches, updates, and configuring OS-level firewall settings. While AWS manages the host OS (the layer directly on the physical hardware), the guest OS that runs your specific workload is your responsibility. AWS manages the foundational

infrastructure, which includes network connectivity (physical cabling and routing), compute hardware (physical servers and storage), and the virtualization hypervisor (such as Nitro or Xen) that abstracts the hardware for user instances.

13. B. AWS Security Groups are stateful firewalls, not stateless. Being stateful means they automatically track the state of network connections. If you define an inbound rule to allow traffic (such as HTTPS on port 443), the security group will automatically allow the corresponding outbound response traffic regardless of your outbound rules. This behavior simplifies management because you do not need to manually configure rules for return traffic. In contrast, Network Access Control Lists (NACLs) are stateless firewalls. With NACLs, if you allow inbound traffic, you must also explicitly define a matching outbound rule for the response to pass through, as the firewall does not "remember" the initial connection.

14. D. Network Access Control Lists (NACLs) are firewalls that operate at the subnet level. Every subnet in your Virtual Private Cloud (VPC) must be associated with a NACL; if you don't explicitly create one, AWS automatically associates the subnet with the default VPC NACL. Because NACLs are applied at the subnet boundary, they act as a "gatekeeper" for all traffic entering or leaving that entire segment of the network. Option A is incorrect. Security groups operate at the instance level, not NACLs. While NACL rules affect instances because instances reside within subnets, the NACL is not directly attached to the instance itself. Option B is also incorrect. Security groups are a separate security resource entirely. They are not the target for NACL associations; rather, they are often used in tandem with NACLs as a second layer of defense. Option C is also incorrect. While NACLs exist within a VPC, they are not applied to the VPC as a whole. You can have multiple NACLs within a single VPC, each protecting different subnets.

15. B. A service control policy (SCP) is a powerful type of policy available when using AWS Organizations. Its primary function is to provide centralized control over the maximum available permissions for all accounts within an Organizational Unit (OU) or the entire organization. SCPs do not grant access, which makes Option A incorrect. Instead, they act as "guardrails" or a "maximum security envelope." They define a boundary of what actions an administrator in a member account is allowed to perform. If an action is explicitly denied in an SCP, no IAM policy in the member account (not even one assigned to the root user) can override that denial. This is crucial for enforcing mandatory security and compliance rules across an entire enterprise. Option C is also incorrect. The management account (formerly master account) has specific administrative functions within AWS Organizations, but SCPs are designed to govern the member accounts within the organization, not lock down the management account itself in this specific way. Option D is also incorrect. While an SCP uses the same JSON syntax as an IAM policy, it doesn't define the operational permissions users will have. It defines the limits of those permissions. The actual permissions are still granted by standard IAM policies within the member accounts.

16. D. You should not use consecutive rule numbers when creating NACL rules. NACL rules are evaluated in order and in the future, you will need to insert new rules. You should space rule numbers like 100, 110, 120, and so on, so you have space to insert new rules in the future where they need to go for proper evaluation. The rest of the options are best practice when using NACLs and should be done.

17. B. As of the writing of this book, the default quota for security groups is 60 inbound rules and 60 outbound rules separately, for a total of 120 rules combined.

18. A, C. To authenticate the AWS CLI for programmatic access using an IAM user, two primary pieces of information are strictly required to sign and verify your requests: `AWS_ACCESS_KEY_ID` (acts as the "username" for your programmatic identity), and `AWS_SECRET_ACCESS_KEY` (acts as the "password" and is used to cryptographically sign requests to prove they came from you). While `aws configure` also prompts for the AWS Region and Default Output Format, these are considered configuration values rather than authentication values. Authentication specifically refers to the identity verification process, which is handled by the access key pair (Options A and C). As a result, Options B and D are incorrect. `AWS_SESSION_TOKEN` is only required when using short-term (temporary) credentials, such as those provided by assuming an IAM role via AWS STS or via federation. For standard IAM user credentials, only the Access Key ID and Secret Access Key are required. Therefore, Option E is incorrect.

19. D. AWS tags are primarily metadata—labels consisting of user-defined keys and values—designed to help manage, identify, and organize resources. While they are highly effective for administrative and security tasks, they do not have the technical capability to change or override the fundamental default settings, configurations, or service limits of AWS Resources. For example, tagging an EC2 instance will not change its default network timeout or override its instance type limitations. Options A, B, and C are all benefits of AWS tags. Therefore, they are all incorrect answers.

20. B. The most significant security advantage of an IAM role is that it provides temporary security credentials via the AWS Security Token Service (STS). Unlike IAM users, which rely on long-term passwords or permanent access keys that can be leaked or stolen, IAM roles provide credentials that automatically expire after a short duration (usually 1 to 12 hours). This reduces the "blast radius" if credentials are ever compromised, as they will quickly become useless without needing manual rotation.

Compute and Containers

THE AWS CERTIFIED CLOUDOPS ENGINEER ASSOCIATE (SOA-C03) EXAM OBJECTIVES COVERED IN THIS CHAPTER MAY INCLUDE, BUT ARE NOT LIMITED TO THE FOLLOWING:

✓ **Domain 3: Deployment, Provisioning, and Automation**

- 3.1 Provision and maintain cloud resources
- 3.2 Automate the management of existing resources

The previous chapter established the foundational elements every CloudOps engineer must know before operating workloads and infrastructure at scale: the hierarchy of AWS's global infrastructure, the principles behind secure landing zones, the tagging strategies that keep environments governable, and the CLI tooling that enables consistent automation. With that groundwork in place, we now turn to the core of SOA-C03 Domain 3—Deployment, Provisioning, and Automation—where compute, containers, and operational tooling converge. This domain is where CloudOps engineers demonstrate their ability not only to launch resources, but to manage them throughout their lifecycle with precision, consistency, and automation-first thinking.

In the CloudOps cycle—Deploy → Monitor → Sustain → Secure → Optimize—compute and container services represent the "deploy" moment, the point where workloads take shape as EC2 instances, Lambda functions, ECS tasks, or EKS clusters. But these resources do not exist in isolation. Their operational health, compliance posture, and long-term sustainability depend on the systems and processes wrapped around them. Provisioning is only the beginning; CloudOps engineers must ensure that what they deploy can be monitored effectively, patched consistently, accessed securely, and remediated automatically. Domain 3 tests this holistic understanding: the ability to provision resources and to automate their ongoing management in a way that supports the entire CloudOps cycle.

For this reason, before diving into the specifics of AWS compute and container services, we begin with the operational substrate that makes all of them manageable: AWS Systems Manager and AWS Config. These services form the control plane and governance layer for modern CloudOps. Systems Manager provides secure access, patching, configuration enforcement, automation runbooks, and fleet-wide visibility—capabilities that eliminate the need for traditional SSH/RDP workflows and enable consistent, scalable operations across compute and container environments. AWS Config complements this by recording resource state, detecting drift, and enforcing compliance through rules and conformance packs. Together, they establish the operational foundation upon which all compute and container services rely. Understanding them first is essential for mastering the provisioning and automation responsibilities at the core of the SOA-C03 exam.

With this broader context in place, we now turn to the operational foundations that make every compute and container service manageable in practice: the systems and governance tools that underpin day-to-day CloudOps.

Systems Operations Fundamentals

Modern CloudOps work begins long before an EC2 instance is launched or a container task is scheduled. The real challenge is operating those resources *consistently* once they exist—ensuring they can be accessed securely, patched automatically, configured predictably, and governed according to organizational standards. Another critical element of this approach is *scalability*. CloudOps teams must deliver all of this at scale, a core expectation of the Operational Excellence (OE) pillar introduced in Chapter 1. The OE best practices of "Design for Operations," "Understand Operational Health," and "Respond to Events" illustrated in Figure 1.2, all emphasize that effective operations require systems that can manage entire fleets, not individual hosts. AWS provides two core services that make this possible across compute and container environments: AWS Systems Manager and AWS Config. These services form the operational layer you—as a CloudOps engineer—rely on to maintain consistency at scale, enforce desired state, and uphold compliance without resorting to manual access or ad hoc scripts.

Let's dive into these two services, which feature prominently in the SOA-C03 exam.

AWS Systems Manager

To enable cloud operations, AWS offers a fully managed service—AWS Systems Manager (SSM)—that helps customers safely manage and operate their IT infrastructure and workloads at scale.

AWS Systems Manager (Systems Manager) was formerly known as Amazon Simple Systems Manager (SSM) and Amazon EC2 Systems Manager (SSM). The original abbreviated name of the service, "SSM," is still reflected in various AWS Resources.

AWS refers to SSM as "Centralized Operations Management," a definition rooted in three strategic drivers that shape modern CloudOps. First, it breaks the silos created by legacy operations management tools by providing a single pane of glass to view real-time operational data—such as resource configuration changes, inventory, and patch compliance—and manage infrastructure across AWS, on-premises, and multi-cloud environments. Second, it accelerates cloud adoption and modern application development by replacing manual, ticket-driven processes with a scalable, consistent, API-driven mechanisms for configuration, access, and automation. Third, it unlocks the speed and agility required to match cloud scale and elasticity by automating routine operational tasks—such as rotating certificates, increasing service limits, taking backups, and resizing instances—through standardized workflows powered by the SSM Agent. Together, these drivers position SSM as the operational hub for CloudOps teams, enabling consistent, compliant, and automated management across heterogeneous environments. Before exploring the core SSM capabilities, let's briefly review how Systems Manager is set up.

Setting Up SSM

For CloudOps teams to use Systems Manager, each compute resource must be prepared to operate as a managed node. In Systems Manager terminology, a *node* is any machine-level compute resource—such as an EC2 instance, an on-premises server, or a virtual machine running in another cloud—that you want Systems Manager to operate on. Once the required prerequisites are met and the resource successfully registers with Systems Manager, it becomes a *managed node*, meaning it can receive commands, participate in automation workflows, report inventory, and be governed by configuration and patching policies through the SSM Agent.

A node is any compute resource that the SSM Agent can run on and manage. Once registered, it becomes a managed node and can participate in all SSM capabilities. Just as important is what a node is not: Systems Manager does not manage Kubernetes pods, containers, Lambda functions, or ECS tasks. SSM manages the host operating system, not the workloads running inside it. Kubernetes worker nodes can be managed nodes, but individual pods cannot.

To become a managed node, three foundational requirements must be met in the following order.

1. Install and run the SSM Agent. The agent is preinstalled on most AWS-provided AMIs (the concept of AMI is covered later in the chapter), including Amazon Linux 2023, Ubuntu Server, SUSE, macOS, and Windows Server, but must be manually installed on some Linux distributions and all hybrid or multi-cloud nodes.

2. Attach the correct IAM permissions. Nodes require the `AmazonSSMManagedInstanceCore` policy, which grants the minimum permissions needed for Systems Manager to function. This includes access to SSM core APIs, Parameter Store (read-only), and the EC2 Messages service used for agent communication. Keep in mind that CloudWatch Logs and S3 permissions must be attached separately if session logging or command output storage is needed.

- **For EC2 instances,** this policy must be attached to the instance profile (the IAM role assigned to the instance).
- **For hybrid, on-premises, or multi-cloud nodes,** this policy must be attached to the IAM role associated with the activation. During a hybrid activation, you specify an IAM role that the SSM Agent will assume when the node registers with Systems Manager. This role provides the node with an AWS identity and the permissions required to communicate with SSM. Without it, hybrid nodes cannot register or function as managed nodes.

3. Register the node with Systems Manager. Registration happens automatically for EC2 instances through their instance profile, or manually via a hybrid activation for on-premises and multi-cloud environments. Hybrid activations generate an Activation Code and Activation ID, which the SSM Agent uses to register the machine as a managed node.

Systems Manager communicates using outbound HTTPS only, meaning no inbound ports need to be opened. For private environments, VPC endpoints (covered in Chapter 10) can optionally be used to keep Systems Manager traffic within the AWS network. With these prerequisites in place, Systems Manager can operate consistently across heterogeneous environments, enabling the capabilities described in the following sections.

Core SSM Capabilities for CloudOps

Systems Manager provides the operational building blocks that CloudOps teams use to manage fleets consistently and at scale. Each capability solves a specific operational challenge—configuration management, secure access, remote execution, patching, compliance, and workflow automation—while integrating through the SSM Agent and a unified API. The following sections introduce the core capabilities you must understand for the SOA-C03 exam, each with a practical CLI example to reinforce how CloudOps engineers use these tools in real environments.

Parameter Store

Parameter Store solves the problem of centralized, versioned configuration management across AWS, on-premises, and multi-cloud environments. Without it, configuration values—AMI IDs, application settings, feature flags, environment variables, or automation inputs—tend to drift across instances and deployments, leading to inconsistent behavior and operational complexity. Parameter Store provides a single, authoritative source for configuration data that can be referenced by automation workflows, CI/CD pipelines, and runtime environments, ensuring consistency at scale.

To accommodate diverse data requirements, Parameter Store supports three distinct types: `String` for standard text, `StringList` for comma-separated values, and `SecureString` for sensitive data encrypted via AWS KMS. Organizations can choose between the `Standard` tier, which provides up to 10,000 parameters at no cost (though you still pay for API interactions) with a max value of 4 KB for a single parameter, and the `Advanced` tier, which increases capacity to 100,000 parameters, doubles the size limit to 8 KB, and enables parameter policies for automated expiration and TTL-based notifications. For simplified management, you can also enable intelligent-tiering, which allows Systems Manager to automatically shift parameters from `Standard` to `Advanced` if their size increases or if policies are added.

Storing and Retrieving Nonsensitive Parameters

The following command shows how to store an AMI ID for fleet-wide use.

```
aws ssm put-parameter \
  --name "/app/prod/base-ami-id" \
  --value "ami-0a1b2c3d4e5f67890" \
  --type "String" \
  --overwrite
```

In this command:

- `--name`: The hierarchical name of the parameter.
- `--value`: The configuration value to store (in this case, an AMI ID).
- `--type String`: Stores the value as plain text (not encrypted).
- `--overwrite`: Allows updating the parameter if it already exists.

When you run the command, the AWS CLI returns a JSON object confirming the version of the parameter and the tier used.


```
{
  "Version": 4,
  "Tier": "Standard"
}
```


In this response:

- `Version`: This indicates the current iteration of the parameter. Since we used the `--overwrite` flag, if the parameter already existed, this number would increment (e.g., to 2 or 3). If it is a new parameter, it starts at 1.
- `Tier`: By default, parameters are created in the `Standard` tier, which is free for up to 10,000 parameters per account per Region.

In a bash script or terminal, use the `get-parameter` command. To get only the value (and not the full JSON metadata), use the `--query` flag:

```
# Retrieve the AMI ID as a plain string
AMI_ID=$(aws ssm get-parameter \
    --name "/app/prod/base-ami-id" \
    --query "Parameter.Value" \
    --output text)
echo "The AMI ID is: $AMI_ID"
```

Storing and Retrieving Sensitive Parameters

If you are storing a password or API key, change the `--type` to `SecureString`. This encrypts the data at rest using AWS Key Management Service (KMS).

```
aws ssm put-parameter \
    --name "/app/prod/db-password" \
    --value <your-db-password> \
    --type "SecureString" \
    --overwrite
```

Never pass plaintext secrets directly on the command line! Values may be visible in shell history, process listings, and AWS CloudTrail logs. In production, read the value from a prompt, file, or AWS Secrets Manager. More details on how to protect secrets are provided in Chapter 9.

When retrieving a `SecureString`, you must add the `--with-decryption` flag. Without it, the AWS CLI will return the encrypted ciphertext instead of the actual password.

```
DB_PASSWORD=$(aws ssm get-parameter \
    --name "/app/prod/db-password" \
    --with-decryption \
    --query "Parameter.Value" \
    --output text)
```

Using `SecureString` provides a robust security layer for sensitive data by ensuring that information is encrypted at rest using AWS KMS, which prevents unauthorized access to the underlying values. This configuration allows for granular access control through IAM policies, ensuring that only authorized users or services can decrypt the data, while also maintaining a complete audit trail of every access and decryption request via AWS CloudTrail.

For more information, visit: `https://docs.aws.amazon.com/cli/latest/reference/ssm/put-parameter.html` and `https://docs.aws.amazon.com/cli/latest/reference/ssm/get-parameter.html`.

Session Manager

Session Manager solves the problem of secure, auditable, port-less access to nodes. Instead of opening SSH ports, managing key pairs, or exposing instances to the Internet, Session Manager provides encrypted, IAM-controlled access through the SSM Agent. This works identically across EC2, on-premises servers, and multi-cloud VMs.

```
aws ssm start-session \
  --target i-0123456789abcdef0
```

In this command:

- `--target`: Instance or managed node ID.

When you run aws `ssm start-session`, the AWS CLI acts as an interactive wrapper for the underlying `StartSession` API. While the API response itself is a JSON object containing a `SessionId` and an encrypted `TokenValue`, the CLI—provided the Session Manager plugin is installed—immediately consumes that JSON to negotiate a WebSocket connection. Consequently, instead of seeing the raw JSON output, a CloudOps engineer is directly presented with an active terminal prompt on the target instance.

For Session Manager to be auditable, you must explicitly enable session logging by configuring the `SSM-SessionManagerRunShell` preferences document to send session output to S3 or CloudWatch Logs.

You first create a file `SessionManagerRunShell.json` similar to the following snippet:

```
{
  "schemaVersion": "1.0",
  "description": "Document to store regional settings for Session Manager",
```

```
  "sessionType": "Standard_Stream",
  "inputs": {
    "s3BucketName": "cloudops-engineer-soa-c03-guide-bucket",
    "s3KeyPrefix": "Chapter03",
    "s3EncryptionEnabled": true,
    "cloudWatchLogGroupName": "MyLogGroupName",
    "cloudWatchEncryptionEnabled": true,
    "cloudWatchStreamingEnabled": false,
    "kmsKeyId": "MyKMSKeyID",
    "runAsEnabled": true,
    "runAsDefaultUser": "MyDefaultRunAsUser",
    "idleSessionTimeout": "20",
    "maxSessionDuration": "60",
    "shellProfile": {
        "windows": "MyCommands",
        "linux": "MyCommands"
    }
  }
}
```

And then you run the following command:

```
aws ssm update-document \
    --name "SSM-SessionManagerRunShell" \
    --content "file://SessionManagerRunShell.json" \
    --document-version "\$LATEST"
```

Without this configuration, sessions leave no audit trail. For regulated environments, also enable KMS encryption for session data. To learn more, visit `https://docs.aws.amazon.com/systems-manager/latest/userguide/getting-started-configure-preferences-cli.html`.

The SSM Agent lives on the target instance (the EC2 instance or on-premises server). It is the listener that executes commands and must have the correct IAM role to communicate with AWS, whereas the Session Manager plugin lives on the client machine. It is an extension for the AWS CLI that turns the JSON response from the API into an interactive terminal session. You do not need the plugin to use Session Manager via the AWS Management Console; the browser handles that connection for you. The plugin is strictly for CLI-based access.

For more information, visit: `https://docs.aws.amazon.com/cli/latest/reference/ssm/start-session.html`.

Run Command

Run Command solves the problem of executing commands remotely across fleets without SSH, custom orchestration, or configuration drift. It allows CloudOps teams to run shell commands, scripts, and automation tasks across thousands of nodes in AWS, on-premises, or multi-cloud environments.

```
aws ssm send-command \
  --document-name "AWS-RunShellScript" \
  --targets "Key=tag:Role,Values=webserver" \
  --parameters commands="uptime" \
  --comment "Check uptime across fleet"
```

In this command:

- `--document-name "AWS-RunShellScript"`: Tells SSM to use the standard AWS-managed document for running shell commands.
- `--targets "Key=tag:Role,Values=webserver"`: Identifies the target instances based on their resource tags. Any managed node tagged with `Role:webserver` will receive the command.
- `--parameters commands="uptime"`: The specific Linux command to run on those targets (in this case, checking how long the system has been running).
- `--comment`: A user-defined label for tracking this specific invocation in the command history.

The command returns a `Command` object in JSON format confirming that the request was successfully sent.

`send-command` returns a receipt/ID; it *does not return the execution output* (`stdout`) in the initial response.

```
{
    "Command": {
        "CommandId": "a1b2c3d4-5678-90ab-cdef-EXAMPLE2026",
        "DocumentName": "AWS-RunShellScript",
        "DocumentVersion": "$DEFAULT",
        "Comment": "Check uptime across fleet",
        "ExpiresAfter": "2026-03-23T13:34:00.000000+00:00",
        "Parameters": {
            "commands": [
                "uptime"
            ]
        },
        "InstanceIds": [],
        "Targets": [
            {
```

```
                "Key": "tag:Role",
                "Values": [
                    "webserver"
                ]
            }
        ],
        "Status": "Pending",
        "StatusDetails": "Pending",
        "RequestedDateTime": "2026-03-23T11:34:00.000000+00:00",
        "TargetCount": 0,
        "CompletedCount": 0,
        "ErrorCount": 0,
        "DeliveryTimedOutCount": 0,
        "ServiceRole": "",
        "MaxConcurrency": "50",
        "MaxErrors": "0",
        "CloudWatchOutputConfig": {
            "CloudWatchLogGroupName": "",
            "CloudWatchOutputEnabled": false
        }
    }
}
```


Since `send-command` is asynchronous, you must use the `CommandId` from the previous output to fetch the results using:

```
aws ssm list-command-invocations --command-id "<COMMAND-ID>" -details
```

For more information, visit: `https://docs.aws.amazon.com/cli/latest/reference/ssm/send-command.html` and `https://docs.aws.amazon.com/cli/latest/reference/ssm/list-command-invocations.html`.

State Manager

State Manager solves the problem of configuration drift by enforcing a desired state across fleets. It ensures that instances maintain required configurations—packages, files, settings, policies—without manual intervention. The following command uses State Manager to ensure your managed nodes stay in a defined configuration. Specifically, it creates an *association* that automates the update of the SSM Agent.

```
aws ssm create-association \
  --name "AWS-UpdateSSMAgent" \
  --targets "Key=InstanceIds,Values=i-0123456789abcdef0" \
  --schedule-expression "rate(30 days)"
```

In this command:

- `create-association`: Tells Systems Manager to apply a specific configuration (an SSM Document) to a target and keep it that way.

- `--name "AWS-UpdateSSMAgent"`: Uses a predefined AWS document designed to check the current version of the SSM Agent and update it if a newer version is available.
- `--targets "Key=InstanceIds,Values=i-0123456789abcdef0"`: Limits this rule to one specific instance. (In a real-world fleet, you would likely target a tag like `Key=tag:OS,Values=Linux`.)
- `--schedule-expression "rate(30 days)"`: Defines when and how often a Systems Manager (SSM) association should run. Supports rate expressions (e.g., `"rate(30 days)"`) and cron expressions (`"cron(0 0 1 * * ?)"`).

The command returns an `AssociationDescription` object. This confirms the rule has been created. Because it is a "state" rule, SSM will now periodically check that instance to ensure the agent is up to date.


```
{
    "AssociationDescription": {
        "Name": "AWS-UpdateSSMAgent",
        "AssociationId": "12345678-abcd-1234-abcd-1234567890ab",
        "AssociationVersion": "1",
        "Date": "2026-03-23T16:15:00.000000-04:00",
        "LastUpdateAssociationDate": "2026-03-23T16:15:00.000000-04:00",
        "Overview": {
            "Status": "Pending",
            "DetailedStatus": "Creating"
        },
        "DocumentVersion": "$DEFAULT",
        "Parameters": {},
        "Targets": [
            {
                "Key": "InstanceIds",
                "Values": [
                    "i-0123456789abcdef0"
                ]
            }
        ],
        "ScheduleExpression": "rate(30 days)",
        "LastExecutionDate": null,
        "LastSuccessfulExecutionDate": null
    }
}
```


For more information, visit: `https://docs.aws.amazon.com/cli/latest/reference/ssm/create-association.html`.

For the exam, remember that `send-command` is a one-time action (e.g., "Run this script now"), whereas `create-association` is a persistent policy (e.g., "Make sure this agent is always the latest version, checking every 30 days").

Patch Manager

Patch Manager solves the problem of patching at scale. Instead of manually updating instances or relying on inconsistent OS-level tooling, Patch Manager automates patch baselines, maintenance windows, and compliance reporting. The following command uses Run Command to trigger a Patch Manager operation across a fleet of instances.

```
aws ssm send-command \
  --document-name "AWS-RunPatchBaseline" \
  --targets "Key=tag:PatchGroup,Values=prod-servers" \
  --parameters Operation=Scan \
  --comment "Scan entire production fleet for missing patches"
```

In this command:

- `--document-name "AWS-RunPatchBaseline"`: This specifies the core SSM Command document that acts as a blueprint for patching. It tells the SSM Agent how to interface with the native package manager (like `yum` or `apt`) to evaluate the instance against its assigned patch baseline.
- `--targets "Key=tag:PatchGroup,Values=prod-servers"`: This identifies the target group using resource tags. Every managed node that has a tag key of `PatchGroup` with the value `prod-servers` will be included in this operation.
- `--parameters Operation=Scan`: This instructs the document to only check for missing updates and report compliance status. It will not download or install any software, allowing you to audit your fleet's security posture without making changes.
- `--comment`: Attaches a descriptive label to the command execution, making it easier to identify this specific run in your AWS Systems Manager history.

The command returns a `Command` object confirming that the request is in a `Pending` state.


```
{
    "Command": {
        "CommandId": "h8i9j0k1-2233-4455-6677-EXAMPLE2026",
        "DocumentName": "AWS-RunPatchBaseline",
        "DocumentVersion": "$DEFAULT",
        "Comment": "Scan entire production fleet for missing patches",
        "ExpiresAfter": "2026-03-23T18:52:00.000000+00:00",
        "Parameters": {
            "Operation": [
                "Scan"
            ]
        },
        "InstanceIds": [],
        "Targets": [
            {
```

```
                "Key": "tag:PatchGroup",
                "Values": [
                    "prod-servers"
                ]
            }
        ],
        "Status": "Pending",
        "StatusDetails": "Pending",
        "RequestedDateTime": "2026-03-23T16:52:00.000000+00:00",
        "TargetCount": 0,
        "CompletedCount": 0,
        "ErrorCount": 0,
        "DeliveryTimedOutCount": 0,
        "MaxConcurrency": "50",
        "MaxErrors": "0",
        "CloudWatchOutputConfig": {
            "CloudWatchLogGroupName": "",
            "CloudWatchOutputEnabled": false
        }
    }
}
```

For more information, visit: `https://docs.aws.amazon.com/systems-manager/latest/userguide/patch-manager-ssm-documents.html`.

Inventory & Compliance

Inventory & Compliance solves the problem of visibility across heterogeneous fleets. It collects metadata—installed packages, network configuration, OS details, application versions—and evaluates compliance against patch baselines and configuration rules. This capability is essential for CloudOps teams that need consistent, audit-ready insight into their environments, regardless of whether nodes run in AWS, on-premises, or other clouds. The following command uses SSM Inventory to manually upload custom metadata to a specific managed node.

```
aws ssm put-inventory \
  --instance-id i-0123456789abcdef0 \
  --items '{
    "TypeName": "Custom:AppInfo",
    "SchemaVersion": "1.0",
    "CaptureTime": "2026-03-23T00:00:00Z",
    "Content": [
      {
        "Name": "webapp",
        "Version": "1.2.3"
      }
    ]
  }'
```

In this command:

- `--instance-id`: Specifies the target node (e.g., `i-0123456789abcdef0`) where the metadata will be stored.
- `--items`: Defines the metadata payload:
  - `TypeName`: A unique name for the custom inventory type. It must start with Custom: (e.g., `Custom:AppInfo`).
  - `SchemaVersion`: The version of the inventory schema, typically `1.0`.
  - `CaptureTime`: A timestamp indicating when the data was collected.
  - `Content`: A JSON array containing your custom key-value pairs (e.g., app name and version).

If the command is successful, the AWS CLI typically returns no output in the terminal. However, the underlying API response includes a simple message to confirm that the inventory record was accepted and stored by Systems Manager:

```
{
    "Message": "Successfully put inventory"
}
```

For more information, visit: `https://docs.aws.amazon.com/cli/latest/reference/ssm/put-inventory.html`.

Automation

Automation solves the problem of orchestrating complex operational workflows—patching, remediation, provisioning, configuration—without custom scripts or "breakable" pipelines. It ties together Parameter Store, Run Command, State Manager, Patch Manager, and Inventory into repeatable, auditable runbooks. The following command uses AWS Systems Manager Automation to perform a workflow-based task—in this case, stopping a specific EC2 instance.

```
aws ssm start-automation-execution \
  --document-name "AWS-StopEC2Instance" \
  --parameters InstanceId=i-0123456789abcdef0
```

In this command:

- `start-automation-execution`: Unlike `send-command` (which runs scripts inside an OS), this triggers an Automation workflow that interacts with the AWS infrastructure (APIs) externally.
- `--document-name "AWS-StopEC2Instance"`: This specifies an AWS-managed automation document that contains the logic to safely stop an instance. It handles the API calls to EC2 on your behalf.

- `--parameters InstanceId=i-0123456789abcdef0`: Passes the required input (the specific instance ID) to the automation document so it knows which resource to target.

The command returns an `AutomationExecutionId`. This is a unique identifier for the specific job we just started.

```
{
    "AutomationExecutionId": "7b8c9d0e-1234-5678-90ab-EXAMPLE2026"
}
```

While AWS provides many predefined automation documents—such as `AWS-StopEC2Instance`, `AWS-RestartEC2Instance`, and `AWS-RunPatchBaseline`—you are not limited to these managed runbooks. As a CloudOps engineer, you can—and are encouraged to—create fully customized automation documents using the `aws ssm create-document` command. A complete example of a custom Automation document is presented in Chapter 6, where we build a remediation workflow end-to-end.

Figure 3.1 illustrates the SSM Documents page from the AWS Management Console. We filter documents whose type is `Automation` and prefix equals `AWS-Restart`. Your own automation documents are listed in the "Owned by me" tab.

For more information, visit: `https://docs.aws.amazon.com/cli/latest/reference/ssm/start-automation-execution.html`.

For the exam, it's important to understand the difference between `start-automation-execution` and `send-command`. The former (`start-automation-execution`) handles Control Plane/AWS Resource management (e.g., stopping instances, creating AMIs, or updating CloudFormation). It communicates directly with AWS APIs and can work even if the SSM Agent is offline. The latter (`send-command`) initiates data plane/OS-level tasks (e.g., shell scripts, checking disk space, or patching) and requires an active SSM Agent on the target to function.

FIGURE 3.1 Filtering SSM Automation Documents.

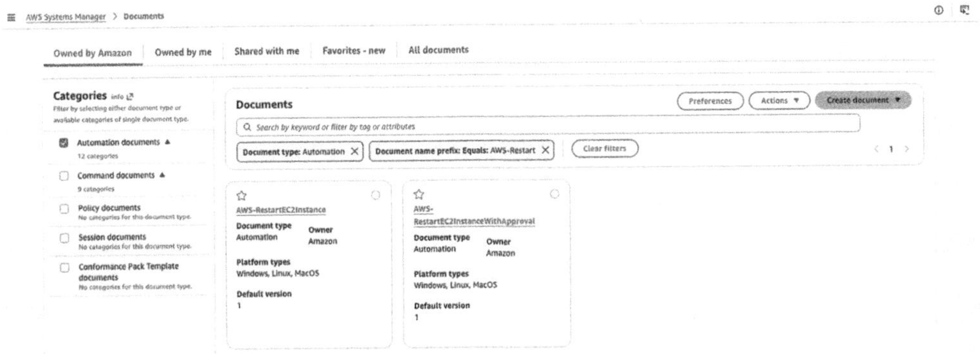

TABLE 3.1 Run Command vs. Automation

Feature	Run Command	Automation
Scope	Guest OS/software level	AWS Infrastructure/Service Level
How it works	SSM Agent must be running	Interacts with AWS APIs
Example use	Running `df -h` or `yum update`	Stopping an EC2 or creating a snapshot
Exam keyword	"Managed Node"/"Scale"	"Workflow"/"Runbook"/"Remediation"

Use Table 3.1 to internalize the differences between Run Command (`send-command`) and Automation (`start-automation-execution`).

Think of SSM Automation as the "Orchestrator." While Run Command is limited to the OS level, an Automation runbook can combine AWS API actions with OS-level scripts by invoking Run Command as a single step in a larger workflow. If an exam scenario requires coordinating infrastructure changes and OS-level commands together, SSM Automation is the correct answer.

AWS Config

AWS Config is the foundational service for continuous configuration monitoring, compliance evaluation, and change tracking across AWS Resources. While Systems Manager focuses on the state of your nodes, AWS Config focuses on the state of your AWS environment. It records configuration changes over time, evaluates those configurations against compliance rules, and provides a historical timeline that CloudOps engineers can use for troubleshooting, auditing, and governance.

AWS Config plays a central role in the Sustain and Secure phases of the CloudOps cycle. It ensures that resources remain compliant with organizational policies—such as enforcing encryption, restricting public access, or validating tagging standards—and it provides the forensic visibility needed to understand when and how a resource drifted from its intended state.

At its core, AWS Config performs three key functions:

Resource Recording AWS Config continuously records configuration changes for supported AWS Resources. This includes details such as security group rules, IAM policy attachments, S3 bucket settings, VPC route tables, and more. Each change is captured as a configuration item and stored in a timeline that CloudOps engineers can query at any time.

Compliance Evaluation AWS Config evaluates resources against Config Rules, which define the desired state of your environment. AWS provides many *managed rules*—such as checking whether S3 buckets block public access or whether IAM users have MFA enabled—but CloudOps teams can also create *custom rules* using Lambda functions for organization-specific policies.

Change Tracking and Troubleshooting AWS Config maintains a complete history of configuration changes, enabling CloudOps engineers to answer questions like:

"When did this security group become open to the world?"
"Who modified this IAM policy?"
"Why did this resource drift from the baseline?"

This historical visibility is essential for root-cause analysis and audit readiness.

Prerequisites for Enabling AWS Config

Before AWS Config can begin recording configuration changes, a few foundational components must be in place. AWS Config relies on an IAM role, a delivery channel, and the configuration recorder working together, and understanding this relationship is essential for your CloudOps team of engineers.

AWS Config uses a service-linked role named `AWSServiceRoleForConfig`, which the service automatically assumes (upon enablement) to record resource configurations and deliver snapshots to S3 and SNS. This role is created with the AWS-managed policy `AWSConfigServiceRolePolicy`, granting the read-only and delivery permissions AWS Config requires. Because this is a service-linked role, users do not need `iam:PassRole` to enable AWS Config; they only need permission to create or use the service-linked role.

To retrieve the exact ARN of your `AWSServiceRoleForConfig` role, use the following command:

```
aws iam get-role \
  --role-name AWSServiceRoleForConfig \
  --query "Role.Arn" --output text
```

In addition to the role, AWS Config requires a delivery channel, which defines where configuration snapshots are stored and how notifications are sent. The delivery channel usually points to an S3 bucket for snapshots and optionally an SNS topic for change notifications. Importantly, the delivery channel must exist before the configuration recorder can be started; otherwise, AWS returns an error.

You can create a delivery channel with the following command, provided you have the necessary permissions:

```
aws configservice put-delivery-channel \
  --delivery-channel name=default,s3BucketName=my-config-bucket
```

When you configure a delivery channel, AWS Config does not validate whether the S3 bucket policy allows the service to write objects. The `put-delivery-channel` command will succeed even if the bucket is misconfigured. However, AWS Config will later fail to deliver configuration snapshots unless the bucket policy explicitly grants the `config.amazonaws.com` service principal permission to `s3:PutObject`. To verify that delivery is actually working, you should always run `aws configservice describe-delivery-channel-status` and check for the `lastStatus` field.

Only after the delivery channel is created and the recorder is started will AWS Config begin capturing configuration items, evaluating rules, and delivering compliance data. Together, these prerequisites form the operational foundation of AWS Config.

You can create Config Rules at any time—even before the recorder is running—but they will not evaluate until the recorder and delivery channel are fully configured. This subtle distinction often appears in exam scenarios and is critical for understanding how AWS Config behaves in real CloudOps environments.

Enabling AWS Config and Starting the Recorder

With the IAM role, delivery channel, and required permissions in place, we can now proceed to enable AWS Config and activate the configuration recorder.

```
aws configservice put-configuration-recorder \
  --configuration-recorder '{
      "name": "default",
      "roleARN": "arn:aws:iam::123456789012:role/aws-service-role/config.
amazonaws.com/AWSServiceRoleForConfig"
  }' \
  --recording-group '{
      "allSupported": true,
      "includeGlobalResourceTypes": true
  }'
```

In this command:

- `--configuration-recorder`: Defines the identity and permissions for the recorder. We are using a JSON object with the following keys:
  - `name`: Identifies the recorder. In nearly all cases, this must be default. AWS Config only supports one recorder per Region, and most tools expect it to be named `default`.

  - `roleARN`: The Amazon Resource Name (ARN) of the IAM role that AWS Config assumes to perform its work. By using the Service-Linked Role (SLR) ARN you are using a role that AWS manages automatically for you.
- `--recording-group`: Defines the scope—what specific resources should be "on the map" for tracking. We are using a JSON object with the following keys:
  - `allSupported`: A Boolean (`true` or `false`). When `true`, AWS Config records every supported resource type in that Region (e.g., EC2, S3, RDS).
  - `includeGlobalResourceTypes`: A Boolean (`true` or `false`). When `true`, AWS Config includes global resources—specifically IAM users, groups, roles, and customer-managed policies. This can only be set to `true` if `allSupported` is also true.

After running this command, the recorder exists in a "CREATED" state but is essentially "OFF." It will not record a single change until you tell it to start.

```
aws configservice start-configuration-recorder \
  --configuration-recorder-name default
```

Once the recorder is running, AWS Config begins capturing configuration changes and evaluating rules.

For more information, visit: `https://docs.aws.amazon.com/cli/latest/reference/configservice/put-configuration-recorder.html` and `https://docs.aws.amazon.com/cli/latest/reference/configservice/start-configuration-recorder.html`.

Creating Config Rules

With AWS Config enabled, CloudOps engineers can define the desired state of their environment using Config Rules. These rules evaluate resources continuously and flag non-compliant configurations.

AWS provides two types of rules:

- Managed rules, which are predefined by AWS
- Custom rules, which are powered by Lambda functions you write

Both types are used heavily in compliance frameworks and Conformance Packs.

Creating a Managed Config Rule

The following example creates a Managed Config Rule that prohibits public reads from an S3 bucket:

```
aws configservice put-config-rule \
  --config-rule '{
    "ConfigRuleName": "s3-bucket-public-read-prohibited",
    "Source": {
```

```
      "Owner": "AWS",
      "SourceIdentifier": "S3_BUCKET_PUBLIC_READ_PROHIBITED"
    }
  }'
```

To list all rules and filter for those owned by AWS, use the `describe-config-rules` command with a query:

```
aws configservice describe-config-rules \
    --query 'ConfigRules[?Source.Owner==`AWS`].ConfigRuleName'
```

Creating a Custom Config Rule

Custom rules allow CloudOps engineers to enforce organization-specific policies. The following example creates (or updates) a Custom Config Rule that uses an AWS Lambda function to evaluate whether your EC2 instances have a specific tag:

```
aws configservice put-config-rule \
  --config-rule '{
    "ConfigRuleName": "ec2-require-environment-tag",
    "Description": "Ensures all EC2 instances have the Environment tag.",
    "Scope": {
      "ComplianceResourceTypes": [
        "AWS::EC2::Instance"
      ]
    },
    "Source": {
      "Owner": "CUSTOM_LAMBDA",
      "SourceIdentifier": "arn:aws:lambda:us-east-1:123456789012:function:Check
EnvironmentTag",
      "SourceDetails": [
        {
          "EventSource": "aws.config",
          "MessageType": "ConfigurationItemChangeNotification"
        }
      ]
    },
    "InputParameters": "{\"requiredTagKey\":\"Environment\"}"
  }'
```

In this command:

- `put-config-rule`: Defines the logic and scope for a compliance check.
- `"Owner": "CUSTOM_LAMBDA"`: Specifies that this is a Custom Rule (not an AWS Managed Rule), meaning it relies on code you've written in a Lambda function.
- `"SourceIdentifier"`: The ARN of the Lambda function that performs the actual evaluation logic.

- `"MessageType": "ConfigurationItemChangeNotification"`: Sets this as a change-triggered rule. The Lambda will run every time an EC2 instance is created or modified.
- `"Scope"`: Limits the rule to only evaluate `AWS::EC2::Instance` resource types.
- `"InputParameters"`: Passes a JSON string (`{"requiredTagKey": "Environment"}`) to the Lambda function, telling it exactly which tag key to look for.

For this command to work, you must have already created the Lambda function and granted AWS Config the `lambda:InvokeFunction` permission to call it.

Custom rules are essential for enforcing internal standards such as naming conventions, encryption requirements, or tag compliance.

For more information, visit: `https://docs.aws.amazon.com/cli/latest/reference/configservice/put-config-rule.html`.

Conformance Packs for Compliance Frameworks

While individual rules are useful, most organizations need to evaluate compliance against entire frameworks such as:

- CIS Benchmarks
- NIST 800-53
- PCI DSS
- HIPAA

AWS provides Conformance Packs, which bundle multiple Config Rules (managed or custom) into a single, deployable compliance baseline. Conformance Packs offer:

- Consistent governance across accounts and Regions
- Centralized compliance reporting
- A scalable way to enforce regulatory or internal standards

For CloudOps engineers working in regulated environments, Conformance Packs are indispensable.

Cost Considerations

AWS Config incurs charges for recording configuration items, evaluating Config Rules (including Conformance Packs), and storing configuration history and snapshots in S3. Because Config evaluates resources continuously, costs scale with the number of resources, the frequency of configuration changes, and the number of rules deployed across accounts and Regions. CloudOps engineers should design rules intentionally, avoid unnecessary evaluations, and use aggregation where possible to keep costs predictable and aligned with operational needs. For more information, visit: `https://aws.amazon.com/config/pricing/`.

Compute

Compute services form the foundation of application execution in AWS, and CloudOps engineers must understand how workloads are deployed, monitored, sustained, secured, and optimized across different compute models. Amazon EC2 is the starting point for this journey: it provides the most control over operating systems, networking, storage, and lifecycle behavior, making it the baseline against which other compute abstractions—such as Image Builder, Lambda, and container services—are understood. Before exploring higher-level compute options, it is essential to establish how EC2 instances are launched, maintained, and governed throughout their lifecycle.

Amazon Elastic Compute Cloud

Amazon Elastic Compute Cloud (Amazon EC2) provides flexible virtual machine compute capacity and remains the backbone of many traditional, hybrid, and lift-and-shift workloads. It offers full control over the operating system, networking, storage, and lifecycle, making it ideal for applications that require customization, predictable performance, or integration with legacy components. EC2 fits naturally into the Deploy phase of the CloudOps cycle, where engineers define Amazon Machine Images (AMIs), instance types, networking, and IAM roles to launch consistent and governed compute environments. At the same time, EC2 instances follow their own instance lifecycle—from pending to running, stopping, stopped, shutting down, and terminated—and CloudOps engineers must understand these transitions to manage availability, automation, and cost effectively.

Once deployed, EC2 instances must be continuously monitored using CloudWatch metrics (covered in Chapter 6), VPC Flow Logs (covered in Chapter 10), and health checks to detect performance issues, network reachability problems, or OS-level failures. The Sustain phase focuses on keeping systems healthy and consistent over time through patching, configuration management, and lifecycle operations. Patching is a core sustainment activity because it prevents drift and maintains operational integrity, but it also directly contributes to the Secure phase by remediating vulnerabilities and reducing attack surface. EC2 then supports the Optimize phase through right-sizing, storage tuning, and selecting the appropriate purchasing model to balance performance and cost.

EC2's flexibility means CloudOps engineers must apply strong governance, tagging, and automation to avoid misconfigurations and cost overruns. Understanding the separation between the AWS control plane and the instance data plane is essential for troubleshooting, as many operational issues originate from OS-level changes rather than AWS infrastructure. The EC2 lifecycle also plays a role here: for example, EBS-backed instances can be stopped and started without losing data, while instance store volumes are lost on stop or termination, and Auto Scaling groups may replace instances automatically based on lifecycle hooks and health checks.

From a cost perspective, EC2 costs are driven by instance type, storage, data transfer, and purchasing model. Right-sizing, using Savings Plans, and cleaning up unused EBS volumes and snapshots are essential CloudOps practices. Spot Instances offer deep discounts but require fault-tolerant workloads, while Reserved Instances and Savings Plans provide predictable long-term savings for steady-state usage.

With EC2 lifecycle responsibilities defined, the next step is ensuring instances launch from secure, consistent, and fully patched images, which is where EC2 Image Builder becomes essential.

EC2 Image Builder

EC2 Image Builder provides a structured, automated approach to creating, hardening, testing, and distributing Amazon Machine Images (AMIs). Instead of manually patching servers and capturing snapshots, CloudOps engineers use Image Builder to produce golden AMIs—standardized, secure, and fully validated images that serve as the foundation for EC2 deployments. This dramatically improves provisioning consistency and reduces configuration drift, ensuring that every instance begins its lifecycle from a known-good baseline.

Golden AMI pipelines are the core of Image Builder. A pipeline defines how an image is built, which components are applied, how it is tested, and where it is distributed. Components can include OS patches, security hardening steps, application dependencies, or compliance controls. Recipes define the structure of the image, while infrastructure configurations specify the build environment. Once a pipeline is created, Image Builder automatically rebuilds AMIs on a schedule—daily, weekly, or monthly—ensuring that new instances always launch with the latest patches and security controls already applied.

Hardening and compliance are first-class capabilities in Image Builder. CloudOps engineers can embed CIS benchmarks, logging agents, and vulnerability remediation directly into the image. This shifts security left: instead of securing instances after launch, the baseline image itself is secure. Image Builder integrates with Systems Manager (SSM) to run patching steps, execute compliance checks, and validate the final image. SSM Automation documents can also be used to create AMIs directly, providing a lightweight alternative for teams that need ad hoc or CI/CD-driven image creation.

Image Builder plays a critical role in provisioning consistency. When EC2 instances are launched from a golden AMI—whether through Launch Templates, Auto Scaling Groups, or Control Tower Account Factory—they inherit the same OS version, patches, configuration, and security posture. This reduces the operational burden on CloudOps teams, simplifies troubleshooting, and ensures that the EC2 lifecycle begins with a predictable, compliant baseline. In large environments, Image Builder pipelines become the authoritative source of truth for how servers should look at boot.

The next three sections walk you through different ways to create AMIs, which you need to know for the exam. Each method addresses a different operational scale and level of automation.

- Creating an AMI directly from EC2
- Creating an AMI using SSM Automation
- Creating a golden AMI pipeline with Image Builder

Creating an AMI Directly from EC2

CloudOps engineers often need to capture an AMI directly from a running instance—for example, before a major change, during a patch-and-capture workflow, or when preparing a baseline image prior to adopting Image Builder. To run the `aws ec2 create-image` command, you must have permissions such as `ec2:CreateImage`, `ec2:DescribeInstances`, and `ec2:CreateTags` (if tags are applied automatically).

The following command creates a new AMI from an existing EC2 instance:

```
aws ec2 create-image \
  --instance-id i-0123456789abcdef0 \
  --name "webserver-2026-04-01" \
  --description "Baseline webserver AMI with patches applied" \
  --no-reboot
```

In this command:

- `--instance-id`: Identifies the EC2 instance to capture. Must be in running or stopped state.
- `--name`: A human-readable name for the AMI.
- `--description`: Optional metadata describing the AMI's purpose.
- `--no-reboot`: Prevents the instance from rebooting before snapshot creation. Reduces downtime but may lead to inconsistent filesystem state.

The AWS CLI returns a single `ImageId` in JSON format. This confirms that the request was received and the imaging process has started in the background.

```
{
  "ImageId": "ami-0abcd1234ef567890"
}
```

This AMI ID is used in launch templates, Auto Scaling groups, and distribution workflows. This method is best for simple, non-recurring tasks or when you have manually configured a "perfect" instance and want to capture its state immediately.

For more information, visit: `https://docs.aws.amazon.com/cli/latest/reference/ec2/create-image.html`.

Creating an AMI Using SSM Automation

Systems Manager (SSM) provides a simple, flexible way to create AMIs without building a full Image Builder pipeline. This is ideal for ad hoc AMI creation, CI/CD workflows, or environments transitioning toward Image Builder. Required permissions include `ssm:StartAutomationExecution`, `ssm:GetAutomationExecution`, and `ec2:CreateImage`.

The following command initiates a runbook-based workflow that automates the creation of an AMI:

```
aws ssm start-automation-execution \
  --document-name "AWS-CreateImage" \
  --parameters '{
    "InstanceId": ["i-0123456789abcdef0"],
    "NoReboot": ["true"]
  }'
```

In this command:

- `--document-name "AWS-CreateImage"`: Specifies the AWS-managed automation document designed specifically to handle AMI creation.
- `--parameters`: Passes the following inputs as JSON lists.
  - `InstanceId`: The required source instance to be imaged.
  - `NoReboot`: An optional flag indicating whether to reboot the instance before creating the image.

For the exam, be aware that `ssm start-automation-execution` initiates a runbook-based workflow. Unlike the direct `ec2 create-image command`, this is a Control Plane operation that can include multiple steps (like verifying the instance state) defined in the automation document.

The command returns a unique `AutomationExecutionId` in JSON format. It does not return the `ImageId` yet, as the automation job is just beginning.

```
{
  "AutomationExecutionId": "12345678-aaaa-bbbb-cccc-1234567890ab"
}
```

You can query the execution to retrieve the AMI ID once complete.

While `ec2 create-image` and `ssm start-automation-execution` both result in an AMI, the SSM Automation approach is preferred in CloudOps because:

- **Extensibility:** The `AWS-CreateImage` document can be configured to perform additional tasks, such as rebooting the instance automatically or ensuring the instance is in a specific state before imaging.
- **Tracking:** You can track the progress of each step in the automation (e.g., "Stopping instance," "Creating snapshot," "Starting instance") via the Automation executions dashboard.

- **Permissions:** You can grant a user permission to run this automation without giving them direct `ec2:CreateImage` permissions, providing separation of duties, better security, and abstraction.

Creating a Golden AMI Pipeline with EC2 Image Builder

Image Builder pipelines automate the creation, hardening, testing, and distribution of AMIs. This is the preferred method for enterprise environments because it is the most scalable and "hands-off" solution for maintaining compliant, secure images on a recurring schedule. Required permissions include `imagebuilder:CreateImagePipeline`, `imagebuilder:GetImageRecipe`, `iam:PassRole`, and `ec2:RunInstances` (for build hosts).

The following command creates an Image Pipeline in EC2 Image Builder, which provides a fully automated, scheduled framework for building and maintaining golden AMIs:

```
aws imagebuilder create-image-pipeline \
  --name "webserver-pipeline" \
  --image-recipe-arn arn:aws:imagebuilder:us-east-1:123456789012:recipe/
webserver-recipe/1.0.0 \
  --infrastructure-configuration-arn arn:aws:imagebuilder:us-east-
1:123456789012:infrastructure-configuration/webserver-infra \
  --schedule '{
    "ScheduleExpression": "cron(0 0 * * ? *)"
  }'
```

In this command:

- `create-image-pipeline`: Sets up the automation engine that orchestrates the entire image creation lifecycle, including building, testing, and distributing the AMI.
- `--image-recipe-arn`: Links the pipeline to a specific Image Recipe. This recipe defines the source parent image (e.g., Amazon Linux 2) and the specific software components or security hardening scripts to be installed.
- `--infrastructure-configuration-arn`: Specifies the Infrastructure Configuration, which defines the underlying AWS Resources (like EC2 instance type, VPC subnets, and IAM roles) used to perform the build and test phases.
- `--schedule`: Sets a recurring trigger using a `cron` expression. In this example (`cron(0 0 * * ? *)`), the pipeline is configured to automatically run and generate a new AMI every day at midnight UTC.

The AWS CLI returns a JSON object containing the unique identifiers for the new pipeline. Unlike `ec2 create-image` or `ssm start-automation-execution`, it returns the resource ARN and a client token.


```
{
  "requestId": "b7c1c1c3-1234-5678-9abc-0abc123def45",
  "clientToken": "webserver-pipeline-20260401",
```

```
  "imagePipelineArn": "arn:aws:imagebuilder:us-east-
1:123456789012:image-pipeline/webserver-pipeline"
}
```

Unlike the manual or runbook-based methods, an Image Pipeline ensures your fleet stays secure by automatically regenerating images whenever the parent AMI is updated or on your custom schedule. This is the most operationally efficient way to handle large-scale, cross-account image management.

For more information, visit: `https://docs.aws.amazon.com/cli/latest/reference/imagebuilder/create-image-pipeline.html`.

Use Table 3.2 to internalize the differences between these three methods to create AMIs.

As golden AMIs and automated image pipelines help standardize and streamline virtual machine provisioning, many modern workloads move even further up the abstraction stack by eliminating servers altogether. This is where AWS Lambda enters the picture.

AWS Lambda (Serverless Compute)

AWS Lambda provides fully managed, event-driven compute that removes almost all traditional server responsibilities from CloudOps teams. There are no instances to launch, patch, harden, right-size, or monitor at the OS level. Instead, Lambda shifts operational focus toward function lifecycle management, event orchestration, and observability, allowing engineers to concentrate on application logic rather than infrastructure maintenance.

From an operational perspective, Lambda dramatically simplifies the Deploy and Sustain phases of the CloudOps cycle. Functions are deployed as versioned resources, each represented by an immutable versioned ARN. Aliases provide stable routing to specific versions, enabling safe deployments, blue/green patterns, and controlled rollouts without managing servers or AMIs. This eliminates configuration drift and ensures consistent execution environments across all invocations.

TABLE 3.2 AMI Creation Methods Comparison

Feature	Directly from EC2	SSM Automation	EC2 Image Builder Pipeline
Effort level	High (Manual)	Medium (Scripted)	Low (Automated)
Best use case	Ad hoc/one-off tasks	Repeatable updates/scripts	Enterprise "golden AMIs"
Automation	None (manual trigger)	Runbook-based	Full lifecycle/scheduled
Consistency	Low (prone to error)	High (repeatable steps)	Highest (recipe-driven)
Exam keyword	"Quick snapshot"	"Patching before image"	"Compliance"/"Distribution"

Monitoring and troubleshooting focus on function-level metrics such as duration, concurrency, throttles, and errors, all surfaced through CloudWatch. Logs are automatically captured by CloudWatch Logs, and CloudWatch Lambda Insights provides deeper visibility into cold starts, memory usage, and performance anomalies. Security responsibilities shift toward IAM permissions, environment variable protection, and ensuring that functions access only the resources they need. Because AWS manages the underlying runtime and patching, CloudOps teams primarily validate that functions run with least privilege and follow secure coding practices.

Cost optimization is equally straightforward: Lambda charges based on the number of requests and compute duration (memory allocated multiplied by execution time). CloudOps engineers tune memory settings, monitor concurrency, and use Provisioned Concurrency only when predictable latency is required. The result is a compute model that minimizes operational overhead while still providing strong controls for governance, security, and observability.

Containers

Containers provide a lightweight, portable execution environment that packages application code, dependencies, and runtime configuration into a single immutable artifact—a container image. Unlike virtual machines, containers share the host OS kernel, making them faster to start, easier to scale, and more efficient to operate. For CloudOps engineers, containerized workloads introduce a new operational lifecycle: building container images, storing and scanning them, orchestrating workloads across clusters, and automating deployments. AWS provides a suite of services—Amazon Elastic Container Service, Amazon Elastic Container Registry, Amazon Elastic Kubernetes Service, and Image Builder for Containers—that together form a complete operational ecosystem for running containers at scale.

Amazon Elastic Container Service

Amazon Elastic Container Service (Amazon ECS) provides a fully managed container orchestration platform that simplifies how CloudOps engineers deploy, scale, and operate containerized workloads. Unlike Kubernetes-based systems, ECS abstracts away much of the cluster complexity, allowing teams to focus on task definitions, service configuration, and container image lifecycle management. ECS supports two launch types—Fargate (serverless containers) and EC2 (self-managed container hosts)—giving CloudOps engineers flexibility in how much infrastructure they want to manage.

Operationally, ECS revolves around task definitions, which specify the container image, CPU and memory requirements, environment variables, IAM roles, logging configuration, and networking mode. Because task definitions reference container images by tag or digest, CloudOps engineers must ensure that images stored in Amazon ECR follow predictable versioning and immutability practices. ECS services then maintain the desired number of running tasks, handle rolling updates, and integrate with Application Load Balancers, CloudWatch Logs, and CloudWatch metrics for observability.

ECS reduces operational overhead by handling placement, health checks, and scaling. With Fargate, the operational burden drops even further—there are no EC2 hosts to patch, secure, or scale. CloudOps responsibilities shift toward monitoring service stability, validating task definition revisions, managing IAM roles for tasks, and ensuring that container images are built, scanned, and deployed consistently. ECS integrates tightly with ECR image scanning, CloudWatch Container Insights, and Systems Manager for runtime configuration, making it a practical and exam-relevant orchestration choice for many AWS environments.

Amazon Elastic Container Registry

Amazon Elastic Container Registry (Amazon ECR) is the central container image registry for AWS, and it plays a critical role in how CloudOps engineers build, store, secure, and distribute container images. ECR repositories store versioned container images, typically tagged by semantic version, build number, or Git commit hash. Because ECS and EKS both pull images directly from ECR, maintaining a clean, secure, and well-organized registry is essential for provisioning consistency and operational reliability.

ECR supports image scanning, which detects vulnerabilities in container layers using AWS-managed or enhanced scanning engines. CloudOps engineers rely on these scans to enforce compliance, identify outdated dependencies, and ensure that only hardened images are deployed. Lifecycle policies help automatically expire old or unused images, reducing storage costs and preventing clutter. ECR also supports cross-account access through resource policies, enabling centralized image management in multi-account landing zones—a common pattern in enterprise CloudOps.

Pushing images to ECR is a straightforward workflow: authenticate with `aws ecr get-login-password`, build the image locally, tag it with the repository URI, and push it using Docker or a CI/CD pipeline. CloudOps engineers ensure that build pipelines produce immutable images, avoid the pitfalls of mutable latest tags, and use digests for deterministic deployments. Because ECS (and EKS, covered next) reference images by tag or digest, ECR becomes the authoritative source of truth for container artifacts across the organization.

Amazon Elastic Kubernetes Service

Amazon Elastic Kubernetes Service (Amazon EKS) provides a managed Kubernetes control plane, allowing CloudOps engineers to run Kubernetes workloads without managing the underlying cluster control components. While EKS reduces operational burden by handling the API server, `etcd`, and control plane scaling, CloudOps teams still manage worker nodes (unless using Fargate), node groups, networking, and cluster add-ons. EKS is more flexible and powerful than ECS but requires deeper operational knowledge, especially around networking, IAM integration, and container image management.

Container images remain central to EKS operations. Kubernetes deployments, daemonsets, and statefulsets all reference images stored in ECR or external registries. CloudOps engineers must ensure that images are versioned, scanned, and immutable.

Furthermore, they must verify that pods and nodes have the necessary permissions to pull these images. While IAM Roles for Service Accounts (IRSA) remains a valid and established approach, EKS Pod Identity has emerged as a newer, simpler alternative for granting pods access to AWS services.

Pod Identity streamlines the workflow by eliminating the requirement for OIDC providers and allowing roles to be reused across different clusters. Both IRSA and Pod Identity are effective methods, but Pod Identity is generally the more straightforward option for clusters running on EC2 instances. EKS integrates with ECR seamlessly, and using ECR as the primary registry simplifies authentication, auditing, and compliance.

Operational responsibilities in EKS include managing cluster upgrades, node group lifecycle, VPC Container Network Interface (CNI) behavior, and observability through CloudWatch Container Insights or Prometheus/Grafana stacks. Because Kubernetes is declarative, CloudOps engineers focus on maintaining clean manifests, validating deployment strategies (rolling updates, blue/green, canary), and ensuring that cluster add-ons such as CoreDNS, kube-proxy, and the VPC CNI plugin remain healthy. EKS Fargate reduces node management further by running pods on serverless compute, but image management, IAM permissions, and workload configuration remain CloudOps responsibilities.

Automating Container Image Creation

Container images are the foundational artifacts consumed by ECS, EKS, and Fargate workloads. While orchestration platforms run containers, CloudOps engineers are responsible for ensuring that images are built consistently, scanned for vulnerabilities, stored securely, and deployed in a predictable manner. AWS provides several mechanisms to automate this lifecycle, ranging from simple CLI-based builds to fully managed pipelines using Systems Manager Automation or Image Builder for Containers. This section walks through each workflow using the same operational pattern: what the command does, which permissions are required, how each flag works, and what output to expect.

Building and Pushing Images with Docker and the AWS CLI

The following commands authenticate Docker to Amazon ECR, build a container image locally, tag it with the correct repository URI, and push it to ECR. This is the foundational workflow used in CI/CD pipelines and day-to-day CloudOps operations.

The following IAM permissions are required to perform this workflow:

- `ecr:GetAuthorizationToken`
- `ecr:BatchCheckLayerAvailability`
- `ecr:InitiateLayerUpload`
- `ecr:UploadLayerPart`

- `ecr:CompleteLayerUpload`
- `ecr:PutImage`

These permissions allow authentication to ECR and pushing image layers and manifests.

Authenticating Docker to ECR

```
aws ecr get-login-password \
  --region us-east-1 \
  | docker login \
      --username AWS \
      --password-stdin 123456789012.dkr.ecr.us-east-1.amazonaws.com
```

In this command:

- `aws ecr get-login-password`: This part of the command calls the AWS API to retrieve a temporary, base64-encoded authentication token.
- The pipe (|): It takes that secret token and passes it directly to the next command without displaying it on your screen or saving it to your shell history.
- `docker login`: This is the standard Docker command to authenticate.
  - `--username AWS`: For Amazon ECR, the username is always literally the string `AWS`.
  - `--password-stdin`: Tells Docker to read the password (the token from the first command) from the standard input (the pipe).
  - `123456789012.dkr.ecr.us-east-1.amazonaws.com`: This is the unique URI for your private ECR registry, which includes your AWS Account ID and Region.

If your AWS credentials are valid and you have the `ecr:GetAuthorizationToken` permission, the output is a single, successful confirmation line from Docker: "Login Succeeded."

Security tokens for ECR are only valid for 12 hours. This command is the standard way to refresh your session. In a CI/CD pipeline (like GitHub Actions or Jenkins), you would run this at the start of your build script to ensure the pipeline has permission to push the newly built image to your registry.

For more information, visit: `https://docs.aws.amazon.com/cli/latest/reference/ecr/get-login-password.html`.

With Docker authenticated to ECR, the next step is to build the container image locally.

Building the Container Image

The following command builds the container image using the `Dockerfile` in the current directory. Modern versions of Docker use BuildKit as the default build engine, which provides parallelized build steps, clearer progress reporting, and more efficient caching.

The following output reflects what CloudOps engineers typically see when building images locally.

```
docker build -t webapp:1.0.0 .
```

In this command:

- `docker build`: Instructs the Docker Engine to create a new image by executing the steps defined in a Dockerfile.
- `-t webapp:1.0.0`: The `tag` flag. It names the image `webapp` and assigns it the version `1.0.0`. Tagging is critical for version control and ensuring the correct code is deployed.
- `.` (the dot): Specifies the build context. It tells Docker to look for the `Dockerfile` and any required application files in the current directory.

The output shows the step-by-step progress of the build. Each instruction in your `Dockerfile` (like `FROM`, `RUN`, or `COPY`) is executed as a layer.

```
[+] Building 4.2s (7/7) FINISHED
 => [internal] load build definition from Dockerfile                   0.1s
 => => transferring dockerfile: 150B                                   0.0s
 => [internal] load .dockerignore                                      0.1s
 => [internal] load metadata for docker.io/library/alpine:latest       1.2s
 => [1/3] FROM docker.io/library/alpine:latest                         0.5s
 => [2/3] COPY . /app                                                  0.2s
 => [3/3] RUN apk add --no-cache python3                               2.0s
 => exporting to image                                                 0.1s
 => => exporting layers                                                0.1s
 => => writing image sha256:a1b2c3d4e5f6...                            0.0s
 => => naming to docker.io/library/webapp:1.0.0                        0.0s
```

Docker BuildKit is enabled by default in modern Docker releases. If you see older-style output (e.g., "Successfully built…"), it usually means that BuildKit was disabled via environment variables or daemon settings.

With the image built locally, the next step is to tag it with the ECR repository URI so it can be pushed to Amazon ECR.

Tagging the Image

This command assigns the ECR repository URI to the locally built image:

```
docker tag webapp:1.0.0 \
  123456789012.dkr.ecr.us-east-1.amazonaws.com/webapp:1.0.0
```

In this command:

- `docker tag`: Tells Docker to create an additional name for an existing image.

- `webapp:1.0.0`: The source image you already built locally.
- `123456789012.dkr.ecr.us-east-1.amazonaws.com/webapp:1.0.0`: The target tag. For Amazon ECR to accept a push, the image name must start with the full URI of your registry (Account ID + Region + `.amazonaws.com`) followed by the repository name and version.

The Docker tag command follows the "no news is good news" principle. If it works, it returns no output and simply brings you back to the command prompt.

You cannot push an image to ECR unless it is tagged with the Registry URI. If you try to push `webapp:1.0.0` directly, Docker will try to send it to Docker Hub instead of AWS.

With the container image tagged for ECR, the final step is to push it to the registry.

Pushing the Image to ECR

The following command uploads your locally built and tagged container image to your Amazon ECR private repository.

```
docker push \
  123456789012.dkr.ecr.us-east-1.amazonaws.com/webapp:1.0.0
```

In this command:

- `docker push`: Instructs the Docker CLI to transfer the image data from your local machine to a remote registry.
- `123456789012.dkr.ecr.us-east-1.amazonaws.com/webapp:1.0.0`: This is the full destination path. It targets the specific AWS account (`123456789012`), Region (`us-east-1`), and repository (`webapp`) with the version tag `1.0.0`.

The output displays the progress of each image layer as it is compressed and uploaded. If a layer already exists in the repository (e.g., from a previous build), Docker will skip it and report it as "Layer already exists," saving time and bandwidth.

```
The push refers to repository [://123456789012.dkr.ecr.us-east-1.amazonaws.com]
a1b2c3d4e5f6: Pushed
b2c3d4e5f6g7: Layer already exists
c3d4e5f6g7h8: Pushing [==================>                    ]  45.2MB/80MB
1.0.0: digest: sha256:7f8e9a0b... size: 1572
```

With the manual build-and-push workflow complete, the next step is to automate this process using Systems Manager Automation.

Automating Image Builds with SSM Automation

While Docker-based builds on a developer workstation are common, many organizations—especially those operating under compliance frameworks—require container images to be built inside AWS, using ephemeral, controlled, auditable environments. AWS Systems Manager Automation provides the framework for this pattern.

Unlike AMI creation, AWS does not provide a fully managed Automation runbook for building and pushing container images. Instead, as a CloudOps engineer, you can create a custom automation document that performs the same steps as the manual Docker workflow in the previous sections:

1. Authenticate to ECR.
2. Build the image.
3. Tag the image.
4. Push the image.

Creating a Custom SSM Automation Runbook

The following AWS Systems Manager (SSM) Automation runbook automates a secure, temporary build pipeline by launching an ephemeral EC2 instance that installs Docker and Git, clones a specified repository, builds a Docker image, and pushes it to an Amazon ECR repository. To maximize cost efficiency and security, the runbook includes error-handling logic that automatically terminates the instance upon completion or if any intermediate step fails, ensuring you only pay for the compute resources used during the build.

Save this runbook locally as `build-and-push.yaml`.

```
schemaVersion: '0.3'
description: Build a Docker image and push to ECR with auto-termination on
failure.
parameters:
  RepositoryUri:
    type: String
  ImageTag:
    type: String
  GitRepoUrl:
    type: String

mainSteps:
  - name: LaunchInstance
    action: aws:runInstances
    inputs:
      ImageId: ami-0c02fb55956c7d316
      InstanceType: t3.micro
      MinInstanceCount: 1
      MaxInstanceCount: 1
      IamInstanceProfileName: SSMInstanceProfile
```

```
    outputs:
      - Name: InstanceIdList
        Selector: "$.InstanceIds"
        Type: StringList

  - name: WaitUntilRunning
    action: aws:waitForAwsResourceProperty
    onFailure: step:TerminateInstance # If the instance fails to start/respond,
kill it
    inputs:
      Service: ec2
      Api: DescribeInstances
      InstanceIds: "{{LaunchInstance.InstanceIdList}}"
      PropertySelector: "$.Reservations[0].Instances[0].State.Name"
      DesiredValues:
        - running

  - name: BuildAndPushImage
    action: aws:runCommand
    onFailure: step:TerminateInstance # If the build fails, skip to termination
    inputs:
      DocumentName: AWS-RunShellScript
      InstanceIds: "{{LaunchInstance.InstanceIdList}}"
      Parameters:
        commands:
          - |
            sudo yum update -y
            sudo yum install -y docker git
            sudo service docker start
            git clone "{{GitRepoUrl}}" /tmp/app
            cd /tmp/app
            docker build -t localimage:latest .
            aws ecr get-login-password --region us-east-1 | docker login
--username AWS --password-stdin {{RepositoryUri}}
            docker tag localimage:latest {{RepositoryUri}}:{{ImageTag}}
            docker push {{RepositoryUri}}:{{ImageTag}}

  - name: TerminateInstance
    action: aws:changeInstanceState
    isEnd: true # This ends the automation after this step
    inputs:
      InstanceIds: "{{LaunchInstance.InstanceIdList}}"
      DesiredState: terminated
```

Figure 3.2 illustrates the workflow of the SSM automation document as it appears from the AWS Management Console.

Another custom runbook you can use as a reference is available at: `https://docs.aws.amazon.com/systems-manager/latest/userguide/automation-document-instance-recovery-example.html`.

FIGURE 3.2 The `BuildAndPushContainerImage` runbook.

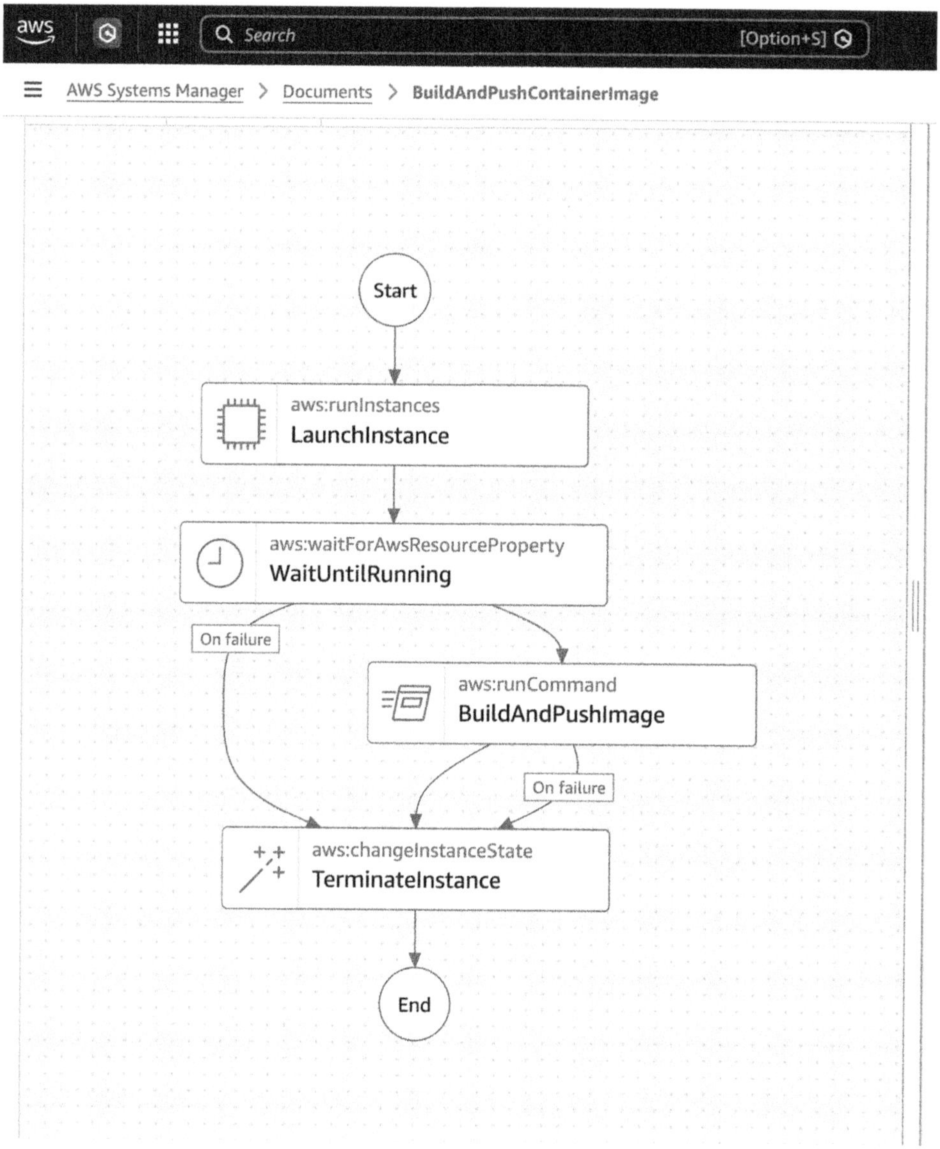

Registering the Runbook with SSM

Just because the runbook is saved locally, this doesn't mean Systems Manager can access it and use it. The following command ensures SSM is fully aware of this custom runbook.

```
aws ssm create-document \
  --name "BuildAndPushContainerImage" \
  --document-type "Automation" \
  --content file://build-and-push.yaml \
  --document-format YAML
```

For more information, visit: `https://docs.aws.amazon.com/cli/latest/reference/ssm/create-document.html`.

Once the runbooks is registered with SSM, you can execute it.

Starting the Automation Execution

You learned about the command `aws ssm start-automation-execution` early in this chapter. We use the same command to trigger the automation workflow we just created. The command tells AWS to start executing the steps in our runbook using the specific parameters (ECR URI, container image tag, and GitHub URL) we provided.

```
aws ssm start-automation-execution \
  --document-name "BuildAndPushContainerImage" \
  --parameters '{
    "RepositoryUri": ["123456789012.dkr.ecr.us-east-1.amazonaws.com/webapp"],
    "ImageTag": ["2026-04-01"],
    "GitRepoUrl": ["https://github.com/example/webapp.git"]
  }'
```

In this command:

- `--document-name "BuildAndPushContainerImage"`: The required name of the Automation runbook to be executed.
- `--parameters`: A key-value map containing the inputs required by the specific runbook. This includes:
  - `RepositoryUri`: The destination ECR repository address.
  - `ImageTag`: The version label for the Docker image.
  - `GitRepoUrl`: The source code repository for the build.

SSM Automation cannot use your local Docker image or local filesystem. The build occurs on an ephemeral EC2 instance inside AWS, so the build context must come from a remote source such as a Git repository or an S3 bucket.

With the Automation workflow in place, the next step is to explore how Image Builder provides a more structured, pipeline-oriented approach to container image creation.

Using EC2 Image Builder for Container Pipelines

The SSM Automation workflow in the previous section provides a flexible, script-driven way to build container images inside AWS. However, it still requires you to manage the build logic, the EC2 lifecycle, and the sequencing of steps. For organizations that want a more structured, pipeline-oriented approach, EC2 Image Builder offers a fully managed framework for defining, building, testing, and distributing container images.

Image Builder for Containers extends the same concepts used for AMI pipelines—recipes, components, infrastructure configurations, and schedules—to container image creation. Instead of orchestrating EC2 instances manually or writing custom Automation documents, you define a container recipe and an image pipeline, and Image Builder handles the rest.

This approach is ideal when you want:

- Consistent, repeatable builds
- Versioned container recipes
- Automated security updates
- Scheduled rebuilds
- Optional vulnerability scanning
- Integration with ECR as the target repository

Where SSM Automation gives you full control over the build steps, Image Builder gives you a declarative pipeline that abstracts away the underlying infrastructure.

To begin using this pipeline-driven model, you start by defining a *container recipe*—a declarative blueprint that specifies the base image, Dockerfile template, and any components Image Builder should apply during the build.

Creating the Container Recipe

A container recipe defines the base image, the Dockerfile template, and the build components that modify or harden the image. This is the declarative equivalent of the Dockerfile-based build process in the previous section "Building and Pushing Images with Docker and the AWS CLI."

To create a container recipe you need the following permissions:

- `imagebuilder:CreateContainerRecipe`
- `iam:PassRole` (for the Image Builder service role)

The following command creates a container recipe in EC2 Image Builder, which serves as a blueprint for building Docker images. It defines the base image, the software components to install, and the final destination repository.

```
aws imagebuilder create-container-recipe \
  --container-type DOCKER \
  --name "webapp-container-recipe" \
  --semantic-version "1.0.0" \
  --components '[
    {
```

```
      "componentArn": "arn:aws:imagebuilder:us-east-1:aws:component/
update-linux/1.0.0"
    }
  ]' \
  --dockerfile-template-uri "s3://mybucket/dockerfiles/webapp.Dockerfile" \
  --parent-image "public.ecr.aws/amazonlinux/amazonlinux:latest" \
  --target-repository '{
    "service": "ECR",
    "repositoryName": "webapp"
  }'
```

In this command:

- `--container-type`: The type of container to create, e.g., DOCKER.
- `--name`: Sets the unique identifier for the recipe (e.g., `"webapp-container-recipe"`).
- `--semantic-version`: Assigns a semantic version (`major.minor.patch`) to the recipe.
- `--components`: An array of software components to be installed during the build process; here, it includes a managed update component.
- `--dockerfile-template-uri`: The S3 URI pointing to the custom Dockerfile used to build the container.
- `--parent-image`: The base image (e.g., Amazon Linux) that Image Builder uses to start the build.
- `--target-repository`: The destination Amazon ECR repository where the final, built image will be stored.

The command returns a JSON object confirming the creation of the recipe. It provides a unique Amazon Resource Name (ARN) and a `ClientToken`.

```
{
    "requestId": "a1b2c3d4-5678-90ab-cdef-EXAMPLE11111",
    "clientToken": "a1b2c3d4-5678-90ab-cdef-EXAMPLE22222",
    "containerRecipeArn": "arn:aws:imagebuilder:us-east-
1:123456789012:container-recipe/webapp-container-recipe/1.0.0"
}
```

In this response:

- `containerRecipeArn`: This is the most important field. You will need this ARN to create an image pipeline or to manually start a build.
- `requestId`: A unique ID for the specific API call, useful for AWS support or CloudTrail auditing.
- `clientToken`: A unique case-sensitive identifier you can provide to ensure the idempotency of the request.

The `imagebuilder create-container-recipe` command only saves the definition. It does not start the build process or create any resources in ECR yet.

For more information, visit: `https://docs.aws.amazon.com/cli/latest/reference/imagebuilder/create-container-recipe.html`.

With the recipe defined, the next step is to create a pipeline that uses it to produce container images automatically.

Creating the Container Pipeline

A container pipeline defines when and how Image Builder should build new images. Pipelines can run on a schedule, on demand, or in response to changes in the recipe or components. This replaces the manual triggering of SSM Automation executions from the previous section, and provides a fully managed, repeatable workflow for container image creation.

To create a container pipeline you need the following permissions:

- `imagebuilder:CreateImagePipeline`
- `iam:PassRole`

The following command creates an Image Pipeline in EC2 Image Builder, which automates the building and maintenance of your container images based on the recipe we just created.

```
aws imagebuilder create-image-pipeline \
  --name "webapp-container-pipeline" \
  --container-recipe-arn arn:aws:imagebuilder:us-east-
1:123456789012:container-recipe/webapp-container-recipe/1.0.0 \
  --infrastructure-configuration-arn arn:aws:imagebuilder:us-east-
1:123456789012:infrastructure-configuration/container-build-infra \
  --schedule '{
    "scheduleExpression": "cron(0 3 * * ? *)"
  }'
```

In this command:

- `--name`: Names the pipeline (e.g., `"webapp-container-pipeline"`).
- `--container-recipe-arn`: Links the pipeline to the specific blueprint (recipe) that defines your base image and components.
- `--infrastructure-configuration-arn`: Specifies the infrastructure (instance type, subnet, IAM role) used to run the build.
- `--schedule`: Sets a `scheduleExpression` (cron) to run the build automatically—in this case, every day at 3:00 AM UTC.

The output is a JSON response confirming the unique Amazon Resource Name (ARN) for your new pipeline.

```
{
    "requestId": "b2c3d4e5-6789-0abc-def1-EXAMPLE33333",
    "clientToken": "b2c3d4e5-6789-0abc-def1-EXAMPLE44444",
    "imagePipelineArn": "arn:aws:imagebuilder:us-east-
1:123456789012:image-pipeline/webapp-container-pipeline"
}
```

The recipe is just a static definition; the pipeline is the engine that actually executes that definition on a schedule or manual trigger.

If you want to manually start a build right now without waiting for the 3:00 AM schedule, use:

```
aws imagebuilder start-image-pipeline-execution \
    --image-pipeline-arn arn:aws:imagebuilder:us-east-1:123456789012:image-
pipeline/webapp-container-pipeline
```

For more information, visit: https://docs.aws.amazon.com/cli/latest/reference/imagebuilder/start-image-pipeline-execution.html.

With the pipeline created, you—as a CloudOps engineer—now have built a fully managed, repeatable mechanism for producing hardened, versioned container images without managing EC2 lifecycles or writing custom Automation logic.

Summary

This chapter began by establishing the operational foundation required for managing compute and container workloads at scale. "Systems Operations Fundamentals" introduced AWS Systems Manager and AWS Config as the core services that enable centralized operations, secure access, configuration enforcement, patching, automation, and compliance monitoring. These services shift the CloudOps mindset away from managing individual instances and toward managing fleets, where automation, visibility, and governance are the primary levers of operational excellence. By grounding the CloudOps engineers in these fundamentals first, this chapter ensures that every subsequent compute or container service is understood within the broader context of lifecycle management.

Building on that foundation, the "Compute" section explored the core AWS compute services—EC2, EC2 Image Builder, and related operational tooling—through the lens of deployment, provisioning, and automation. Rather than focus solely on launching instances, the section emphasized the full lifecycle: secure access without SSH, patching and configuration with Systems Manager, drift detection with Config, and automated remediation. This reinforces the idea that compute resources are not isolated units but components of a managed, monitored, and continuously maintained environment. The section also highlighted how CloudOps engineers use automation to ensure consistency across environments, reduce operational risk, and support scalable architectures.

Finally, the "Containers" section extended these operational principles into the world of containerized workloads. The section began with the manual Docker workflow, then showed how to automate the same process using SSM Automation. It concluded with Image Builder pipelines for fully managed, declarative container image creation. Together, these subsections illustrate the progression from hands-on container builds to automated workflows and finally to pipeline-driven, infrastructure-abstracted image creation. You should now understand not only how to deploy compute and container workloads, but how to operate them securely, consistently, and at scale—aligning directly with the domains tested in the SOA-C03 exam.

Exam Essentials

Understand why systems operations is critical to CloudOps. CloudOps is not about launching individual resources—it is about operating entire fleets consistently, securely, and predictably. The exam expects you to understand how operational tooling such as AWS Systems Manager and AWS Config provide centralized visibility, automation, and governance across enterprise-scale compute and container environments. These services form the operational backbone that enables patching, configuration enforcement, secure access, and compliance monitoring at scale.

Know Systems Manager Parameter Store types and tiers. Utilize Systems Manager Parameter Store as a centralized, secure repository for managing configuration data like database strings or encrypted secrets. Parameters are categorized into three types: `String` for plain text, `StringList` for comma-separated values, and `SecureString` for sensitive data encrypted via AWS KMS. You must distinguish between the `Standard` tier, which is free and supports up to 10,000 parameters at 4 KB each, and the `Advanced` tier, which allows for 100,000 parameters at 8 KB each and introduces parameter policies for expiration and TTL. To simplify management, you can enable intelligent-tiering to automatically switch between these tiers based on the specific count or size requirements of your request.

Master AWS Config recording, rules, and conformance packs. Deploy AWS Config as a regional governance service to record configuration history and detect resource drift. You must specifically understand the difference between managed rules (predefined best practices) and custom rules (logic written in AWS Lambda or other supported languages) to evaluate your infrastructure's compliance. While rules can be triggered by configuration changes or periodic schedules, conformance packs are the key to scaling these controls across an entire AWS Organization. These packs bundle multiple rules and remediation actions into a single immutable YAML template, allowing you to establish a common security baseline that member accounts cannot modify or delete.

Know the difference between AWS Systems Manager and AWS Config. Systems Manager is an operations service: it executes actions such as patching, running commands, enforcing desired state, and automating workflows. AWS Config is a governance service: it records configuration changes, evaluates resources against compliance rules, and detects drift. A common exam trap is confusing "who changed something" (CloudTrail), "what changed" (Config), and "how to fix it" (Systems Manager). Keep these roles clearly separated.

Understand how EC2 Image Builder enables automated AMI creation and governance. EC2 Image Builder provides a structured, pipeline-driven approach to creating, hardening, testing, and distributing Amazon Machine Images (AMIs). Instead of manually building images or scripting the process with SSM Automation, Image Builder uses recipes, components, and infrastructure configurations to produce versioned, compliant AMIs on a schedule. The exam expects you to know when EC2 Image Builder is the right choice—specifically when you need repeatable, centrally governed image creation with integrated testing and distribution.

Master the container image build workflow. The exam expects you to understand the full container image lifecycle: building, tagging, pushing, and storing images in ECR. You should know the manual Docker workflow, how to authenticate to ECR, and how to automate the build process using SSM Automation. The key concept is that container builds inside AWS typically use ephemeral EC2 instances, and Automation documents orchestrate the sequence of steps required to produce a reproducible image.

Know when to use SSM Automation vs EC2 Image Builder. SSM Automation gives you full control over the build steps and is ideal for custom workflows, compliance-driven environments, or scenarios where you need to orchestrate EC2 instances directly. EC2 Image Builder provides a higher-level, declarative pipeline for producing versioned, hardened container images without managing infrastructure. The exam may test your ability to choose the right tool: SSM Automation for procedural builds, EC2 Image Builder for scheduled, declarative (recipe-driven) pipelines.

Review Questions

1. A CloudOps team manages 800 EC2 instances across three environments (development, staging, production). They need to apply OS patches to production instances during a specific maintenance window, while allowing development instances to patch immediately. Which combination of Systems Manager features should they configure?
   A. Create separate patch baselines per environment and assign maintenance windows to production.
   B. Use Run Command with a tag filter to patch all instances simultaneously.
   C. Use AWS Config Rules to detect missing patches and auto-remediate with Lambda.
   D. Create a single patch baseline and use Amazon EventBridge to schedule patching.

2. A company runs 300 EC2 instances tagged by environment (dev, staging, prod). A CloudOps engineer needs to collect diagnostic logs from all production instances and store the output in S3, without opening inbound ports. Which approach meets these requirements?
   A. Use Systems Manager Run Command with a tag-based target and configure output to an S3 bucket.
   B. Use EC2 Instance Connect to SSH into each instance and run the command manually.
   C. Create a Lambda function that uses the EC2 API to execute commands on each instance.
   D. Use AWS Config to evaluate log collection compliance and trigger remediation.

3. A team wants to build container images using a Git repository as the build context inside AWS. Which command must be included in the Automation document?
   A. `docker pull`
   B. `docker run`
   C. `git clone`
   D. `aws s3 sync`

4. A CloudOps team needs to automate remediation when an EC2 instance drifts from its approved configuration. What should they use?
   A. AWS Config + SSM Automation
   B. AWS Lambda + CloudTrail
   C. Amazon EventBridge Scheduler
   D. AWS CloudFormation StackSets

5. A CloudOps team currently builds container images using a custom SSM Automation document that launches an EC2 instance, runs a build script, and pushes to ECR. They want to add automated vulnerability scanning, scheduled rebuilds, and version-controlled build definitions without managing EC2 lifecycle logic. Which approach should they adopt?

   A. Add scanning steps to the existing SSM Automation document.

   B. Replace the workflow with an EC2 Image Builder container pipeline.

   C. Use AWS CodeBuild with a `buildspec.yml` file.

   D. Use AWS Lambda to orchestrate the build steps.

6. A CloudOps engineer's CI/CD pipeline fails when pushing a container image to ECR with the error "no basic auth credentials." The pipeline runs `docker build`, `docker tag`, and `docker push` in sequence. What is the most likely cause?

   A. The `docker tag` command used an incorrect repository URI.

   B. The ECR repository does not exist in the target Region.

   C. The pipeline did not run `aws ecr get-login-password` and `docker login` before pushing.

   D. The IAM role lacks the `ecr:PutImage` permission.

7. A company's security policy requires that all EC2 access be controlled through IAM policies, be fully auditable in CloudTrail, and not require any inbound ports to be open on security groups. Which access method meets all three requirements?

   A. AWS Systems Manager Session Manager

   B. EC2 Instance Connect

   C. SSH with key pairs stored in AWS Secrets Manager

   D. AWS Systems Manager Run Command

8. A CloudOps team discovers that several EC2 instances are not appearing in the Systems Manager Fleet Manager console. They need to continuously monitor all instances for SSM Agent compliance and receive alerts when instances become non-compliant. Which approach should they implement?

   A. Use Amazon Inspector to scan instances for the SSM Agent.

   B. Create a CloudWatch alarm based on SSM Agent metrics.

   C. Enable an AWS Config managed rule to evaluate SSM Agent compliance and configure SNS notifications.

   D. Use Systems Manager Inventory to track installed software.

9. A CloudOps engineer runs an SSM Run Command against instances tagged `Role:webserver`, but three instances show a status of "Undeliverable." The instances are running in a public subnet with Internet access, and the SSM Agent is installed and running. What is the most likely cause?

   A. The Run Command document is incompatible with the instance operating system.

   B. The instances do not have an IAM instance profile with the `AmazonSSMManagedInstanceCore` policy.

   C. The instances are not tagged correctly for the Run Command target filter.

   D. The SSM Agent version is outdated and needs to be updated.

10. A company currently creates AMIs by manually configuring an EC2 instance and running `aws ec2 create-image` each month. They want to automate this process so that AMIs are rebuilt on a schedule with consistent hardening steps and automated testing before the image is made available. Which approach should they adopt?

    A. Write a shell script that runs `aws ec2 create-image` on a cron schedule.

    B. Create an SSM Automation document that configures the instance and creates the AMI.

    C. Create an EC2 Image Builder pipeline with a recipe, test components, and a build schedule.

    D. Use AWS Lambda to launch an instance, configure it, and create an AMI monthly.

11. A CloudOps engineer needs to verify that a specific configuration file exists on all 1,000 managed instances and collect the file contents centrally for audit. The output must be stored in S3 and the engineer needs to identify which instances are missing the file. Which approach is most operationally efficient?

    A. Use Run Command with `AWS-RunShellScript`, target by tag, and configure S3 output.

    B. Use Session Manager to connect to each instance and check manually.

    C. Use AWS Config to create a custom rule that checks for the file.

    D. Use SSM Inventory to collect file metadata from all instances.

12. A team wants to terminate an EC2 instance automatically if a container build fails during an SSM Automation workflow. What should they configure?

    A. `aws:runInstances`

    B. `aws:waitForAwsResourceProperty`

    C. `aws:runCommand`

    D. `onFailure: step:TerminateInstance`

13. A CloudOps engineer wants to build a Docker image inside AWS using an ephemeral EC2 instance launched by SSM Automation. Which step performs the build?

    A. `aws:runInstances`

    B. `aws:waitForAwsResourceProperty`

    C. `aws:runCommand`

    D. `aws:changeInstanceState`

14. A CloudOps team wants to detect when an EC2 instance becomes non-compliant with CIS benchmarks and automatically trigger a remediation workflow. What should they use?

    A. Amazon Inspector

    B. AWS Config with remediation

    C. AWS CloudTrail

    D. AWS Trusted Advisor

15. A CloudOps engineer uses EC2 user data to install application dependencies at launch. After scaling out, they discover that some instances failed to install dependencies because the user data script exited with errors, but the instances still joined the Auto Scaling group. How should they ensure only properly configured instances serve traffic?

    A. Add error handling to the user data script and signal `cfn-signal` to the Auto Scaling group.

    B. Use AWS Config to detect instances missing the dependencies and terminate them.

    C. Replace user data with an SSM Automation document triggered by EventBridge.

    D. Use a golden AMI with dependencies pre-installed and remove the user data script.

16. A team needs to schedule nightly container image builds without managing EC2 instances. What should they use?

    A. SSM Run Command

    B. AWS Batch

    C. EC2 Image Builder pipeline

    D. AWS Lambda

17. A CloudOps team is creating an EC2 Image Builder container recipe. They need the recipe to use a custom Dockerfile stored in S3, install security updates via a managed component, build from an Amazon Linux base image, and push the result to an ECR repository. Which combination of recipe fields must they configure?

    A. `parent-image`, `componentArn`, and `target-repository` only

    B. `dockerfile-template-uri`, `parent-image`, `componentArn`, and `target-repository`

    C. `dockerfile-template-uri` and `target-repository` only

    D. `parent-image` and `componentArn` only

18. A company wants to detect when an EC2 instance's security group changes and automatically revert it. What should they use?
   A. CloudTrail + Athena
   B. CloudWatch Logs Insights
   C. AWS Config + SSM Automation
   D. AWS Trusted Advisor

19. A compliance team needs a complete history of configuration changes to EC2 instances, including security group updates. Which service provides this?
   A. CloudWatch Logs
   B. AWS Config
   C. AWS Systems Manager Inventory
   D. AWS CloudTrail

20. A company wants to track who changed an EC2 instance's IAM role and when. Which service provides this?
   A. AWS Config
   B. Amazon Inspector
   C. AWS Systems Manager Inventory
   D. AWS CloudTrail

Answers to Review Questions

1. A. Patch Manager supports multiple patch baselines scoped by tags or patch groups. Maintenance windows let you define when patching occurs for specific targets, so production can be restricted to approved windows, while development patches immediately through on-demand operations. Run Command (Option B) can execute patching commands, but patching all instances simultaneously ignores the requirement for environment-specific timing. It also bypasses Patch Manager's baseline and compliance tracking. AWS Config (Option C) can detect missing patches via managed rules, but using Lambda for remediation adds unnecessary complexity. Patch Manager with maintenance windows is the purpose-built solution for scheduled patching. A single patch baseline (Option D) cannot enforce different approval rules per environment. EventBridge can trigger actions on a schedule but does not provide the maintenance window controls needed for environment-specific patching.

2. A. Run Command supports tag-based targeting to scope execution to production instances and natively supports S3 output for centralized log collection. It communicates through the SSM Agent without requiring inbound ports. EC2 Instance Connect (Option B) still requires SSH (port 22) to be open, which violates the no-inbound-ports requirement. Connecting to each instance individually is also impractical at scale. The EC2 API (Option C) does not include the ability to execute OS-level commands on instances. Lambda could invoke Run Command via the SSM API, but that adds unnecessary indirection. AWS Config (Option D)

evaluates resource configuration compliance but cannot execute commands on instances or collect log files.

3. C. `git clone` retrieves the build context. `docker pull` retrieves images (Option A), `docker run` executes containers (Option B), and `s3 sync` is irrelevant for Git repositories (Option D).

4. A. AWS Config detects drift and Automation remediates it. Lambda is possible but not the recommended pattern (Option B), EventBridge cannot remediate resources (Option C), and StackSets deploy infrastructure but do not correct drift (Option D).

5. B. EC2 Image Builder container pipelines provide built-in scheduling, version-controlled recipes, automated testing and scanning components, and handle EC2 lifecycle management internally. This meets all stated requirements with the least operational overhead. Adding scanning steps to the SSM Automation document (Option A) is possible but does not address the requirement to eliminate EC2 lifecycle management. The team would still need to handle instance launch, cleanup, and failure scenarios. CodeBuild (Option C) can build container images and supports `buildspec` files, but it does not natively provide image pipeline scheduling, recipe versioning, or the integrated testing framework that Image Builder offers. Lambda (Option D) has a 15-minute execution timeout and limited storage, making it unsuitable for container image builds. It also cannot run Docker natively.

6. C. The "no basic auth credentials" error specifically indicates that Docker has not been authenticated to the ECR registry. The pipeline must run `aws ecr get-login-password` piped to `docker login` before pushing. An incorrect repository URI (Option A) would produce a "repository does not exist" or name resolution error, not "no basic auth credentials." A missing repository (Option B) would produce a "repository not found" error, not an authentication error. Missing IAM permissions (Option D) would produce an "AccessDeniedException" after authentication succeeds, not "no basic auth credentials."

7. A. Session Manager provides interactive shell access controlled entirely through IAM policies, logs all session activity to CloudTrail, and communicates through the SSM Agent without requiring any inbound security group rules. It meets all three requirements. EC2 Instance Connect (Option B) requires port 22 to be open for SSH access, which violates the no-inbound-ports requirement. SSH with key pairs (Option C) requires port 22 to be open regardless of where the keys are stored. Secrets Manager secures the keys but does not eliminate the need for inbound ports. SSM Run Command (Option D) executes commands without inbound ports and is auditable, but it does not provide interactive shell access. It runs predefined commands rather than allowing ad hoc terminal sessions.

8. C. AWS Config provides the `ec2-instance-managed-by-systems-manager` managed rule that continuously evaluates whether EC2 instances are managed by Systems Manager. Combined with SNS notifications on compliance changes, this provides the continuous monitoring and alerting the CloudOps team needs. Amazon Inspector (Option A) scans for software vulnerabilities and network exposure, but does not evaluate whether the SSM Agent is installed or running. CloudWatch (Option B) does not publish a native metric for SSM Agent status. You would need custom metrics, which adds operational overhead and does not provide a compliance evaluation framework. Systems Manager Inventory

(Option D) collects metadata from managed instances, but it only works on instances that already have the SSM Agent running. It cannot detect instances that are missing from Systems Manager.

9. B. Without an IAM instance profile that includes the `AmazonSSMManagedInstanceCore` policy, the SSM Agent cannot authenticate with the Systems Manager service and the instance never registers as a managed node. The chapter covers this as one of the three required prerequisites: install the agent, attach IAM permissions, and register the node. Document incompatibility (Option A) would produce a "Failed" status with an error message, not "Undeliverable." That status specifically indicates the service could not reach the instance. Tag filtering (Option C) determines which instances are targeted, but an instance that does not match the filter simply would not appear in the command results at all. It would not show "Undeliverable." An outdated SSM Agent (Option D) might lack support for newer features, but it would still register with Systems Manager and receive commands. The "Undeliverable" status indicates that the instance is not reachable as a managed node, not that the agent version is old.

10. C. EC2 Image Builder pipelines provide scheduled builds, recipe-driven configuration with reusable components for hardening, and integrated test components that validate the image before it becomes available. This matches the progression from manual to fully automated that the chapter covers in Table 3.2. A shell script with cron (Option A) can schedule the image capture, but it does not provide built-in hardening steps, component-based configuration, or automated testing. The CloudOps team would need to build all of that logic themselves. SSM Automation (Option B) can configure an instance and create an AMI, and it supports repeatable steps. However, it does not natively provide scheduled execution, integrated test components, or recipe-driven configuration. It is a good fit for ad hoc or CI/CD-driven builds but not for a fully managed pipeline. Lambda (Option D) has a 15-minute execution timeout and cannot run EC2 configuration tasks or Docker builds natively. It is not designed for AMI creation workflows.

11. A. Run Command can execute a shell script across all 1,000 instances simultaneously using tag-based targeting. S3 output captures the results centrally, and the command status per instance identifies which ones failed. This is the most direct and scalable approach. Connecting to 1,000 instances individually via Session Manager (Option B) is not operationally feasible and does not provide centralized output collection. Config custom rules (Option C) evaluate resource configurations via the AWS API, not OS-level filesystem state. A custom rule cannot check whether a specific file exists on an instance. SSM Inventory (Option D) can collect file metadata if configured with a custom inventory type, but it collects metadata (filename, size, modification date) rather than file contents. It also does not natively store collected data in S3 for audit.

12. D. `onFailure` ensures cleanup by terminating the instance. `runInstances` launches instances (Option A), `waitForAwsResourceProperty` waits for readiness (Option B), and `runCommand` executes commands but does not handle failure paths (Option C).

13. C. `aws:runCommand` executes the build steps. `runInstances` launches the instance (Option A), `waitForAwsResourceProperty` waits for readiness (Option B), and `changeInstanceState` terminates the instance (Option D).

14. B. AWS Config evaluates compliance and can trigger remediation actions when combined with services such as SSM Automation, EventBridge, and Lambda. Inspector (Option A) scans vulnerabilities but does not enforce remediation, CloudTrail (Option C) logs API calls only, and Trusted Advisor (Option D) provides recommendations but cannot remediate.

15. D. A golden AMI with dependencies pre-installed eliminates the runtime installation step entirely, removing the failure mode. This aligns with the chapter's Image Builder pipeline pattern for producing hardened, tested, immutable AMIs. Adding `cfn-signal` (Option A) requires the Auto Scaling group to be managed through CloudFormation with a `CreationPolicy`, which adds complexity. It addresses the symptom (failed instances joining the group) but not the root cause (runtime dependency installation that can fail). Using AWS Config (Option B) to detect and terminate non-compliant instances is reactive and introduces a delay between launch and termination. During that window, unhealthy instances could serve traffic. Replacing user data with SSM Automation (Option C) adds complexity and still performs runtime installation, which can fail for the same reasons (network issues, package repository outages).

16. C. Image Builder pipelines support scheduled container builds. Run Command (Option A) cannot schedule builds, Batch (Option B) runs jobs but not image pipelines, and Lambda (Option D) cannot build images.

17. B. All four fields are required for this scenario. `dockerfile-template-uri` points to the custom Dockerfile in S3, `parent-image` specifies the Amazon Linux base, `componentArn` references the managed security update component, and `target-repository` defines the ECR destination. Option A omits `dockerfile-template-uri`. Without it, Image Builder would use its default Dockerfile generation rather than the team's custom Dockerfile stored in S3. Option C omits `parent-image` and `componentArn`. The recipe needs a base image to build from and a component reference to install security updates. Option D omits both `dockerfile-template-uri` and `target-repository`. Without the Dockerfile URI the custom Dockerfile is not used, and without target-repository the built image has no push destination.

18. C. AWS Config detects drift and Automation remediates it. CloudTrail + Athena (Option A) only analyze logs, Logs Insights (Option B) queries logs but cannot remediate, and Trusted Advisor (Option D) provides recommendations only.

19. B. AWS Config records configuration changes over time. CloudWatch Logs (Option A) stores logs but not configuration state, Inventory (Option C) collects metadata only, and CloudTrail (Option D) logs API calls but not full configuration history.

20. D. AWS CloudTrail logs API calls, including IAM role changes. Config (Option A) tracks configuration state but not who changed it, Inspector (Option B) scans vulnerabilities, and Inventory (Option C) collects metadata only.

Databases

THE AWS CERTIFIED CLOUDOPS ENGINEER ASSOCIATE (SOA-C03) EXAM OBJECTIVES COVERED IN THIS CHAPTER MAY INCLUDE, BUT ARE NOT LIMITED TO THE FOLLOWING:

✓ **Domain 1: Monitoring, Logging, Analysis, Remediation, and Performance Optimization**

- 1.3 Implement performance optimization strategies for compute, storage, and database resources

✓ **Domain 2: Reliability and Business Continuity**

- 2.1 Implement scalability and elasticity
- 2.2 Implement highly available and resilient environments
- 2.3 Implement backup and restore strategies

✓ **Domain 3: Deployment, Provisioning, and Automation**

- 3.2 Automate the management of existing resources

Building on the foundations of compute and container services, this chapter turns to databases—the backbone of modern applications that power business logic, analytics, and customer experiences. For the SOA-C03 exam, you must show not only familiarity with AWS database services but also the ability to apply operational strategies that ensure performance, scalability, and resilience.

A key focus is performance optimization, where you'll learn to fine-tune workloads for efficiency, reliability, and cost. From query optimization and indexing in relational systems to partitioning and throughput tuning in NoSQL, AWS provides built-in mechanisms to minimize latency and maximize responsiveness—skills essential for CloudOps engineers balancing speed, reliability, and budget.

Equally important is scalability and elasticity. Modern applications must expand and contract seamlessly to meet demand. We explore how RDS and Aurora handle vertical and horizontal scaling, how DynamoDB leverages on-demand capacity and auto scaling, and how ElastiCache supports distributed caching to reduce load on primary data stores—all embodying AWS's principle of elastic infrastructure.

Finally, no operational strategy is complete without backup and restore. AWS offers automated backups, snapshots, and point-in-time recovery to ensure durability and business continuity. By mastering these capabilities across RDS, Aurora, DynamoDB, and ElastiCache, you'll gain a comprehensive toolkit for reliable database operations in AWS.

Understanding Database Types

Databases are the engines that store, organize, and serve application data. For the SOA-C03 exam, candidates are not expected to be professional database administrators or data engineers, but they must understand the fundamentals of how different database models operate. This knowledge is essential for implementing performance optimization, scalability, and backup strategies across AWS services. The two main paradigms—relational databases and NoSQL databases—offer distinct approaches to structuring and retrieving data, and AWS provides managed services for both.

Relational databases follow a schema-driven model, where data is organized into tables with defined relationships. They excel at enforcing consistency and supporting complex queries, but they can introduce overhead when scaling horizontally. NoSQL databases, by contrast, are schema-flexible and designed for massive scale and high-velocity workloads. They trade rigid structure for agility, allowing developers to model data in ways that align with application access patterns. Understanding these differences is crucial for exam candidates, because AWS services like Amazon RDS and DynamoDB embody these paradigms in practice.

Importantly, the boundary between relational and NoSQL is not absolute. With proper design and cost optimization, NoSQL databases can store relational data effectively. For example, DynamoDB allows developers to consolidate related entities into a single table with multiple attributes, reducing the need for traditional joins. While joins are considered computationally expensive in relational systems, DynamoDB's design patterns make them less costly by discouraging normalization and favoring denormalized, access-optimized schemas. This shift from normalized relational design to denormalized NoSQL patterns is a key concept for CloudOps engineers preparing for SOA-C03.

Relational Databases

Relational databases (RDBMS) organize data into structured tables with rows and columns, enforcing relationships through primary and foreign keys. They are ideal for workloads requiring strict consistency, transactional integrity, and complex queries. A defining characteristic of relational databases is their support for the ACID properties—Atomicity, Consistency, Isolation, and Durability—which ensure that transactions are processed reliably. Atomicity guarantees that a transaction is all-or-nothing, Consistency enforces valid states before and after transactions, Isolation prevents concurrent transactions from interfering with each other, and Durability ensures that committed changes persist even in the event of failures. This ACID compliance makes RDBMS particularly well-suited for mission-critical applications where correctness and reliability of data are paramount.

NoSQL Databases

NoSQL databases are schema-flexible (or even schemaless) and designed for scale, speed, and adaptability. They support diverse data models—key-value, document, graph, or wide-column—and are optimized for predictable data access patterns. In AWS, Amazon DynamoDB exemplifies this approach, offering single-digit millisecond latency at virtually any scale. Unlike traditional RDBMS, DynamoDB best practices discourage normalization; instead, related data is stored together in denormalized structures, often within a single table. This design minimizes the need for joins and enables efficient queries, turning what was once computationally expensive into a cost-optimized strategy. For exam candidates, grasping this shift is critical to understanding how NoSQL can be used not only for unstructured data but also for relational workloads when modeled correctly.

Amazon Relational Database Service (RDS)

As a CloudOps engineer, relational databases are among the most critical components you manage in AWS, powering transactional systems, analytics platforms, and enterprise applications. Amazon Relational Database Service (Amazon RDS) simplifies this responsibility by handling undifferentiated tasks such as provisioning, patching, and maintenance, allowing you to focus on operational excellence. With support for engines like MySQL, PostgreSQL, MariaDB, Oracle, Microsoft SQL Server, and IBM Db2, RDS enables you to configure instances for performance, scale elastically to meet demand, and implement robust backup and restore strategies. Mastering these operational levers equips you to optimize workloads, ensure resilience, and align with best practices for scalability and durability in the cloud.

Overview of Amazon RDS

Before diving into the operational details, it's important to understand what makes Amazon RDS a managed service, which engines it supports, and the kinds of tasks you'll be expected to perform as a CloudOps engineer. These three aspects form the foundation of working with Amazon RDS and will guide how you approach performance, scalability, and durability in the chapters ahead.

Managed Relational Database Service

Amazon RDS is a fully managed service, which means AWS takes care of the infrastructure "plumbing" that traditionally consumes a DBA's time: hardware provisioning, OS installation, patching, and database engine maintenance. As a CloudOps engineer, this frees you to focus on the operational levers that directly impact performance, elasticity, and resilience. To make this distinction clear, Table 4.1 compares operational responsibilities across three deployment models: on-premises, Amazon EC2 (IaaS), and Amazon RDS (PaaS).

Supported Database Engines

Amazon RDS supports multiple popular relational engines: MySQL, PostgreSQL, MariaDB, Oracle, Microsoft SQL Server, and most recently IBM Db2. This breadth allows you to migrate existing workloads into AWS with minimal friction, while still benefiting from managed operations. Each engine retains its familiar query language and features, but Amazon RDS standardizes the operational layer across them.

Operational Tasks

Your role as a CloudOps engineer is not to become a DBA, but to master the operational levers Amazon RDS provides. These include:

- **Performance optimization** through parameter groups, indexing, and monitoring with Performance Insights.
- **Scalability and elasticity** via instance resizing, read replicas, and Multi-AZ deployments.
- **Backup and restore** using automated backups, snapshots, and point-in-time recovery.

By understanding these tasks, you'll be able to run relational workloads in AWS with confidence, ensuring they remain performant, scalable, secure, and resilient.

TABLE 4.1 Database Operational Responsibility Comparison

Responsibility	On-Premises (Self-Managed)	Amazon EC2 (IaaS)	Amazon RDS (PaaS)
Rack and Stack	You	AWS	AWS
Power and Cooling	You	AWS	AWS
Server Maintenance	You	AWS	AWS
OS Installation	You	You	AWS
OS Patches	You	You	AWS
DB Engine Installation	You	You	AWS
DB Engine Patches	You	You	AWS
Backups	You	You	AWS automates, but you configure retention, PITR, snapshot policies
High Availability	You	You (manual setup)	AWS provides Multi-AZ failover, but you enable and choose deployment
Scaling	You	You (resize EC2)	AWS provides instance classes, replicas, serverless options—you configure thresholds and policies
App Optimization	You	You	You (always your responsibility)

Performance Optimization Strategies

Optimizing performance in Amazon RDS is not about tweaking knobs in isolation. As a CloudOps engineer, you'll follow a logical progression: first configure the database engine itself, then observe how queries behave, then monitor system-level metrics, next ensure storage can sustain throughput, and finally manage connections efficiently. Each step builds on the previous one, creating a holistic performance strategy.

Parameter Groups and Engine-Specific Tuning

Amazon RDS *parameter groups* act as configuration templates that define the runtime settings for your database instances. They provide granular control over the associated database engine's behavior while ensuring repeatability, reusability, and standardized patterns across environments.

Each parameter group is tied to a specific engine family and version (for example, `mysql8.0` or `postgres15`) and can only be applied to compatible instances. Parameters may be static (requiring a restart) or dynamic (applied immediately).

AWS exposes parameter groups so you don't have to edit OS-level configuration files inside each DB instance. This aligns with Amazon RDS being a fully managed service: you don't get unrestricted administrative control, but you get just enough to tune the performance of your database engine safely and consistently.

While the full list of parameters varies by engine, for the exam you should be familiar with the ones listed in Table 4.2.

TABLE 4.2 Static vs. Dynamic Parameter Comparison

Parameter Type	Common Examples	Notes
Static	• `character_set_server` (MySQL/MariaDB) • `innodb_log_file_size` (MySQL/MariaDB) • `shared_buffers` (PostgreSQL) • `max_server_memory` (SQL Server)	Require a DB restart to take effect. Plan changes during maintenance windows.
Dynamic	• `max_connections` (often dynamic, though it may have limits based on instance class) • `innodb_lock_wait_timeout` (MySQL/MariaDB) • `work_mem` (PostgreSQL) • `log_destination` (PostgreSQL)	Can be applied immediately without downtime. Useful for quick tuning and troubleshooting.

From an operational perspective, parameter groups allow you to standardize configurations across multiple Amazon RDS instances, reducing drift and simplifying management. Every modification is tracked via AWS CloudTrail, giving you an audit trail for compliance and governance.

How to Use Parameter Groups

As a CloudOps engineer, you'll typically follow this four-step process:

1. **Create a custom parameter group**—always recommended for production workloads.
2. **Modify parameters as needed**—align settings with KPIs or SLOs (e.g., query latency, connection limits).
3. **Link the parameter group to your Amazon RDS instance**—ensuring the instance inherits the configuration.
4. **Apply changes**—immediately for dynamic parameters, or during maintenance windows for static ones.

Make sure you have the necessary IAM permissions to use parameter groups. These include:

- `rds:CreateDBParameterGroup`
- `rds:ModifyDBParameterGroup`
- `rds:DeleteDBParameterGroup`
- `rds:ResetDBParameterGroup`
- `rds:DescribeDBParameterGroups`
- `rds:ModifyDBInstance.`

The following example shows you how to create and apply a custom parameter group:

```
# Step 1: Create a custom parameter group
aws rds create-db-parameter-group \
    --db-parameter-group-name my-custom-pg \
    --db-parameter-group-family mysql8.0 \
    --description "Custom MySQL parameter group"

# Step 2: Modify parameters (example: increase max_connections)
aws rds modify-db-parameter-group \
    --db-parameter-group-name my-custom-pg \
    --parameters
"ParameterName=max_connections,ParameterValue=500,ApplyMethod=immediate"

# Step 3: Link the parameter group to your Amazon RDS instance
aws rds modify-db-instance \
    --db-instance-identifier mydbinstance \
    --db-parameter-group-name my-custom-pg
```

Monitoring Amazon RDS with Performance Insights and Amazon CloudWatch Metrics

Once you've set consistent configurations with parameter groups, the next step is to watch how your database performs under real workloads. Configurations alone cannot guarantee performance; you need observability to understand query patterns, database load, and system bottlenecks. Most importantly, your job—as a CloudOps engineer—is to build mechanisms that enable automatic responses, whenever thresholds are breached or performance bottlenecks emerge, ensuring issues are detected, acted upon, and resolved before they impact end users.

Amazon RDS provides *Performance Insights* to help you with just that. Amazon RDS Performance Insights is a powerful tool for database observability, which integrates seamlessly with Amazon CloudWatch alarms to provide proactive, data-driven notifications for performance bottlenecks. This synergy allows for the swift identification and resolution of database issues, before they impact your customers.

Amazon RDS Performance Insights

Performance Insights (PI) provides a single pane of glass in the form of a dashboard that visualizes the database load, measured in Average Active Sessions (AAS), over time. This metric is crucial because it helps identify if the database demand exceeds the available CPU capacity (vCPUs). Key features include:

Visual Troubleshooting It aggregates complex performance data into a single graph, allowing you to slice and dice the load by dimensions such as SQL queries, wait events (e.g., CPU utilization, I/O latency, locks), hosts, users, and databases.

Root Cause Analysis (RCA) When a bottleneck occurs, you can drill down to identify exactly which SQL statements are causing the high load, facilitating targeted query optimization or resource scaling.

Fully Managed Performance Insights requires no configuration or maintenance to start collecting performance data, providing a free tier with seven days of data retention.

While Amazon RDS Performance Insights is excellent for troubleshooting and root cause analysis, it does not inherently offer an alarming mechanism within its own dashboard. That's where Amazon CloudWatch comes into play. Its native integration with Amazon CloudWatch provides a proactive alerting capability. Amazon RDS Performance Insights automatically publishes key metrics to Amazon CloudWatch, which can then be used to set up alarms that you (or your team) can act upon. Here is how the integration works:

1. **Publish Metrics**—When enabled for an Amazon RDS instance, Performance Insights automatically sends four primary metrics to Amazon CloudWatch, as illustrated in Table 4.3: `DBLoad`, `DBLoadCPU`, `DBLoadNonCPU`, and `DBLoadRelativeToNumVCPUs`.
2. **Configure Alarms**—You can configure Amazon CloudWatch alarms on these metrics using the console or Metric Math expressions. For example, an alarm can be set to trigger when `DBLoadCPU` exceeds the number of available vCPUs for a sustained period, indicating CPU contention.

3. **Notify and Respond**—When an alarm breaches a defined threshold, it can publish a notification to an Amazon SNS topic, which can then alert on-call teams via email or SMS, or integrate with third-party incident management tools like PagerDuty.

The metrics in Table 4.3 are essential numerical values you need to know to monitor the overall database health. These metrics will help you determine whether a performance bottleneck exists in your Amazon RDS instance.

Once you confirm that a bottleneck exists, how do you identify its root cause? Dimensions are the answer and are the mechanism you use to refine (or dice) your view of the metrics, helping you move from general observation to specific root cause identification. Performance Insights *Dimensions* are critical for a CloudOps engineer to perform effective RCA by filtering and categorizing the metric data (similar to using a GROUP BY in SQL). A dimension like "Wait Events" transforms the generic `DBLoadNonCPU` number into actionable insight, telling you why the database is waiting (e.g., waiting for I/O versus waiting on locks). Table 4.4 details how these filters allow you to pinpoint specific problematic SQL queries, users, or hosts and determine the correct configuration change required for remediation.

TABLE 4.3 Amazon CloudWatch Metrics for Amazon RDS Performance Insights

Metric Name (Console/ API Name)	Description	Tuning Insight
DBLoad (`db.load.avg`)	The total measure of database activity in Average Active Sessions (AAS).	High `DBLoad` indicates overall workload pressure; consider scaling instance size or optimizing queries.
DBLoadCPU (`db.load.avg + CPU filter`)	The portion of `DBLoad` actively consuming CPU cycles.	High `DBLoadCPU` suggests a CPU bottleneck. Tune inefficient SQL queries or scale up the DB instance size by increasing available vCPUs.
DBLoadNonCPU (`db.load.avg + non-CPU filter`)	The portion of `DBLoad` actively consuming non-CPU cycles (i.e., waiting for non-CPU resources such as I/O, locks, network).	High `DBLoadNonCPU` means the bottleneck is not the CPU. Use the Wait Events dimension for root cause analysis (RCA).
DBLoadRelativeToNumVCPUs (`DBLoadRelativeToNumVCPUs`)	Ratio of `DBLoad` to number of vCPUs (the DB instance capacity limit).	A `DBLoadRelativeToNumVCPUs > 1` means there are more active sessions than available vCPUs; scale up or distribute workload.

TABLE 4.4 Amazon RDS Performance Insights Dimensions

Dimension Name (Console/ API Name)	Description	Usage in PI/RCA
Wait Events (**db.wait_event.name**)	Used to filter DBLoadNonCPU by the specific cause of the wait (e.g., io:wait, lock:wait).	This is the primary RCA tool. It tells you why you have a bottleneck (e.g., slow storage, query conflicts).
Top SQL (**db.sql.statement**)	Used to filter DBLoad to identify which exact queries consume the most Average Active Sessions (AAS).	Focuses optimization efforts (adding indexes, rewriting queries) on the specific SQL statements causing the most load.
Hosts (**db.host.name**)	Used to filter DBLoad by the client machine's IP address or name.	Helps trace the source of high DBLoad back to a specific application server or client host for further investigation.
Users (**db.user.name**)	Used to filter DBLoad by the database user account used for connections.	Allows you to pinpoint which specific user account is generating the problematic workload. Often used for auditing or access control adjustments.
Databases (**db.name**)	Used to filter DBLoad when multiple databases exist on a single RDS instance.	Helps isolate performance issues to a specific database schema within a shared instance.

You can (and should) programmatically use Performance Insights dimensions through the AWS SDKs (Python boto3, Java, etc.) or the AWS CLI, using dedicated Performance Insights API actions rather than standard CloudWatch metrics calls.

The two primary API actions you will use are:

1. `get-resource-metrics`—Retrieves time-series data for specified metrics, allowing you to optionally aggregate (group by) dimensions.
2. `describe-dimension-keys`—Summarizes the top dimension values (e.g., the top ten SQL statements or wait events) contributing the most to a specific metric over a time range.

The following code snippet shows how you would use the `get-resource-metrics` AWS CLI command to retrieve the average number of active sessions waiting specifically for an I/O event type (`db.wait_event.type = 'I/O'`) on your database instance:

```
# Define necessary variables (replace with your values)
DB_RESOURCE_ID="your-db-instance-prod-01-resource-id"
REGION="us-east-1"
SERVICE_TYPE="RDS"
END_TIME=$(date -u +"%Y-%m-%dT%H:%M:%SZ")
START_TIME=$(date -u -d '1 hour ago' +"%Y-%m-%dT%H:%M:%SZ")

aws pi get-resource-metrics \
    --region $REGION \
    --service-type $SERVICE_TYPE \
    --identifier $DB_RESOURCE_ID \
    --start-time $START_TIME \
    --end-time $END_TIME \
    --period-in-seconds 300 \
    --metric-queries '
        [
            {
                "Metric": "db.load.avg",
                "GroupBy": {
                    "Group": "db.wait_event",
                    "Limit": 10
                },
                "Filter": {
                    "db.wait_event.type": "I/O"
                }
            }
        ]
    ' \
    --output json
```

For a complete reference of the `aws pi get-resource-metrics` command, visit: `https://docs.aws.amazon.com/cli/latest/reference/pi/get-resource-metrics.html`.

Selecting Storage Types

When provisioning Amazon RDS instances, the choice of Amazon Elastic Block Store (EBS) volume type directly affects performance, cost, and reliability. Amazon RDS relies on Amazon EBS for persistent block storage, with three options: General Purpose SSD (`gp3`/`gp2`), Provisioned IOPS SSD (`io1`/`io2`/`io2 Block Express`), and Magnetic volumes. This last type (Magnetic volumes) is legacy storage maintained only for backward compatibility and is not recommended for any new deployments. Selecting between `gp3` (recommended over `gp2`) and Provisioned IOPS is a critical optimization skill, as the wrong choice can cause poor latency, `DBLoad` bottlenecks, and operational failures even if the instance size is correct. General Purpose SSD (`gp3`) suits most moderate, bursty workloads, offering 3,000 baseline IOPS and 125 MiB/s throughput at low cost, with flexibility to provision IOPS and throughput independently. Provisioned IOPS SSD (`io1/io2 Block Express`) is best for consistently high, predictable performance and low latency, supporting up to 64,000 IOPS for `io2` or 256,000 for `io2 Block Express` at higher cost but with guaranteed stability. Beyond initial selection, tuning IOPS and throughput requires ongoing monitoring; Amazon CloudWatch metrics and Performance Insights help identify bottlenecks and correlate query load with storage performance. For the exam, ensure that you understand the metrics listed in Table 4.5, as they reveal how well the storage layer sustains workload demand.

Detailed coverage of Amazon EBS and the aforementioned volume types is provided in Chapter 5.

Modifying Configurations to Increase Performance

Modifying the configuration of an Amazon RDS instance is the primary way you, as a CloudOps engineer, remediate performance bottlenecks identified through monitoring. The transition from *identifying* a problem to *fixing* it programmatically is a core SOA-C03

TABLE 4.5 Amazon CloudWatch Metrics for Amazon RDS Storage Volumes

Metric Name	Description	Tuning Insight
`ReadIOPS`	Number of read I/O operations per second.	High sustained values may require Provisioned IOPS SSDs for predictable throughput.
`WriteIOPS`	Number of write I/O operations per second.	Elevated write activity suggests tuning write-intensive workloads or scaling IOPS capacity.
`ReadLatency`	Average time for each read operation.	High latency indicates storage bottlenecks; consider upgrading to `io1/io2` volumes.
`WriteLatency`	Average time for each write operation.	Persistent delays suggest insufficient IOPS; provision more or optimize schema/indexing.
`DiskQueueDepth`	Number of outstanding I/O requests waiting to be processed.	A deep queue signals saturation; increase IOPS or switch to higher-performance volumes.
`FreeStorageSpace`	Amount of available storage space in bytes.	Low free space can degrade performance; expand storage or monitor growth proactively.

objective. Configuration changes generally fall into two categories: immediate actions (like scaling resources) and structural changes (like adding an RDS Proxy). Performance Insights itself provides immediate, actionable intelligence to guide these modifications, ensuring that changes are targeted and effective.

A key feature for proactive cloud operations is the Performance Insights Recommendations pane. Instead of manually interpreting every metric and dimension, this console feature uses machine learning to analyze the dominant wait events and offer specific, plain-English suggestions. For example, if PI detects a high volume of a specific lock wait event (`lock:wait`), the recommendation might be to review the SQL statement identified in the Top SQL dimension and add a database index. You can retrieve these recommendations programmatically using the AWS CLI `aws pi get-performance-insights-recommendations` command and integrate them into an automated ticketing system or operations dashboard.

When scaling compute resources, the modification workflow is straightforward using the AWS CLI. If monitoring identifies a CPU bottleneck (high `DBLoadCPU` or `DBLoadRelativeToNumVCPUs > 1.0`), you can modify the instance class. This requires an intentional, brief outage, which is a key operational consideration for the exam.

```
# Action: Scale up the instance size to increase vCPUs and RAM
aws rds modify-db-instance \
    --db-instance-identifier my-prod-db-instance \
    --db-instance-class db.r6g.xlarge \
    --apply-immediately
```

Sometimes, Performance Insights may recommend adjusting memory parameters to mitigate performance issues related to memory pressure (low `FreeableMemory` metric in CloudWatch). You use the `aws rds modify-db-parameter-group` command to change how memory is allocated for buffering or caching.

```
# Action: Adjust a specific memory parameter (e.g., changing sort_buffer_size)
# Note: You must update a custom parameter group, not the default one.
aws rds modify-db-parameter-group \
    --db-parameter-group-name custom-mysql-parameter-group \
    --parameters "ParameterName=sort_buffer_size,ParameterValue=2097152,ApplyMe
thod=pending-reboot"

# Action: Reboot the instance for 'pending-reboot' parameters to take effect
aws rds reboot-db-instance \
    --db-instance-identifier my-prod-db-instance
```

RDS Proxy

To optimize connection handling and application resilience without scaling the main database instance, you should leverage Amazon RDS Proxy. This fully managed proxy sits between the application and the database, pooling and reusing database connections. This approach significantly reduces the overhead associated with establishing new connections for serverless or high-churn applications, which often cause a high `DatabaseConnections` count in Amazon CloudWatch metrics. The RDS Proxy is a key strategy for mitigating performance issues related to connection saturation.

Finally, Amazon RDS Proxy addresses the operational challenge of failover times and connection management. During a Multi-AZ failover event, connections are rerouted to the standby instance transparently via the proxy, minimizing application downtime from over a minute to typically under 30 seconds. You, as a CloudOps engineer, can manage this via the CLI to deploy and link the proxy to the database cluster, effectively abstracting connection management away from the primary DB instance's performance profile.

```
# Action: Create an RDS Proxy to pool connections
aws rds create-db-proxy \
    --db-proxy-name my-rds-proxy \
    --engine-family MYSQL \
    --auth '[{"AuthScheme":"SECRETS","SecretArn":"arn:aws:secretsmanager:
us-east-1:123456789012:secret:rds-creds-xxxx","IAMAuth":"DISABLED"}]' \
    --role-arn arn:aws:iam::123456789012:role/rds-proxy-role \
    --vpc-subnet-ids subnet-xxxxxxxx subnet-yyyyyyyy
```

When you configure Amazon RDS Proxy, you provide the ARN to tell the proxy *where* to find the database credentials within AWS Secrets Manager. The RDS Proxy service internally retrieves the actual username and password securely; you never expose the sensitive value in the CLI command itself.

Scalability and Elasticity

The first general design principle of the AWS Well-Architected Framework is: "Stop guessing your capacity needs." In traditional environments, teams often over-provisioned hardware to avoid running out of resources. Back two decades ago, when I was working as an Application Architect in a large, global manufacturing enterprise, before requesting new hardware the general consensus was to "Go big, and hope for the best!" Capacity planning was more art than science—a mix of spreadsheets, gut feelings, and long approval cycles. We would spend weeks estimating peak workloads, then justify the purchase of expensive servers that might sit underutilized most of the year. The risk of under-provisioning was considered high, so the safer bet was always to overspend.

With Amazon RDS, you don't need to guess anymore. Instead, you can scale your database vertically (up/down), or—better yet—horizontally (in/out), and design for elasticity so that your system adapts to demand. Let's explore the main strategies.

Vertical Scaling (Instance Classes)

Vertical scaling, or "scaling up," increases computing power by changing the instance class (e.g., from `db.t3.small` to `db.r5.large`). Storage and instance type are decoupled, so modifying storage incurs no downtime. Predictable workloads may benefit from switching storage types (General Purpose SSD to Provisioned IOPS), while unpredictable workloads can use Amazon RDS storage autoscaling with a defined maximum threshold. For more details, see: `https://docs.aws.amazon.com/AmazonRDS/latest/UserGuide/USER_PIOPS.Autoscaling.html`.

This strategy is best for temporary CPU or memory bottlenecks or short-term growth when horizontal scaling isn't feasible. However, it is limited by the largest available instance type and requires a brief outage during resizing, making it unsuitable for workloads needing continuous availability. In Multi-AZ setups, the standby is upgraded first before failover, while Single-AZ instances remain unavailable throughout the scaling operation.

Horizontal Scaling with Read Replicas

Horizontal scaling ("scaling out") involves adding more instances to distribute the workload. For read-heavy applications, *read replicas* are the most common solution. You create read replica copies of your primary database instance, and configure your application to direct all read traffic to these replicas. This offloads the primary instance, allowing it to focus exclusively on write operations.

After you create a read replica from a source DB instance, the source becomes the primary DB instance. When you make updates to the primary DB instance, Amazon RDS automatically replicates them to the read replica. The replication process is *asynchronous*. This means that when data is written to the primary instance, the transaction is immediately committed without waiting for the replica(s) to catch up. The changes are sent in the background, resulting in a slight delay (replication lag) between the primary and the replica(s). If the primary fails before the latest transaction has been copied to the replica, that data can be lost. For this reason, the data on the replica is *eventually consistent*. This asynchronous nature ensures the primary database's write performance is maximized and not impacted by network latency or replica processing speeds. As illustrated in Figure 4.1, you can create read replicas in the same Availability Zone of your primary Amazon RDS instance, or a different Availability Zone in the same or a different region.

This approach is best suited for applications with a high ratio of read operations to write operations, such as e-commerce websites or content platforms. It is also a key implementation of the Well-Architected Reliability Pillar principle to "scale horizontally to increase aggregate workload availability" and minimize the risk of single points of failure.

It is not well suited for write-heavy applications, as all write operations still have to go through the single primary instance. Additionally, because replication is asynchronous, a read from a replica might not immediately reflect the most recent write to the primary.

The following snippet shows how to create a read replica in a different Availability Zone (AZ) using the AWS CLI:

```
aws rds create-db-instance-read-replica \
    --db-instance-identifier my-read-replica \
    --source-db-instance-identifier my-database-instance \
    --db-instance-class db.r5.large \
    --availability-zone us-east-1a
```

FIGURE 4.1 Amazon RDS read replicas.

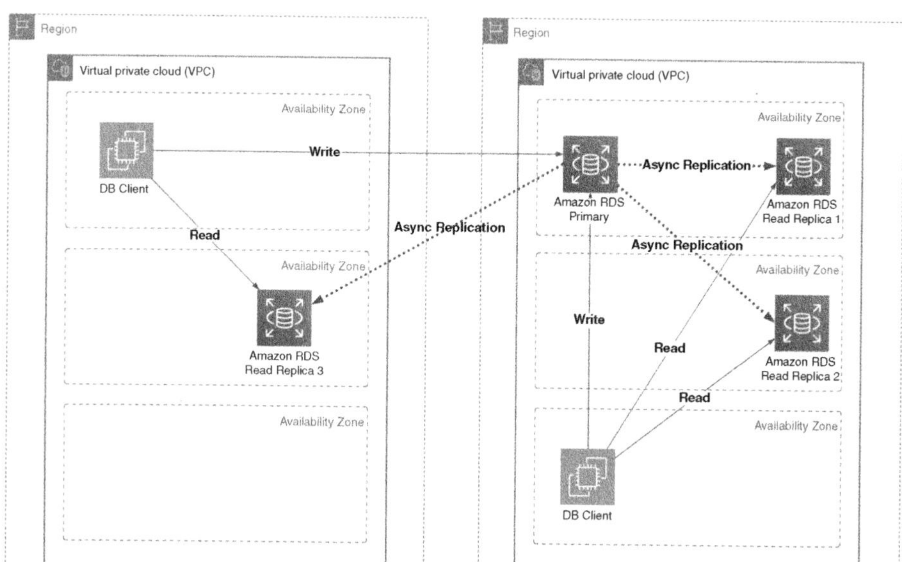

To learn more, visit: `https://docs.aws.amazon.com/cli/latest/reference/rds/create-db-instance-read-replica.html`.

Read replicas are billed the same way as standard DB instances, meaning you pay the regular hourly rate for the instance class you choose for the replica. For example, if your primary database is a `db.m6g.large` and you create a read replica of the same class, the replica will incur the same hourly cost as that instance type. Importantly, AWS does not charge for the data transfer that happens when the source DB instance replicates changes to its read replicas within the same region. This makes scaling reads with replicas cost-effective, since you only pay for the compute and storage of the replica itself, not for the replication traffic.

For the exam, be aware of the following:

- **Supported engines:** MySQL, PostgreSQL, MariaDB, Oracle, SQL Server, and Db2.
- **DNS endpoints:** Each read replica has its own endpoint; applications must direct queries accordingly.

- **Traffic distribution:** Use Amazon Route 53 weighted records or application logic to balance queries.
- **Disaster recovery:** Read replicas can be promoted to primaries, but they are *not* a substitute for Multi-AZ high availability, which leverages *synchronous replication* instead, to ensure the standby copy is always up-to-date, guaranteeing zero data loss during failover.
- **Global scaling:** As previously mentioned, read replicas can be deployed across regions for global applications. Unlike in-region replicas (where replication traffic is free), cross-region replication incurs data transfer charges. You pay for the network traffic that moves changes from the primary DB instance to the replica in another region.

Command Query Responsibility Segregation (CQRS) Pattern

The CQRS pattern is a critical architectural design approach that perfectly complements horizontal scaling using read replicas. It advocates for separating the application's command (write/update) operations from its query (read) operations into distinct application components. The command model operates on the primary database, while the query model reads data from a separate data store, such as a read replica or even a different type of database system. This clear separation of duties allows you to optimize both sides independently for performance and availability. To learn more, visit: `https://docs.aws.amazon.com/prescriptive-guidance/latest/modernization-data-persistence/cqrs-pattern.html`.

Horizontal Scaling with Partitioning

Partitioning (or *sharding*) is an advanced horizontal scaling technique that involves manually splitting your data into multiple, smaller databases (shards) based on a specific business logic key, such as a customer ID range.

This strategy is best suited for extremely large databases that require improved write performance and storage capacity beyond what a single Amazon RDS instance (even the largest one) can provide. It offers massive scalability for both reads and writes.

It is not well suited for most standard workloads due to its significant operational complexity. AWS does not natively automate this within the RDS service itself; it requires careful application-level design, management of data consistency across shards, and a complex implementation strategy.

Multi-AZ Deployments for High Availability

Multi-AZ deployments are crucial for building resilient systems, though their primary focus is high availability and disaster recovery, not performance scaling. When you enable

Multi-AZ, AWS creates a redundant, *synchronously* replicated standby copy of your primary database in a separate, isolated Availability Zone.

This configuration is best suited for production workloads that require high durability and minimal downtime (high availability) in the event of an infrastructure failure. It provides automatic failover with typical recovery times of under 60 seconds, ensuring business continuity with minimal administrative intervention.

It is not well suited as a performance scaling solution. The standby replica is not used to serve read traffic; it simply waits to be promoted in a disaster scenario. Furthermore, the synchronous replication introduces a very slight increase in write latency compared to a Single-AZ deployment, which might be a concern for ultra-low latency write-intensive systems.

You enable Multi-AZ simply by modifying your instance:

```
aws rds modify-db-instance \
    --db-instance-identifier my-database-instance \
    --multi-az \
    --apply-immediately
```

For the exam, make sure you understand that Amazon RDS Multi-AZ Deployments and read replicas are complementary solutions designed for different architectural goals: Multi-AZ Deployments for reliability and read replicas for performance scaling. The key differences between the two are summarized in Table 4.6.

TABLE 4.6 Amazon RDS Read Replicas vs. Multi-AZ Deployments

Feature	Amazon RDS Read Replicas	Amazon RDS Multi-AZ Deployments
Primary Purpose	Horizontal scalability (offload read traffic)	High availability with automatic failover/failback (disaster recovery)
Replication Type	Asynchronous (potential for slight data lag)	Synchronous (ensures zero data loss)
Accessibility	Directly accessible via its own endpoint	Standby is not directly accessible; it's passive
Supported Operations	Read-only (SELECT queries); can be promoted to standalone DB for writes	Full read/write on primary; standby is not accessible until failover

Feature	Amazon RDS Read Replicas	Amazon RDS Multi-AZ Deployments
Automated Failover?	No, manual promotion is required if primary fails	Yes, automatic failover to standby in another AZ (typically 60–120s)
Deployment Scope	Same-AZ, Cross-AZ, or Cross-Region with extra cost for replication traffic	Cross-AZ (within the same region only)
Application Impact	Requires application logic to direct queries	DNS record updates automatically after failover (transparent to app)
Typical Use Case	Reporting, analytics, heavy read-intensive apps	Production workloads requiring resilience, disaster recovery, and uptime guarantees

Multi-AZ DB Cluster Deployment for High Availability and Read Scaling

Building upon the foundational concept of high availability provided by the traditional Multi-AZ instance configuration (one primary and a redundant, synchronously replicated standby copy in a separate AZ), the Amazon RDS Multi-AZ DB cluster deployment was introduced to specifically address the limitations regarding performance scaling.

While a traditional Multi-AZ instance deployment excels at high durability by using a non-readable standby replica, the Multi-AZ DB cluster deployment leverages a different architecture that features one primary writer instance and two readable standby instances (for MySQL and PostgreSQL-compatible engines) spread across three distinct Availability Zones. This configuration maintains the same high-durability and near-zero data loss RPO (Recovery Point Objective) as the original setup but introduces the significant advantage of horizontal read scaling.

The primary benefit of the Multi-AZ DB cluster is the separation of concerns between write operations and read-heavy workloads. The primary instance manages all transactional writes, while application-side configurations can direct analytical queries, reporting, and other read-intensive tasks to a separate "reader endpoint" that intelligently load balances connections across the two readable standby replicas. This design ensures that resource contention between critical write transactions and demanding read queries is eliminated. Furthermore, failover times in a Multi-AZ DB cluster are often significantly faster than a traditional Multi-AZ instance deployment, typically achieving recovery times of under 35 seconds, thus improving both performance and operational resilience for demanding production environments.

Backup and Restore Strategies

For a CloudOps engineer, mastering backup and recovery processes is essential. These capabilities directly support the Reliability pillar of the AWS Well-Architected Framework, ensuring that systems can withstand failures and recover quickly. Amazon RDS delivers highly durable, managed backup solutions, designed to meet strict Recovery Point Objective (RPO) and Recovery Time Objective (RTO) requirements. A clear understanding of how automated backups, manual snapshots, and advanced recovery options work together is critical for operational excellence and exam success. In this section, we focus on four key strategies: automating backup and retention policies, manual snapshots and point-in-time recovery, cross-region snapshot copy for disaster recovery, and integration with AWS backup.

Automating Backup and Retention Policies

Amazon RDS enables automated backups by default, taking daily snapshots and streaming transaction logs to Amazon S3 every five minutes. With a configurable retention period of 1–35 days, these backups support point-in-time recovery, allowing restoration to any specific second within the window, up to the `LatestRestorableTime` (usually within the last five minutes). Manual snapshots are retained indefinitely until explicitly deleted, making them ideal for long-term retention, compliance requirements, or preserving data before major changes.

To modify the automated backup retention window for an existing DB instance using the AWS CLI, you use the `modify-db-instance` command.

```
aws rds modify-db-instance \
    --db-instance-identifier my-database-instance \
    --backup-retention-period 14 \
    --apply-immediately
```

In this command:

- `--db-instance-identifier my-database-instance`: The unique name of your existing RDS database instance, whose backup retention window you want to modify.
- `--backup-retention-period 14`: The number of days you want AWS to retain automated backups. In this case, 14 days. A value of 0 disables automated backups entirely.
- `--apply-immediately`: A flag that applies the change right away. For backup window changes, this typically does not cause an outage.

Manual Snapshots and Point-in-Time Recovery

While automated backups handle day-to-day recovery, manual DB snapshots are user-initiated backups that you control explicitly. These snapshots are retained indefinitely until you manually delete them, making them ideal for long-term archival, compliance requirements, or creating a reliable baseline before a major application upgrade.

You can initiate a manual snapshot at any time using the AWS CLI `create-db-snapshot` command:

```
aws rds create-db-snapshot \
    --db-snapshot-identifier manual-snapshot-pre-upgrade-20251209 \
    --db-instance-identifier my-database-instance
```

In this command:

- `--db-snapshot-identifier manual-snapshot-pre-upgrade-20251209`: A unique name you assign to the new manual snapshot for easy identification.
- `--db-instance-identifier my-database-instance`: The unique name of the source Amazon RDS instance you are taking a snapshot of.

To restore from a specific manual snapshot, you use the `restore-db-instance-from-db-snapshot` command. Like the PITR command, this always creates a new database instance (you cannot restore over an existing one).

```
aws rds restore-db-instance-from-db-snapshot \
    --db-snapshot-identifier manual-snapshot-pre-upgrade-20251209 \
    --db-instance-identifier my-restored-instance-from-snapshot \
    --db-instance-class db.t3.medium \
    --engine postgres
```

In this command:

- `--db-snapshot-identifier manual-snapshot-pre-upgrade-20251209`: The identifier of the specific manual snapshot you want to restore from.
- `--db-instance-identifier my-restored-instance-from-snapshot`: The unique name for the new Amazon RDS instance that will be created with the data from the snapshot.
- `--db-instance-class db.t3.medium`: The desired compute/memory class for the new restored instance. This can be different from the original instance.
- `--engine postgres`: The database engine type (e.g., `postgres`, `mysql`, `oracle`). This must match the engine type of the snapshot.

If you need to perform a point-in-time recovery using automated backups (restoring to a specific second), you use the `restore-db-instance-to-point-in-time` command instead:

```
aws rds restore-db-instance-to-point-in-time \
    --source-db-instance-identifier my-database-instance \
    --target-db-instance-identifier my-database-instance-restored \
    --restore-to-time 2025-12-08T14:30:00Z
```

In this command:

- `--source-db-instance-identifier my-database-instance`: The identifier of the source instance whose data you want to restore.
- `--target-db-instance-identifier my-database-instance-restored`: The unique name for the new RDS instance that will be created with the restored data.
- `--restore-to-time 2025-12-08T14:30:00Z`: The precise point in time (UTC format required, ending in Z) to which you want to restore the data. This time must be within your backup retention window.

For a complete reference of `restore-db-instance-to-point-in-time` visit: `https://docs.aws.amazon.com/cli/latest/reference/rds/restore-db-instance-to-point-in-time.html`.

Cross-Region Snapshot Copy for Disaster Recovery

A robust disaster recovery (DR) strategy often requires storing backups in a separate geographical region, adhering to the principle of isolation. Amazon RDS allows you to copy both manual and automated snapshots across AWS regions.

This process is initiated from the target (destination) region and involves "pulling" the snapshot from the source region. A critical consideration for encrypted snapshots is that AWS KMS keys are region-specific, so you must specify a valid KMS key for the destination region.

To copy a snapshot across regions using the AWS CLI:

```
aws rds copy-db-snapshot \
  --source-db-snapshot-identifier arn:aws:rds:us-east-1:123456789012:snapshot:
source-snapshot-id \
  --target-db-snapshot-identifier target-snapshot-copy-id \
  --kms-key-id arn:aws:kms:us-west-2:123456789012:key/my-us-west-2-kms-key-id \
  --source-region us-east-1 \
  --region us-west-2
```

In this command:

- `--source-db-snapshot-identifier arn:aws:rds:us-east-1:123456789012:snapshot:source-snapshot-id`: The full ARN (Amazon Resource Name) of the snapshot located in the source region (`us-east-1`).
- `--target-db-snapshot-identifier target-snapshot-copy-id`: The unique name for the new snapshot copy created in the destination region.
- `--kms-key-id arn:aws:kms:us-west-2:123456789012:key/my-us-west-2-kms-key-id`: If the source or destination snapshot is encrypted, you must provide the ARN of a valid KMS encryption key available in the destination region (`us-west-2`).

- `--source-region us-east-1`: Specifies the AWS region where the original snapshot resides. The command itself is run from `us-west-2` (implicitly set via environment variables or the `--region` parameter).

While Amazon RDS provides a managed foundation for relational databases, Amazon Aurora builds on this by offering a cloud-native engine designed for high performance and scalability.

Amazon Aurora

Amazon Aurora is a fully managed relational database engine (compatible with MySQL and PostgreSQL) that operates within the Amazon RDS ecosystem. It is offered as two distinct engine choices alongside traditional options like MySQL, PostgreSQL, MariaDB, Oracle, Microsoft SQL Server, and IBM Db2, as illustrated in Figure 4.2.

However, Aurora's architecture, cost, and operational models diverge so significantly from standard Amazon RDS engines that it requires its own dedicated treatment in this chapter.

Overview of Amazon Aurora

Aurora was designed from the ground up to exploit the elasticity, fault tolerance, and distributed nature of the AWS cloud. Unlike conventional Amazon RDS engines that directly rely on centralized block storage and asynchronous replication, Aurora introduces a cloud-native architecture with shared, distributed storage that extends beyond the limitations of a single SAN (Storage Area Network). This architecture results in near-instantaneous failover and performance optimizations that rival commercial-grade databases.

We treat Aurora as a separate section in the "Databases" chapter not only because of its unique architecture, but also because SOA-C03 exam scenarios often test you on Aurora-specific features—such as its replication model, global database capabilities, and compatibility layers—that do not apply to other RDS engines. Understanding Aurora as a

FIGURE 4.2 Amazon RDS engine options.

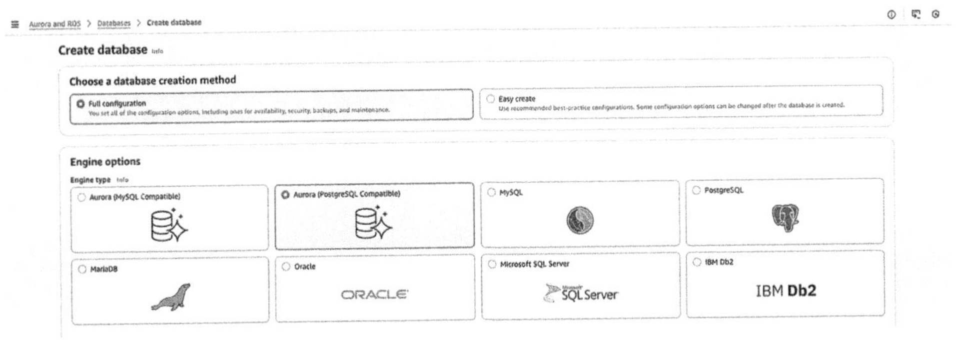

distinct paradigm helps you, as a CloudOps engineer, reason about operational trade-offs, migration paths, and performance tuning strategies in real-world cloud environments.

Aurora Architecture

Aurora's architecture is purpose-built for the cloud, and this is where it diverges most significantly from traditional relational databases. "A picture is worth a thousand words," right? Let's focus on the key aspects of Amazon Aurora's architecture with an illustration. Figure 4.3 shows the main components of the architecture.

Separation of compute and storage Aurora decouples the database engine (compute layer) from the underlying storage. The storage layer is distributed, fault-tolerant, and self-healing, automatically replicating data across six copies spread across three Availability Zones (AZs).

FIGURE 4.3 Amazon Aurora architecture.

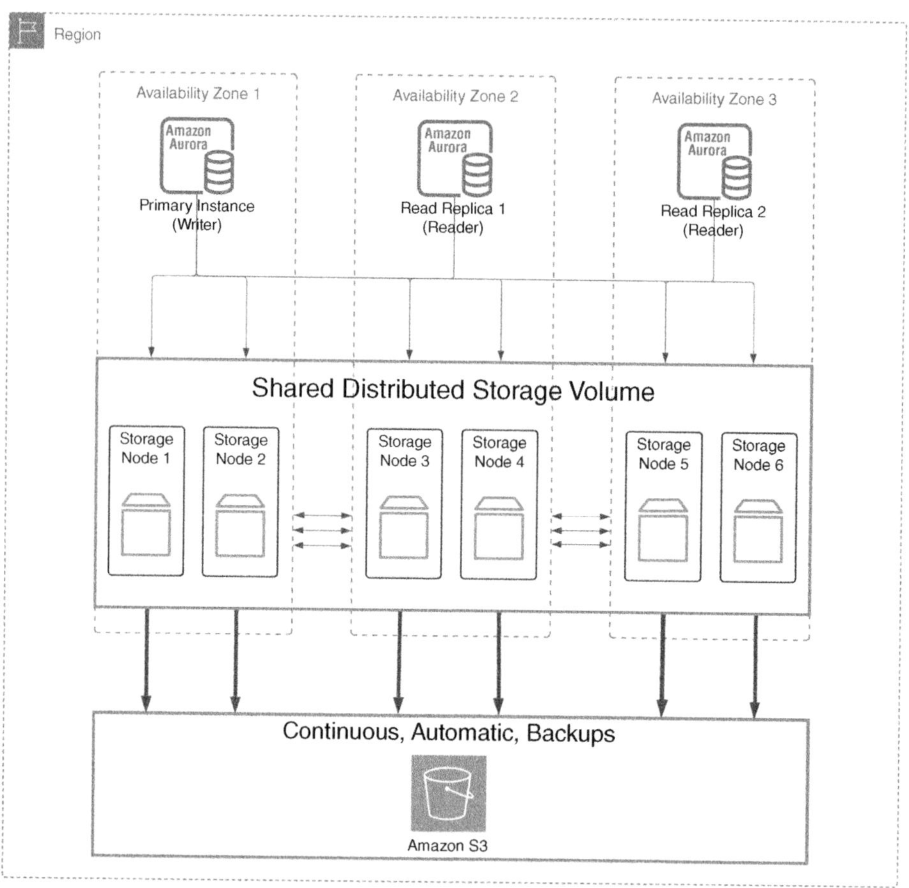

If an Availability Zone goes down, your data remains intact and available. This design ensures durability and high availability without manual intervention.

Shared distributed storage volume As shown in Figure 4.3, all Aurora instances (primary and read replicas) in a cluster share the same storage volume. This means read replicas don't require full data duplication; they simply attach to the same distributed storage, reducing replication lag to milliseconds, which is significantly faster than the eventual consistency model of standard Amazon RDS MySQL or PostgreSQL read replicas.

Continuous backups and Point-in-Time Recovery (PITR) Aurora performs continuous, automatic backups to Amazon S3 without performance impact, eliminating the need for traditional backup windows. This enables granular point-in-time recovery with a one-second granularity.

High throughput and scalability Aurora can elastically scale up to 256 TiB per database cluster (128 TiB for earlier engine versions), and supports up to 15 low-latency read replicas, making it suitable for workloads with heavy read traffic.

Compatibility with MySQL and PostgreSQL

Aurora is designed as a drop-in replacement for existing MySQL and PostgreSQL workloads, facilitating straightforward migration with minimal application code changes. Here's what you need to know for the exam:

MySQL Compatibility As of the writing of this book, Aurora MySQL is compatible with MySQL 5.7 and MySQL 8.0. Applications that work with MySQL drivers and schema structure work seamlessly with Aurora. To learn when to expect the general availability of Aurora MySQL releases, based on MySQL's major and minor releases, visit: `https://docs.aws.amazon.com/AmazonRDS/latest/AuroraMySQLReleaseNotes/AuroraMySQL.release-calendars.html`.

PostgreSQL Compatibility As of the writing of this book, Aurora PostgreSQL is compatible with PostgreSQL versions 11 and higher, including releases like PostgreSQL major version 17 and various minor versions within 12, 13, 14, 15, and 16. This compatibility allows organizations to leverage Aurora's performance benefits without retraining developers on a new database dialect. To learn when to expect the general availability of Aurora PostgreSQL releases, based on PostgreSQL's major and minor releases, visit: `https://docs.aws.amazon.com/AmazonRDS/latest/AuroraPostgreSQLReleaseNotes/aurorapostgresql-release-calendar.html`.

Data Migration Services AWS provides streamlined migration tools, such as AWS Database Migration Service (DMS)—covered in Chapter 7—to move databases into Aurora from on-premises servers or standard Amazon RDS instances.

Key Differentiators from Amazon RDS

While Aurora and Amazon RDS are both managed services, Aurora offers distinct advantages over standard RDS engines (like standard MySQL on RDS, or PostgreSQL on RDS). Table 4.7 summarizes the key differences you need to know for the exam.

TABLE 4.7 Amazon Aurora vs. Amazon RDS

Feature	Amazon Aurora	Amazon RDS (MySQL/ PostgreSQL)
Performance	Up to 5x the throughput of standard MySQL and up to 3x the throughput of standard PostgreSQL on the same hardware, thanks to its optimized storage engine and distributed architecture.	Standard performance; constrained by traditional engine architecture and Provisioned IOPS/storage.
Storage Architecture	Cloud-native, distributed, self-healing storage (shared volume).	Traditional file system on EBS volumes.
Storage Scaling	Automatically scales storage from 10 GiB to 256 TiB in 10 GiB increments; pay only for what you use.	Requires manually provisioning specific EBS volume sizes and types (e.g., gp3, io2).
Replication Lag	Asynchronous replication in the range of milliseconds for Aurora read replicas (using the shared, distributed storage volume).	Asynchronous replication results in seconds to minutes for Cross-AZ.
High Availability	Aurora's six-way replication across AZs and continuous S3 backups provide resilience beyond standard RDS Multi-AZ deployments. Failover is automatic, nearly instantaneous (< 30s typically) due to the shared storage model.	Failover times can be longer (often 60s+) as the new primary needs to perform crash recovery and attach volumes.
Global Database (Cross-Region)	Natively supports Aurora Global Database for fast cross-region disaster recovery (RPO < 1s, RTO < 1 min).	Cross-region replication possible but requires manual setup; can have higher lag and slower disaster recovery times.
Serverless Option	Offers Aurora Serverless v1 and v2 for on-demand capacity scaling for intermittent workloads.	RDS Custom is available, but no true "serverless" scaling of the compute layer like Aurora Serverless provides.

Performance Optimization Strategies

Amazon Aurora is designed to deliver high performance with minimal operational overhead, but to truly optimize its performance, you need to understand not only its architecture, but also the strategies AWS provides for monitoring, tuning, and scaling. We begin with the foundation—the storage engine—and progressively move into monitoring, query acceleration, cluster tuning, and finally how RDS Proxy complements Aurora in real-world workloads.

Aurora Storage Engine

Aurora's performance starts with its cloud-native storage engine. Unlike traditional RDS engines that rely on centralized or specialized storage, Aurora uses a distributed, log-structured system that replicates data six ways across three Availability Zones (as shown in Figure 4.3), ensuring durability, fault tolerance, and minimal replication lag without extra hardware.

A log-structured design appends changes as redo log records instead of overwriting blocks. This sequential writing is more efficient than random updates; it making writes faster and recovery simpler since the log itself contains a complete record of changes.

This approach reduces write amplification, where a single logical write triggers multiple physical writes in block-based systems. By appending compact log entries, Aurora lowers I/O overhead, improves durability, and delivers predictable latency under heavy workloads, boosting throughput for write-intensive applications.

Aurora storage is elastic, automatically scaling in 10 GiB increments up to 256 TiB per cluster. This eliminates downtime for capacity planning and ensures workloads don't stall due to storage limits, a key advantage over traditional RDS instances that require manual resizing.

With Aurora's storage foundation established, the next step is monitoring performance using Amazon CloudWatch metrics, which provide visibility into replication, compute, and storage activity.

Monitoring Aurora with CloudWatch Metrics

While Performance Insights is available for Aurora, we've already explained it in the Amazon RDS section. For Aurora, the exam emphasis is on CloudWatch metrics that are unique or critical to Aurora's architecture. These metrics allow CloudOps engineers to detect replication lag, connection saturation, and resource bottlenecks.

Table 4.8 provides a consolidated list of these key Amazon CloudWatch metrics that every SOA-C03 candidate should know for the exam:

For a full list of all Amazon CloudWatch metrics for Amazon Aurora, visit: `https://docs.aws.amazon.com/AmazonRDS/latest/AuroraUserGuide/Aurora.AuroraMonitoring.Metrics.html`.

For exam readiness, it's also important to know how to query these metrics programmatically. AWS CLI provides two main commands—`get-metric-statistics` and `get-metric-data`. The former is used for retrieving aggregated statistics (Average,

TABLE 4.8 Amazon Aurora Metrics

Metric Name (Console/API Name)	Description	Tuning Insight
`AuroraReplicaLag`	Replication lag (seconds) for each Aurora replica.	Alerts if replicas fall behind; critical for failover readiness and read scaling.
`AuroraReplicaLagMaximum`	Maximum replication lag across all replicas.	Identifies worst-case lag; useful for monitoring cluster health under heavy load.
`AuroraReplicaLagMinimum`	Minimum replication lag across all replicas.	Confirms best-case replication health; useful for tuning replica placement.
`CPUUtilization`	Percentage of CPU used by the DB instance.	High values indicate compute bottlenecks; scale vertically or add replicas.
`DatabaseConnections`	Number of active connections to the cluster.	Connection saturation suggests adding RDS Proxy or scaling instance class.
`FreeableMemory`	Amount of available memory for queries and caching.	Low memory can cause query slowdowns; tune parameters or scale instance size.
`VolumeReadIOPs/ VolumeWriteIOPs`	Number of read/write I/O operations per second.	High IOPS indicates storage pressure; optimize queries or consider workload split.
`Deadlocks`	Number of deadlocks detected in the cluster.	Frequent deadlocks point to query contention; optimize schema and indexing.
`CrossRegionReplication Latency`	Latency of replication traffic across regions (Aurora Global Database).	Critical for disaster recovery; monitor to ensure that global workloads remain resilient.

Maximum, Minimum, Sum) for one metric at a time; the latter is best suited for retrieving multiple metrics at once or performing metric math.

The following example shows how to retrieve the maximum replica lag (in seconds) for an Aurora cluster named `my-aurora-cluster`.

```
aws cloudwatch get-metric-statistics \
    --namespace AWS/RDS \
    --metric-name AuroraReplicaLag \
    --dimensions Name=DBClusterIdentifier,Value=my-aurora-cluster \
    --start-time 2025-12-11T14:00:00Z \
    --end-time 2025-12-11T15:00:00Z \
    --period 60 \
    --statistics Maximum \
    --region us-east-1
```

In this command:

- `--namespace AWS/RDS`: Aurora metrics are published under the RDS namespace.
- `--metric-name AuroraReplicaLag`: Queries replication lag.
- `--dimensions`: Filters by cluster identifier.
- `--start-time / --end-time`: Defines the query window (ISO 8601 UTC).
- `--period 60`: Aggregates into one-minute intervals.
- `--statistics Maximum`: Returns the worst-case lag value.
- `--region us-east-1`: Ensures that query runs in the correct AWS region.

The output is returned in JSON format and looks like this:

```
{
  "Label": "AuroraReplicaLag",
  "Datapoints": [
    {
      "Timestamp": "2025-12-11T14:01:00Z",
      "Unit": "Seconds",
      "Maximum": 2.0
    },
    {
      "Timestamp": "2025-12-11T14:02:00Z",
      "Unit": "Seconds",
      "Maximum": 1.0
    },
    {
      "Timestamp": "2025-12-11T14:03:00Z",
      "Unit": "Seconds",
      "Maximum": 0.0
    }
  ]
}
```

The next example shows how to retrieve the average CPU utilization and the maximum number of database connections for the Aurora cluster.

```
aws cloudwatch get-metric-data \
    --metric-data-queries '[
      {
        "Id":"cpu1",
        "MetricStat":{
"Metric":{"Namespace":"AWS/RDS","MetricName":"CPUUtilization","Dimensions":
[{"Name":"DBClusterIdentifier","Value":"my-aurora-cluster"}]},
          "Period":60,
          "Stat":"Average"
        }
      },
      {
        "Id":"conn1",
        "MetricStat":{
"Metric":{"Namespace":"AWS/RDS","MetricName":"DatabaseConnections",
"Dimensions":[{"Name":"DBClusterIdentifier","Value":"my-aurora-cluster"}]},
          "Period":60,
          "Stat":"Maximum"
        }
      }
    ]' \
    --start-time 2025-12-11T14:00:00Z \
    --end-time 2025-12-11T15:00:00Z \
    --region us-east-1
```

In this command:

- `--metric-data-queries`: JSON array of metrics to query.
- Each query has an `Id` (label), a `MetricStat` (metric name, namespace, dimensions), a `Period`, and a `Stat` key.
- Multiple metrics can be requested in one call (here: `CPUUtilization` and `DatabaseConnections`).
- Supports metric math (e.g., subtracting one metric from another).

The output is another JSON document that looks like this:

```
{
  "MetricDataResults": [
    {
      "Id": "cpu1",
      "Label": "CPUUtilization",
      "Timestamps": ["2025-12-11T14:01:00Z", "2025-12-11T14:02:00Z"],
      "Values": [15.0, 20.0],
      "StatusCode": "Complete",
    },
    {
      "Id": "conn1",
      "Label": "DatabaseConnections",
```

```
      "Timestamps": ["2025-12-11T14:01:00Z", "2025-12-11T14:02:00Z"],
      "Values": [120, 150],
      "StatusCode": "Complete",
    }
  ]
}
```


To learn more about the structure of this output, visit: `https://docs.aws.amazon.com/AmazonCloudWatch/latest/APIReference/API_MetricDataResult.html`.

Use `get-metric-statistics` for simple, single-metric historical stats. Use `get-metric-data` when you need multiple metrics, math expressions, or advanced queries in one call.

Once your Aurora workloads can be monitored effectively, the next logical step is to accelerate queries—especially those scanning large datasets.

Aurora Parallel Query

Aurora Parallel Query lets analytical (OLAP) queries run directly on transactional (OLTP) databases without a separate warehouse. Traditional engines struggle to use all CPU cores efficiently because the compute layer must wait for the full dataset from storage before processing.

Aurora changes this dynamic. The Parallel Query feature pushes computationally intensive parts of a query—specifically data filtering and projection (selecting certain columns/rows) and aggregation (like calculating `SUM()` or `AVG()` over large datasets)—down to the specialized Aurora storage layer. This architecture allows the storage nodes, rather than the primary compute instance, to perform the heavy lifting in parallel. Only the final, significantly smaller, filtered result set is returned to the compute instance, drastically reducing network traffic and speeding up query completion times, often by a factor of ten or more for complex analytical queries.

You can enable this feature using a custom DB cluster parameter group. It must be enabled at the cluster level.

```
# First, identify your DB cluster parameter group name
aws rds modify-db-cluster-parameter-group \
    --db-cluster-parameter-group-name my-custom-cluster-pg \
    --parameters
"ParameterName=aurora_parallel_query,ParameterValue=ON,ApplyMethod=
pending-reboot"
```

In this command:

- `--parameters "ParameterName=...,ParameterValue=...,ApplyMethod=pending-reboot"`: This is how you change individual settings within a parameter group.

- `ParameterName=aurora_parallel_query,ParameterValue=ON`: This specific key-value pair enables the feature.
- `ApplyMethod=pending-reboot`: For this specific parameter change to take effect, the Aurora cluster needs to be rebooted during a maintenance window.

Once enabled, Aurora determines automatically (using its cost optimizer) whether a specific query would benefit from parallel execution. An administrator typically doesn't need to rewrite SQL queries to take advantage of this feature.

Cluster Tuning Best Practices

Effective Aurora tuning involves managing the compute instances, the shared storage, and the cluster parameters. Here are some of the guidelines to know for the exam:

Read Scaling with Aurora Replicas The simplest optimization is horizontal read scaling: distribute traffic across up to 15 Aurora Replicas using the cluster reader endpoint for automatic load balancing.

Use Appropriate Instance Types Aurora relies on ample RAM, so use memory-optimized R-series instances (e.g., `db.r5.large`, `db.r6g.large`) for best price-performance.

Monitor Cluster Volume I/O Metrics You don't provision IOPS, but pay per request. High I/O costs with low CPU often signal inefficient queries—monitor `VolumeReadIOPS` and `VolumeWriteIOPS` to detect full table scans versus index lookups.

Parameter Group Configuration Use custom DB Cluster and parameter groups to tune engine settings. Avoid defaults to track and apply changes consistently.

Scalability and Elasticity

Amazon Aurora provides robust mechanisms for both horizontal (read scaling) and vertical (compute scaling) elasticity that significantly exceed the capabilities of equivalent Amazon RDS engines. As a CloudOps engineer it is your job to understand how to implement these strategies using the AWS toolset. In the exam, scalability questions often test whether you can recommend the right Aurora feature for a given scenario. Let's build this knowledge step by step.

Read Replica Scaling

The most direct form of Aurora scalability is horizontal scaling with Aurora Replicas. These replicas offload read-heavy traffic from the writer, boosting throughput without affecting transactions.

Unlike RDS replicas, Aurora replicas share the same distributed storage as the writer, removing I/O overhead and keeping replication lag to milliseconds—ideal for sensitive read operations.

In addition to increasing performance for read operations, an Aurora replica can also serve as a potential failover target, ordered by priority. As a CloudOps engineer, you can easily add an Aurora replica to your cluster using the AWS CLI's `create-db-instance` command.

```
aws rds create-db-instance \
    --db-instance-identifier my-aurora-replica-01 \
    --engine aurora-mysql \
    --db-cluster-identifier my-aurora-cluster \
    --db-instance-class db.r6g.large \
    --availability-zone us-east-1a \
    --promotion-tier 1
```

In this command:

- `--db-instance-identifier`: A unique name for this specific replica instance.
- `--engine aurora-mysql`: Specifies the engine type.
- `--db-cluster-identifier`: A crucial flag used to associate this new instance with your existing Aurora cluster, linking it to the shared storage volume.
- `--db-instance-class`: Defines the compute/memory capacity (vertical scaling of the replica itself). R-series instances are recommended for Aurora.
- `--availability-zone`: Specifies the physical location within a region.
- `--promotion-tier 1`: Defines the failover priority. Tiers 0 through 15 are valid. Lower numbers indicate higher priority. If the primary instance fails, Aurora attempts to promote the lowest-numbered, available replica first (e.g., tier 0 is highest priority).

Once replicas are created, the most important operational concept is the *reader endpoint*. This is the endpoint that Aurora consumers (the client applications, services, or processes that need to read data from the database) should use to read data from the Aurora cluster.

Instead of connecting directly to the individual instance endpoints (e.g., `my-aurora-replica-01.xxxxxxxx.rds.amazonaws.com`), you provide your application configuration with the single, stable reader endpoint URL (e.g., `my-aurora-cluster.cluster-ro-xxxxxxxx.us-east-1.rds.amazonaws.com`).

The reader endpoint is a DNS name managed by AWS that automatically handles internal load balancing and connection routing across all available Aurora Replicas within that cluster. If a replica becomes unhealthy, Aurora automatically removes it from the endpoint's rotation until it recovers. This provides automatic high availability for your read path without requiring complex application-side logic.

You can easily determine the reader endpoint URL for your cluster using the AWS CLI's `describe-db-clusters` command:

```
aws rds describe-db-clusters \
    --db-cluster-identifier my-aurora-cluster \
    --query 'DBClusters.ReaderEndpoint' \
    --output text
```

In this command:

- `--db-cluster-identifier`: The name of your Aurora cluster.
- `--query 'DBClusters.ReaderEndpoint'`: Uses JMESPath syntax to filter the extensive JSON output and return only the specific `ReaderEndpoint` URL string from the first cluster found in the results.
- `--output text`: Formats the output as plain text, making it easy to copy and paste the URL directly into application configuration files or scripts.

Once read scaling is understood, the next logical step is elastic compute scaling, which Aurora Serverless v2 provides.

Aurora Serverless v2

While read replicas handle static scaling of read capacity, modern cloud operations demand solutions for intermittent or unpredictable workloads where provisioning a fixed instance size is inefficient. This is where Aurora Serverless v2 provides true compute elasticity.

Aurora Serverless v2 doesn't require you to manually manage instance classes like `db.r6g.large`. Instead, you define a minimum and maximum capacity range using Aurora Capacity Units (ACUs). The database seamlessly and instantaneously scales its compute and memory capacity in fine-grained increments (0.5 ACU at a time) based on workload demand, often without impacting active connections. This is a game-changer for cost optimization in environments with variable traffic patterns (e.g., testing environments, multi-tenant apps, or seasonal workloads).

As a CloudOps engineer you use parameter groups to enable this scaling model and CloudWatch alarms to monitor ACU consumption against predefined thresholds.

To create an Aurora Serverless v2 cluster you use the AWS CLI's `create-db-cluster` command as follows:

When provisioning resources, security best practices dictate using secure storage for secrets (e.g., credentials, API keys, etc.) like AWS Secrets Manager. Never pass plaintext passwords via command-line flags!

```
aws rds create-db-cluster \
    --db-cluster-identifier my-serverless-v2-cluster \
    --engine aurora-mysql \
    --master-username admin \
    --manage-master-user-password \
    --serverless-v2-scaling-configuration MinCapacity=0.5,MaxCapacity=4.0
```

In this command:

- `--db-cluster-identifier`: Specifies the unique name for your cluster (e.g., `my-serverless-v2-cluster`).
- `--engine`: Defines the database engine to use. In this case, `aurora-mysql` specifies the MySQL-compatible edition of Amazon Aurora.

- `--master-username`: Sets the administrator login name for the database (e.g., `admin`).
- `--manage-master-user-password`: Enables AWS-managed credentials. Instead of you providing a password, RDS automatically generates a strong password and stores it securely in AWS Secrets Manager.
- `--serverless-v2-scaling-configuration`: Configures the scaling limits for the Serverless v2 cluster using ACUs.
  - `MinCapacity=0.5`: The minimum compute power the cluster will maintain.
  - `MaxCapacity=4.0`: The maximum compute power the cluster can scale up to during high load.

One ACU provides approximately 2 GiB of memory along with corresponding CPU and networking I/O bandwidth.

It's important for the exam to understand that running the previous command creates the Aurora Serverless v2 cluster (the storage and management layer). To actually use the database, you must follow up by creating a DB Instance within this cluster:

```
aws rds create-db-instance \
    --db-cluster-identifier my-serverless-v2-cluster \
    --db-instance-identifier my-instance-1 \
    --db-instance-class db.serverless \
    --engine aurora-mysql
```

A crucial operational benefit of Aurora Serverless v2 is its flexibility. Yes, it is possible to transform an existing Aurora Provisioned cluster into an Aurora Serverless v2 cluster (and vice versa) with minimal downtime. This is accomplished first by defining the scaling configuration with the `modify-db-cluster` command (step 1 in the following snippet), and then by changing the instance class of the existing primary and replica instances to `db.serverless` via a `modify-db-instance` command (steps 2 and 3).

For the exam, make sure you understand that:

- The `modify-db-cluster` command with `--serverless-v2-scaling-configuration` tells the entire cluster's control plane how to manage the scaling boundaries (Min/Max ACUs) *for all* instances set to `db.serverless`.
- The `modify-db-instance` command with the `--db-instance-class db.serverless` flag tells AWS which type of compute to use for that specific database node.

The underlying shared storage architecture remains exactly the same, making the transition seamless.

```
# 1. Update the CLUSTER-level configuration first.
# This sets the "blueprint" (Min/Max ACUs) for the entire cluster.
# Note: --db-cluster-identifier points to the Aurora Provisioned cluster.
aws rds modify-db-cluster \
    --db-cluster-identifier my-new-serverless-v2-cluster \
    --serverless-v2-scaling-configuration MinCapacity=0.5,MaxCapacity=16.0 \
    --apply-immediately

# 2. Convert the PRIMARY instance to the serverless class.
# Note: --db-instance-identifier is the name of the individual node,
# but this node MUST belong to the cluster modified in Step 1.
aws rds modify-db-instance \
    --db-instance-identifier my-primary-provisioned-instance \
    --db-instance-class db.serverless \
    --apply-immediately

# 3. Convert the REPLICA instance to the serverless class.
# Note: Like the primary, this individual node must be a member
# of 'my-new-serverless-v2-cluster' to inherit the scaling rules.
aws rds modify-db-instance \
    --db-instance-identifier my-replica-provisioned-instance \
    --db-instance-class db.serverless \
    --apply-immediately
```

The `MaxCapacity` in the `--serverless-v2-scaling-configuration` flag defines the maximum number of ACUs that the Aurora Serverless v2 cluster is allowed to scale up to.

Here are the key details you should know for the exam:

The Limit Setting the `MaxCapacity` puts an upper bound on how much compute power and memory your cluster can use, which is critical for cost control and predictability.

Operational Impact Even if your workload suddenly spikes and requires more resources, the cluster will not scale beyond this configured maximum value. This will likely result in increased CPU utilization, higher latency, connection throttling, or query failures if the limit is insufficient for peak load.

Value Range The allowed range for `MaxCapacity` typically runs from 0.5 ACUs up to 256 ACUs, depending on region and engine type.

When managing the scaling configuration, as a CloudOps engineer, you must balance performance requirements (setting a high enough `MaxCapacity` to handle peak demand) with cost management needs (setting a limit that prevents unexpectedly high AWS bills).

Aurora Global Database

For organizations requiring extreme fault tolerance across geographic regions or needing to serve read traffic with minimal latency to a global user base, Aurora offers the Global Database feature. This extends the concept of shared storage across AWS regions.

An Aurora Global Database consists of one primary cluster in one region (e.g., `us-east-1`) and up to five secondary read-only clusters in different regions (e.g., `us-west-2`, `eu-west-1`) in the same partition. Data is replicated with minimal impact on performance, achieving a Recovery Point Objective (RPO) of typically less than one second and a Recovery Time Objective (RTO) of less than one minute in a disaster scenario.

This setup is crucial for exam scenarios where Business Continuity Plans (BCPs) demand near-zero data loss and rapid cross-region failover.

Setting this up involves creating the global database structure, then adding a secondary region cluster.

```
# 1. Create the global database structure from the primary cluster
#    (must already exist)
aws rds create-global-cluster \
    --global-cluster-identifier my-global-db-cluster \
    --source-db-cluster-identifier arn:aws:rds:us-east-
1:123456789012:cluster:my-primary-cluster

# 2. Add a secondary region cluster (in a different region)
aws rds create-db-cluster \
    --db-cluster-identifier my-secondary-cluster-dr \
    --engine aurora-mysql \
    --global-cluster-identifier my-global-db-cluster \
    --region us-west-2
```

The secondary cluster must use the exact same `--engine` and `--engine-version` as the primary.

As with any new standalone Aurora cluster, the secondary cluster created in step 2 initially contains only the shared storage volume. It has no compute capacity until you provision at least one database instance. You must attach a database instance to the secondary cluster before it can serve reads or accept any connections.

```
aws rds create-db-instance \
    --db-cluster-identifier my-secondary-cluster-dr \
    --db-instance-identifier my-secondary-instance-1 \
    --db-instance-class db.r6g.large \
    --engine aurora-mysql \
    --region us-west-2
```

If `my-primary-cluster` was created in `us-east-1` with the `--manage-master-user-password` flag, Aurora Global Database does not automatically replicate the secret to `us-west-2`. This is because Secrets Manager is a regional service, and it does not participate in Aurora Global Database replication. You must use the Secrets Manager `replicate-secret-to-regions` command if you want your DR applications to find the password locally.

Having explored how Aurora scales and adapts to workloads, the next critical capability to master is Amazon Aurora Backup and Restore Strategies, which ensure durability, recovery, and operational resilience.

Backup and Restore Strategies

Reliable backup and restore capabilities are foundational elements of a CloudOps engineer's responsibilities, crucial for meeting Recovery Point Objectives (RPOs) and Recovery Time Objectives (RTOs) required for the SOA-C03 exam. Amazon Aurora streamlines these operations compared to traditional database systems by leveraging its cloud-native storage architecture, primarily backing up data to Amazon S3 automatically and efficiently.

Continuous Backups to Amazon S3

As shown in Figure 4.3, Amazon Aurora takes continuous, incremental backups of your entire cluster volume to Amazon S3 automatically. This is a background operation that does not cause any performance degradation or I/O latency to your primary database workload.

CloudOps engineers enable this simply by setting `BackupRetentionPeriod` when creating or modifying an Aurora cluster. This period defines how far back you can restore your data. The default retention is one day, but it can be configured up to 35 days.

The benefit of continuous, incremental backup is efficiency: only changes (redo logs) are shipped to S3, rather than full data snapshots, making the process fast and highly durable.

This command configures a seven-day retention period using the AWS CLI:

```
aws rds modify-db-cluster \
    --db-cluster-identifier my-aurora-cluster \
    --backup-retention-period 7 \
    --apply-immediately
```

In this command:

- `--backup-retention-period 7`: Sets the number of days of continuous backup history to retain. This is the operational window for point-in-time recovery.
- `--apply-immediately`: Applies the retention change immediately rather than waiting for the next maintenance window.

The continuity of these backups directly feeds into Aurora's powerful recovery feature, which allows administrators to restore the database to virtually any desired moment within that retention window.

Point-in-Time Recovery

Point-in-Time Recovery (PITR) is the primary restore method for day-to-day operations and accidental data modification events (like a mistakenly committed `DELETE` statement).

Because Aurora continuously streams changes to Amazon S3, you can restore a cluster with a one-second granularity to any point in time within your configured backup retention window (up to 35 days). This eliminates data loss scenarios and dramatically improves RPOs compared to traditional hourly or daily snapshot schedules.

The restore operation creates a new, independent Aurora cluster starting from the specified point in time.

To perform a PITR restore to a specific time, you would use the following CLI command, specifying the exact time in UTC format:

```
aws rds restore-db-cluster-to-point-in-time \
    --source-db-cluster-identifier my-aurora-cluster \
    --target-db-cluster-identifier my-aurora-cluster-restored-pitr \
    --restore-to-time 2025-12-01T14:35:00Z \
    --use-latest-restorable-time
```

In this command:

- `--source-db-cluster-identifier`: The original cluster you are recovering data from.
- `--target-db-cluster-identifier`: The name for the new cluster that will contain the restored data.
- `--restore-to-time`: The specific timestamp (UTC) you want to restore to.
- `--use-latest-restorable-time` (or `--restore-to-latest-time`): A useful flag to recover the database right up to the second before failure, maximizing RPO. Note: You can omit `--restore-to-time` entirely if you just want the absolute latest possible restoration.

While PITR is ideal for granular recovery, sometimes a CloudOps engineer needs a static, long-term archive copy of the entire database cluster for compliance or auditing purposes, which is where manual snapshots come in.

Cluster Snapshots

Aurora automatically takes a daily system snapshot within the maintenance window, but a CloudOps engineer can also take manual cluster snapshots on demand. These are full data copies stored durably in Amazon S3, separate from the continuous backup stream.

Manual snapshots persist indefinitely, even if you delete the source Aurora cluster, making them perfect for compliance archives or as a safe base point before implementing major schema changes.

To create a manual snapshot:

```
aws rds create-db-cluster-snapshot \
   --db-cluster-snapshot-identifier my-aurora-cluster-manual-archive-20251201 \
   --db-cluster-identifier my-aurora-cluster
```

In this command:

- `--db-cluster-snapshot-identifier`: A unique name for your new snapshot archive.
- `--db-cluster-identifier`: The name of the cluster you are snapshotting.

Snapshots are powerful not just for disaster recovery, but also as a mechanism for rapid development and testing cycles using Aurora's cloning capabilities.

Fast Database Cloning

Fast database cloning is a performance optimization feature unique to Aurora that leverages the *copy-on-write* (CoW) protocol of the underlying shared storage system. This feature allows a CloudOps engineer to create a near-instantaneous, writable copy of an existing Aurora cluster.

When you initiate a clone of an Aurora cluster, AWS doesn't actually duplicate all terabytes of data immediately. Instead, it creates a virtual copy that shares the exact same physical storage pages as the source cluster. You only incur storage charges for new data written to either the source or the clone after the clone operation is performed; the initial clone shares the vast majority of the storage footprint.

This feature is incredibly fast—cloning multi-terabyte databases takes minutes instead of hours—and is a key tool for Dev/Test environments where rapid iteration is crucial for operational efficiency.

To create a fast clone:

```
aws rds restore-db-cluster-to-point-in-time \
    --source-db-cluster-identifier my-production-cluster \
    --target-db-cluster-identifier my-dev-test-cluster-clone \
    --restore-type copy-on-write \
    --use-latest-restorable-time
```

In this command:

- `--source-db-cluster-identifier`: The identifier of the existing Aurora cluster you want to clone.
- `--target-db-cluster-clone-identifier`: The identifier of your new, cloned cluster.
- `--restore-type copy-on-write`: This specific flag tells Aurora to use the fast cloning, copy-on-write (CoW) protocol instead of a standard restoration from backup.
- `--use-latest-restorable-time`: Ensures that the clone reflects the most current state of the source data. You can also specify a specific `--restore-to-time` if you want a clone of the database as it existed in the past.

A CloudOps engineer must understand the operational trade-offs between using a fast clone and performing a standard data restore (either from a snapshot or PITR). The choice depends entirely on your use case, as described in Table 4.9.

Choose fast cloning when:

- You need a temporary copy of production data for testing a new feature or running a quick batch job.
- You prioritize RTO (recovery time) in a non-DR scenario where costs need to be minimized.

TABLE 4.9 Fast Cloning vs. Standard Restore

Use Case	Fast Database Clone	Standard Restore (PITR or Deep Snapshot Restore)
Speed	Minutes, regardless of database size (e.g., five minutes for 10 TiB).	Hours, proportional to database size.
Cost Model	Only pay for new data changes/writes in either source or clone.	Pay for full storage capacity immediately upon restore completion.
Primary Use Case	Dev/Test environments, rapid prototyping, ephemeral testing, running ad hoc queries on recent production data.	Disaster recovery (DR), production data corruption events, long-term compliance archives.
Data Integrity	Shares storage pages; changes to one might theoretically impact the underlying shared storage blocks, although AWS manages isolation well.	Creates a fully isolated, independent copy from a specific point in time.

- The cloned environment is short-lived.

Choose a standard restore/PITR when:

- You have a production outage and need to recover the main database to a clean state immediately. This creates a fully independent, guaranteed-isolated copy.
- You need a compliance archive that must exist independently of the source cluster's lifecycle.

Having explored Amazon Aurora as a cloud-native, highly performant relational database, you next learn about Amazon DynamoDB—another cloud-native, but schema-flexible NoSQL database engineered for massive scalability and performance at any scale.

Amazon DynamoDB

Amazon DynamoDB is a fully managed, serverless NoSQL key-value and document database service designed to run high-performance, highly scalable applications with single-digit millisecond latency at any scale. For a CloudOps engineer preparing for the AWS SOA-C03 exam, operational excellence with DynamoDB involves understanding its unique architecture, performance levers, serverless scaling model, and backup and restore strategies.

Overview of Amazon DynamoDB

Amazon DynamoDB offloads the operational heavy lifting—managing host servers, OS patching, hardware failures, and cluster scaling—entirely to AWS, allowing cloud operations teams to focus purely on monitoring application performance, data modeling, and backup and recovery best practices.

The SOA-C03 exam doesn't require deep expertise in DynamoDB's data engineering. However, as a CloudOps engineer, you'll need a strong grasp of core NoSQL principles and how DynamoDB applies them. This foundation is essential for optimizing performance, managing scale, and designing effective backup and restore strategies. The next section walks you through these key concepts.

A Mini Crash Course in NoSQL

For a CloudOps engineer accustomed to relational databases (like MySQL or Aurora), NoSQL introduces a shift in thinking about data structure and access. Relational databases use rigid, predefined schemas with tables and rows. NoSQL databases like Amazon DynamoDB are *schemaless* or *schema-on-read*, meaning the structure of the data can vary item by item within the same table.

The fundamental components in DynamoDB translate roughly as follows: a *Table* is similar to a relational table, a Row is called an *Item*, and a Column is called an *Attribute*. The key difference is flexibility: one item representing a `User` might have attributes for `email` and `login_count`, while the next item in the same table might only have `user_id` and `last_seen`. This flexibility accelerates development and schema evolution.

The most important NoSQL construct in DynamoDB is the primary key, which is composed of a partition key (`HASH` attribute) and an optional sort key (`RANGE` attribute). The partition key determines the physical location (partition) where data is stored. Accessing data via this key is extremely fast and efficient, which is essential for achieving DynamoDB's guaranteed performance.

Because of this partitioning mechanism, efficient data retrieval relies entirely on knowing the primary key structure before you need the data. You design your application's required access patterns first, and then you model your data structure to fit those queries efficiently, rather than normalizing data into many small tables as you would in a relational system. This focus on access patterns over rigid normalization is critical to DynamoDB's operation and performance.

Key-Value and Document Model

DynamoDB is fundamentally a NoSQL database. It supports both a key-value store model, where data is retrieved using a unique primary key, and a document model, where items can be complex, nested JSON objects. This model provides schema flexibility, allowing different items within the same table to have varying attributes.

Schemaless Design and Access Patterns

The term "schemaless" means you do not pre-define all attributes and their data types upfront as you would in a relational database like Aurora. The operational implication is that database changes can be deployed without complex schema migrations.

As previously mentioned, Amazon DynamoDB requires you to design your access patterns first, before modeling your data. Efficient operations (like `GetItem`, `PutItem`, `Query`) use the primary key (partition key and optional sort key) to locate data quickly. This approach is crucial for the performance of your DynamoDB database. Inefficient operations (`Scan`), which read every single item in the table, must be avoided in production environments as they impact performance and cost.

ACID Transactions in DynamoDB

While many NoSQL databases struggle with complex, multi-item updates, Amazon DynamoDB supports ACID (Atomicity, Consistency, Isolation, Durability) compliant transactions. These allow you to coordinate inserts, updates, or deletes across multiple items within a single request, ensuring all changes succeed or all fail together, in a *transaction* manner. This feature simplifies application logic for financial or inventory-based workloads that require data consistency guarantees.

When reading data outside of a transaction context, a CloudOps engineer needs to consider data consistency models. By default, DynamoDB provides eventual consistency for reads, meaning a read request might not see the result of a very recent write operation immediately (consistency within a second or two). However, you can explicitly request *strongly consistent* reads for critical operations where you must read the most recent data. Strongly consistent reads have slightly higher latency and consume more Read Capacity Units (RCUs) than eventually consistent reads.

The "Single-Table" Design Pattern

For the SOA-C03 exam, be aware of a common data modeling strategy in DynamoDB called the "single-table design." Unlike relational databases where you normalize data into many specific tables (e.g., Users table, Orders table, Products table), a DynamoDB single-table design often consolidates related entities into one large table.

This pattern leverages generic partition key (PK) and sort key (SK) attributes. For instance, a User item might have PK: `USER#123` and SK: `PROFILE`. An order associated with that user might have PK: `USER#123` and SK: `ORDER#A456`.

This approach keeps related items physically close together on the same storage partition. The primary benefit is performance efficiency: you can retrieve all related items (the user profile and their orders) using a single, fast `Query` operation, which is critical for minimizing latency and managing I/O costs at scale. With a relational database you would have to design entity relationships between the tables, with foreign keys. The resulting query would require "expensive" joins to retrieve the same data, at the cost of extra latency.

To learn more, visit: `https://aws.amazon.com/blogs/compute/creating-a-single-table-design-with-amazon-dynamodb/`.

Understanding the underlying structure and design principles of DynamoDB leads naturally into the critical operational decision of how to configure its performance and indexing strategies. A CloudOps engineer must continuously weigh trade-offs—whether to use strongly consistent reads for performance, choose on-demand capacity for elasticity, or enable PITR for RPO guarantees—to optimize performance, cost, scale, and design effective backup and restore strategies that align with business needs.

Performance Optimization Strategies

Performance tuning in DynamoDB is less about tuning server hardware and more about capacity planning, data modeling, indexing, and caching. Operational metrics focus on consumed capacity, throttling events, and latency.

Provisioned vs. On-Demand Capacity

A crucial early decision for a CloudOps engineer is selecting the correct capacity mode, which dictates how you pay for and manage throughput. Amazon DynamoDB measures the speed of data operations using abstract units:

- **Read Capacity Units (RCUs):** One RCU represents one strongly consistent read request (or two eventually consistent read requests) for an item up to 4 KB in size per second.
- **Write Capacity Units (WCUs):** One WCU represents one write request for an item up to 1 KB in size per second.

The capacity mode is a table-level setting, not a database-level one, allowing different tables in the same account to use different configurations. You configure your table capacity using any of these two modes:

- **On-Demand Capacity Mode (default):** AWS manages all scaling automatically and instantaneously based on actual usage. You pay per request, and DynamoDB adapts to virtually any traffic volume without capacity planning. This is excellent for unpredictable workloads or test environments, prioritizing elasticity over cost control for stable workloads.
- **Provisioned Capacity Mode:** You specify the exact number of RCUs and WCUs needed upfront. This offers predictable performance and is more cost-effective for stable, predictable workloads. This mode requires the use of auto scaling to handle unexpected traffic spikes within defined boundaries.

For example, to create a table using the `PROVISIONED` mode, you explicitly specify the mode and provide initial capacity values. The following command also illustrates the required flags for defining the table structure using the `UserID` attribute name:

```
aws dynamodb create-table \
    --table-name UserOrdersTableProvisioned \
    --attribute-definitions AttributeName=UserID,AttributeType=S \
    --key-schema AttributeName=UserID,KeyType=HASH \
    --billing-mode PROVISIONED \
    --provisioned-throughput ReadCapacityUnits=100,WriteCapacityUnits=100
```

In this command:

- `--attribute-definitions AttributeName=UserID,AttributeType=S`: Defines the *names* and *data types* for every attribute you intend to use as part of a primary key or secondary index key. In this case, we declare an attribute named `UserID` as a String (S).
- `--key-schema AttributeName=UserID,KeyType=HASH`: Specifies *which* of the defined attributes actually functions as the partition key (`HASH`) for the main table. The partition key determines the physical location (partition) where data is stored.
- `--billing-mode PROVISIONED`: Explicitly sets the table to use the provisioned capacity model.
- `--provisioned-throughput ReadCapacityUnits=100,WriteCapacityUnits=100`: Defines the baseline RCU and WCU limits for the table. You will be billed for this capacity 24/7, regardless of usage. The values specified here set the initial throughput that your table can sustain.

You can specify the capacity mode at table creation or switch between modes using the `update-table` command after the table is operational.

Indexing: Global and Local Secondary Indexes

In DynamoDB, the performance of your application hinges entirely on how effectively you retrieve data. Unlike relational databases that can efficiently perform ad hoc queries on any column, DynamoDB requires indexes tailored to specific data access patterns. Misusing access patterns can lead to performance bottlenecks and throttling events.

To illustrate how indexing works, we need a table that holds different types of related data in a single-table design pattern. As shown in Table 4.10, we shift from simple attribute names like `UserId` to a more generic `PK`, single-table pattern where attribute values define the item type.

TABLE 4.10 Single-Table Design Example

PK (Partition Key)	SK (Sort Key)	Type	Data	Status	GSI1PK	GSI1SK
`USER#123`	`#PROFILE#`	User	...	Active	(None)	(None)
`USER#123`	`ORDER#A456`	Order	...	Shipped	`ORDER#A456`	2025-12-01
`USER#456`	`ORDER#B789`	Order	...	Pending	`ORDER#B789`	2025-12-02

In this design, the attributes are named PK and SK (partition key and sort key), which are generic placeholders whose values define the entity type and relationship. The item with SK value `#PROFILE#` represents the user's details, whereas items with SK values starting with `ORDER#` represent that user's orders. This keeps related data on the same physical partition for efficient retrieval.

Designing Indexes for Access Patterns and Performance

Indexes in DynamoDB are not general-purpose data structures; they are specialized look-up tables optimized for specific queries your application needs to perform efficiently. The primary goal of index design is to make every query a highly efficient "Key-Value lookup" or `Query` operation, avoiding expensive full-table scans.

The operational process for designing indexes follows these critical steps:

1. **Identify Data Access Patterns**

   The CloudOps team collaborates with developers to list all the ways the application needs to fetch data (e.g., "Get a user's profile," "Find all open orders for user X," "Find all orders shipped on a specific date Y").

2. **Map to Keys/Indexes**

   The data modeler designs a primary key (`PK/SK`) to satisfy the most frequent patterns. Secondary indexes (LSIs and GSIs) are used to satisfy alternative access patterns identified in Step 1.

3. **Monitor Impact**

   CloudOps engineers monitor CloudWatch metrics like `ReadThrottleEvents` and `Latency` after deployment to confirm that index usage is efficient and capacity limits are not prematurely hit.

With DynamoDB there are two types of secondary indexes you need to know for the exam: Local Secondary Index (LSI), and Global Secondary Index (GSI).

Local Secondary Index (LSI)

An LSI shares the *same partition key* (`PK` or `UserID` in our previous example) as the base table but uses a different sort key attribute (e.g., Status attribute).

Use Case and Design You want to efficiently find all items within a user's partition that have a specific status. The LSI allows filtering/sorting by `Status` after querying the PK.

Performance Impact LSIs are strongly consistent with the base table (data is immediately available after a write) but add to the cost of every write on the base table.

As of the writing of this book, an LSI comes with a strict 10 GB limit on item collection size per partition key value and must be defined at table creation.

Global Secondary Index (GSI)

A GSI has a *different partition key and sort key* from the base table. This creates an entirely separate physical index that is eventually consistent with the main table.

Use Case and Design You want to find *all* orders across your entire application that were created on a specific date (`2025-12-02`), regardless of which user placed them. The base table cannot efficiently answer this because dates are not part of the primary key structure. The GSI is designed with its own PK/SK pair (`GSI1PK`, `GSI1SK` in the previous table), which we populate with `Order ID` and `Date` attributes. This allows us to query across all user partitions using a different index key.

Performance Impact GSIs are essential when querying on non-key attributes but maintain their own independent provisioned capacity units (RCUs/WCUs), which must be monitored and scaled separately from the main table. Queries against a GSI are eventually consistent.

Unlike LSIs, we can add a GSI to an existing table using the `update-table` command:

```
# Add the GSI to an existing table
aws dynamodb update-table \
    --table-name UserOrdersTableProvisioned \
    --attribute-definitions AttributeName=GSI1PK,AttributeType=S AttributeName=
GSI1SK,AttributeType=S \
    --global-secondary-index-updates '
        [
            {
                "Create": {
                    "IndexName": "OrdersByDateGSI",
                    "KeySchema": [
                        {"AttributeName": "GSI1PK", "KeyType": "HASH"},
                        {"AttributeName": "GSI1SK", "KeyType": "RANGE"}
                    ],
                    "Projection": {"ProjectionType": "ALL"},
                    "ProvisionedThroughput": {"ReadCapacityUnits": 1,
"WriteCapacityUnits": 1}
                }
            }
        ]
    '
```

In this command:

- `--update-table`: Modifies table settings online.
- `--attribute-definitions`: We must ensure the new GSI key attributes (`GSI1PK`, `GSI1SK`) are declared as available key types.
- `--global-secondary-index-updates`: Requires a JSON structure defining a `Create`, `Update`, or `Delete` action for an index.
- `"ProvisionedThroughput"`: Requires its own dedicated capacity units because it is a separate physical index.

Query and Scan Best Practices

The most important performance best practice is to optimize for `Query` operations and avoid `Scan` operations in production. A `Query` uses your defined primary key or GSI key to efficiently access data within a specific partition. A `Scan`, however, reads every single item in the entire table, which is slow, expensive, and consumes excessive capacity units, leading to throttling.

Caching with DynamoDB Accelerator (DAX)

To reduce read latency from milliseconds to microseconds for read-heavy workloads, CloudOps engineers deploy Amazon DynamoDB Accelerator (DAX). DAX is a fully managed, API-compatible in-memory caching service. It sits in front of your DynamoDB tables; the key operational benefit is that you simply switch your application endpoint from the DynamoDB endpoint to the DAX cluster endpoint, requiring minimal application code changes.

The operational flow involves two primary scenarios when an application requests data through the DAX endpoint:

- **Cache Hit:** If the requested item is in the cache, DAX immediately returns the data from its in-memory store (microseconds latency).
- **Cache Miss:** If the requested item is not in the cache (a cache miss), DAX automatically forwards the request to the underlying DynamoDB table. It waits for the response from DynamoDB, caches that data in memory for subsequent requests, and then returns the item to the application. This operation takes milliseconds, similar to a standard DynamoDB call.

This managed caching logic ensures that popular data is served with extreme speed, while DAX seamlessly handles the complexities of fetching fresh data when needed.

Regardless of your chosen capacity mode or indexing strategy, ensuring that the database can handle spikes in traffic requires leveraging DynamoDB's robust scalability and elasticity features.

Scalability and Elasticity

Amazon DynamoDB is inherently serverless in its underlying design, managing data distribution across partitions automatically. The primary operational concern for scalability lies in how you configure and monitor throughput limits, which differs based on your chosen capacity mode.

Auto Scaling for Throughput

On-Demand Capacity Mode leverages a completely managed, instantaneous serverless scaling mechanism handled entirely by AWS. There are no RCU/WCU limits to manage, so auto scaling logic is redundant.

In contrast, DynamoDB auto scaling helps CloudOps engineers manage traffic spikes for provisioned tables. It dynamically adjusts the table's provisioned capacity (RCUs and WCUs) in response to actual traffic patterns, within defined minimum and maximum range limits that you define. This mitigates throttling events, while managing costs more effectively than staying statically provisioned at peak capacity 24/7.

The following snippet shows an example CLI command to register a scalable target for a DynamoDB table's Read capacity.

```
aws application-autoscaling register-scalable-target \
    --service-namespace dynamodb \
    --resource-id table/MyAppTable \
    --scalable-dimension dynamodb:table:ReadCapacityUnits \
    --min-capacity 100 \
    --max-capacity 1000
```

In this command:

- `--service-namespace dynamodb`: Specifies that we are targeting the DynamoDB service.
- `--resource-id table/MyAppTable`: Identifies the specific table resource (must be a `PROVISIONED` table).
- `--scalable-dimension dynamodb:table:ReadCapacityUnits`: Designates the metric we are scaling (Read Capacity). A similar command is used for Write Capacity Units.
- `--min-capacity` and `--max-capacity`: Defines the auto scaling boundaries. DynamoDB will automatically increase capacity if load is near the current provisioned limit (default target utilization is 70%) and will decrease it when idle, staying within these bounds.

Monitoring and Alerting for GSI Throttling Events

A critical task for a CloudOps engineer is proactively monitoring for throttling events, especially on Global Secondary Indexes (GSIs), which maintain independent capacity limits (if provisioned). Throttling occurs when the application traffic exceeds the configured RCU/WCU limits, resulting in failed API calls and application errors.

You can set up a CloudWatch Alarm using the AWS CLI to alert your CloudOps team when GSI throttles occur:

```
aws cloudwatch put-metric-alarm \
    --alarm-name GSILatencyAlarm-OrdersByDateGSI \
    --metric-name ReadThrottleEvents \
    --namespace AWS/DynamoDB \
    --statistic Sum \
    --period 60 \
    --threshold 5 \
    --comparison-operator GreaterThanOrEqualToThreshold \
    --dimensions Name=TableName,Value=UserOrdersTableProvisioned
Name=IndexName,Value=OrdersByDateGSI \
    --evaluation-periods 1 \
    --alarm-actions arn:aws:sns:us-east-1:123456789012:MySNSTopicForOps
```

In this command:

- `--alarm-name`: A unique, descriptive name for the alarm.
- `--metric-name ReadThrottleEvents`: The specific metric indicating a throttle occurred.
- `--period 60, --threshold 5, --evaluation-periods 1`: Configures the alarm to fire if more than five throttling events occur in a single 60-second period.
- `--dimensions Name=TableName,Value=... Name=IndexName, Value=...`: Crucial flag: This scopes the alarm specifically to the GSI named `OrdersByDateGSI`.
- `--alarm-actions arn:aws:sns...`: Specifies the action to take when the alarm state is reached (e.g., sending a notification to an SNS Topic that alerts an operations team).

For the exam, be sure that you are familiar with the relevant metrics available in Amazon CloudWatch to assess performance, availability, and throughput health. Table 4.11 summarizes these metrics.

Partitioning and Hot Key Management

Amazon DynamoDB distributes your data across internal physical partitions based on your partition key design. Scalability limitations often manifest as a *hot partition*—when one partition key receives disproportionately high traffic compared to others. This is typically a design flaw and causes throttling for that specific partition even if the overall table capacity is sufficient.

A single partition has hard limits (around 3,000 RCUs and 1,000 WCUs), and if a specific PK value exceeds this limit, operations are throttled. It is your job, as a CloudOps engineer, to proactively monitor the CloudWatch metrics for per-partition utilization, and design partition keys that distribute traffic evenly.

DynamoDB tables are designed to scale to virtually unlimited total RCU/WCU *if the traffic is perfectly distributed.* AWS simply adds more physical partitions behind the scenes as your total data size or total even traffic grows. However, each individual physical partition has a specific throughput ceiling (currently 3,000 RCUs and 1,000 WCUs). This ceiling is enforced per partition to maintain performance guarantees. For example, if you direct all 50,000 of your total provisioned RCUs for your table to a single user's data (a single partition key value), the requests exceeding 3,000 RCU for that key will be throttled.

The following guidelines can help you mitigate the risk of hot partitions:

Optimize Partition Key Design Avoid sequential values or popular static attributes that clump traffic. Use high-cardinality, randomly accessed identifiers (UUIDs, hashed values) that naturally spread load across partitions.

TABLE 4.11 Amazon DynamoDB Metrics

Metric Name (Console/API Name)	Description	Tuning Insight
`ConsumedReadCapacityUnits`	Number of RCUs used in all successful read operations.	Use with `ProvisionedReadCapacityUnits` to check the current utilization rate and validate if auto scaling is working correctly (should hover around 70%).
`ReadThrottleEvents`	The number of read requests that were throttled (failed) due to insufficient capacity.	A non-zero value here is a high-priority alert. Indicates auto scaling failed to keep up, max capacity limit was hit, or a hot partition exists.
`WriteThrottleEvents`	The number of write requests that were throttled (failed) due to insufficient capacity.	A non-zero value is a critical alert. Indicates a need to increase WCU limits or investigate hot partitions.
`OnlineIndexConsumedWriteCapacity`	The WCU consumed by updates propagating from a base table to its GSI.	Used to monitor the cost and throughput required by your GSIs separately from the main table.
`Latency`	End-to-end latency of API calls (e.g., `PutItem`, `GetItem`, `Query`) in milliseconds.	Spikes in latency often correlate with throttling events or network issues. Should remain in single-digit milliseconds.
`SystemErrors`	Number of server-side errors encountered by DynamoDB.	A non-zero value indicates an AWS service issue that needs immediate attention/investigation via the AWS Health Dashboard.

Implement Write Sharding For high-volume single entities (like a live event counter), append a random suffix to the partition key (e.g., `EVENT#123#1`, `EVENT#123#2`) to manually distribute writes across multiple partitions.

Leverage DAX (for Reads) Deploy the DynamoDB Accelerator caching service to absorb millions of read requests per second for popular items, preventing those reads from ever hitting the physical partition limits.

Use Asynchronous Processing (for Writes) If immediate consistency is not required, use SQS or Kinesis streams to buffer writes during traffic spikes and process them at a controlled pace into DynamoDB, smoothing out the load on partitions.

Global Tables for Multi-Region Scale

For cross-region high availability, disaster recovery, and low-latency access for global users, consider implementing *Global Tables*. This provides a fully managed, multi-master, Multi-Region database solution where DynamoDB handles the complex data replication automatically. Changes in one region are replicated to all others almost instantly (typically within a second). This ensures that RTO (Recovery Time Objective) and RPO (Recovery Point Objective) goals are met for mission-critical, globally distributed applications.

To enable Global Tables for our existing `UserOrdersTableProvisioned` (assuming PITR is already enabled in all participating regions), you use the `update-table` command to add the desired replica regions:

```
# Command must be run in the 'primary' region first
aws dynamodb update-table \
    --table-name UserOrdersTableProvisioned \
    --replica-updates \
        'Create={RegionName=us-west-2}' \
        'Create={RegionName=eu-west-1}'
```

In this command:

- `--table-name`: Specifies the name of the existing DynamoDB table you want to modify. In modern Global Tables (v2019.11.21), the "Global Table" name is simply the name of the base table.
- `--replica-updates`: This is the primary parameter used to manage regional copies of your table. It accepts a list of operations (`Create`, `Update`, or `Delete`) to be performed on replicas.
- `Create={RegionName=...}`: This is a specific action within the `--replica-updates` list.
    - `Create`: Tells DynamoDB to initialize a new replica in a new region.
    - `RegionName`: Defines which AWS region (e.g., `us-west-2`) will host the new replica.

Unlike Route 53 or IAM, DynamoDB does not have a single global endpoint. Every command must be directed to a specific region.

Regardless of the operational configurations for scaling, a robust backup and restore plan is necessary to meet business continuity and compliance requirements, which leads us to the next section.

Backup and Restore Strategies

AWS provides several methods for ensuring business continuity and compliance with Amazon DynamoDB data, moving beyond simple snapshots to continuous recovery options tailored for modern cloud operations. For a CloudOps engineer managing operational data, these strategies are critical for meeting defined Recovery Point Objectives (RPOs) and Recovery Time Objectives (RTOs).

Point-in-Time Recovery (PITR)

PITR is the foundational restore method for day-to-day operations and accidental data modification events (like a mistakenly executed `DELETE` operation). When enabled, DynamoDB provides continuous, incremental backups of your table data with one-second granularity, up to the last 35 days.

As a CloudOps engineer, PITR allows for restores to any specific second within that window, minimizing RPO (Recovery Point Objective) to near zero. This feature prevents data loss from human error and is a core part of operational reliability. PITR must be explicitly enabled per-table, as it is not active by default.

PITR is charged hourly for each table it is enabled on, regardless of whether you perform a restore operation. The cost is a flat rate per hour, and it is highly cost-effective for operational recovery needs.

To enable PITR using the AWS CLI for our single-table design (`UserOrdersTableProvisioned`), use this command:

```
aws dynamodb update-continuous-backups \
    --table-name UserOrdersTableProvisioned \
    --point-in-time-recovery-specification PointInTimeRecoveryEnabled=True
```

In this command:

- `--table-name`: Specifies the target table (`UserOrdersTableProvisioned`).
- `--point-in-time-recovery-specification PointInTimeRecoveryEnabled=True`: Specifies the configuration object that turns the continuous backup feature on.

When you perform a restore using PITR, it creates a new table with the original data at the specified timestamp. This new table can then be used to resume application operations or extract corrupted data.

On-Demand Backups

For long-term retention or archival purposes beyond the 35-day PITR window, you can take explicit, on-demand backups (snapshots) of a table. These backups retain data indefinitely until manually deleted and do not impact table performance or throughput while they are being created.

These manual backups are useful for compliance requirements that mandate retaining data for seven years, for instance, where continuous PITR costs would be excessive.

You are charged based on the total size of the compressed data stored for the duration of the backup's lifecycle (similar to S3 storage costs). The first 100 GB per month is often free, but charges apply after that threshold. There is also a charge if you copy these snapshots to a different region.

To create an on-demand backup for our table:

```
aws dynamodb create-backup \
    --table-name UserOrdersTableProvisioned \
    --backup-name UserOrdersTableArchive2025Q4
```

In this command:

- `--table-name`: Specifies the target table (`UserOrdersTableProvisioned`).
- `--backup-name UserOrdersTableArchive2025Q4`: A unique identifier for the specific backup archive we are creating.

These on-demand backups can also serve as the basis for cross-region disaster recovery strategies, ensuring geographical resilience.

Cross-Region Backup and Restore

While Global Tables provide active-active availability across regions, a simpler, more cost-effective DR strategy is managing backups across regions. AWS allows you to copy both continuous backups (PITR data) and on-demand snapshots to different AWS regions.

This feature ensures that even in the unlikely event of a widespread regional outage, your data is available for restoration elsewhere, fulfilling high-durability compliance requirements and robust business continuity plans (BCPs). The restore process from a cross-region backup is identical to a standard restore operation; you simply specify the source region and the target region for the new table creation. Keep in mind that this involves two costs:

- **Data Transfer:** A charge for transferring the backup data out of the source region (standard data transfer charges apply).
- **Storage:** Storage costs for the duplicate backup copy in the destination region. This is generally more cost effective than running a fully operational Global Table 24/7 if passive DR is sufficient.

The next and final section of this chapter introduces Amazon ElastiCache—another schema-flexible service, but one that persists data in memory to deliver extremely low latency for caching and real-time enterprise-scale workloads.

Amazon ElastiCache

This section provides a comprehensive guide to Amazon ElastiCache, a fully managed, in-memory caching service that accelerates application performance by reducing database load and delivering microsecond latency. Caching is particularly relevant to the SOA-C03 exam because it sits at the intersection of three pillars of the AWS Well-Architected Framework: performance efficiency, operational excellence, and reliability. It accelerates performance by reducing latency, minimizes operational overhead by reducing backend database load, and improves reliability by abstracting primary data stores during potential failures. Similarly to Amazon RDS, Amazon Aurora, and Amazon DynamoDB, we cover fundamental concepts, performance tuning, scalability best practices, and robust backup strategies that you need to know for the exam.

Overview of Amazon ElastiCache

Caching is one of the most effective strategies for performance acceleration. By storing frequently accessed data in memory, ElastiCache reduces the need for repeated queries to backend databases such as Amazon RDS, Aurora, or DynamoDB. This not only improves response times, but also offloads read pressure from primary data stores.

Supported Engines

Amazon ElastiCache supports three popular open-source in-memory engines, allowing you to choose the best fit for your application needs:

Redis OSS (Open Source Software) A high-performance, single-threaded, in-memory data structure store that supports a wide range of data structures (strings, hashes, lists, sets, sorted sets, etc.). It offers advanced features like persistence, replication, high availability (Multi-AZ), pub/sub messaging, and geospatial indexes.

Memcached A simple, high-performance, multi-threaded key-value store. It is best suited for simple caching of objects, horizontally scaling across multiple nodes for large datasets, and use cases where data partitioning and threading simplicity are prioritized over advanced data types and persistence.

Valkey A high-performance, drop-in replacement for Redis OSS, stewarded by the Linux Foundation. It supports all the same features as Redis OSS (data structures, persistence, Multi-AZ, pub/sub) and offers performance and memory efficiency improvements.

Deployment Options

As illustrated in Figure 4.4, AWS offers two distinct deployment options that cater to different operational needs and control requirements:

Amazon ElastiCache Serverless Supporting the "Use serverless architectures" design principle of the Performance Efficiency pillar of the AWS Well-Architected Framework, this option provides zero infrastructure management, automatic scaling (vertical and horizontal),

FIGURE 4.4 Amazon ElastiCache engines and deployment options.

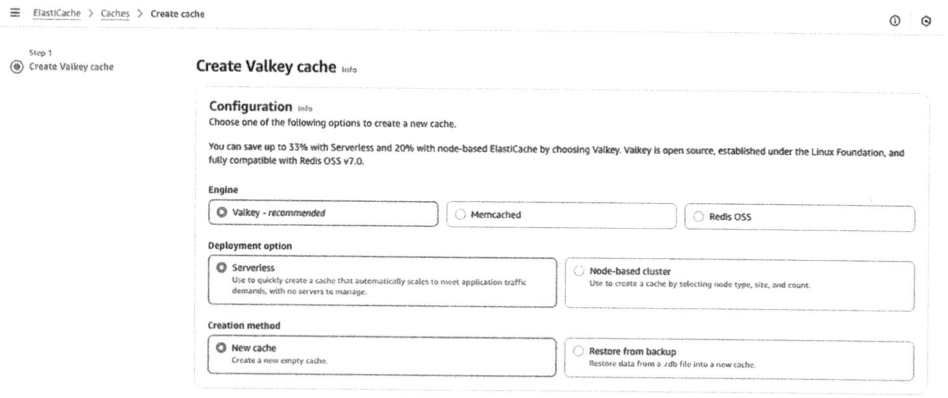

ElastiCache > Caches > Create cache

Step 1
Create Valkey cache

Create Valkey cache Info

Configuration Info
Choose one of the following options to create a new cache.

You can save up to 33% with Serverless and 20% with node-based ElastiCache by choosing Valkey. Valkey is open source, established under the Linux Foundation, and fully compatible with Redis OSS v7.0.

Engine
Valkey - *recommended*
Memcached
Redis OSS

Deployment option
Serverless
Use to quickly create a cache that automatically scales to meet application traffic demands, with no servers to manage.
Node-based cluster
Use to create a cache by selecting node type, size, and count.

Creation method
New cache
Create a new empty cache.
Restore from backup
Restore data from a .rdb file into a new cache.

FIGURE 4.5 Amazon ElastiCache Node-based cluster configuration page.

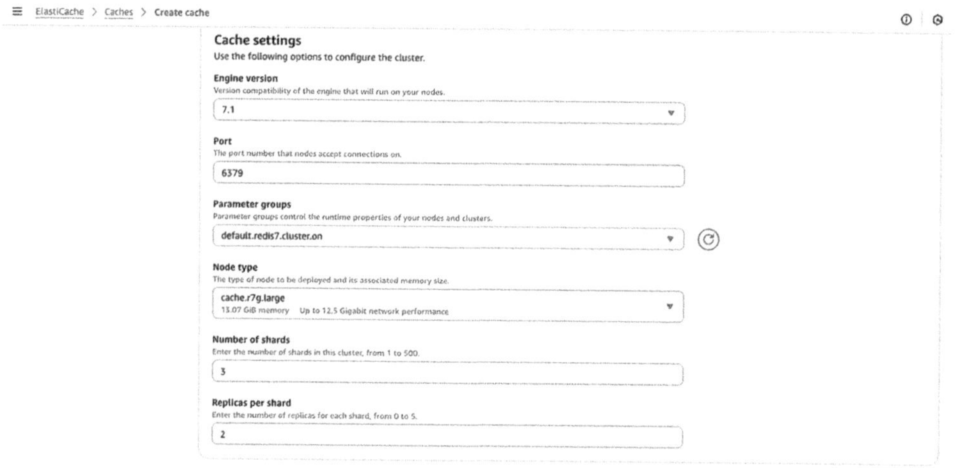

ElastiCache > Caches > Create cache

Cache settings
Use the following options to configure the cluster.

Engine version
Version compatibility of the engine that will run on your nodes.
7.1

Port
The port number that nodes accept connections on.
6379

Parameter groups
Parameter groups control the runtime properties of your nodes and clusters.
default.redis7.cluster.on

Node type
The type of node to be deployed and its associated memory size.
cache.r7g.large
13.07 GiB memory Up to 12.5 Gigabit network performance

Number of shards
Enter the number of shards in this cluster, from 1 to 500.
3

Replicas per shard
Enter the number of replicas for each shard, from 0 to 5.
2

and a 99.99% availability SLA without requiring capacity planning. You simply select your cache engine, provide a cache name, and you are ready to go! When your Amazon ElastiCache Serverless instance is deployed, you receive a single endpoint. Serverless is ideal for new workloads, unpredictable traffic patterns, or teams that want to minimize operational overhead. You pay only for the data stored and the compute consumed (ECPUs).

Node-Based Clusters This option gives CloudOps engineers fine-grained control over the environment. As shown in Figure 4.5, you manually select the node type (instance size), the number of shards, the number of replicas per shard, and their placement across Availability Zones. This model is better for predictable workloads, where you can forecast capacity requirements to optimize costs, potentially using reserved instances. While it requires more hands-on management (e.g., planning scaling events), it offers maximum flexibility and cost control for stable workloads.

For the exam, it is important to know that unlike node-based clusters (Redis OSS, Valkey, Memcached)—where clients need to be topology-aware—ElastiCache Serverless abstracts network concerns away. As illustrated in Figure 4.6, cache consumer applications (Client App 1, Client App 2, Client App 3) connect once to the provided serverless endpoint, and the serverless architecture handles routing behind the scenes with Amazon Route 53.

FIGURE 4.6 Amazon ElastiCache Serverless architecture.

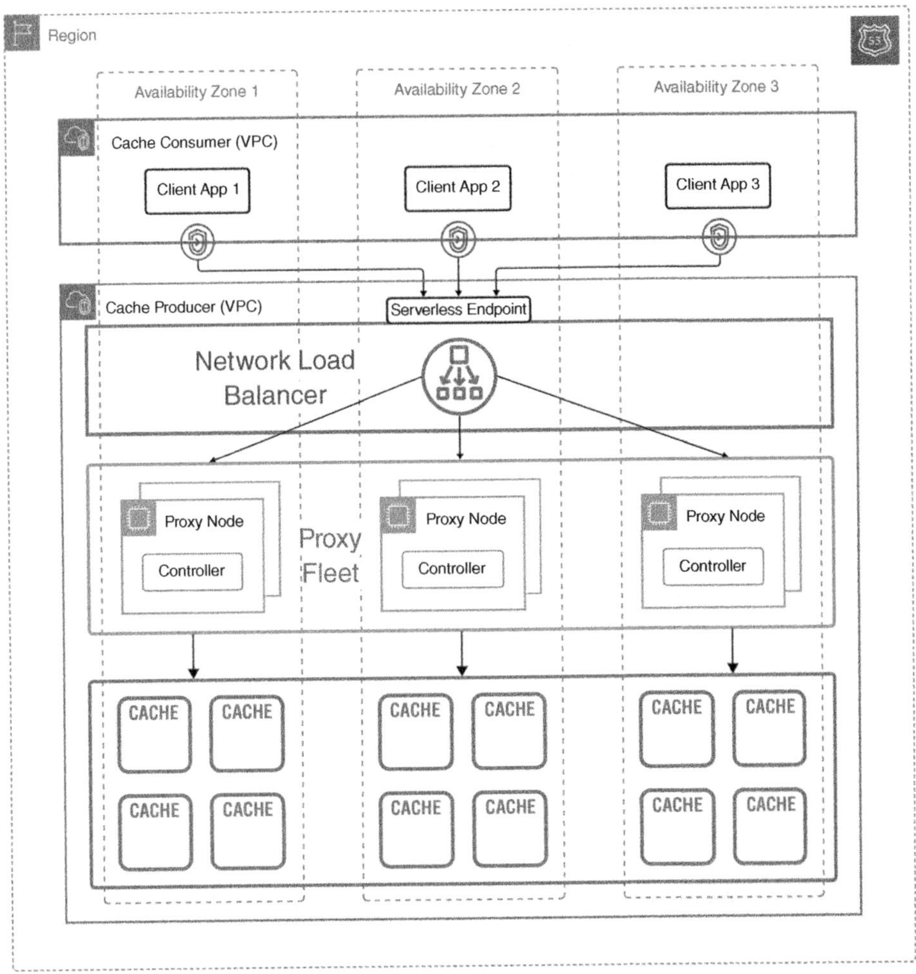

An ElastiCache Serverless endpoint is *unique* and operates globally within a region, providing a single, simplified connection point that abstracts away the underlying Multi-AZ complexity, automatically handling replication and failover for high availability, so that your application uses one endpoint for all data and compute across AZs without needing to know node details.

The endpoint remains valid even during failover. If a primary node in one AZ fails, ElastiCache Serverless promotes a replica in another AZ transparently, without requiring client reconfiguration. As a result, you don't need to manage multiple endpoints or update connection strings when scaling horizontally or vertically.

Integration with AWS Databases

Amazon ElastiCache seamlessly integrates with most AWS database services, most commonly with Amazon RDS (relational databases) and Amazon DynamoDB (NoSQL). The typical implementation involves the application checking the cache first ("cache-aside" pattern) before querying the primary database if the data is not found in memory.

Understanding which engine to use is crucial for performance. The next section dives into specific strategies for optimizing performance once ElastiCache is deployed.

Performance Optimization Strategies

Optimizing Amazon ElastiCache performance goes beyond initial setup; it involves careful engine selection, resilient deployment, proactive monitoring, and disciplined data access patterns to ensure minimal latency. For CloudOps engineers, this means designing clusters that can scale horizontally, survive Availability Zone disruptions, and integrate seamlessly with backend data stores, all while maintaining operational efficiency and reliability under heavy workloads.

In-Memory Data Access

The fundamental performance advantage of ElastiCache is rooted in its in-memory nature. Data access is direct and avoids the disk I/O bottlenecks inherent in traditional databases. To maximize this benefit, engineers should strive for high "cache hit ratios"—the percentage of data requests that are successfully fulfilled by the cache rather than the underlying database. Efficient client-side libraries and consistent use of appropriate data structures are key to achieving high throughput.

Here is an example of deploying a production-ready Redis OSS cluster using the AWS CLI, which leverages a replication group for high availability:

```
aws elasticache create-replication-group \
    --replication-group-id MyRedisCluster \
    --replication-group-description "A cluster for session caching" \
    --engine redis \
    --cache-node-type cache.m6g.large \
```

```
--num-cache-clusters 2 \
--automatic-failover-enabled \
--cache-subnet-group-name custom-app-subnet-group \
--security-group-ids sg-0a1b2c3d4e5f67890
```

In this command:

- `--replication-group-id`: Indicates a unique identifier for the cluster.
- `--engine`: Specifies the desired engine (`redis` or `memcached`).
- `--cache-node-type`: Defines the instance size for the nodes.
- `--num-cache-clusters`: Specifies the total number of nodes; for Redis OSS with `--automatic-failover-enabled`, this sets the primary node and its replicas (e.g., one primary and one replica).
- `--automatic-failover-enabled`: Ensures high availability with a primary and a replica across AZs.
- `--cache-subnet-group-name`: Specifies a custom-created subnet group where the cache nodes will be launched within your VPC. Note: Using custom subnet groups and security groups in a non-default VPC is highly encouraged for production environments for better security and network control.
- `--security-group-ids`: Associates a specific security group (SG) with the cluster for controlled network access.

For clarity, as a CloudOps engineer, you should distinguish between two primary CLI deployment commands:

- `create-replication-group`: The standard, production-ready command for Redis OSS, enabling high availability, replication, and automatic failover.
- `create-cache-cluster`: Primarily used for Memcached deployments (which scale horizontally without replication features) or single-node Redis OSS instances that lack high availability features.

Choosing the Right Engine

The selection between Redis OSS and Memcached is the first and most critical performance optimization decision you need to make. This choice is rarely arbitrary and should align with specific application requirements:

- **Memcached** is a simple, high-throughput, in-memory key-value cache that scales horizontally and linearly across nodes. It offers no native backup or restore—data is lost if nodes restart. Amazon ElastiCache Serverless now adds backup/restore for Memcached, improving resilience when durability is needed.
- **Redis OSS** or **Valkey** deliver persistence, rich data structures support, and high availability. They support use cases like sessions, analytics, queues, and leaderboards, with Multi-AZ failover and snapshots for durability. Valkey is often preferred over Redis OSS for cost and open-source governance.

For the latest information about Amazon ElastiCache supported in-memory engines, visit: `https://docs.aws.amazon.com/AmazonElastiCache/latest/dg/engine-versions.html`.

Monitoring with CloudWatch and Enhanced Metrics

Once the correct engine is selected and deployed, continuous monitoring via Amazon CloudWatch is essential for identifying bottlenecks and ensuring the cache performs as expected. Amazon ElastiCache Enhanced Metrics offer even more granular visibility into resource usage at a per-node level. The key metrics in Table 4.12 provide crucial operational insights.

For a complete reference of Amazon ElastiCache metrics published to Amazon CloudWatch, visit: `https://docs.aws.amazon.com/AmazonElastiCache/latest/dg/CacheMetrics.html`.

Best Practices for Cache Key Design

A simple, descriptive, and consistent cache key design is vital for efficient data retrieval and maintenance. Keys should be easy to manage and partition effectively. A common practice is to use a hierarchical structure (e.g., `user:{user_id}:session` or `product:{product_id}:details`). Avoid excessively long keys, as they consume valuable memory and slightly increase latency.

Effective key design often simplifies the approach to managing large datasets, which brings us to the next critical topic: scaling the cache environment.

Scalability and Elasticity

Amazon ElastiCache provides features that allow the cache environment to grow or shrink seamlessly in response to demand, ensuring high availability and consistent performance. As a CloudOps engineer, understanding the operational differences in how serverless and node-based deployments handle scaling is critical for the SOA-C03 exam, as it directly impacts your management responsibilities, monitoring strategies, and response to production load changes. The approach to achieving scalability and elasticity differs considerably between these two options.

Serverless vs. Node-Based: Horizontal and Vertical Scaling

The main operational difference between deployment models lies entirely in who manages the scaling and how it is executed.

With ElastiCache Serverless Caching, AWS handles all scaling automatically and transparently. The service constantly monitors memory, compute, and network utilization and instantly scales the underlying infrastructure—both vertically (scaling up the size of a node) and horizontally (scaling out by adding nodes)—without any downtime or manual intervention. Your job as a CloudOps engineer is to simply monitor application performance metrics (listed in Table 4.12) and the resulting costs. There is no need to manually plan or execute capacity changes in advance.

TABLE 4.12 Amazon ElastiCache Metrics

Metric Name (Console, API Name)	Description	Tuning Insight
CPU Utilization (`CPUUtilization`)	CPU utilization for the server instance (cache node) as a whole, including other operating system and management processes. Recommended for hosts with two vCPUs or less.	Persistently high CPU usage may indicate the need to scale up to a larger node type, optimize complex Redis OSS or Valkey operations (using `EngineCPUUtilization`), or scale out horizontally.
Bytes Used For Cache (`BytesUsedForCache`)	The amount of memory currently used by the cache data itself.	Use this to set proactive alarms. High utilization indicates memory pressure and potential for evictions.
Cache Hits (`CacheHits`) and Cache Misses (`CacheMisses`)	The number of successful key lookups (hits) versus failed lookups (misses) that necessitated a database call.	The cache hit ratio (hits/(hits and misses)) should be consistently high (ideally > 90%). A low ratio suggests ineffective caching strategies or key design.
Valkey or Redis OSS Single Thread Utilization (`EngineCPUUtilization`)	CPU utilization of the Valkey or Redis OSS engine single thread. The `EngineCPUUtilization` metric provides a more precise visibility of the process than `CPUUtilization`.	For Redis OSS or Valkey cache node types with four vCPUs or more, use the `EngineCPUUtilization` metric to monitor and set thresholds for scaling.
Evictions (`Evictions`)	The number of times that items are removed from the cache to free up memory for new items, based on the eviction policy (e.g., `volatile-lru`).	A high rate of evictions is a strong indicator of memory pressure. This signals that the cluster is too small and requires scaling up the node size or scaling out the cluster capacity.

In contrast, scaling in node-based clusters fundamentally depends on whether you are using the Valkey/Redis OSS or Memcached engine:

- For **Memcached,** scaling is exclusively horizontal. Because Memcached nodes are peer-to-peer and do not support complex data replication (like primary/replica models), you scale simply by adding or removing individual nodes from the cluster. This is typically done using the AWS CLI command `modify-cache-cluster` and adjusting the `--num-cache-nodes` parameter. All clients must use a client-side hashing algorithm to distribute data consistently across all nodes in the cluster.
- For **Valkey** and **Redis OSS**, scaling offers both vertical and horizontal options:
  - **Vertical Scaling** (scaling up node size) is achieved using `modify-replication-group` and adjusting the `--cache-node-type` parameter.
  - **Horizontal Scaling** involves two distinct operations: increasing read throughput by adding replicas to existing primary nodes (`increase-replica-count`), or increasing overall cluster capacity and write throughput in `cluster mode enabled` setups by adding or removing primary shards (node groups) using the specific `modify-replication-group-shard-configuration` command.

In summary, the operational approach to scaling is highly engine-dependent: Memcached only scales horizontally via node count adjustments, whereas Valkey/Redis OSS offers a robust mix of vertical scaling and sophisticated horizontal scaling options through replicas and sharding configuration commands.

Multi-AZ with Automatic Failover

High availability is a built-in feature in both deployment models, but managed differently.

For ElastiCache Serverless, high availability is a default feature with a 99.99% SLA. Data is automatically stored redundantly across a minimum of three Availability Zones, and the service handles all failover and node replacements internally and transparently to the application.

For node-based clusters, Multi-AZ with automatic failover must be explicitly enabled during cluster creation and is only available for Valkey and Redis OSS engines. Memcached does not support Multi-AZ automatic failover in the same capacity. Resilience is achieved by simply spreading nodes across multiple AZs and accepting potential data loss on node failure. For Valkey/Redis OSS, enabling Multi-AZ requires provisioning at least one replica node in a different AZ from the primary. The CloudOps engineer has control over AZ placement to ensure application resilience.

Scaling Patterns for Read-Heavy Workloads

Read-heavy workloads are handled efficiently in both deployment options.

For *ElastiCache Serverless*, read traffic is automatically distributed across the underlying, managed replicas. The system instantly adjusts capacity to accommodate fluctuating read demands. CloudOps engineers primarily monitor metrics like `CacheHits`, `CacheMisses`, and `Evictions` to validate the application's caching strategy, while AWS handles the underlying resource adjustment in response to metrics like `CPUUtilization` or `BytesUsedForCache`.

For *Node-based clusters*, you can manually provision up to five read replicas per primary node to serve read traffic, distributing the load and improving overall read throughput. The application logic typically needs to manage distributing reads across the replica endpoints for optimal performance.

Summary of Serverless vs. Node-Based Scaling Differences

The key differences you need to know for the exam are listed in Table 4.13.

While single-region availability (Multi-AZ) ensures high availability within a region, proactive backup strategies and cross-region replication are essential for protecting the data stored within the cache and preparing for full regional outages, which we cover next.

Backup and Restore Strategies

Although ElastiCache is primarily a transient cache layer, the ability to back up and restore data is vital, especially when the cache holds critical state information like active user sessions or pre-computed results that take a long time to regenerate.

TABLE 4.13 Serverless vs. Node-based Scaling Comparison

Feature	ElastiCache Serverless	ElastiCache Node-Based
Horizontal Scaling	Fully automatic, transparent (AWS managed)	Manual via CLI commands (`modify-cache-cluster`, `modify-replication-group-shard-configuration`), IaC, SDK, CDK, Console
Vertical Scaling	Fully automatic, transparent (AWS managed)	Manual via CLI commands (`modify-replication-group`), IaC, SDK, CDK, Console
Multi-AZ with Automatic Failover	Automatic by default across three AZs (99.99% SLA)	Manual configuration required (Valkey/Redis OSS only); Memcached has no auto-failover
Cross-Region with Automatic Failover	Not available as an automatic feature	Not an automatic feature; requires manual operation to promote a secondary cluster in a Global Datastore setup (next section)
Scaling Patterns	Pay-per-use, scales with unpredictable traffic, no capacity planning	Fixed node sizes, best for predictable workloads where capacity can be forecasted

Backup and Restore

Amazon ElastiCache for Valkey and Redis OSS supports point-in-time snapshots, stored securely in Amazon S3, which can be restored into new clusters pre-populated with the chosen data. This provides durable backup and recovery options for workloads that need persistence. In contrast, traditional ElastiCache for Memcached does not support snapshots or backups, reflecting its design as a lightweight, purely in-memory cache optimized for speed and simplicity rather than durability—data is lost if nodes are restarted or replaced. However, ElastiCache Serverless now extends backup and restore capabilities to Memcached, a major enhancement that improves resilience by allowing cached states to be safeguarded and recovered when durability and recovery are critical.

Snapshot Management

You can configure automatic daily snapshots during a specified maintenance window or take manual snapshots at any time. These manual snapshots persist until you explicitly delete them, unlike automatic snapshots, which adhere to a configured retention period (up to 35 days).

To manually create a snapshot using the AWS CLI, use this code:

```
aws elasticache create-snapshot \
    --snapshot-name my-manual-backup-001 \
    --replication-group-id MyRedisCluster
```

In this command:

- `--snapshot-name`: A unique name for your new snapshot.
- `--replication-group-id`: The source cluster you are backing up (`MyRedisCluster`).

Disaster Recovery with Cross-Region Snapshots

For robust disaster recovery, AWS allows you to copy manual snapshots to different AWS regions. This mitigates the risk of a regional outage. A snapshot copied to another region can then be used to seed a new ElastiCache cluster there, ensuring data availability even during major regional disruptions.

Global Datastore for Cross-Region Disaster Recovery and Low-Latency Local Reads

ElastiCache Global Datastore for Valkey and Redis OSS supports global enterprises needing *low-latency local reads* and cross-region disaster recovery. It replicates data from a primary Redis OSS cluster to up to two read-only secondary clusters in other regions, enabling sub-second latency and improved responsiveness. In case of primary region failure, a secondary can be promoted to primary in under a minute, with automation possible via Lambda and Route 53 for efficient failover.

In this section you learned how Amazon ElastiCache leverages the power of in-memory, schema-flexible data management for ultra-low latency use cases, but broader persistence requirements call for dedicated storage services. The next chapter shifts to AWS storage solutions—object, block, and file—that deliver scalability, durability, and high availability, all of which are foundational to CloudOps engineering in the SOA-C03 exam.

Summary

This chapter covered the core operational aspects of AWS managed databases, emphasizing the choice between traditional RDBMS and scalable NoSQL systems. The key lesson is aligning application data models and access patterns with the right service—structured SQL for transactional integrity or flexible schemas for speed and scale in Amazon DynamoDB and Amazon ElastiCache.

Amazon RDS automates management of engines like MySQL, PostgreSQL, Oracle, Microsoft SQL Server, and IBM Db2. Essential exam topics include using parameter groups for tuning, Multi-AZ for high availability, read replicas for scaling, and distinguishing automated backups for PITR from snapshots for long-term archiving.

Amazon Aurora, AWS's cloud-native relational database, delivers higher performance and faster failover than Amazon RDS. Aurora Serverless v2 is especially important for unpredictable workloads, automatically scaling capacity to optimize cost and efficiency without disruption.

Amazon DynamoDB provides a serverless, schemaless key-value store with millisecond performance at scale. Success depends on proper data modeling and understanding secondary indexes: LSIs support strong consistency within a partition, while GSIs enable flexible queries across the table with eventual consistency.

Amazon ElastiCache (Valkey, Redis OSS, Memcached) adds high-speed caching to reduce database load. ElastiCache Serverless eliminates manual capacity planning by auto scaling throughput and storage, letting teams focus on application performance instead of infrastructure.

Exam Essentials

Know the differences between relational and NoSQL databases. Relational databases (e.g., MySQL, PostgreSQL, Oracle) store data in structured tables with predefined schemas, use SQL for complex queries, and enforce ACID properties—ideal for ERP, CRM, and transactional systems. In contrast, NoSQL databases (e.g., DynamoDB, MongoDB, Cassandra) use flexible models like key-value or document, scale horizontally, and power modern apps such as real-time web, mobile, and big data analytics where flexibility and availability matter more than strict consistency.

Know what parameter groups are and how they can be used to optimize Amazon RDS performance. Parameter groups are containers for engine configuration values applied to Amazon RDS instances of the same type. They enable CloudOps engineers to fine-tune settings such as memory limits, query timeouts, and logging beyond AWS defaults, optimizing database behavior for workload needs and improving latency and throughput.

Understand the benefits provided by Amazon RDS Performance Insights. Amazon RDS Performance Insights is a managed monitoring tool that visualizes database load, identifies bottlenecks (CPU, I/O, locks), and highlights resource-heavy queries for targeted tuning and cost-efficient right-sizing. It collects data with minimal impact, offering seven days of free retention with options for longer periods.

Understand when to use Amazon RDS horizontal scaling and when to implement Multi-AZ. Amazon RDS horizontal scaling improves performance with read replicas for read-heavy workloads, while multi-AZ ensures high availability by synchronously replicating data to a standby instance for near-zero loss and automatic failover.

Know the difference between Amazon RDS automated backups and snapshots. Amazon RDS automated backups support point-in-time recovery within a 1–35 day retention window, while snapshots are user-initiated full backups that persist until deleted, which is ideal for archiving or compliance. Both use incremental storage, but automated backups are AWS-managed for continuous recovery, whereas snapshots are user-managed.

Understand when to use Amazon Aurora vs. Amazon RDS (with the same database engine). Use Amazon Aurora for mission-critical workloads needing superior performance and high availability, and Amazon RDS for predictable, cost-effective use cases. Aurora's cloud-native design delivers faster throughput (five times MySQL, three times PostgreSQL), rapid failover under 30 seconds, and durable storage scaling to 256 TiB with six copies, while RDS provides broader engine support and simpler management for less intensive workloads.

Understand when to use Amazon Aurora Serverless v2. Amazon Aurora Serverless v2 is ideal for variable or unpredictable workloads, automatically scaling compute without disrupting connections ensuring resources match demand. Common uses include dev/test, Multi-Tenant SaaS, and new apps with unknown demand. You pay only for Aurora Capacity Units (ACUs) consumed, avoiding over-provisioning.

Understand when to use Amazon Aurora Global Database. Aurora Global Database is ideal for workloads that demand low-latency global reads and fast cross-region disaster recovery. It replicates storage from the primary region to secondary regions with typically sub-second lag, allowing applications in distant geographies to read locally without impacting the writer. It also provides a managed cross-region DR strategy, enabling a secondary region to be promoted to full read/write capability in under a minute if the primary becomes unavailable. Use it when your application must stay globally responsive and resilient, but avoid it for workloads that don't require multi-region reads or rapid cross-region failover.

Know the difference between a GSI and LSI, and why they matter to Amazon DynamoDB performance optimization. In Amazon DynamoDB, Global Secondary Indexes (GSIs) and Local Secondary Indexes (LSIs) both enhance queries but differ in scope and consistency. GSIs act like separate tables with their own keys, support queries across partitions, and are eventually consistent. LSIs share the base table's partition key with a different sort key, allow strongly consistent reads within a partition, must be defined at creation, and have a 10 GB limit per partition key.

Understand the operational benefits of Amazon ElastiCache Serverless. Amazon ElastiCache Serverless removes infrastructure management, auto-scales with demand, and offers a single endpoint where you pay only for data stored and throughput consumed. It's ideal for unpredictable workloads, ensuring consistent in-memory performance without manual intervention.

Understand when to use Amazon ElastiCache Global Datastore. Amazon ElastiCache Global Datastore is designed for applications that require low-latency, cross-region reads and fast disaster recovery for Redis OSS or Valkey workloads. It asynchronously replicates data from a primary region to up to two secondary regions, allowing users in distant geographies to read from a local replica with minimal latency impact. In the event of a regional outage, a secondary cluster can be manually promoted to full read/write capability in under a minute, providing a rapid recovery option. Use Global Datastore when you need globally distributed caching performance or cross-region resilience, but not for workloads that require multi-region writes or strict consistency guarantees.

Review Questions

1. A CloudOps engineer is investigating a performance degradation on a production Amazon RDS for a PostgreSQL instance. The Performance Insights dashboard shows that the DB load (Average Active Sessions) is significantly higher than the number of available vCPUs. The engineer identifies that the majority of the load is categorized under the CPU wait event, but the Top SQL list shows multiple different queries all contributing small, equal amounts to the total load. The engineer suspects that a specific legacy application server is malfunctioning and sending an excessive volume of short, rapid requests to the database. Which Performance Insights dimension should the engineer use to confirm if the load is originating from a specific application server's IP address?

   A. Wait Events

   B. SQL

   C. Hosts

   D. Users

2. A new AWS engineer on your team attempts to modify a setting in the `default.mysql8.0` parameter group assigned to a newly launched development database instance. They find that the console interface prevents them from saving any changes and throws an error when using the AWS CLI. Why can the engineer not modify parameters within the `default.mysql8.0` parameter group?

   A. The engineer lacks the necessary IAM permissions to edit default parameter groups, which are restricted to the AWS root user.

   B. Default parameter groups are read-only and maintained by AWS; you must create a custom parameter group to modify any engine settings.

   C. The instance must first be stopped before modifying a default parameter group, which is an action prevented in the current development environment.

   D. Default groups only allow dynamic parameter changes, and the setting the engineer tried to change was static.

3. A production Amazon RDS for PostgreSQL instance has a persistent performance bottleneck. Performance Insights consistently registers a `DBLoad` of 10.5 average active sessions (AAS), while the instance only has eight vCPUs. The database administration team has already confirmed that all comprehensive query optimization efforts have been exhausted for this stable OLTP workload. Which two of the following approaches are valid strategies to address the performance capacity constraint caused by the high `DBLoad` relative to available vCPUs? (Select TWO.)

   A. Terminate all active user sessions immediately using database functions.

   B. Migrate the database to a different engine like Amazon Aurora PostgreSQL.

   C. Review query execution plans again to find additional optimization opportunities.

   D. Scale the RDS instance class vertically to a larger size with more vCPUs (e.g., to a `db.r5.4xlarge`).

   E. Implement Amazon RDS Proxy to efficiently manage connection pooling and reduce connection CPU overhead.

4. You are a CloudOps engineer monitoring a production RDS for PostgreSQL instance using Amazon Performance Insights. You observe that the `DBLoad` metric is significantly higher than the instance's vCPU count. Upon inspecting the breakdown, you notice that `DBLoadNonCPU` is consistently high, while `DBLoadCPU` remains low. Which of the following actions should you take first to diagnose the specific cause of this bottleneck?

   A. Immediately scale up the RDS DB instance class (e.g., from `db.m5.large` to `db.m5.xlarge`) using the `aws rds modify-db-instance` command to increase available vCPUs.

   B. Modify the database parameter group to increase the `max_connections` parameter, as high non-CPU load often indicates a connection pooling bottleneck.

   C. Inspect the Wait Events dimension in the Performance Insights dashboard to identify the specific type of resource contention (e.g., I/O waits, locks, network).

   D. Analyze the Top SQL dimension to identify inefficient queries that may be consuming excessive CPU resources and causing the load.

5. A database administrator is architecting an Amazon RDS solution for a mission-critical application that demands both extremely high availability (RPO near-zero, automatic failover) and scalable read performance to handle a growing number of concurrent analytical queries during peak usage. The current single-instance deployment needs modification to meet these stringent production requirements. Which of the following approaches is the most comprehensive and resilient solution that addresses both high availability and dedicated read scaling for an application utilizing a supported engine like PostgreSQL or MySQL?

   A. Implement an Amazon RDS Multi-AZ DB cluster deployment with one primary and two readable standby instances across three Availability Zones, leveraging the dedicated reader endpoint for analytical queries.

   B. Configure a traditional Amazon RDS Multi-AZ instance deployment and, concurrently, establish one or more read replicas (configured as Single-AZ) in different Availability Zones to offload read traffic.

   C. Vertically scale the current RDS instance to the largest available instance class and implement advanced database performance tuning, as Multi-AZ and read replicas introduce too much replication lag for real-time analytics.

   D. Migrate the transactional write operations to a Single-AZ RDS instance for maximum write performance and the analytical read workloads to a data warehouse solution like Amazon Redshift.

6. A financial services company utilizes Amazon RDS in the `us-east-1` region for its primary transaction database. Due to strict regulatory compliance requirements, the company must maintain a robust disaster recovery plan that includes recovering the database in a geographically separate region (`us-west-2`) with a recovery time objective (RTO) and recovery point objective (RPO) within defined limits. Manual data transfer is too slow and error-prone. Which Amazon RDS feature should the company use to efficiently and reliably achieve its cost-optimized cross-regional disaster recovery objectives?

   A. Configure a real-time, synchronous Amazon RDS Multi-AZ DB cluster replication between `us-east-1` and `us-west-2`.

   B. Implement Amazon RDS cross-region read replicas and promote the replica in `us-west-2` during a disaster scenario.

C. Utilize the Amazon RDS Cross-Region Snapshot Copy feature to regularly replicate automated or manual snapshots to the `us-west-2` region.

D. Vertically scale the primary RDS instance in `us-east-1` to the largest memory-optimized size available to improve durability and prevent regional outages.

7. A CloudOps engineer needs to design a high-availability solution for an Amazon Aurora MySQL database within a single AWS region. The business requires the lowest possible Recovery Point Objective (RPO) and rapid, automatic failover (typically < 30 seconds). Which Amazon Aurora architecture feature best meets these strict requirements?

A. Deploying a Multi-AZ Aurora cluster with a primary writer instance and multiple Aurora replicas.

B. Utilizing a single-instance Aurora cluster with continuous backups enabled.

C. Configuring a manual, Cross-AZ read replica and performing a manual failover if the primary fails.

D. Implementing cross-region snapshots to restore the database in a secondary region.

8. An application team notices high CPU utilization on the primary Aurora MySQL instance, but application monitoring reveals that the application is primarily performing read operations (90% reads, 10% writes). How should a CloudOps engineer optimize performance while minimizing operational overhead?

A. Modify the instance class to a larger size (vertical scaling) to provide more CPU capacity.

B. Enable Aurora Parallel Query to push read operations down to the storage layer.

C. Provision and route traffic to an additional Aurora replica and use the reader endpoint.

D. Configure auto scaling policies on the primary instance's CPU utilization metric.

9. A CloudOps engineer is monitoring a performance issue in an Aurora cluster using Amazon CloudWatch. They are observing a high value for the `VolumeReadIOPS` metric, but the `CPUUtilization` metric is surprisingly low. What is the most likely cause of this operational behavior?

A. The Aurora instance class is undersized (CPU-bound) and cannot process the incoming I/O requests fast enough.

B. The application is executing inefficient queries that force full table scans rather than efficient index lookups.

C. The Aurora storage subsystem is experiencing throttling because it hit the 128 TiB storage limit.

D. The application is experiencing high replication lag to the Aurora replicas, causing I/O backpressure.

10. A CloudOps engineer needs to select the most appropriate Amazon Aurora deployment model for a new development environment that experiences highly variable, intermittent workloads, and requires strict cost optimization. The solution must support standard database engine interactions and scale compute capacity automatically and instantaneously without manual intervention. Which combination of cluster-level configuration and instance-level setting must be implemented together to meet these requirements? (Select TWO.)
    - **A.** Provisioning a standard Aurora cluster using a fixed R-series instance type.
    - **B.** Implementing Amazon Aurora Serverless v2 for automatic, fine-grained scaling.
    - **C.** Utilizing Aurora Global Database to manage Multi-Region compute capacity on demand.
    - **D.** Configuring the cluster to use the `db.serverless` instance class within defined ACU ranges.
    - **E.** Migrating the workload to Amazon DynamoDB On-Demand capacity mode.

11. A CloudOps engineer is tasked with enhancing the resilience and global presence of a mission-critical financial application currently running on a single-region Amazon Aurora cluster. The operational requirements demand a highly available, Multi-Region architecture that provides low latency global reads and a minimal Recovery Point Objective (RPO) and Recovery Time Objective (RTO) in the event of a regional failure. Which two actions should the CloudOps engineer take to meet these operational requirements? (Select TWO.)
    - **A.** Create several cross-region standard MySQL read replicas and manage manual failover via Lambda functions.
    - **B.** Deploy an Aurora Global Database topology, connecting the source region to a new secondary region replica cluster.
    - **C.** Enable Point-in-Time Recovery (PITR) and configure cross-region backup replication policies.
    - **D.** Utilize Aurora Serverless v2 to distribute capacity across multiple Availability Zones automatically.
    - **E.** Use the `FailoverDBCluster` API call to promote the secondary region in case of a disaster, achieving RTO < 1 minute.

12. A CloudOps engineer is designing a new DynamoDB table for an application's user profiles. The application requires retrieving user data based on their `UserID` (the primary key), but it also needs to frequently query user profiles based on a non-key attribute: the user's `EmailAddress`. The engineer anticipates high read volumes for both data access patterns and needs consistent, low-latency performance for all queries. Which DynamoDB feature should the engineer implement to satisfy the requirement of querying the `EmailAddress` attribute efficiently?
    - **A.** Implement a Local Secondary Index (LSI) on the `EmailAddress` attribute.
    - **B.** Use a `Scan` operation with a filter expression on the `EmailAddress` attribute.
    - **C.** Implement a Global Secondary Index (GSI) on the `EmailAddress` attribute.
    - **D.** Deploy Amazon DynamoDB Accelerator (DAX) to cache the results of all scan operations.

13. A CloudOps engineer is monitoring a production DynamoDB table configured in `PROVISIONED` capacity mode. The engineer observes a sharp increase in the `ReadThrottleEvents` CloudWatch metric. The application reports HTTP 400 `ProvisionedThroughputExceeded` errors. The engineer verifies that the table's overall `ConsumedReadCapacityUnits` is below the configured `MaxCapacity` limit set in the auto scaling policy. What is the most likely cause of these throttling events?
    - **A.** The application is executing inefficient `Scan` operations, consuming too many RCUs.
    - **B.** The database is experiencing a "hot partition" because too many requests are targeting a single partition key value.
    - **C.** The table has been automatically switched to the `PAY_PER_REQUEST` billing mode, causing a temporary limit reduction.
    - **D.** The CloudOps engineer forgot to enable Point-in-Time Recovery (PITR), which causes throttling events.
14. A CloudOps engineer is tasked with enabling a robust data recovery solution for a critical production DynamoDB table. The Recovery Point Objective (RPO) requirement is to lose no more than one second of data in the event of an accidental deletion or data corruption event. Which feature should the engineer enable to satisfy this RPO requirement?
    - **A.** Enable Point-in-Time Recovery (PITR) for the target table.
    - **B.** Configure On-Demand Backups (snapshots) taken every 15 minutes via AWS Backup.
    - **C.** Implement a Global Table with a replica in a different AWS region.
    - **D.** Manually export table data to Amazon S3 hourly using AWS Glue jobs.
15. A global e-commerce platform needs to provide low-latency reads for users in Europe and Asia while maintaining a single source of truth in the United States. Which features of Amazon ElastiCache Global Datastore should they leverage? (Select TWO.)
    - **A.** Use "Active-Active" replication to allow local writes in the primary and secondary regions simultaneously.
    - **B.** Promote a secondary regional cluster to primary in under a minute if the primary region experiences degradation.
    - **C.** Implement cross-region snapshots to automatically back up the secondary clusters to their local S3 buckets.
    - **D.** Utilize "Local Reads" in secondary regions to access data with typically less than one second of replication latency.
    - **E.** Disable "Encryption in Transit" for cross-region traffic to achieve the lowest possible inter-regional latency.
16. A startup's application experiences unpredictable, spiky traffic patterns throughout the day and the team wants a hands-off solution for their Amazon ElastiCache for Redis OSS instance. They choose Amazon ElastiCache Serverless. Which two statements accurately describe how this service manages capacity? (Select TWO.)
    - **A.** The user must manually define CloudWatch metrics to trigger scaling policies for memory usage.
    - **B.** The service automatically and continuously adjusts capacity based on real-time workload demands.

C. Users pay for provisioned capacity units (ECPUs) rather than managing underlying node types and sizes.

D. Scaling out requires a scheduled maintenance window during which the cache endpoint becomes unavailable.

E. It is primarily designed for workloads with static, predictable performance requirements.

17. A development team is using a node-based Amazon ElastiCache for Memcached cluster and needs to increase its total memory capacity due to cache hit rate drops. They want to accomplish this with the least disruption. Which two actions can they take? (Select TWO.)

A. Change the node size (e.g., from `cache.m5.large` to `cache.m5.xlarge`) to vertically scale each existing node.

B. Migrate the entire workload to Amazon ElastiCache Serverless, which provides virtually unlimited, on-demand memory capacity.

C. Add new nodes to the existing cluster to horizontally distribute the data load across more instances.

D. Convert the Memcached cluster into a Redis OSS cluster to utilize more efficient data structures for storage.

E. Enable the "Multi-AZ with Auto-Failover" feature, which automatically doubles the available RAM.

18. A company wants to reduce the read latency of its high-traffic DynamoDB table from milliseconds to microseconds. The development team has limited time and prefers a solution that requires minimal changes to the existing application code. Which strategies should the CloudOps engineer recommend? (Select TWO.)

A. Configure Amazon RDS Proxy to manage the connection pooling for the DynamoDB table requests.

B. Deploy an Amazon ElastiCache for Redis OSS cluster and implement a "lazy loading" caching pattern in the application logic.

C. Leverage DAX because it is API-compatible with DynamoDB, allowing the application to point to a new endpoint without rewriting complex CRUD logic.

D. Use Amazon Redshift as a caching layer by enabling its automated materialized views for the DynamoDB source.

E. Provision a DynamoDB Accelerator (DAX) cluster and update the application to use the DAX client SDK.

19. A CloudOps engineer is designing a caching layer for a complex application that retrieves data from both Amazon DynamoDB and several Amazon RDS databases. The solution must support advanced data structures like sorted sets for a real-time leaderboard. Which approach provides the best balance of flexibility and performance? (Select TWO.)

A. Use Amazon ElastiCache for Redis OSS, as it can cache data from multiple diverse sources, including RDS and DynamoDB.

B. Deploy a DAX cluster to handle all database types because it provides microsecond write-through capabilities for any RDS engine.

C. Use Amazon EBS with Provisioned IOPS to cache frequently accessed queries from both RDS and DynamoDB.

D. Implement Amazon ElastiCache for Redis OSS specifically to leverage advanced data types (like Sorted Sets and Hashes) not natively supported by DAX.

E. Configure Amazon RDS Multi-AZ with readable standby instances to serve as a high-speed caching layer for DynamoDB traffic.

20. An e-commerce application uses Amazon DynamoDB to store its product catalog. During seasonal sales, a CloudOps engineer must implement a caching solution that ensures that the cache remains synchronized with catalog updates automatically while also reducing the costs associated with high read volume. Which configurations meet these requirements? (Select TWO.)

A. Utilize DAX, as its write-through caching mechanism automatically updates the cache whenever an item is written to the underlying DynamoDB table.

B. Use Amazon ElastiCache for Memcached with a "write-back" strategy to ensure the fastest possible database updates.

C. Deploy a DAX cluster to handle eventually consistent reads, which reduces the load on the DynamoDB provisioned read capacity units (RCUs).

D. Enable Amazon RDS Multi-AZ to automatically invalidate the cache whenever a failover occurs between regions.

E. Use AWS DMS to continuously sync an Amazon ElastiCache cluster with the DynamoDB table to maintain strong consistency for all read operations.

Answers to Review Questions

1. C. The Hosts dimension is the only dimension that isolates the originating client IP address or hostname. While Wait Events (A) identifies why the database is bottlenecked (e.g., CPU) and SQL (B) identify what query is running, neither attributes lead to a specific physical server. Similarly, Users (D) only shows the database account name (e.g., admin), which may be shared across many servers.

2. B. AWS default parameter groups serve as unchangeable templates with standard settings. To implement specific configurations or custom values, users are required to create and associate their own custom parameter groups.

3. D, E. Since query optimization efforts are exhausted and the load consistently exceeds the available vCPU capacity (10.5 AAS > 8 vCPUs), scaling the instance size is a direct and valid way to provide the necessary hardware resources to meet demand. Reducing the CPU overhead associated with establishing and tearing down (disconnecting and closing) numerous database connections via RDS Proxy is a capacity management strategy that can free up CPU resources to handle the existing query load more efficiently.

4. C. `DBLoadNonCPU` represents time that database sessions spend waiting for resources other than the CPU. When this metric is high, the bottleneck is external to the main processor. To perform a proper Root Cause Analysis (RCA), you, as the CloudOps engineer, must determine which non-CPU resource is the issue. The Wait Events dimension is the primary tool in Performance Insights that categorizes these waits.

5. A. The Multi-AZ DB cluster deployment (with two readable standbys) is the specific RDS option that consolidates both requirements: it provides high availability with automatic, near-zero data loss failover (typically under 35 seconds) and offers dedicated, readable standby instances via a reader endpoint for horizontal read scaling. Traditional Multi-AZ instances do not allow reading from the standby, while standard read replicas use asynchronous replication, making the Multi-AZ DB cluster the optimal and most modern approach for this specific set of high-bar requirements.

6. C. The Amazon RDS Cross-Region Snapshot Copy feature provides an efficient, managed way to transfer point-in-time backups (snapshots) of the database to a different AWS region for cost-effective, long-term disaster recovery archiving. While setting up a cross-region read replica (Option B) offers better RPO/RTO metrics for operational recovery, the snapshot copy is a foundational, reliable, and often regulatory-compliant mechanism designed specifically for robust and efficient cross-regional data restoration as a core component of a disaster recovery plan.

7. A. A Multi-AZ Aurora cluster with Aurora Replicas provides automatic, near-instantaneous failover capability (RTO < 30s) because all replicas share the same underlying storage volume. This configuration offers built-in high availability superior to options requiring manual intervention (C, D) or single points of failure (B).

8. C. The most effective and standard operational pattern for read-heavy workloads is horizontal scaling using Aurora Replicas. By adding replicas and directing read traffic to the reader endpoint, you distribute the load and alleviate pressure on the writer instance's CPU.

9. B. Aurora charges for I/O requests, and a high volume of I/O with low CPU usage suggests that the CPU isn't doing much computational work, but is simply moving large amounts of data. This pattern usually indicates inefficient database queries forcing full table scans that fail to utilize indexes effectively.

10. B, D. Aurora Serverless v2 is designed specifically for highly variable workloads by automatically and instantaneously scaling its compute capacity. Options B and D are two ways of describing the Aurora Serverless v2 implementation: using the service name itself (B) and specifying the underlying required instance class and configuration parameters (D). Option A is incorrect, as it requires manual intervention and fixed costs. Option C uses Global Database features, which are for Multi-Region HA, not compute elasticity optimization. Option E changes the database service entirely, which is not an Aurora solution.

11. B, E. The Aurora Global Database architecture (B) is the native AWS solution designed for cross-region resilience with minimal RPO/RTO goals. This configuration allows for rapid disaster recovery promotion of the secondary cluster (E), meeting the requirement for RTO < 1 minute. Option A describes a manual, less efficient replication method with higher RPO/RTO than Global Database. Option C is a backup strategy, not an active/passive highly available architecture. Option D is related to compute scaling within a region, not cross-region disaster recovery.

12. C. An `EmailAddress` is an attribute that is different from the table's primary `UserID`, making it a non-key attribute that requires a Global Secondary Index (GSI) for efficient querying. An LSI shares the same partition key as the base table, making it unsuitable for a different primary access pattern.

13. B. Throttling that occurs when overall table capacity is technically available often points to a "hot partition." This bottleneck happens when traffic to a single partition key value exceeds the per-partition hard limit (3,000 RCUs or 1,000 WCUs), causing requests targeting that specific partition to fail.

14. A. Point-in-Time Recovery (PITR) is a managed feature providing a continuous backup stream with one-second granularity, perfectly matching the RPO requirement. On-demand snapshots or manual exports (B, D) would inherently result in data loss between backup intervals.

15. B, D. Amazon ElastiCache Global Datastore supports promoting a secondary cluster to primary for fast disaster recovery and provides low-latency local reads in secondary regions. This setup ensures high availability and improved performance for globally distributed users.

16. B, C. Amazon ElastiCache Serverless automatically handles all scaling operations, eliminating manual management. Users only pay for the capacity consumed based on actual requests and storage used, making it ideal for variable workloads.

17. A, C. Both vertical scaling (changing node size) and horizontal scaling (adding nodes) are valid methods to increase total capacity in a node-based cluster. These operations are core features of the Memcached engine on Amazon ElastiCache designed for seamless capacity adjustments.

18. C, E. DAX is purpose-built as an API-compatible cache for Amazon DynamoDB, meaning that it requires very little code change—typically just changing the endpoint in the SDK. Unlike Amazon ElastiCache, which requires manual "side-cache" logic (checking the cache, then the database, then updating the cache), DAX handles cache population and invalidation transparently.

19. A, D. Amazon ElastiCache for Redis OSS is a versatile service that supports many data sources beyond Amazon DynamoDB and provides specialized data structures like sorted sets for leaderboards. DAX is specialized only for Amazon DynamoDB and does not offer the same flexibility for complex data types or multi-source caching.

20. A, C. DAX employs a write-through mechanism to ensure the cache and the primary table stay in sync during updates. Offloading eventually consistent reads to DAX can significantly lower a table's provisioned read capacity (RCUs), directly reducing costs for read-heavy workloads.

Chapter 5

Storage and Data Management

THE AWS CERTIFIED CLOUDOPS ENGINEER ASSOCIATE (SOA-C03) EXAM OBJECTIVES COVERED IN THIS CHAPTER MAY INCLUDE, BUT ARE NOT LIMITED TO THE FOLLOWING:

✔ **Domain 1: Monitoring, Logging, Analysis, Remediation, and Performance Optimization**

- 1.3 Implement performance optimization strategies for compute, storage, and database resources

✔ **Domain 2: Reliability and Business Continuity**

- 2.3 Implement backup and restore strategies

✔ **Domain 3: Deployment, Provisioning, and Automation**

- 3.2 Automate the management of existing resources

In Chapter 4, you learned the different types of AWS services that support the databases, where data is made accessible for your workloads. We introduced the concept of data access pattern, as a key element AWS database engineers should consider in designing the data architecture of their applications. This chapter expands on that foundation by exploring the broader landscape of storage and data management services in AWS—where data lives before, after, and beyond the database layer. Understanding how data is stored, accessed, transferred, and synchronized is essential to building resilient, performant, and cost-effective architectures.

AWS offers three primary types of storage: object, block, and file. Each serves distinct use cases and data access patterns. Amazon Simple Storage Service (Amazon S3) is the official AWS service for object storage. Designed for scalability, durability (99.999999999% i.e., 11 nines), and global availability (99.99% i.e., four nines), Amazon S3 is ideal for storing unstructured data such as backups, media assets, logs, and data lake objects. For block-level storage, Amazon Elastic Block Store (Amazon EBS) provides persistent volumes for EC2 instances, supporting high-performance workloads like databases and transactional systems. File storage is addressed through Amazon Elastic File System (Amazon EFS), which offers scalable, shared access across multiple instances, and Amazon FSx, which delivers fully managed file systems for Windows File Server, Lustre, NetApp ONTAP, and OpenZFS—each tailored to specific enterprise or High-Performance Computing (HPC) requirements. These services are central to SOA-C03's task 1.3, which emphasizes "*performance optimization strategies for compute, storage, and database resources*." Choosing the right storage type and configuration directly impacts throughput, latency, and cost efficiency.

Beyond storage itself, AWS provides robust services for data movement and hybrid integration. AWS Storage Gateway extends cloud storage into on-premises environments by presenting familiar block, file, or tape interfaces while asynchronously transferring data to Amazon S3. This enables organizations with legacy systems—such as applications that write to iSCSI targets or file shares—to modernize their backup and archival workflows without disrupting existing tooling. AWS DataSync further simplifies and accelerates large-scale data migration and synchronization between on-premises storage and AWS services, or between AWS services themselves. Together, these services operationalize hybrid data workflows, ensure that data is securely and efficiently moved to the right storage tier, and directly support SOA-C03's task 2.3 on "*implementing backup and restore strategies*." Whether you're replicating data across regions, synchronizing file systems, or automating archival to Amazon S3 Glacier, these tools help ensure data availability, durability, and recovery readiness.

As you progress through this chapter, you'll examine how to evaluate storage performance metrics, apply lifecycle policies, and design backup and restore workflows that align with operational excellence. Remember, operational excellence is your main focus as an AWS CloudOps engineer! You'll learn how to optimize storage configurations with focus on throughput and latency, implement cross-region replication, and use AWS Backup to centralize and automate data protection across workloads. These capabilities not only fulfill exam objectives—they empower you to build and support architectures that are resilient, scalable, and cost-aware.

Understanding Storage Types

In traditional IT environments, two storage types are prevalent: *block storage* and *file storage*. Block storage operates at the raw storage device level and manages data as a set of numbered, fixed-size blocks. File storage operates at the OS (Operating System) level and manages data as a hierarchical structure of files and folders.

Block and file storage can be either directly attached to a server (also referred to as DAS—Direct Attached Storage) or distributed over a network (NAS—Network Attached Storage). This latter scenario (NAS) is your main focus as a CloudOps engineer, as it enables workloads in your organization to scale, be fault-tolerant, and adaptive to changes, which are all key responsibilities of cloud operations.

Network block storage is accessed by clients in the form of a Storage Area Network (SAN)—using protocols such as iSCSI or Fibre Channel. Conversely, network file storage uses NAS file servers, which leverage protocols such as NFS (Network File System) or SMB (Server Message Block).

The terms "SAN" and "NAS" are similar, but they denote different things. A simple way to distinguish NAS from SAN is how they appear to the client's operating system. NAS looks like a file server—you connect to shared folders over the network, just like mapping a network drive. SAN, on the other hand, presents storage as if it were a local disk. It shows up in disk management tools alongside your computer's own drives. You are responsible for formatting it, assigning a file system, and mounting it just like any other physical disk.

Whether DAS or NAS, block and file storage are tightly coupled to the server (compute) and the OS that is using the storage—an architectural constraint that limits scalability, fault tolerance, and operational excellence. This tight coupling introduces single points of failure and complicates recovery, making it harder to meet the reliability and performance efficiency expectations outlined in the AWS Well-Architected Framework. This is where the concept of *object storage* comes into play: by decoupling data from compute and operating systems, object storage enables distributed access, automatic replication, and virtually unlimited scalability.

By design, object storage is independent of a server, and it is accessed over the Internet. Instead of managing data as fixed-sized blocks or files using iSCSI, or NFS protocols, data is managed as objects using an Application Programming Interface (API) built on standard HTTP verbs. But, what are objects? Are they limited in size like blocks? Are they logically accessible in a hierarchical structure similar to a file system? Can they be modified like a file, or overwritten like a block? The answers to these questions are provided in the next section, which introduces Amazon Simple Storage Service (Amazon S3), the AWS service specifically designed for object storage.

Amazon Simple Storage Service (S3)

Amazon S3 provides object storage with high durability, availability, scalability, security, and performance.

Objects are any type of data (structured, semi-structured, unstructured), which live in containers called *buckets*. Buckets are folders with no file system hierarchy. You can have multiple buckets in your AWS account, but you can't create a bucket inside another Amazon S3 bucket. There is no limit to the number of objects in a bucket. As a result, Amazon S3 provides virtually unlimited scalability.

Exam Tip

Even though a bucket can contain an unlimited number of objects, individual objects have a maximum size of 50TB. Objects larger than 5 GB must be uploaded using Multipart Upload, and it is recommended for objects larger than 100 MB for improved throughput and quick recovery from network issues. Multipart Upload is covered in a dedicated section later in this chapter.

Each object contains both data (e.g., image, document, video) and metadata (key-value pairs describing the object itself). Data and metadata are stored together as a single, atomic unit, ensuring consistency and avoiding partial updates or mismatches.

Amazon S3 is optimized for read operations and is built with a minimalistic feature set by design. It provides a simple and robust abstraction for data storage without having to manage the complex details you'd normally face with traditional storage systems. For example, with Amazon S3, you don't need to manage hardware or file systems, or worry about running out of space—a single bucket can hold as many objects as you need. You also don't have to think about keeping your data safe or copying it across AZs (Availability Zones). Amazon S3 automatically stores multiple copies of each object across different servers and AZs in the same region to ensure durability and availability of your data. And if your application starts sending more requests, Amazon S3 scales behind the scenes by splitting your bucket into partitions, so it can handle high traffic and many users at once—no manual setup required.

"Simplexity" in Amazon S3—Simplicity First, Complexity Managed

Amazon S3—as the name suggests—promotes simplicity by delivering a clean, minimalistic abstraction for object storage that conceals massive architectural complexity. This aligns with the concept of "*Simplexity*," introduced by Werner Vogels (Amazon CTO) at re:Invent 2024—the art of designing systems that are simple to use but deeply complex under the hood.

As a CloudOps engineer, you benefit from this elegant simplicity:

- **Unlimited scalability:** A single bucket can store billions of objects without capacity planning.
- **Automated durability:** Objects are transparently replicated across multiple Availability Zones in the same region.
- **Performance optimization:** Buckets are auto-partitioned to handle high request rates and concurrency.
- **Operational abstraction:** No need to manage file systems, devices, or replication logic.

Amazon S3's minimal feature set is intentional—it reduces cognitive load while enabling powerful automation, cost optimization, and lifecycle control. Behind the scenes, AWS orchestrates distributed storage, failure recovery, eventual consistency, and dynamic scaling—all invisible to the user.

To learn more about "Simplexity," visit: `https://www.allthingsdistributed.com/2025/03/in-s3-simplicity-is-table-stakes.html`.

Let's now deep dive into Amazon S3's building blocks: buckets, objects, and the operations you will perform on these resources as a CloudOps engineer—with a focus on reliability, optimization, and automation workflows across your cloud infrastructure.

Buckets

A bucket in Amazon S3 serves as the fundamental container for storing objects such as files, metadata, and versioned data. Buckets form the top-level namespace for Amazon S3. As a result, each bucket name must be globally unique across all AWS accounts, and across all AWS regions within a given partition. This means that no two buckets—regardless of which AWS account or region they belong to—can share the same name within the same partition.

A partition is a grouping of regions. For example: the commercial AWS partition `aws`, the U.S. Government AWS partition `aws-us-gov`, the AWS European Sovereign Cloud `aws-eusc`, and China's `aws-cn` partition.

This global bucket name uniqueness is not arbitrary; it is a deliberate design choice rooted in how Amazon S3 handles object addressing and routing. Amazon S3 bucket names are directly incorporated into DNS-based endpoints (e.g., `https://my-bucket.s3.amazonaws.com`), which are resolved globally. To ensure that DNS resolution consistently maps to the correct bucket, AWS enforces a single, flat namespace across the entire partition. If duplicate bucket names were allowed, it would create ambiguity in routing requests and could lead to data being sent to the wrong account or region.

When you create a bucket at least two elements are required: a name and a region. You may wonder why do you need to choose a region for your bucket when its name is globally unique in its partition. The reason is that while the bucket name must be unique across all accounts and regions in a partition, the actual data and infrastructure behind that bucket are regionally scoped. Choosing a region determines where your data physically resides, how it's replicated for durability, and what latency and compliance characteristics apply. This regional placement is critical for optimizing performance (e.g., by creating a bucket in a region close to your users), implementing reliability (e.g., by creating a bucket in a secondary region for disaster recovery), meeting regulatory requirements (e.g., data sovereignty), and controlling costs—especially when designing architectures that span multiple geographic zones.

The bucket name must conform to the following rules:

- **Length:** Between 3 and 63 characters.
- **Characters:** Only lowercase letters (`a-z`), numbers (`0-9`), periods (`.`), and hyphens (`-`) are allowed.
- **Start and end:** Must begin and end with a lowercase letter or a number.
- **Invalid patterns:**
  - Cannot contain two adjacent periods (`..`).
  - Cannot be formatted as an IP address (e.g., `192.168.1.5`).
- **Uniqueness:** Bucket names are globally unique across all AWS accounts and regions within a partition.
- **Invalid prefixes:** `xn--`, `sthree-`, `amzn-s3-demo-`.
- **Invalid suffixes:** `-s3alias`, `--ol-s3`, `.mrap`, `--x-s3`, `--table-s3`.
- **Amazon S3 Transfer Acceleration:** Buckets used with Amazon S3 Transfer Acceleration can't have periods (`.`) in their names.

You can create an Amazon S3 bucket with the AWS CLI using two different sets of commands: the high-level `aws s3` commands and the lower-level `aws s3api` commands. As a CloudOps engineer, it is recommended that you become familiar with both, although the choice depends on your need for simplicity versus granular control, as summarized in Table 5.1.

To create a bucket with `aws s3` use the following command and replace the **user input placeholders** (in bold font) with your own information:

```
aws s3 mb s3://my-unique-bucket-name
```

TABLE 5.1 Comparison of AWS CLI S3 APIs

Feature	`aws s3` (High-Level)	`aws s3api` (API-Level)
Simplicity	High, uses simple URI syntax (e.g., `s3://bucket`) and abstracts complexity.	Lower, requires explicit parameter flags such as: `--bucket`.
Region Handling	Automatic; handles `LocationConstraint` based on your CLI configuration.	Manual; requires explicit: `--create-bucket-configuration` for regions outside of `us-east-1`.
Control Level	Basic S3 operations (move, copy, sync, make bucket).	Granular, direct mapping to S3 REST API for advanced features (ACLs, specific configurations).

To create a bucket in a specific region, you simply use the `--region` flag, and the CLI manages the underlying API request:

```
aws s3 mb s3://my-region-specific-bucket
    --region us-west-2
```

To create a bucket with `aws s3api`, use the following command:

```
aws s3api create-bucket \
  --bucket my-unique-bucket-name \
  --region us-east-2 \
  --create-bucket-configuration LocationConstraint=us-east-2
```

Notice how in this last example we had to explicitly specify the bucket region, since we opted to use a region other than `us-east-1`.

A successful creation will output a message similar to:
`make_bucket: my-unique-bucket-name`.

Objects

Objects are the units of data stored in Amazon S3 buckets. From a user standpoint, an object is nothing but a file that contains any type of data—structured (e.g., a comma-separated value CSV file), semi-structured (e.g., a JavaScript Object Notation JSON file), and unstructured (e.g., a video in MP4 format). As of the writing of this book, an object is limited to a size of 50 TB, and there is no limit to the number of objects a bucket can contain.

This flexibility in object content and format isn't coincidental—it reflects Amazon S3's foundational design principle: simplicity. By abstracting away file type constraints and allowing unlimited number of objects in a bucket, Amazon S3 empowers users to store virtually any data as-is, whether structured, semi-structured, or unstructured. This design choice aligns with the two general design principles of the AWS Well-Architected Framework you learned in Chapter 1.

There cannot be orphaned Amazon S3 objects. This is because an object must always exist within a bucket, as a bucket is the fundamental container for objects. If an object is truly "lost" or missing, it's likely due to a data corruption event, a user error, or a misconfiguration.

Each Amazon S3 object comprises two components: the object data (the actual content being stored) and associated *metadata* (information describing the object). The data portion is opaque to Amazon S3, meaning the service treats it as an uninterpreted sequence of bytes. Amazon S3 does not inspect, validate, or differentiate the content based on its format—whether it's text, binary, image, or any other type—and applies the same storage and retrieval mechanisms regardless of the data type. The metadata of an object comes in two forms: system-defined metadata, which governs internal behaviors like storage class (discussed in the next section) and encryption, and user-defined metadata, which allows custom key-value annotations to support application logic, indexing, and resource tagging.

Another important aspect of Amazon S3 objects, and a key difference when compared to blocks and files, is their *immutability*. Once an object is written to Amazon S3, its contents cannot be modified in place; any change requires uploading a new version or replacing the object entirely. This immutability simplifies consistency across distributed systems and supports versioning, auditability, and data integrity—core tenets of operational excellence in SOA-C03.

Understanding Object Key and Object URI

In Amazon S3, every object is uniquely identified within a bucket by its object key, which acts as the full path to the object. Despite appearances, Amazon S3 does not use folders or directories in the traditional sense—all objects reside in a flat namespace within a bucket. The use of slashes (/) in object keys is purely conventional and helps simulate a folder-like structure for organizational or UI purposes, especially in the AWS Management Console.

For example, an object with the key `report.pdf` is stored directly in the bucket with no implied hierarchy. In contrast, an object with the key `2025/financials/q3/report.pdf` appears nested in folders, but is still just a single key in a flat structure. The full Object URI combines the bucket name and key, such as `s3://my-bucket/report.pdf` or `s3://my-bucket/2025/financials/q3/report.pdf`, enabling precise referencing and access control.

Operations

Amazon S3 supports a comprehensive set of operations for both objects and buckets. These operations include Create, Read, Update, Delete, and List (CRUDL), and they can be performed manually using the AWS Management Console, or programmatically via Infrastructure-as-Code (IaC) tools such as AWS CloudFormation, AWS Cloud Development Kit (CDK), HashiCorp Terraform, and others.

Enabling Automation with "Programmability"

In accordance to the AWS Well-Architected general principle "Automate with architectural experimentation in mind," you—as a CloudOps engineer—should have a bias for automation. You learned in Chapter 1 how automation is accomplished by mechanisms that enable repeatability, consistency, and adherence to standards with code. As a result, we recommend you always seek ways to automate cloud operations with a programmable approach, rather than using the AWS Management Console, unless no other options are available.

Whether you're managing objects or provisioning buckets, each action you initiated with IaC results in one or more specific Amazon S3 API call(s). Table 5.2 includes the main operations you are likely to perform in your day-to-day job. For a complete reference, visit the Amazon S3 REST API at: `https://docs.aws.amazon.com/AmazonS3/latest/API/API_Operations_Amazon_Simple_Storage_Service.html`.

Notice how Amazon S3 operations span two architectural layers: Data Plane and Control Plane. The Data Plane handles object-level operations within a region, with strong read-after-write consistency (more to follow in the upcoming sections). The Control Plane manages bucket-level operations and metadata.

Durability and Availability

In cloud operations, understanding the difference between *durability* and *availability* is essential for designing resilient and performant storage architectures. Durability refers to the long-term integrity of your data—how safely it is preserved over time, whereas availability measures how quickly, and reliably that data can be accessed when needed. As a CloudOps engineer, selecting the appropriate type of storage—also referred to as a *storage class*—is a strategic decision that directly impacts both metrics. For example, Amazon S3 Standard

TABLE 5.2 Amazon S3 Operations (Not Exhaustive)

Separation of Concerns	Operation	AWS Resource	API Call	HTTP Verb	HTTP Resource URI	Description
Data Plane	Create	Object	`PutObject`	`PUT`	`/bucket-name/object-key`	Upload object
	Read	Object	`GetObject`	`GET`	`/bucket-name/object-key`	Read object
	Update	Object	`PutObject`	`PUT`	`/bucket-name/object-key`	Overwrite object
	Delete	Object	`DeleteObject`	`DELETE`	`/bucket-name/object-key`	Delete object
Control Plane	List	Bucket	`ListObjectsV2`	`GET`	`/bucket-name?list-type=2`	List objects
	Create	Bucket	`CreateBucket`	`PUT`	`/bucket-name`	Create bucket
	Read	Bucket	`HeadBucket`	`HEAD`	`/bucket-name`	Check bucket exists
	Update	Bucket	`PutBucketPolicy`	`PUT`	`/bucket-name?policy`	Set policy
	Delete	Bucket	`DeleteBucket`	`DELETE`	`/bucket-name`	Delete bucket
	List	Bucket	`ListBuckets`	`GET`	`/ (root endpoint)`	List buckets

offers high durability and availability, while classes like Amazon S3 Glacier Deep Archive prioritize durability over immediate access.

Amazon S3 is engineered for 99.999999999% (11 nines) durability, meaning that data is redundantly stored across multiple Availability Zones to withstand hardware failures and disasters. Availability, such as the 99.99% offered by Amazon S3 Standard, ensures that your data is accessible nearly all the time. While durability protects against data loss, availability ensures business continuity—especially critical for applications with real-time access requirements or small recovery objectives.

These concepts directly align with two SOA-C03 tasks: "Implement performance optimization strategies for storage resources" and "Implement backup and restore strategies." Choosing the right storage class allows CloudOps engineers to optimize access latency, retrieval costs, and fault tolerance. Durability underpins backup integrity, while availability governs restore speed—making both metrics foundational to operational excellence.

The next section reviews Amazon S3's storage classes in detail.

Storage Classes

For the exam, make sure you have a good understanding of the Amazon S3 storage classes. The S3 storage classes as of the writing of this book are described in Table 5.3.

Data Consistency

Amazon S3 provides strong *read-after-write consistency* for all object operations within a region. This means that after a successful write (PUT), overwrite (PUT), or delete (DELETE) of an object, any subsequent read (GET) or list (LIST) request made within that same region is guaranteed to return the latest version of the object. Each object—including its data and metadata—is stored and retrieved as a single, atomic unit. There's no lag, no eventual propagation: once the operation is acknowledged, the object is consistently visible across all Availability Zones in that region.

However, the handling of a bucket name operates under a different consistency model due to its unique, global nature. As you learned at the begin of the chapter, Amazon S3 bucket names must be unique across all AWS accounts and regions within a partition (e.g., `aws`). The system relies on a global DNS and metadata coordination process to manage this unique namespace. When a bucket is created or deleted, this global change must propagate across all these systems worldwide to prevent naming conflicts. Because this is a massive, distributed update, it does not happen instantaneously. This is why you must wait for a period—sometimes up to an hour or more—before you can reuse a deleted bucket name.

The observed delay in a bucket name's availability is not in conflict with Amazon S3's strong read-after-write consistency model, but rather a necessary side effect of its global design. Amazon S3's architecture effectively separates the management of the global bucket namespace from the management of data (the actual objects in a bucket) within a regional bucket. The global namespace, which is only updated occasionally, operates under an

TABLE 5.3 Amazon S3 Storage Classes

Storage Class	Primary Use Case	Access Speed	Availability (SLA)	Notes
S3 Express One Zone	High-performance data requiring single-digit millisecond access	Single-digit milliseconds	99.95%	Data is stored in a single Availability Zone; one-hour minimum storage duration
S3 Standard	Frequently accessed data	Milliseconds	99.99% (99.9% SLA)	General-purpose, flexible, and robust storage
S3 Intelligent-Tiering	Data with unpredictable access patterns	Milliseconds	99.9% (99% SLA)	Automatically moves data to the most cost-effective tier
S3 Standard-Infrequent Access (S3 Standard-IA)	Infrequently accessed data requiring millisecond access	Milliseconds	99.9% (99% SLA)	Has a 30-day minimum storage duration and retrieval fees
S3 One Zone-Infrequent Access (S3 One Zone-IA)	Infrequently accessed, re-creatable data	Milliseconds	99.5% (99% SLA)	Stores data in a single Availability Zone; has a 30-day minimum storage duration and retrieval fees
S3 Glacier Instant Retrieval	Archive data with rare access but needs immediate retrieval	Milliseconds	99.9% (99% SLA)	Has a 90-day minimum storage duration and retrieval fees
S3 Glacier Flexible Retrieval	Backup and archive data accessed infrequently	Minutes to hours	99.99% (99% SLA)	Has a 90-day minimum storage duration
S3 Glacier Deep Archive	Long-term archive data	Hours	99.99% (99% SLA)	Has a 180-day minimum storage duration; lowest cost for archive data
S3 on Outposts	Hybrid cloud storage to keep data on-premises	Varies	Varies	Extends AWS storage services to on-premises environments

eventually consistent model. The regional object data, which is written and read frequently, benefits from the performance and reliability of a strongly read-after-write consistent model. This dual-consistency model allows Amazon S3 to offer both a globally unique identifier for accessibility, and highly consistent data access for application workloads.

So remember: in Amazon S3 object data is regional and strongly consistent, whereas a bucket name is global and eventually consistent. For you, as a CloudOps engineer, this distinction is essential when implementing SOA-C03 tasks like automating storage provisioning, orchestrating backups, and optimizing performance (all covered in the next two sections). This important distinction ensures that high-performance and low-latency object workflows are reliable and immediate, while bucket name operations may require safeguards against propagation delays.

Optimizing Amazon S3 Performance

Now that you understand how data consistency work in Amazon S3, and what storage classes are best suited for your workloads' availability and data retention needs, this section takes a deep dive into some of the ways to optimize performance.

Object Lifecycle Management

Amazon S3 Object Lifecycle Management enables automated transfers and deletions of objects between storage classes based on defined configurations, helping optimize storage costs and performance. By intelligently moving data between storage classes—such as from S3 Standard to S3 Glacier Flexible Retrieval—organizations can reduce expenses while maintaining access patterns aligned with business needs. Lifecycle configurations are especially relevant in environments with large volumes of aging data, such as logs, backups, or archival content. The visual in Figure 5.1 illustrates the allowed transitions between S3 storage classes.

FIGURE 5.1 Supported object lifecycle transitions.

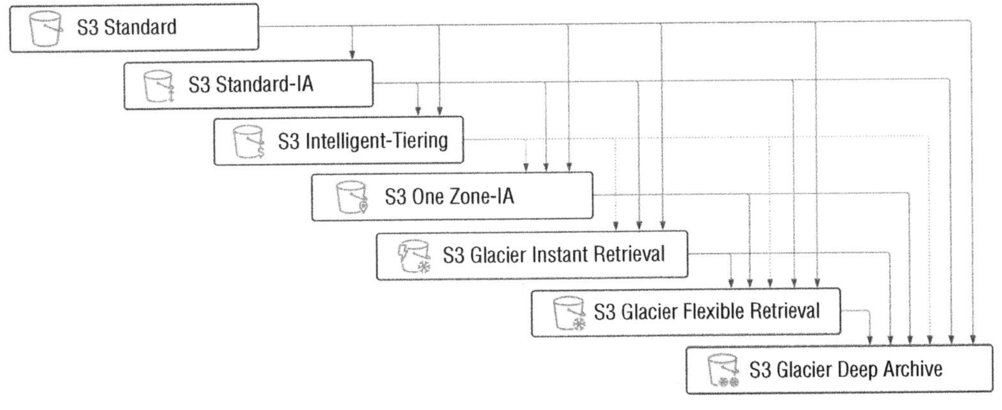

As of the writing of this book, Amazon S3 Express One Zone does not support automated lifecycle transitions to any other S3 storage class, nor can objects in other classes transition into Express One Zone. However, you can use S3 Lifecycle to expire (delete) objects in S3 Express One Zone based on their age.

Object lifecycle configurations in Amazon S3 are composed of rules that define actions on objects over time. These rules fall into two categories:

- **Transition rules,** which move objects to a different storage class after a specified number of days.
- **Expiration rules,** which permanently delete objects after a defined period.

Rules can apply to an entire bucket or be scoped using filters—either by object (key) prefixes (e.g., `logs/`, `images/`) or by object tags (e.g., `project:telemetry`). This flexibility allows fine-grained control over data retention and cost optimization strategies across different workloads.

The next two examples show lifecycle configurations in XML. Lifecycle configurations can also be defined in JSON, or even in HCL (HashiCorp Configuration Language) if you are using Terraform.

The first uses a prefix filter to transition objects in the `logs/` folder to Glacier after 30 days and expires them after 365 days:

```
<LifecycleConfiguration>
  <Rule>
    <ID>LogsTransitionAndExpire</ID>
    <Filter>
      <Prefix>logs/</Prefix>
    </Filter>
    <Status>Enabled</Status>
    <Transition>
      <Days>30</Days>
      <StorageClass>GLACIER</StorageClass>
    </Transition>
    <Expiration>
      <Days>365</Days>
    </Expiration>
  </Rule>
</LifecycleConfiguration>
```

The second example uses a tag filter to transition objects tagged with `project:telemetry` to S3 Intelligent-Tiering after 60 days:

```
<LifecycleConfiguration>
  <Rule>
    <ID>ProjectAlphaTransition</ID>
    <Filter>
```

```
      <Tag>
        <Key>project</Key>
        <Value>telemetry</Value>
      </Tag>
    </Filter>
    <Status>Enabled</Status>
    <Transition>
      <Days>60</Days>
      <StorageClass>INTELLIGENT_TIERING</StorageClass>
    </Transition>
  </Rule>
</LifecycleConfiguration>
```

To apply these lifecycle configurations using the AWS CLI first save your XML configuration to a local file (e.g., `lifecycle.xml`), then execute the following command:

```
aws s3api put-bucket-lifecycle-configuration \
  --bucket your-bucket-name \
  --lifecycle-configuration file://lifecycle.xml
```

Replace **`your-bucket-name`** with the actual name of your Amazon S3 bucket. This command will apply the lifecycle rules defined in the XML file to the specified bucket. To learn more about the `put-bucket-lifecycle-configuration` CLI command, visit: `https://docs.aws.amazon.com/cli/latest/reference/s3api/put-bucket-lifecycle-configuration.html`.

You can verify your object lifecycle configuration with this:

```
aws s3api get-bucket-lifecycle-configuration \
  --bucket your-bucket-name
```

This ensures your lifecycle configurations are correctly applied and visible for auditing or troubleshooting.

For the SOA-C03 exam be aware of scenarios where an object could be eligible for multiple lifecycle rules if its characteristics (such as prefix or tags) match more than one rule's filter. When this happens, Amazon S3 resolves conflicts by applying a specific order of precedence, which is designed to prevent unexpected behavior and unintended actions.

Here's what you need to know.

Expiration over transition If an object is subject to both an expiration (deletion) rule and a transition rule, the expiration rule takes precedence. For example, an object is in the `documents/` prefix and has `project:archive` as a tag.

Rule A: Filter by prefix `documents/`, action is: expire after 90 days.

Rule B: Filter by tag `project:archive`, action is: transition to `GLACIER` after 180 days.

Resolution: Since expiration takes precedence over transition, the object will be permanently deleted after 90 days.

Transition over delete marker creation If an object in a versioned bucket is subject to both an expiration (deletion marker creation) rule and a transition rule, the transition rule takes precedence.

You'll learn about object versioning in the upcoming sections. For the time being, just know that when you delete an object in a bucket with versioning enabled, Amazon S3 does not actually delete the object, but rather adds a *delete marker* that hides the latest version from `GET` operations, while preserving all previous versions for recovery or auditing.

For example, an object in a versioned bucket is in the `documents/` prefix.

Rule A: Filter by prefix `documents/`, action is: expire the current version (i.e., create delete marker) after 90 days.
Rule B: Filter by prefix `documents/`, action is: transition the current version to `GLACIER` after 90 days.
Resolution: Since transition takes precedence over delete marker creation, the current version of the object will be moved to `GLACIER` after 90 days, and the delete marker will not be created. This means the object remains accessible (though in `GLACIER`) and is not hidden by a delete marker.

Shorter time interval over longer time interval If an object is subject to multiple rules for the same action (i.e., expiration or transition) but with different time intervals, Amazon S3 will choose the shortest duration to take action. This prevents objects from being stored longer than you intend. For example, an object is in the `tmp/` prefix.

Rule A: Filter by prefix `tmp/`, action is: expire after 30 days.
Rule B: Filter by prefix `tmp/`, action is: expire after 60 days.
Resolution: Amazon S3 will delete the object after 30 days, following the shorter expiration time.

Transition to lower-cost storage over higher-cost storage If two transition rules with the same number of days apply to an object, Amazon S3 will transition the object to the lower-cost storage class. For example, an object is in the `logs/` prefix.

Rule A: Filter by prefix `logs/`, action is: transition to `STANDARD_IA` after 180 days.
Rule B: Filter by prefix `logs/`, action is: transition to `GLACIER` after 180 days.
Resolution: Since `GLACIER` is a lower-cost storage class than `STANDARD_IA`, the object will be transitioned to `GLACIER`.

In summary, Amazon S3 Object Lifecycle Management is a powerful tool for automating storage optimization. By defining transition and expiration rules filtered by prefixes or tags, you—as a CloudOps engineer—can reduce costs and streamline data retention. Understanding rule precedence and conflict resolution ensures reliable outcomes. The next section explores Object Multipart Upload, a key performance optimization for handling large files efficiently in Amazon S3.

What's the "Temperature" of Your Data?

Think of your data like molecules in motion. At high temperatures, molecules zip around rapidly—constantly moving, colliding, and interacting. As the temperature drops, their motion slows. At absolute zero (0 Kelvin, or –273.15°C), molecular motion theoretically ceases altogether. This physical principle offers a powerful metaphor for understanding data access patterns in Amazon S3.

- **Hot Data:** Like high-energy molecules, hot data is accessed frequently and must be available with low latency. Examples include active application content, real-time analytics, and user-uploaded media. Store this data in S3 Standard or S3 Intelligent-Tiering (frequent tier) for optimal performance.
- **Warm Data:** Warm data is accessed occasionally—perhaps weekly or monthly. It's still important, but not mission-critical. Think of archived logs, historical reports, and infrequently used documents. Suitable storage classes include S3 Standard-IA or S3 Intelligent-Tiering (infrequent tier).
- **Cold Data:** Cold data is rarely accessed—maybe once a year, or only for compliance. Like molecules near absolute zero, this data is nearly motionless. Examples include legal records, backups, and scientific archives. Store it in S3 Glacier Flexible Retrieval, or S3 Glacier Deep Archive for maximum cost savings.

Understanding the "temperature" of your data helps you design smarter object lifecycle configurations. By aligning storage class transitions with data access patterns, you can reduce costs without sacrificing availability where it matters.

Object Multipart Uploads

As an AWS CloudOps engineer, you may be tasked with transferring large datasets from on-premises environments to Amazon S3—whether it's nightly backups, media archives, or analytics payloads. These transfers must be fast, fault-tolerant, and scalable. But operational excellence demands more than just performance—it requires a bias for automation and mechanisms that streamline repetitive tasks. Amazon S3's Multipart Upload capability embodies this principle. It allows large objects to be uploaded in discrete parts, enabling parallelism, granular retries, and efficient resource usage. This approach offers several key advantages:

- **Improved throughput** by uploading parts in parallel.
- **Quick recovery from network issues,** since smaller parts reduce the impact of failures.
- **Pause and resume flexibility,** allowing uploads to span time without automatic expiration.
- **Streaming uploads,** where you can begin transferring data before knowing the final object size.

For SOA-C03 candidates, understanding this feature is foundational to building resilient, cost-aware, and automation-friendly storage pipelines.

Multipart Uploads can be initiated and managed through several interfaces—not just the AWS CLI. You can use the AWS SDKs (e.g., Python Boto3, Java, Node.js), the REST API directly, or the AWS CLI. The CLI (`aws s3 cp`) offers a high-level abstraction that automatically initiates the multipart lifecycle, streams the file in parts, and completes the process. Behind the scenes, it performs the same API calls you'd manually invoke: `CreateMultipartUpload`, multiple `UploadPart` operations, and a final `CompleteMultipartUpload`. You don't need to split the file into chunks; the CLI reads byte ranges from the original file and handles part logic internally.

AWS recommends using Multipart Upload for any file larger than 100 MB, and it becomes mandatory for files over 5 GB. This threshold ensures optimal performance and reliability, especially in environments with variable network conditions or long-distance transfers.

Here's the high-level CLI in action:

```
# Automatically triggers multipart upload for large files
aws s3 cp /Users/me/tmp/largefile.zip \
  s3://my-bucket/largefile.zip

# Optional: hint expected size to optimize multipart behavior
aws s3 cp /Users/me/tmp/largefile.zip \
  s3://my-bucket/largefile.zip \
  --expected-size 500MB
```

This approach aligns with the CloudOps principle of automation—reducing manual effort while maintaining performance. It's the recommended path for most use cases. However, there are scenarios where full control over the upload lifecycle is required—such as distributed systems, custom retry logic, bandwidth shaping, or integration with external orchestration tools. In these cases, the manual approach is not just viable—it's essential. And while it's not managed by AWS, you can still automate it using scripts, pipelines, or SDKs.

To manually control the upload process, you can split a large file into smaller chunks using Bash. This is useful when you want to upload parts individually or simulate multipart behavior for testing.

```
# Split /Users/me/tmp/largefile.zip into 50MB chunks
cd /Users/me/tmp
split -b 50M largefile.zip part_

# Resulting files: part_aa, part_ab, part_ac, ...
# Rename them for clarity (optional)
mv part_aa part1.zip
```

```
mv part_ab part2.zip
mv part_ac part3.zip
```

Then use the low-level CLI to upload each part:

```
# Step 1: Initiate the multipart upload
# This returns an UploadId, which you'll use for all subsequent part uploads
aws s3api create-multipart-upload \
  --bucket my-bucket \
  --key largefile.zip
```

Capture the `UploadId` from the response and use it in the next steps:

```
# Step 2: Upload each part using the UploadId
aws s3api upload-part \
  --bucket my-bucket \
  --key largefile.zip \
  --part-number 1 \
  --body /Users/me/tmp/part1.zip \
  --upload-id <UploadId>

aws s3api upload-part \
  --bucket my-bucket \
  --key largefile.zip \
  --part-number 2 \
  --body /Users/me/tmp/part2.zip \
  --upload-id <UploadId>
```

Each `upload-part` response returns an `ETag`—a unique identifier for that part. You'll need to collect these to build the `parts.json` manifest.

The `parts.json` file is a manifest that tells Amazon S3 how to reassemble the uploaded parts into a single object. It contains a list of all uploaded parts, each identified by its `PartNumber` and the corresponding `ETag`. This file is required when completing the Multipart Upload.

Example structure:

```
{
  "Parts": [
    {
      "ETag": "\"d41d8cd98f00b204e9800998ecf8427e\"",
      "PartNumber": 1
    },
    {
      "ETag": "\"9b74c9897bac770ffc029102a200c5de\"",
      "PartNumber": 2
    }
  ]
}
```

You can build this file manually by copying the `ETag` and `PartNumber` from each `upload-part` response, or automate it using a script that parses the CLI output and appends entries to a JSON array.

Finally, complete the upload:

```
# Step 3: Complete the multipart upload using the manifest
aws s3api complete-multipart-upload \
  --bucket my-bucket \
  --key largefile.zip \
  --upload-id <UploadId> \
  --multipart-upload file://Users/me/tmp/parts.json
```

This manual approach gives you full control over part size, sequencing, retry logic, and monitoring. It's especially useful when integrating with CI/CD pipelines, custom schedulers, or edge devices. The illustration in Figure 5.2 compares these two approaches, showing how the CLI simplifies the multipart lifecycle while the API offers granular control.

While Multipart Upload optimizes how large files are broken down and transferred, it doesn't address geographic latency. That's where Amazon S3 Transfer Acceleration comes in. By routing uploads through Amazon CloudFront's globally distributed edge locations, Transfer Acceleration reduces roundtrip time and speeds up uploads from distant clients. This is especially useful for mobile apps, global teams, or IoT devices operating far from the Amazon S3 bucket's region. The next section explores how Transfer Acceleration complements Multipart Upload—forming a layered strategy for high-performance, globally distributed storage pipelines.

FIGURE 5.2 Multipart Upload comparison.

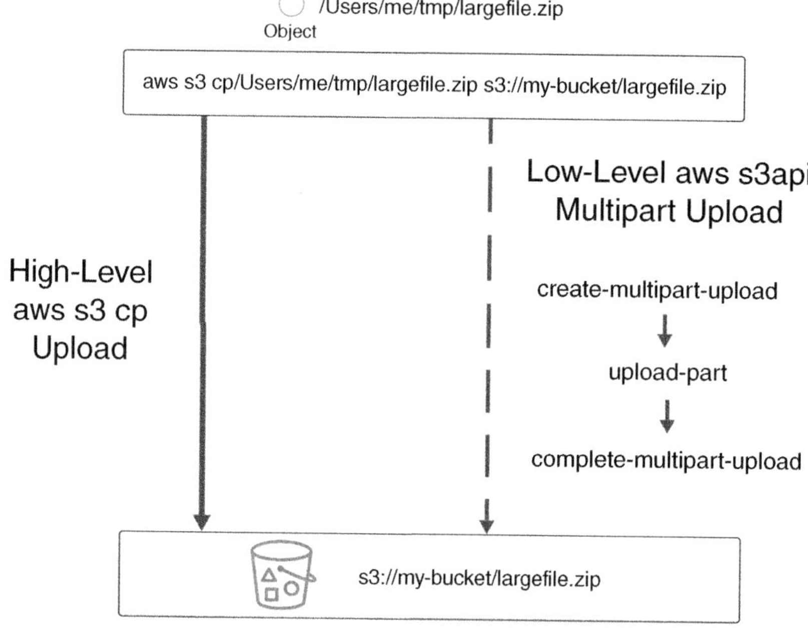

Amazon S3 Transfer Acceleration

Amazon S3 Transfer Acceleration (S3TA) is a performance-boosting feature designed to speed up uploads to Amazon S3 buckets, especially for geographically dispersed users. By leveraging Amazon CloudFront's globally distributed edge locations, Transfer Acceleration minimizes latency and maximizes throughput, making it ideal for applications that require fast, reliable data transfer. Key benefits include accelerated uploads over long distances, seamless integration with existing S3 workflows, and no need to modify your application logic—just enable the feature on your bucket and use the designated endpoint. This can dramatically reduce the time it takes to move large files into Amazon S3, improving user experience and operational efficiency.

Under the hood, S3 Transfer Acceleration works by routing upload traffic through optimized network paths. When a user initiates an upload to an Amazon S3 bucket with Transfer Acceleration enabled, the request is first directed to the nearest CloudFront edge location. From there, it travels over Amazon's high-speed backbone network to the target Amazon S3 bucket, bypassing congested public Internet routes. This architecture reduces roundtrip times and packet loss, especially for uploads originating far from the bucket's AWS Region. Additionally, since the request doesn't traverse the public Internet, it benefits from enhanced security, consistent throughput, and reduced exposure to unpredictable network congestion or routing anomalies. The accelerated endpoint follows the format `bucketname.s3-accelerate.amazonaws.com`, and AWS automatically handles the routing logic, ensuring optimal performance without additional configuration.

Transfer Acceleration is particularly useful for global applications, such as media uploads from mobile devices, large-scale data ingestion from remote offices, or IoT telemetry streaming. It's also a strategic asset for backup and restore workflows, where minimizing transfer time can be critical during recovery scenarios. The next section explores how to implement robust backup and restore solutions using Amazon S3, including snapshots, versioning, and cross-region replication. These techniques, when combined with Transfer Acceleration, can help ensure data durability, availability, and rapid recovery across diverse operational contexts.

Implementing Backup and Restore

A well-architected backup and restore strategy is a key aspect to operational resilience in the cloud. This section explores how to implement such a strategy using Amazon S3 features like object versioning, and automated backup workflows. These capabilities align directly with the Reliability pillar of the AWS Well-Architected Framework—specifically the design principle to "automatically recover from failure." By enabling versioning and automating backups, you create a safety net that supports rapid recovery and minimizes data loss. This approach also reinforces the Failure Management practice area, which emphasizes proactive preparation, detection, and recovery mechanisms to ensure business continuity. Let's dive into the tools and configurations that make this possible.

Versioning Amazon S3 Buckets

Amazon S3 *Versioning* is a data governance and protection feature that allows you to preserve, retrieve, and restore every version of every object stored in an Amazon S3 bucket. By default, Amazon S3 overwrites objects with the same key. With versioning enabled, Amazon S3 stores multiple copies (versions) of an object, each with a unique version ID, offering a powerful safety net against accidental data loss or corruption. The main benefits include:

Accidental Deletion Recovery If a user or application accidentally deletes an object, the previous versions remain intact and can be easily restored. A *delete marker* is created as the latest version, but the actual data is preserved.

Protection Against Overwrites When an object is overwritten (via a PUT operation with the same object key), the original data is not lost. The previous state is stored as a noncurrent version.

Auditing and Compliance Versioning maintains a complete history of changes to your objects, which is crucial for auditing purposes and meeting regulatory compliance requirements for data retention.

Easy Rollbacks If a change introduces an error or data corruption, you can quickly revert to a previous, working version of the object, minimizing downtime.

Integration with Object Lifecycle Configurations You can use Amazon S3 Object Lifecycle Configurations to automatically manage storage costs by transitioning older, noncurrent versions to lower-cost storage classes (like S3 Glacier Flexible Retrieval) or permanently deleting them after a specified period.

Just like Transfer Acceleration, Versioning is enabled at the bucket level. Once enabled, Amazon S3 automatically generates a unique, system-generated version ID for every object uploaded to that bucket. Here's what you need to know for the SOA-C03 exam:

Uploading a New Object The object receives a unique version ID. Version IDs are Unicode, UTF-8 encoded, URL-ready, and opaque strings that are no more than 1,024 bytes long.

Enabling S3 Versioning on a bucket doesn't affect existing objects—they retain their original content, permissions, and a `null` version ID. New uploads receive unique version IDs, allowing multiple versions of the same object key to coexist.

Overwriting an Object The new object becomes the current version with a new version ID. The previous object is retained as a `noncurrent` version with its original version ID.

Deleting an Object Instead of permanent removal, Amazon S3 places a delete marker as the new current version. When you try to GET the object, Amazon S3 returns a `404 Not Found` HTTP error because the delete marker is the current version. However, the actual object data and all its previous versions remain in the bucket. To permanently delete an object, you must specify the version ID in the delete request.

The following example shows how to enable versioning on a bucket named `my-versioned-bucket`.

```
aws s3api put-bucket-versioning \
  --bucket my-versioned-bucket \
  --versioning-configuration Status=Enabled
```

After versioning the bucket, the new object `object.txt` will have its first version ID (e.g., `versionId1`).

```
echo "This is the first version." > object.txt
aws s3 cp object.txt s3://my-versioned-bucket/object.txt
```

To overwrite the object:

```
echo "This is the second version." > object.txt
aws s3 cp object.txt s3://my-versioned-bucket/object.txt
```

After overwriting the object, the previous version is preserved, and the new object becomes the current version with a new version ID (e.g., `versionId2`).

To list all the versions of the object:

```
aws s3api list-object-versions \
  --bucket my-versioned-bucket \
  --prefix object.txt
```

To recover a specific version, use its version ID:

```
aws s3api get-object \
  --bucket my-versioned-bucket \
  --key object.txt \
  --version-id versionId1 recovered_old_object.txt
```

To delete the object:

```
aws s3 rm s3://my-versioned-bucket/object.txt
```

The operation created a delete marker, rather than deleting the object. To permanently delete a specific version, you must explicitly provide the version ID:

```
aws s3api delete-object \
  --bucket my-versioned-bucket \
  --key object.txt \
  --version-id versionId2
```

In addition to implementing object backups and recovery, Versioning is particularly useful in scenarios such as collaborative content editing, regulatory compliance, and application rollback strategies. For example, software deployment pipelines can store configuration files or binaries in versioned buckets (e.g., `terraform.tfstate`) to ensure traceability and rollback capability. Similarly, healthcare or financial institutions can use Versioning to maintain immutable records for auditing purposes.

With Versioning in place, you've laid the groundwork for resilient data protection. The next step is to automate your backup workflows—leveraging lifecycle rules, replication, and scheduled tasks to ensure consistent, scalable, and cost-effective backups. The next section explores how to build these automation patterns using Amazon S3.

Automating Backups for Amazon S3 Buckets

Ensuring the safety and recoverability of data stored in Amazon S3 is the foundation of reliable cloud operations. While Amazon S3 provides eleven nines of durability, human error, application flaws, or malicious actions remain real threats to data integrity. Fortunately, AWS offers powerful, interconnected tools to automate your backup strategy, ensuring your data is protected without constant manual intervention.

The most effective backup strategies for Amazon S3 data typically rely on a layered approach using dedicated AWS services and native S3 features.

AWS Backup

For most organizations, the most straightforward and robust path to automated S3 backups is AWS Backup. This fully managed service acts as a central command center for data protection across the AWS ecosystem.

Instead of manually scripting backups for each bucket, you define a comprehensive "backup plan." This plan dictates the frequency of backups—perhaps every hour for critical data or daily for routine information—and how long they must be retained. Once a plan is assigned to your S3 buckets (via tags or explicit selection), AWS Backup takes over, executing the backups automatically and storing them in secure, encrypted backup vaults.

AWS Backup offers two recovery methods: periodic snapshots for long-term archiving and continuous backups. With continuous backups, you gain point-in-time recovery (PITR) capabilities, allowing you to restore your bucket's state to any specific second within a 35-day window—an invaluable safeguard against rapid data corruption events. Furthermore, features like Vault Lock ensure immutability, making your backups tamper-proof for compliance purposes.

Detailed coverage of AWS Backup is provided in Chapter 7.

Amazon S3 Replication

For mission-critical data that demands virtually instant redundancy, S3 Replication is the ideal mechanism. This native S3 feature operates in near real-time, automatically copying new objects from a source bucket to a destination bucket.

Whether you choose Cross-Region Replication (CRR) to create an off-site copy for disaster recovery or Same-Region Replication (SRR) for compliance requirements, the automation is seamless. Once a replication rule is configured, every new upload is immediately mirrored, offering the highest level of protection against regional outages with minimal RTOs and RPOs.

Cost Optimization Through Versioning and Object Lifecycle Configurations

As you learned in the previous section—within the S3 bucket itself—Versioning is a fundamental safety net. By enabling it, S3 preserves previous iterations of an object every time it's modified or deleted, shielding you from accidental data loss.

To manage the cost and complexity of storing these numerous versions, object lifecycle configurations provide automated housekeeping. These rules act as intelligent data managers, automatically transitioning older (noncurrent) versions of objects to cheaper storage classes like S3 Glacier Flexible Retrieval as they age. They can also automate the permanent expiration of these versions after a defined period, ensuring you retain data for as long as necessary without incurring unnecessary costs.

Integrating External Data

Finally, if the data you need to back up resides outside of AWS—perhaps on a local file server or another cloud provider—AWS offers tools such as AWS DataSync to automate its ingestion into Amazon S3. AWS DataSync is covered in more detail at the end of this chapter.

By combining these services, you can build an automated, multi-layered backup strategy that is resilient, cost-effective, and fully managed.

Amazon Elastic Block Store (EBS)

Amazon EBS provides persistent, block-level, network-attached storage volumes that can be connected to Amazon EC2 instances, enabling high-performance, low-latency data access and resilient workload operations.

While the underlying network infrastructure is abstracted from the user, AWS internally uses a *dedicated*, high-speed network for EBS traffic. This separation from the general data network is an important architectural choice that provides several benefits:

Flexibility and Persistence The dedicated, high-speed storage network connection allows Amazon EBS volumes to be independent of the physical host (compute) running the EC2 instance. This means that volumes can be easily detached from one instance and attached to another (within the same Availability Zone), and data persists even after the associated Amazon EC2 instance is terminated.

Reliable Performance On modern, EBS-optimized instances (especially those built on the AWS Nitro System), this dedicated connection ensures consistent and predictable throughput and IOPS (Input/Output Operations per Second) performance, as EBS traffic does not contend with other network traffic (such as application or management traffic).

Scalability This setup allows AWS to offer SAN-like performance and scalability in the cloud, without the user needing to manage complex physical storage area networks (SANs), host bus adapters (HBAs), or switches.

Each Amazon EBS volume is automatically replicated within its Availability Zone to protect against component failure, offering high availability and durability.

An Amazon EBS volume can only be attached to an EC2 instance if both are located in the same Availability Zone. Both the EC2 instance and the EBS volume are tied to a specific Availability Zone.

Once an EBS volume is attached to an EC2 instance, it becomes visible to the operating system as a block device. At this point, the volume can be formatted with a file system (e.g., ext4, XFS, NTFS), and the file system can then be mounted to a directory path, making it accessible for read/write operations. This process allows workloads running on the instance to interact with the volume as if it were a local disk.

You can attach multiple EBS volumes to a single instance. Generally, an EBS volume can only be attached to one instance at a time. However, the EBS Multi-Attach feature allows a single `io1` or `io2` volume to be attached to up to 16 Nitro-based instances within the same Availability Zone. A Nitro-based instance is an Amazon EC2 instance built on the AWS Nitro System, using specialized hardware to deliver improved performance and security. The `io1` and `io2` volume types are discussed in the next section. To learn more about the Amazon EBS Multi-Attach feature, visit: `https://docs.aws.amazon.com/ebs/latest/userguide/ebs-volumes-multi.html`.

Volume Types

Amazon EBS volumes are available in a variety of types that differ in supported sizes, performance characteristics, and prices. Table 5.4 shows the volume types available as of the writing of this book.

Here are a few highlights you need to know for the exam:

- `gp2` is the older generation of volumes with performance that scales with volume size (3 IOPS/GiB, bursting up to 3,000 IOPS, max 16,000 IOPS). They are generally more expensive for the same level of performance compared to `gp3`, which offers a lower storage price and allows independent scaling of performance metrics.
- `gp3` is the most flexible and cost-efficient volume type for general workloads, allowing you to provision performance (IOPS and throughput) and storage capacity independently.
- `io2 Block Express` offers the highest durability (99.999%) and performance, ideal for production, mission-critical, enterprise-grade databases.
- `st1` and `sc1` are HDD-based and optimized for throughput rather than IOPS, suitable for sequential workloads and archival, respectively.

TABLE 5.4 Amazon EBS Volume Types Comparison

Volume Type	Use Cases	Volume Size	Max Throughput	IOPS Performance	Approx. Cost (USD/month)
`gp3` (General Purpose SSD)	Boot volumes, dev/test environments, medium-sized databases, virtual desktops	1 GiB-64 TiB	Up to 2,000 MiB/s	Up to 80,000 IOPS	$0.08/GB + $0.005/IOPS + $0.04/MBps
`io2` Block Express (Provisioned IOPS SSD)	Mission-critical databases, latency-sensitive apps, high IOPS workloads	4 GiB-64 TiB	Up to 4,000 MiB/s	Up to 256,000 IOPS	$0.125/GB + $0.032-$0.065/IOPS
`io1` (Provisioned IOPS SSD)	I/O-intensive databases, sustained IOPS workloads, Multi-Attach scenarios	4 GiB-16 TiB	Up to 1,000 MiB/s	Up to 64,000 IOPS	$0.125/GB + $0.065/IOPS
`st1` (Throughput Optimized HDD)	Big data, log processing, data warehousing, streaming workloads	125 GiB-16 TiB	Up to 500 MiB/s	Up to 500 IOPS	$0.045/GB
`sc1` (Cold HDD)	Infrequently accessed data, backups, archival storage	125 GiB-16 TiB	Up to 250 MiB/s	Up to 250 IOPS	$0.015/GB

Elasticity

As the name suggests, Amazon EBS is designed to be elastic—able to dynamically scale, adapt, and respond to changing workload demands in real time and without disruption. This elasticity is not just a technical convenience; it's a foundational capability that directly supports the AWS Well-Architected Framework's general design principle: "Stop guessing your capacity needs." For SOA-C03 candidates, understanding EBS elasticity means recognizing how storage can be right-sized dynamically, reducing operational overhead and improving cost efficiency.

Elasticity allows you, as a CloudOps engineer, to modify EBS volumes—size, performance, and type—while the volume remains attached and active. This is especially relevant in production environments where I/O patterns may fluctuate, datasets may grow unpredictably, and performance requirements may evolve over time. Whether you're scaling a transactional database, tuning throughput for a batch job, or migrating to a more cost-effective volume type, Amazon EBS elasticity ensures that storage remains aligned with real-time requirements.

More specifically, this elasticity means:

Increase Capacity You can provision more block storage space for an existing volume on-the-fly as your data needs grow.

Tune Performance You can adjust performance characteristics (like IOPS and throughput) independently of the storage size, allowing you to scale performance up or down to meet demand and optimize costs.

Change Volume Type You can switch between different volume types (e.g., from `gp2` to `gp3`, or between SSD and HDD-backed volumes) while the volume is still attached and in use by an EC2 instance.

Automated Scaling You can use services like Amazon CloudWatch and AWS Lambda to automate volume changes based on predefined performance metrics or schedules, ensuring your resources always align with workload requirements.

These modifications can be made without stopping the instance or detaching the volume, ensuring continuous application availability. For SOA-C03 scenarios, expect questions that test your ability to apply these features in operational contexts—such as resizing volumes for performance spikes, migrating to `gp3` for cost savings, or integrating Amazon EBS into CI/CD pipelines.

Cost Models

When evaluating Amazon EBS, it's critical to understand the pricing model tied to performance. Modern SSD volumes such as `gp3`, `io1`, and `io2` use a provisioned-based model: you explicitly pay for the IOPS and throughput you configure, independent of volume size. This ensures predictable performance and billing, making them ideal for enterprise workloads that demand guaranteed performance and consistency.

By contrast, older *burst-capable* volumes like `gp2`, `st1`, and `sc1` rely on a credit bucket system. These volumes accumulate performance credits when idle and consume them during bursts. Costs are tied to volume size, not provisioned performance (IOPS, throughput), which can make them cheaper for workloads with spiky demand but unpredictable under sustained load. Once credits are depleted, performance drops back to baseline, potentially impacting applications.

The key difference is guaranteed vs. opportunistic performance. Provisioned models guarantee what you pay for, while burst-capable models trade cost for variability. This is an important distinction you need to know for the exam and is summarized in Table 5.5.

Exam Tip

For the exam, remember that `gp3` includes baseline performance (3,000 IOPS and 125 MiB/s) with storage cost, with additional fees only for performance above baseline. This distinguishes it from `io1`/`io2`, where all IOPS are explicitly provisioned and charged separately.

TABLE 5.5 Amazon EBS Performance Models Comparison

Volume Type(s)	Performance Model	Mechanism	Cost Implications
`gp2`, `st1`, `sc1`	Burst-capable	Performance above baseline is achieved by "spending" I/O credits accumulated in a burst bucket when demand is low. Performance is throttled to baseline if the bucket is empty.	Cost is based solely on storage capacity (per GiB). To increase performance, you must provision more storage, which might lead to paying for unnecessary space.
`gp3`, `io1`, `io2`	Provisioned	You explicitly define the desired IOPS and throughput, and the volume consistently delivers that performance level (or very close to it) indefinitely, without the need for credits or a burst bucket.	Cost is a combination of storage capacity (per GiB) plus additional fees for explicitly provisioned IOPS and throughput above the baseline, allowing for more precise cost optimization by separating storage needs from performance needs.

Optimizing Amazon EBS Performance

For you as a CloudOps engineer, optimizing Amazon EBS performance begins with understanding four metrics: *IOPS*, *Throughput*, *Latency*, and *Volume Queue Length*.

- **IOPS** measures how many read/write operations a volume can handle per second. The Amazon CloudWatch metrics you should monitor for IOPS are `VolumeReadOps` and `VolumeWriteOps`.
- **Throughput** reflects the volume's ability to transfer large blocks of data efficiently. The Amazon CloudWatch metrics you should monitor for throughput are `VolumeReadBytes` and `VolumeWriteBytes`.
- **Latency** captures the delay between issuing a request and receiving a response. The Amazon CloudWatch metrics you should monitor for latency are `VolumeAverageReadLatency` and `VolumeAverageWriteLatency`.
- **Volume Queue Length** (also referred to as "Queue Depth") indicates how many I/O operations can be pending at once. A persistently high queue depth suggests the volume is struggling to keep up with requests (i.e., it's experiencing a *bottleneck)*. The Amazon CloudWatch metric you should monitor for Volume Queue Length is `VolumeQueueLength`.

These metrics are influenced by volume type, EC2 instance configuration, and workload characteristics—and they're central to both exam success and real-world optimization. For a detailed walkthrough of these metrics, visit: `https://docs.aws.amazon.com/ebs/latest/userguide/ebs-io-characteristics.html`.

Two decades ago, I learned this the hard way. I spent hours configuring RAID 0 (striping) across two 7,200 RPM (Revolutions Per Minute) "old-fashion" hard drives, chasing performance gains for a database workload that constantly bottlenecked. It was a painful exercise of striping, BIOS tweaks, and hope (for the best). Fast forward to today, and AWS offers Provisioned IOPS SSDs (`io1`, `io2`) that deliver high IOPS out of the box—no RAID 0 "gymnastics" required. These volumes scale linearly with size and provisioned IOPS, and while RAID 0 (striping) still requires manual configuration, it's often unnecessary. With `io2 Block Express`, AWS provides up to 256,000 IOPS and 4,000 MiB/s throughput in a single volume, making RAID configurations largely obsolete for most high-performance workloads.

Even RAID 1 (mirroring) for durability is no longer a concern. Amazon EBS automatically replicates volumes within the same Availability Zone to protect against hardware failures. This built-in replication ensures high availability and durability without the complexity of managing RAID arrays. For you as a SOA-C03 candidate, this is a crucial takeaway: Amazon EBS volumes are resilient by design, and AWS handles the heavy lifting behind the scenes.

So how do you choose a volume type that not only withstands failure, but also sustains your workload in line with the principles we introduced in Chapter 1—specifically, the Sustain phase of the CloudOps lifecycle in Figure 1.1? In the next section, you learn the important aspects you need to know to help you select a volume type that best suits your workload block-storage requirements.

Selecting the Right Volume Type

First and foremost, you need to have a good understanding of what performance metric you want to monitor for your workload to maintain a consistent and reliable performance after deployment. This typically comes down to choosing between IOPS or throughput. These two metrics represent distinct dimensions of Amazon EBS performance, and selecting the wrong one can lead to inefficiencies, or unexpected expenses.

IOPS is the metric to watch when your application performs frequent, small, random read/write operations—that is, transactional databases, key-value stores, or messaging queues. These workloads demand rapid responsiveness and low latency, and they benefit from SSD-backed volumes like `io1`, `io2`, or `gp3`, where you can provision IOPS directly. On the other hand, throughput becomes critical when your workload involves large, sequential data transfers—such as log processing, big data analytics, or media streaming. In these use cases, maximizing MiB/s is more important than IOPS, and volume types like `st1` (Throughput Optimized HDD) or `gp3` with high throughput settings are better suited.

Exam Tip

For the exam, it's important that you're not just familiar with the `gp3` volume type, but also aware of the recent enhancements AWS has introduced. Historically, `gp3` volumes supported up to 16,000 IOPS and 1,000 MiB/s throughput, making them a flexible and cost-effective choice for general-purpose workloads. However, AWS has doubled the throughput ceiling to 2,000 MiB/s and raised the IOPS limit to 80,000, bringing `gp3` much closer to the performance territory once reserved for `io1` and `io2` volumes. These changes significantly expand the use cases for `gp3`, allowing it to sustain more demanding workloads—such as high-volume web servers, containerized applications, and even some database tiers—while keeping an eye on your wallet and avoiding the need to provision more expensive `io2` volumes. To learn more, visit: `https://aws.amazon.com/about-aws/whats-new/2025/09/amazon-ebs-size-provisioned-performance-gp3-volumes/`.

The SOA-C03 exam is designed to test not just your technical knowledge, but your ability to make strategic trade-offs—balancing performance, resilience, and cost across a range of AWS services. Amazon EBS is a prime example of this balancing act. You'll encounter scenarios where multiple volume types could technically satisfy the workload requirements, but only one offers the optimal blend of performance, efficiency, and cost. This is where your judgment comes into play.

As you walk through the EBS decision tree in Figure 5.3, always ask yourself: "Can this volume type (e.g., `gp3`) meet the performance target on its own, without introducing unnecessary complexity or overspending—unless the workload demands higher IOPS or lower latency that justify a move to `io2` or `io2 Block Express`?" If the answer is yes, you've identified a solution that's not only technically sound, but also frugal and sustainable.

FIGURE 5.3 Amazon EBS volume types decision tree.

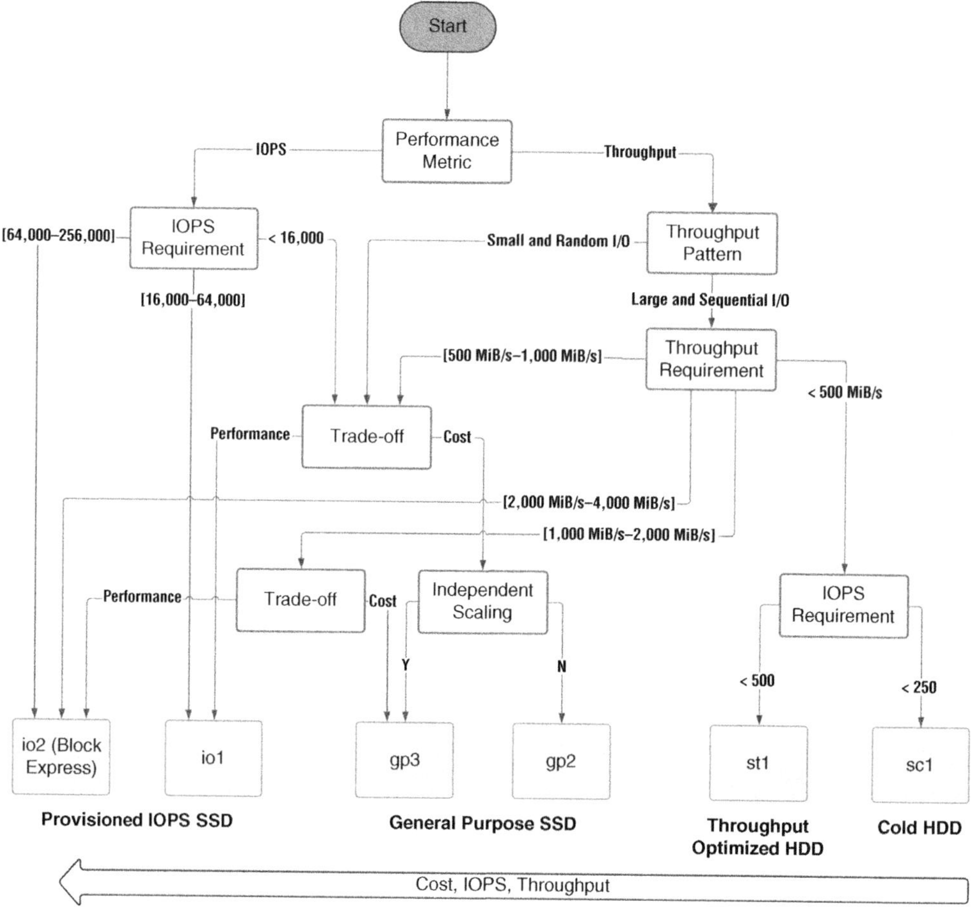

It reflects a deeper understanding of AWS's evolving capabilities and aligns perfectly with Phase 3 of the CloudOps lifecycle, where optimization and cost-awareness converge to sustain long-term operational health.

Once you've navigated the Amazon EBS Volume Types decision tree and selected the volume that best aligns with your workload—whether it's `gp3` for balanced performance or `io2` for high IOPS—you can further enhance EBS performance through three key strategies. First, choose an EBS-optimized instance to ensure dedicated throughput between EC2 (compute) and EBS (block-storage). Next, fine-tune your volume configuration by adjusting performance parameters like IOPS and throughput (especially for `gp3` and `io2`). Finally, optimize your application's I/O patterns to reduce latency and maximize parallelism, ensuring that your architecture extracts the full potential of the underlying block-storage. Let's deep dive into these strategies.

Selecting an EBS-Optimized Instance

Upon choosing the best EBS volume type with the decision tree—whether it's `gp3` for general-purpose workloads or `io2 Block Express` for high-performance production databases—the next step is to select an Amazon EC2 instance that can fully support your volume's IOPS, throughput, and size requirements.

This is where Amazon EBS-optimized instances come into play. As the name suggests, these instances are optimized by enabling dedicated bandwidth solely for Amazon EBS I/O operations, and separate from the general network traffic of the instance. This dedicated throughput minimizes contention and enables the instance to fully utilize the IOPS and throughput provisioned on the EBS volume, ensuring consistent, predictable, and reliable performance, especially for I/O-intensive workloads.

Some instance types are EBS-optimized by default, and there is no need for you to enable this feature. If you try to disable EBS optimization (we show you how shortly), no change will happen.

Exam Tip

For the exam, know that all Nitro-based instances are EBS-optimized by default. AWS Nitro-based instances are relevant to EBS optimization because their architecture fundamentally offloads and accelerates storage I/O functions to dedicated hardware, maximizing available bandwidth and performance for the main instance CPU and memory. To learn more about Nitro-based instances, visit: `https://aws.amazon.com/ec2/nitro`.

Other instance types support EBS optimization, and you can enable it for an additional hourly fee. Some older instance types do not support EBS optimization. To find the most current list of EBS-optimized instance types, refer to the official AWS documentation: `https://docs.aws.amazon.com/AWSEC2/latest/UserGuide/ebs-optimized.html#current`.

If you prefer to use the AWS CLI, here is the command to list the instance types that are EBS-optimized by default:

```
aws ec2 describe-instance-types \
    --filters Name=ebs-info.ebs-optimized-support,Values=default  \
    --query 'InstanceTypes[].{InstanceType:InstanceType,
"MaxBandwidth(Mb/s)":EbsInfo.EbsOptimizedInfo.MaximumBandwidthInMbps,
MaxIOPS:EbsInfo.EbsOptimizedInfo.MaximumIops,
"MaxThroughput(MB/s)":EbsInfo.EbsOptimizedInfo.MaximumThroughputInMBps}' \
    --output=table
```

If you want to list the instance types that optionally support EBS optimization, here is the AWS CLI command:

```
aws ec2 describe-instance-types \
    --filters Name=ebs-info.ebs-optimized-support,Values=supported \
    --query 'InstanceTypes[].{InstanceType:InstanceType,
"MaxBandwidth(Mb/s)":EbsInfo.EbsOptimizedInfo.MaximumBandwidthInMbps,
MaxIOPS:EbsInfo.EbsOptimizedInfo.MaximumIops, "MaxThroughput(MB/s)":EbsInfo.
EbsOptimizedInfo.MaximumThroughputInMBps}' \
    --output=table
```

To turn EBS optimization on or off for an Amazon EC2 instance whose type supports this feature, use the following commands and replace the **user input placeholders** (in bold font) with your own information:

```
aws ec2 modify-instance-attribute \
    --instance-id i-1234567890abcdef0 \
    --ebs-optimized

aws ec2 modify-instance-attribute \
    --instance-id i-1234567890abcdef0 \
    --no-ebs-optimized
```

For older instances that support optional optimization, you must stop the instance before running the aforementioned commands.

For the exam remember the following important principle.

> An instance's EBS performance is limited by two factors: the maximum IOPS and throughput supported by the instance type, and the combined (aggregated) performance of its attached volumes. The lower of these two determines the actual performance.

To reach peak EBS performance, the instance must be paired with volumes that can deliver at least as much IOPS and throughput as the instance allows.

Your job as a CloudOps engineer is to make sure you provision volumes that can meet or exceed the instance's EBS performance limits—without overprovisioning or creating bottlenecks. This means selecting the right volume types, configuring IOPS and throughput appropriately, and ensuring that the total performance of all attached volumes aligns with what the instance can actually sustain. If the volumes are underpowered, the instance won't reach its full potential. If they're overpowered, you're wasting resources. EBS optimization is about finding the right balance—matching volume performance to instance capabilities so that your workloads run efficiently and reliably, in accordance with your workload's specifications. Whether you're supporting a mission-critical transactional database, a batch job, or a development environment, the goal is to avoid underprovisioning (which causes bottlenecks), and overprovisioning (which wastes resources). As a CloudOps engineer, you ensure that the instance and its volumes are aligned to deliver consistent performance without unnecessary cost.

Each EC2 instance type supports specific performance thresholds for EBS IOPS and throughput, defined by *baseline* and *maximum* levels. The baseline represents the default IOPS and throughput the instance can sustain under normal conditions, whereas the maximum defines the upper limit achievable under optimal configuration. These limits vary by instance family and size, and AWS updates them regularly to reflect improvements in infrastructure.

For example, as of the writing of this book, the `m8a.8xlarge` instance is EBS-optimized and can sustain up to 40,000 IOPS and 1,250 MB/s throughput indefinitely, which corresponds to 10,000 Mbps of dedicated EBS bandwidth. These limits represent the maximum performance the instance can achieve when paired with appropriately provisioned volumes.

In this specific example, we focus exclusively on maximizing IOPS—not throughput. We also assume your trade-off is on cost savings—you want the most inexpensive Amazon EBS volume(s) to achieve 40,000 IOPS on an `m8a.8xlarge` instance. With this performance requirement the only viable volume types are `gp2` and `gp3`.

To reach the full 40,000 IOPS using `gp2`, you must provision at least three separate volumes, because each `gp2` volume is capped at 16,000 IOPS regardless of size. Although `gp2` scales linearly at three IOPS per GiB, the per-volume ceiling means that a single large volume—even one sized at 13,333 GiB—cannot exceed 16,000 IOPS. To achieve higher aggregate performance, you must stripe multiple `gp2` volumes together (for example, in RAID 0). Each volume must be sized to unlock its maximum IOPS potential:

$$\text{Size}_{\text{per volume}} = \frac{16{,}000\ \text{IOPS}}{3\ \text{IOPS/GiB}} \approx 5{,}334\ \text{GiB}$$

With three such volumes, the combined performance is as follows:

$$3 \times 16{,}000 = 48{,}000\ \text{IOPS}$$

which comfortably meets the 40,000 IOPS target. The trade-off, however, is significant overprovisioning of storage capacity—about 16,002 GiB total.

A better alternative is to use a single `gp3` volume, provisioned with the exact IOPS required by the workload, up to the instance type's maximum limit. Unlike `gp2`, `gp3` decouples performance from volume size, allowing CloudOps engineers to provision up to 80,000 IOPS and 2,000 MiB/s throughput (i.e., 16,000 Mbps bandwidth). However, AWS enforces a practical constraint (described shortly in the "Volume Tuning" section): the volume must be sized to support the requested IOPS at a ratio of 500 IOPS per GiB. In our example, to fully utilize the 40,000 IOPS supported by an `m8a.8xlarge` instance, the `gp3` volume must be at least:

$$\text{Size}_{\text{per volume}} = \frac{40{,}000 \text{ IOPS}}{500 \text{ IOPS/GiB}} = 80 \text{ GiB}$$

This ensures the volume meets AWS's internal performance thresholds and avoids throttling. You can then provision 40,000 IOPS, 1,250 MiB/s throughput, with a `gp3` volume size of 80 GiB or more, all without requiring RAID or overprovisioning.

Some EC2 instances allow *bandwidth weighting* between EBS and networking. This feature enables you to optimize how the available bandwidth is allocated between block storage traffic and network traffic. If your instance supports this feature, be careful—prioritizing network throughput may reduce EBS bandwidth. Monitor CloudWatch metrics like `EBSIOBalance%` and `EBSByteBalance%` to detect bottlenecks. A consistently low balance percentage suggests that your instance is underprovisioned for EBS traffic.

Figure 5.4 illustrates the two block-storage options just discussed in the example. Our instance type `m8a.8xlarge` supports the bandwidth weighting feature and is configured using the AWS CLI with `--bandwidth-weighting=ebs-1`. This configuration further increases the baseline bandwidth available for EBS operations and decreases the baseline bandwidth for networking. Attached to the instance:

- **Option 1:** Three `gp2` volumes sized 5,334 GiB each
- **Option 2:** A single `gp3` volume sized 80 GiB

Notice how in Option 2, you can independently scale volume size and performance. The illustration includes two distinct slider controls: one for adjusting the volume size in GiB, and another for jointly configuring the volume IOPS and throughput. This visual separation reinforces a key architectural advantage of `gp3` volumes—the decoupling of size from performance. Unlike `gp2`, where IOPS and throughput scale linearly with volume size, `gp3` allows you to provision performance independently. This means you can fine-tune IOPS and throughput without increasing volume size, enabling cost-effective and performance-optimized architectures.

Volume Tuning

After ensuring that your Amazon EC2 instance can effectively leverage the full performance of your attached EBS volumes through optimization, the next step is tuning the volumes themselves to match your workload specific requirements.

Amazon EBS performance is measured primarily by IOPS and throughput (MiB/s), and the tuning strategy heavily depends on the volume type selected.

FIGURE 5.4 Scaling gp2 vs. gp3 volume types.

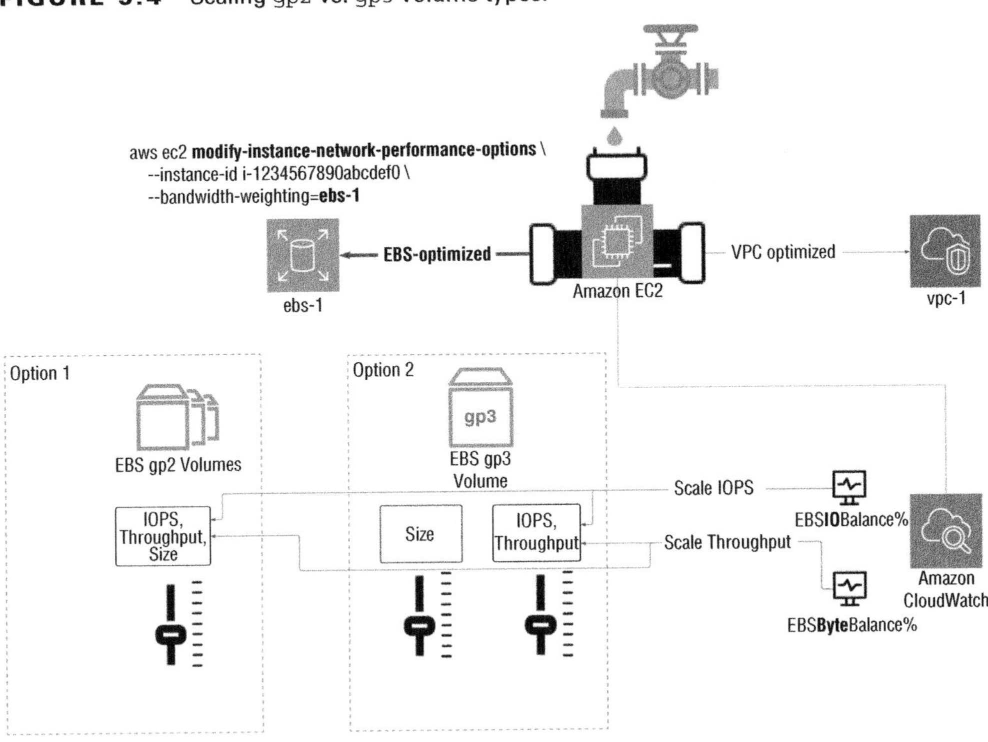

For transactional workloads with frequent, small, random I/O read/write operations, each SSD-backed EBS volume type enforces a baseline performance ratio—typically expressed as provisioned IOPS per 1 GiB of volume size. This ratio doesn't apply to HDD-backed volume types such as `st1` and `sc1`, because these volume types are throughput-focused, and throughput is the key performance metric to watch for workloads characterized by large and sequential I/O operations.

Volume tuning is the art and science of balancing volume type with sizing (for `gp2`), or explicit provisioning of performance (for `gp3`, `io1` and `io2`). Table 5.6 illustrates how SSD-backed volumes can be tuned, and how the tuning strategy is strongly related to the IOPS ratio per GiB.

For HDD-backed volume types such as `st1` and `sc1`, make sure the volume size is large enough to support the desired throughput limits, as their performance is burst-based and tied to volume size.

Regardless of workload type, to make your volume tuning strategy effective, you as a CloudOps engineer must continuously monitor key metrics provided via Amazon CloudWatch. By analyzing these metrics, you can identify performance bottlenecks and proactively adjust your EBS configuration to meet demand.

Table 5.7 shows the key metrics you need to know for the exam.

TABLE 5.6 Comparison of SSD-Backed Volume Types IOPS Ratio Per 1 GiB

Volume Type	IOPS Ratio per 1 GiB	Volume Tuning Strategy
`gp3` (General Purpose SSD)	Up to 500:1 (when provisioning additional IOPS)	Provision IOPS and throughput independently of volume size based on your specific workload needs. Use the baseline 3,000 IOPS/125 MiB/s for general use cases and increase up to 80,000 IOPS/2,000 MiB/s total at a ratio of 500 IOPS per GiB with volumes 160 GiB and larger for a fee (500 IOPS × 160 GiB = 80,000 IOPS).
`gp2` (General Purpose SSD)	3:1	Performance scales with volume size (3 IOPS/GiB). To increase IOPS, increase the volume size. Monitor `BurstBalance` metric and increase volume size if the volume frequently runs out of credits.
`io2 Block Express` (Provisioned IOPS SSD)	1,000:1	Provision IOPS for demanding, latency-sensitive applications like large databases. Attach to Nitro-based instances to achieve maximum performance up to 256,000 IOPS with volumes 256 GiB and larger (1,000 IOPS × 256 GiB = 256,000 IOPS).
`io2` (Provisioned IOPS SSD)	500:1	Suitable for performance-intensive workloads. Attach to Nitro-based instances for full performance potential up to 64,000 IOPS with volumes 128 GiB and larger (500 IOPS × 128 GiB = 64,000 IOPS).
`io1` (Provisioned IOPS SSD)	50:1	Provision IOPS for I/O-hungry applications. Attach to Nitro-based instances for full performance potential up to 64,000 IOPS with volumes 1,280 GiB and larger (50 IOPS × 1,280 GiB = 64,000 IOPS). The ratio is lower than io2, so consider io2 for better price-performance and durability.

As mentioned in the "Elasticity" section, a key feature of Amazon EBS is its ability to dynamically tune volumes without detaching them or stopping the instance. You can change the volume type, increase its size, tweak IOPS, and throughput on-the-fly with no downtime, provided you are using current-generation EBS volumes (i.e., `gp3`, `io1`, `io2 (Block Express)`, `st1`, `sc1`) attached to EBS-optimized instance types (e.g., AWS Nitro-based instances).

TABLE 5.7 Key CloudWatch Metrics for EBS Performance Monitoring

Metric Name	Description	Tuning Insight
`VolumeReadOps/ VolumeWriteOps`	The total number of read/write operations completed in a specified period of time.	Helps confirm if your application demand matches your provisioned IOPS. To calculate the average read/ write operations per second (read/ write IOPS) for the period, divide the total read/write operations in the period by the number of seconds in that period.
`VolumeReadBytes/ VolumeWriteBytes`	The total bytes transferred for read/ write operations in a specified period of time.	Used to calculate actual throughput (MiB/s) requirements.
`VolumeTotalOps/ VolumeTotalBytes`	The aggregate of read/ write operations and bytes in a specified period of time.	Provides overall I/O activity summary. `VolumeTotalBytes` = `VolumeWriteBytes` + `VolumeReadBytes` `VolumeTotalOps` = `VolumeWriteOps` + `VolumeReadOps`
`VolumeQueueLength`	The number of pending I/O requests waiting to be fulfilled by the volume in a specified period of time.	A consistently high queue length suggests the volume cannot keep up with demand and needs more performance (IOPS/throughput).
`BurstBalance`	(For `gp2`, `st1`, `sc1` only) Percentage of I/O credits (for `gp2`) or throughput credits (for `st1` and `sc1`) remaining in the burst bucket.	If this metric consistently drops below 20–30%, your volume is exhausting its burst capacity and needs a performance upgrade (e.g., move to `gp3` or increase `gp2` size).
`EBSIOBalance%`	(For `gp2` only on Nitro-based instances) Percentage of I/O credits remaining in the burst bucket.	A low percentage indicates that your workload requires more consistent IOPS than the current volume configuration can provide at its baseline rate.

(*Continued*)

TABLE 5.7 (Continued)

Metric Name	Description	Tuning Insight
`EBSBytesBalance%`	(For `st1`, `sc1` only on Nitro-based instances) Percentage of throughput credits remaining in the burst bucket.	A low percentage indicates that your workload requires more consistent throughput than the current volume configuration can provide at its baseline rate.

With reference to Table 5.7, `EBSIOBalance%` and `EBSBytesBalance%` are EC2 instance metrics (AWS/EC2 namespace) that monitor instance-level EBS bandwidth limits. All other metrics are EBS volume metrics (AWS/EBS namespace).

From a CloudOps perspective, you can programmatically make these changes using the AWS CLI, IaC tools (like HashiCorp Terraform), the AWS CDK, or even direct calls to the AWS API.

The following AWS CLI command changes a `gp2` volume to `gp3` and sets specific performance values. To use this command, replace the **user input placeholders** (in bold font) with your own information:

```
aws ec2 modify-volume \
    --volume-id vol-0abcdef1234567890 \
    --volume-type gp3 \
    --iops 4000 \
    --throughput 200
```

Amazon EBS does not support reducing volume size. You can only expand a volume size using the live modification feature. To use a smaller volume, you must create a new volume and migrate the data using application-level tools.

Changes typically take effect within a few minutes, although the volume status will show as `optimizing` during the transition.

For example, you can implement a self-healing mechanism to upgrade a `gp2` volume to a `gp3` with 4,000 IOPS and 200 MiB/s throughput when the Amazon CloudWatch metric `EBSIOBalance%` drops below 20%. Here is the general architecture of how this solution would work:

1. Create a CloudWatch alarm. The alarm monitors the `EBSIOBalance%` (for Nitro instances) or `BurstBalance` (for older instances) metric for your specific `gp2` volume and is configured to transition to the `ALARM` state when the balance drops below your specified threshold (e.g., < 20%) for a certain duration (e.g., five consecutive minutes). When the alarm state changes to `ALARM`, it triggers an action. You can configure the alarm to directly invoke an AWS Lambda function.

2. Invoke an AWS Lambda function. The Lambda function receives the event from the Amazon CloudWatch alarm, which contains information about the volume that triggered it (e.g., the dimension `VolumeId`). The function uses the AWS SDK (e.g., boto3 for Python) to call the `modify-volume` API operation. The API call modifies the volume's configuration from `gp2` to `gp3` and explicitly sets the desired performance parameters:

- `VolumeType: gp3`
- `Iops: 4000`
- `Throughput: 200`

The Lambda function's IAM role must have the necessary permissions to describe and modify Amazon EBS volumes (`ec2:ModifyVolume`, `ec2:DescribeVolumes`).

3. Change Amazon EBS Volume. Thanks to the Amazon EBS Volumes' elasticity feature, this modification happens on-the-fly, without any downtime or the need to stop the Amazon EC2 instance (assuming it is a compatible, current-generation instance type).

This setup allows for a robust, automated, and self-healing infrastructure that dynamically scales to meet performance demands, avoiding performance bottlenecks associated with an empty burst bucket.

`EBSIOBalance%` is an EC2 instance-level metric (Nitro instances only) that monitors aggregate burst balance across all attached volumes. `BurstBalance` is the EBS volume-level metric for monitoring a specific `gp2`, `st1`, or `sc1` volume.

Application-Level Optimization

Once you've selected the right EBS volume type, attached it to an EBS-optimized instance, and tuned the volume, the next step is application-level optimization. This is where performance bottlenecks often remain, and the SOA-C03 exam expects you to know how to address them. Think of it as fine-tuning how the operating system and the application itself interact with Amazon EBS, so you can unlock the full potential of the provisioned performance. Application-level optimization falls into two broad categories: OS configuration and application logic.

OS Configuration This category focuses on how the operating system manages I/O. File system choices matter: modern file systems like XFS or ext4 are recommended, and mount options such as `noatime` (to avoid unnecessary metadata writes) can reduce overhead. Aligning file system block sizes with EBS characteristics ensures that reads and writes are efficient. For throughput-heavy workloads, larger block sizes (256 KB or 1 MB) reduce I/O overhead, while latency-sensitive workloads benefit from smaller blocks. RAID striping

(RAID 0) across multiple EBS volumes can also be used to aggregate performance, though you should remember it sacrifices durability. These OS-level tweaks are about ensuring the operating system doesn't become the bottleneck.

Application Logic This category is about how the workload itself issues I/O. Applications should be designed to issue multiple concurrent requests rather than serializing them, since Amazon EBS volumes perform best with parallel I/O. Write-heavy workloads benefit from batching small writes into larger sequential operations, which aligns with EBS throughput models. Read-heavy workloads can be optimized with caching layers such as Redis or Amazon ElastiCache, reducing repeated disk reads. Architectural patterns like CQRS (Command Query Responsibility Segregation) take this further by separating write paths from read paths, allowing writes to be optimized for sequential throughput, while reads are offloaded to caches or replicas. This reduces contention and ensures provisioned IOPS are used efficiently.

For the exam, the key takeaway is that infrastructure-level optimization sets the baseline, but application-level optimization ensures workloads actually consume that performance. OS configuration handles the mechanics of how data is written and read, while application logic determines the patterns of those operations. Together, they form the complete optimization picture. Expect scenario questions where the correct answer isn't "increase the volume size," but rather "tune the file system" or "implement CQRS with caching." Recognizing these distinctions is what sets apart an SOA-C03 candidate who understands Amazon EBS in theory from one who can optimize it in practice.

Implementing Backup and Restore

Implementing robust backup and restoration processes is crucial for data durability and disaster recovery within AWS, and this is a key topic for the SOA-C03 exam. While Amazon EBS volumes themselves are zonal resources (meaning they exist within a single Availability Zone), the mechanisms used to back them up—snapshots and AMIs—are regional, leveraging the durability of Amazon S3 across multiple AZs.

Snapshots

An Amazon EBS *snapshot* is a point-in-time, incremental backup of an Amazon EBS volume. The first snapshot of a volume is a full copy of the data; subsequent snapshots only store the changes (or "blocks") that have occurred since the previous snapshot, making them highly efficient in terms of storage and cost. These incremental changes are stored durably in Amazon S3 within the region, ensuring that your data is protected even if the original EBS volume fails.

Creating a Snapshot

You can take a snapshot of a single volume, or if your EC2 instance has multiple volumes attached, you can capture them all together using a multi-volume snapshot. This is especially useful when you need consistency across volumes, such as for a database with separate data and log disks.

Snapshot creation is asynchronous. That means the snapshot request is accepted right away, but the snapshot stays in a `pending` state until all the data is copied into Amazon S3. Depending on how much data has changed on the volume, this transfer can take hours.

The good news: you can keep using the volume while the snapshot is being created, and it won't affect the backup process. Just remember that the snapshot only captures the data that was actually written to the volume at the moment you requested it. Any data still sitting in application or operating system caches won't be included.

If you create a snapshot of a volume that serves as the root device for an Amazon EC2 instance, it is best practice to stop the instance before taking the snapshot.

Single Volume

To create a snapshot of a single EBS volume with the Amazon CLI use the following command and replace the **user input placeholders** (in bold font) with your own information:

```
aws ec2 create-snapshot \
    --volume-id vol-0abcdef1234567890 \
    --description "My first volume snapshot"
```

The command immediately returns a snapshot ID, while the creation process happens in the background.

Multi Volume

For workloads like databases, where multiple volumes (e.g., data and logs) need to be backed up at the exact same moment to maintain data integrity, AWS provides multi-volume snapshots. This functionality ensures crash consistency across all specified volumes.

To create a snapshot of a multi EBS volume with the Amazon CLI use the following command and replace the **user input placeholders** (in bold font) with your own information:

```
aws ec2 create-snapshots \
    --instance-specification InstanceId=i-1234567890abcdef0 \
    --description "Snapshot of all volumes on my instance id"
```

Creating an AMI from a Snapshot

Upon creating a snapshot, you can restore it into a new volume, or you can use it to create an Amazon Machine Image (AMI). The latter option packages the necessary boot data with the snapshot, allowing you to launch fully functional Amazon EC2 instances.

Creating an AMI from an EBS snapshot is how you make a bootable image ready to launch an EC2 instance. AMIs and snapshots are regional resources; they exist across all Availability Zones within that region.

You use the `aws ec2 register-image` command to link a snapshot to a new AMI ID, as shown in the following command.

```
aws ec2 register-image \
    --name "MyBootableAMI" \
    --architecture x86_64 \
    --virtualization-type hvm \
    --root-device-name /dev/sda1 \
    --block-device-mappings "DeviceName=/dev/sda1,Ebs={SnapshotId=snap-
0fedcba9876543210}"
```

Copying a Snapshot

As noted earlier, snapshots are regional resources tied to the region where they were created. To use a snapshot in a different region (e.g., for cross-region disaster recovery or migration), you must copy it from your source region to your destination region, and—of course—you need permissions to copy it to the destination region.

The following AWS CLI command shows you how to copy a snapshot from a region to another. Replace the **user input placeholders** (in bold font) with your own information:

```
aws ec2 copy-snapshot \
    --source-snapshot-id snap-0abcdef1234567890 \
    --source-region us-east-1 \
    --destination-region us-west-2 \
    --description "Copy for DR"
```

Encrypting a Snapshot

If your source Amazon EBS volume is already encrypted, any snapshot created from it is automatically encrypted using the same AWS KMS key.

If you have an unencrypted volume and want to create an encrypted snapshot, you must use the copy operation to achieve this. You copy the unencrypted snapshot within the same region and specify the `kms-key-id` and the `encrypted` flag.

The following AWS CLI command shows you how to copy and encrypt a snapshot. Replace the **user input placeholders** (in bold font) with your own information:

```
aws ec2 copy-snapshot \
    --source-snapshot-id snap-0abcdef1234567890 \
    --source-region us-east-1 \
    --destination-region us-east-1 \
    --description "Encrypting existing snapshot" \
    --encrypted \
    --kms-key-id arn:aws:kms:us-east-1:123456789012:key/your-custom-cmk-id
```

Sharing a Snapshot

Snapshots can be shared with other AWS accounts or made public (use caution with public sharing). Sharing allows other principals to restore data from your snapshot without needing access to your AWS account credentials. When sharing, you modify the snapshot's permissions.

```
aws ec2 modify-snapshot-attribute \
    --snapshot-id snap-0abcdef1234567890 \
    --attribute createVolumePermission \
    --operation-type add \
    --user-ids 123456789012
```

You can't share snapshots that are encrypted with the default AWS managed key (`aws/ebs`). You can only share snapshots that are encrypted with a customer managed key (CMK) you create in AWS Key Management Service (AWS KMS). If you need to share an encrypted snapshot using the default key, you must first copy it and re-encrypt it using a custom CMK.

Restoring a Volume from a Snapshot

Upon creating a snapshot, you can restore it into a new volume, which is a fundamental operation in AWS EBS management. The process varies slightly depending on the target destination (Availability Zone in the same or a different region), and whether the snapshot is encrypted. Let's see how this restoration process work for each of these use cases.

1. Restoring a snapshot to a volume in the same region. In the same region, the process is straightforward. Snapshots are regional resources, so you can restore them to a volume in any Availability Zone within that region.

Scenario A: Unencrypted Snapshot (Same Region) Use the `create-volume` command and specify an Availability Zone where you need the new volume to reside.

```
aws ec2 create-volume \
    --availability-zone us-east-1a \
    --snapshot-id snap-0abcdef1234567890 \
    --volume-type gp3
```

Scenario B: Encrypted Snapshot (Same Region) The process is identical to restoring an unencrypted snapshot. The new volume automatically inherits the encryption status and uses the same KMS key as the source snapshot. You just need to ensure your IAM user has permission to use that KMS key.

2. Restoring a snapshot to a volume in a different region. To restore a snapshot in a different region, you must first copy the snapshot to the destination region.

Scenario A: Unencrypted Snapshot (Different Region) Copy the unencrypted snapshot to the destination region (`us-west-2`), as illustrated in Step 2 in Figure 5.5. This makes the snapshot available as a new resource ID in the destination region.

```
aws ec2 copy-snapshot \
    --source-region us-east-1 \
    --source-snapshot-id snap-0abcdef1234567890 \
    --description "Copy for DR" \
    --region us-west-2
```

FIGURE 5.5 Restoring an unencrypted volume cross-region.

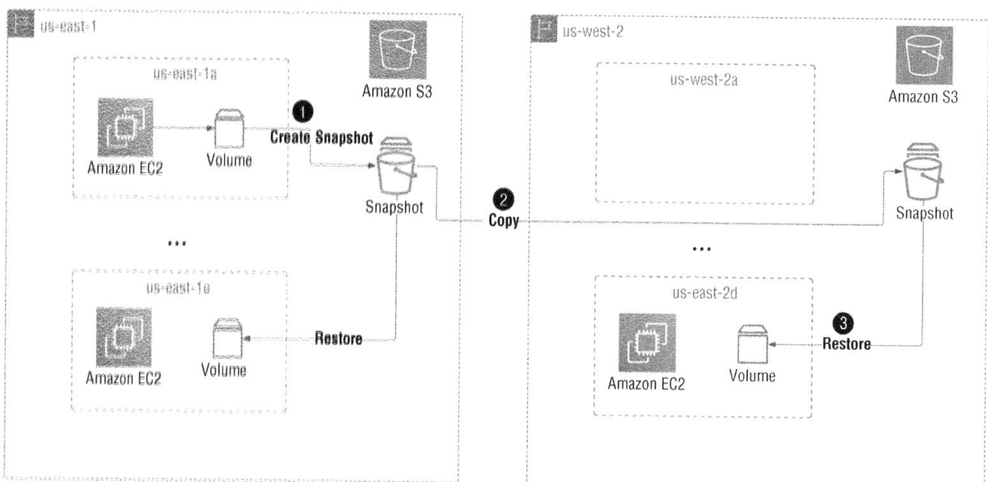

Once the new snapshot (`snap-0fedcba9876543210`) is available in the `us-west-2` region, create the volume using the destination region's snapshot ID. This step is illustrated in Step 3 in Figure 5.5. Make sure you run this command targeting the destination region's endpoint.

```
aws ec2 create-volume \
    --availability-zone us-west-2d \
    --snapshot-id snap-0fedcba9876543210 \
    --volume-type gp3 \
    --region us-west-2
```

Upon successful completion, the `aws ec2 create-volume` command restores the unencrypted volume from the snapshot in the `us-west-2d` Availability Zone. The restored volume can now be attached to a new instance in the same Availability Zone in `us-west-2`.

Scenario B: Encrypted Snapshot (Different Region) When your snapshot is encrypted, you must copy the snapshot and specify a new KMS key in the destination region for re-encryption (`us-west-2`), as AWS KMS keys are regional resources.

AWS KMS keys are region-specific, so the original key from `us-east-1` cannot be used in `us-west-2`.

The good news is that you do not need to decrypt the snapshot manually. AWS handles automatically the decryption of your snapshot in the source region (`us-east-1`) and the re-encryption process during the cross-region `aws ec2 copy-snapshot` operation, but you must specify a new AWS KMS key in the destination region (`us-west-2`) for the copy. This action is illustrated in Step 3 in Figure 5.6.

FIGURE 5.6 Restoring an encrypted volume cross-region.

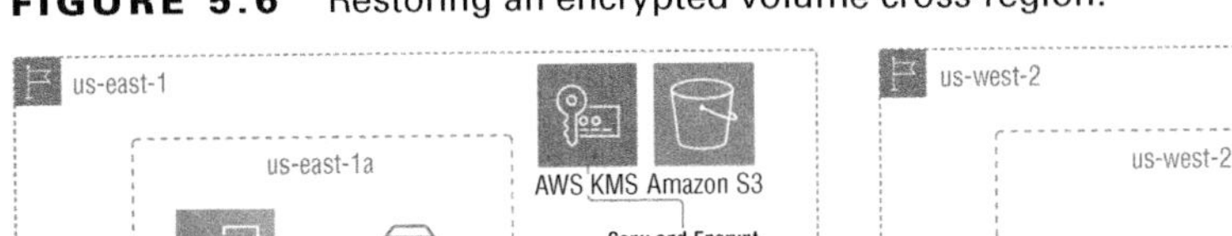

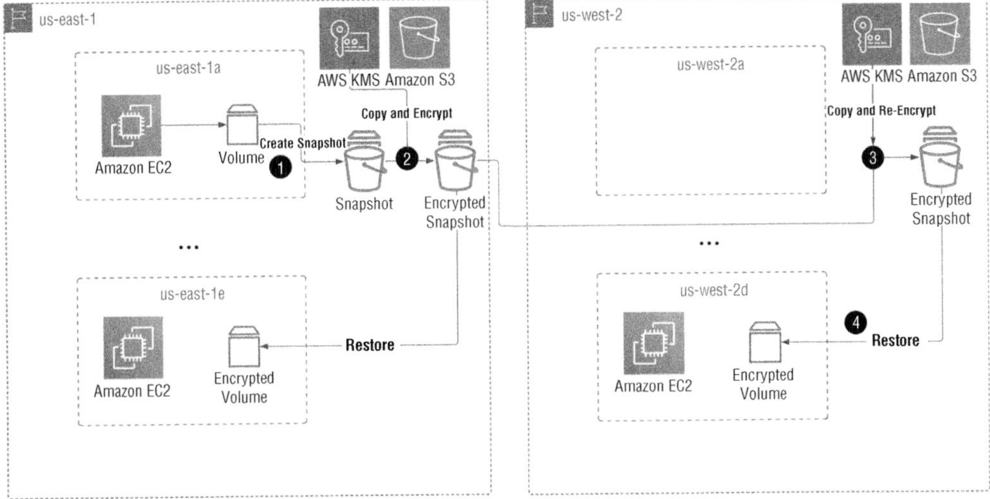

Make sure the IAM principal (user or role) performing this action has the necessary permissions for both the source KMS key (`kms:Decrypt`) in `us-east-1` and the destination KMS key (`kms:Encrypt`, `kms:GenerateDataKey`, etc.) in `us-west-2`.

```
aws ec2 copy-snapshot \
    --source-region us-east-1 \
    --source-snapshot-id snap-0abcdef1234567890 \
    --description "Encrypted copy for DR in us-west-2" \
    --region us-west-2 \
    --encrypted \
    --kms-key-id arn:aws:kms:us-west-2:123456789012:key/
your-destination-kms-key-id
```

Use the new, re-encrypted snapshot ID (`snap-0fedcba9876543210`) to create the volume in the destination region (`us-west-2`). The new volume is automatically encrypted with the destination KMS key, as illustrated in Step 4 in Figure 5.6:

```
aws ec2 create-volume \
    --availability-zone us-west-2d \
    --snapshot-id snap-0fedcba9876543210 \
    --volume-type gp3 \
    --region us-west-2
```

Upon successful completion, the `aws ec2 create-volume` command restores the encrypted volume from the snapshot in the `us-west-2d` Availability Zone. The restored encrypted volume can now be attached to a new instance in the same Availability Zone in `us-west-2`.

Launching an EC2 Instance Using an AMI Created from a Snapshot

Once you get an AMI ID back from the `aws ec2 register-image` command (e.g., `ami-0a1b2c3d4e5f67890`), you can launch an instance, ensuring you point it to a specific subnet that is located in the desired Availability Zone. The regional nature of the AMI handles the cross-AZ availability automatically.

```
aws ec2 run-instances \
    --image-id ami-0a1b2c3d4e5f67890 \
    --instance-type t2.micro \
    --key-name MyKeyPair \
    --security-group-ids sg-0123456789abcdef \
    --subnet-id subnet-0abcdef1234567abc \
    --placement AvailabilityZone=us-east-1b
```

Automating Snapshots and Backups for Amazon EBS Volumes

Manually creating snapshots is impractical for production environments. AWS offers two primary services for automating the process, ensuring compliance with backup policies without manual intervention.

AWS Backup

AWS Backup is a fully managed, centralized backup service that simplifies the management of backups across multiple AWS services (Amazon EBS, Amazon RDS, Amazon DynamoDB, Amazon EFS, etc.). It's the recommended, enterprise-grade solution.

To use AWS Backup, you define a backup plan that specifies resources to back up, backup frequency (e.g., daily at 5 AM), retention periods, and a backup vault for secure storage.

Use AWS Backup when your organization requires a single, unified strategy for backing up heterogeneous AWS data stores (Amazon EBS volumes, Amazon RDS databases, Amazon EFS file systems, etc.) and needs robust compliance reporting and cross-service management.

The following AWS CLI command illustrates an example of a backup-plan creation. Replace the **user input placeholders** (in bold font) with your own information:

```
aws backup create-backup-plan \
    --backup-plan '{
        "BackupPlanName": "DailyEBSBackup",
        "Rules": [{
            "RuleName": "Daily",
            "TargetBackupVaultName": "Default",
            "ScheduleExpression": "cron(0 12 * * ? *)",
            "Lifecycle": {"DeleteAfterDays": 30}
        }]
    }'
```

Amazon Data Lifecycle Manager

Amazon Data Lifecycle Manager (Amazon DLM) is a specific automation tool focused only on the lifecycle of Amazon EBS volumes and snapshots. You create lifecycle policies that automate the creation, retention, and deletion of snapshots based on tags.

Amazon DLM is simpler to set up for Amazon EBS-only backups if you don't need the broader capabilities of AWS Backup. Policies can also be associated with AMIs to manage their lifecycle alongside snapshots. Use Amazon DLM when you only need to manage the lifecycle of Amazon EBS volumes and their associated snapshots or AMIs in a simple, EBS-specific way.

The following AWS CLI command illustrates an example of a lifecycle-policy creation. Replace the **user input placeholders** (in bold font) with your own information:

```
aws dlm create-lifecycle-policy \
    --execution-role-arn arn:aws:iam::123456789012:role/AWSDataLifecycleRole \
    --description "12-hour snapshot policy" \
    --state ENABLED \
    --policy-details '{
        "ResourceTypes":["VOLUME"],
        "TargetTags":[{"Key":"Backup","Value":"True"}],
        "Schedules":[{
            "Name":"12HourSchedule",
            "CreateRule":{"Interval":12, "IntervalUnit": "HOURS"},
            "RetainRule":{"Count":14}
        }]
    }'
```

Amazon Elastic File System (EFS)

Amazon Elastic File System (Amazon EFS) is a fully managed cloud-native NFS file system designed to provide simple, scalable, elastic, shared file storage for use with AWS Cloud services and on-premises resources. For you, preparing for the AWS Certified CloudOps Engineer—Associate (SOA-C03) exam, understanding Amazon EFS is essential, particularly its performance optimization features and operational aspects, including its storage classes.

Amazon EFS operates on the standard Network File System (NFS) protocol versions 4.0 and 4.1. Its key value proposition is elasticity; it automatically grows and shrinks storage capacity as you add and remove files, eliminating the need for complex capacity planning.

Amazon EFS is only available for Linux and macOS instances. If you need a cloud-native file system that supports Windows instances, then the service to use is Amazon FSx for Windows File Server (discussed later in the chapter).

Understanding EFS Performance Modes

A key decision when provisioning an Amazon EFS file system is selecting the right performance mode to match your application's needs. You must make this choice when creating the file system, as it cannot be changed later. At the time of writing this book, two performance modes are available:

General Purpose (Recommended) This is the default mode and is suitable for most file workloads, including general-purpose applications, web serving, content management, and high-performance computing. It offers a balance of throughput and latency for applications with average traffic patterns.

Max I/O (Legacy) This is a previous generation performance type that is designed for highly parallelized workloads that can tolerate higher latencies than the General Purpose mode. Max I/O mode is not supported for file systems that use Elastic throughput (explained next).

Throughput Modes and the Role of Provisioned Throughput

Unlike performance modes, throughput modes can be changed after the file system is created. There are three throughput modes:

Elastic Throughput (Recommended) Elastic Throughput mode is designed for workloads with highly variable or unpredictable performance demands. Instead of provisioning throughput in advance, EFS automatically delivers the level of throughput your application requires, scaling up during bursts and scaling down when demand falls. This mode is particularly effective when throughput patterns are difficult to forecast or when an application's sustained throughput is only a small fraction of its peak demand. By adapting in real time, Elastic Throughput removes the need for capacity planning while ensuring consistent performance during sudden spikes.

Provisioned Throughput For workloads that require consistent, high levels of throughput independent of the file system's size, you can provision a specific level of throughput in MiB/s. This allows you to scale performance before you scale storage, ensuring consistent performance for demanding applications like critical databases or enterprise applications. For the exam, remember that this provides predictable performance when your file system's storage size isn't large enough to support the required performance.

Bursting Throughput In this mode, your available throughput scales with the amount of data stored in your EFS file system. A larger file system earns credits which allow it to burst to higher throughput levels for short periods. This is a cost-effective option for workloads with occasional bursts of high activity.

EFS Storage Classes and Lifecycle Policies

Just like Amazon S3, Amazon EFS offers multiple storage classes designed to optimize costs based on data access patterns. Understanding these is vital for cost optimization, a core CloudOps engineer responsibility.

There are three EFS storage classes:

Standard Storage This is the primary storage class for frequently accessed data, offering the highest performance and the lowest latency for file operations. Data stored here is replicated across multiple Availability Zones for high durability and availability.

EFS Infrequent Access (EFS IA) This lower-cost storage class is optimized for data that is accessed less frequently. It provides the same high durability and availability as Standard storage but at a significantly lower price point, with a small charge upon first access after the data has transitioned to the class. The trade-off is a slightly elevated first-byte latency when retrieving data that has been moved to this class.

EFS Archive This even lower-cost class is designed for data that is rarely accessed and typically stored for compliance or long-term retention. It offers substantial cost savings but with higher latency for retrieval compared to EFS IA.

Lifecycle policies are the automation mechanism that defines when data transitions from Standard storage to EFS IA (or EFS Archive). You can configure the policy to automatically move files that haven't been accessed for a specified duration (e.g., 7, 14, 30, 60, or 90 days). The data seamlessly returns to Standard storage upon subsequent access. Utilizing EFS IA is a primary method for cost optimization within EFS.

Managing Amazon EFS with the AWS CLI

Amazon Elastic File System (EFS) is designed to be simple to use, but as a CloudOps engineer you'll often need to manage it programmatically. In the next sections, you'll learn the basic Amazon EFS operations you need to know for the exam.

Creating an Amazon EFS File System

The starting point is creating the file system itself. You can create a new Amazon EFS file system and enable the default lifecycle policy (move to IA after 30 days) using a single command:

```
aws efs create-file-system \
    --performance-mode generalPurpose \
    --throughput-mode bursting \
    --tags Key=Name,Value=MyTestEFS \
    --lifecycle-policies "TransitionToIA=AFTER_30_DAYS"
```

Managing Mount Targets

Once a file system is created, you must create mount targets in the desired subnets (one per Availability Zone) to make it accessible to EC2 instances.

```
# Create a mount target in a specific subnet with a given Security Group ID
aws efs create-mount-target \
    --file-system-id fs-abcdef1234567890a \
    --subnet-id subnet-0a1b2c3d \
    --security-groups sg-0a1b2c3d4e5f67890
```

Modifying Throughput Mode

If your application requirements change, you can update the throughput mode from bursting to provisioned:

```
aws efs update-file-system \
    --file-system-id fs-abcdef1234567890a \
    --throughput-mode provisioned \
    --provisioned-throughput-in-mibps 100
```

Mounting an EFS File System to an Instance

Mounting an Amazon EFS file system to an EC2 instance is straightforward using the standard Linux mount command with the EFS mount helper utility. The `amazon-efs-utils` package should be installed on your Linux instance first.

Before mounting an Amazon EFS file system with the EFS mount helper, you need an *EFS Access Point*. An Access Point is an application-specific entry path into your file system that enforces a consistent root directory, user and group IDs, and POSIX permissions for all clients that mount through it. This allows CloudOps teams to provide isolated, predictable access for each workload without manually managing directory structures or permissions on the file system itself.

You can create an Access Point using the AWS CLI by specifying the File system ID (for example, `fs-abcdef1234567890a`) and defining the POSIX identity and root directory settings you want the application to use. A minimal example looks like this:

```
aws efs create-access-point \
  --file-system-id fs-abcdef1234567890a \
  --posix-user Uid=1000,Gid=1000 \
  --root-directory Path="/app",CreationInfo={OwnerUid=1000,OwnerGid=1000,
    Permissions=755}
```

In the command:

- `--file-system-id fs-abcdef1234567890a` specifies the Amazon EFS file system where the access point will be created. This ensures the access point is associated with the correct file system.
- `--posix-user Uid=1000,Gid=1000` defines the POSIX identity that all clients will assume when connecting through this access point. This enforces consistent ownership for all file operations, regardless of the client's local user.
  - `Uid=1000` sets the user ID.
  - `Gid=1000` sets the group ID.
- `--root-directory Path="/app",CreationInfo={OwnerUid=1000, OwnerGid=1000,Permissions=755}` configures the directory that becomes the root for any client mounting through the access point.

- `Path="/app"` tells EFS to use `/app` as the entry point. If the directory does not exist, EFS will create it.
- `CreationInfo={...}` defines how that directory should be created if it doesn't already exist:
  - `OwnerUid=1000` sets the directory owner.
  - `OwnerGid=1000` sets the directory group.
  - `Permissions=755` applies standard POSIX permissions (`rwxr-xr-x`), allowing the owner full access while granting read/execute access to others.

The command returns an Access Point ID such as `fsap-0123456789abcdef`. This identifier is then used in the following `sudo mount` command to ensure the client connects through the correct entry point with the appropriate permissions and directory structure.

Here is how you mount a file system using its File System ID (`fs-abcdef1234567890a`) and the newly created access point (`fsap-0123456789abcdef`).

Mounting Using the EFS Mount Helper (Recommended)

The mount helper handles DNS resolution and automatically attempts to use the recommended NFSv4.1 protocol with TCP.

```
sudo mount \
    -t efs \
    -o tls,accesspoint=fsap-0123456789abcdef \
    fs-abcdef1234567890a:/ \
    /mnt/efs/fs1
```

In the `mount` bash command:

- `tls`: Ensures that data is encrypted in transit. This is a crucial security best practice.
- `accesspoint`: Mounts the file system through a specific EFS Access Point, which can enforce specific POSIX user identities and restrict directory access, a valuable security feature for multi-tenant environments.

Mounting Manually Using the Standard Linux Mount Command

For scenarios where the `mount` helper isn't available, you can use the standard `mount` command, specifying the DNS name provided by AWS and recommended options.

```
sudo mount -t nfs4 \
    -o rsize=1048576,wsize=1048576,hard,timeo=600,retrans=2,noresvport \
    fs-abcdef1234567890a.efs.us-east-1.amazonaws.com:/ \
    /mnt/efs/fs2
```

This command specifies several performance-enhancing options like `rsize` (read buffer size) and `wsize` (write buffer size) for optimized data transfer, which are good to be aware of for the exam.

By understanding these performance, cost-optimization, and operational aspects of EFS, you will be well-prepared for the scenarios presented in the SOA-C03 exam.

Amazon FSx

While previous sections of this chapter provided thorough coverage of core AWS storage services like Amazon S3 (object storage), Amazon EBS (block storage), and Amazon EFS (file storage), your journey toward the SOA-C03 AWS certification requires a comprehensive understanding of more specialized file storage solutions. For example, you just learned that Amazon EFS only supports Linux and macOS instances. What if your workload requires Windows-based file storage? The Amazon FSx family of products extends AWS's file storage portfolio, offering fully managed file systems built for specific enterprise workloads. For you as a CloudOps engineer, mastering Amazon FSx is essential for optimizing performance, ensuring robust recovery strategies, and maintaining a strong bias for automation in diverse, specialized use cases. Each FSx product is purpose-built, offering distinct optimization and recovery strategies that you need to understand well for the exam.

Amazon FSx is comprised of four main services:

- Amazon FSx for Windows File Server
- Amazon FSx for NetApp ONTAP
- Amazon FSx for OpenZFS
- Amazon FSx for Lustre

Amazon FSx for Windows File Server

Amazon FSx for Windows File Server provides a fully managed, highly reliable, and scalable file system built on Windows Server. It offers native compatibility with the Server Message Block (SMB) protocol and Windows NTFS, and it seamlessly integrates with Active Directory (AD), making it ideal for migrating Windows-based applications, home directories, and SQL Server deployments that require shared storage.

An Amazon FSx for Windows File Server consists of a Windows file server that clients connect to, with attached storage volumes, and it uses an in-memory cache to accelerate access to frequently used data.

As shown in Figure 5.7, if the requested data is already in the in-memory cache, the file server sends it straight to the client over the network. This use case is referred to as "cache hit" because no disk read or write is needed. As a result, your file server's performance depends only on the network I/O limits and the cache size.

If the data is not in cache, the file server must read or write it to disk first (disk I/O), then deliver it to the client over the network. In this case, performance depends on both the network I/O limits and the disk I/O limits. Figure 5.8 illustrates this use case, also known as "cache miss."

FIGURE 5.7 Cache hit use case with Amazon FSx for Windows File Server file system.

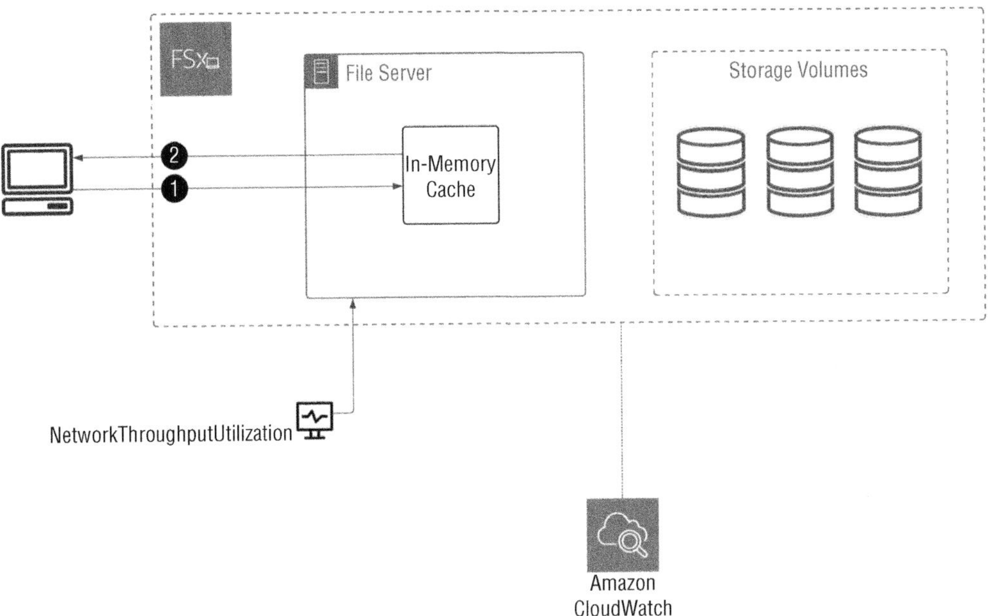

FIGURE 5.8 Cache miss use case with Amazon FSx for Windows File Server file system.

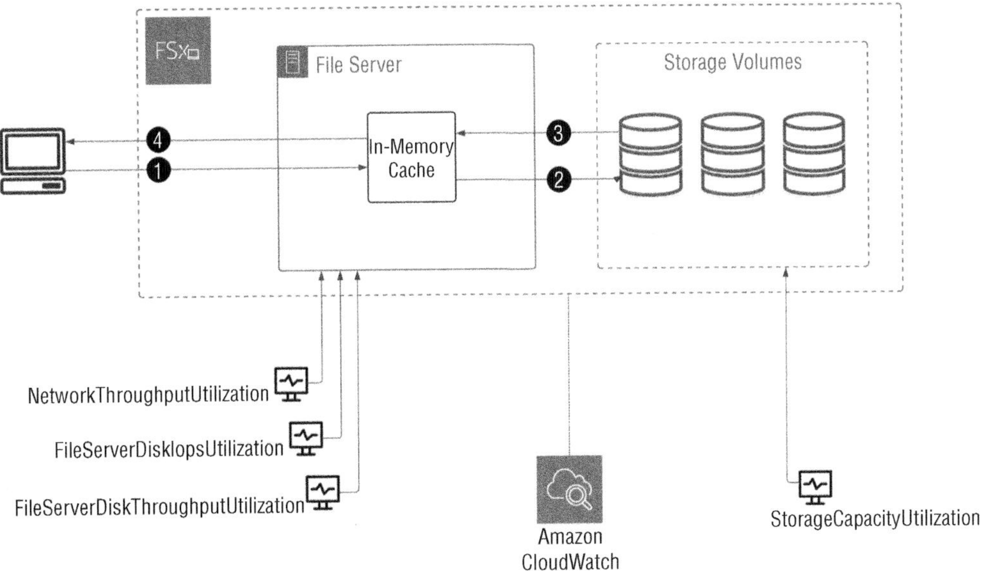

Performance Optimization Strategies

For the SOA-C03 exam, you should focus on key Amazon FSx for Windows File Server metrics that directly inform performance and scaling decisions. The most important metrics to watch for effective file server tuning during performance optimization are listed in Table 5.8.

These four metrics provide clear, actionable insights into network bandwidth, disk throughput, disk I/O, and storage capacity, which are the main tunable dimensions for FSx for Windows File Server performance.

To ensure your Windows workloads run efficiently, reliably and cost-effectively, focus on the following optimization strategies that leverage both AWS features and native Windows Server capabilities:

Scalability For Amazon FSx for Windows File Server, IOPS, throughput, and storage capacity are loosely coupled and can be scaled independently, providing granular control over performance and cost. By default, three IOPS are included per GiB of SSD storage (baseline), but you can provision additional SSD IOPS independently of storage capacity up to a higher ratio (capped at 500 IOPS per GiB). This higher ratio is available when using the "User-provisioned" SSD IOPS mode. In User-provisioned mode, you can provision additional SSD IOPS independently of storage capacity up to 500 IOPS per GiB (maximum 400,000 IOPS per file system). You pay for the total provisioned IOPS in this mode. The maximum achievable IOPS is ultimately constrained by the file system's provisioned throughput capacity level. AWS offers a table of supported throughput capacities (e.g., 32, 64, 128 ... up to 12,288 MBps), and each level is associated with a corresponding maximum number of achievable IOPS. Higher throughput levels come with higher maximum IOPS limits and a larger amount of cache memory. To learn more, visit: `https://docs.aws.amazon.com/fsx/latest/WindowsGuide/performance.html#impact-throughput-cap-performance`.

Remember that HDD storage does not support user-provisioned IOPS; this feature is exclusive to SSD-based file systems.

Storage Type Selection Choose SSD storage for latency-sensitive workloads like databases, and leverage cost-optimization features such as data deduplication and compression for general-purpose file shares.

Multi-AZ Deployment Deploying in Multi-AZ provides high availability and automatic failover, which is a key component for reliable production workloads like SQL Server Failover Cluster Instances (FCI).

TABLE 5.8 Amazon CloudWatch FSx for Window File Server Key Metrics

Metric Name	Description	Tuning Insight
`NetworkThroughputUtilization`	The percentage of the provisioned network throughput capacity currently in use by clients.	A value consistently approaching 100% indicates a network bottleneck between clients and the file server. Provisioning a higher throughput capacity is the primary action.
`FileServerDiskThroughputUtilization`	The percentage of the disk throughput capacity being consumed between the file server and its storage volumes.	High utilization (near 100%) suggests the file server's internal I/O pipeline is a constraint. The tuning action is to increase the file system's overall throughput capacity.
`FileServerDiskIopsUtilization`	The percentage of the provisioned disk I/O capacity being consumed by the file server.	High utilization suggests the workload is constrained by disk I/O operations. Consider increasing the provisioned SSD IOPS or scaling storage size to improve latency.
`StorageCapacityUtilization`	The used physical storage capacity as a percentage of the total provisioned capacity.	A consistently high percentage indicates the need to increase the storage capacity to avoid operational impacts on performance and availability. This is key for capacity planning.

Backup and Recovery Strategies

Operational excellence requires a robust plan for data protection and quick recovery. Implement these strategies using automation to ensure data integrity and meet RPO/RTO requirements:

Automated and User-Initiated Backups Amazon FSx automatically takes daily backups, stored in highly durable Amazon S3. For specific recovery points, you can use the AWS CLI or AWS SDKs to create user-initiated backups.

Shadow Copies Leverage the Windows-native Distributed File System (DFS) Shadow Copies feature to allow end-users to restore previous versions of files themselves, reducing the operational burden on the CloudOps team.

Shadow copies are not enabled by default on Amazon FSx for Windows File Server. You must explicitly enable and configure them using PowerShell commands.

Infrastructure-as-Code (IaC) Automate the deployment and configuration of your file systems and backup policies using AWS CloudFormation or Terraform, ensuring consistency and repeatability across environments.

Amazon FSx for NetApp ONTAP

Amazon FSx for NetApp ONTAP provides fully managed shared storage with the features, performance, and APIs of NetApp ONTAP file systems, delivering enterprise-grade data management capabilities on AWS. Beyond simple file storage, ONTAP brings a rich set of capabilities such as multiprotocol access (SMB, NFS, and dual-protocol support), high-performance snapshots and clones, inline data reduction, thin provisioning, and advanced replication technologies like SnapMirror. These features make FSx for ONTAP an ideal choice for lift-and-shift migrations of on-premises NetApp environments, as well as for modern applications that depend on ONTAP's mature data management, security, and interoperability.

Performance Optimization Strategies

Leverage NetApp's intelligent tiering and data efficiency features to manage performance and control costs across your enterprise workloads. Monitor these specific CloudWatch metrics to ensure optimal performance (see Table 5.9). All of these metrics take one dimension (`FileSystemId`)—except `StorageCapacityUtilization`, which takes `FileSystemId`, `StorageTier`, and `DataType`.

To ensure that your NetApp ONTAP file system runs efficiently, reliably and cost-effectively, focus on the following optimization strategies:

Scalability For Amazon FSx for NetApp ONTAP, throughput and IOPS are loosely coupled to storage capacity and can be scaled independently for granular control. By default, three

TABLE 5.9 Amazon CloudWatch FSx for NetApp ONTAP Key Metrics

Metric Name	Description	Tuning Insight
`NetworkThroughputUtilization`	The percentage of the file system's network throughput capacity currently in use.	If this consistently hits 100%, your application is being throttled by the file server's network pipe. Scale up throughput capacity to resolve.
`FileServerDiskThroughputUtilization`	The percentage of the underlying disk throughput capacity being utilized.	High disk utilization with low network utilization suggests your storage type (SSD) or IOPS are the bottleneck rather than the network.
`StorageCapacityUtilization`	The percentage of the primary (SSD) storage tier currently consumed.	When this reaches 80%+, consider enabling Autogrow or increasing storage capacity to prevent "out of space" errors.
`DataReadBytes / DataWriteBytes`	The total number of bytes read from or written to the file system during the period.	Divide the Sum by the Period (seconds) to calculate your actual throughput in MBps. Useful for right-sizing your provisioned throughput.

SSD IOPS are provisioned per GiB of SSD storage, but you can provision additional SSD IOPS independently. The max IOPS is ultimately tied to the provisioned throughput capacity.

Intelligent Tiering Data is automatically tiered across high-performance SSD and lower-cost capacity storage tiers, allowing you to achieve SSD performance while paying for SSD storage for only a fraction of your data.

Storage Efficiency Leverage built-in ONTAP features like compression and deduplication to automatically reduce storage consumption and costs for both your file systems and backups.

Snapshots and Cloning Use ONTAP-specific features like Snapshots (point-in-time copies) and FlexClone (writable copies of data that share blocks) for efficient development, testing, and data management workflows.

Backup and Recovery Strategies

FSx for NetApp ONTAP offers advanced data replication and backup capabilities essential for enterprise compliance and disaster recovery. Automate these processes for reliable operations:

SnapMirror Replication Utilize NetApp SnapMirror technology to replicate data to another FSx for ONTAP file system, potentially in a different AWS Region, for cross-region disaster recovery with low RPO (Recovery Point Objective) and RTO (Recovery Time Objective).

Volume Backups Beyond SnapMirror, leverage standard Amazon FSx volume backups, which are incremental and highly durable, to meet data retention and compliance needs.

Operational Excellence Use tools like the NetApp BlueXP Workload Factory to assess and implement well-architected practices, using infrastructure-as-code to manage and optimize your ONTAP environments.

Amazon FSx for OpenZFS

Amazon FSx for OpenZFS offers fully managed file storage built on the OpenZFS file system, providing rich data management features like snapshots, data cloning, and compression, with high performance and low latency. It's an excellent choice for general-purpose file serving, Oracle databases, and workloads requiring POSIX compatibility.

Performance Optimization Strategies

OpenZFS offers unique, built-in capabilities that you can optimize for high performance. Monitor and scale throughput capacity dynamically to meet application needs, using the key CloudWatch metrics listed in Table 5.10 for insight.

To ensure your FSx for OpenZFS file system runs efficiently, reliably and cost-effectively, focus on the following optimization strategies:

TABLE 5.10 Amazon CloudWatch FSx for OpenZFS Key Metrics

Metric Name	Description	Tuning Insight
`ReadLatency, WriteLatency`	The latency of read and write operations in milliseconds.	These are crucial for latency-sensitive applications like databases. High latency suggests a need to increase the file system's *throughput capacity* or scale storage size to increase IOPS/performance.
`StorageCapacityUtilization`	The used physical storage capacity as a percentage of the total provisioned capacity.	A consistently high percentage indicates the need to scale the *storage capacity*, as performance for OpenZFS scales with the amount of provisioned storage.
`FileServerCacheHitRatio`	The percentage of I/O operations served from the memory cache (ARC—Adaptive Replacement Cache).	A low cache hit rate means more I/O is going to disk storage. To improve performance and reduce latency, consider scaling the file system to acquire a larger memory cache.

Scalability For FSx for OpenZFS, IOPS and throughput are loosely coupled to storage capacity. By default, three IOPS are included per GiB of storage, but you can provision additional SSD IOPS independently from the storage capacity. The throughput capacity can also be scaled independently from the storage, allowing for flexible performance tuning.

ZFS Optimization Benefit from ZFS's inherent features like data compression (Zstandard and LZ4), thin provisioning, and high-performance caching to reduce costs and improve performance.

Backup and Recovery Strategies

Leverage the speed of OpenZFS snapshots and integrate them into your automated backup routines to ensure rapid recovery times for critical data:

Automated Daily Backups FSx for OpenZFS automatically takes durable, incremental daily backups to Amazon S3.

Snapshots and Replication Use OpenZFS snapshots for point-in-time recovery and share them across accounts and regions for disaster recovery purposes.

Automation Automate the creation, deletion, and restoration of snapshots and file systems using the AWS CLI or SDKs, ensuring your recovery procedures are consistent and tested regularly.

Amazon FSx for Lustre

Amazon FSx for Lustre is optimized for compute-intensive workloads such as machine learning (ML), high-performance computing (HPC), video processing, and financial simulations, where speed and massive scalability are paramount. It is built on the popular open-source Lustre file system and integrates natively with Amazon S3, making it the ideal high-performance storage layer for MLOps training datasets that demand low latency and high throughput.

Performance Optimization Strategies

Optimizing FSx for Lustre involves selecting the right storage class and leveraging its unique S3 integration capabilities to maximize data throughput for compute-intensive tasks. Key Amazon CloudWatch metrics help monitor performance and capacity, as listed in Table 5.11.

To ensure your FSx for Lustre file system runs efficiently, reliably and cost-effectively, focus on the following optimization strategies:

Scalability For most FSx for Lustre deployments, performance (throughput and IOPS) is tightly coupled with storage capacity. Scaling the file system size linearly increases the available baseline throughput and IOPS. For Intelligent-Tiering, total file system throughput is provisioned independently of storage capacity, and metadata IOPS can be provisioned separately.

TABLE 5.11 Amazon CloudWatch FSx for Lustre Key Metrics

Metric Name	Description	Tuning Insight
`DataReadBytes`, `DataWriteBytes`	Total number of bytes read from or written to the file system.	Use the Sum divided by the Period to find MB/s. If this hits your provisioned throughput limit, your HPC jobs will stall.
`StorageCapacityUtilization`	The used physical storage capacity as a percentage of the total provisioned capacity.	For `PERSISTENT` file systems, a high percentage indicates the need to scale the storage capacity, which also linearly increases performance capabilities.
`MetaDataOperations`	The number of metadata operations per second (e.g., open, close, stat).	High metadata operations are common in HPC. If this metric spikes, it indicates heavy file system navigation, which might require specific software configuration tuning or ensuring sufficient metadata performance is provisioned.

Storage Class and Tiers Select between SSD-based storage for low-latency, IOPS-intensive workloads like ML model training, or cost-effective HDD-based storage for throughput-intensive workloads like data analytics.

S3 Integration (Data Repositories) Link your FSx for Lustre file system to an S3 bucket to provide a high-performance file interface to your data lake. Data Repository Association (DRA) features allow you to automatically sync data and even evict file contents from the file system to S3 to optimize storage consumption and cost.

Backup and Recovery Strategies

Data durability in FSx for Lustre depends heavily on your chosen deployment type. Focus on these strategies to protect persistent data and automate environment recovery:

Persistent vs. Scratch Understand the difference between `PERSISTENT` file systems (data replicated, failed components replaced automatically) and `SCRATCH` (temporary storage, no data replication). Choose the appropriate type based on your workload's durability requirements.

Backups For persistent file systems not linked to an S3 data repository, use automatic daily or user-initiated backups. Data is stored in Amazon S3 for high durability.

Automation Use the AWS CLI or SDK to automate the creation and linking of FSx for Lustre file systems to Amazon S3 data repositories, streamlining the setup of HPC and MLOps environments.

Selecting a File Share Storage Solution

Choosing the right AWS shared file storage solution—whether Amazon EFS or one of the Amazon FSx family products—is a critical decision for CloudOps engineers. The ideal choice depends entirely on the workload's operating system, required protocols, performance profile, cost, and data management feature needs. Each service is purpose-built to excel in specific use cases.

Table 5.12 provides a high-level comparison of the key AWS shared storage services to help guide your selection for diverse workloads. Use it as a cheat sheet to consolidate your knowledge as you prepare for the exam.

Storage Types Comparison

Table 5.13 summarizes the three storage types you learned in this chapter. Use it as a quick reference to remember the key differences between each storage type, and how each storage type maps to one or more AWS service(s).

TABLE 5.12 File Storage AWS Services Comparison

Service	Primary Use Case(s)	Supported Protocols	Performance Profile and Scalability (Max IOPS)	Cost Insight
Amazon EFS	Linux-based general-purpose file shares, web serving, container storage, big data analytics.	NFS (v4.0, v4.1)	Automatically scales throughput and capacity on demand (pay-as-you-use model). Higher latency than FSx services.	**Generally cost-effective for variable workloads.** Pay-per-use, automatically tiered for savings on less-accessed data.
FSx for Windows File Server	Lift-and-shift of Windows apps, home directories, SQL Server shared storage, VDI.	SMB (2.0-3.1.1)	High performance and low latency. Throughput, IOPS, and storage capacity scaled independently. (Max ~400,000 IOPS.)	**Moderate to high cost.** Separate charges for storage (SSD/HDD), provisioned throughput, and additional IOPS. HDD can reduce costs.
FSx for NetApp ONTAP	Enterprise lift-and-shift, databases, advanced data management (SnapMirror, clones, tiering), hybrid cloud.	SMB, NFS, iSCSI	High performance and low latency. Throughput and IOPS loosely coupled with capacity. (Max 1.2+ million IOPS with scale-out.)	**High cost (feature rich).** Separate charges for SSD storage, low-cost capacity pool, throughput, and additional IOPS/requests. Pricing is premium.
FSx for OpenZFS	General-purpose file serving, Oracle databases, ZFS features (snapshots, cloning).	NFS (v3, v4.0, v4.1)	High performance and very low latency. Performance (IOPS/Throughput) loosely coupled with capacity. (Max ~400,000 IOPS.)	**Moderate cost.** Separate charges for storage (SSD), provisioned throughput, and additional IOPS. Generally more cost-effective than ONTAP for similar performance.
FSx for Lustre	High-Performance Computing (HPC), machine learning (ML), video processing.	POSIX-compliant (custom)	Extremely high performance, massive throughput (GB/s). Performance tightly coupled with capacity for most types. (Max millions of IOPS.)	**High cost (performance optimized).** All-inclusive pricing per GB varies based on the required performance level (MBps per TiB). Priced for massive scale and speed.

TABLE 5.13 Storage Types Comparison

Storage Type	Block	File	Object
AWS Service	Amazon EBS	Amazon EFS, Amazon FSx	Amazon S3
Data Format	Fixed-size blocks	Hierarchical files	Flat objects and metadata
Data Access Method	iSCSI / Nitro (low-level)	NFS (Linux) / SMB (Windows)	HTTP API over Internet
Data Access Latency	Low (~100–500 µs)	Low-Medium (~100–500 µs) FSx Lustre (~1–10 ms) EFS	High (~10–100+ ms)
Data Addressing Scheme	Offset-based (block ID + offset)	Path-based (`/folder/file.txt`)	URI-based (`https://bucket/key`)
Mutability	Yes	Yes	No
Scalability	Elastic	Elastic	Virtually unlimited
Cost Model	GiB/month + provisioned IOPS	GB/month (standard + IA tiers)	GB/month + requests + storage class

So far you learned about the core AWS storage services you need to master for the exam. Once you have a good understanding on where and how to store your data, the next logical step in your certification journey is to understand how to reliably, securely and efficiently move that data into (and out of) those storage locations. This is where dedicated data movement services like the AWS DataSync, and AWS Storage Gateway become essential tools for you as a CloudOps engineer. These services provide managed solutions for data ingestion and migration with a focus on operational excellence and Amazon S3 performance optimization.

AWS DataSync

In enterprise environments, your data often resides across diverse locations—on-premises file servers, edge devices, and external cloud platforms. Migrating this data into AWS, or synchronizing it across hybrid architectures, requires a solution that is secure, scalable, and operationally efficient. AWS DataSync is engineered to meet this need.

As a fully managed service, AWS DataSync simplifies and accelerates the transfer of large volumes of file and object data between supported sources and AWS storage services. It supports a wide range of storage systems, including:

- On-premises file systems:
  - Network File System (NFS)
  - Server Message Block (SMB)
  - Hadoop Distributed File System (HDFS)
- Cloud-based and self-managed object stores:
  - Google Cloud Storage, Azure Blob Storage, Azure Files, Wasabi Cloud Storage
  - Amazon S3-compatible storage on AWS Snow Family devices
- AWS-native destinations:
  - Amazon S3 (object storage)
  - Amazon EFS (file storage)
  - Amazon FSx for Windows File Server, Lustre, OpenZFS, and NetApp ONTAP

Security is integral to AWS DataSync's design. All data is encrypted in transit using TLS, and access to AWS Resources is governed by IAM roles, ensuring fine-grained control and compliance with your organization's enterprise security policies.

Common use cases for AWS DataSync include data migration to AWS, data archival to free up on-premises storage capacity, data replication to AWS for business continuity, and data transfer to the cloud for analysis and processing.

Data Movement and S3 Performance Optimization

AWS DataSync is an essential tool for implementing and optimizing S3 performance strategies, particularly for large-scale data ingestion. It uses a purpose-built, optimized network protocol that can achieve up to 10× faster transfer speeds than standard command-line tools like `rsync` or simple API calls. AWS DataSync is fundamentally different from manual tools like `scp` or `rsync`. While those are manual utilities designed for individual file transfers, AWS DataSync is an enterprise-grade service designed for large-scale, automated data movement and synchronization.

AWS DataSync is engineered for performance, performing data verification, compression, and parallelization automatically. An `scp` or `rsync` operation requires manual scripting for features like automatic retries, integrity checks, and bandwidth management, all of which are built-in features of DataSync tasks. AWS DataSync is your best choice for high-throughput, reliable, secure and automated data pipelines expected in an enterprise cloud environment.

AWS DataSync is purpose-built for *file* and *object* data movement only—not for database migration or streaming ingestion. DataSync supports transfers to Amazon S3, Amazon EFS, and all Amazon FSx file system types (Windows File Server, Lustre, OpenZFS, and NetApp ONTAP). In the exam, consider AWS DataSync a strong candidate in scenarios involving automated, high-volume transfers to any of these three destinations from on-premises systems, other cloud providers, or AWS storage services.

Hybrid Cloud Scenarios and Performance AWS DataSync's primary function is moving data between on-premises data centers and AWS storage services. To facilitate this, you deploy a software agent (as a VM or EC2 instance) within your local network, which connects to NFS, SMB, HDFS, or S3-compatible storage systems.

Multi-Cloud Scenarios AWS DataSync supports other cloud providers like Google Cloud Storage, Azure Blob Storage, and Azure Files as *source* locations for transfers into AWS. You can deploy an agent in that cloud environment or use agentless "Enhanced mode" for object storage to pull data efficiently into AWS.

Intra-AWS Scenarios and Optimization AWS DataSync can also be used exclusively within the AWS cloud to move data between different AWS storage services (e.g., copy objects from one S3 bucket to another bucket configured with Glacier Deep Archive as the default storage class, or enabling high-speed cross-region replication of EFS file systems).

Automation and Operational Excellence

AWS DataSync is built with operational efficiency and speed in mind. Its primary purpose is automation and acceleration. When migrating data from on-premises environments (or other clouds), you deploy a software agent which acts as the data mover.

Operational excellence is evident in how AWS DataSync manages the entire transfer process via a *task*. This task defines the source, destination, and key settings like bandwidth limits and scheduling. These tasks are designed to be resilient, automatically recovering from network interruptions and performing comprehensive data integrity verification (checksums) both during and after the transfer, ensuring data accuracy without manual checks.

For the IaC focus of the SOA-C03 exam, AWS DataSync tasks, agents, and locations can all be provisioned and managed entirely using AWS CloudFormation (covered in Chapter 8) or similar tools. This allows for automated deployment of data pipelines that can be integrated into your overall infrastructure management strategy.

Automation is further extended through Amazon EventBridge integration (covered in Chapter 6). AWS DataSync can send events for task success, failure, or various status changes, allowing you to trigger subsequent automated actions like kicking off an AWS Step Functions state machine to process the newly arrived data in Amazon S3, ensuring seamless data ingestion and workflow integration. It effectively eliminates manual intervention for large-scale, recurring data movement operations while maximizing S3 ingestion performance.

AWS Storage Gateway

AWS Storage Gateway is a hybrid storage service that extends AWS storage into on-premises environments, enabling organizations to modernize gradually while maintaining compatibility with existing applications. For CloudOps engineers, it represents the operational bridge between legacy systems and cloud-native storage, providing predictable performance, secure connectivity, and seamless integration with Amazon S3, EBS snapshots, and AWS Backup. For the SOA-C03 exam, you're expected to understand the gateway types, their use cases, deployment patterns, and the operational signals that keep hybrid storage healthy.

Gateway Types

Storage Gateway comes in three variants, each designed to solve a specific hybrid storage use case. As a CloudOps engineer, you must be able to distinguish these use cases, and understand how they behave operationally, especially when troubleshooting performance, connectivity, or data-movement issues.

Table 5.14 illustrates the three Gateway types.

Deployment Patterns

Storage Gateway supports several deployment patterns that allow CloudOps engineers to align hybrid storage with the operational realities of on-premises environments.

TABLE 5.14 AWS Storage Gateway Types

Gateway Type	Use Case	Key CloudOps Considerations
S3 File Gateway	Provides NFS/SMB access to objects stored in Amazon S3	Manages local caching for low-latency reads, integrates with S3 lifecycle policies, supports Active Directory for SMB, and is ideal for replacing on-prem file servers
Volume Gateway	Exposes cloud-backed iSCSI block volumes to on-prem systems	Offers cached and stored modes, uses EBS snapshots, and AWS Backup for backup and disaster recovery, and requires careful monitoring of cache and upload buffer performance
Tape Gateway	Acts as a virtual tape library for backup applications	Integrates with existing backup software, automatically moves tapes to S3 Glacier tiers, and simplifies long-term archival without physical media

The most common pattern is deploying the gateway as a virtual appliance on VMware, Hyper-V, or KVM, which provides low-latency access to local applications while seamlessly extending storage into AWS. This pattern is ideal for file-server modernization, block-storage backup workflows, and tape-replacement scenarios where workloads must continue running on-premises but benefit from cloud durability and lifecycle management.

A second pattern uses the hardware appliance, which is purpose-built for environments without virtualization infrastructure or where predictable, appliance-level performance and support are required.

A third pattern places the gateway on Amazon EC2, enabling cloud-side workflows such as cross-Region replication, cloud-to-cloud backup, or disaster recovery failover where the gateway must operate entirely within AWS. This approach is especially useful when on-premises infrastructure is unavailable or when hybrid workflows need to be tested without impacting production systems.

Across all patterns, CloudOps engineers must ensure stable connectivity to AWS endpoints, correct IAM permissions for accessing S3 or EBS snapshots, and proper sizing of cache and upload buffers to maintain consistent performance and reliable data movement.

Monitoring and Performance

Operational excellence with Storage Gateway depends on continuous visibility into cache behavior, data-transfer performance, and gateway health. CloudWatch metrics such as `CacheHitPercent`, `CachePercentDirty`, `CloudBytesUploaded`, and `FilesFailingUpload` help identify bottlenecks, diagnose latency issues, and ensure that data is being uploaded to AWS reliably. CloudTrail provides a full audit trail of API activity, while CloudWatch Logs capture detailed gateway events, giving CloudOps teams the insight needed to troubleshoot hybrid storage workflows, validate backup operations, and maintain predictable performance across both on-premises and cloud environments.

Table 5.15 describes the metrics you need to know for the exam.

AWS Transfer Family

AWS Transfer Family functions as a comprehensive, fully managed suite of services that facilitates file transfers using industry-standard protocols, allowing you to move data directly into and out of AWS storage without the heavy lifting of managing server infrastructure. AWS Transfer Family supports the following protocols out-of-the-box:

- **SFTP** (Secure File Transfer Protocol), which provides secure transfers over SSH and is commonly used for B2B data exchange.
- **FTPS** (File Transfer Protocol Secure), which adds security via SSL/TLS encryption.
- **FTP** (File Transfer Protocol) to support legacy system integrators, although it is not recommended due to lack of encryption in-transit capabilities.
- **AS2** (Applicability Statement 2), which caters to enterprise B2B document exchange, de-facto standard for compliance-heavy supply chain logistics.

TABLE 5.15 Amazon CloudWatch Storage Gateway Key Metrics

Metric Name	Description	Tuning Insight
`CacheHitPercent`	The percentage of read requests served directly from the local cache rather than being fetched from the cloud.	A low percentage indicates the *local cache disk is too small* for the active dataset ("hot" data). Increase the local cache storage to improve performance and reduce latency.
`CachePercentDirty`	The percentage of data currently residing in the local cache that has not yet been successfully uploaded to AWS.	If this remains high (e.g., above 80%), it suggests your *outbound network bandwidth* cannot keep up with local write speeds. Consider increasing bandwidth or scheduling uploads during off-peak hours.
`IOWaitPercent`	The percentage of time the gateway's CPU is waiting for disk I/O operations to complete.	High values (typically *>20%)* indicate that the underlying local hardware (virtual or physical disks) is *too slow* for the workload. Upgrade to SSD/NVMe or add more virtual disks to resolve.
`CloudBytesUploaded`	The total number of bytes the gateway successfully sent to the cloud backend (S3/Glacier) during the period.	Monitor this against your *bandwidth rate limits.* If this hits a flat line below your expected speed, it may indicate a network throttling issue or an ISP bottleneck.
`FilesFailingUpload`	The number of files that encountered errors when trying to sync from the gateway to the cloud.	Any value *greater than zero* requires immediate attention. Use CloudWatch Logs to identify the specific files and check for S3 permission (IAM) issues or connectivity drops.
`FileSharesUnavailable`	The count of file shares on the gateway that are currently in an "Unavailable" state.	Typically indicates that the gateway *cannot reach the S3 endpoint* or lacks the necessary permissions to access the bucket. Check your VPC endpoints and IAM roles immediately.

Additionally, the recently introduced Web Apps feature exposes a simple, browser-based interface for end-users to interact with Amazon S3 data seamlessly, integrating with IAM Identity Center for user access management.

AWS Transfer Family is out-of-scope for the SOA-C03 exam, so this section is optional for exam preparation. However, it remains highly relevant for CloudOps engineers because many organizations still rely on SFTP, FTPS, and FTP for partner integrations and legacy data-transfer workflows. Understanding Transfer Family helps you design secure, scalable file-ingestion pipelines that bridge traditional protocols with modern AWS storage services.

Automation and Operational Excellence

Amazon Transfer Family offers CloudOps engineers a fully managed, highly available alternative to self-managed SFTP, FTPS, and FTP servers. Instead of provisioning, securing, patching, and scaling EC2 instances running `scp` or `rsync` endpoints, you simply configure users, keys, and an S3 or EFS backend while AWS handles the infrastructure, availability, and scaling. The service integrates cleanly with IaC tools such as CloudFormation, the AWS SDKs, and Terraform, enabling consistent, repeatable deployments across environments.

Operational excellence is further supported through CloudTrail auditing, CloudWatch metrics and logs, and the ability to build automated ingestion pipelines using Managed Workflows. These workflows allow you to trigger serverless processing steps—such as decrypting, scanning, or tagging uploaded files—without maintaining any event-handling infrastructure, making Transfer Family a powerful component in automated, end-to-end data-processing architectures.

Summary

In this chapter you learned how Amazon S3 establishes the foundation of AWS storage with its durability, availability, scalability, and flexible cost models. For SOA-C03 preparation, you should focus on how storage classes—Standard, Intelligent-Tiering, and Glacier—map to workload access patterns to optimize both performance and cost. Backup and recovery features such as versioning, lifecycle policies, and cross-region replication were emphasized as operational best practices, ensuring resilience and compliance in real-world scenarios.

The discussion then moved to Amazon Elastic Block Store (EBS), which provides block-level storage for EC2 instances. Here, we introduced a decision tree designed to help you select the right EBS volume type for your workloads—whether General Purpose SSD for balanced performance, Provisioned IOPS SSD for latency-sensitive databases, or HDD options for throughput-oriented applications. Snapshots were highlighted as the foundational resource of backup and recovery, enabling point-in-time restoration and automation for disaster recovery. This structured approach ensures you can confidently match workload requirements to the optimal EBS solution.

From block storage, the chapter transitioned to Amazon Elastic File System (EFS), which delivers elastic, shared file storage on AWS, accessible across multiple EC2 instances. You learned to distinguish between performance modes and throughput options, both of which are frequently tested in optimization scenarios. Backup and recovery strategies included EFS replication and AWS Backup integration, reinforcing the importance of resilience for shared workloads—a common exam theme around high availability and business continuity.

The chapter next explored Amazon FSx, which provides managed file systems tailored to specialized workloads. FSx for Windows File Server offers native SMB compatibility for enterprise environments, while FSx for Lustre integrates with S3 to accelerate compute-intensive tasks. Automated daily backups and AWS Backup integration were emphasized as recovery mechanisms, while performance optimization was achieved through native protocol support and high-throughput design. For the exam, you should be prepared to identify which FSx option best aligns with workload requirements in scenario-based questions.

At this point, the chapter shifted focus from storage services to data movement and hybrid storage management. AWS DataSync was introduced as the managed service for fast, automated, and secure data transfer between on-premises systems and AWS storage services such as S3, EFS, and FSx. For CloudOps engineers, DataSync is essential for large-scale migrations, recurring data ingestion, and cross-environment synchronization, offering built-in encryption, scheduling, verification, and performance tuning without the operational burden of custom transfer tooling.

Finally, the chapter examined hybrid storage patterns using AWS Storage Gateway, which extends cloud storage into on-premises environments through file, block, and tape-based interfaces. You learned how File Gateway, Volume Gateway, and Tape Gateway enable organizations to modernize gradually while maintaining compatibility with existing applications. For SOA-C03 exam, the focus is on understanding each gateway type and its integration with S3, EBS snapshots, and archival tiers, while day-to-day CloudOps responsibilities include monitoring cache health, upload buffer performance, and connectivity to ensure predictable, resilient hybrid storage workflows.

With these foundations established, you are now prepared to move into the next chapter: "Monitoring, Logging, and Remediation," where operational visibility and corrective actions become the focus.

Exam Essentials

Know the differences between object, block, and file storage. Object storage (Amazon S3) manages data as objects with metadata and is ideal for scalability and durability. Block storage (Amazon EBS) provides raw volumes for Amazon EC2, optimized for performance and low latency. File storage (Amazon EFS and FSx) organizes data hierarchically and supports shared access across instances, making it suitable for workloads requiring traditional file system semantics.

Know that Amazon S3 provides durable, scalable object storage with multiple storage classes to optimize performance and cost. Standard is used for frequently accessed data, Intelligent-Tiering adapts to changing data access patterns, and Glacier supports archival. Backup and recovery are reinforced through versioning, lifecycle policies, and cross-region replication.

Understand that Amazon EBS delivers block-level storage for EC2 instances and supports different volume types for workload optimization. General Purpose SSD (`gp2`, `gp3`) balances cost and performance. Provisioned IOPS SSD (`io1`, `io2`, `io2 Block Express`) is designed for latency-sensitive databases with consistently high, and predictable IOPS, whereas HDD options (`st1`, `sc1`) serve throughput-oriented workloads, with large and sequential I/O. Snapshots provide point-in-time backup and recovery, ensuring resilience in disaster recovery scenarios.

Know that Amazon EBS `gp3` volumes provide independent scaling of IOPS, throughput, and volume capacity. This flexibility allows workloads to be optimized without overprovisioning storage size, a critical exam concept. Backup remains centered on snapshots, which capture consistent recovery points across scaling configurations.

Understand that Amazon EFS offers elastic, shared file storage accessible across multiple Linux EC2 instances. EFS is a regional service with a region-level fault isolation boundary, automatically replicating data across multiple Availability Zones for durability and high availability. In addition, optional cross-region replication can be configured for disaster recovery. Backup and recovery are further supported through AWS Backup integration, ensuring continuity for shared workloads.

Know that Amazon FSx delivers managed file systems tailored to specialized workloads. Amazon FSx for Windows File Server provides SMB compatibility for enterprise environments, FSx for Lustre accelerates compute-intensive tasks (such as training complex Machine Learning models) with native Amazon S3 integration, FSx for OpenZFS offers low-latency performance with snapshot and clone features, and FSx for NetApp ONTAP supports enterprise protocols with tiering, deduplication, and replication. Across all FSx options, automated backups and AWS Backup integration ensure recovery, while native protocol support and advanced features optimize performance.

Know that AWS DataSync accelerates and automates large data transfers from on-premises storage, other clouds or AWS storage to AWS. Parallel transfer mechanisms, encryption, and validation optimize performance while maintaining security. Synchronization ensures datasets remain current, supporting reliable recovery points for disaster recovery.

Know the three types of AWS Storage Gateway and their use cases. File Gateway provides NFS/SMB access backed by Amazon S3, making it the right choice for modernizing on-premises file servers and enabling low-latency access to cloud-stored objects. Volume Gateway exposes iSCSI block volumes that use EBS snapshots for backup and disaster recovery, with cached and stored modes that determine whether primary data resides on-premises or in AWS. Tape Gateway delivers a virtual tape library that integrates with existing backup software and automatically archives tapes to S3 Glacier, eliminating physical media while preserving established backup workflows. Understanding these three patterns ensures that you can quickly identify the correct gateway for hybrid storage, migration, and backup scenarios on the exam.

Review Questions

1. A critical financial database requires the highest level of consistent performance with extremely low latency (single-digit milliseconds) and guarantees of high durability (99.999%). Which EBS volume type is the appropriate choice?
   - A. Throughput Optimized HDD (`st1`)
   - B. General Purpose SSD (`gp3`)
   - C. Cold HDD (`sc1`)
   - D. Provisioned IOPS SSD (`io2`)
2. A data archival solution requires an Amazon S3 bucket configuration where data accessed one to two times per month moves to one storage class after 30 days, then to a cheaper class after 90 days, where is permanently deleted after one year of aging. Which S3 features and storage classes are necessary to implement this at the lowest cost? (Select THREE.)
   - A. S3 Versioning
   - B. S3 Lifecycle Policies
   - C. S3 Standard-IA
   - D. S3 Glacier Instant Retrieval
   - E. S3 Glacier Deep Archive
3. An application requires persistent storage that survives instance termination and provides consistent IOPS for a database workload. The storage must be accessible from a single EC2 instance. Which storage service should you use?
   - A. Amazon S3
   - B. Amazon EFS
   - C. Amazon EBS
   - D. Amazon FSx for OpenZFS
4. A company is migrating an on-premises application built on Microsoft Windows Server that requires a shared file system using the SMB protocol and Active Directory integration. Which AWS service should you use?
   - A. Amazon EFS
   - B. Amazon S3
   - C. Amazon FSx for Lustre
   - D. Amazon FSx for Windows File Server

5. A CloudOps engineer needs to perform a large-scale, one-time migration of 50TB of data from an on-premises NFS file server to Amazon EFS. The engineer needs the process to be automated, efficient, and monitored. Which service is best suited for this task?

   A. AWS Direct Connect

   B. AWS VPN

   C. AWS DataSync

   D. AWS Storage Gateway

6. A CloudOps engineer needs to increase the performance and capacity of an existing production Amazon EBS volume without causing application downtime. Which modification parameters can be adjusted dynamically while the volume is in use? (Select THREE.)

   A. Availability Zone

   B. IOPS performance

   C. Volume type

   D. Encryption status

   E. Volume size

7. To protect against accidental file deletion in an S3 bucket and allow for easy recovery of deleted objects, which feature should you enable?

   A. S3 Object Lock

   B. S3 Versioning

   C. S3 Transfer Acceleration

   D. S3 Bucket Policies

8. A team of scientists needs a very high-performance file system for short-term (temporary) computational analysis on a Linux cluster. They require extremely fast access to data while the job is running. Which AWS service fits this requirement?

   A. Amazon EFS (General Purpose)

   B. Amazon EBS (`gp3`)

   C. Amazon FSx for Lustre

   D. Amazon EFS (Max I/O)

9. A CloudOps engineer needs storage for a database workload that requires 8,000 IOPS but only 250 MiB/s throughput. The engineer wants to provision exactly these performance characteristics without overprovisioning. Which Amazon EBS volume type allows independent configuration of both IOPS and throughput?

   A. Provisioned IOPS SSD (`io1`)

   B. Provisioned IOPS SSD (`io2`)

   C. General Purpose SSD (`gp3`)

   D. Throughput Optimized HDD (`st1`)

10. A manufacturing company has an on-premises data center with limited storage capacity. They need to move large amounts of legacy backup data to Amazon S3 for long-term archiving, but their existing backup software only supports writing to local iSCSI targets. The solution must provide a local cache for low-latency access to the most recent backups while asynchronously backing up the full dataset to AWS. Which service should the CloudOps engineer implement to meet these requirements?
    - **A.** AWS Storage Gateway (File Gateway)
    - **B.** AWS DataSync
    - **C.** AWS Storage Gateway (Volume Gateway)
    - **D.** Amazon FSx for Windows File Server

11. A logging application primarily performs large, sequential writes. A CloudOps engineer is tasked with maximizing throughput (MiB/s) at the lowest cost possible. Which Amazon EBS volume types are suitable for this workload? (Select TWO.)
    - **A.** General Purpose SSD (`gp3`)
    - **B.** Provisioned IOPS SSD (`io2`)
    - **C.** Throughput Optimized HDD (`st1`)
    - **D.** Cold HDD (`sc1`)
    - **E.** General Purpose SSD (`gp2`)

12. What are the primary protocols used by Amazon EFS and Amazon FSx for Windows File Server? (Select TWO.)
    - **A.** NFS
    - **B.** iSCSI
    - **C.** HTTP API
    - **D.** SMB
    - **E.** FTP

13. A large data file must be uploaded to Amazon S3. To ensure maximum throughput and fault tolerance during the upload process, which method is the best technical implementation?
    - **A.** S3 Transfer Acceleration
    - **B.** Using a single, standard PUT request
    - **C.** S3 Multipart Uploads
    - **D.** S3 Versioning

14. A media production team needs to upload large video files (multiple gigabytes) from various global locations to a central Amazon S3 bucket in a distant AWS Region. They require the fastest possible upload speeds and resilience against network interruptions. Which Amazon S3 features should a CloudOps engineer recommend enabling/using? (Select TWO.)

    A. S3 Versioning

    B. S3 Transfer Acceleration

    C. S3 Replication

    D. S3 Multipart Uploads

    E. S3 Lifecycle Policies

15. A distributed web application running on multiple Linux EC2 instances across different Availability Zones requires a single, shared directory for persistent session state. Which AWS service provides a highly available, scalable shared file system for this purpose?

    A. Amazon EBS

    B. Amazon S3

    C. Amazon FSx for Windows File Server

    D. Amazon EFS

16. A large organization needs to facilitate ongoing, incremental replication of data from an on-premises NFS file server to an Amazon S3 bucket. The solution needs to be secure, monitored, and capable of handling incremental updates efficiently. Which services and methods are explicitly designed to facilitate this scenario? (Select TWO.)

    A. AWS Direct Connect

    B. AWS DataSync

    C. S3 Multipart Uploads

    D. S3 Transfer Acceleration

    E. S3 Replication

17. A shared web content management system running on an EC2 Auto Scaling group requires a unified data repository for user-uploaded assets (images/videos). The system needs high availability and must be simple to implement without requiring complex Amazon S3 API code changes. Which storage solution meets these criteria?

    A. Attach a dedicated EBS volume to each instance.

    B. Use Amazon EFS as a shared file system for all instances.

    C. Use Amazon S3 and require application code changes to use API calls.

    D. Use Amazon FSx for Windows File Server (if using Windows instances).

18. To ensure fast disaster recovery and point-in-time backups, a CloudOps engineer implements regular automated backups of Amazon EBS volumes and EFS file systems. Which AWS features are explicitly used for these backup operations? (Select TWO.)
    - A. S3 Versioning
    - B. EBS Snapshots
    - C. EFS Backups (via AWS Backup or EFS automated backups)
    - D. EFS Lifecycle Policies
    - E. AWS DataSync
19. An application team reports slow performance when accessing a newly deployed Amazon FSx for Windows File Server file system. The configuration is correct, in the same VPC/AZ, using SSD storage. Which configuration settings are the most likely causes of a performance bottleneck that a CloudOps engineer can immediately address? (Select TWO.)
    - A. The client EC2 instance type has insufficient network bandwidth.
    - B. The file system's provisioned throughput capacity is too low for the workload.
    - C. The application is configured to use the NFS protocol instead of SMB.
    - D. The allocated storage capacity is insufficient (affecting disk IOPS for the workload).
    - E. The client's security group does not allow enough network bandwidth.
20. A CloudOps engineer is configuring a transfer using AWS DataSync between an on-premises file system and Amazon S3. Which settings are critical for optimizing the transfer performance and network management? (Select THREE.)
    - A. Security Group rules
    - B. Bandwidth throttling limits
    - C. VPC endpoint configuration
    - D. EC2 Instance Type of the DataSync agent
    - E. Task execution configuration (e.g., maximizing bandwidth use)

Answers to Review Questions

1. D. `io2` (Provisioned IOPS SSD) volumes are engineered for the most demanding transactional workloads requiring explicit performance guarantees, extremely low latency, and the highest durability (five nines, 99.999%).
2. B, C, E. S3 Lifecycle Policies (B) provide the automation needed to transition data between classes, while S3 Standard-IA (C) is the cost-optimized tier for data accessed one to two times per month after the first 30 days, and S3 Glacier Deep Archive (E) offers the lowest-cost storage for the final long-term archival phase before deletion.

3. C. Amazon EBS provides persistent block storage that survives instance termination (when using non-ephemeral volumes), delivers consistent and provisionable IOPS (with `gp3` or `io2` types) for database workloads, and is designed to attach to a single EC2 instance, which matches the requirement.

4. D. Amazon FSx for Windows File Server is a managed Windows file system that supports the native SMB protocol and Active Directory integration, making it ideal for Windows application migrations.

5. C. AWS DataSync is an online data transfer service specifically designed for migrating large datasets from on-premises file systems (NFS/SMB) to AWS storage services like EFS, automating the logistics and optimizing performance.

6. B, C, E. Amazon EBS supports dynamic modification of volume size, volume type, and IOPS/throughput performance while the volume is attached and in use, with no downtime required. Encryption status cannot be changed dynamically. Availability Zone (AZ) cannot be changed dynamically either, because an EBS volume must reside in the same AZ where its attached instance resides.

7. B. S3 Versioning enables recovery from accidental deletions by preserving previous object versions and placing a delete marker instead of permanently removing data.

8. C. Amazon FSx for Lustre is optimized for HPC workloads requiring massive throughput and low latency, and it can be configured as a temporary scratch file system linked to S3.

9. C. `gp3` volumes allow independent configuration of IOPS (3,000–80,000) and throughput (125–2,000 MiB/s) as separate parameters. The engineer can provision exactly 8,000 IOPS and 250 MiB/s without overprovisioning either metric. `io1` and `io2` volumes couple throughput to IOPS—throughput is calculated based on provisioned IOPS and I/O size (up to 1,000 MiB/s for `io2`). To achieve 8,000 IOPS, the throughput would be determined by the IOPS-to-throughput ratio, not independently configured. `st1` volumes are throughput-optimized HDDs designed for sequential workloads, not IOPS-intensive database operations. As a result, Options A, B, and D are incorrect.

10. C. AWS Storage Gateway (Volume Gateway) (C) is the specific solution designed to provide iSCSI targets to on-premises applications. In Cached Volume mode, it stores the full dataset in S3 while maintaining a local cache of frequently accessed data, perfectly matching the backup software's requirements.

11. A, C. `st1` (C) is an HDD explicitly designed for high-throughput, sequential workloads like logging at a very low price point. `gp3` (A) is the modern SSD choice because it allows you to provision high throughput (up to 2,000 MiB/s) independently of storage size at a lower cost than previous SSD generations. In contrast, `io2` (B) is the most expensive tier and is over-engineered for simple logging; `sc1` (D) is designed for infrequent access (cold data) and would likely bottleneck under active logging writes; and `gp2` (E) is less efficient because its throughput is locked to volume size, often forcing you to pay for unused storage just to increase performance.

12. A, D. Amazon EFS uses the NFS protocol. Amazon FSx for Windows File Server uses the SMB protocol.

13. C. Multipart Uploads maximize throughput by enabling parallel uploads of chunks and provide fault tolerance by allowing individual part retries, making it the superior method for large file technical implementation.

14. B, D. S3 Transfer Acceleration optimizes transfer path over the AWS global network for distant clients. Multipart Uploads improve reliability for large files by allowing concurrent uploads of smaller parts and enabling individual part retries upon failure.

15. D. Amazon EFS is specifically designed as a regional, highly available NFS file system that can be mounted concurrently by many Linux EC2 instances, providing the necessary shared access across AZs.

16. A, B. AWS DataSync (B) is the primary service explicitly designed for this task. It automates moving data between on-premises storage (like NFS) and AWS, handles incremental updates by only copying changed files, and includes built-in encryption and monitoring via CloudWatch. AWS Direct Connect (A) provides the secure, dedicated, and consistent network connection required to facilitate large-scale, ongoing data replication between an on-premises data center and AWS.

17. B. Amazon EFS is the ideal choice here because it provides a standard NFS interface, allowing it to be mounted as a local directory on all EC2 instances in your Auto Scaling group simultaneously. This allows the application to read and write user assets exactly like a local file system, satisfying the "no complex S3 API code changes" requirement. It also provides built-in high availability by storing data across multiple Availability Zones.

18. B, C. EBS Snapshots are the fundamental mechanism for creating point-in-time, incremental backups of EBS volumes. EFS file systems have integrated automated backup capabilities (often managed through AWS Backup) for data protection.

19. A, B. Amazon FSx for Windows File Server (A) is a network-attached file system. If the EC2 instance has low baseline or burst network throughput, SMB traffic will bottleneck immediately. On Amazon FSx for Windows File Server (B), the Throughput Capacity is a specific, provisioned setting (independent of storage size) that determines the baseline and burst speeds for your file system. If your application's demand exceeds this MBps limit, FSx will throttle the I/O, leading to increased latency and slow performance. This is the primary FSx tuning knob and a classic cause of slow performance.

20. B, C, E. Bandwidth throttling limits (B) allow control over network usage. This is critical for network management. It allows you to cap the amount of network bandwidth AWS DataSync consumes, ensuring the migration doesn't saturate your connection and disrupt other critical business traffic. To optimize performance and security, you can use Interface VPC endpoints (C) to keep data traffic within the AWS private network rather than traversing the public Internet. This reduces latency and improves the reliability of the transfer. Task execution configuration (E) manages internal parameters like parallelism to maximize the transfer speed. AWS DataSync tasks have specific settings—such as transferring only changed data or adjusting the maximum bandwidth used for a specific run—that are essential for optimizing speed and efficiency.

Monitoring, Logging, and Remediation

THE AWS CERTIFIED CLOUDOPS ENGINEER ASSOCIATE (SOA-C03) EXAM OBJECTIVES COVERED IN THIS CHAPTER MAY INCLUDE, BUT ARE NOT LIMITED TO THE FOLLOWING:

✓ **Domain 1: Monitoring, Logging, Analysis, Remediation, and Performance Optimization**

- 1.1 Implement metrics, alarms, and filters by using AWS monitoring and logging services
- 1.2 Identify and remediate issues by using monitoring and availability metrics
- 1.3 Implement performance optimization strategies for compute, storage, and database resources

This chapter covers the most important aspects of cloud operations, which are the capabilities that enable your team to observe the behavior of your workloads, including its underlying infrastructure on AWS, and—most importantly—the tools you can leverage to proactively respond to any deviation from expected performance or reliability. In modern cloud environments, operational excellence depends on your ability to detect signals early, interpret them accurately, and act decisively. AWS reinforces this mindset in the Well-Architected Framework, reminding us that "AWS best practices emerge from our experience running thousands of systems at Internet scale. We prefer to use data to define best practice." Data is the foundation of observability, and the services in this chapter exist to help you collect, analyze, and operationalize that data at scale.

To build this data-driven operational posture, you need a clear understanding of how AWS surfaces telemetry across metrics, logs, traces, and events. This chapter begins by grounding you in the core monitoring and logging services—starting with Amazon CloudWatch, the central nervous system of AWS observability. CloudWatch provides the primitives you rely on every day: metrics that quantify system behavior, logs that capture detailed execution context, alarms that turn signals into actionable insights, and dashboards that help you visualize trends and anomalies. From there, you'll explore CloudTrail for auditing API activity and CloudWatch Logs for deep log analytics, completing the triad of services that underpin visibility in AWS.

Once you understand how to observe your workloads, the next step is learning how to act on that information. The second part of this chapter transitions from monitoring to automated remediation, showing how to route events with Amazon EventBridge and orchestrate responses with Systems Manager Automation runbooks. These capabilities allow your CloudOps team to close the loop between detection and correction, reducing mean time to resolution and enabling consistent, scalable operational workflows. By the end of this chapter, you'll have a cohesive understanding of how AWS monitoring, logging, and automation services work together—and why Amazon CloudWatch sits at the center of every resilient, well-operated architecture.

Monitoring and Logging on AWS

Monitoring and logging on AWS revolve around three foundational services that give you visibility into every dimension of your workloads. Amazon CloudWatch provides the operational telemetry you rely on day-to-day—metrics, alarms, dashboards, and application signals that quantify system health and performance. AWS CloudTrail complements this by recording every API call and control-plane action across your accounts, enabling governance, auditing, and security investigations. Amazon CloudWatch Logs then delivers the log-level depth needed to troubleshoot applications, analyze patterns, and retain operational history at scale. Together, these services form the core of AWS observability, ensuring you can detect, understand, and act on signals across your environment.

Yet the real power of these tools emerges only when CloudOps engineers collaborate closely with application teams and product owners to identify which signals truly matter for the business. With AWS surfacing vast amounts of telemetry, it's easy to get lost in the noise. The discipline lies in selecting the few metrics that accurately reflect user experience, reliability, and performance. This minimalist, targeted approach is what enables meaningful service level objectives (SLOs), sharpens the effectiveness of CloudWatch alarms and dashboards, and ultimately sets the stage for deeper Application Performance Monitoring (APM) insights through Application Signals.

Amazon CloudWatch

By now, you've seen Amazon CloudWatch appear throughout earlier chapters as a key enabler of performance optimization across compute, storage, and database services. In this section, we shift from using CloudWatch as a supporting tool to understanding it as a first-class observability platform—one that every CloudOps engineer must know how to implement, configure, and integrate deeply within the AWS ecosystem. Amazon CloudWatch is designed to give you real-time insight into the behavior of your workloads, unifying telemetry from AWS Resources (infrastructure), applications, and custom instrumentation into a single pane of glass. Its strength lies in the breadth of its capabilities and the consistency of its data model, allowing you to monitor application performance, assess operational health, and track resource utilization with precision.

Core Components

The following sections break down the components that enable Amazon CloudWatch's observability capabilities—metrics, logs, resolution, alarms, application signals, and dashboards. These are the building blocks you will rely on to develop a robust, efficient, and enterprise-scale observability strategy.

Metrics

Metrics are the backbone of Amazon CloudWatch and the primary signals a CloudOps engineer relies on to understand how a workload is behaving. A *metric* is simply a measurement tracked over time—`CPUUtilization` for an EC2 instance, `FreeStorageSpace` for an RDS database, or any custom value your application emits. Each metric is made up of individual data points, and those data points form a time-ordered series that CloudWatch can graph, analyze, and alarm on. If you think of your system as a living organism, metrics are its vital signs.

Most AWS services automatically publish a *standard* set of metrics at no additional cost (five-minute intervals), giving you immediate visibility into core resources like EC2, EBS, and RDS. When you need higher-resolution telemetry or application-specific insights, you can enable (for a charge) detailed monitoring (one-minute interval) or publish your own custom metrics.

While standard metrics are automatically pushed by AWS, *custom* metrics must be proactively sent by your application. This is typically done by the application calling the `PutMetricData` API or by the CloudWatch Agent collecting application-level data via `StatsD`. Alternatively, you can use Metric Filters to transform log entries into numerical metrics after they are written.

Amazon CloudWatch doesn't impose strict timing rules on custom data—you can send data points in any order and at whatever frequency your workload requires. CloudWatch then stores and aggregates these values so you can retrieve statistics such as averages, percentiles, or maximums across any time window.

Every metric lives in the region where it was created and is uniquely identified by its namespace, metric name, and optional dimensions (such as `InstanceId` or `AutoScalingGroupName`). Metrics aren't manually deleted. Instead, they age out automatically after 15 months if no new data is published. However, the availability of specific data points depends on their resolution: high-resolution (sub-minute) data is retained for three hours, one-minute data for 15 days, five-minute data for 63 days, and one-hour data for 455 days. Each data point includes a timestamp and can optionally specify a unit of measure, helping CloudWatch interpret and visualize the data correctly. As a CloudOps engineer, understanding how metrics are structured—and how AWS services publish them—is essential for building reliable alarms, dashboards, and automation workflows throughout your observability strategy.

Namespaces

A *namespace* in Amazon CloudWatch acts as a logical container for metrics, ensuring that data from different systems never gets mixed together. For a CloudOps engineer, this isolation is essential: it prevents metrics from unrelated applications or environments from being aggregated into the same graphs, alarms, or statistics. Each application, workload, or domain can have its own namespace, giving you clean boundaries and predictable organization as your observability footprint grows.

Amazon CloudWatch does not provide a default namespace, so every metric you publish—especially custom metrics—must explicitly specify one. Namespace names must use valid ASCII characters, be no more than 255 characters long, and include at least one non-whitespace character. You can use alphanumeric characters along with symbols such as periods, hyphens, underscores, slashes, hashes, colons, and spaces. This flexibility allows teams to adopt naming conventions that reflect their architecture nomenclature, such as grouping metrics by application, environment, or business domain.

AWS services follow a consistent naming pattern for their own namespaces: `AWS/service`. For example, Amazon EC2 publishes metrics under `AWS/EC2`, and other services follow similar conventions. Understanding namespaces—and using them intentionally—is key to keeping your CloudWatch environment organized, scalable, and easy to navigate as you build dashboards, alarms, and automation workflows throughout your CloudOps practice.

Dimensions

Dimensions add context to your CloudWatch metrics. They are simple name/value pairs—such as `InstanceId=i-1234567890` or `AutoScalingGroupName=web-asg`—that become part of a metric's identity. You can attach up to 30 dimensions to a single metric, and each unique combination creates a distinct variation of that metric. For a CloudOps engineer, dimensions are how you slice, categorize, and organize telemetry so you can answer precise operational questions.

Think of dimensions as the attributes that describe what a metric refers to. They help you structure your monitoring strategy by grouping metrics in meaningful ways—by instance, by environment, by application component, or by any other category that matters to your workload. Because dimensions are part of the metric's unique identifier, adding a new name/value pair doesn't just annotate the metric. It creates a new metric stream that CloudWatch tracks independently.

AWS services automatically attach relevant dimensions to the metrics they publish. This is what allows you to filter CloudWatch results so effectively. For example, when you query the `AWS/EC2` namespace and specify the `InstanceId` dimension, CloudWatch returns statistics only for that specific instance. If you omit dimensions entirely, CloudWatch aggregates data across all matching resources—this is useful for example when you want a fleet-level view of `CPUUtilization` or `NetworkIn` metrics.

Automatic aggregation applies only to certain AWS-generated metrics (e.g., `AWS/EC2`). Custom metrics never aggregate across dimensions. CloudWatch treats every unique combination of custom metrics' dimensions as a completely separate metric. For example, if you publish a custom metric called `LoginLatency` with a dimension `ServerID=Server-01`, CloudWatch will not automatically aggregate it into an "average" `LoginLatency` metric for all servers.

Understanding how dimensions shape metric filtering is an essential skill you need to master to build accurate dashboards, alarms, and automation workflows.

Logs

Logs provide the "story" behind the metrics. While a metric tells you CPU is at 100%, the logs tell you which process is causing the spike. For the exam, be aware of the following two log categories:

- **Log Groups:** A collection of logs that share retention and access policies (e.g., `/aws/lambda/MyFunction`).
- **Log Streams:** A sequence of log events from a specific source (e.g., a specific EC2 instance ID).

By centralizing text-based data from EC2 instances, AWS CloudTrail, and application-level events into Log Groups and Log Streams, CloudWatch Logs enables you to perform near real-time analysis and deep forensic troubleshooting.

This visibility is further enhanced by Log Insights, which supports three query languages (Logs Insights QL, OpenSearch PPL, and OpenSearch SQL) for analyzing log data. An optional natural language feature can help generate queries, allowing CloudOps engineers to rapidly query millions of log lines without needing to master complex query syntax.

To export logs from EC2 to CloudWatch, the instance requires the Unified CloudWatch Agent installed and an IAM role with `logs:CreateLogGroup`, `logs:CreateLogStream`, and `logs:PutLogEvents` permissions.

Resolution

Resolution determines the granularity of your data and the speed at which your alarms can react. For a CloudOps engineer, this involves choosing between Standard Resolution, where data is stored at one-minute granularity, and High Resolution, which allows for sub-minute tracking down to one-second intervals. This choice directly impacts your budget: after the AWS Free Tier (which provides ten free metrics), the price for a metric begins at $0.30 per month for the first 10,000 metrics, with tiered volume discounts dropping the price as low as $0.02 per month for larger fleets.

It is critical to distinguish these storage types from the Basic Monitoring cadence provided for free by AWS services, which publishes data every five minutes. While the base cost for a custom metric remains the same regardless of its resolution, the cost of the associated automation changes. High-Resolution Alarms are priced at $0.30 per month, triple the $0.10 cost of a standard resolution alarm. By opting for higher granularity, you empower your architecture to detect and remediate transient spikes within seconds, but you must balance this against the increased volume of API request costs and the premium on rapid-fire alerting.

Pricing varies by region and is subject to change. The figures discussed reflect typical U.S. region pricing as of 2026. Always consult the AWS CloudWatch Pricing page for current rates in your region. For more information, visit: `https://aws.amazon.com/cloudwatch/pricing/`.

Alarms

Alarms act as the proactive watchdog for your infrastructure, moving beyond simple data collection to provide a mechanism for real-time response. They function by continuously evaluating your metrics against a defined "line in the sand," or threshold, to determine if your environment is operating within healthy parameters. For a CloudOps engineer, an alarm is the primary link between visibility and action. It is the component that monitors the numerical stories told by your metrics and, upon detecting a breach, initiates the automated logic required to notify a team or remediate a failure. By shifting the burden of constant dashboard monitoring to this automated evaluation layer, you ensure that your Cloud operations team is alerted only when specific, meaningful conditions are met, allowing you to maintain high availability with minimal manual intervention.

Application Signals

Application Signals provide an automated, "set-and-forget" approach to application performance management (APM) by discovering and monitoring your services on AWS without manual instrumentation. For a CloudOps engineer, this means you no longer need to write custom code to track basic request volumes, error rates, or latencies. Application Signals identifies these "golden signals" for you. This data then flows into Service Level Objectives (SLOs), which allow you to move away from low-level infrastructure alerts and toward business-centric monitoring. By defining SLOs, you set a clear performance target—such as ensuring 99.9% of requests are successful—and use Amazon CloudWatch to track your "error budget," providing a high-level summary of whether your application is meeting the actual reliability expectations of your end-users.

To enable this powerful visibility, specific permissions must be granted to the IAM entities interacting with the service. For you, as a CloudOps engineer, this involves ensuring the `CloudWatchApplicationSignalsReadOnlyAccess` or `CloudWatchApplicationSignalsFullAccess` managed policies are attached to the relevant users or roles. Furthermore, the underlying compute resources require appropriate IAM permissions. For EC2 instances, attach the `CloudWatchAgentServerPolicy` to the instance role. For Lambda functions, the `CloudWatchLambdaApplicationSignalsExecutionRolePolicy` is automatically attached when enabling Application Signals. For EKS clusters, permissions are managed through the CloudWatch Observability EKS add-on. Without these permissions, the automated discovery and telemetry streaming will fail, leaving a gap in your application's performance visibility.

Dashboards

Dashboards serve as the essential visualization layer that synthesizes raw telemetry into a unified operational command center. For a CloudOps engineer, a dashboard is more than just a collection of graphs; it is a strategic tool that provides at-a-glance visibility into the health of complex, distributed environments. By aggregating metrics from different regions and multiple AWS accounts into a single pane of glass, you can correlate infrastructure spikes with application performance in real time. This centralized view ensures that when a system breach occurs, you are not navigating blindly between services, but are instead empowered with a comprehensive overview that facilitates rapid decision-making.

The power of these visualizations is significantly enhanced by AI-driven insights, which fundamentally transform how CloudOps engineers approach Root Cause Analysis (RCA). With CloudWatch Investigations, Amazon CloudWatch applies generative-AI agents to analyze incident-related telemetry and surface the most relevant signals, accelerating root-cause exploration. CloudWatch Investigations sift through logs and traces to surface potential hypotheses for a failure the moment an alarm fires, effectively doing the heavy lifting of "connecting the dots" between a metric spike on a dashboard and the underlying code or configuration error.

Beyond immediate troubleshooting, these AI capabilities streamline Problem Management by automating the post-incident process. Amazon CloudWatch uses machine learning to generate interactive incident reports, providing executive summaries and automated timelines that help teams understand the "why" behind an outage. By integrating with Amazon Q, dashboards can even suggest specific Systems Manager Automation runbooks for remediation. For SOA-C03 candidates, mastering these AI-enhanced dashboards means shifting from manual log-diving to a high-velocity workflow where data is automatically correlated to accelerate resolution and prevent future recurrence.

Configuring Monitoring with Amazon CloudWatch

As a CloudOps engineer, your primary goal is to ensure the health, performance, and security of your infrastructure and workloads. As mentioned earlier, Amazon CloudWatch is the "central nervous system" of your AWS environment. It transforms raw data into actionable insights, allowing you to move from reactive firefighting to proactive remediation.

Imagine you are managing a fleet of EC2 instances for a high-traffic retail site. To maintain high availability, you don't just need to know if an instance is "up" or "down." You need to know why it might be slowing down before it fails. Amazon CloudWatch operates on a three-tier lifecycle.

1. **Collect:** Gathering metrics (numbers) and logs (text).
2. **Monitor:** Visualizing that data on dashboards.
3. **Act:** Triggering alarms or automated scripts when thresholds are breached.

Metrics are time-series data points. Your job as a CloudOps engineer is to effectively leverage both standard metrics, which are automatically published by AWS services for foundational visibility, and custom metrics, which you explicitly define and publish to track specialized application-level behavior. Each of these types is explored in the following sections to help you build a complete observability strategy.

Standard Metrics

Standard metrics are the out-of-the-box performance indicators automatically published by over 80 AWS services, such as Amazon EC2, Amazon RDS, and Amazon S3. For a CloudOps engineer, these are the primary building blocks for visibility, providing essential data like CPU utilization and network throughput without requiring any manual installation or code changes. Most of these metrics are available for free through *Basic Monitoring*, which typically publishes data at a five-minute cadence. However, if your workload requires faster detection, you can enable *Detailed Monitoring* to receive these same metrics at a one-minute interval for an additional per-metric charge.

To enhance your visibility beyond the five-minute default, you can easily shift a specific instance into Detailed Monitoring using the AWS CLI. This action tells the EC2 service to start publishing the same standard metrics at a one-minute cadence, which is key for workloads where performance spikes need to be identified and remediated much faster.

```
aws ec2 monitor-instances \
    --instance-ids i-0123456789abcdef0
```

In this command:

- `--instance-ids` identifies the specific server(s) you want to upgrade to one-minute monitoring. Once this command is executed, the "producer" (the EC2 service) will increase its publishing frequency for that instance.

Exam Tip

For the SOA-C03 exam, it is vital to remember that while the metrics themselves are often free under basic monitoring, any automated actions you build on top of them—such as alarms—will incur standard monthly costs.

To explore which metrics a specific service is currently reporting to your account, you can use the CLI to filter the registry by its unique service namespace.

```
aws cloudwatch list-metrics \
    --namespace "AWS/EC2"
```

In this command:

- `--namespace` acts as a filter to narrow down the thousands of available metrics to just the service you are investigating. Standard AWS namespaces always begin with the `AWS/`prefix (e.g., `AWS/EC2`, `AWS/RDS`, `AWS/S3`). This command returns the metadata—the Metric Name and Dimensions—confirming that the service is successfully publishing data before you attempt to configure an alarm or a dashboard.

To see how much CPU one of your instances is using, you can query the `AWS/EC2` namespace.

```
aws cloudwatch get-metric-statistics \
    --namespace AWS/EC2 \
    --metric-name CPUUtilization \
    --dimensions Name=InstanceId,Value=i-0123456789abcdef0 \
    --start-time 2026-01-16T10:00:00Z \
    --end-time 2026-01-16T10:50:00Z \
    --period 300 \
    --statistics Average
```

In this command:

- `--namespace` specifies the container for the metric. `AWS/EC2` is the reserved name for EC2 metrics.
- `--metric-name` indicates the specific measurement you want to retrieve (e.g., `CPUUtilization`, `NetworkIn`).

- `--dimensions` filters the data. In this example, it ensures you are only seeing data for one specific instance rather than the aggregate of all instances in the region.
- `--start-time` is the timestamp for the beginning of the data slice you want to retrieve (must be in ISO 8601 format).
- `--end-time` is the timestamp for the end of the data slice.
- `--period` is the granularity, in seconds, of the returned data points. 300 seconds (five minutes) matches the standard monitoring interval.
- `--statistics`: is the mathematical method used to aggregate the data. Common values include `Average`, `Sum`, `Minimum`, `Maximum`, and `SampleCount`.

Custom Metrics

Standard EC2 metrics only see what the hypervisor sees (CPU, Network, Disk I/O). They cannot see "inside" the operating system to track RAM usage or disk space. Furthermore, AWS doesn't know your application's business logic. To track these, you must publish custom metrics.

Custom metrics are published to Amazon CloudWatch when your application or a script explicitly calls the `PutMetricData` API. This is usually triggered by code execution—for example, every time a user completes a checkout, your application "pushes" a data point.

Suppose you want to track how many successful checkouts your application processes in real-time.

```
aws cloudwatch put-metric-data \
    --namespace "RetailApp/OrderSystem" \
    --metric-name SuccessfulCheckouts \
    --dimensions OrderType=Digital \
    --value 1 \
    --unit Count
```

In this command:

- `--namespace` is the custom name for your metric container. Avoid starting this with `AWS/` as that is reserved for AWS services.
- `--metric-name` is the name of the custom data point you are creating.
- `--dimensions` is a name/value pair that acts as a unique identifier. Note: Custom metrics do not automatically aggregate; `OrderType=Digital` will be stored separately from `OrderType=Physical`.
- `--value` is the numerical value of the data point you are submitting.
- `--unit` specifies the type of measurement. Using the correct unit (e.g., `Count`, `Bytes`, `Seconds`, `Percent`) ensures that CloudWatch graphs and alarms scale correctly.

Amazon CloudWatch Metric Alarms

In the CloudOps lifecycle, Amazon CloudWatch Alarms serve as the essential bridge between passive data collection and active infrastructure management. While standard and custom metrics provide the raw numerical story of your environment—ranging from hypervisor-level

CPU utilization to deep, application-specific transaction counts—alarms provide the critical rationale for when those numbers actually matter. By defining a specific threshold within a namespace, such as our previously configured `RetailApp/OrderSystem`, an alarm transforms an abstract data point into a meaningful operational boundary. This allows CloudOps engineers to stop staring at dashboards and instead rely on the system to "speak up" only when performance deviates from the established baseline.

In the following sections the core components of an alarm are introduced, along with an example, which is used throughout the chapter to demonstrate how they work together.

Alarm States

The health of the resources—whose metrics (standard or custom) are monitored by Amazon CloudWatch—is expressed through three distinct alarm states, which act as the current status of your operational requirements. When a metric remains within your defined boundaries, the alarm sits in the `OK` state, signaling that the system is healthy. Conversely, when the metric crosses the threshold according to your logic, it enters the `ALARM` state, indicating a breach that requires attention. However, if the data stream is interrupted—perhaps because the CloudWatch Agent stopped reporting or an instance was terminated—the alarm enters the `INSUFFICIENT_DATA` state. For the SOA-C03 exam, mastering these states is vital, as they provide the immediate context needed to determine if you are facing a performance crisis or simply a loss of visibility.

Alarm Evaluation

To ensure that these state changes are accurate and not the result of momentary statistical "noise," CloudWatch utilizes a sophisticated evaluation process based on the "`M` out of `N`" logic. When you configure an alarm, you define a Period (the duration of a single data bucket, such as 60 seconds) and an Evaluation Period (the total number of buckets to examine, or `N`). By setting the Datapoints to Alarm (or `M`), you determine how many of those buckets must be in a breaching state to trigger a change. This mathematical windowing allows you to create a "buffer"—for instance, requiring two out of three minutes to be over a threshold—which ensures that the system only reacts to sustained trends rather than transient spikes that would otherwise trigger unnecessary operational alerts.

Alarm Actions

Standard metric alarms operate with high-resolution visibility into specific resources, which grants them a unique set of native, hardware-level capabilities that are often the first line of defense for a CloudOps engineer. Because these alarms are tied directly to resource dimensions—such as a specific `InstanceId`—they possess the unique authority to execute EC2 instance actions without any intermediary logic. This means an alarm detecting a system failure can autonomously reboot, stop, terminate, or even recover an instance, the latter of which automatically migrates a virtual machine to new underlying hardware if the original host fails.

Beyond hardware resets, metric alarms are the primary engine behind auto-scaling actions, where they directly invoke scaling policies to add or remove capacity in response to real-time demand. For communication and tracking, they natively integrate with Amazon SNS to push notifications across email or SMS and can interface directly with AWS

Systems Manager to generate OpsItems or incidents. Most significantly, metric alarms can now perform direct Lambda Invocations, allowing you to execute custom code for rapid remediation the moment a threshold is crossed.

Configuring Amazon CloudWatch Metric Alarms

When you configure an alarm via the CLI, you are defining the mathematical rules for the `ALARM` state. In the following examples, we utilize "`M` out of `N`" alarm logic to ensure mathematical accuracy and reduce false positives. This logic evaluates a sliding window of 180 seconds; if any 120 seconds (not necessarily consecutive) within that window violate the threshold, the alarm state changes to `ALARM`.

This alarm monitors the total volume of successful transactions by leveraging the custom metric `SuccessfulCheckouts`. We want to identify if business activity has dropped below a critical threshold. The alarm will change to the `ALARM` state if the total number of successful checkouts drops below five for two or more 60-second periods within a three-minute evaluation window.

```
aws cloudwatch put-metric-alarm \
    --alarm-name "LowOrderVolume-Standard" \
    --metric-name "SuccessfulCheckouts" \
    --namespace "RetailApp/OrderSystem" \
    --dimensions Name=OrderType,Value=Digital \
    --statistic "Sum" \
    --period 60 \
    --threshold 5 \
    --comparison-operator "LessThanThreshold" \
    --evaluation-periods 3 \
    --datapoints-to-alarm 2 \
    --alarm-actions "arn:aws:sns:us-east-1:123456789012:LowOrderVolume-Topic"
```

In this command:

- `--alarm-name` is a unique, descriptive name for the alarm.
- `--metric-name` & `--namespace` points the alarm to the specific metric data it should watch.
- `--dimensions` is the "identity match." By specifying `Name=OrderType, Value=Digital`, we tell Amazon CloudWatch to look specifically in the bucket where our local script is pushing digital transaction counts.
- `--statistic` is the aggregation method used to evaluate the threshold. Using `Sum` over three minutes checks the total number of orders in that window.
- `--period` is the length of time (60), in seconds, to evaluate the metric for each data point.
- `--threshold` is the value that the metric is compared against to determine if the alarm should trigger.
- `--comparison-operator` is the mathematical logic used (e.g., `LessThanThreshold`, `GreaterThanOrEqualToThreshold`).

- `--evaluation-periods` (N) is the total evaluation window size (three periods).
- `--datapoints-to-alarm` (M) is the number of breaches (two) required within the evaluation window to trigger the alarm.
- `--alarm-actions` is the Amazon Resource Name (ARN) of the action to execute when this alarm transitions to the `ALARM` state from any other state. In this case we are pushing an event to an Amazon SNS topic. Other actions could also be executing an auto-scaling policy, an EC2 recovery action, a Lambda function, a SSM integration, or even an Amazon Q Developer operational investigation.

To learn more, visit: `https://docs.aws.amazon.com/cli/latest/reference/cloudwatch/put-metric-alarm.html`.

Configuring the Unified CloudWatch Agent

In your journey toward the SOA-C03 certification, you will quickly realize that standard AWS metrics only tell half the story. While AWS can see the "outside" of your resources (like CPU load or network traffic), it cannot see "inside" the operating system. To monitor memory (RAM) usage, disk space, or application logs, you must bridge the gap using the Unified CloudWatch Agent.

Think of the Unified CloudWatch Agent as a specialized "reporting officer" stationed inside your instances and clusters. Its job is to gather granular data and ship it back to the CloudWatch "headquarters" for analysis. Your job, as a CloudOps engineer, is to master the centralized deployment and lifecycle management of this agent using AWS Systems Manager (SSM).

In the following sections you learn how to install and configure the Unified CloudWatch Agent on EC2 instances, ECS clusters, and Amazon Elastic Kubernetes Service (Amazon EKS) clusters.

Monitoring Amazon EC2 Instances with the CloudWatch Agent

For standalone EC2 instances, the CloudWatch Agent is managed as a binary package controlled via AWS Systems Manager (SSM) to allow for automated, fleet-wide administration.

Defining the CloudWatch Agent Configuration

Before using the agent, we must first draft a comprehensive JSON blueprint that instructs it on which specific OS-level performance counters to track and which log file paths to ingest. The agent is effectively a blank slate until it receives this instruction manual, which maps local system data to CloudWatch namespaces and determines the frequency of data collection. The following snippet shows an example of a JSON configuration that we saved as `metrics-config.json`.

```
{
  "metrics": {
    "namespace": "CWAgent",
    "metrics_collected": {
```

```
      "mem": { "measurement": ["mem_used_percent"] },
      "disk": { "measurement": ["disk_used_percent"], "resources": ["/"] }
    }
  },
  "logs": {
    "logs_collected": {
      "files": {
        "collect_list": [
          {
            "file_path": "/var/log/messages",
            "log_group_name": "/ec2/system-logs",
            "log_stream_name": "{instance_id}"
          }
        ]
      }
    }
  }
}
```

Key components of the JSON:

- `namespace`: The custom container in CloudWatch where these metrics will appear (defaults to `CWAgent`).
- `metrics_collected`: Specific OS-level data points (like `mem_used_percent`) that the hypervisor cannot see.
- `logs_collected`: Defines the local file paths to be streamed to CloudWatch Logs, the destination Log Group, and the Log Stream (using `{instance_id}` as a dynamic variable).

This example omits the optional `agent` section, which means the CloudWatch agent will use default values: 60-second metrics collection interval, the instance's region for the CloudWatch endpoint, and standard (non-debug) logging. You can add an `agent` section to customize these settings, such as setting `metrics_collection_interval` below 60 seconds for high-resolution metrics. For more information, visit: `https://docs.aws.amazon.com/AmazonCloudWatch/latest/monitoring/CloudWatch-Agent-Configuration-File-Details.html`.

Authorizing the Agent with IAM

Before the agent can successfully transmit data, the EC2 instance must be granted the appropriate permissions through an IAM Instance Profile. The `CloudWatchAgentServerPolicy` is the AWS-managed policy specifically designed for this agent. It provides the essential permissions required to create log groups, create log streams, and put log events, alongside the ability to publish custom metric data. For a CloudOps engineer, attaching this policy is a non-negotiable step, as omitting it will result in "Access Denied" errors, leaving your dashboards empty despite the agent service running locally.

In addition to `CloudWatchAgentServerPolicy`, ensure that the `AmazonSSMManagedInstanceCore` policy is attached so you can manage the agent remotely via Systems Manager.

Storing the Configuration in SSM Parameter Store

In this stage, we will use the CLI to upload our local JSON file into a centralized, cloud-based repository so that it can be shared across an entire fleet of instances without manually copying files to each server. By using a POSIX-like path for the parameter name, we establish a structured hierarchy that makes it easy to manage configurations for different environments, such as separating production settings from development settings.

```
aws ssm put-parameter \
    --name "/Monitoring/Config/WebServers" \
    --type "String" \
    --value file://metrics-config.json \
    --overwrite
```

In this command:

- `--name` is a unique identifier (POSIX path) for hierarchical organization.
- `--type "String"` specifies the data format as a simple string.
- `--value` points to the local file (`file://`) containing the JSON data.
- `--overwrite` allows replacing an existing parameter version to support updates.

Installing the CloudWatch Agent via SSM

With the configuration stored in the cloud, we will use the following SSM `send-command` to remotely trigger the installation of the CloudWatch Agent software package onto our target EC2 instances. This command leverages the AWS-managed package repository to ensure the latest version of the agent is downloaded and installed across our fleet simultaneously, removing the need for manual SSH access or individual package management.

```
aws ssm send-command \
    --document-name "AWS-ConfigureAWSPackage" \
    --document-version "latest" \
    --targets '[{"Key":"InstanceIds","Values":["i-0123456789abcdef0"]}]' \
    --parameters '{"action":["Install"],"name":["AmazonCloudWatchAgent"]}' \
    --timeout-seconds 600 \
    --max-concurrency "1" \
    --max-errors "0" \
    --region us-east-1
```

In this command:

- `--document-name` points to the `AWS-ConfigureAWSPackage` script for automated package management.
- `--document-version` ensures that the most recent version of the document is used.
- `--targets` identifies the specific EC2 instances that will receive the software.
- `--parameters` is set to `["Install"]` and the name is set to the official package `["AmazonCloudWatchAgent"]`.
- `--timeout-seconds` is the maximum time before the command fails.
- `--max-concurrency` is the number of instances the agent runs at a time.
- `--max-errors` when set to `"0"`, it fails immediately if any instance errors.
- `--region` is the region where SSM and EC2 resources exist.

Starting the Agent

We will now execute a command that "marries" the installed software with the stored configuration by instructing the agent to fetch its settings from the SSM path and initiate the monitoring service. This step is critical because it moves the agent from an idle state to an active state, where it begins streaming RAM, disk, and log data to the CloudWatch Dashboard for the first time.

```
aws ssm send-command \
    --document-name "AmazonCloudWatch-ManageAgent" \
    --targets '[{"Key":"InstanceIds","Values":["i-0123456789abcdef0"]}]' \
    --parameters '{
        "action": ["configure"],
        "mode": ["ec2"],
        "optionalConfigurationSource": ["ssm"],
        "optionalConfigurationLocation": ["/Monitoring/Config/WebServers"],
        "optionalRestart": ["yes"]
    }'
```

In this command:

- `--document-name` points to `AmazonCloudWatch-ManageAgent`, the document for agent lifecycle tasks.
- `--targets` identifies the specific EC2 instance(s) where the CloudWatch agent will start.
- `--parameters`:
  - `action` is set to `["configure"]` to load settings.
  - `mode` is set to `["ec2"]` to indicate the CloudWatch agent will run on an EC2 instance.
  - `optionalConfigurationSource` is set to `["ssm"]` to pull from Parameter Store.

- `optionalConfigurationLocation` is the POSIX path name whose value is the agent JSON configuration.
- `optionalRestart` is set to `["yes"]` to ensure that the agent starts immediately.

Verifying EC2 Agent Status

In the final stage of our agent deployment on an EC2 instance, we will send a query to the instance to confirm that its service is currently "running." This will also verify that the CloudWatch agent has successfully ingested the specific configuration version we intended. This verification step is a CloudOps best practice to ensure that our automation worked as expected, and that there are no "silent failures" where the agent is installed but not actually reporting data.

```
aws ssm send-command \
    --document-name "AmazonCloudWatch-ManageAgent" \
    --targets '[{"Key":"InstanceIds","Values":["i-0123456789abcdef0"]}]' \
    --parameters '{"action": ["status"]}'
```

In this command:

- `--document-name` points to `AmazonCloudWatch-ManageAgent`, the document for agent lifecycle tasks.
- `--targets` identifies the specific EC2 instance(s) where the query be sent.
- `--parameters`:
    - `action` is set to `["status"]` to return the current state (running) and identify which configuration is active.

The expected outcome, if everything works, is that the CloudWatch agent is running, the IAM permissions are in place, and the instance is online.

As shown in the following snippet, the command produces a successful SSM command invocation, whose payload contains the current CloudWatch agent status on the target EC2 instance.

```
{
  "status": "running",
  "starttime": "2026-01-18T10:00:00Z",
  "version": "1.3000.0"
}
```

To learn more, visit: `https://docs.aws.amazon.com/cli/latest/reference/ssm/send-command.html`.

Monitoring Amazon ECS and EKS Clusters with the CloudWatch Agent

In this section, we move beyond individual instances to cover the installation of the CloudWatch Agent in containerized compute environments, specifically focusing on Amazon ECS and Amazon EKS (Managed Kubernetes). Here, the agent is not managed as a standalone server binary but is instead deployed as a containerized "daemon" process that provides visibility into shared cluster resources and high-density container workloads.

Enabling Container Insights

In this initial stage, we will use the CLI to enable Container Insights at the cluster level to prepare the AWS control plane to receive and aggregate specialized performance data. This action activates the collection of granular metrics such as `CpuUtilized` and `MemoryUtilized` at the cluster, node, and task levels for observability dashboards.

```
aws ecs update-cluster-settings \
    --cluster "Production-ECS-Cluster" \
    --settings name=containerInsights,value=enabled
```

In this command:

- `--cluster` specifies the unique name of the ECS cluster you are configuring.
- `--settings` is a key-value pair where `name=containerInsights` and `value=enabled` activate automated metric collection.

Deploying the Agent as an ECS Daemon Service

To capture OS-level metrics from the EC2 instances supporting your ECS cluster, we will now deploy the agent using the `DAEMON` scheduling strategy.

```
aws ecs create-service \
    --cluster "Production-ECS-Cluster" \
    --service-name "cwagent-daemon" \
    --task-definition "cwagent-task-def" \
    --scheduling-strategy "DAEMON"
```

In this command:

- `--cluster` is the cluster where the agent service will reside.
- `--service-name` is a unique identifier for the agent service.
- `--task-definition` is the JSON definition containing the agent image and IAM roles.
- `--scheduling-strategy "DAEMON"` is a critical flag. Forces ECS to launch one copy of this task on every EC2 instance in the cluster.

Deploying the Agent on EKS (Managed Add-on)

For Amazon EKS worker nodes, we will use the EKS add-on feature to deploy the agent across the cluster as a Kubernetes DaemonSet in a single managed operation.

```
aws eks create-addon \
    --cluster-name "Production-EKS-Cluster" \
    --addon-name "amazon-cloudwatch-observability" \
    --region us-east-1
```

In this command:

- `--cluster-name` identifies the EKS cluster for deployment.
- `--addon-name` specifies `amazon-cloudwatch-observability`, the unified 2026 package for metrics and logs.
- `--region` is the AWS Region where your cluster nodes are located.

Verifying Cluster Metric Collection

In the final stage of cluster setup, we will verify that our agents are successfully communicating with the CloudWatch API by querying the specialized `ContainerInsights` namespace.

```
aws cloudwatch list-metrics \
    --namespace "ECS/ContainerInsights" \
    --metric-name "CpuUtilized"
```

In this command:

- `--namespace` uses `ContainerInsights` for EKS metrics or `ECS/ContainerInsights` for ECS metrics. Note that EKS metrics use dimensions like `ClusterName`, `Namespace`, `PodName`, and `NodeName` to differentiate from ECS metrics.
- `--metric-name` checks for a specific metric (e.g., `CpuUtilized`) to prove data ingestion has begun.

If everything works, the command produces an output similar to the following snippet, which includes a list of metrics to confirm the agent is successfully pushing data.


```
{
    "Metrics": [
        {
            "Namespace": "ECS/ContainerInsights",
            "MetricName": "CpuUtilized",
            "Dimensions": [
                {
                    "Name": "ClusterName",
                    "Value": "Production-ECS-Cluster"
                }
            ]
        },
        {
            "Namespace": "ECS/ContainerInsights",
            "MetricName": "CpuUtilized",
            "Dimensions": [
                {
                    "Name": "ClusterName",
                    "Value": "Production-ECS-Cluster"
                },
                {
```

```
                    "Name": "ServiceName",
                    "Value": "web-frontend-service"
                }
            ]
        }
    ]
}
```


There are a few observations you need to be aware of for the exam:

- **Metrics array:** Contains every unique combination of dimensions that has reported data in the last two weeks.
- **Dimensions:** These are the critical identifiers for your cluster monitoring. In `ECS/ContainerInsights`, you will see metrics sliced by `ClusterName`, `ServiceName`, and even `TaskId` if granular monitoring is enabled.
- **Namespace:** Confirms that the data is stored in the correct containerized monitoring bucket.
- **Empty result:** If the output is an empty metrics array, it indicates that either Container Insights is not enabled or the agent lacks the IAM permissions (`cloudwatch:PutMetricData`) to publish data points.

Identification vs. Retrieval

If a question asks how to verify if a metric is available, use `list-metrics`. If it asks for the highest value over the last hour, use `get-metric-statistics`. The `aws cloudwatch list-metrics` command confirms the agent is communicating by returning metadata (Names/Dimensions), but provides no numerical values. To view actual performance, use `aws cloudwatch get-metric-statistics`. This retrieves data points (numerical values/timestamps) for analysis and troubleshooting.

Alarms Troubleshooting

In the current landscape of AWS cloud operations, your value as a CloudOps engineer is measured by your ability to move away from manual monitoring and shift toward self-healing architectures. This strategy is fully aligned with two important design principles of the AWS Well-Architected Framework. The first principle states, "Safely automate where possible" and is part of the Operational Excellence pillar. The second principle states, "Automatically recover from failure" and is part of the Reliability pillar. To realize this strategy a deep mastery of Amazon CloudWatch Alarms is required. As you learned in the previous sections, alarms are the primary mechanism for detecting issues and triggering remediation. Whether you are dealing with a simple metric crossing a threshold or complex, multi-layered dependencies, Amazon CloudWatch Alarms act as the "trigger" for your automation.

Amazon CloudWatch Composite Alarms

The journey of automated remediation begins with the concept of metric alarms, which you previously learned. These alarms watch a single metric—such as the `CPUUtilization` (standard metric) of an EC2 instance or the `SuccessfulCheckouts` (custom metric) of your application—and change state based on a defined threshold. While powerful, relying solely on single metric alarms in a complex environment often leads to "alarm fatigue." For instance, if a network outage occurs, you might receive 50 individual alarms for 50 different instances, even though there is only one root cause.

To solve this, AWS provides *composite alarms*. A composite alarm does not watch the change of state for a single metric directly; instead, it watches the change of state for multiple metrics altogether. This allows you to create sophisticated "AND/OR" performance or failure detection logic. You might create a composite alarm that only fires if both orders are low and system latency is elevated, ensuring that you only wake up a CloudOps engineer when a performance spike is actually impacting business outcomes (true positive).

Unlike metric alarms, composite alarms are designed for high-level decision-making and the reduction of operational noise, which fundamentally changes how they interact with other AWS services. Because a composite alarm evaluates a Boolean expression (like Alarm A AND Alarm B) rather than a single resource, it lacks the direct "dimension awareness" required to natively reboot a specific server or trigger a scaling group. Instead, its invokable actions are focused on high-tier orchestration and notification.

More specifically, when a composite alarm enters the `ALARM` state, it primarily leverages SNS notifications to alert CloudOps engineers or incident response teams only when a true system-wide failure is confirmed (a true positive). Like their metric-based counterparts, they can directly trigger AWS Lambda functions to begin complex, multi-service recovery workflows and can automatically create incidents or OpsItems in Systems Manager (SSM). The narrative of a composite alarm is one of intelligence; it acts as the "brain" that suppresses individual alerts and only initiates high-stakes actions when the combined state of your infrastructure warrants a critical intervention.

Table 6.1 compares these two types of alarms. Use it as a reference for the exam.

Configuring Amazon CloudWatch Composite Alarms

In the following sections, you walk through the steps to configure a composite alarm. We follow a best practice designed to transform raw metric data into a sophisticated, automated execution chain for rapid remediation.

Establishing a Baseline

Before you can build complex logic, you must establish your base-layer metric alarms.

TABLE 6.1 Metric Alarm vs. Composite Alarm Comparison

Feature	Metric Alarm	Composite Alarm
Primary Goal	Monitor specific resource performance	Reduce noise by aggregating alarm states
Native EC2 Actions	Yes (reboot, stop, terminate, recover)	No (cannot natively reboot an instance)
Auto-Scaling Actions	Yes (standard for scaling policies)	No (not natively supported for auto-scaling)
Lambda Integration Actions	Yes (direct invocation)	Yes (direct invocation)
SNS/SSM Integration Actions	Yes	Yes
Amazon Q Developer Operational Investigation Actions[1]	Yes	No

[1]Amazon Q Developer integration with CloudWatch alarms may vary by region and requires additional setup. Verify current availability in AWS documentation.

Let's build on the previously introduced custom metric alarm `LowOrderVolume-Standard` to design a composite alarm that takes into account low order sales *and* the application performance latency.

To bridge these concepts, we must first address how the underlying application performance data reaches the cloud. Unlike standard AWS metrics, application-level latency is not captured automatically. It requires a proactive "heartbeat" of data generated from within the resource itself. To accomplish this, a local monitoring script resides on the instance, continuously calculating response times and executing the following `put-metric-data` command at regular intervals:

```
aws cloudwatch put-metric-data \
    --namespace "RetailApp/OrderSystem" \
    --metric-data '{
        "MetricName": "Latency",
        "Dimensions": [{ "Name": "InstanceId", "Value":
"i-0123456789abcdef0" }],
        "Unit": "Milliseconds",
        "Value": 650,
        "StorageResolution": 60
    }'
```

In the previous example, the local script pushed a latency data point for the instance with a value of 650 ms. This repetitive cycle ensures the metric is initialized in the Amazon CloudWatch registry and maintains a constant stream of telemetry, tagged with the specific `InstanceId` dimension that allows for precise, resource-level targeting.

The following custom metric alarm monitors the time it takes for the application to respond to user requests. We want to identify if the user experience is degrading, which often indicates a bigger problem such as an impending system failure. The alarm will change to the `ALARM` state if the average response time exceeds `500 ms` (500 ms) for two or more 60-second periods within a three-minute evaluation window.

Unlike with `LowOrderVolume-Standard`, instead of simply publishing a notification to the Amazon SNS `LowOrderVolume-Topic`, we will attach a native EC2 action to this alarm. Because this is a metric alarm with a specific `InstanceId` dimension, Amazon CloudWatch knows exactly which resource to target if a reboot is required to clear the latency.

```
aws cloudwatch put-metric-alarm \
    --alarm-name "HighAppLatency-Standard" \
    --metric-name "Latency" \
    --namespace "RetailApp/OrderSystem" \
    --dimensions Name=InstanceId,Value=i-0123456789abcdef0 \
    --statistic "Average" \
    --period 60 \
    --threshold 500 \
    --comparison-operator "GreaterThanThreshold" \
    --evaluation-periods 3 \
    --datapoints-to-alarm 2 \
    --alarm-actions "arn:aws:automate:us-east-1:ec2:reboot"
```

In this command:

- `--alarm-name` is the unique identifier for managing this alarm.
- `--metric-name` & `--namespace` pinpoint the data source in the `RetailApp/OrderSystem` namespace.
- `--dimensions` specifies the `InstanceId`. This is required for native actions like reboot so CloudWatch knows which specific instance to reset.
- `--statistic` is the aggregation method (`Sum` for counts, `Average` for latency).
- `--period` is the 60-second granularity of each evaluated data point.
- `--threshold` is the value (5 orders or 500 ms) compared against the metric.
- `--comparison-operator` is the logic for the breach (`LessThanThreshold` or `GreaterThanThreshold`).
- `--evaluation-periods` (N) is the total window size (three periods).
- `--datapoints-to-alarm` (M) is the number of breaches (two) required within that window to trigger the alarm.

- `--alarm-actions` is the ARN of the service to invoke when this alarm transitions to the ALARM state from any other state. Using `arn:aws:automate:us-east-1:ec2:reboot` triggers a control plane EC2 `RebootInstances` API operation on the specific instance identified in the alarm's `InstanceId` dimension, causing AWS to perform a managed reboot of that instance.

Layering Intelligence with Composite Alarms

Once you have these baseline alarms (`LowOrderVolume-Standard` and `HighAppLatency-Standard`), you can aggregate them into a composite alarm. This is particularly useful for identifying "invokable actions" that should only occur under multi-factor conditions. The core of a composite alarm is the Alarm Rule, which uses Boolean logic. Note that because a composite alarm has no dimensions of its own, it cannot natively "reboot" an instance; instead, it triggers broader orchestration.

The following example shows how you can trigger a high-priority incident only if both "child" alarms fire simultaneously.

```
aws cloudwatch put-composite-alarm \
    --alarm-name "CriticalBusinessImpact-Composite" \
    --alarm-rule "ALARM(LowOrderVolume-Standard) AND
ALARM(HighAppLatency-Standard)" \
    --alarm-actions "arn:aws:sns:us-east-1:123456789012:HighPriorityAlerts" \
    --actions-suppressor "arn:aws:cloudwatch:us-east-1:123456789012:alarm:
MaintenanceWindowActive"
```

In this command:

- `--alarm-rule` is the Boolean AND expression requiring both child alarms to be active.
- `--alarm-actions` is the high-priority ARN invoked only when the complex condition is met.
- `--actions-suppressor` is a feature that prevents actions if a specific "suppressor" alarm (like a maintenance flag) is active, reducing noise during planned work.

To learn more, visit: `https://docs.aws.amazon.com/cli/latest/reference/cloudwatch/put-composite-alarm.html`.

As a summary, the components that make up a composite alarm are as follows:

- **Child alarm 1** (`LowOrderVolume-Standard`): Triggers if total checkouts drop below five for two out of three periods (60-second periods).
- **Child alarm 2** (`HighAppLatency-Standard`): Triggers if `i-0123456789abcdef0` exceeds 500 ms for two out of three periods (each period is 60 seconds, totaling two minutes of breach within a three-minute window).
- **Composite alarm logic:** Uses the AND operator in the alarm-rule, meaning it only enters the ALARM state if both of these specific conditions are met simultaneously. To learn more, visit: `https://docs.aws.amazon.com/AmazonCloudWatch/latest/monitoring/Create_Composite_Alarm.html`.

Exam Tip

For the exam, remember that child alarms do not lose their own actions just because they are part of a composite alarm. A child alarm action is good for low-impact local remediation (like rebooting a single instance). A composite alarm action is good for high-impact business notification (like paging the on-call CloudOps engineer) only when a combination of factors indicates a true failure.

In our example, if the latency was high for two minutes, but the checkout volume remained healthy (e.g., ten orders per minute), the child latency alarm (`HighAppLatency-Standard`) would fire—causing the instance to reboot—but the composite alarm would remain `OK`. This demonstrates how composite alarms prevent "alert fatigue" by requiring multiple points of failure before escalating to a critical incident.

This decoupling allows you to attempt an automated fix (the reboot) quietly in the background without necessarily escalating the situation to a critical business alert unless the automated fix fails to solve the broader business problem (the low order volume).

Identifying and Troubleshooting the Remediation Path

Your job as a CloudOps engineer is not done once the command is sent. You must be able to identify where a break in the remediation chain occurred by inspecting the alarm history.

CloudWatch retains alarm history for 30 days. When troubleshooting remediation issues, ensure you're investigating events within this timeframe. For longer-term alarm history analysis, use Amazon EventBridge (covered in detail later) to capture alarm state changes and send them to CloudWatch Logs.

```
aws cloudwatch describe-alarm-history \
    --alarm-name "CriticalBusinessImpact-Composite" \
    --history-item-type "Action" \
    --start-date 2026-01-20T12:00:00Z
```

In this command:

- `--alarm-name` filters history specifically for the composite alarm.
- `--history-item-type` setting this to `"Action"` is the primary troubleshooting filter. It limits the output to logs of attempted executions.
- `--start-date` is an ISO 8601 timestamp to narrow the search to the specific window when the failure occurred.

To learn more, visit: `https://docs.aws.amazon.com/cli/latest/reference/cloudwatch/describe-alarm-history.html`.

When you run this command, you will receive a JSON response. To troubleshoot, you must identify these specific keys:

- `HistoryItemType`: Should be `Action`.
- `HistorySummary`: A brief description. Look for "Successfully executed action" vs. "Failed to execute action."

- `HistoryData`: A nested JSON string (which you may need to parse) containing:
  - `actionState`: If this says `Failed`, the issue is likely IAM permissions. The alarm's service role might be missing, for example, the permissions: `ssm:StartAutomationExecution` or `sns:Publish`.
  - `error`: Provides a detailed reason for failure, such as "Resource not found" or "Access Denied."
  - `stateUpdateTimestamp`: Use this to correlate the exact second the alarm fired with the logs in Amazon EventBridge or SSM.

To master the automated remediation lifecycle for the SOA-C03 exam, you must visualize the operational flow as a continuous chain. The process begins when a CloudWatch Alarm detects a breach and triggers the appropriate action—whether that means rebooting an unhealthy instance, opening an OpsItem, or notifying your CloudOps team of degraded business metrics. From there, Amazon CloudWatch captures every transition in the alarm's history, giving you a chronological record you can interrogate to validate that the remediation path behaved as expected. By reviewing these state changes and correlating them with application behavior, you build the insights required to troubleshoot complex operational scenarios under exam conditions. The next step is learning how to surface these signals visually. This is where Amazon CloudWatch Dashboards come into play, allowing you to transform raw alarm activity, performance metrics, and application KPIs into a unified operational view that makes patterns—and problems—visible.

Building Dashboards

By this point in the chapter, you've created meaningful metrics, configured the Unified CloudWatch Agent, built alarms that detect operational anomalies, and learned how to troubleshoot them. The final step in your CloudWatch journey is to bring all of this telemetry together into a single, coherent operational view. CloudWatch Dashboards give CloudOps engineers the ability to visualize the health and performance of their workloads in real time, across multiple AWS accounts and Regions, using fully customizable and shareable dashboards. For SOA-C03 candidates, dashboards are not just a convenience—they are an essential tool for situational awareness, operational readiness, and cross-team collaboration.

A CloudWatch Dashboard is essentially a canvas where you assemble widgets that display metrics, alarms, logs, and even custom text. You can leverage several specialized widget types to represent your data:

- **Line (Graph):** The standard for comparing time-series data from multiple sources to identify outliers and trends.
- **Table:** Provides a structured, tabular view of multiple metrics or resources, allowing for quick sorting and comparison of current values.
- **Number (Graph):** Displays the single most recent value for a critical metric.
- **Gauge (Graph):** Visualizes a metric relative to a minimum and maximum threshold (e.g., Disk % Used).

- **Metric Explorer:** A dynamic widget that automatically discovers and visualizes metrics based on tags or properties, ensuring that as you scale your fleet, new resources are automatically reflected on the dashboard.
- **Query Result (Logs):** Displays the output of a CloudWatch Logs Insights query directly on the board.
- **Text:** Allows for adding static documentation, runbook links, or section headers using Markdown.

For a complete reference of CloudWatch widgets, visit: `https://docs.aws.amazon.com/AmazonCloudWatch/latest/monitoring/create-and-work-with-widgets.html`.

The power of dashboards comes from their flexibility: you can mix metrics from different services, overlay multiple time series on the same graph, and combine data from multiple accounts and regions using AWS Organizations and CloudWatch cross-account observability. This means your operations team can monitor the entire `RetailApp` ecosystem—compute, storage, databases, and application-level KPIs—from a single pane of glass, regardless of where those resources live.

To make this concrete, consider the metrics you created earlier in this chapter: `RetailApp/OrderSystem SuccessfulCheckouts` and `RetailApp/OrderSystem Latency`. These two metrics represent the heartbeat of the order-processing workflow. On a dashboard, you might place them side by side: a line graph showing successful checkouts over time, and another showing application latency. When read together, these metrics tell a story. A drop in successful checkouts accompanied by a spike in latency is a strong signal of application degradation—something your `LowOrderVolume-Standard` and `HighAppLatency-Standard` alarms are already watching for. Dashboards allow you to visualize these relationships continuously, not just when an alarm fires.

Dashboards also shine when you need to correlate signals across services. For example, you might add widgets showing EC2 CPU utilization, Application Load Balancer request counts, DynamoDB read/write capacity usage, or even custom metrics emitted by the Unified CloudWatch Agent. When these signals are displayed together, CloudOps engineers can quickly identify whether a performance issue originates in the application layer, the infrastructure layer, or an external dependency. This holistic visibility is exactly what the SOA-C03 exam expects you to understand: dashboards are not just visualizations—they are operational decision-making tools.

Another key capability is cross-account and cross-region dashboards. In large organizations, workloads are often distributed across multiple accounts for security and governance reasons, and across regions for latency or resilience. CloudWatch allows you to pull metrics from these disparate environments into a single dashboard, provided you've enabled cross-account observability. This means your operations team can monitor the entire `RetailApp` deployment—whether it spans `us-east-1`, `us-west-2`, or multiple business units—without switching consoles or losing context. For exam purposes, remember that dashboards can reference any metric you have permission to view, regardless of where it originates.

While a dashboard can view metrics from anywhere, the alarms you build must reside in the same region as the metric they are monitoring. Dashboards are for visibility (global), but alarms are for detection (regional).

Finally, dashboards are shareable and versionable, which makes them ideal for team-based operations. You can grant read-only access to stakeholders, embed dashboards in operational runbooks, or export them as JSON for version control. Many CloudOps teams treat dashboards as living artifacts: they evolve as the application evolves, and they are refined during Game Days—the AWS Well-Architected practice of testing systems under controlled failure conditions. Game Days often reveal blind spots in observability, and dashboards are one of the first places teams apply those lessons.

With dashboards in place, you've completed the study of the monitoring capabilities provided by Amazon CloudWatch. The next step is to explore the logs that enable the diagnostic depth behind those metrics with Amazon CloudWatch Logs.

Amazon CloudWatch Logs

Amazon CloudWatch metrics tell you what is happening. Amazon CloudWatch Logs tell you why. Logs provide the granular, line-by-line detail that helps CloudOps engineers understand the root cause of anomalies surfaced by alarms and dashboards. For SOA-C03 candidates, CloudWatch Logs is a foundational service because it bridges the gap between high-level signals and low-level diagnostics, enabling both troubleshooting and automation.

Amazon CloudWatch Logs ingests, stores, indexes, and analyzes log data from virtually any source: EC2 instances, Lambda functions, containerized workloads, on-premises servers, and even custom applications. Earlier in this chapter, you learned how to configure the Unified CloudWatch Agent to publish system-level logs. This section explores how those logs are organized, queried, and used to drive operational insights.

CloudWatch Logs encrypts all log data at rest by default using AES-GCM. For additional control, you can use AWS KMS customer-managed keys to encrypt log groups and manage key rotation policies.

Core Components

By now, you've already seen how CloudWatch organizes log data into log groups and log streams, and how the Unified CloudWatch Agent publishes system-level and application-level logs into that structure. In this section, we build on that foundation and focus on the components that make CloudWatch Logs more than just a storage layer—the features that turn raw log lines into operational insight.

At the core of CloudWatch Logs is the *log event*, the individual timestamped entry that captures what your workload was doing at a specific moment. These events are indexed as they arrive, which allows CloudOps engineers to search, filter, and analyze them with minimal latency. This indexing is what makes CloudWatch Logs useful during incident response: when your `HighAppLatency-Standard` alarm fires, you can immediately pivot into the relevant log group and inspect slow requests, dependency failures, or stack traces without waiting for ingestion delays.

CloudWatch Logs also gives you control over *retention policies*, allowing you to define how long log data should be kept based on compliance, cost, or operational needs. Short-lived application logs might only need a few days of retention, while audit-sensitive logs may require months or years. For the SOA-C03 exam, remember that retention is configured at the log-group level and can be changed at any time without interrupting ingestion.

Amazon CloudWatch Logs retains log data indefinitely by default, meaning every new log group starts with a "Never Expire" policy unless you explicitly choose a shorter retention period.This default is safe from a data-preservation standpoint, but it has direct cost implications: CloudWatch Logs charges for ingestion (commonly around $0.50 per GB ingested) and for storage (commonly around $0.03 per GB per month). If you leave retention at "Never Expire," logs accumulate in relatively expensive hot storage, and costs grow predictably over time. Setting an appropriate retention window is both an operational best practice and a FinOps expectation for the SOA-C03 exam.

Another key capability is *metric filters*, which allow you to extract numerical signals from log data and convert them into CloudWatch metrics. This is where logs and metrics converge. For example, if your `RetailApp` logs contain entries like `CheckoutFailed`, you can create a metric filter that counts these occurrences and emits a metric such as `RetailApp/OrderSystem FailedCheckouts`. That metric can then feed an alarm, appear on a dashboard, or trigger an EventBridge rule. Metric filters are a powerful way to turn unstructured log data into structured operational signals.

For real-time processing, CloudWatch Logs supports *subscription filters*, which continuously stream log events to downstream consumers such as Lambda, Kinesis Data Streams, or OpenSearch. This enables advanced use cases like anomaly detection, custom alerting, or centralized log analytics across multiple accounts. Subscription filters are especially relevant in multi-account environments, where logs from many workloads need to be aggregated into a single analytics pipeline.

Finally, CloudWatch Logs includes Logs Insights, a purpose-built query engine—Logs Insights QL—that lets you search, aggregate, and visualize log data using a SQL-like query language. Logs Insights is optimized for speed and cost-efficiency, making it ideal for investigating issues surfaced by your alarms or dashboards. When your `LowOrderVolume-Standard` alarm fires, a Logs Insights query can quickly reveal whether checkout failures correlate with specific endpoints, user segments, or dependency timeouts.

To learn more about Logs Insights QL, visit: `https://docs.aws.amazon.com/AmazonCloudWatch/latest/logs/CWL_AnalyzeLogData_Tutorials.html`.

Together, these components transform CloudWatch Logs from a passive repository into an active diagnostic platform—one that complements your metrics, alarms, and dashboards, and prepares you for the next layer of observability: AWS CloudTrail, where you'll gain visibility into the control-plane actions that shape your AWS environment.

AWS CloudTrail

While CloudWatch Logs captures application and system telemetry, AWS CloudTrail captures control-plane activity—the API calls that configure, modify, or operate your AWS Resources. CloudTrail is essential for governance, auditing, security investigations, and compliance. For SOA-C03 candidates, CloudTrail represents the visibility layer that ensures operational actions are accountable and traceable.

CloudTrail records every API call made through the AWS Management Console, CLI, SDKs, and many AWS services. Each event includes the identity of the caller, the action performed, the parameters passed, the response returned, and the timestamp. This makes CloudTrail the authoritative source for answering questions like these:

- Who terminated an EC2 instance
- When was a security group modified
- Which IAM role assumed privileges
- What automation triggered a particular change

CloudTrail logs can be delivered to S3 for long-term retention, to CloudWatch Logs for real-time analysis, or to EventBridge for automated responses. This last capability is especially important: CloudTrail events can trigger EventBridge rules that enforce governance or initiate remediation workflows. For example, you can automatically detect and revert unauthorized IAM changes, or notify security teams when sensitive resources are modified.

CloudTrail also integrates with CloudTrail Lake, which provides SQL-based querying across years of audit data without managing storage or indexing. This is useful for compliance audits, forensic investigations, and operational reviews.

With CloudTrail, you now have full visibility into both the data plane (CloudWatch Logs) and the control plane (CloudTrail). This completes the observability foundation needed to understand and trust the signals that drive automated remediation.

The next section builds directly on this foundation. You'll learn how to turn CloudWatch alarms and log-derived signals into automated, event-driven workflows using Amazon EventBridge and Systems Manager Automation.

Advanced Automatic Remediation Techniques

Earlier in this chapter, in the "Alarms Troubleshooting" section, we explored the simplest form of automatic remediation: attaching a direct action to a CloudWatch alarm. Restarting an EC2 instance when a status check fails is a perfect example of this pattern. It's fast, intuitive, and works well for isolated, single-resource issues where the corrective action is straightforward. But as soon as remediation requires additional context, coordination across multiple services, or conditional logic, this direct-action model begins to show its limits. Real-world CloudOps environments rarely present problems that can be solved by a single API call, and AWS expects SOA-C03 candidates to understand when this simple approach is no longer sufficient.

This section builds on that foundation and introduces the techniques needed to remediate complex, multi-signal operational scenarios—the kind that benefit from event-driven architectures. These scenarios require capturing meaningful events the moment they occur, enriching them with the right context, routing them intelligently, and invoking automation workflows capable of performing multi-step corrective actions. And because the AWS Well-Architected Framework encourages teams to "improve through Game Days," these advanced remediation pipelines should be validated under controlled failure conditions using Game Days—AWS's approach to chaos engineering. Game Days give CloudOps engineers the confidence that their event-driven remediation logic behaves correctly under stress, scales predictably, and recovers gracefully.

This is where Amazon EventBridge becomes essential. EventBridge provides the event-driven backbone that connects CloudWatch alarms, operational signals, and Systems Manager Automation runbooks into a cohesive, scalable remediation pipeline. The sections that follow walk through this pipeline step by step: starting with EventBridge as the routing fabric, then exploring how events are enriched and delivered, and finally showing how Automation runbooks implement the logic that closes the loop.

Amazon EventBridge

Modern cloud environments are constantly in motion. Workloads may generate unpredictable traffic patterns, user interactions may spike without warning, and microservices may communicate in bursts rather than steady flows. Meanwhile, the underlying infrastructure adjusts to support this activity—adding or removing compute capacity, shifting workloads, and responding to health signals. In the cloud, this often means horizontal scaling (scale-out and scale-in) rather than vertical scaling (scale-up and scale-down), because distributing load across multiple smaller instances is faster, safer, and more resilient than resizing a single server. Do you remember the first general design principle—"Stop guessing your capacity needs"—of the AWS Well-Architected Framework (WAF) you learned in Chapter 1? With so many independent components changing state in real time, CloudOps engineers need a way for systems to react the moment something meaningful happens. This is the essence of Event-Driven Architectures.

Event-Driven Architectures

An *event-driven architecture (EDA)* is a design approach where systems communicate by producing and consuming events—small, self-contained messages that describe something that happened. Instead of services polling each other or relying on tightly coupled integrations, each component simply produces (or emits) events and reacts to events that matter to it.

This model is essential in modern applications because it enables:

Loose Coupling Producers don't need to know who consumes their events, making systems easier to evolve and safer to change. This is a true enabler of another general design principle of the AWS WAF—"Consider evolutionary architectures."

Real-Time Responsiveness Systems react immediately when something happens—ideal for remediation, scaling, and operational automation. Reacting instantly to events aligns with the cloud philosophy of scaling based on demand rather than prediction. It also reinforces the idea that operational responses should be automated, not manual or scheduled—in full alignment with the Operational Excellence design principle of the AWS WAF "Safely automate where possible."

High Scalability Event streams naturally fan out to many consumers without adding load to the producer. This is exactly what the AWS WAF encourages ("Use managed services," another design principle of the Operational Excellence pillar): rely on managed, elastic services that scale automatically and remove undifferentiated heavy lifting.

Operational Resilience In an EDA, failures in one component don't cascade. Events can be retried, buffered, or rerouted. Chapter 7 covers this exam domain in detail. Operational resilience directly reflects the AWS WAF's Operational Excellence design principle "Anticipate failure," and build systems that recover automatically.

For you, as a CloudOps engineer preparing for the SOA-C03 exam, the key insight is this:

> Event-driven architectures let you automate operational responses the moment an event occurs, without polling or manual intervention.

Amazon EventBridge is AWS's native service for building these architectures, enabling your CloudOps team to respond to operational signals "here and now," the moment they occur.

Core Components

Amazon EventBridge provides the backbone for event-driven CloudOps workflows. Figure 6.1 illustrates how these components interact: event sources produce events, event buses receive them by means of rules, which match them using event patterns, and targets act on them. Once you understand these relationships, the remediation patterns you'll build later become intuitive.

Pipes and Schedulers—The Other EventBridge Engines

Amazon EventBridge includes three engines, all shown in Figure 6.1:

- **Event Buses:** The routing fabric (the focus of this chapter)
- **Pipes:** Point-to-point data movement for stream and queue-based sources
- **Schedulers:** Time-based invocation for cron-like automation

Pipes are ideal when you need to move records from sources like DynamoDB Streams or SQS directly into a target with optional filtering or enrichment. Schedulers are ideal when you need to trigger actions at specific times or intervals. Both are powerful, but neither is used in CloudWatch-driven remediation, which is fundamentally event-driven, not time-driven or stream-driven.

This chapter focuses on Event Buses because they are the engine that powers CloudWatch → EventBridge → SSM Automation remediation workflows.

Event Buses

Readers with an enterprise background will recognize the conceptual similarity between an event bus in Amazon EventBridge and a traditional on-premises enterprise service bus (ESB), such as IBM Integration Bus (formerly known as IBM WebSphere Message Broker). Both act as central communication backbones. But EventBridge is the cloud-native evolution of that idea: fully managed, serverless, highly scalable, and intentionally lightweight.

Unlike ESBs, which often acted as transformation engines and workflow coordinators, EventBridge is designed to be a stateless routing fabric. It receives events, evaluates them against rules, and forwards them to the appropriate targets without performing heavy mediation or multi-step processing. This simplicity is a feature, not a limitation—it keeps EventBridge predictable, elastic, and easy to reason about in automated remediation workflows.

EventBridge provides three types of event buses, each serving a distinct purpose:

Default Event Bus This is the built-in bus that every AWS account receives automatically. All AWS service events—including CloudWatch alarm state changes—flow here without any configuration. For CloudOps engineers, this is the bus that powers most remediation workflows.

FIGURE 6.1 Amazon EventBridge core components.

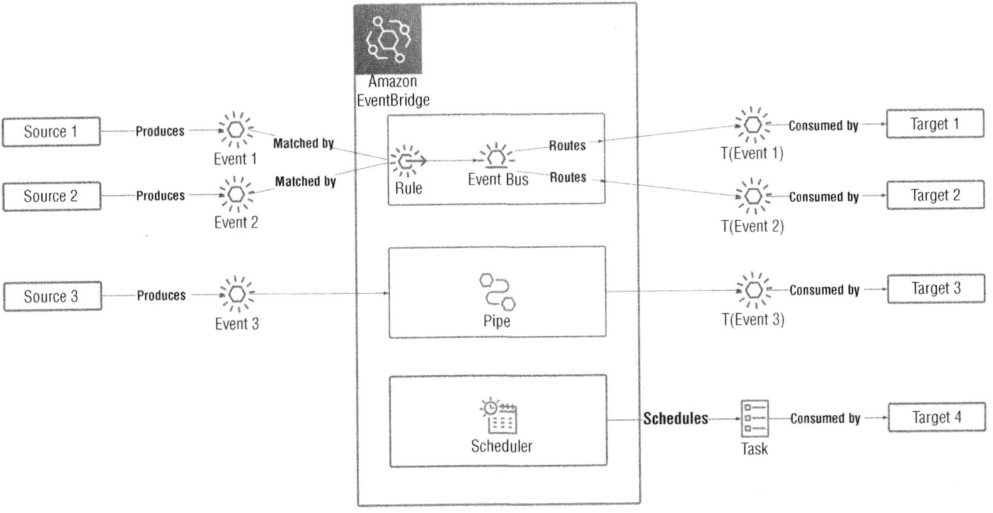

Custom Event Buses These are application-specific buses you create to decouple microservices or domain-driven components. They allow teams to publish their own business events without mixing them with AWS service events. In large systems, custom buses help maintain separation of duties and reduce noise.

Partner Event Buses Many SaaS providers integrate directly with EventBridge. When you authorize a partner, AWS provisions a dedicated partner event bus in your account where that provider can publish events natively. This eliminates the need for webhooks, polling, or custom adapters—a major departure from the ESB era.

Together, these three bus types give EventBridge a clean, scalable structure: AWS services publish to the default event bus, your applications publish to custom event buses, and SaaS vendors publish to partner event buses. Amazon EventBridge then routes all of these events using the same stateless, declarative model.

Events

An *event* is a structured JSON document describing something that happened in your environment. Amazon CloudWatch alarm transitions, EC2 state changes, auto-scaling activities, and Systems Manager notifications all appear as events on the EventBridge bus. Each event captures a precise moment when the system signals that something has become meaningful or actionable.

For CloudOps engineers, it's helpful to think of an event as the system's "here and now"[1]—a snapshot of state, the exact instant (when) and component localization (where) something requires attention. This mindset makes it easier to reason about automated remediation: you're not polling for conditions or waiting for scheduled checks; you're responding to the system the moment it tells you, "An action is required here and now."

Amazon CloudWatch alarm events are especially important in remediation workflows. They contain:

- The alarm name
- The previous and new state
- Timestamps
- Metric dimensions (for metric alarms)
- Only the state of child alarms (for composite alarms)

This last point becomes critical in the upcoming sections: composite alarms do *not* include metric dimensions, which is why an SSM Automation runbook—not EventBridge—must retrieve contextual data (e.g., a dimension such as an instance ID) to respond to an event.

[1] Optional for curious readers: the idea of an event marking the "here and now" echoes a classic concept from concurrency theory in computer science, where a token in a Petri Net represents a precise point in time and causality. You don't need to know Petri Nets to use EventBridge, but the metaphor helps illustrate why events are such a natural trigger for automated remediation.

Event Sources

In enterprise ESB environments, "sources" were often adapters: JDBC connectors, MQ listeners, SOAP endpoints, FTP pollers, and so on. They required configuration, maintenance, and sometimes entire teams to keep them running.

EventBridge flips that model on its head.

An *event source* in EventBridge is any AWS service, SaaS provider, or application that emits events onto an event bus. There is no adapter layer to manage. AWS services natively publish events in a consistent JSON format, and CloudWatch alarms automatically send state-change events to the default event bus without any configuration.

Common event sources include:

- CloudWatch alarms
- EC2 instance state changes
- Auto-scaling lifecycle events
- Systems Manager notifications
- DynamoDB Streams (via Pipes)
- SaaS partners (e.g., Zendesk, ServiceNow, Datadog)

For CloudOps engineers, the important mental shift is this:

> EventBridge doesn't "pull" from sources—sources "push" events into EventBridge.

This push-based model eliminates polling, reduces latency, and ensures that remediation workflows begin the moment the system changes state.

Rules

A *rule* determines which events EventBridge should match. Conceptually, a rule consists of an event pattern (the filter) and one or more targets (the actions).

However, AWS separates these responsibilities across two API calls:

- `put-rule` defines what to listen for (the event pattern)
- `put-targets` attaches what to do (the targets associated with that rule)

This separation is intentional. It allows:

- Multiple targets to be attached to the same rule.
- Targets to be added or removed without modifying the rule's filter.
- EventBridge to remain stateless and scalable.

Rules are stateless, meaning they evaluate each event independently.

This is why EventBridge cannot enforce AND logic across multiple alarms—something we address later using composite alarms and SSM automation.

Event Patterns

If you've worked with ESBs (I did a couple of decades ago!), you may remember XPath filters, XSLT transforms, message selectors, or content-based routing rules. EventBridge

Event Patterns serve a similar purpose—but with a simpler, declarative, JSON-based approach.

An *event pattern* defines the conditions under which a rule should match an incoming event. It is essentially a filter that inspects the event's fields and determines whether the rule should trigger.

Patterns can match on:

- Source (e.g., `aws.cloudwatch`)
- `detail-type` (e.g., CloudWatch Alarm State Change)
- `detail.alarmName`
- `detail.state.value`
- Any other field in the event JSON

Unlike ESB filters, event patterns are:

- Stateless
- Declarative
- Schema-aware
- Zero-maintenance

There is no scripting language, no transformation engine, and no runtime to tune. EventBridge simply evaluates the pattern against the event and decides whether to forward it to the target.

For example, a CloudOps rule that listens for a composite alarm entering the `ALARM` state might use this event pattern:

```
{
  "source": ["aws.cloudwatch"],
  "detail-type": ["CloudWatch Alarm State Change"],
  "detail": {
    "alarmName": ["CriticalBusinessImpact-Composite"],
    "state": { "value": ["ALARM"] }
  }
}
```

This is the cloud-native equivalent of a content-based router—but without the operational overhead of an ESB.

Event Targets

An *event target* is the action EventBridge takes when a rule matches an event. This is where the event leaves the routing fabric and enters the system that performs the work. In ESB terms, this is the "service endpoint" or "consumer."

EventBridge supports a wide range of targets, including SSM Automation runbooks, Lambda functions, Step Functions state machines, SNS topics, SQS queues, API destinations, and even other event buses.

This is also where EventBridge performs its only form of event shaping. Unlike ESBs, which often performed complex, multi-step transformations on the bus itself, EventBridge supports only lightweight, declarative shaping through input paths and *input transformers*. These mechanisms allow you to extract fields, rename them, or repackage them into a smaller JSON payload before delivering them to the target. They never mutate the original event, never orchestrate, and never perform procedural logic. They exist solely to ensure the target receives exactly the context in the format it needs—nothing more.

For example, if a CloudWatch alarm event includes the alarm name under `detail.alarmName`, an EventBridge rule can use an `InputPathsMap` such as:

```
"InputPathsMap": {
  "alarm": "$.detail.alarmName"
}
```

and then pass a compact payload like so:

```
"InputTemplate": "{\"AlarmName\": <alarm>}"
```

The result is a tiny, purpose-built JSON object—`{"AlarmName": "HighCPU"}`—that the target runbook or Lambda function receives without needing to parse the full CloudWatch alarm event. This illustrates the core idea: simple extraction, simple reshaping, no logic, and no transformation engine.

In automated remediation workflows, the most important target is AWS Systems Manager (SSM) Automation. This is where the operational logic lives. EventBridge routes the event, but the SSM Automation runbook performs the investigation and remediation. Before a runbook receives an event, EventBridge can apply just enough declarative shaping—extracting fields, injecting static values (the topic of the next section), or packaging the event into a simpler structure—to ensure the runbook receives the right context in the right format. This is not ESB-style transformation; it is lightweight input preparation that keeps EventBridge stateless and predictable. This leads directly into the next section, where you learn how EventBridge shapes events just enough for SSM Automation to do its job.

Enriching, Routing, and Delivering Events

While native reboots are an effective way to remediate unhealthy single instances, complex architectures often require an orchestrated process in response to events. Orchestration typically takes the form of coordinated actions including events enrichment, transformation, routing and delivery to selected targets.

With reference to our previously configured Amazon CloudWatch composite alarm `CriticalBusinessImpact-Composite`, let's see how Amazon EventBridge can be leveraged to automatically remediate (reboot) an unhealthy instance.

First and foremost, we need to change the action of our standard metric alarm `HighAppLatency-Standard`, which was a child of `CriticalBusinessImpact-Composite`. The former was configured to directly reboot the unhealthy instance with the flag `--alarm-actions "arn:aws:automate:us-east-1:ec2:reboot"` as a response to the state change to `ALARM`. Instead of rebooting the instance, let's update the alarm to publish a message to a new topic, as shown in the following CLI command.

```
aws cloudwatch put-metric-alarm \
    --alarm-name "HighAppLatency-Standard" \
    --metric-name "Latency" \
    --namespace "RetailApp/OrderSystem" \
    --dimensions Name=InstanceId,Value=i-0123456789abcdef0 \
    --statistic "Average" \
    --period 60 \
    --threshold 500 \
    --comparison-operator "GreaterThanThreshold" \
    --evaluation-periods 3 \
    --datapoints-to-alarm 2 \
    --alarm-actions "arn:aws:sns:us-east-1:123456789012:HighAppLatency-Topic"
```

After this change is applied, if both `HighAppLatency-Standard` and `LowOrderVolume-Standard` transition to the `ALARM` state, each alarm publishes its own notification to its respective Amazon SNS topic (`HighAppLatency-Topic` and `LowOrderVolume-Topic`) within the same account. This behavior is shown in Step 1 of Figure 6.2.

In Step 1, both child alarms enter the `ALARM` state, which causes the `CriticalBusinessImpact-Composite` alarm to transition to `ALARM` as well. The composite alarm behaves this way because it is configured to fire only when both underlying alarms are in `ALARM`. This transition is shown in Step 2 of Figure 6.2.

Every Amazon CloudWatch alarm state change is emitted as a JSON event, which allows Amazon EventBridge to detect when our composite alarm transitions to `ALARM` and route that event to a remediation workflow. We begin by creating a rule (`RemediateCriticalImpact`) that listens for the specific state-change event from the composite alarm, as shown in Step 3 of Figure 6.2.

```
aws events put-rule \
    --name "RemediateCriticalImpact" \
    --event-pattern '{
        "source": ["aws.cloudwatch"],
        "detail-type": ["CloudWatch Alarm State Change"],
        "detail": {
            "alarmName": ["CriticalBusinessImpact-Composite"],
            "state": { "value": ["ALARM"] }
        }
    }' \
    --state ENABLED
```

In this command:

- `--name` is the unique identifier for the EventBridge rule.
- `--event-pattern` is a JSON filter that defines which events the rule "catches."
  - `source: ["aws.cloudwatch"]` ensures we only listen to events from the CloudWatch service.

FIGURE 6.2 Automatic remediation with Amazon EventBridge and built-in SSM runbook.

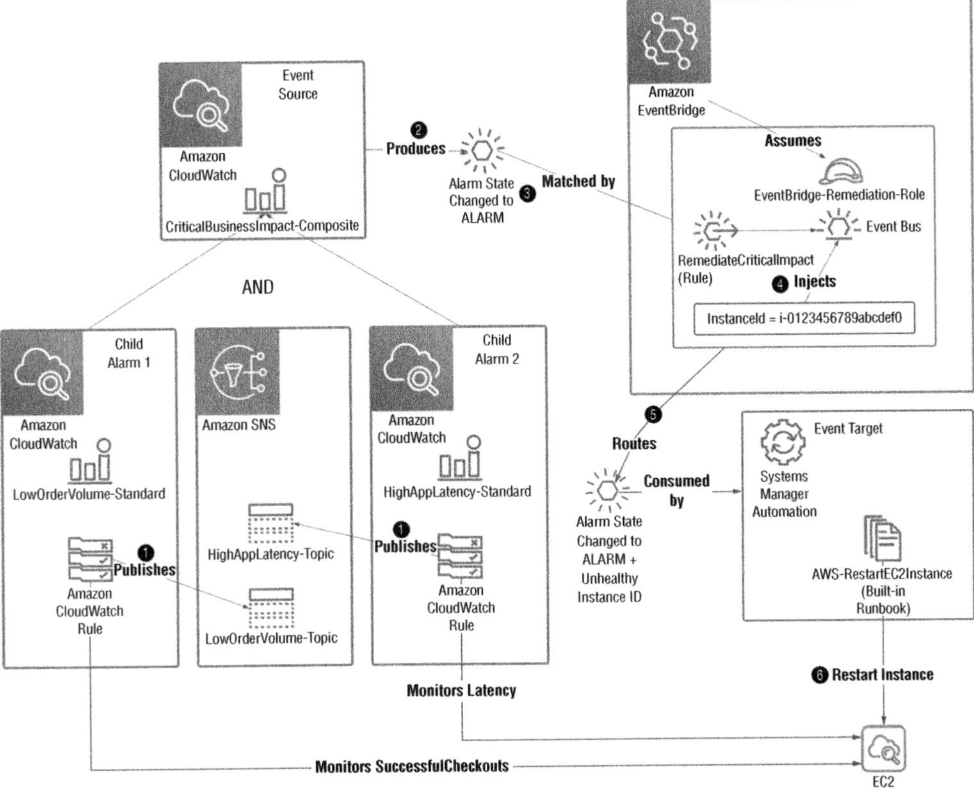

  - `detail-type: ["CloudWatch Alarm State Change"]` filters for the specific event type triggered when an alarm's status moves between OK, `ALARM`, or `INSUFFICIENT_DATA`.
  - `alarmName: ["CriticalBusinessImpact-Composite"]` ensures this rule only reacts to our high-priority business alarm.
  - `state {"value": ["ALARM"]}` is the most critical filter; it ensures remediation only runs when the system enters a failure state, and not when it recovers back to OK.
- `--state` is the state of the EventBridge rule. When `ENABLED`, EventBridge matches all events against the rule, except for AWS management events delivered through CloudTrail. When `DISABLED`, EventBridge does not match any events against the rule. When `ENABLED_WITH_ALL_CLOUDTRAIL_MANAGEMENT_EVENTS`, EventBridge matches all events against the rule, including AWS management events delivered through CloudTrail.

To learn more, visit: `https://docs.aws.amazon.com/cli/latest/reference/events/put-rule.html`.

The rule is then associated with an invokable action. Through the following `aws events put-targets` command, this action both enriches the event with the unhealthy instance ID (Step 4) and supplies EventBridge with the IAM role (`EventBridge-Remediation-Role`) required to invoke the SSM Automation runbook. Once enriched, the event is delivered to the built-in runbook `AWS-RestartEC2Instance` (Step 5), where the SSM Automation document performs the restart of the application stack (Step 6).

```
aws events put-targets \
  --rule "RemediateCriticalImpact" \
  --targets '[
    {
      "Id": "RebootTarget",
      "Arn": "arn:aws:ssm:us-east-1:123456789012:automation-definition/
AWS-RestartEC2Instance",
      "RoleArn": "arn:aws:iam::123456789012:role/EventBridge-Remediation-Role",
      "Input": "{\"InstanceId\": [\"i-0123456789abcdef0\"]}"
    }
  ]'
```

In this command:

- `--rule` points to the rule previously created.
- `--targets` is a JSON array defining what happens when the rule matches.
  - `Id: RebootTarget` is a unique tracking ID for this specific target within the rule.
  - `Arn` is the Amazon Resource Name for the SSM Automation document (i.e., `AWS-RestartEC2Instance`).
  - `RoleArn` provides EventBridge with the temporary credentials needed to start the SSM Automation. Without this flag, the execution will fail because EventBridge does not have permission to act on your resources by default.
  - `Input` is a JSON string that provides parameters to the target. We use this to inject the specific `InstanceId` (e.g., `i-0123456789abcdef0`) that the SSM runbook needs to act upon. This "hardcoding" of the ID in the target is how we solve the problem of composite alarms lacking their own resource dimensions.

To learn more, visit: `https://docs.aws.amazon.com/cli/latest/reference/events/put-targets.html`.

For the official reference of the `AWS-RestartEC2Instance` built-in runbook, visit: `https://docs.aws.amazon.com/systems-manager-automation-runbooks/latest/userguide/automation-aws-restartec2instance.html`.

In the previous example, we manually "injected" the unhealthy instance ID to demonstrate how EventBridge can enrich an event with additional context—useful for understanding the mechanics of automated remediation.

Composite alarms don't work with metric dimensions. They evaluate only the state of other "child" alarms, not the underlying metrics, so concepts like namespaces, metric names, statistics, and dimensions don't apply. Had we used a metric alarm such as `HighAppLatency-Standard`, the value of the instance ID could have been easily retrieved by leveraging the `InstanceId` dimension of the `Latency` metric.

In real CloudOps workflows, however, the recommended approach is to move the logic to extract the unhealthy instance ID out of the EventBridge rule and into an SSM Automation runbook, which is the topic we explore in the following section.

Implementing Systems Manager Automation Runbooks

EventBridge is excellent at capturing, enriching, and routing events, but it is not the right place to perform investigative logic. In enterprise-scale CloudOps environments the recommended pattern is to keep EventBridge *stateless* and let AWS Systems Manager (SSM) Automation perform the heavy lifting.

This is especially important when working with composite alarms, because composite alarms do not expose metric dimensions such as `InstanceId`. They evaluate only the state of their child alarms. That means the EventBridge rule triggered by a composite alarm cannot extract the unhealthy instance ID directly.

Instead, the remediation workflow should:

1. Allow the composite alarm to trigger the EventBridge rule.
2. Pass the metric alarm name (e.g., `HighAppLatency-Standard`) into the runbook.
3. Let the SSM Automation runbook call CloudWatch to retrieve the instance ID.
4. Perform the remediation action (e.g., restart the instance).

This pattern keeps the system stateless, deterministic, and aligned with AWS best practices. The architecture of this pattern is illustrated in Figure 6.3.

You may wonder why SSM Automation is the right place for instance ID extraction?

The answer is simple: because Systems Manager Automation is specifically designed for operational logic:

- It can call AWS APIs directly.
- It can parse JSON responses.
- It can orchestrate multi-step workflows.
- It can enforce IAM boundaries cleanly.
- It can run safely under automation-specific execution roles.

Most importantly, it can perform investigative steps—like calling the `DescribeAlarms` CloudWatch API—without introducing state, drift, or race conditions. This is exactly the kind of architecture you, as an SOA-C03 candidate, are expected to recognize. Let's see how this pattern works.

FIGURE 6.3 Automatic remediation with Amazon EventBridge and custom SSM runbook.

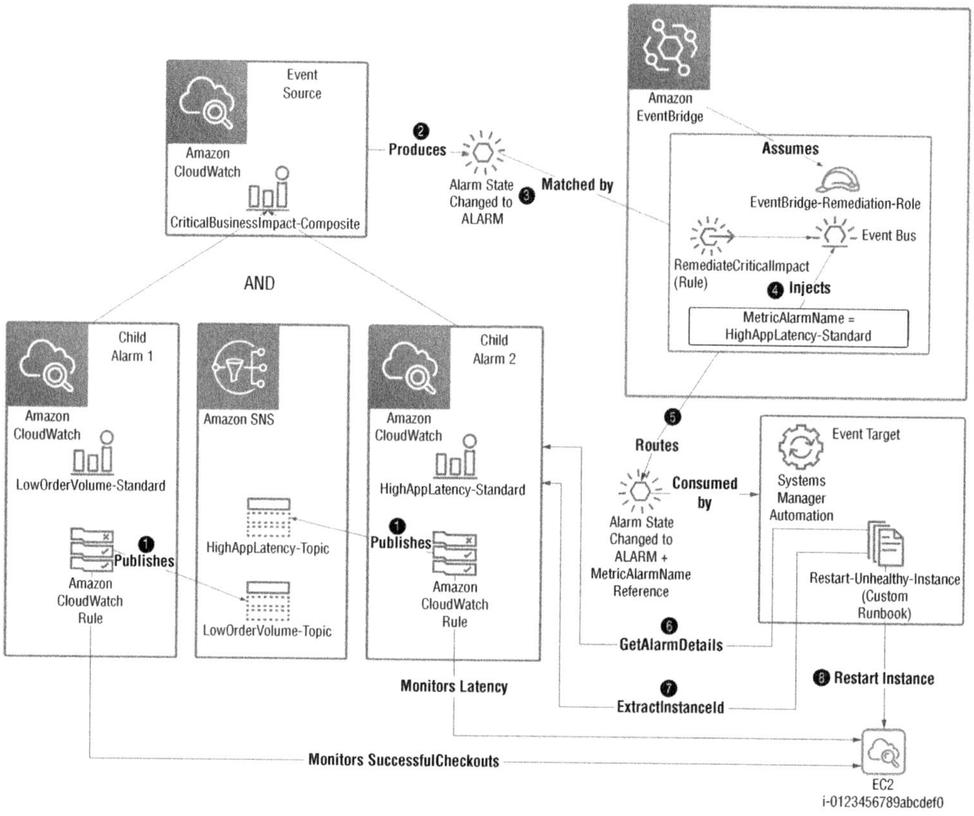

The composite alarm `CriticalBusinessImpact-Composite` remains the "gatekeeper" and the EventBridge rule `RemediateCriticalImpact` doesn't change. With reference to Figure 6.3, Steps 1-3 are identical to the ones in Figure 6.2. This is the "beauty" of the EventBridge rules design, where targets can be added or removed without modifying the rule's filter.

```
aws events put-rule \
  --name "RemediateCriticalImpact" \
  --event-pattern '{
    "source": ["aws.cloudwatch"],
    "detail-type": ["CloudWatch Alarm State Change"],
    "detail": {
      "alarmName": ["CriticalBusinessImpact-Composite"],
      "state": { "value": ["ALARM"] }
    }
  }'
```

When `CriticalBusinessImpact-Composite` enters the `ALARM` state, the remediation workflow begins. Here is what's different from the architecture in Figure 6.2. We still use a SSM Automation runbook as a target, but we inject a reference to the `MetricAlarmName` (with value `HighAppLatency-Standard`) into the event instead of the unhealthy `InstanceID` (with value `i-0123456789abcdef0`). Step 4 in Figure 6.3 shows this event enrichment.

More specifically, we move the remediation logic into SSM Automation by configuring a custom runbook to perform three steps:

1. `GetAlarmDetails` (Step 6): Calls the CloudWatch's API `DescribeAlarms` to retrieve the definition of the custom metric alarm `HighAppLatency-Standard`.
2. `ExtractInstanceId` (Step 7): Extracts the `InstanceId` dimension.
3. `RestartInstance` (Step 8): Restarts the unhealthy instance.

The following code details each step. Save the file as `restart-unhealthy-instance.yaml`.

```
description: Restart the unhealthy instance that triggered the metric alarm
schemaVersion: '0.3'

parameters:
  MetricAlarmName:
    type: String
    description: "Name of the metric alarm to inspect (for example,
HighAppLatency-Standard)"

mainSteps:
  - name: GetAlarmDetails
    action: aws:executeAwsApi
    inputs:
      Service: cloudwatch
      Api: DescribeAlarms
      AlarmNames:
        - "{{ MetricAlarmName }}"
    outputs:
      - Name: AlarmData
        Selector: "$.MetricAlarms[0]"
        Type: Object

  - name: ExtractInstanceId
    action: aws:executeScript
    inputs:
      Runtime: python3.8
      Handler: extract_instance
      Script: |
        def extract_instance(event, context):
            dims = event["AlarmData"]["Dimensions"]
            for d in dims:
```

```
                if d["Name"] == "InstanceId":
                    return {"InstanceId": d["Value"]}
            raise Exception("InstanceId dimension not found")
      InputPayload:
        AlarmData: "{{ GetAlarmDetails.AlarmData }}"
    outputs:
      - Name: InstanceId
        Selector: "$.InstanceId"
        Type: String

  - name: RestartInstance
    action: aws:executeAwsApi
    inputs:
      Service: ec2
      Api: RebootInstances
      InstanceIds:
        - "{{ ExtractInstanceId.InstanceId }}"
```

Next, we create the SSM Automation runbook (`Restart-Unhealthy-Instance`) resource with the following command:

```
aws ssm create-document \
  --name "Restart-Unhealthy-Instance" \
  --document-type "Automation" \
  --content file://restart-unhealthy-instance.yaml \
  --document-format YAML
```

In this command:

- `--name` sets the official name of the Automation runbook in Systems Manager. This name must *exactly match* the name embedded in the ARN used by EventBridge. If the names differ (even by capitalization or hyphens), EventBridge will fail to invoke the runbook. This is why the runbook must be created *before* attaching it as an EventBridge target.
- `--document-type` is the value `Automation` tells SSM that the uploaded document is an Automation runbook, not a command document, a session document, or a policy document. Automation documents support API calls, script execution, conditional branching, output passing, and multi-step workflows. `Automation` is the correct document type for remediation workflows.
- `--content` is a flag that points to the local YAML file containing the runbook definition. The `file://` prefix tells the CLI to load the contents from disk. The file must contain valid YAML following the Automation schema. This is where the logic lives: retrieving the metric alarm, extracting the instance ID, and restarting the instance.
- `--document-format` is a flag that specifies the format of the uploaded document. SSM supports JSON (default) and YAML.

For the sake of completeness, we also detail the process to create the IAM role EventBridge needs to assume to execute the runbook.

EventBridge does not run Automation runbooks by default. It must assume an IAM role that grants `ssm:StartAutomationExecution` on the runbook.

EventBridge needs a role it can assume when it triggers the runbook. The following command creates that role and defines who is allowed to assume it.

```
aws iam create-role \
  --role-name EventBridge-Remediation-Role \
  --assume-role-policy-document '{
    "Version": "2012-10-17",
    "Statement": [
      {
        "Effect": "Allow",
        "Principal": { "Service": "events.amazonaws.com" },
        "Action": "sts:AssumeRole"
      }
    ]
  }'
```

In this command:

- `--role-name` is the name of the IAM role (`EventBridge-Remediation-Role`) that EventBridge will assume to execute the runbook.
- `--assume-role-policy-document:` is the trust policy, which tells AWS, "EventBridge is allowed to assume this role."
  - `Principal.Service: events.amazonaws.com` identifies EventBridge as the trusted service.
  - `Action: sts:AssumeRole` grants EventBridge permission to assume this role when the rule fires.

After having verified that EventBridge can assume the role, the next step is to define what the role is allowed to do. In this automatic remediation workflow, it only needs one permission: start the Automation runbook. In the following command, we attach the Permissions policy with this single permission (following the principle of least privilege) to the newly created IAM role `EventBridge-Remediation-Role`.

```
aws iam put-role-policy \
  --role-name EventBridge-Remediation-Role \
  --policy-name InvokeAutomation \
  --policy-document '{
    "Version": "2012-10-17",
    "Statement": [
      {
        "Effect": "Allow",
        "Action": "ssm:StartAutomationExecution",
```

```
        "Resource": "*"
      }
    ]
  }'
```

In this command:

- `--policy-name` is a friendly name for the inline policy.
  - `Action: ssm:StartAutomationExecution` is the only permission EventBridge needs to run the remediation.
  - `Resource: "*"` allows starting any runbook. (In production, you would scope this to the specific runbook ARN.)

Now that the remediation logic has been packaged into the `Restart-Unhealthy-Instance` SSM Automation runbook—and we have a valid ARN that EventBridge can reference—we also ensured that EventBridge has a valid IAM role it can assume with the necessary permission to start the runbook. With these prerequisites in place, the final step is to wire the remediation workflow together by attaching the runbook as the target of the composite alarm rule and passing the name of the metric alarm (`HighAppLatency-Standard`) as input. This is so the runbook knows which alarm to inspect when extracting the unhealthy instance ID.

```
aws events put-targets \
  --rule "RemediateCriticalImpact" \
  --targets '[
    {
      "Id": "InvokeRunbook",
      "Arn": "arn:aws:ssm:us-east-1:123456789012:automation-definition/
Restart-Unhealthy-Instance",
      "RoleArn": "arn:aws:iam::123456789012:role/EventBridge-Remediation-Role",
      "Input": "{\"MetricAlarmName\": \"HighAppLatency-Standard\"}"
    }
  ]'
```

In this command:

- `--rule` associates the target with the rule created earlier.
- `--targets` is a JSON array defining one or more actions to take when the rule matches.
  - `Id: InvokeRunbook` is a unique tracking ID for this specific target within the rule.
  - `Arn` is the ARN of the SSM Automation runbook.
  - `RoleArn` is the IAM role EventBridge assumes to invoke the runbook.
  - `Input` is a JSON string that provides parameters to the target. Here we inject the metric alarm name `MetricAlarmName: HighAppLatency-Standard` so the runbook knows which alarm to inspect.

When you step back and look at the full remediation workflow, a clear pattern emerges—one that aligns perfectly with how AWS wants CloudOps engineers to think. EventBridge stays in its lane as a stateless event router, doing nothing more than reacting to the composite alarm and forwarding the right inputs. The composite alarm itself remains a pure logical evaluator, responsible only for determining when multiple conditions are simultaneously true. And the deeper operational logic—retrieving the instance ID, calling CloudWatch APIs, and performing the actual remediation—lives where it belongs: inside Systems Manager Automation.

This separation of responsibilities is exactly what makes the design reliable. There's no Lambda function to maintain, no Step Functions workflow to orchestrate, and no Parameter Store value that might drift or become stale. Each service does one job, and does it deterministically, which eliminates race conditions and keeps the workflow predictable even under stress.

The most important principle, though, is understanding why the runbook must retrieve the instance ID. Composite alarms simply don't carry metric dimensions—they were never designed to. Only metric alarms expose the underlying dimensions like `InstanceId`, so the runbook is the natural place to query CloudWatch and extract that information. Once you internalize that, the architecture becomes clear: EventBridge triggers, SSM investigates, and remediation happens cleanly and consistently.

This is the CloudOps mindset AWS wants you to bring into SOA-C03: keep the system stateless, let each service do the job it was built for, and always retrieve operational context from the source of truth.

Summary

Mastering the monitoring, logging, and remediation domain for the SOA-C03 exam requires a shift from viewing AWS services in isolation to seeing them as a unified, self-healing ecosystem. The foundation of this system is Amazon CloudWatch, which serves as the primary repository for both standard metrics vended by AWS services and custom metrics pushed from your applications. By deploying and authorizing the Unified CloudWatch Agent, you extend this visibility deep into the operating system, capturing critical internal data like memory utilization and system logs that standard hypervisor monitoring cannot reach.

Once your telemetry stream is established, you move from observation to detection by configuring a hierarchy of metric and composite alarms. Using "M out of N" evaluation logic, you define precise thresholds that filter out transient spikes, ensuring that your system only reacts to sustained performance breaches. While standard metric alarms provide a granular "heartbeat" for individual resources, composite alarms allow you to layer Boolean logic across multiple signals. This reduces "alarm fatigue" by ensuring high-priority alerts are only triggered when a specific combination of failures—such as high latency paired with low order volume—indicates a genuine business-critical crisis.

When an alarm state change is detected, the operational best practice is to move beyond simple notifications toward Advanced Automatic Remediation. This transition is managed by Amazon EventBridge, acting as a stateless routing fabric that "catches" alarm events and delivers them to specialized targets. For you, as a CloudOps engineer, the most robust target is an SSM Automation runbook. By keeping EventBridge stateless and moving the investigative logic into the runbook, you create an orchestration chain capable of fetching relevant insights from a failure and executing complex recovery steps, such as native EC2 reboots or application stack restarts.

Maintaining this complex environment requires a disciplined approach to troubleshooting and visibility. When the remediation chain fails, your first line of defense is the CloudWatch Alarm History, which confirms if an action was successfully initiated, followed by AWS CloudTrail to audit the underlying API calls for permission errors. To provide a single pane of glass for the entire CloudOps team, you synthesize these metrics, logs, and alarm states into AI-enhanced dashboards. Using a variety of widgets—from Metric Explorers for dynamic fleets to Logs Insights for real-time forensic analysis—you empower your organization with the high-velocity data needed to correlate events and accelerate root cause analysis.

Ultimately, the goal of this chapter is to equip you with the skills to build an architecture that is not only observable but inherently resilient. By integrating CloudWatch Logs for the "why" behind the metrics and Application Signals for tracking Service Level Objectives (SLOs), you move from reactive firefighting to a proactive, data-driven operational model. For the SOA-C03 exam, remember that the true mark of a CloudOps expert is the ability to connect these dots: for example, using EventBridge and SSM Automation to ensure that when a system fails, the first person to know isn't the customer, but the automated remediation script that has already resolved the issue.

Exam Essentials

Understand Amazon CloudWatch's core components. Amazon CloudWatch provides a unified observability layer built from several foundational building blocks. Metrics capture numerical time-series data such as `CPUUtilization` or `RequestCount`, while namespaces group related metrics (for example, `AWS/EC2` or `AWS/Lambda`) to keep data organized. Dimensions act as key-value pairs—like `InstanceId` or `FunctionName`—that let you slice and filter metrics with precision. Logs store raw application and system events, enabling deep troubleshooting and analytics through CloudWatch Logs Insights. Resolutions determine how granular your metrics are, ranging from standard one-minute intervals to high-resolution metrics at one-second granularity. Alarms continuously evaluate metric conditions and trigger automated actions or notifications when thresholds are breached. Application Signals (SLOs) provide service-level indicators and error-budget tracking for modern applications, helping teams measure reliability against defined objectives. Finally,

Dashboards offer customizable visualizations that bring metrics, alarms, and logs together into a single operational view, making it easier to monitor system health at a glance.

Understand Amazon CloudWatch custom metrics. Custom metrics let you publish your own application-specific measurements into CloudWatch when AWS's built-in metrics aren't enough. They allow you to track exactly what matters to your workload—such as queue depth, checkout latency, or cache hit rate—using your own namespaces, metric names, and dimensions. You can push data at whatever frequency your system requires, including high-resolution (one-second) granularity, and then build alarms, dashboards, and automation workflows around those signals just like any native AWS metric. Custom metrics give CloudOps teams full control over observability, enabling deeper insight into application behavior and faster, more targeted remediation.

Understand Amazon CloudWatch metric alarms. Metric alarms act as CloudWatch's real-time sentinels: they watch a single metric, compare it against a threshold, and transition between `OK`, `ALARM`, and `INSUFFICIENT_DATA` states based on the data points they receive. Their behavior is shaped by settings such as period, evaluation periods, and data points to alarm, which together determine how quickly an alarm fires. When an alarm fires (enters the `ALARM` state), it can perform several native actions: send notifications through SNS, invoke a Lambda function, trigger auto-scaling policies, initiate EC2 recovery actions (reboot, stop, terminate, or recover), create OpsItems in Systems Manager OpsCenter, or start an Incident Manager response plan. What they cannot do is *directly* invoke an SSM Automation runbook. Instead, every alarm emits a state-change event to Amazon EventBridge, and this event stream becomes the automation gateway. By creating an EventBridge rule that listens for a specific alarm entering `ALARM`, CloudOps engineers can target an SSM Automation runbook and pass only the fields the workflow needs. This event-driven pattern keeps remediation clean, decoupled, and fully aligned with AWS's recommended operational guidelines.

Know that composite alarms are unaware of dimensions. Composite alarms never evaluate metrics directly, which means they have no access to namespaces, metric names, statistics, or dimensions such as `InstanceId`, `QueueName`, or `FunctionName`. They operate purely on the state of other alarms—`OK`, `ALARM`, or `INSUFFICIENT_DATA`—and nothing more. As a result, a composite alarm cannot tell which specific resource triggered a child alarm, nor can it extract identifiers from `reasonData` the way a standard metric alarm can. This design keeps composite alarms focused on high-level health signals and forces any remediation workflow to obtain resource-level details from the underlying metric alarms or another authoritative source.

Know how to configure the Unified CloudWatch Agent. Configuring the Unified CloudWatch Agent is a foundational skill for a CloudOps engineer, as it extends visibility beyond basic hypervisor metrics into the operating system's internal health. The process begins with a JSON configuration file that explicitly defines which OS-level metrics, such as RAM and disk utilization, and which specific log files should be ingested. To manage this at scale, the configuration is typically uploaded to the AWS Systems Manager (SSM) Parameter Store, allowing you to centrally store and version your monitoring blueprints.

By using the `AmazonCloudWatch-ManageAgent` SSM document, you can remotely push this configuration to your entire fleet, ensuring that every instance is authorized via the `CloudWatchAgentServerPolicy` to stream high-resolution telemetry and logs into your centralized dashboards.

Know the difference between Amazon CloudWatch and Amazon CloudWatch Logs. CloudWatch is primarily a metrics engine designed for quantitative analysis; it tracks time-series data like CPU percentages or request counts to help you understand what is happening at a glance. In contrast, CloudWatch Logs is a specialized service for qualitative data, capturing the raw, text-based output from your applications and operating systems. While a metric might alert you that a server is failing, CloudWatch Logs allows you to dive into the Log Groups and Log Streams to read the specific error messages and stack traces that explain why it failed. Think of CloudWatch as the dashboard of your car and CloudWatch Logs as the detailed diagnostic report from the engine's computer.

Understand how Amazon EventBridge and AWS Systems Manager Automation enable automatic remediation. EventBridge and SSM Automation work together to form one of AWS's most powerful remediation pipelines. EventBridge acts as the event router: it listens for operational signals—such as a CloudWatch alarm entering `ALARM`—and forwards only the relevant context to the right target. SSM Automation is the execution engine on the other side, running predefined runbooks that perform safe, repeatable operational tasks like restarting an instance, rotating credentials, or isolating a resource. The magic comes from the decoupling: EventBridge decides when remediation should happen, and SSM Automation decides how it should happen. This clean separation keeps workflows predictable, auditable, and operationally sound, making it easy for CloudOps engineers to build reliable, event-driven self-healing patterns across their environments.

Review Questions

1. An application running on a fleet of EC2 instances is experiencing intermittent memory leaks. A CloudOps engineer has installed the Unified CloudWatch Agent on all instances. The engineer can see standard CPU and network metrics in the console, but the custom memory metrics are missing. What is the most likely cause of this issue?

   A. The EC2 instances are missing the `AmazonSSMManagedInstanceCore` managed policy.

   B. The CloudWatch Agent configuration file does not have the `metrics_collection` section defined for memory.

   C. The instances are using Basic Monitoring, which does not support memory metrics.

   D. The IAM instance profile is missing the `cloudwatch:PutMetricData` permission.

2. A company wants to reduce "alarm fatigue" by only alerting the on-call engineer if the `CPUUtilization` is over 80% and the application `Latency` is over 500 ms. You decide to use a composite alarm. How should you configure the remediation actions?

   A. Attach the SNS notification to both child alarms and the composite alarm.

   B. Attach a native EC2 reboot action directly to the composite alarm.

   C. Attach the SNS notification only to the composite alarm and leave child alarm actions empty or for low-priority logging.

   D. Use an EventBridge Rule to transform the composite alarm's `InstanceId` dimension into a reboot command.

3. You are troubleshooting a standard metric alarm that is stuck in the `INSUFFICIENT_DATA` state. The alarm monitors a custom metric `SuccessfulCheckouts` pushed by a local script. You verify that the script is running every 60 seconds. What should you check next? (Select TWO.)

   A. Verify that the `Namespace` in the script matches the `Namespace` in the alarm configuration.

   B. Verify that the `Statistic` used in the alarm is `Average` instead of `Sum`.

   C. Check if the `Dimensions` in the `put-metric-data` command exactly match the `Dimensions` defined in the alarm.

   D. Ensure that the `Detailed Monitoring` is enabled on the EC2 instance.

   E. Check if the `Period` of the alarm is set to exactly one second.

4. A CloudOps engineer needs to implement an automated reboot for an EC2 instance if a composite alarm named `SystemCritical-Composite` triggers. Since the composite alarm has no dimensions, which architectural pattern is the most robust and scalable?

   A. Use an EventBridge Input Transformer to extract the `InstanceId` from the composite alarm's `reasonData`.

   B. Trigger an SNS topic that sends a message to an SQS queue for manual processing.

C. Trigger an SSM Automation runbook via EventBridge that fetches the target `InstanceId` from the SSM Parameter Store.

D. Add a native `arn:aws:automate:us-east-1:ec2:reboot` action to the composite alarm.

5. You have an alarm configured with a `Period` of 60 seconds, `Evaluation Periods` of 3, and `Datapoints to Alarm` of 2. In which scenario will the alarm change to the `ALARM` state? (Select TWO.)

A. The metric breaches the threshold for three consecutive minutes.

B. The metric breaches the threshold for one minute, is `OK` for one minute, then breaches again for one minute.

C. The metric breaches the threshold for 60 seconds total over a five-minute window.

D. The metric is in `INSUFFICIENT_DATA` for two out of three minutes.

E. The metric breaches the threshold once and then the instance is terminated.

6. A CloudOps engineer is using CloudWatch Logs Insights to investigate a performance spike. They want to identify the specific process causing the issue. Which of the following is a prerequisite for this investigation?

A. CloudTrail must be enabled in all regions.

B. The Unified CloudWatch Agent must be configured to collect specific log files (e.g., `/var/log/messages`).

C. An IAM role with `logs:DescribeLogGroups` must be attached to the dashboard.

D. The `CPUUtilization` metric must have a Resolution of one second.

7. You want to create a CloudWatch Dashboard that displays the `HighAppLatency-Standard` alarm state alongside an application error log count. The application is deployed across `us-east-1` and `us-west-2`. What should you do to meet this requirement?

A. You must create two separate dashboards, as CloudWatch Dashboards are region-specific.

B. You can add widgets from both regions to a single dashboard if you have the correct permissions.

C. You must use a third-party application because dashboards can only display metrics, not alarm states or log query results.

D. You must use an EventBridge Rule to sync metrics between regions before they can be displayed.

8. An automated remediation rule in EventBridge is failing to trigger an SSM Automation runbook. You check the CloudWatch Alarm History and see the message: "Successfully executed action." Where should you investigate next? (Select TWO.)

A. The IAM Trust Relationship of the EventBridge service role.

B. The `AlarmRule` syntax in the composite alarm.

C. The permissions of the `RoleArn` specified in the EventBridge Target.

D. The Execution History of the SSM Automation in the Systems Manager console.

E. The `put-metric-data` command in the local monitoring script.

9. How does Amazon EventBridge handle the payload when routing a CloudWatch Alarm state change to a target?

   A. It "pulls" the dimensions from the metric and automatically injects them into the target.

   B. It acts as a "push" fabric, delivering a JSON payload containing the `detail` of the state change.

   C. It transforms the JSON into a CSV format by default for better compatibility.

   D. It only sends the `AlarmName` and discards all other metadata.

10. A CloudOps engineer needs to ensure that an automated remediation action does not run during a weekly Sunday maintenance window from 02:00 to 04:00. What is the most efficient way to achieve this?

    A. Use a Lambda function to delete and re-create the alarm every Sunday.

    B. Configure an Actions Suppressor on the alarm and link it to a "Maintenance" alarm that is active during that window.

    C. Change the `threshold` of the alarm to a very high value during the window.

    D. Use `disable-alarm-actions` via a cron job on a management instance.

11. A CloudOps engineer is configuring the Unified CloudWatch Agent to collect application logs. The agent is running, but the Log Group in the console shows no new data. Upon inspecting the agent logs, the engineer sees `AccessDeniedException` when attempting to call `CreateLogStream`. Which policy should be added to the IAM role?

    A. `CloudWatchReadOnlyAccess`

    B. `AmazonSSMManagedInstanceCore`

    C. `CloudWatchAgentServerPolicy`

    D. `CloudWatchApplicationSignalsFullAccess`

12. You have a composite alarm that monitors three different microservices. You notice that the composite alarm is in the `INSUFFICIENT_DATA` state even though two of the three child alarms are in the `OK` state. What is the most likely reason?

    A. One of the child alarms is in the `INSUFFICIENT_DATA` state.

    B. The composite alarm rule uses an `OR` operator instead of an `AND` operator.

    C. The child alarms are using high-resolution metrics.

    D. The composite alarm is missing a `Dimension` for `InstanceId`.

    E. The `Actions Suppressor` is currently active for the composite alarm.

13. An organization requires Detailed Monitoring for a critical production instance to get one-minute metric granularity. Which CLI command should the CloudOps engineer use to enable this?

    A. `aws cloudwatch put-metric-alarm --alarm-name "Granular" --period 60`

    B. `aws ec2 monitor-instances --instance-ids i-0123456789abcdef0`

    C. `aws ssm send-command --document-name "AWS-ConfigureAWSPackage" --parameters "action=Install"`

D. `aws ec2 modify-instance-attribute --instance-id i-0123456789abcdef0 --attribute monitoring`

E. `aws cloudwatch put-metric-data --namespace AWS/EC2 --value 1`

14. A CloudOps engineer is building an EventBridge Rule to trigger a remediation Lambda function. The engineer wants the Lambda to receive the Alarm Name and the New State Reason from the CloudWatch Alarm event. Which EventBridge feature should be used to simplify the JSON input for the Lambda?

A. Event Bus Schema Registry

B. Dead Letter Queue (DLQ)

C. Input Transformer

D. API Destinations

E. Event Replay

15. An EC2 instance has a local script pushing a custom metric `MemorySwapUsage` using the CLI. The CloudOps engineer wants to create an alarm that triggers if the swap usage is high for at least five consecutive minutes. How should the alarm be configured?

A. `Period: 300, EvaluationPeriods: 1, DatapointsToAlarm: 1`

B. `Period: 60, EvaluationPeriods: 5, DatapointsToAlarm: 5`

C. `Period: 60, EvaluationPeriods: 1, DatapointsToAlarm: 5`

D. `Period: 300, EvaluationPeriods: 5, DatapointsToAlarm: 1`

E. `Period: 60, EvaluationPeriods: 5, DatapointsToAlarm: 1`

16. You are reviewing CloudTrail logs to find out who deleted a critical CloudWatch Alarm. You see many events, but cannot find the deletion event. What is the most likely reason?

A. CloudWatch Alarm deletions are only logged in CloudWatch Logs, not CloudTrail.

B. The event is a "Data Event," and you only have "Management Events" enabled.

C. You are looking for the event `DeleteAlarms` in the wrong AWS Region.

D. CloudTrail only logs API calls made via the Management Console, not the CLI.

E. The alarm was deleted by a composite alarm action, which isn't logged.

17. A CloudOps engineer is using SSM Automation to remediate an issue. The runbook fails at a step that calls `ec2:TerminateInstances`. The engineer confirms the SSM service role has the `AmazonSSMAutomationRole` policy. What is the most likely issue?

A. The instance has Termination Protection enabled.

B. The `RoleArn` in the EventBridge target is incorrect.

C. The EC2 instance is missing the SSM Agent.

D. The SSM runbook `schemaVersion` is 0.3 instead of 1.2.

E. The `PutMetricData` permission is missing from the instance profile.

18. Which CloudWatch Dashboard widget type would be best for comparing the `CPUUtilization` of ten different EC2 instances over the last 24 hours to find outliers?

   A. Gauge

   B. Number

   C. Line

   D. Query Result (Logs)

   E. Text

19. A company wants to track the "error budget" for their checkout service. They want to know the percentage of successful requests over a rolling 30-day period. Which CloudWatch feature should they use?

   A. Metric Math

   B. Service Level Objectives (SLOs) via Application Signals

   C. Composite Alarms

   D. Detailed Monitoring

   E. Log Insights

20. A CloudOps engineer needs to run a custom Python script to perform a complex database failover whenever a metric alarm triggers. Which is the most decoupled and serverless way to achieve this?

   A. Set the `AlarmAction` to an EC2 Instance action.

   B. Use an EventBridge Rule to trigger an AWS Lambda function.

   C. Add the Python script to the `UserData` of the EC2 instance.

   D. Configure the alarm to send an email via SNS to the DBA.

   E. Use the `aws cloudwatch set-alarm-state` command in a loop.

Answers to Review Questions

1. D. While the agent may be configured correctly, it acts as a "producer." Without the `cloudwatch:PutMetricData` permission, the agent cannot push data to the CloudWatch API, resulting in a 403 Access Denied error (often silent in logs). Options A, B, and C are incorrect. Option A is for SSM management, not data pushing. Option B is possible, but Option D is the most common "missing link" in exam scenarios. Option C refers only to standard AWS-vended metrics.

2. C. The rationale of a composite alarm is to suppress noise. By only putting the high-priority action (SNS) on the composite, you ensure the engineer is only paged when the "AND" logic is satisfied. Options A, B, and D are incorrect. Option A would increase fatigue, not reduce it. Option B is wrong because composite alarms do not support native EC2 actions (reboot/recover). Option D is wrong because composite alarms do not have an `InstanceId` dimension to transform.

3. A, C. Metrics are uniquely identified by their Name, Namespace, and Dimensions. If any of these differ between the producer (script) and the consumer (alarm), CloudWatch treats them as different metrics, leading to `INSUFFICIENT_DATA`. Options B, D, and E are incorrect. Statistic choice in Option B doesn't cause `INSUFFICIENT_DATA`. Detailed monitoring (Option D) is for standard AWS metrics, not custom metrics. Custom metrics (Option E) usually use 60s (Standard) or 1s (High Res), but mismatching names/dimensions is the root cause of data not being found.

4. C. This is the "Self-Aware" remediation pattern. Since the composite alarm is "blind" to dimensions, the SSM Automation runbook pulls the "Single Source of Truth" from the Parameter Store to identify the target. Options A, B, and D are incorrect. Composite alarms (Option A) don't include dimensions in their payload. Option B is not automated remediation. Composite alarms (Option D) do not support native reboot actions.

5. A, B. Option A would trigger it. Option B is "M out of N" logic. Within a window of three minutes (N), we need two minutes (M) to be breaching. They do not have to be consecutive. Options C, D, and E are incorrect. Option C exceeds the evaluation window. `INSUFFICIENT_DATA` (Option D) is not a breach. Option E requires two data points; one is not enough.

6. B. Metrics tell you what (CPU is high), but logs tell you why. To see the "story," the agent must be configured to push the text-based log data into CloudWatch Logs. Option A, C, and D are incorrect. CloudTrail tracks API calls, not OS-level processes (Option A). Option C is a viewing permission, not a collection requirement. Resolution doesn't provide the process name (Option D).

7. B. CloudWatch Dashboards are a "Global" visualization tool. They can aggregate metrics, alarms, and Log Insights results from multiple regions or accounts into a single pane of glass. Options A, C, and D are incorrect. Dashboards are not limited to one region (Option A). There is no need to use a third-party application because dashboards support Alarms and Logs Insights widgets (Option C). No syncing is required (Option D).

8. C, D. If CloudWatch says "Successfully executed," it means it successfully handed the event to EventBridge. If nothing happened after that, the issue is either EventBridge lacks permission to start SSM (Option C) or the SSM Runbook itself failed during execution (Option D). Options A, B, and E are incorrect. Option A is about the role's Trust Policy, whereas Option C is about the role's Permission Policy. The trust relationship allows EventBridge to assume the role (Option A). Even if EventBridge successfully assumes the role (the trust is fine), it will still fail if the role itself doesn't have a permission policy that explicitly allows the `ssm:StartAutomationExecution` action. Options B and E occur before the "Successfully executed action" step in the chain.

9. B. EventBridge is a push-based router. It takes the JSON emitted by the source (CloudWatch) and delivers it to the target. Options A, C, and D are incorrect. Option A It doesn't "pull" data; it receives what is pushed. It remains JSON (Option C). It sends a full, rich metadata payload (Option D).

10. B. The Actions Suppressor is the modern way to silence alarm actions without disabling the alarm's ability to track state. It is cleaner than manual CLI toggles. Options A, C, and D are incorrect. Options A and C are manual workarounds that risk breaking the configuration. Option D works, but Option B is the built-in, best-practice feature designed for this exact scenario.

11. C. `CloudWatchAgentServerPolicy` is the AWS-managed policy specifically designed for the agent. It includes permissions to create log groups, create log streams, and put log events (and metric data). Options A, B, and D are incorrect. Option A is read-only. Option B manages the SSM connection, not CloudWatch data. Option D is for Application Signals, a different feature set.

12. A. By default, if any child alarm is in `INSUFFICIENT_DATA`, the composite alarm may also move to that state depending on the logic, as it cannot definitively evaluate the rule. Options B, C, D, and E are incorrect. Operator choice affects the state (`OK`/`ALARM`), but not the presence of data (Option B). High resolution is supported (Option C). Composite alarms never have dimensions (Option D). Suppressors silence actions, not state evaluation (Option E).

13. B. `monitor-instances` is the specific EC2 API command to toggle an instance from Basic Monitoring (five mins) to Detailed Monitoring (one min). Options A, C, D, and E are incorrect. Alarms don't enable monitoring; they only watch existing data (Option A). Option C installs software (the agent), but doesn't enable the AWS-vended detailed monitoring. Option D is a generic attribute command; the specific `monitor-instances` API is preferred for this task. You cannot manually push data into the `AWS/` reserved namespaces (Option E).

14. C. The Input Transformer allows you to use `InputPathsMap` to extract specific keys (like `$.detail.alarmName`) and map them to a simplified `InputTemplate` that the Lambda function receives. Options A, B, D, and E are incorrect. Option A helps with discovery, not transformation. Option B handles failures. Option D is for sending events to third-party APIs. Option E is for reprocessing past events.

15. B. To check for consecutive minutes at one-minute granularity, you set the Period to 60s and require that five out of five (M out of N) evaluation periods be in breach. Options A, C, D, and E are incorrect. A single five-minute period is an average, not five distinct consecutive checks (Option A). N must be greater than or equal to M (Option C). Option D would look at a 25-minute window. Option E would trigger if only one minute out of five was bad (not consecutive).

16. C. CloudWatch is a Regional service. API calls like `DeleteAlarms` are logged by CloudTrail in the specific region where the alarm resided. Options A, B, D, and E are incorrect. API calls are always CloudTrail's domain (Option A). Creating/deleting alarms is a management event (Option B). CloudTrail logs all API calls (CLI, SDK, Console) (Option D). Composite alarms don't delete other alarms (Option E).

17. A. Termination Protection is a specific EC2 attribute that prevents the `TerminateInstances` API call from succeeding, regardless of the IAM permissions held by the caller. Options B, C, D, and E are incorrect. If the runbook started, the `RoleArn` worked (Option B). SSM Automation (control plane) doesn't require the agent for API actions like termination (Option C). 0.3 is the standard modern schema version (Option D). Finally, Option E is for monitoring, not remediation.

18. C. Line charts are designed to show time-series data for multiple metrics simultaneously, making it easy to visually identify which instance is behaving differently (the outlier) over time. Options A, B, D, and E are incorrect. Option A shows a single value against a max/min. Option B shows a single current value. Option D is for text logs. Option E is for static documentation.

19. B. Application Signals allows you to define SLOs specifically to track reliability targets (like 99.9% success rate) and monitor your "Error Budget" directly. SLOs track success rate over configurable time windows: a rolling window (e.g., the last seven or 28 days) or a calendar-aligned window (e.g., monthly). Options A, C, D, and E are incorrect. Option A can calculate percentages, but doesn't have the built-in "Error Budget" tracking. Option C is for state aggregation. Option D is for one-minute granularity. Option E is for log analysis.

20. B. EventBridge providing a bridge to Lambda is the gold standard for decoupled, serverless remediation. It allows you to run custom code without managing servers. Options A, C, D, and E are incorrect. Native actions (Option A) are limited (Reboot/Stop). UserData (Option C) only runs at launch. Option D is manual remediation. Option E is a testing command, not a remediation workflow.

Reliability and Business Continuity

THE AWS CERTIFIED CLOUDOPS ENGINEER ASSOCIATE (SOA-C03) EXAM OBJECTIVES COVERED IN THIS CHAPTER MAY INCLUDE, BUT ARE NOT LIMITED TO THE FOLLOWING:

✓ **Domain 2: Reliability and Business Continuity**

- 2.1 Implement scalability and elasticity
- 2.2 Implement highly available and resilient environments
- 2.3 Implement backup and restore strategies

Reliability on AWS is built on a simple idea: workloads must perform correctly and recover quickly when something goes wrong. That recovery capability—*resilience*—is the foundation of reliable operations and the starting point for business continuity. In this chapter, we shift from service-specific features you explored earlier to the AWS-native services and operational patterns that keep entire workloads available during failures, disruptions, and regional events. You'll learn how AWS implements resilience at scale, how centralized backup and disaster recovery services protect your data and workloads, and how migration and replication tools support business continuity with minimal downtime. These are the mechanisms SOA-C03 candidates are expected to understand, operate, and troubleshoot in real-world environments.

Architecting for Resilience

Resilience is the operational backbone of reliability on AWS. A workload isn't considered reliable simply because it performs correctly under normal conditions—it must continue to function, or recover quickly, when components fail, when demand surges, or when an Availability Zone becomes impaired. This is where the concept of Fault Isolation Boundaries, introduced in Chapter 2, becomes essential. AWS designs not only Availability Zones but entire Regions as independent fault domains, each with isolated power, networking, and control planes. This prevents failures from cascading across the AWS global infrastructure. Understanding these boundaries helps CloudOps engineers design workloads that can withstand both AZ-level disruptions and the far rarer—but higher-impact—scenario of a Region-level impairment. Multi-AZ architectures, health checks, and routing controls provide resilience within a Region, while Multi-Region patterns and global routing services extend resilience across Regions.

Beyond architectural patterns, AWS provides dedicated services that help CloudOps engineers measure, validate, and continuously improve resilience across their workloads. Tools like AWS Resilience Hub allow teams to assess their resilience posture against best practices, while AWS Fault Injection Service (FIS) enables controlled experiments that reveal how systems behave under real-world failure scenarios. Together, these capabilities turn resilience from a set of design principles into an operational discipline. As you move through the rest of this chapter, you'll see how resilience underpins high-availability patterns, centralized backup orchestration, disaster recovery strategies, and even data migration workflows. By grounding these topics in the concept of Fault Isolation Boundaries, you'll gain a clearer understanding of how AWS builds reliability from the infrastructure up, and how you—as a CloudOps engineer—can operate workloads that remain available even when the unexpected occurs.

We begin this exploration by introducing the key site reliability engineering terms every CloudOps engineer should be familiar with, regardless of which cloud they operate.

Site Reliability Engineering Concepts

The AWS Well-Architected Framework defines *resilience* (or resiliency) as "the ability of a workload to recover from infrastructure or service disruptions, dynamically acquire computing resources to meet demand, and mitigate disruptions, such as misconfigurations or transient network issues." However, resilience remains a theoretical concept until it is measured and managed through site reliability engineering (SRE). For a CloudOps engineer, SRE provides a measurement-driven approach to transform "resilient design" into "reliable performance." This journey begins with *service level indicators* (SLIs), the raw, quantitative measurements of your system's behavior. Imagine monitoring an application behind an Application Load Balancer: your SLIs are the granular metrics like request latency (e.g., milliseconds to serve a page), error rate (e.g., percentage of 5XX responses), or availability (e.g., uptime of your target EC2 instances). These are the vital signs that indicate whether your resilient architecture is actually holding up under pressure.

While SLIs tell you what is happening, *service level objectives* (SLOs) define what *should* be happening to maintain reliability. An SLO is an internal target, such as "99.9% of successful requests over a trailing 30-day period." For the AWS SOA-C03 exam, it is crucial to understand that SLOs are the bridge between technical SLIs and business requirements. They create an *error budget*—the margin of allowable failure. If your resilient Multi-AZ deployment is performing well, your error budget remains full, allowing you to deploy new features. If failures occur, the budget is consumed, signaling that the team must stop new releases and focus on hardening the environment. If these internal objectives are missed significantly, you risk breaching the service level agreement (SLA), which is the formal, legally binding contract with your customers that outlines the financial penalties or service credits owed when reliability falls below a commercial threshold.

To truly build a foundation of reliability, you must also define the boundaries of recovery through RTO (*Recovery Time Objective*) and RPO (*Recovery Point Objective*). Within the reliability framework, RTO and RPO are categorized as Disaster Recovery objectives, often informed by SLAs and compliance requirements, which represent business-critical recovery targets. RTO is your "timer for downtime," representing the maximum acceptable time to restore a service after a failure (e.g., "The system must be back online within two hours using Amazon Route 53 Application Recovery Controller"). RPO is your "data loss window," defining how much data the business can afford to lose in time (e.g., "We must be able to restore data to within 15 minutes of the failure using Amazon RDS Snapshots"). Together, these concepts ensure that resilience isn't just a configuration, but a measurable, contractually-backed standard of operational excellence.

To learn more, visit: `https://aws.amazon.com/what-is/sre/`.

High Availability vs. Fault Tolerance

While the SRE metrics allow you to measure the success of a resilient system, the architecture itself must be built to meet these targets through specific design patterns. Understanding how to achieve these objectives requires a clear distinction between strategies that aim for constant uptime versus those that prioritize seamless survival of hardware failures.

High availability (HA) and fault tolerance (FT) are often mentioned together, but they represent two distinct approaches to resilience on AWS. *High availability* focuses on minimizing downtime by rapidly detecting failures and shifting traffic or workloads to healthy resources. It accepts that failures will occur and relies on redundancy, health checks, and automated recovery to keep the application reachable. Most AWS managed services—such as RDS Multi-AZ, ECS with multiple tasks, or auto-scaling groups—are designed around this model. For CloudOps engineers, HA is the default operational strategy: build for failure, detect it quickly, and recover automatically.

Fault tolerance, by contrast, aims to eliminate downtime entirely by ensuring that a failure in one component has no impact on the workload's ability to operate. This requires fully redundant systems running in parallel, often with synchronous replication and no dependency on a single failure domain. Fault-tolerant architectures are more complex and more expensive, and are typically reserved for workloads with strict business continuity requirements, such as financial transaction systems or real-time control systems. On AWS, fault tolerance may involve Multi-AZ synchronous replication, distributed load balancing, or even Multi-Region Active-Active architectures.

For you as a CloudOps engineer, the key is understanding when your workload's business requirements expect you to use HA versus FT, and how these choices map to the Fault Isolation Boundaries you learned in Chapter 2. HA is usually sufficient within a Region, while FT becomes relevant when the business cannot tolerate even brief interruptions—or when Region-level resilience is required. With this distinction clear, we can now explore how AWS implements these two approaches to resilience.

Resilience Patterns

Cloud architects rarely begin by designing full-fledged, fault-tolerant, Multi-Region architectures in a single iteration. Instead, resilience grows in layers as business requirements evolve. You start with the simplest protections against common failures, then progressively add capabilities as the workload matures, traffic increases, or the business demands stronger guarantees. AWS makes this incremental journey intuitive: each resilience pattern builds on the previous one, expanding your Fault Isolation Boundaries and strengthening your operational posture without forcing you to redesign everything from scratch.

This section introduces five resilience patterns, each representing a step forward in architectural maturity. As you move through them, you'll see how AWS helps you implement the three SOA-C03 exam objectives introduced at the beginning of this chapter (i.e., 2.1, 2.2, and 2.3) in a natural progression:

- Implement scalability and elasticity (Patterns 1–2)
- Implement highly available and resilient environments (Patterns 2–3)

- Implement backup and restore strategies (Patterns 4–5)

By the end of this section, you'll have learned a basic framework that helps you design resilient workloads in AWS, and assists you in recognizing which pattern the SOA-C03 exam expects you to choose in a given scenario during the exam.

Pattern 1—Multi-AZ Deployment

Every resilience journey begins with Multi-AZ deployment. It's the simplest, most cost-effective way to protect a workload from the most common type of infrastructure failure: the loss of an Availability Zone. You're not redesigning your application; you're simply placing your compute, data, and networking components across at least two AZs so that a localized outage doesn't take down your entire workload.

In practice, this means:

- Your auto-scaling group spans multiple AZs.
- Your load balancer distributes traffic across them.
- Your database uses Multi-AZ replication.
- Your storage (S3, EFS) is inherently Multi-AZ.

This is also where scalability and elasticity first enter the picture; Auto-scaling groups don't just replace failed instances—they scale (horizontally) your fleet in and out based on demand. Managed services like Amazon DynamoDB and Aurora Serverless v2 scale automatically as well.

For you as a CloudOps engineer, Multi-AZ deployment is the baseline. But while Multi-AZ deployment protects you from AZ failures, it doesn't guarantee that your workload remains stable during a failure. Basic Multi-AZ deployments often exhibit what's known as *bimodal behavior*.

As illustrated in Figure 7.1, under normal conditions ("Normal Mode"), the workload operates in a stable performance mode. But when AZ 1 is lost, the sudden drop in capacity triggers auto-scaling events, load redistribution, and temporary overload on Instance 1, Instance 2, and Instance 3 in AZ 2. The workload shifts into a degraded mode until scaling completes. This oscillation between "Normal Mode" and "Failure Mode" is the sign of bimodal behavior—and it's the limitation that Pattern 2 is designed to eliminate.

Pattern 2—Multi-AZ with Static Stability

Static stability is the idea that your workload should remain healthy even when something breaks—without relying on rapid scaling or emergency provisioning. In other words, the system should continue operating in a single, stable performance mode even under failure conditions.

This pattern builds directly on Multi-AZ deployment but eliminates the bimodal behavior introduced in Pattern 1.

Static stability prevents bimodal behavior by ensuring that the workload has enough preexisting "headroom" capacity to absorb 100% of the loss of an AZ without changing modes.

FIGURE 7.1 Multi-AZ deployment pattern.

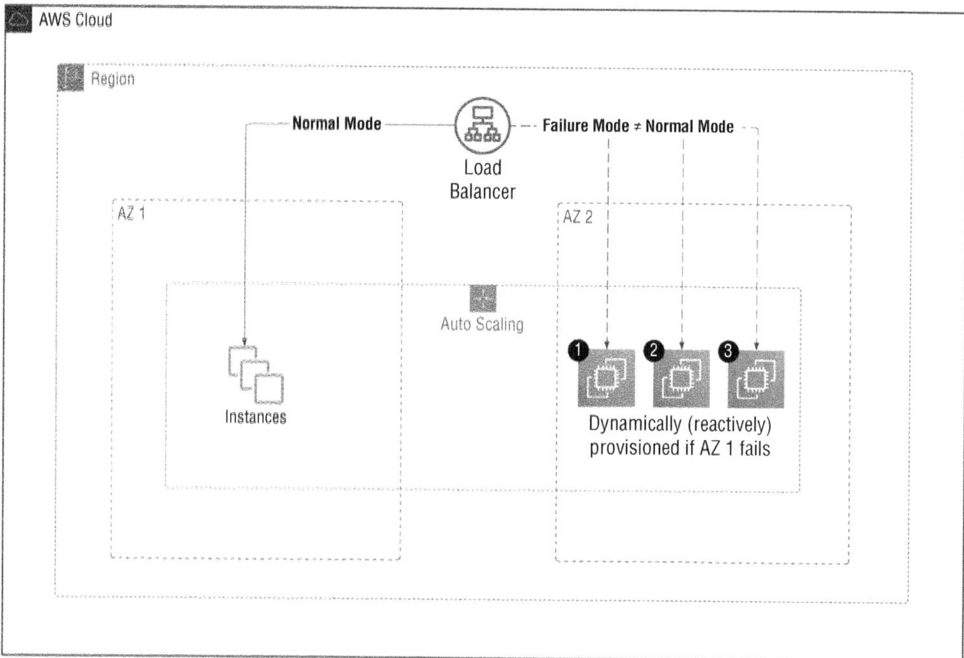

As displayed in Figure 7.2, when AZ 1 fails there are already three EC2 instances in AZ 2 ready to serve requests. No emergency scaling is required. No performance dip occurs. The workload behaves the same before and after the failure.

To make this intuitive, it helps to introduce two common redundancy models:

- **N+1 redundancy** provides one additional unit of capacity (e.g., an extra EC2 instance) beyond what is needed for normal operations.
- **2N redundancy** duplicates the entire environment so that a full standby can take over immediately after a failure occurs.

Multi-AZ with static stability sits between these two models.

It provides more redundancy than simple N+1—because it must absorb the loss of an entire AZ—but it stops well short of the full duplication required for 2N architectures.

In practice this pattern results in:

- Running N+AZ-headroom capacity so the remaining AZ can absorb 100% of the load if one AZ fails.
- Designing services to be stateless, so any instance can serve any request.
- Persisting state to resilient data stores like Amazon DynamoDB, Amazon Aurora, or Amazon S3.
- Using caching, queues, and retries to smooth out transient spikes.
- Maintaining one stable performance mode, even under failure.

FIGURE 7.2 Multi-AZ with static stability pattern.

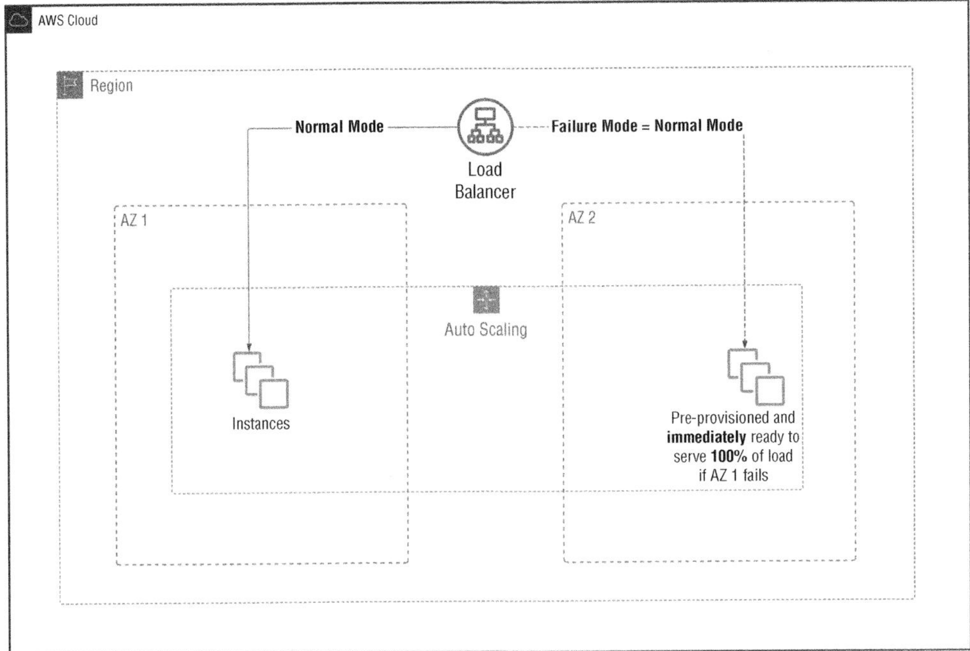

For SOA-C03, this pattern aligns strongly with "Implement highly available and resilient environments." Many exam scenarios describe workloads that collapse when an AZ goes offline. The correct answer often involves adding static stability to eliminate bimodal behavior.

To learn more, visit: `https://docs.aws.amazon.com/wellarchitected/latest/reliability-pillar/rel_withstand_component_failures_static_stability.html`.

Once your individual workloads are stable, the next challenge is scaling resilience across your entire application portfolio.

Pattern 3—Application Portfolio Distribution

The Application Portfolio Distribution pattern is a strategic Multi-Region approach focused on maximizing functional resilience. Rather than trying to maintain a complex active-active state for every single component, this pattern involves intentionally distributing different critical digital channels or business applications across separate AWS Regions. By isolating functions—such as hosting a payment processing API in `us-east-1` and an order fulfillment portal in `us-west-2`—you effectively contain the blast radius of rare but high-impact regional service disruptions.

From an operational perspective, this pattern requires moving beyond Multi-AZ deployments to manage a distributed portfolio that provides continuous service even if one "leg" of the business becomes unavailable. If a region-wide event occurs, your customers retain access to business-critical services through alternative channels hosted in healthy regions, ensuring that the business never experiences a total blackout. This approach is particularly effective for large-scale organizations that provide multiple digital interfaces, as it allows for a "graceful degradation" of service rather than a complete failure.

Implementing this pattern demands high-level technical orchestration, as cloud engineers must account for cross-region data synchronization, consistent deployment pipelines (e.g., via AWS CodePipeline), and unified observability. While it introduces higher complexity and cost compared to single-region architectures, it significantly strengthens your reliability posture. Using tools like AWS Resilience Hub can help you define and track recovery objectives (RTO/RPO) for each channel in your portfolio, ensuring that your distributed infrastructure meets the rigorous standards of the AWS Well-Architected Framework's Reliability pillar.

For the SOA-C03 exam, this pattern deepens the objective "Implement highly available and resilient environments" by shifting the focus from application resilience to business capability resilience. Once critical functions are diversified across regions, the natural next step is to formalize regional recovery strategies (Pattern 4) and eventually evolve toward globally active architectures (Pattern 5).

Pattern 4—Multi-AZ Deployment with Regional DR

This pattern introduces a new dimension: geographic redundancy. While Multi-AZ protects you from localized failures, it does not protect you from Region-wide outages, data corruption, or catastrophic events.

As illustrated in Figure 7.3, Multi-AZ deployment with Regional DR extends your resilience posture by adding a secondary (DR) Region that can take over if the primary Region becomes unavailable.

FIGURE 7.3 Multi-AZ deployment with Regional DR pattern.

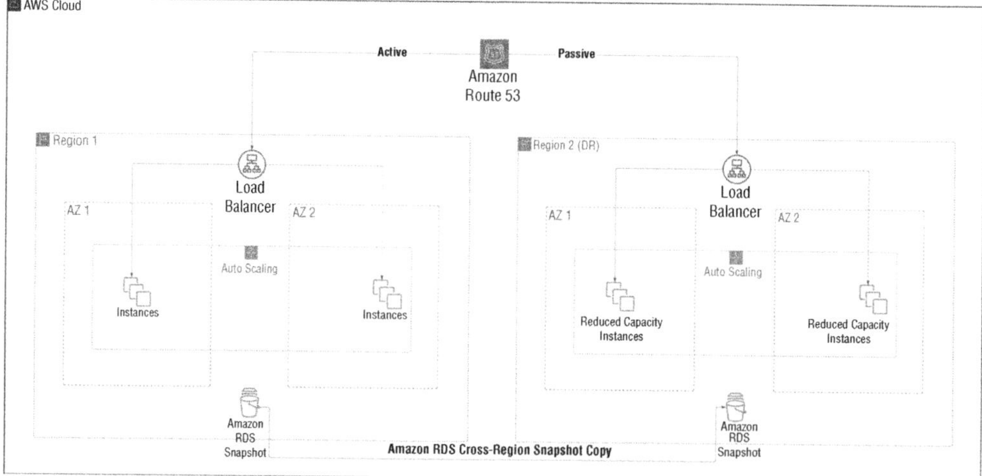

This pattern is implemented by leveraging the database and storage services you learned in Chapters 4 and 5, including:

- **Cross-Region backups** using Amazon S3 CRR, AWS Backup, or Amazon RDS Cross-Region Snapshot Copy (as shown in Figure 7.3).
- **Cross-Region replication** using Amazon Aurora Global Database, Amazon DynamoDB Global Tables, or Amazon RDS Read Replicas.
- **DR strategies** such as Backup & Restore, Pilot Light, Warm Standby, or Multi-Site Active-Active (all covered later in this chapter).
- **Failover routing** using Route 53 health checks and DNS failover (covered in the next section).

This is where the SOA-C03 objective "Implement backup and restore strategies" becomes central. You, as a CloudOps engineer, must understand RTO/RPO trade-offs, replication mechanisms and costs, and the operational steps required to bring up a DR Region.

This pattern also marks the transition from High Availability to Fault Tolerance because it introduces regional failover. At this point, the architecture no longer assumes the Region is a reliable fault-isolation boundary. Instead, it prepares to continue operating even if the entire Region becomes unavailable.

But even Regional DR still treats the secondary Region as a backup. The next pattern removes that distinction entirely.

Pattern 5—Multi-Region Active-Active Deployment

Pattern 5 represents the highest level of resilience on AWS: a globally distributed, continuously operating architecture where multiple Regions actively serve traffic at the same time. Unlike Multi-AZ deployment with Regional DR (Pattern 4), which relies on restoring or promoting resources after a failure, Pattern 5 assumes that every Region is already live, already capable of handling requests, and already maintaining its own copy of the data needed to operate.

To achieve this, Pattern 5 relies on continuous, asynchronous cross-region replication. This is a fundamental shift from the backup-and-restore mechanisms used in Pattern 4. Because synchronous replication is only possible within a Region (due to latency constraints), all Multi-Region data propagation in Pattern 5 is asynchronous. Services such as DynamoDB Global Tables, Aurora Global Database, S3 Cross-Region Replication, and Multi-Region event streaming patterns provide low-lag, eventually consistent replication that keeps Regions loosely synchronized while allowing each to serve traffic independently. This design requires applications to tolerate eventual consistency, handle conflict resolution, and avoid assumptions about strict ordering across Regions.

In this pattern, backups and snapshots still exist—but they are not part of the active-active replication path. They serve long-term retention, compliance, and disaster recovery needs, not live data propagation. Active-active architectures depend on continuous replication, not restore-based mechanisms. As a result, Pattern 5 delivers true fault tolerance: if an entire Region becomes unavailable, traffic simply shifts to the remaining Regions with minimal disruption, because they were already operating and already holding the necessary data.

FIGURE 7.4 Multi-Region Active-Active deployment pattern.

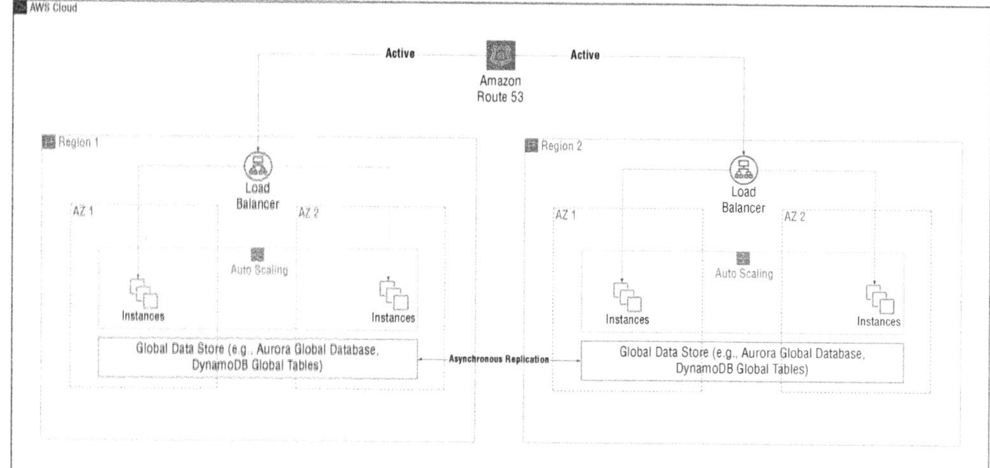

Figure 7.4 illustrates a Multi-Region Active-Active deployment pattern in which each Region independently serves production traffic, while maintaining continuous, asynchronous cross-region replication. Database services such as DynamoDB Global Tables, and Aurora Global Database keep data loosely synchronized across Regions with low-lag, eventually consistent replication. Global routing via Route 53 (latency-based or weighted routing) directs users to the nearest healthy Region, and if one Region becomes unavailable, traffic seamlessly shifts to the others without requiring recovery operations. This pattern represents true fault tolerance through continuous operation rather than restore-based failover (Pattern 4).

To understand how AWS detects failures and orchestrates these routing decisions in practice, we now turn to the underlying mechanisms that make both Regional and global resilience possible: Elastic Load Balancing (ELB) and Amazon Route 53 health checks.

Configuring and Troubleshooting Elastic Load Balancing (ELB) and Amazon Route 53 Health Checks

Resilience on AWS depends on two complementary mechanisms: *ELB health checks*, which operate inside a Region, and *Amazon Route 53 health checks*, which operate globally. These two mechanisms work together to detect failures quickly and route traffic safely, forming the operational foundation for the resilience patterns you explored earlier. For you as a CloudOps engineer preparing for the SOA-C03 exam, understanding how these health checks are configured, how they behave under failure, and how to troubleshoot them is essential to building and operating resilient workloads.

This section walks you through how ELB and Route 53 health checks work, how to configure them, and how to diagnose the most common failure scenarios. Along the way, you'll see AWS CLI examples with explanations of each flag and exam-relevant insights that reflect real operational tasks.

ELB Health Checks

ELB health checks give the load balancer a continuous understanding of whether a compute target is ready to serve traffic. These checks are always performed against targets inside a *target group*, never directly against an auto-scaling group. When a target becomes unhealthy, the load balancer simply stops routing traffic to it; nothing is terminated as a direct result of an ELB health check.

Before creating the Target Group, it's important you understand what AWS means by "target." The `--target-type` flag determines what kind of compute resource the load balancer will be sending traffic to. Choosing `instance` means routing traffic directly to EC2 instances using their instance IDs. Choosing `ip` allows the load balancer to route traffic to IP addresses, which is essential for ECS tasks, containers, hybrid workloads, and on-premises servers reachable through Direct Connect or VPN.

When you're using `--target-type ip`, the IP address must be from RFC 1918 ranges, RFC 6598 (100.64.0.0/10), or VPC subnets. Publicly Internet-routable IPs are not supported.

Choosing `lambda` allows an Application Load Balancer to invoke a Lambda function directly in response to an HTTP(S) request. These three modes cover the full spectrum of compute backends supported by ELB.

Creating a Target Group

With that foundation in place, we can create a Target Group. The following command creates one that expects HTTPS traffic on port 443:

```
aws elbv2 create-target-group \
  --name mytg \
  --protocol HTTPS \
  --port 443 \
  --vpc-id vpc-1234567890abcdef \
  --target-type instance
```

In this command:

- `--name` assigns a human-readable name to the Target Group.
- `--protocol` defines the protocol the load balancer uses when forwarding traffic to targets. Common values: `HTTP`, `HTTPS`, `TCP`, `UDP`, `TCP_UDP`.
- `--port` specifies the port on which the targets receive traffic.
- `--vpc-id` ensures that the Target Group is created in the correct VPC network.
- `--target-type` determines what kind of compute resource the load balancer will route traffic to. Valid values: `instance`, `ip`, `lambda`.

Registering Targets

After creating the Target Group, the next step is registering one or more targets so the load balancer has something to probe and route traffic to. For a `target-type instance`, this means attaching EC2 instance IDs:

```
aws elbv2 register-targets \
  --target-group-arn arn:aws:elasticloadbalancing:us-east-
1:123456789012:targetgroup/mytg/<id> \
  --targets Id=i-0123456789abcdef0
```

In this command:

- `--target-group-arn` identifies the Target Group where the targets will be registered.
- `--targets` specifies one or more targets to register. The structure depends on the target type:
  - For `instance`: `Id=i-xxxx`
  - For `ip`: `Id=10.0.1.25`
  - For `lambda`: `Id=arn:aws:lambda:`... You can register multiple targets by repeating the `Id=` structure.

Configuring Health Checks

Once the Target Group exists and has registered targets, the next step is configuring its health check. This is where you define how the load balancer determines whether a target is healthy. In a zero-trust posture, HTTPS is the preferred protocol because it ensures encryption in transit. The following command configures the health check:

```
aws elbv2 modify-target-group \
  --target-group-arn arn:aws:elasticloadbalancing:us-east-
1:123456789012:targetgroup/mytg/<target-group-id> \
  --health-check-protocol HTTPS \
  --health-check-path /health \
  --health-check-port 443 \
  --health-check-interval-seconds 15 \
  --healthy-threshold-count 3 \
  --unhealthy-threshold-count 2
```

In this command:

- `--target-group-arn` identifies the specific Target Group you want to modify. Every Target Group has a unique ARN, and this flag tells ELB which one to update.
- `--health-check-protocol` defines the protocol the load balancer uses when performing health checks. Common values: `HTTP, HTTPS, TCP, UDP, TCP_UDP.` Using `HTTPS` ensures that the probe performs a TLS handshake before sending the request.

- `--health-check-path` specifies the exact URL path the load balancer calls to determine target health. Example: `/health`, `/status`, `/readyz`. Only applies to `HTTP/HTTPS` health checks.
- `--health-check-port` tells the load balancer which port to use for health checks. You can specify a number (e.g., `443`) or the keyword traffic-port to reuse the Target Group's main port.
- `--health-check-interval-seconds` sets how frequently the load balancer sends health check requests. Shorter intervals detect failures faster but increase probe traffic.
- `--healthy-threshold-count` defines how many consecutive successful health checks are required before a target is marked healthy. This prevents flapping during recovery.
- `--unhealthy-threshold-count` defines how many consecutive failed health checks are required before a target is marked unhealthy. This prevents marking a target unhealthy due to a single transient failure.

An HTTPS health check is considered successful only when two conditions are met: the load balancer must complete a TLS handshake with the target, and the target must respond to the configured path with an HTTP status code matching the configured success codes (default: 200). If either condition fails—whether due to a timeout, or a 4xx/5xx response—the health check is considered failed.

Understanding Health Check Types

Although HTTPS is the most secure and most commonly recommended option, ELB supports several other health check types. As shown in Table 7.1, each one exists for a specific class of workloads, and understanding these options helps engineers choose the right mechanism for the architecture they are supporting.

TABLE 7.1 ELB Health Check Types

Health Check Type	What It Validates	When It's Used
HTTPS	TLS handshake + HTTP 2xx/3xx response	Secure, encrypted, application-level readiness checks
HTTP	HTTP status code matching the configured success codes (default: 200)	Simple application-level checks without TLS
TCP	Ability to complete a TCP handshake	Non-HTTP protocols (databases, custom services)

(Continued)

TABLE 7.1 (Continued)

Health Check Type	What It Validates	When It's Used
UDP/TCP_UDP	Ability to send/receive UDP traffic	DNS, SIP, and other UDP-based workloads
Lambda (implicit)	Successful Lambda invocation	ALB routing directly to Lambda functions
GENEVE	Appliance responsiveness via GENEVE encapsulation	Gateway Load Balancer for firewalls/IDS/IPS

These types exist because AWS load balancers support a wide variety of workloads, from classic web applications to network appliances and serverless functions. Even though the SOA-C03 exam does not require deep networking knowledge, it does expect candidates to recognize which health check type aligns with which workload.

Shallow vs. Deep Health Checks (A Critical Operational Distinction)

AWS uses the terms *shallow* and *deep* health checks in its official guidance, particularly in the AWS Networking & Content Delivery blog.

A *shallow health check* (also called a *local health check*) verifies only that the instance itself is reachable and responsive. It checks that the process is running, the port is open, and the instance can return a basic `200 OK`. Shallow checks do not validate downstream dependencies such as databases, caches, or internal services. Because they reflect only the health of the instance, shallow checks are the correct choice for auto-scaling groups.

A *deep health check* (also called a *dependency health check*) validates actual application readiness. It may confirm that the application can connect to its database, that internal services are reachable, or that startup routines have completed. Deep checks are more expressive but also more fragile. If a dependency fails, a deep check will fail—even if the instance itself is perfectly healthy.

AWS explicitly warns against using deep health checks as the ASG's health source. Doing so can cause the ASG to terminate healthy instances during dependency outages, potentially triggering cascading failure.

To learn more, visit: `https://aws.amazon.com/blogs/networking-and-content-delivery/choosing-the-right-health-check-with-elastic-load-balancing-and-ec2-auto-scaling/`.

Creating an Auto-Scaling Group that Consumes ELB Health Checks

To integrate ELB health checks with auto-scaling, the auto-scaling group (ASG) must be configured to consume the health status reported by the load balancer. This is controlled by the `--health-check-type` flag. Choosing `EC2` means the ASG relies on EC2 system status checks, while choosing `ELB` means the ASG uses the Target Group's health status. The following command creates an ASG that uses ELB health checks:

```
aws autoscaling create-auto-scaling-group \
  --auto-scaling-group-name my-asg \
  --launch-template LaunchTemplateName=my-template,Version=1 \
  --min-size 2 \
  --max-size 6 \
  --desired-capacity 3 \
  --vpc-zone-identifier "subnet-aaa,subnet-bbb" \
  --target-group-arns arn:aws:elasticloadbalancing:us-east-
1:123456789012:targetgroup/mytg/<id> \
  --health-check-type ELB \
  --health-check-grace-period 300
```

In this command:

- `--auto-scaling-group-name` assigns a name to the ASG.
- `--launch-template` specifies the launch template that defines AMI, instance type, Security Groups, and user data.
- `--min-size` is the minimum number of instances the ASG must maintain.
- `--max-size` is the maximum number of instances the ASG is allowed to scale to.
- `--desired-capacity` is the number of instances the ASG launches immediately.
- `--vpc-zone-identifier` is a comma-separated list of subnet IDs where the ASG will launch instances.
- `--target-group-arns` tells the auto-scaling group to automatically register any instances it launches into the specified Target Group(s) ARN(s). It does not register existing instances—those must be registered manually using `aws elbv2 register-targets`.
- `--health-check-type` determines which health check system the ASG uses to replace instances.
  - EC2 uses EC2 system status checks.
  - `ELB` uses ELB Target Group health checks.
- `--health-check-grace-period` gives new instances time to boot and initialize before health checks apply. Prevents premature termination during startup.

The health check grace period tells the ASG how long to wait before evaluating a newly launched instance's health. Choose a value that is slightly longer than your application's slowest expected startup time. Lightweight apps may need only 30–60 seconds, while more complex applications often require 120–300 seconds or more. Setting the grace period too short is a common cause of launch/terminate loops, especially when using HTTPS or deep health checks.

EC2 health checks evaluate the instance itself (hardware, hypervisor, and OS-level reachability). ELB health checks evaluate whatever your application's health check endpoint returns. By default this is shallow—a simple `200 OK` confirming the process is running. If your application implements deeper logic (database checks, dependency checks, startup readiness), ELB will surface those failures as well. Use EC2 checks when you want the ASG to replace only truly unhealthy instances, and use ELB checks when application-level readiness should drive replacement decisions.

Amazon Route 53 Health Checks

Amazon Route 53 health checks operate at a completely different layer. While ELB health checks operate inside a Region and evaluate individual compute targets, Route 53 health checks operate globally and evaluate publicly reachable endpoints. They are used for DNS-based failover, Multi-Region routing, and external endpoint monitoring.

A Route 53 health check is configured by providing the endpoint's IP address or domain name, the protocol, the port, and the path to probe. The following example creates an HTTPS health check:

```
aws route53 create-health-check \
  --caller-reference "$(date +%s)" \
  --health-check-config '{
      "IPAddress": "203.0.113.10",
      "Port": 443,
      "Type": "HTTPS",
      "ResourcePath": "/health",
      "RequestInterval": 30,
      "FailureThreshold": 3
  }'
```

In this command:

- `--caller-reference` is a unique string that ensures the request is idempotent. Route 53 uses this value to prevent accidental duplicate health check creation. Using a timestamp (as shown) is a common best practice.

- `--health-check-config` is a JSON structure that defines *how* Route 53 performs the health check. Contains all the protocol, endpoint, and threshold settings.

Inside `--health-check-config`:

- `IPAddress` is the public IP address Route 53 will probe. Must be reachable from the Internet because Route 53 health checkers operate globally.
- `Port` is the port number Route 53 uses when sending the health check request. For HTTPS, this is typically 443.
- `Type` is the protocol used for the health check. Determines how Route 53 validates health (e.g., TLS handshake + HTTP status code for HTTPS). Valid values include HTTP, HTTPS, TCP, HTTP_STR_MATCH, and HTTPS_STR_MATCH.
- `ResourcePath` is the URL path Route 53 requests when performing HTTP/HTTPS checks. Must return a 2xx or 3xx status code to be considered healthy.
- `RequestInterval` determines how frequently Route 53 sends health check requests (in seconds). Valid values: 10 or 30 seconds.
- `FailureThreshold` is the number of consecutive failed checks required before Route 53 marks the endpoint unhealthy. Higher values reduce false positives; lower values detect failures faster.

Troubleshooting Health Check Failures

When a health check fails—whether in ELB or Route 53—the key to resolving the issue is understanding which system is reporting the failure and what that system is actually measuring. ELB health checks operate inside the VPC and evaluate the reachability and responsiveness of individual compute targets. Route 53 health checks originate from AWS's global health-checker fleet and evaluate publicly reachable endpoints. Because these systems observe different parts of the architecture, they fail for different reasons and require different investigative approaches.

For ELB health checks, the most reliable starting point is always the load balancer's own perspective. The `describe-target-health` command reveals exactly what the load balancer sees when it probes a target:

```
aws elbv2 describe-target-health \
  --target-group-arn arn:aws:elasticloadbalancing:us-east-
1:123456789012:targetgroup/mytg/<target-group-id>
```

If the response shows a state of `unhealthy` with a reason such as `Target.ResponseCodeMismatch`, the load balancer is reaching the instance but receiving an unexpected status code—often a 500 error or a redirect. A `Target.Timeout` reason suggests the instance is reachable but too slow to respond, which may indicate startup delays, overloaded resources, or a misconfigured health check path. TLS-related failures appear before the HTTP request is even sent, and they typically point to target not configured for TLS, or unsupported protocol versions. In all these cases, the load balancer's diagnostic output provides the most direct clue about what to investigate next.

If the load balancer cannot reach the instance at all, the investigation shifts to network reachability. A simple `curl` command from within the instance can confirm whether the application is responding locally. If it is, the problem almost always lies in the network path between the load balancer and the instance—usually a missing security-group rule, a restrictive NACL, or a routing misconfiguration. These issues are common in Multi-AZ deployments where engineers assume that Security Groups allow traffic from the load balancer by default, when in fact they must explicitly allow inbound traffic from the load balancer's Security Group.

Startup time is another frequent culprit. Many applications take longer to initialize than the health check interval allows, especially when they perform dependency (deep health) checks or warm caches, or they establish database connections. If the ASG is consuming ELB health checks, this can lead to a launch-and-terminate loop where instances are replaced before they ever become healthy. Increasing the health check grace period usually resolves this pattern.

Route 53 health check failures require a different mindset because the probes originate from AWS's global health-checker fleet rather than from inside the VPC. The first question is always whether the endpoint is reachable from the public Internet. If it is not, the issue may be as simple as a firewall rule blocking AWS health-checker IP ranges—a surprisingly common oversight. Route 53 publishes these IP ranges in the `ip-ranges.json` document under the `ROUTE53_HEALTHCHECKERS` service key. Because this list changes over time, AWS recommends consuming it programmatically rather than hard-coding individual addresses. Any firewall protecting your endpoint must allow inbound traffic from these ranges; otherwise, Route 53 will consistently mark the endpoint as unhealthy even if it is functioning normally.

TLS issues are another frequent cause of Route 53 failures. Route 53 is strict about certificate validity, hostname matching, and intermediate certificates, and a misconfigured certificate chain can cause global failures even when the endpoint appears healthy in a browser. Latency also plays a role. If the endpoint responds slowly, Route 53 may time out before receiving a response, marking the endpoint unhealthy even though it eventually responds. In these cases, increasing the request interval or failure threshold can help, but the long-term fix is improving the endpoint's responsiveness.

Across both systems, the pattern is the same: start with the perspective of the system reporting the failure, interpret what it is actually measuring, and follow the signal outward. ELB failures usually point to application responsiveness, TLS configuration, or VPC-level networking. Route 53 failures usually point to public reachability, firewall rules, certificate chains, or latency. Understanding these distinctions allows you, as a CloudOps engineer, to troubleshoot quickly and confidently, and prepares you to recognize the underlying causes of health check failures in exam scenarios.

Disaster Recovery

High Availability and Disaster Recovery (DR) share foundational practices—monitoring, multi-location deployments, and automated failover—but they serve different purposes within a resilient architecture. Availability focuses on keeping individual components healthy and responsive, while disaster recovery prepares for large-scale events that can take an entire workload offline. After establishing a resilient, highly available architecture, the next step is to design a disaster recovery strategy that can restore the entire workload in a different location when necessary.

The level of availability you build directly shapes your disaster recovery approach. A workload running on a single instance in one Availability Zone requires a full failover to another AZ if that zone becomes unavailable, whereas a Multi-Region Active-Active deployment can withstand even a regional outage simply by routing traffic to the remaining Regions. Data strategy also diverges between availability and DR: continuous replication supports high availability, but it can also propagate corruption or accidental deletions. To protect against these scenarios, disaster recovery requires point-in-time backups that allow you to restore clean data even when replication cannot.

As you move from resilience into disaster recovery, the focus naturally shifts from how a system stays healthy to how a system comes back when everything goes wrong. The concepts you've just explored—SRE principles, HA vs. FT, resilience patterns, and the mechanics of ELB and Route 53 health checks—form the operational backbone that DR strategies build upon. With that foundation in place, you're now ready to explore the four canonical AWS disaster recovery strategies: Backup & Restore, Pilot Light, Warm Standby, and Multi-Region Active-Active. These patterns represent progressively stronger (and more complex) approaches to recovering entire workloads, and they are central to both real-world CloudOps and the SOA-C03 exam.

DR Strategies

Before diving into the four DR strategies themselves, it's helpful to refresh the two recovery-focused service level objectives (SLOs) that guide every disaster recovery decision: Recovery Time Objective (RTO) and Recovery Point Objective (RPO). Both are measured in units of time. RTO defines how long a workload can be unavailable before the business is harmed, while RPO defines how much time's worth of data the business can afford to lose. For example, if a workload has an RTO of one hour and an RPO of five minutes, the business can tolerate up to one hour of downtime but no more than five minutes of lost data. The figures referenced in this section use illustrative data to help you visualize these concepts. The SOA-C03 exam expects you to treat RTO and RPO as business-driven SLOs that directly constrain which DR strategies are acceptable.

To make these constraints concrete, the diagram in Figure 7.5 plots Recovery Cost against RTO. The curve shows diminishing returns: early investments dramatically reduce downtime, while later investments yield smaller improvements. The vertical long-dash line represents the Acceptable Recovery Cost, and the horizontal dotted line represents the maximum acceptable RTO. Only the bolded portion of the curve—the segment that lies below the RTO threshold and to the left of the cost limit—represents DR strategies that satisfy both constraints. In the illustrative example, Warm Standby is the only strategy that falls inside this feasible region. Backup & Restore is too slow, Pilot Light still exceeds the RTO requirement, and Multi-Site Active-Active meets the RTO target but violates the cost boundary. This visual reinforces a key SOA-C03 insight: the "right" DR strategy is the one that meets the recovery SLOs, not the one with the lowest theoretical downtime.

FIGURE 7.5 RTO vs. cost.

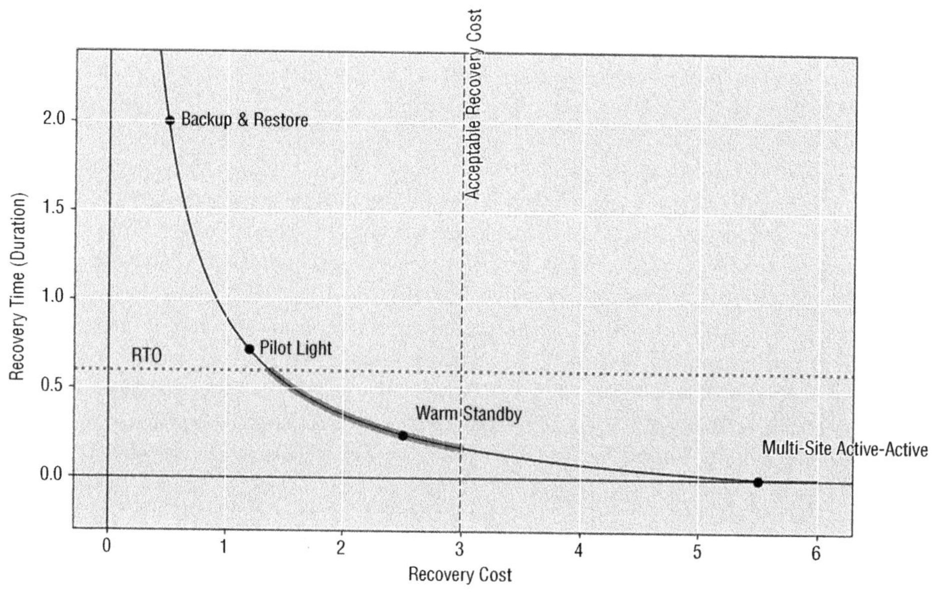

FIGURE 7.6 RPO vs. cost.

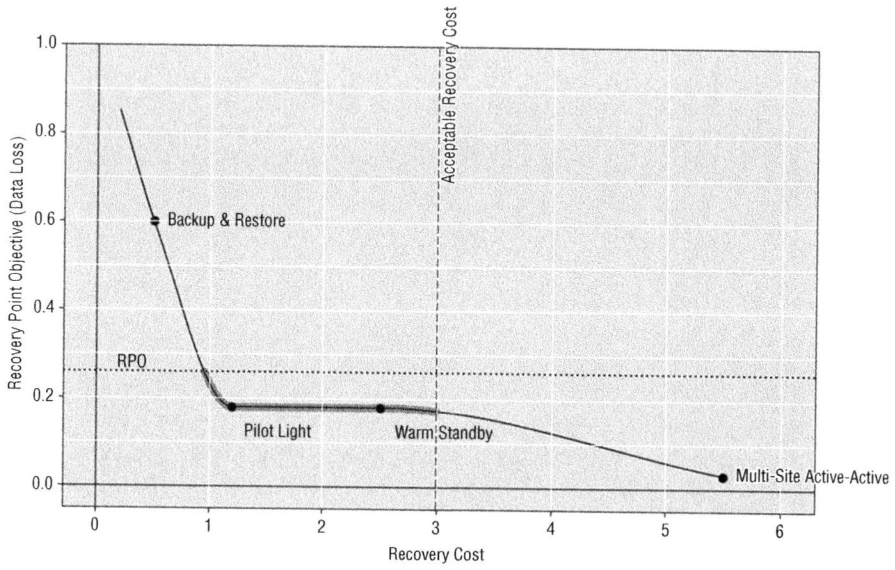

The diagram in Figure 7.6 mirrors the first but focuses on RPO, again measured in time units. Here, the curve drops more quickly—RPO improves earlier and more sharply than RTO as you invest in replication and continuous data protection. The vertical long-dash line again marks the Acceptable Recovery Cost, and the horizontal dotted line marks the maximum acceptable RPO. The bolded segment highlights the portion of the curve that satisfies both constraints. In the illustrative example, Pilot Light and Warm Standby both fall within the acceptable region, while Backup & Restore exceeds the RPO limit and Multi-Site Active-Active exceeds the cost limit. This contrast with the RTO diagram is intentional: it shows that RPO and RTO improve at different rates, and that a strategy acceptable for one may not be acceptable for the other.

Taken together, these two visuals give you a unified framework for DR strategy selection. They show that each strategy corresponds to a specific point on both curves, and that the "right" choice depends entirely on where the acceptable region lies for your workload. In the illustrative example, Warm Standby is the only strategy that satisfies both RTO and RPO constraints within the cost boundary—making it the correct answer in an SOA-C03 scenario. This is exactly how the exam frames DR questions: not as memorization of definitions, but as reasoning about trade-offs, constraints, and time-based recovery SLOs. With this visual foundation in place, you're now ready to examine each DR strategy in detail and understand how and why it fits into the broader recovery landscape.

Backup & Restore

Backup & Restore is the most cost-efficient DR strategy and is often the right choice when your primary goal is protecting against data loss or corruption. As a CloudOps engineer, you should recognize that this approach can also provide regional protection by replicating backups to another AWS Region, or by compensating for workloads that run in a single Availability Zone without built-in redundancy.

Because Backup & Restore does not maintain any pre-provisioned infrastructure in the recovery Region, you must be prepared to rebuild everything during recovery—infrastructure, configuration, and application code. For the SOA-C03 exam, remember that the only reliable way to do this quickly and consistently is to use Infrastructure-as-Code (IaC). Services like AWS CloudFormation, the AWS Cloud Development Kit (CDK), or third-party tools like HashiCorp Terraform allow you to redeploy environments without manual steps, reducing the risk of configuration drift and helping you stay within your RTO.

A common pitfall—both in real operations and on the exam—is backing up only user data. Backup & Restore requires you to also preserve application artifacts, including configuration files, deployment packages, and any Amazon Machine Images (AMIs) used to launch Amazon EC2 instances. Without these, recovery becomes slow, error-prone, and may exceed your RTO.

To streamline recovery even further, CloudOps teams automate the redeployment of application code and configuration using AWS CodePipeline or similar CI/CD tooling (GitHub Actions, GitLab, etc.). This ensures that once the infrastructure is restored, the application stack can be rebuilt and validated with minimal intervention—an operational pattern the SOA-C03 exam strongly favors in full alignment with the "Safely automate where possible" Operational Excellence principle you learned in Chapter 1.

To put this DR strategy into action, the next section introduces a key AWS service that fully automates and centralizes your backups, simplifying the operational burden of securing your backups and ensuring you can reliably restore data to a clean point in time. This capability is especially critical in scenarios involving data corruption, accidental deletion, or ransomware, where the ability to recover known-good data is just as important as restoring infrastructure. By integrating this service into your Backup & Restore workflow, you, as a CloudOps engineer, gain a predictable, auditable, and exam-relevant foundation for meeting both RTO and RPO commitments.

AWS Backup

We briefly covered AWS Backup as part of the backup and restore strategies for databases and storage services you learned in Chapters 4 and 5. In this section, we expand that foundation and examine AWS Backup as a dedicated, centralized service for orchestrating data protection across your entire AWS environment—an essential capability for CloudOps engineers preparing for the SOA-C03 exam.

AWS Backup is a fully managed, centralized backup service that allows CloudOps engineers to define, automate, and enforce data-protection policies across AWS services and hybrid workloads. It provides a single control plane for creating backup plans, scheduling backups, managing retention, and orchestrating restores across multiple accounts and Regions. AWS Backup helps ensure that backups are consistent, encrypted, and governed by policies rather than ad-hoc scripts or service-specific mechanisms.

A core benefit for CloudOps teams is that AWS Backup standardizes backup operations across a wide range of AWS services, including Amazon S3, EBS, RDS, Aurora, DynamoDB, EFS, FSx, EC2, and even on-premises VMware workloads via AWS Backup Gateway. This breadth allows you to apply tag-based backup policies, enforce compliance centrally, and avoid the operational drift that often occurs when each service is backed up independently. Backups are stored in backup vaults, which provide encryption, access control, and isolation boundaries for recovery points.

AWS Backup also includes features that directly support resilience and security objectives tested on the SOA-C03 exam. These include cross-region and cross-account backup, immutable backups using Backup Vault Lock, and automated backup auditing to verify that workloads meet organizational data-protection requirements. These capabilities are especially important in scenarios involving ransomware, accidental deletion, or data corruption, where clean, point-in-time recovery is essential.

AWS Backup Vault Lock is the specific feature designed to provide WORM (Write Once, Read Many) immutability. In "compliance mode," even the root user cannot delete backups or shorten the retention period.

Finally, AWS Backup provides a consistent mechanism for restoring resources through restore jobs, allowing CloudOps engineers to recover data and infrastructure in a predictable, auditable way. Restore plans and automated restore testing help validate that backups are usable and that recovery workflows meet RTO and RPO commitments. For you as a CloudOps engineer, AWS Backup represents the preferred, policy-driven approach to protecting and restoring AWS workloads at scale.

Implementing Backup & Restore with AWS Backup

To see how AWS Backup works in practice, imagine a landing zone hosting three Amazon EC2 instances and an Amazon Aurora Database Cluster. Figure 7.7 illustrates this setup.

With AWS Backup, you can apply a single, tag-based backup policy that captures all four resources on a defined schedule, stores their recovery points in encrypted backup vaults, and replicates them to a secondary Region for disaster recovery. In the event of a regional outage, data corruption, or ransomware event, AWS Backup provides the recovery points needed to rebuild the EC2 instances from their AMIs and restore the Aurora cluster to a clean point in time. This gives your CloudOps team a predictable, auditable path to meet RTO and RPO commitments without relying on ad hoc scripts or service-specific tooling.

With this foundation in place, the next sections explore how AWS Backup orchestrates these backups and restores in 11 steps, and how you can use it to implement a resilient, exam-ready DR strategy.

Phase 1: Setup and Orchestration

Phase 1 addresses the administrative "control plane" of your backup strategy. In this stage, we establish the governance required to automate data protection across account boundaries and regions. By creating vaults, we define the secure storage locations for our recovery points, and by configuring the backup plan, we create the "instruction set" that AWS Backup will follow. This phase ensures that our landing zone resources are not just backed up, but are categorized and managed according to a centralized policy that removes the need for manual, resource-by-resource intervention.

Step 1: Create the Source and Target Backup Vaults

Backup Vaults are the logical containers for your recovery points. Because they are regional, you need one in your production region and one in your DR region.

```
# Create Source Vault in Region 1
aws backup create-backup-vault \
    --backup-vault-name SourceVault \
    --region us-east-1

# Create Target Vault in Region 2
aws backup create-backup-vault \
    --backup-vault-name TargetVault \
    --region us-west-2
```

In this command:

- `--backup-vault-name` is the unique name you assign to your container.
- `--region` is the regional boundary where the vault's metadata and underlying S3 storage will reside.

FIGURE 7.7 Backup & Restore example architecture.

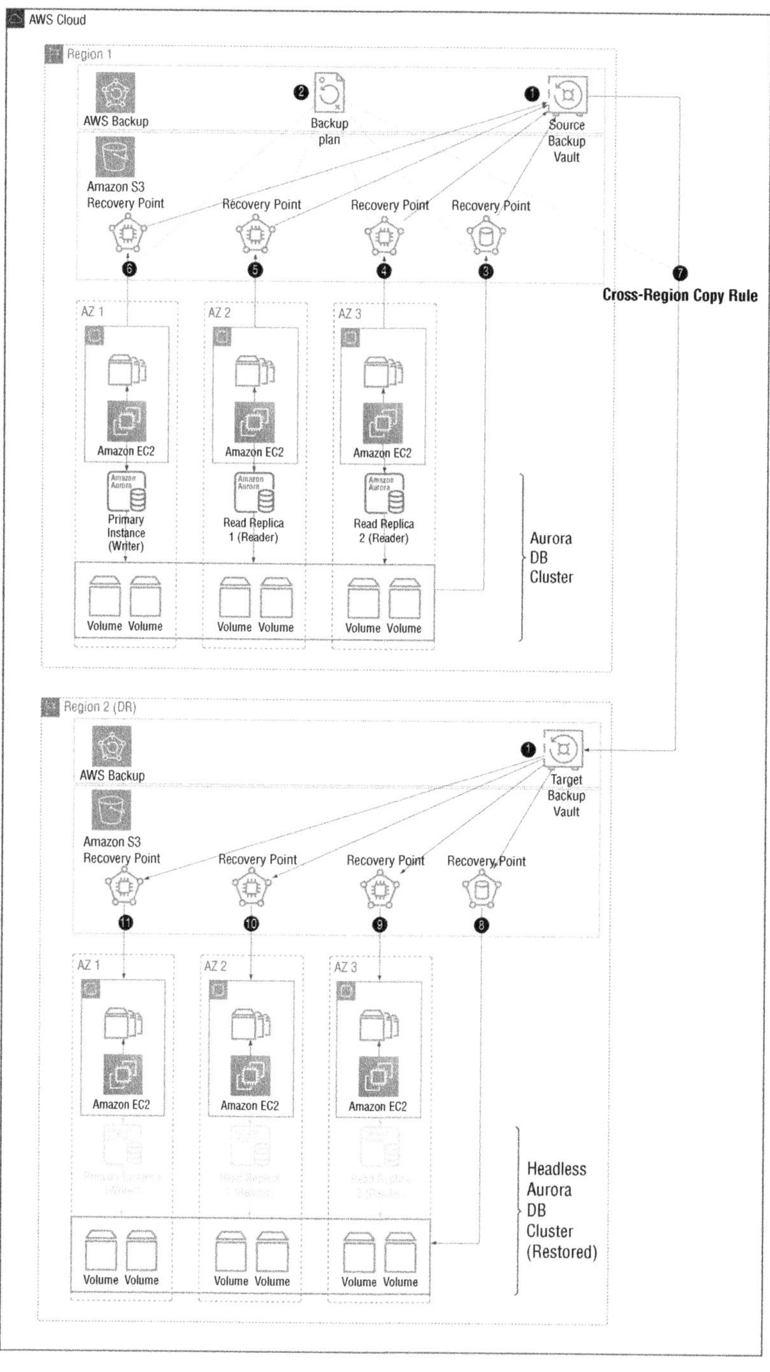

Step 2: Create a Backup Plan and Assign Resources to the Backup Plan

The *backup plan* acts as the central brain and orchestrator of your data protection lifecycle. It does not simply schedule snapshots; it manages the creation of recovery points, governs their retention, and initiates the Cross-Region Copy necessary for your Backup & Restore or more advanced DR strategies.

The following command creates the plan and includes a `CopyActions` block, which tells AWS Backup to replicate every recovery point to the DR region immediately after it is created.

```
aws backup create-backup-plan \
    --region us-east-1 \
    --backup-plan '{
        "BackupPlanName": "LZ-DR-Orchestrator",
        "Rules": [
            {
                "RuleName": "DailyDRRule",
                "TargetBackupVaultName": "SourceVault",
                "ScheduleExpression": "cron(0 5 * * ? *)",
                "StartWindowMinutes": 60,
                "CompletionWindowMinutes": 120,
                "Lifecycle": {
                    "DeleteAfterDays": 35
                },
                "CopyActions": [
                    {
                        "DestinationBackupVaultArn": "arn:aws:backup:us-west-
2:123456789012:backup-vault:TargetVault",
                        "Lifecycle": {
                            "DeleteAfterDays": 35
                        }
                    }
                ]
            }
        ]
    }'
```

In this command:

- `--backup-plan` is a flag that accepts the JSON definition that defines the "backup policy."

The JSON keys used are as follows:

- `BackupPlanName`: A user-defined string used to identify the plan in the console.
- `RuleName`: A unique name for the specific backup rule within the plan.
- `TargetBackupVaultName`: Specifies the vault where recovery points are initially stored in the source region.
- `ScheduleExpression`: Uses a CRON expression to define when the orchestrator should trigger (e.g., daily at 5:00 AM).

- `StartWindowMinutes`: The time period (in minutes) during which a backup job must start.
- `CompletionWindowMinutes`: The time period allowed for a backup job to successfully finish.
- `Lifecycle`: Controls the age of recovery points before they are deleted or moved to cold storage. In this example, recovery points are automatically deleted after 35 days to manage costs.
- `CopyActions`: This is the engine of your DR strategy. It instructs the orchestrator to copy the recovery point to the `DestinationBackupVaultArn` (your Target Vault in Region 2).
- `DestinationBackupVaultArn`: The full ARN of the vault in Region 2 that will receive the replicated backup.

For a complete reference, visit: `https://docs.aws.amazon.com/cli/latest/reference/backup/create-backup-plan.html`.

Once the plan is created, you must assign your resources using a backup selection. As you learned in Chapter 2, tags are the gold standard for CloudOps. It allows the backup plan to automatically "discover" your three EC2 instances and Aurora cluster as long as they have the correct tag.

```
aws backup create-backup-selection \
    --backup-plan-id "a1b2c3d4-5678-90ab-cdef-EXAMPLE11111" \
    --backup-selection '{
        "SelectionName": "LZ-Tag-Selection",
        "IamRoleArn": "arn:aws:iam::123456789012:role/service-role/
AWSBackupDefaultServiceRole",
        "Conditions": {
            "StringEquals": [
                {
                    "ConditionKey": "aws:ResourceTag/Backup",
                    "ConditionValue": "LZ-DR"
                }
            ]
        }
    }'
```

In this command:

- `--backup-plan-id` must be the system-generated UUID, not the `LZ-DR-Orchestrator` name.
- `--backup-selection` is a flag that accepts a JSON structure that defines which resources are governed by the plan.

The JSON keys used are detailed here:

- `SelectionName`: A display name for this specific selection rule (e.g., `LZ-Tag-Selection`).

- `IamRoleArn`: The ARN of the IAM role AWS Backup assumes to create snapshots. It must have policies like `AWSBackupServiceRolePolicyForBackup`.
- `Conditions`: This key defines a set of rules used to assign resources to a backup plan based on their tags. `Conditions` supports operators such as `StringEquals`, `StringLike`, `StringNotEquals`, `StringNotLike` and requires a resource to match all specified rules (AND logic) to be included. Inside the `Conditions` block you define the following hierarchy:
  - `StringEquals`: This is a condition operator used for exact matching. It filters your resources to include only those where the tag value exactly matches your specified criteria. It contains a list of objects, each consisting of:
    - `ConditionKey`: The specific tag key you want to check. When using `Conditions`, you must include the `aws:ResourceTag/` prefix before the tag name (e.g., `aws:ResourceTag/Backup`) to tell AWS Backup to look at the resource's tags.
    - `ConditionValue`: The specific tag value that must be present for the resource to be selected. For instance, if your key is `Backup`, and you only want to back up resources tagged for disaster recovery, your value would be `LZ-DR`.

For a complete reference, visit: `https://docs.aws.amazon.com/cli/latest/reference/backup/create-backup-selection.html`.

You can also assign resources by explicitly listing their Amazon Resource Names (ARNs) within the `Resources` key of the JSON. However, this is not a best practice because it is a manual process. If you replace an instance or scale your environment, you must manually update the backup plan, which creates a high risk of "backup gaps."

Phase 2: Backup Cycle (Region 1)

Phase 2 focuses on the active generation and replication of recovery points. This is where the theoretical plan meets the physical data. During this phase, the orchestrator communicates with the zonal resources (EC2/EBS) and the regional database (Aurora) to capture a consistent point-in-time snapshot of the entire landing zone. Crucially, this phase handles the transformation of zonal data into regional, durable objects stored in Amazon S3, and then executes the cross-region copy rule to ensure that a localized disaster in Region 1 cannot destroy your only path to recovery.

Steps 3–6: Create Recovery Points (Aurora and EC2)

One of the most powerful features of AWS Backup for EC2 is how it leverages the Amazon Machine Image (AMI) concept.

When the orchestrator triggers a backup for an EC2 instance, it creates a specialized AMI. This recovery point automatically packages multi-volume, crash-consistent EBS snapshots along with the Instance Metadata (the "blueprint" of the CPU, RAM, and Networking). Because it captures the entire instance state, you do not need to manually create EBS snapshots for each volume. AWS Backup handles the synchronization of all attached disks for you.

- **Step 3:** AWS Backup automatically creates Aurora Recovery Point, which captures the shared volume across three AZs.
- **Steps 4–6:** AWS Backup automatically creates EC2 Recovery Points (AZ 3, 2, 1). AWS Backup leverages AMIs to package crash-consistent EBS snapshots with Instance Metadata, eliminating the need for manual EBS snapshots.

Step 7: Cross-Region Copy Rule

As illustrated in Figure 7.7, AWS Backup automatically executes the Cross-Region Copy Rule, replicating these four recovery points to the Target Vault in Region 2.

Phase 3: Manual Restoration (Region 2)

Phase 3 addresses the "Data Plane" recovery and the re-materialization of resources in your DR region. This is the most critical stage for meeting your RTO, as it involves taking the regional S3 objects and "pinning" them back into specific Availability Zones in Region 2. This phase goes beyond mere data copying; it requires reapplying the network context—Security Groups, subnets, and instance types—to ensure that the restored environment is functional. We also address the specific technical requirement of Aurora, where the shared storage volume is restored first, followed by the manual provisioning of compute nodes to bring the database back online.

Step 8: Restore Aurora Cluster Shared Volume

When restoring Aurora, AWS Backup restores the Regional Shared Storage Volume (the cluster) into Region 2 (`us-west-2`).

```
aws backup start-restore-job \
    --region us-west-2 \
    --recovery-point-arn "arn:aws:backup:us-west-2:123456789012:recovery-
point:AURORA-ID" \
    --metadata '{
        "DBClusterIdentifier": "dr-cluster",
        "DBSubnetGroupName": "dr-subnets"
    }'
```

In this command:

- `--region`: Specifies the target region where the restore job should execute (e.g., your DR region).
- `--recovery-point-arn`: The unique Amazon Resource Name of the backup you want to restore from the Target Vault.
- `--metadata`: A JSON string containing resource-specific configuration required to re-create the resource.

The JSON keys used are detailed here:

- `DBClusterIdentifier`: The unique name for the restored Aurora DB cluster in the new region.

- `DBSubnetGroupName`: Connects the regional cluster to a specific set of subnets defined in the DR VPC.

For the exam, be aware that restoring the cluster volume does not create the database instances (compute nodes). In this state your Aurora cluster is referred to as "headless"—it has the body (data) but no head (processor) to handle SQL queries. After this job completes and the cluster is in an available state, you must *manually* create the primary (writer) instance using the Amazon RDS API or CLI to make the database functional. Figure 7.7 shows the headless Aurora DB Cluster at the bottom of the figure.

As you learned in Chapter 4, the command to create a DB instance in your Aurora DB cluster is as follows:

```
aws rds create-db-instance \
    --db-instance-identifier dr-primary-instance \
    --db-cluster-identifier dr-cluster \
    --db-instance-class db.r6g.large \
    --engine aurora-mysql
```

Steps 9, 10, and 11: Restore EC2 Instances in AZ 3, 2, and 1

Restoring an EC2 recovery point uses the AMI metadata to transform regional S3 data back into a Zonal EC2/EBS resource.

```
aws backup start-restore-job \
    --region us-west-2 \
    --recovery-point-arn "arn:aws:backup:us-west-2:123456789012:recovery-
point:EC2-AZ1-ID" \
    --metadata '{
        "SubnetId": "subnet-dr-app-az1",
        "SecurityGroupIds": "[\"sg-dr-app-server\"]",
        "InstanceType": "t3.medium"
    }'
```

The JSON keys used are detailed here:

- `SubnetId`: This is the key that converts a regional backup back into a Zonal resource by pinning it to a specific Availability Zone.
- `SecurityGroupIds`: Reattaches the virtual firewall rules (Security Groups) required for the instance in the new region.
- `InstanceType`: Allows you to specify the compute hardware (e.g., `t3.medium`) for the restored instance.

For a complete reference, visit: `https://docs.aws.amazon.com/cli/latest/reference/backup/start-restore-job.html`.

Automating DR Orchestration with AWS Backup Restore Testing

AWS Backup becomes far more powerful when paired with its Restore Testing capability. AWS Backup Restore Testing allows you to schedule automated "dry run" restores of your landing zone, giving you a repeatable way to validate that your DR posture actually meets your defined RTO and RPO. In a practical scenario—such as the landing zone in Figure 7.7—AWS Backup can automatically restore these resources into an isolated test VPC on a daily or weekly cadence. This continuous validation ensures that recovery points are usable, infrastructure definitions are correct, and your team can trust that clean, point-in-time data is available when a real disaster occurs. For the SOA-C03 exam, remember that automated restore testing is one of the strongest ways to prove DR readiness without impacting production.

With reference to the Phase 3 in the previous example, instead of manually typing metadata for four separate resources (three EC2 instances and an Aurora Cluster) during an emergency, you preconfigure a *restore testing plan*. This plan acts as the "restoration orchestrator" in Region 2. When a disaster is declared, or according to a test schedule, it automatically maps the regional recovery points back into zonal resources using the networking context you defined. The next section shows an alternative approach to Phase 3, which is a fully automated, repeatable way to restore your four recovery points in Region 2.

Phase 3b: Automated Restoration (Region 2)

The following command creates a restore testing plan to pre-map networking metadata. This resource eliminates the need to manually type metadata for four separate resources during a disaster.

Create the Restore Testing Plan (Region 2)

```
aws backup create-restore-testing-plan \
    --region us-west-2 \
    --restore-testing-plan '{
        "RestoreTestingPlanName": "LZ-DR-Restore-Orchestrator",
        "ScheduleExpression": "cron(0 12 ? * SUN *)",
        "StartWindowHours": 6,
        "RecoveryPointSelection": {
            "Algorithm": "LATEST_WITHIN_WINDOW",
            "IncludeVaults": ["arn:aws:backup:us-west-2:123456789012:backup-
vault:TargetVault"],
            "RecoveryPointTypes": ["SNAPSHOT"],
            "SelectionWindowDays": 7
        }
    }'
```

In this command:

- `--region` is the DR region where the plan resides.
- `--restore-testing-plan` is a flag that accepts a JSON object that defines the core behavior of your automated restoration tests. Here is a breakdown of its primary keys:
    - `RestoreTestingPlanName`: A unique string used to identify the plan. It cannot be changed after creation.

- `ScheduleExpression`: A cron or rate expression (e.g., `cron(0 12 ? * SUN *)`) that determines how often AWS Backup automatically triggers a test restore. In this case, every Sunday at 12:00 PM (noon) UTC.
- `StartWindowHours`: A numerical value in hours (between 1 and 168) representing the time window in which the restore test must begin. If it doesn't start within this window, the test is canceled.
- `RecoveryPointSelection`: A nested object that tells AWS Backup which specific backup (recovery point) to choose for the test. It contains:
  - `Algorithm`: The logic used to pick the backup. Options are `LATEST_WITHIN_WINDOW` (grabs the newest available) or `RANDOM_WITHIN_WINDOW` (picks one at random).
  - `IncludeVaults`: An array of ARNs or names of the backup vaults to search. Using `["*"]` targets all vaults in the current region.
  - `RecoveryPointTypes`: Specifies the type of backup to test. Use `["SNAPSHOT"]` for standard backups or `["CONTINUOUS"]` for point-in-time recovery points.
  - `SelectionWindowDays`: (Optional) An integer defining the look-back period (e.g., seven days) for the algorithm to find a valid recovery point.

For a detailed reference of the `create-restore-testing-plan` command, visit: `https://docs.aws.amazon.com/cli/latest/reference/backup/create-restore-testing-plan.html`.

Once the restore testing plan is created, we add *restore testing selections* to the plan, similarly to how we assigned resources to the backup plan in Step 2.

Create Restore Testing Selections (Automating Steps 8–11)

The following command adds the metadata for the Aurora Cluster to be restored in Region 2. Make sure the value of the `--restore-testing-plan-name` flag matches the friendly name you used for the `RestoreTestingPlanName` key in the previous command.

```
aws backup create-restore-testing-selection \
    --region us-west-2 \
    --restore-testing-plan-name "LZ-DR-Restore-Orchestrator" \
    --restore-testing-selection '{
        "RestoreTestingSelectionName": "Aurora-Mapping",
        "ProtectedResourceType": "RDS",
        "IamRoleArn": "arn:aws:iam::123456789012:role/service-role/
AWSBackupDefaultServiceRole",
        "RestoreMetadataOverrides": {
            "DBSubnetGroupName": "dr-vpc-data-subnet-group",
            "VpcSecurityGroupIds": "[\"sg-dr-database\"]"
        },
        "ProtectedResourceArns": ["*"]
    }'
```

In this command:

- `RestoreTestingSelectionName` is the name of the restore testing selection for the related restore testing plan. Note that this name cannot be changed after the selection is created.
- `ProtectedResourceType` filters by service (e.g., RDS or EC2) to apply valid metadata keys.
- `ProtectedResourceArns`: Using `["*"]` combined with the resource type allows the plan to automatically capture your Aurora cluster recovery point in your Target Vault without needing to list its individual ARN.
- `IamRoleArn`: Unlike the backup process where the role is often set at the plan level, for restore testing, the role is defined within the selection. This allows you to use different roles for different resource types (e.g., a specific role for RDS and another for EC2).
- `RestoreMetadataOverrides` is the "mapping engine" that pins resources to subnets.
  - `DBSubnetGroupName` (RDS): Rematerializes Aurora into the data-tier subnets.
  - `VpcSecurityGroupIds`: Reattaches the virtual firewall rules required for the database tier in Region 2.

The `RestoreMetadataOverrides` object is defined at the selection level. Because you can only provide a single string (instead of an array) for `SubnetId` within that object, every resource captured by that specific selection will be forced into that one subnet (i.e., into a single AZ). Put differently, Multi-AZ restore patterns require multiple selections, each with their own subnet mapping.

The following command configures a targeted restoration rule to automatically test the recovery of a specific EC2 instance into its designated DR subnet in AZ 1 (i.e., `subnet-dr-app-az1`). By applying `RestoreMetadataOverrides` to this individual instance ARN, the testing plan ensures that the server is scheduled to be restored into the correct network tier with the appropriate DR-specific security group for validation.

```
aws backup create-restore-testing-selection \
    --region us-west-2 \
    --restore-testing-plan-name "LZ-DR-Restore-Orchestrator" \
    --restore-testing-selection '{
        "RestoreTestingSelectionName": "EC2-App-Tier-AZ1-Mapping",
        "ProtectedResourceType": "EC2",
        "IamRoleArn": "arn:aws:iam::123456789012:role/service-role/
AWSBackupDefaultServiceRole",
        "ProtectedResourceArns": ["arn:aws:ec2:us-west-2:123456789012:
instance/i-01111111111111111"],
        "RestoreMetadataOverrides": {
```

```
            "SubnetId": "subnet-dr-app-az1",
            "SecurityGroupIds": "[\"sg-dr-app-server\"]",
            "InstanceType": "t3.medium"
        }
    }'
```

In this command:

- `ProtectedResourceType` is set to EC2. This ensures the orchestrator only applies these specific networking overrides to your EC2 instance(s) and not your database cluster.
- `ProtectedResourceArns`: Using `["arn:aws:ec2:us-west-2:123456789012:instance/i-0111111111111111"]` combined with the resource type allows the plan to automatically capture a specific EC2 instance recovery point in the Target Vault.
- `RestoreMetadataOverrides` is where you transform the regional backup back into a zonal resource:
  - `SubnetId`: The critical key that "pins" the instance to a specific subnet.
  - `SecurityGroupIds`: Reattaches the virtual firewall rules required for the application tier in Region 2.
  - `InstanceType`: Allows you to specify the compute hardware. In a 2026 DR scenario, you might downsize to a `t3.medium` to save costs during a drill or keep it at production levels for a real disaster.

To restore the three EC2 instances into their dedicated subnet, you need to repeat the aforementioned command to create three separate selections (one for each AZ) within the plan, each mapping the specific Instance ARN to its corresponding DR Subnet ID.

For a detailed reference of the `create-restore-testing-selection` command, visit: `https://docs.aws.amazon.com/cli/latest/reference/backup/create-restore-testing-selection.html`.

By having the `Aurora-Mapping` and the three `EC2-App-Tier-AZ[1-3]-Mapping` selections in place, the Restore Testing Plan ensures that at the scheduled interval:

- **Step 8 (Aurora Selection)** is triggered, automatically restoring the cluster in the data subnets.
- **Steps 9-11 (EC2 Selections)** are triggered in parallel, automatically restoring the three instances into their respective app subnets.

As a result, Phase 3b provides a preferred, automated and repeatable solution to restore the Aurora Cluster and the three EC2 instances in Region 2.

Integration with AWS Step Functions

AWS Backup becomes even more effective when integrated with AWS Step Functions, enabling CloudOps teams to orchestrate the full sequence of post-restore actions that turn raw recovery points into a functioning environment. AWS Step Functions can call the Amazon RDS API to promote or create the Aurora writer instance, update Route 53 DNS records to point clients to Region 2 endpoints, or trigger application-level health checks before traffic is shifted. This creates a near "one-click" recovery workflow that minimizes human error during high-stress disaster events and ensures that recovery steps are executed consistently every time. As you prepare for the exam, the key takeaway is that AWS Backup is not just a backup service—it is a DR automation engine that, when combined with orchestration tools, delivers predictable, auditable, and highly repeatable recovery outcomes.

Pilot Light

Following the Backup & Restore Disaster Recovery strategy, the next step to reduce RTO and RPO is adopting a *Pilot Light* architecture. In this model, you continuously replicate your data to a secondary Region and maintain a minimal but functional copy of your core infrastructure. Resources required to support data replication—such as databases, distributed storage volumes, and object storage—are *always on*, ensuring that the DR Region has a live, continuously updated data layer. Other components, such as web and application servers, remain "switched off" until needed, which keeps costs low while still enabling rapid recovery.

Figure 7.8 illustrates this pattern with a web application deployed across three Availability Zones in `Region 1`. An ALB distributes traffic to a three-node web tier and a three-node app tier, each spread across `AZ 1`, `AZ 2`, and `AZ 3`. The data layer is an Aurora Global Database with a primary writer in `AZ 1` and read replicas in `AZ 2` and `AZ 3`. Route 53 monitors the ALB endpoint and, if `Region 1` becomes unavailable, fails traffic over to an identical—but powered-down—stack in `Region 2`. In the DR Region, the Web and App tiers remain off, but the Aurora shared storage volume stays continuously hydrated through Asynchronous Cross-Region Continuous Replication.

For SOA-C03 candidates, the key advantage of Pilot Light is that it provides much lower RTO and RPO than Backup & Restore, while still controlling cost. Because the core infrastructure is already deployed in both Regions, recovery primarily involves "switching on" compute resources and scaling them out. This requires CloudOps teams to adopt deployment practices that keep Regions in sync—most commonly through Infrastructure-as-Code (IaC) and automated CI/CD pipelines that push configuration and application updates to both Regions *simultaneously*. Many organizations also use separate AWS accounts per Region to maximize isolation and reduce blast radius in the event of compromised credentials.

Continuous replication is central to achieving low RPO in a Pilot Light DR strategy. AWS services such as Amazon S3 Cross-Region Replication, Amazon RDS Read Replicas, Aurora Global Database, Amazon DynamoDB Global Tables, Amazon DocumentDB Global Clusters, and Amazon ElastiCache Global Datastore provide asynchronous, cross-region data movement with near-real-time lag. Aurora Global Database is particularly powerful for DR: it uses dedicated replication infrastructure, typically maintains sub-second lag, and

FIGURE 7.8 Pilot Light example architecture.

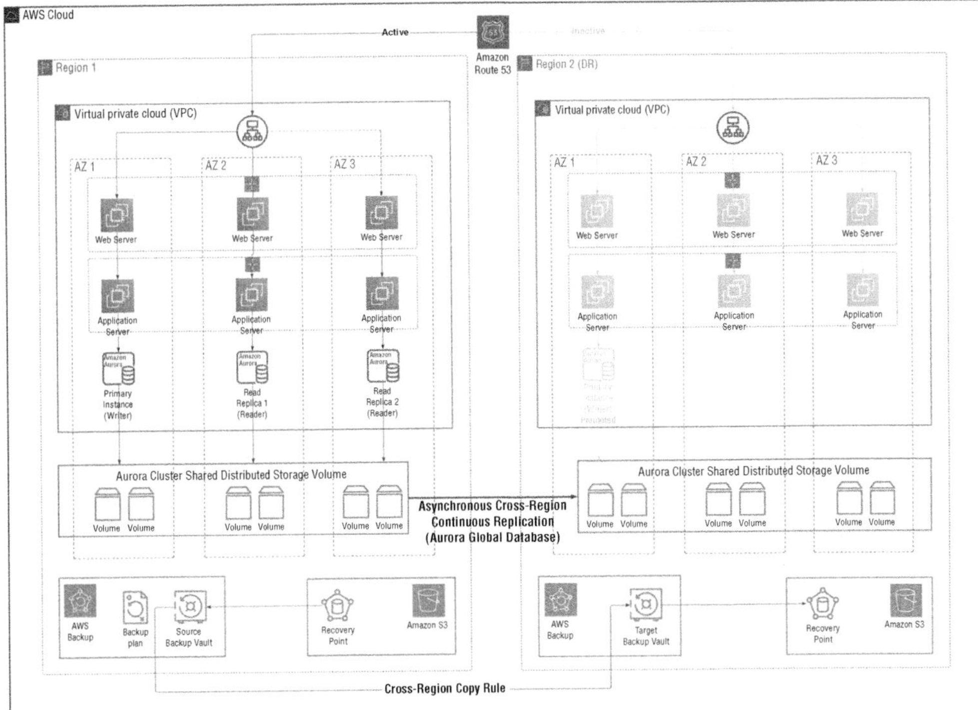

allows a secondary Region to be promoted to full read/write capability in under a minute—even during a complete regional outage.

However, continuous replication alone does not protect against a Data Disaster, for example, in the event of data corruption, malicious deletion, or a ransomware attack where an attacker encrypts or steals your data. In these scenarios, the replicated data in the DR Region may already be compromised. CloudOps engineers must therefore maintain point-in-time backups and versioned storage in the DR Region. As shown in Figure 7.8, AWS Backup is a perfect service for this requirement because it provides automated, policy-driven point-in-time backups that complement continuous replication and ensure you always have clean recovery points available—even when both Regions contain corrupted or encrypted data. It is also a best practice, and highly relevant for SOA-C03 candidates, to store AWS Backup recovery points in a separate AWS account from the one used to restore infrastructure in the DR Region. This cross-account isolation means that even if an attacker compromises your primary account during a ransomware event, your protected vault in the backup account remains intact, giving you a secure, uncompromised path to full recovery.

Finally, Pilot Light requires a scaled-down version of your workload to be deployed in the DR Region. Infrastructure-as-Code (IaC) tools like AWS CloudFormation or HashiCorp Terraform make it possible to deploy full infrastructure in the primary Region and a reduced footprint in the DR Region using conditional logic. Golden AMIs built with EC2 Image

Builder ensure that EC2 instances can be launched quickly and consistently during failover. Traffic can be shifted manually or automatically using Route 53 or AWS Global Accelerator, though you should remember that automatic failover must be used cautiously to avoid false positives. Your job as a CloudOps engineer is to build a DR solution where failover is fast, predictable, and as automated as possible, while still maintaining cost efficiency.

For the exam, it is important to know how to handle the failover of an Aurora Global Database. In the next section, we use the example in Figure 7.8 to show you how.

Aurora Global Database Failover Mechanics

In a Pilot Light architecture, your secondary Region (Region 2) maintains a "headless" Aurora cluster. While the storage volume is continuously updated via sub-second replication, no compute nodes are running to save costs. In the event of a disaster or a DR drill, you must promote this secondary cluster to a Primary role.

Managed Planned Failover (Switchover)

Use this for DR drills or planned regional migrations. It is a "graceful" transition that ensures zero data loss. The orchestrator synchronizes any remaining data in the primary's buffer before swapping roles.

```
aws rds switchover-global-cluster \
    --global-cluster-identifier "LZ-Global-DB" \
    --target-db-cluster-identifier "arn:aws:rds:us-west-2:123456789012:cluster:
dr-cluster" \
    --region us-west-2
```

In this command:

- `--global-cluster-identifier` is the unique name of your Aurora Global Database container that spans both regions.
- `--target-db-cluster-identifier` is the full ARN of the cluster in Region 2 that you want to promote to the new Primary (Writer).
- `--region` specifies the region where the command is issued. It is best practice to run this against the Target Region to ensure that the command succeeds even if the source region is experiencing connectivity issues.

When you use the `switchover-global-cluster` command for a planned drill, the Aurora Global Database orchestrator automatically reverses the replication direction. The old primary cluster is gracefully demoted to a secondary role and immediately begins receiving asynchronous updates from the newly promoted primary in `Region 2`. Your global topology remains intact without any manual reconfiguration.

For more information, visit: `https://docs.aws.amazon.com/cli/latest/reference/rds/switchover-global-cluster.html`.

Unplanned Failover (Emergency Disaster Recovery)

Use this when `Region 1` is completely offline. Because the primary is unreachable, the orchestrator cannot synchronize the last few milliseconds of data. You must "force" the promotion of `Region 2`.

```
aws rds failover-global-cluster \
    --global-cluster-identifier "LZ-Global-DB" \
    --target-db-cluster-identifier "arn:aws:rds:us-west-2:123456789012:cluster:
dr-cluster" \
    --allow-data-loss \
    --region us-west-2
```

In this command:

- `--global-cluster-identifier` is the unique name of the Aurora Global Database that needs emergency intervention.
- `--target-db-cluster-identifier` is the full ARN of the cluster in `Region 2` that you want to promote to the new Primary (Writer).
- `--allow-data-loss` is a mandatory flag for unplanned failovers. It acknowledges that because replication is asynchronous, any transactions that were in transit from `Region 1` at the moment of the crash will be lost.
- `--region` specifies the region where the command is issued. It is best practice to run this against the Target Region to ensure that the command succeeds even if the source region is experiencing connectivity issues.

When you use the `failover-global-cluster` command during a true regional outage (with the `--allow-data-loss flag`), the replication direction is not automatically reversed. Because the primary region was unreachable during the failover, the "link" between the regions is broken to allow the DR region (`Region 2`) to diverge as the new source of truth.The old cluster in `Region 1` is essentially orphaned. Once `Region 1` becomes healthy, you must manually remove the old cluster from the Aurora Global Database and add it back as a new secondary to reestablish replication from `Region 2` back to `Region 1`.

For more information, visit: `https://docs.aws.amazon.com/cli/latest/reference/rds/failover-global-cluster.html`.

Post Failover

For you, as a CloudOps engineer, the critical takeaway you need to remember for the exam is the distinction between a *managed switchover* and an *unplanned failover*. A switchover is an orchestrated, zero-data-loss event used during "game day" drills or maintenance, requiring the primary region to be healthy to synchronize final buffers before swapping roles. Conversely, a failover is an emergency response to a regional outage that requires the mandatory `--allow-data-loss` flag to bypass synchronization with the failed primary. This forces the promotion of the secondary cluster to ensure availability, even if the most recent asynchronous transactions are lost.

Regardless of the method, the Global Writer Endpoint will logically shift to the new region (`Region 2`), but in a true Pilot Light architecture, the database remains inaccessible until you provision at least one compute node (DB instance) to attach to the newly promoted storage volume.

With the Pilot Light foundation in place, the next step is to explore Warm Standby, a strategy that builds on the same principles but keeps more of the workload actively running to further reduce RTO and RPO.

Warm Standby

Warm Standby builds on the Pilot Light pattern by keeping a scaled-down, but fully functional version of your production environment running in the DR Region. As shown in Figure 7.9, this model extends the Pilot Light architecture from Figure 7.8 by powering on only the essential compute resources in `Region 2`—specifically the Web and App tier in `AZ 1`,

FIGURE 7.9 Warm Standby example architecture.

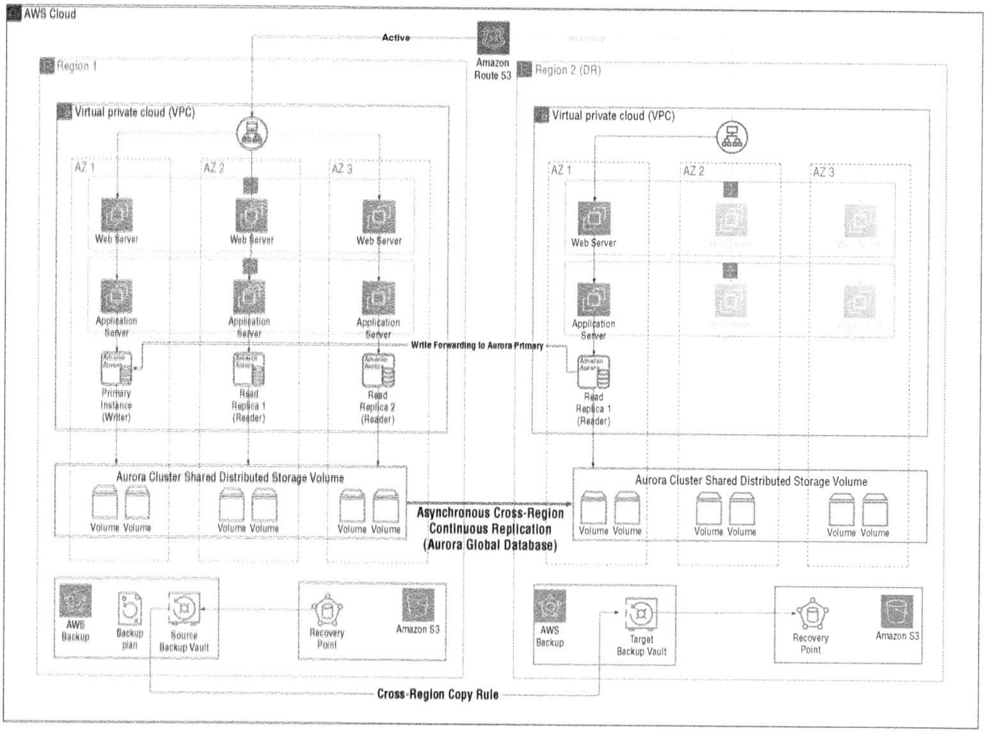

along with an Aurora Read Replica capable of Write Forwarding to the primary Aurora writer in `Region 1` (`AZ 1`). Because part of the workload is already running, Warm Standby significantly reduces recovery time and makes it easier to perform regular or continuous DR testing, which is a key competency for SOA-C03 CloudOps engineers.

The distinction between Pilot Light and Warm Standby is subtle but important. Both patterns maintain a copy of your workload in the DR Region, but Pilot Light cannot process traffic without first turning on additional infrastructure, whereas Warm Standby can immediately handle requests—though at reduced capacity. In Pilot Light, you must power on servers, deploy non-core components, and scale out before the environment becomes usable. In Warm Standby, everything required to serve traffic is already deployed and running; you only need to scale out to reach full production capacity. Your RTO and RPO requirements should guide which approach is appropriate.

Warm Standby continues to rely on the same AWS services used in Backup & Restore and Pilot Light—such as AWS Backup, Amazon S3 Cross-Region Replication, Route 53 health checks, and IaC-driven deployments—but adds the operational requirement of keeping a minimal but active compute footprint online in the DR Region. This ensures that data replication, application health checks, and failover routing remain continuously validated.

To scale the DR Region to full production capacity during a failover, Amazon EC2 auto-scaling plays a central role. Auto-scaling can increase EC2 instance counts, scale ECS tasks, adjust DynamoDB throughput, or expand Aurora replica capacity across Availability Zones. CloudOps engineers can trigger scaling manually through the console, programmatically via the SDK, or automatically by redeploying CloudFormation templates with updated desired-capacity parameters. It is essential to verify that service quotas in the DR Region are high enough to support scaling to full production load.

However, relying on auto-scaling introduces a trade-off. Because scaling actions depend on the AWS Control Plane, they reduce the overall resilience of your DR strategy. Some organizations choose to provision enough capacity in the DR Region to handle full production load without scaling—known as Hot Standby, which corresponds to Resilience Pattern 2 (Multi-AZ with Static Stability) covered earlier, in the "Resilience Patterns" section. This statically stable configuration offers the lowest RTO but at a higher cost. Others deploy only enough resources to handle initial traffic and then rely on auto-scaling to ramp up, balancing cost efficiency with acceptable recovery performance. Warm Standby sits between these extremes, offering a practical blend of readiness, cost control, and operational simplicity for your CloudOps team.

The next section introduces the most advanced DR strategy, where the traditional distinction between primary and DR regions disappears entirely, and workloads operate in a truly distributed environment with no concept of failover or failback—only continuous, concurrent operation across Regions.

Multi-Site Active-Active

Multi-Site Active-Active represents the most advanced and operationally mature disaster recovery strategy, where the workload runs concurrently in multiple regions and users can be served from any of them. This architecture is more complex and costly than Pilot Light or Warm Standby, but it delivers the strongest resilience posture (recovery time for regional outages approaches zero) for workloads that require continuous availability.

Figure 7.10 illustrates this evolution by extending the Warm Standby example from Figure 7.9 into a fully active architecture. `Region 2` is no longer labeled (`DR`), reinforcing that failover and failback no longer exist in this pattern. The figure also shows that all three Aurora Read Replicas in `Region 2` support Write Forwarding to the Aurora Primary Instance in `Region 1`, enabling low-latency local reads while maintaining a single write authority for global consistency. With both regions actively serving traffic, disaster recovery testing focuses on how the system behaves when a region is lost: traffic must be routed away from the impaired region, and the remaining region(s) must absorb the full load.

All the AWS services used in Backup & Restore, Pilot Light, and Warm Standby continue to apply here—point-in-time backups, cross-region replication, health-based routing, and IaC-driven deployments. For traffic management, Amazon Route 53 and AWS Global Accelerator both support Active-Active routing. Global Accelerator provides traffic-dial controls to shift percentages of traffic to each region and leverages the AWS Edge network to reduce latency. Amazon Route 53 offers weighted, latency-based, and geo-proximity routing, enabling fine-grained control over how users are directed to active endpoints.

Near-zero RPO is achieved through asynchronous cross-region replication, with services like Aurora Global Database providing sub-second replication to up to five secondary

FIGURE 7.10 Multi-Site Active-Active example architecture.

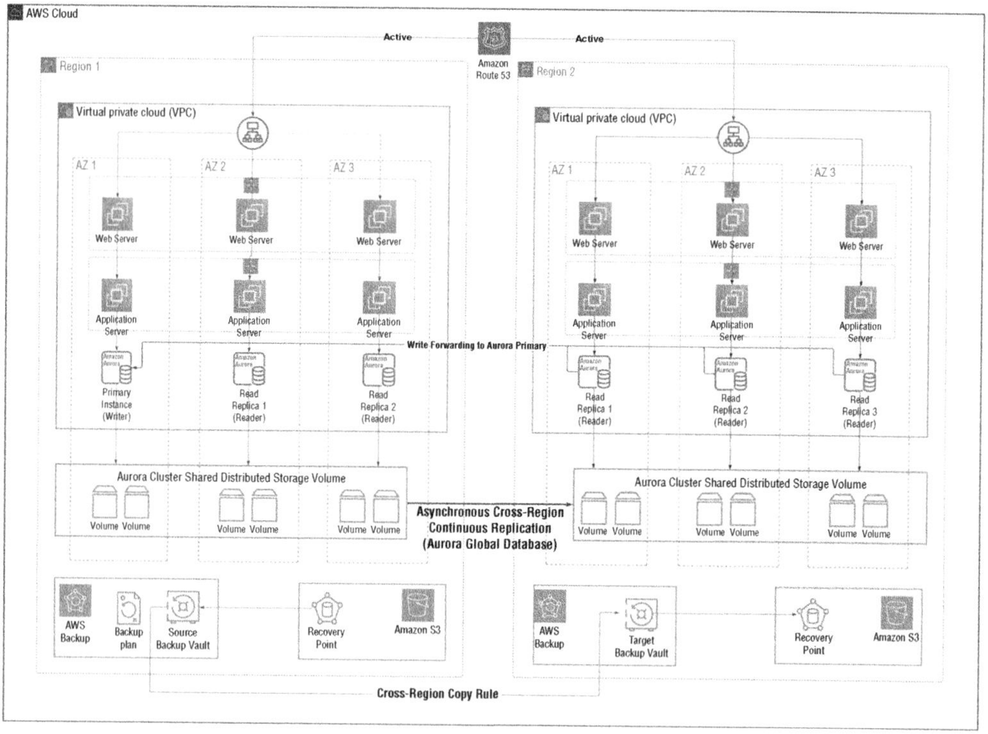

regions. The main design challenge in Active-Active architectures is write consistency across Regions. Three common patterns exist:

- **Write global:** All writes go to one Region; Aurora Global Database fits this model and supports fast promotion and Write Forwarding.
- **Write local:** Each Region accepts writes; DynamoDB Global Tables support this with *last-writer-wins* conflict resolution.
- **Write partitioned:** Each Region handles writes for a subset of data (for example, by user ID); bi-directional S3 replication can support this pattern when replica-modification sync is enabled.

Regardless of the write strategy, point-in-time backups remain mandatory to protect against data disasters, including corruption, deletion, or malicious modification. Multi-Site Active-Active offers the strongest resilience posture, but it requires careful design, continuous validation, and a mature CloudOps practice to operate effectively.

As powerful as Multi-Site Active-Active architectures are, they still rely on accurate, timely, and resilient data movement between regions to keep applications consistent and recoverable. The next section, "Data Migration for Continuity," explores how AWS Database Migration Service (AWS DMS) supports these goals by enabling continuous, low-impact replication across heterogeneous data stores and regions.

Data Migration for Continuity

While data migration is not traditionally categorized as a reliability function, it plays a critical role in maintaining business continuity—especially when workloads must be moved, modernized, or replicated with minimal downtime. AWS Database Migration Service (DMS) is the primary AWS tool for performing these migrations, enabling continuous data replication and supporting heterogeneous database engines across Regions and accounts. Although AWS DMS is not included in the official AWS SOA-C03 exam guide, we include it here for the sake of completeness and because CloudOps engineers must understand how data movement and replication strategies contribute to business continuity and resilience. Whether used for zero-downtime migrations, cross-region replication, or blue/green deployment patterns, AWS DMS provides capabilities that directly support the continuity objectives discussed throughout this chapter.

AWS Database Migration Service (DMS)

As an AWS CloudOps engineer preparing for the SOA-C03 certification, you will encounter scenarios where database migration is not just a technical exercise, but a critical operational responsibility. AWS DMS exemplifies two key AWS Well-Architected design principles: Operational Excellence—"safely automate where possible" and Reliability—"manage change through automation." By automating schema conversion, data replication, and cutover processes, AWS DMS reduces human error and ensures migrations are executed consistently and securely. Its ability to continuously replicate changes from source to target databases—also referred to as *Change Data Capture* (CDC)—allows engineers to manage evolving workloads without manual intervention, directly supporting reliability in dynamic environments. Following the same approach we adopted for the previous database services, we will explore DMS through four lenses—Overview, Performance and Optimization, Scalability and Elasticity, and Backup and Restore Strategies—each designed to equip you with both conceptual clarity and practical guidelines. By the end, you should be able to configure, monitor, and troubleshoot DMS tasks, applying best practices that align with AWS's operational excellence and reliability models.

Overview of AWS DMS

AWS DMS is a managed migration and replication service designed to help you migrate relational databases, data warehouses, NoSQL databases, and other data stores quickly and securely. The source database remains fully operational during the migration, minimizing downtime to applications that rely on the database.

Purpose and Use Cases

The primary purpose of AWS DMS is data mobility, a key operational capability for the SOA-C03 exam. As a CloudOps engineer, you will use DMS for several operational tasks beyond simply moving data to the cloud.

One common scenario is *homogeneous migration*, which involves moving data between identical database engines (e.g., replicating data from an on-premises Oracle database to Amazon RDS for Oracle, or MySQL to Aurora MySQL). This is operationally simpler because the data formats and schemas are inherently compatible.

More complex, and a frequent focus of operational challenges, is *heterogeneous migration*. This task moves data between different database platforms entirely (e.g., migrating an Oracle source database to a PostgreSQL target in RDS). In these scenarios, the data structures and procedural code often differ significantly. DMS only handles the data movement; you—as a CloudOps engineer—will likely pair DMS with the AWS Schema Conversion Tool (AWS SCT) before the data migration begins to automatically convert the schema structure, stored procedures, and functions into a compatible format.

Finally, a critical ongoing operational use case is *continuous replication* (Change Data Capture—CDC). This enables CloudOps teams to keep source and target databases in sync for operational needs or for achieving a near-zero downtime cutover. The CDC process ensures the integrity of ongoing application data while the migration proceeds, which is key to maintaining the Reliability and Operational Excellence pillars of the Well-Architected Framework.

Deployment Options

AWS DMS provides two primary models for deploying and managing the infrastructure required for data replication: AWS DMS Standard and AWS DMS Serverless. In the DMS Standard (provisioned) model, you manually select and manage specific replication instances, such as an `dms.r7i.large` instance type, and are responsible for choosing the engine version and capacity. This option is ideal for steady-state workloads where you require granular control over the compute environment and wish to maintain predictable resource allocation.

Alternatively, AWS DMS Serverless automates the provisioning, monitoring, and scaling of migration resources. This model dynamically adjusts capacity—measured in DMS Capacity Units (DCUs)—to match the real-time demands of your data transaction volume. As of the writing of this book, this includes features like automatic storage scaling to handle large transaction logs or detailed logging without manual intervention. By removing the operational burden of capacity planning and instance management, DMS Serverless ensures high-performance replication while optimizing costs through a pay-for-use billing structure.

Supported Source and Target Databases

AWS DMS supports a wide variety of database and data warehouse engines. Common relational sources include commercial engines like Oracle and SQL Server, and open-source options like MySQL, PostgreSQL, and MariaDB. Target endpoints extend beyond relational databases to NoSQL stores such as Amazon DynamoDB, data warehouses like Amazon Redshift, and even streaming services such as Amazon Kinesis Data Streams. This flexibility is key to integrating different operational data systems within the AWS ecosystem.

For a complete list of supported source databases, visit: `https://docs.aws.amazon.com/dms/latest/userguide/CHAP_Introduction.Sources.html`.

For a complete list of supported target databases, visit: `https://docs.aws.amazon.com/dms/latest/userguide/CHAP_Introduction.Targets.html`.

DMS Migration Task Types

AWS DMS operations fundamentally rely on the concept of a *task*, and every task runs in one of three supported migration types, each with distinct operational considerations that a CloudOps engineer must master for the SOA-C03 exam.

Full Load Only This mode performs a bulk copy of existing data from the source database to the target at the moment the task starts. DMS can execute this load while the source remains online, but because Full Load Only does not capture ongoing changes, the CloudOps engineer may need to schedule a brief application maintenance window during cutover to ensure transactional completeness. This approach is generally suitable for smaller datasets, non-critical workloads, or testing environments where a short downtime window is acceptable.

Full Load and CDC This is the most operationally demanding migration type and the one most closely aligned with AWS's near-zero-downtime migration capabilities. The task first performs the initial full load and then automatically transitions into Change Data Capture (CDC) mode, continuously replicating inserts, updates, and deletes from the source. The CloudOps engineer must ensure that the source database's logging mechanism (such as MySQL binlogs or Oracle archive logs) is correctly configured and retained long enough for DMS to read changes. Monitoring metrics like `CDCLatencySource` becomes essential to ensure the replication stream remains current. This mode is the standard choice for production migrations requiring seamless cutovers and aligns directly with SOA-C03 reliability objectives.

CDC Only In this mode, DMS skips the initial bulk load entirely and begins capturing changes from the source immediately. This is typically used when the initial dataset has already been migrated through another mechanism (such as native database export/import tools or AWS Snow Family services), and DMS is needed only to synchronize ongoing changes before cutover. Operationally, CDC Only carries the same logging and retention requirements as Full Load and CDC, but without the overhead of the initial bulk copy.

Optimizing the configuration of these migration tasks is essential for operational efficiency and reliability. The next section details strategies for ensuring your migrations run smoothly and quickly.

Performance Optimization Strategies

Running an efficient database migration requires careful configuration of the *DMS replication instance* and the specific migration tasks to maximize throughput without overloading the source database. For the SOA-C03 exam, CloudOps engineers must master the operational nuances of tuning AWS DMS to meet specific performance requirements, focusing on optimizing data replication speed and managing a smooth cutover process. The core of this operation is the DMS replication instance, the managed compute engine (an EC2 instance) that runs within your VPC. This instance acts as the essential hub, connecting to both source and target endpoints, processing and transforming data in memory, and using its local storage for caching change data (CDC logs). Selecting the correct size for this instance and managing network latency are foundational operational tasks; the following subsections detail how to achieve these performance objectives through careful configuration of the *task parameters* and proactive monitoring.

Right-Sizing the DMS Replication Instance

Choosing the correct DMS replication instance size is a primary operational decision, as it dictates the CPU, memory, and I/O capacity available for data processing. There is no single formula for selection; instead, you—as a CloudOps engineer— must consider several factors, outlined here.

Workload Type (Compute vs. Memory) Heterogeneous migrations (e.g., Oracle to PostgreSQL) are CPU-intensive due to on-the-fly data conversion and benefit from Compute-Optimized (C-family) instances (e.g., `dms.c5.xlarge`). Homogeneous migrations and migrations involving high volumes of ongoing transactions or Large Objects (LOBs) are typically memory-intensive, favoring Memory-Optimized (R-family) instances (e.g., `dms.r5.xlarge`).

Data Volume and Complexity Large databases, high transaction rates (measured in TPS, transactions per second), and wide tables require more resources. DMS caches changes in memory first; if memory is exhausted, changes are written to disk ("swapping"), which dramatically increases latency.

Number of Concurrent Tasks The total number of tasks running on a single instance shares its CPU and memory. You might run multiple smaller tasks in parallel on one large instance.

Initial Testing The best approach is to begin with a reasonable instance size during testing and monitor CloudWatch metrics (`CPUUtilization`, `MemoryUsed`,

FreeStorageSpace). You can scale the instance class up or down later based on CloudWatch metrics, although the change triggers a reboot of the replication instance.

To learn more, visit: https://docs.aws.amazon.com/dms/latest/userguide/CHAP_ReplicationInstance.Types.html.

Task Settings and Parallelization

Optimization begins within the DMS task configuration using Table Settings and LOB (Large Object) settings. For large-scale migrations, fine-tuning parallelization is crucial. By default, AWS DMS can perform full table loads sequentially. You can introduce parallelism by defining specific settings within a JSON object passed to the CLI or API, allowing DMS to use more resources to extract and load data concurrently.

For example, the MaxFullLoadSubTasks setting within FullLoadSettings determines how many tables or table segments AWS DMS loads in parallel during the full-load phase. Increasing this value increases parallelism and can significantly improve throughput for environments with many tables or large, segmentable tables.

Here is how you would specify task settings, including parallelization parameters, when creating a replication task via the AWS CLI. The settings are provided as a JSON string within the --replication-task-settings flag, shown here with indentation for clarity:

```
aws dms create-replication-task \
  --replication-task-id my-migration-task \
  --replication-instance-arn arn:aws:dms:us-east-1:123456789012:rep:abc
def1234567890 \
  --source-endpoint-arn arn:aws:dms:us-east-1:123456789012:endpoint:source123 \
  --target-endpoint-arn arn:aws:dms:us-east-1:123456789012:endpoint:target123 \
  --migration-type full-load-and-cdc \
  --table-mappings '{"rules": [...]}' \
  --replication-task-settings '{
        "FullLoadSettings": {
            "TargetTablePrepMode": "TRUNCATE_BEFORE_LOAD",
            "MaxFullLoadSubTasks": 49,
            "CommitRate": 10000
        }
    }'
```

In this command:

- --replication-task-id is a unique identifier for the migration task being created.
- --replication-instance-arn is the Amazon Resource Name (ARN) of the specific DMS replication instance that will run this task.
- --source-endpoint-arn is the ARN of the source database endpoint connection.
- --target-endpoint-arn is the ARN of the target database endpoint connection.
- --migration-type defines the type of migration: full-load, cdc, or full-load-and-cdc.

- `--table-mappings` is a JSON structure that defines which tables to include/exclude in the migration.
- `--replication-task-settings` is a JSON structure (as shown previously) used for advanced fine-tuning of the migration behavior, performance, and error handling.

`MaxFullLoadSubTasks` controls how many tables or table segments AWS DMS loads in parallel during the Full Load phase. The default value is 8, and AWS supports up to 49 sub-tasks depending on the source engine and segmentation capabilities. This setting is a key lever for performance tuning. `TargetTablePrepMode` and `CommitRate` are two important settings within an AWS DMS replication task that control how data is prepared and committed during the Full Load phase of a migration. `TargetTablePrepMode` determines the action AWS DMS takes on the target table before the full data load begins (e.g., `TRUNCATE_BEFORE_LOAD`). `CommitRate` manages the frequency of data commits during the full load phase. The setting `"CommitRate": 10000` means DMS collects 10,000 records (rows) in a batch before issuing a single `COMMIT` transaction to the target database. This balances migration throughput speed with memory utilization and transactional safety.

For a complete reference guide to the DMS task settings, visit: `https://docs.aws.amazon.com/dms/latest/userguide/CHAP_Tasks.CustomizingTasks.TaskSettings.html#CHAP_Tasks.CustomizingTasks.TaskSettings.Example`.

Network and Storage Considerations

The performance of DMS is highly dependent on the replication instance's network connection to both source and target databases and its assigned storage.

Network The replication instance should be placed within the same VPC as the AWS-based source or target endpoints to benefit from high-speed, low-latency internal networking. For on-premises sources, ensure a stable, high-bandwidth connection (e.g., AWS Direct Connect or Site-to-Site VPN).

Storage The replication instance uses storage for caching change data during CDC operations (before applying them to the target). Insufficient storage can cause the instance to bottleneck or pause the task. Monitoring the `FreeStorageSpace` metric in CloudWatch is essential for avoiding operational issues.

Monitoring with CloudWatch and DMS Console

As a CloudOps engineer you use the AWS Management Console and Amazon CloudWatch to monitor migrations actively. The DMS console also provides graphical visualization of table status, throughput, and ongoing progress. The metrics in Table 7.2 track the performance and health of individual migration tasks.

Best Practices for Large-Scale Migrations

When dealing with petabyte-scale data migrations or migrating hundreds of tables, standard procedures need scaling up to manage complexity, performance, and operational risk. CloudOps engineers should adopt these best practices to maintain control and ensure a smooth migration.

TABLE 7.2 AWS DMS Task Metrics

Metric Name (Console/API Name)	Description	Tuning Insight
CDC Latency Source (`CDCLatencySource`)	The time difference (in seconds) between a change occurring on the source database and that change being captured by the replication instance.	High values indicate that the source DB is under heavy load or its logs are being generated faster than DMS can read them. Consider using a larger replication instance class (e.g., R5) or optimizing source database I/O.
CDC Latency Target (`CDCLatencyTarget`)	The time difference (in seconds) between a change being captured by the replication instance and that change being applied to the target database.	High latency here indicates a bottleneck on the target database (e.g., slow writes due to insufficient IOPS or schema conflicts). Tune target database performance, disable unnecessary constraints, or consider batching changes more efficiently.
CDC Source Throughput (rows/second) (`CDCThroughputRowsSource`)	The number of rows per second being read from the source database during replication.	Use this to baseline your "normal" replication speed; a sudden drop might indicate a stalled source or network issue.
CDC Target Throughput (rows/second) (`CDCThroughputRowsTarget`)	The number of rows per second being applied to the target database.	If this is significantly lower than the Source Rows metric, your target is falling behind, and you may need to enable Parallel Apply.

(*Continued*)

TABLE 7.2 (Continued)

Metric Name (Console/API Name)	Description	Tuning Insight
Full Load Source Throughput (rows/second) (`FullLoadThroughputRowsSource`)	The number of rows per second being unloaded from the source during the initial migration.	If this is low, consider increasing `MaxFullLoadSubTasks` to process more tables or table segments simultaneously.
Full Load Target Throughput (rows/second) (`FullLoadThroughputRowsTarget`)	The number of rows per second being committed to the target during the initial migration.	If this is low, check the target's write IOPS or consider using `ParallelLoadThreads` to increase the number of concurrent load sessions.

Stage Migrations in Phases Don't treat a large migration as a single event. A sound operational approach involves staging the process: first complete the initial Full Load, pause the application during a brief maintenance window if necessary to verify data integrity, then switch to Continuous Replication (CDC). This modular approach allows you to validate data integrity in manageable chunks and isolate performance issues to specific phases.

Don't Be Afraid to Over-Provision a DMS Replication Instance Large-scale migrations generate significant data throughput and require substantial processing power. Monitor metrics closely during initial testing. Use a larger, memory-optimized (R-family) or compute-optimized (C-family) replication instance (e.g., `dms.r5.2xlarge` or larger) initially. It is generally more cost-effective to use an oversized instance for a shorter, successful migration window than to use an undersized instance that bottlenecks performance, increases latency, and significantly extends the total project timeline.

Disable Target Constraints Temporarily One of the most effective ways to increase the Full Load throughput is to minimize the work the target database has to do. Temporarily disable resource-intensive operations on the target during the initial data load, such as foreign keys, triggers, indexes, and constraints. This turns the load process into simple bulk inserts, which are highly efficient. Crucially, these constraints must be reenabled before the application cutover, typically while the task is paused and preparing to transition to CDC mode.

Use Parallelization Settings (Task Settings) Leverage the JSON task settings discussed earlier (`MaxFullLoadSubTasks`, `CommitRate`) to read and write data in parallel across multiple threads. This maximizes the utilization of the DMS replication instance's CPU and network bandwidth.

Implement Robust Data Validation For large migrations, automated data validation is a necessity. Enable the built-in DMS Data Validation feature and use manual SQL aggregate checks (e.g., `COUNT(*)`, `SUM()`) on critical tables across source and target. Never assume data integrity at scale; always verify it operationally before cutting over production traffic.

Managing these large datasets effectively requires a deep understanding of scaling the service itself. The next section focuses on the scalability and elasticity of the AWS DMS infrastructure.

Scalability and Elasticity

AWS DMS offers operational resilience features, allowing for horizontal scalability of tasks and high availability of the underlying replication instances. For the SOA-C03 exam, CloudOps engineers must understand these distinctions.

The core of DMS operations relies on the replication instance, which has a fixed compute capacity determined by its EC2 instance class (e.g., `dms.r5.large`). This means that true vertical scalability—the ability to seamlessly increase the CPU/memory of a running instance without operational impact—is not a native, seamless feature of the DMS service. To change the size (scale vertically), you typically initiate a modification that results in a brief outage, while the instance type is switched and rebooted.

However, you can achieve overall scalability by having more than one DMS environment running. You can deploy multiple DMS replication instances within your AWS environment, allowing you to distribute the migration workload horizontally across these independent hosts.

Scaling Migration Tasks

You cannot vertically scale a single task across multiple replication instances. Instead, scalability is achieved by using a more powerful replication instance size (vertical scaling of the host itself) or by running multiple smaller, concurrent tasks on a single, sufficiently powerful instance.

Deciding whether to run multiple smaller, concurrent tasks on a single, sufficiently powerful instance, or distributing tasks across entirely separate replication instances, often depends on how you can partition your data logically (e.g., by schema or specific table groups) and whether you need to isolate workloads for performance or security reasons.

High Availability with Multi-AZ Replication Instances

For critical production migrations that demand high availability, you must deploy the DMS replication instance as a Multi-AZ deployment.

This configuration automatically provisions a standby replica of the replication instance in a different Availability Zone. In the event of a failure of the primary instance (due to hardware failure or AZ disruption), AWS DMS automatically fails over to the standby replica. This minimizes disruption to continuous replication tasks. The failover process automatically restarts running tasks on the new primary instance.

You can configure a Multi-AZ DMS replication instance using the AWS CLI:

```
aws dms create-replication-instance \
    --replication-instance-id my-multi-az-instance \
    --replication-instance-class dms.r5.large \
    --engine-version 3.4.6 \
    --vpc-security-group-ids sg-0a1b2c3d4e5f67890 \
    --availability-zone us-east-1a \
    --multi-az
```

In this command:

- `--multi-az` is an essential flag that tells DMS to provision a standby instance for high availability.
- `--replication-instance-class` specifies the compute and memory capacity of the instance. R5 instances are generally preferred for memory-intensive replication tasks.
- `--replication-instance-id` is a unique identifier for the instance.
- `--engine-version` is the desired DMS engine version.
- `--vpc-security-group-ids` is the Security Group(s) to associate with the instance for network access control.
- `--availability-zone` is the specific AZ to launch the primary instance into (optional; often automatically selected in Multi-AZ mode but can be specified if needed).

Handling Ongoing Replication for Dynamic Workloads

For highly dynamic production workloads with many transactions per second (TPS), CloudOps engineers must ensure the DMS replication instance is appropriately sized and that disk I/O on both source and target can keep pace with change data capture and application rates. Monitoring the `CDCLatencyTarget` metric (listed in Table 7.2) is key here. If latency spikes during peak hours, it is a strong indicator that the replication instance is under-provisioned or the target database is experiencing write bottlenecks.

Integration with Other AWS Services (e.g., SCT, Glue)

DMS often works as part of a larger migration ecosystem:

- **AWS Schema Conversion Tool (AWS SCT):** For heterogeneous migrations, SCT handles the schema and code conversion (e.g., stored procedures, functions) that DMS does not cover. DMS handles only the data movement.
- **AWS Glue:** DMS can use AWS Glue Data Catalog integration when the target is Amazon S3, allowing the migrated data to be immediately queryable as a data lake source using services like Amazon Athena or Amazon Redshift Spectrum.

To learn more about AWS SCT, visit: `https://docs.aws.amazon.com/SchemaConversionTool/latest/userguide/CHAP_Welcome.html`.

Ensuring data integrity during these complex transitions is paramount. The next section covers operational strategies for data validation and recovery options.

Backup and Restore Strategies

In the context of DMS, "backup and restore" primarily refers to ensuring the integrity and recoverability of the data being migrated, rather than backing up the DMS service itself (DMS tasks restart automatically upon failure, resuming from where they left off).

Ensuring Data Integrity During Migration

AWS DMS includes a built-in Data Validation feature. When enabled for a task, DMS automatically compares the row counts and checksums between the source and target tables after the initial full load completes and continues to monitor data integrity during CDC. This operational feature significantly reduces manual verification efforts and provides assurance that the migration is accurate. As a CloudOps engineer, you must monitor the validation-specific metrics in CloudWatch (e.g., `ValidationSucceededRecordCount`, `ValidationFailedOverallCount`, and `ValidationSuspendedOverallCount`) to identify and remediate any data discrepancies in real time. `ValidationFailedOverallCount` is the most critical metric; it indicates data that exists on the source but is missing or different on the target. `ValidationSucceededRecordCount` confirms that records match exactly across both environments.

Validation and Verification of Migrated Data

Beyond the automated validation feature, CloudOps engineers should employ manual spot checks and verification scripts. Use SQL queries on both the source and target systems to compare aggregate values (like SUMs, COUNTs, and AVG timestamps) on critical tables to ensure business data integrity matches before a final application cutover.

Rollback and Recovery Options

AWS DMS does not provide a built-in rollback mechanism. If a migration fails or the application cutover is unsuccessful, there is no automatic "rollback" button within DMS that reverts the source database to a previous state. Operational strategy dictates that:

1. The source database is kept operational and untouched during the entire process.
2. If rollback is needed after cutover, traffic is simply pointed back to the original source database instance. The application logic must support switching endpoints quickly (e.g., via Route 53 DNS updates).

Disaster Recovery Considerations in Migration Scenarios

During an ongoing migration, your DR posture changes. You temporarily have two active databases (source and target). A key consideration is that the target database typically does not have "point-in-time recovery" (PITR) enabled until the task is completed and the target is promoted to a fully independent production system (e.g., enabling RDS backups). Ensure the source database's existing DR plan remains robust until the cutover is complete and validated.

Furthermore, DMS migrations themselves should be embedded within broader organizational disaster recovery plans. While DMS tasks can restart automatically, critical DMS replication instances should have their configurations backed up (or better yet, deployed using IaC tools like CloudFormation or Terraform). Scripting migration tasks via the AWS CLI or IaC ensures rapid, consistent redeployment in the event of an unexpected AWS account issue or regional failure, a key operational objective for a CloudOps engineer.

Summary

This chapter introduced the foundations of Reliability and Business Continuity through core SRE concepts—Service Level Indicators (SLIs), Service Level Objectives (SLOs), and recovery objectives (RTO and RPO). Early in the chapter, we also clarified the distinction between High Availability (HA) and Fault Tolerance (FT), reinforcing the chapter's central theme that resilience is a key enabler of reliability. We then explored the five AWS resilience patterns, along with how ELB and Route 53 health checks detect failures and route traffic to healthy endpoints.

The chapter then walked you through the four AWS Disaster Recovery (DR) strategies—Backup & Restore, Pilot Light, Warm Standby, and Multi-Site Active-Active—framed around RTO, RPO, cost, and operational complexity. You learned how to select the right strategy based on business needs, with AWS Backup providing the foundation for point-in-time protection across AWS workloads.

From there, we progressed through Pilot Light and Warm Standby, seeing how pre-provisioned infrastructure accelerates recovery without the cost of full active-active operation. We emphasized quotas, automation, and static stability—key SOA-C03 concepts. The section culminated in Multi-Site Active-Active, where both Regions are fully active and Aurora-based examples illustrated global routing, write-consistency models, and cross-Region asynchronous replication. These examples also showed how AWS managed databases perform automatic failover by remapping stable DNS endpoints (such as the Aurora Cluster Writer Endpoint) to healthy instances, allowing applications to reconnect without configuration changes.

Aurora served throughout as a practical anchor for understanding real-world Multi-AZ and Multi-Region deployments. You learned how failover works, how readers can be promoted to writers, and how replication strategies influence RPO—skills essential for the exam and for day-to-day cloud operations.

The chapter concluded with data migration for continuity, focusing on AWS Database Migration Service (AWS DMS). You learned how DMS enables continuous, low-impact replication and change data capture across engines and Regions, supporting both DR readiness and modernization. By the end, you gained a clear, exam-aligned understanding of how resilience patterns, DR strategies, and data-continuity services work together to support reliable workloads on AWS.

Exam Essentials

Understand SLIs, SLOs, RPO, and RTO. As a CloudOps engineer, you anchor reliability around measurable targets. A Service Level Indicator (SLI) is the metric you observe—such as availability, latency, or error rate. A Service Level Objective (SLO) is the specific performance target you commit to meeting, like "99.9% availability over 30 days." For recovery planning, you use two time-based objectives: the Recovery Time Objective (RTO), which defines how long your workload can be down after a failure, and the Recovery Point Objective (RPO), which defines how much data loss (measured as time) the business can tolerate. Together, these objectives guide your resilience patterns, failover strategies, and DR architecture choices on AWS.

Know the difference between High Availability (HA) and Fault Tolerance (FT). High Availability (HA) assumes that failures will occur and focuses on minimizing downtime through rapid detection and automated recovery. In HA architectures, components can fail, but the system restores service quickly—typically by shifting traffic to healthy resources in another AZ. Fault Tolerance (FT) goes a step further by ensuring that a failure has no impact on service availability. FT architectures run fully redundant components in parallel, often with synchronous replication, so the workload continues operating seamlessly even if an entire node or AZ is lost. In short: HA recovers from failure; FT absorbs it without interruption—a distinction that is essential for designing resilient AWS workloads and for success on the SOA-C03 exam.

Understand the Multi-AZ with Static Stability resilience pattern. Multi-AZ with Static Stability is a resilience pattern where all the compute capacity needed to survive an Availability Zone failure is pre-provisioned and already running across at least two AZs. Instead of relying on auto-scaling or the AWS Control Plane to launch new instances during an outage, you maintain enough headroom in the remaining AZ to absorb the full workload immediately. This ensures that the system continues operating in a single, stable mode before and after the failure, with no emergency scaling, no cold starts, and no performance degradation. For the SOA-C03 exam, remember that static stability is about preexisting capacity, predictable failover behavior, and resilience without dynamic provisioning.

Understand when to use ELB health checks vs. Route 53 health checks. As a CloudOps engineer, you use ELB health checks to monitor the instances or targets behind a load balancer and ensure that only healthy resources receive traffic within a single Region. They operate at the load balancer layer and are ideal for detecting failures of EC2 instances, containers, or IP targets. Route 53 health checks, on the other hand, evaluate the availability of entire endpoints—including load balancers, web servers, or even external URLs—and can trigger DNS-level failover across Regions or between on-premises and AWS. In short, ELB health checks keep traffic flowing to healthy targets inside a Region, while Route 53 health checks enable global or cross-endpoint failover, making them essential for Multi-Region resilience patterns.

Know how AWS Backup simplifies a Backup & Restore DR strategy. AWS Backup simplifies a Backup & Restore strategy by serving as a centralized orchestration engine that replaces fragmented, service-specific snapshot scripts with unified, policy-based governance. For CloudOps engineers, it eliminates manual overhead by automatically managing the entire data lifecycle—from the scheduled creation of crash-consistent AMIs for EC2 and shared storage volumes for Aurora, to the automated execution of Cross-Region Copy Rules for regional resilience. Furthermore, by utilizing Restore Testing Plans, AWS Backup transforms a traditionally manual recovery into an orchestrated event, allowing you to predefine networking metadata and automate the re-materialization of regional backups into functional zonal resources with minimal human intervention.

Know the difference between Pilot Light and Warm Standby DR strategies. The distinction between Pilot Light and Warm Standby lies in the operational readiness of the compute tier and the resulting Recovery Time Objective (RTO). In a Pilot Light strategy, the DR region maintains a live, continuously updated version of the data (such as an Aurora Global Database storage volume), but the application and web servers remain "off" or unprovisioned to minimize costs; recovery requires "lighting" the environment by manually or programmatically launching compute resources. Conversely, a Warm Standby maintains a "scaled-down" but fully functional version of the entire stack (such as a small EC2 fleet and a running database instance) always on in the DR region. While Warm Standby carries a higher ongoing cost, it provides a significantly lower RTO by allowing the infrastructure to handle a small amount of traffic immediately and scale up to production levels via auto-scaling once a failover is triggered.

Understand Aurora Global Database's failover mechanisms. Aurora Global Database provides two distinct regional failover mechanisms: managed planned failover and unplanned failover. A managed planned failover (switchover) is a zero-data-loss orchestration used for DR drills or migrations, where AWS synchronizes all secondary regions with the primary, swaps the regional roles, and automatically reverses the asynchronous replication direction to maintain the global topology. In contrast, an unplanned failover is an emergency response to a regional outage that requires the mandatory `--allow-data-loss` flag to promote a secondary cluster immediately, bypassing synchronization with the unreachable primary. Because an unplanned failover breaks the replication link, engineers must manually reintegrate the original region once it recovers, and regardless of the method, must programmatically provision compute nodes in Pilot Light architectures to turn the restored "headless" Aurora Database Cluster into a functional database.

Understand when to use the Multi-Site Active-Active DR strategy. A Multi-Site Active-Active strategy is the only disaster recovery approach capable of achieving near-zero Recovery Time Objective (RTO) and Recovery Point Objective (RPO), because it eliminates the need for failover entirely. Any strategy that relies on manual or automated failover inherently incurs non-zero RTO and RPO. This pattern is used for mission-critical workloads where users are served from two or more regions simultaneously, providing the highest level of availability and "static stability" against regional outages. While it is the most expensive and operationally complex pattern—often requiring a move to native Multi-Region services like Aurora Global Database with Write Forwarding—it ensures that if one region fails, the remaining sites are already fully provisioned and capable of absorbing the global traffic load without a perceptible interruption of service.

Review Questions

1. A company uses AWS Backup to protect a landing zone with 100 EC2 instances and an Aurora cluster. A new compliance mandate requires that all current and future EC2 instances be automatically enrolled in an immutable backup policy that protects recovery points against accidental deletion or ransomware encryption for at least 90 days. Furthermore, the recovery process must automatically re-create the EC2 instances with their original IAM roles and Security Groups. Which TWO steps should a CloudOps engineer take to enforce the new compliance mandate? (Select TWO.)
   - **A.** Enable S3 Object Lock on the underlying S3 buckets where AWS Backup stores the recovery points.
   - **B.** Configure a Backup Vault with Vault Lock in compliance mode for a minimum duration of 90 days.
   - **C.** Manually create EBS snapshots for each volume to ensure that the IAM metadata is captured outside of AWS Backup.
   - **D.** Assign resources to the backup plan using Tags to ensure that new instances are automatically included in the immutable vault.
   - **E.** Use AWS Lambda to parse the AMI metadata during restoration to manually reattach Security Groups.
   - **F.** Enable S3 Cross-Region Replication (CRR) on the Aurora cluster storage volume.
2. An organization utilizes a Pilot Light DR strategy with an Amazon Aurora Global Database. The primary region (`us-east-1`) becomes unavailable due to a regional service outage. A CloudOps engineer must promote the secondary cluster in `us-west-2` to full read/write capability to restore operations. The secondary cluster in `us-west-2` maintains a continuously replicated storage volume but has no provisioned DB instances in order to minimize costs. Which TWO actions are required to successfully complete this transition? (Select TWO.)
   - **A.** Execute the `aws rds failover-global-cluster` command with the `--allow-data-loss` flag against the secondary region.
   - **B.** Trigger a Managed Planned Failover using the `switchover-global-cluster` command to ensure zero data loss.
   - **C.** Manually call `aws rds create-db-instance` to add a writer node if the secondary cluster was previously "headless."
   - **D.** Use S3 Cross-Region Replication to move the transaction logs from `us-east-1` to `us-west-2` before promotion.
   - **E.** Update the application's connection string to point to the Aurora Cluster's Reader Endpoint in the new primary region.
   - **F.** Rerun the AWS Backup Restore job for the Aurora Shared Volume to populate the new cluster.

3. A company has implemented a Warm Standby DR pattern in Region 2. During a routine audit, the finance department notes that the DR costs are nearly 60% of the production costs. A CloudOps engineer is tasked with reducing costs without reverting to a Pilot Light strategy (the RTO must remain under 15 minutes). Which TWO actions will achieve this? (Select TWO.)

   A. Transition the EC2 instances in Region 2 to Stopped state and use an auto-scaling group with a min-size of 0.

   B. Decrease the instance size of the EC2 and Aurora nodes in Region 2 while maintaining a "scaled-down" but functional fleet.

   C. Switch the DR strategy to Backup & Restore to eliminate the cost of running any standby compute resources.

   D. Use S3 Intelligent-Tiering for the storage of EBS snapshots in the primary region only.

   E. Implement a Multi-Site Active-Active pattern to spread the load and justify the cost of the secondary region.

   F. Use Aurora Serverless v2 in the DR region with a low minimum ACU (Aurora Capacity Unit) setting.

4. A globally distributed application uses Amazon Aurora Global Database to provide low-latency access to users in two regions. App servers in Region 2 (Secondary, DR Region) are successfully performing local read operations, but users are reporting "Database Read-Only" errors when attempting to update their profiles. A CloudOps engineer confirms that the application in Region 2 connects via a read-only connection pool and that Write Forwarding is not enabled on the secondary cluster. Which TWO configurations are necessary to allow Region 2 to process these writes while Region 1 remains the primary writer? (Select TWO.)

   A. Enable Write Forwarding on the secondary Aurora DB cluster in Region 2.

   B. Promote one Read Replica in Region 2 to a Writer role while Region 1 is still active.

   C. Configure the application sessions in Region 2 to set `aurora_replica_read_consistency` and direct write operations to the local cluster endpoint.

   D. Use Amazon Aurora Multi-Master clusters in both regions to allow simultaneous native writes.

   E. Implement a Managed Planned Failover to swap the primary and secondary regional roles every 60 minutes.

   F. Enable Cross-Region Replication (CRR) at the individual DB Instance level for the replicas in Region 2.

5. A CloudOps team is conducting a "game day" to test their Backup & Restore and Warm Standby plans. They need to ensure that the recovery in the DR region is fully automated and that the networking context is preserved without manual intervention during a failover. Which TWO AWS services or features should be prioritized to satisfy these requirements? (Select TWO.)

   A. AWS Backup Restore Testing plans to predefine the mapping of subnets and Security Groups in the DR region.

   B. AWS CloudTrail to log the manual steps taken by engineers during the restoration process for future review.

C. Amazon S3 Transfer Acceleration to speed up the movement of snapshots between regions during the drill.

D. AWS Route 53 Application Recovery Controller (ARC) to manage the traffic shift and monitor regional readiness.

E. AWS Config Rules to automatically delete resources in the primary region once the restore starts in the DR region.

F. EC2 Image Builder to manually create new AMIs in the DR region after the disaster is declared.

6. A CloudOps engineer is tasked with ensuring that all EC2 instances in a production VPC are backed up nightly. The engineer creates a backup plan with the desired schedule but notices that no backups are being created for any of the instances. Upon investigation, the engineer realizes they forgot to define which resources should be governed by the plan. Which action is required to fix this issue and begin the automated backups?

   A. Manually run the `aws ec2 create-snapshot` command for every EBS volume in the VPC.

   B. Create a backup selection and link it to the backup plan using either resource Tags or ARNs.

   C. Enable S3 Cross-Region Replication (CRR) on the instances' root volumes.

   D. Update the backup vault's access policy to allow public "Read" permissions for the EC2 service.

   E. Restart the AWS Backup agent on each of the production EC2 instances.

7. An organization is recovering from a regional disaster using a Backup & Restore strategy. A CloudOps engineer successfully executes a restore job from an Aurora Cluster recovery point in the DR region. However, the application servers are still unable to connect to the database, and the RDS console shows that no database instances exist within the newly restored cluster. What is the next mandatory step to make the database functional?

   A. Run the `aws rds create-db-instance` command to add a writer instance to the restored storage volume.

   B. Initiate a second AWS Backup Restore job specifically for the DB instances using the same recovery point.

   C. Change the DB Subnet Group of the restored cluster to "Public" to allow external connections.

   D. Wait for the Aurora "Storage Auto-scaling" feature to automatically provision a new primary node.

   E. Enable "Write Forwarding" on the restored cluster to redirect traffic back to the original region.

8. A startup needs a Disaster Recovery strategy that minimizes costs during normal operations. They are willing to accept a high Recovery Time Objective (RTO) of 24 hours, meaning they only want to pay for resources in the DR region once a disaster actually occurs. Which DR pattern is the most cost-effective solution for this requirement?

   A. Multi-Site Active-Active

   B. Warm Standby

C. Pilot Light

D. Backup & Restore

E. Amazon Aurora Global Database with Write Forwarding

9. A CloudOps engineer is designing a DR plan for an application consisting of EC2 instances and EBS volumes. The engineer is confused about which resources will be automatically protected across an entire region and which are limited to a single Availability Zone (AZ). Which statement regarding resource scope is correct?

   A. EBS volumes are regional resources and are automatically available in any AZ in the region.

   B. EC2 instances are regional and can be moved between AZs without using AMIs.

   C. AWS Backup recovery points are stored in a regional vault and are durable across multiple AZs.

   D. VPC Security Groups are zonal and must be re-created for every individual subnet.

   E. Amazon Aurora clusters are zonal and cannot survive the failure of a single data center.

10. A team wants to automate their cross-region disaster recovery. They want a solution that not only creates a local backup of their EC2 instances every morning at 2:00 a.m. but also automatically ensures a copy of that backup is sent to a different region's vault immediately after creation. Which component of AWS Backup is responsible for orchestrating both the schedule and the cross-region replication?

    A. The Backup Vault

    B. The Restore Testing plan

    C. The Backup plan

    D. The IAM service-linked role

    E. The AWS Backup Gateway

11. A CloudOps engineer has deployed an Application Load Balancer (ALB) to distribute traffic across three EC2 instances. After the deployment, the ALB console reports that all three targets are in an unhealthy state with the description "Health check failed with HTTP 404 (Not Found)." The application is confirmed to be running on the instances at the root path `/index.html`. Which action will resolve this issue and allow the targets to pass health checks?

    A. Increase the "Health check threshold" to ten consecutive successes to give the instances more time to respond.

    B. Change the "Health check path" in the Target Group settings from the default / to `/index.html`.

    C. Modify the Security Group of the instances to allow all outbound traffic to the ALB's DNS name.

    D. Update the Route 53 record to use a Multi-value Answer routing policy instead of a Simple routing policy.

    E. Replace the ALB with a Network Load Balancer (NLB) to bypass HTTP-level health checks.

12. An organization wants to configure a disaster recovery (DR) strategy where traffic is automatically shifted from a primary region to a secondary region if the primary web application becomes unavailable. A CloudOps engineer decides to use Route 53 Failover Routing to accomplish this. What is a mandatory requirement for Route 53 to successfully trigger this regional shift?
   - A. The primary and secondary regions must be connected via an AWS Site-to-Site VPN.
   - B. A Route 53 Health Check must be created and associated with the Primary record.
   - C. The TTL (Time to Live) for the DNS records must be set to at least 86,400 seconds (24 hours).
   - D. The ALB in the primary region must have "Cross-Zone Load Balancing" disabled.
   - E. The engineer must manually click "Failover" in the Route 53 console when an outage is detected.

13. A CloudOps engineer needs to monitor the health of an internal database server that is located in a private subnet and does not have a public IP address. The engineer wants to use a Route 53 Health Check to notify the team if the database port (3306) stops responding. What must the engineer consider when configuring this specific health check?
   - A. Route 53 public health checkers cannot reach endpoints with private IP addresses.
   - B. The database must be moved to a public subnet to allow the Route 53 service to see it.
   - C. The engineer must install the CloudWatch Agent on the database to forward health status to Route 53.
   - D. Route 53 Health Checks only support HTTP/HTTPS and cannot monitor TCP port 3306.
   - E. The database Security Group must allow inbound traffic from the "Route 53 Health Checker" service tag.

14. To improve the Recovery Time Objective (RTO) during an instance failure, a CloudOps engineer wants to make the ALB detect a failure as quickly as possible. Currently, the ALB takes nearly two minutes to mark an instance as unhealthy. Which combination of settings will result in the fastest detection of a failure?
   - A. Increase the "Healthy threshold" and decrease the "Health check interval."
   - B. Decrease the "Unhealthy threshold" and decrease the "Health check interval."
   - C. Increase the "Timeout" and increase the "Unhealthy threshold."
   - D. Enable "Cross-zone load balancing" and increase the "Healthy threshold."
   - E. Switch the health check protocol from HTTP to HTTPS for more frequent probes.

15. A CloudOps engineer has an auto-scaling group (ASG) that is currently using the default EC2 health check type. Although the Application Load Balancer (ALB) marks an instance as unhealthy due to a web server crash, the ASG continues to keep the instance in service because the underlying EC2 hardware is still functioning. Which sequence of actions must the engineer take to ensure the ASG automatically replaces instances that fail the ALB health check?

A. Manually terminate the unhealthy instances so that the ASG can detect the decrease in "Desired Capacity" and launch replacements.

B. Modify the ASG settings to change the "Health check type" from EC2 to ELB and ensure the "Health check grace period" is sufficient for instance warmup.

C. Create a new Route 53 health check for each instance and link it to the ASG's "Target Tracking" scaling policy.

D. Update the ALB's Target Group to use the TCP protocol instead of HTTP to bypass the need for an ASG health check update.

E. Install the AWS Systems Manager (SSM) agent on the instances to report web server status directly to the ASG.

16. An engineer is designing a health check for a high-traffic web application. The application relies on a backend database and a third-party API. The engineer is concerned that if the backend database experiences a temporary spike in latency, the ALB health check might fail for all instances simultaneously, leading to a "cascading failure" where the entire fleet is terminated. According to AWS best practices, which configuration represents a "shallow" health check that avoids this risk?

A. A health check that queries the database to ensure the connection is active before returning a `200 OK`.

B. A health check that attempts to reach the third-party API to verify external connectivity.

C. A health check that only verifies the local web server is running by hitting a static file like `/health.html`.

D. A health check that performs a full end-to-end transaction to validate the entire application stack.

E. A health check that monitors the CPU utilization of the instance and fails if it exceeds 90%.

17. A CloudOps engineer is setting up a new Application Load Balancer (ALB) and needs to configure the health check for the Target Group. The application is designed to return a status of `200 OK` only when the application is fully initialized and ready to accept traffic. What is the correct sequence of steps to establish and verify this custom health check?

A. Enable "Cross-zone load balancing" in the ALB attributes and wait for the "Initial" state to change to "Healthy."

B. Set the "Unhealthy threshold" to 1 so that the ALB immediately stops sending traffic if a single probe fails during initialization.

C. Create a Simple routing policy in Route 53 and associate it with the ALB's DNS name before configuring the Target Group.

D. Configure the "Health check path" in the Target Group to the application's readiness endpoint (e.g., `/ready`) and monitor the "Target Health" status in the console.

E. Update the instances' Security Group to allow outbound traffic to the Amazon S3 service to fetch the health check script.

18. An organization needs to upgrade a Single-AZ Amazon RDS for MySQL instance to a fault-tolerant architecture. The goal is to survive an Availability Zone (AZ) failure with an RTO (Recovery Time Objective) of less than two minutes. A CloudOps engineer must ensure that the application can automatically reconnect to the database after a failover without requiring any manual changes to the database endpoint (connection string) in the application's configuration files. Which action will correctly implement this fault-tolerant configuration?

   A. Create a Read Replica in a different AZ and instruct the DevOps team to manually update the application's database URL to the replica's endpoint if the primary fails.

   B. Modify the RDS instance settings to enable "Multi-AZ deployment," which provisions a synchronous standby in another AZ and manages the DNS failover automatically.

   C. Use an AWS Lambda function to monitor the primary instance and, upon failure, restore the latest snapshot to a new instance with the same name.

   D. Deploy a second, independent RDS instance in another AZ and use an Application Load Balancer (ALB) to toggle traffic between the two database IP addresses.

   E. Enable "Automated Backups" with a zero-day retention period to force the database to replicate its data blocks to a standby region every hour.

19. A company runs a mission-critical web application in a region with three Availability Zones (`AZ 1`, `AZ 2`, and `AZ 3`). To meet their Service Level Agreement (SLA), the application must be able to handle its full peak load of 100,000 requests per minute even if one AZ becomes completely unavailable. A CloudOps engineer wants to implement a Statically Stable architecture to avoid depending on the EC2 Control Plane's ability to launch new instances during a regional crisis. Which auto-scaling group (ASG) and capacity configuration best achieves this goal?

   A. Deploy the ASG across three AZs and set the "Desired Capacity" to 150% of the total required peak load, distributed equally as 50% in each zone.

   B. Deploy the ASG across three AZs and set the "Minimum Capacity" to 100% of peak load, allowing the ASG to scale out only after a failure is detected.

   C. Deploy the ASG in a single AZ with 100% capacity and rely on a "Cross-Region Replica" to handle overflow traffic during a failure.

   D. Configure the ASG across two AZs and set the "Desired Capacity" to 100% of peak load, split as 50% in `AZ 1` and 50% in `AZ 2`.

   E. Use a "Target Tracking" policy based on CPU utilization to automatically launch new instances in healthy zones once an AZ failure occurs.

20. A CloudOps engineer is architecting a mission-critical database layer that must survive the total loss of an Availability Zone (AZ) without any manual intervention or reliance on the AWS Control Plane to launch new compute capacity during the event. The engineer must choose a Statically Stable Multi-AZ deployment option that ensures the database can perform an automated failover to a "warm," pre-provisioned standby that is already running in a healthy AZ. Which Amazon RDS or Aurora configuration best implements this Static Stability pattern?

   A. Deploy an Amazon Aurora cluster with a single writer instance and configure an Aurora auto-scaling policy to launch a new reader instance only when a zonal failure is detected.

B. Deploy a Single-AZ Amazon RDS instance and rely on an AWS Backup Restore plan to automatically re-create the database in a different AZ during an outage.

C. Deploy an Amazon RDS instance with a Cross-Region Read Replica and use a custom Lambda script to promote the replica to Primary if the source region experiences an AZ failure.

D. Deploy an Amazon Aurora Cluster with at least one reader instance (one writer and one reader across two or three AZs) and ensure that the application uses the Cluster Writer Endpoint.

E. Deploy an Amazon RDS Multi-AZ instance (Mirroring) and configure the application to use the Standby's unique IP address to handle read traffic during normal operations.

Answers to Review Questions

1. B, D. AWS Backup Vault Lock (Option B) is the specific AWS Backup feature for immutability. In "Compliance Mode," even the root user cannot delete backups or shorten the retention period, satisfying the mandate against ransomware and accidental deletion. Tags (Option D) are the best practice for automated resource assignment. Options A, C, E, and F are incorrect. AWS Backup manages its own storage in Amazon S3; users do not apply S3 Object Lock to the service's internal buckets (Option A). AWS Backup already captures IAM/metadata via its AMI-based EC2 recovery points (Option C). Option E proposes a manual, custom solution for a problem that AWS Backup solves natively. S3 CRR is for user-managed buckets, not Aurora's managed storage (Option F).

2. A, C. In an unplanned outage (a true regional outage), `failover-global-cluster` (Option A) is required. The `--allow-data-loss` flag is a mandatory requirement to acknowledge that the secondary may be slightly behind due to asynchronous replication. In a Pilot Light (headless) setup, you must manually create an instance (Option C) to act as the new primary writer. This is because Aurora Global Database only replicates the storage, not the compute. Options B, D, E, and F are incorrect. (Option B) `switchover` only works if the primary region is healthy (planned maintenance). Option D describes a manual data transfer process that contradicts how Amazon Aurora Global Database fundamentally operates. After failover, the application must point to the Writer Endpoint, not the Reader Endpoint (Option E), to perform updates. Aurora Global Database replicates storage continuously; you don't use Backup Restore jobs to populate it during failover (Option F).

3. B, F. Warm Standby requires a small, functional fleet. Scaling down instances (Option B) and using Aurora Serverless v2 (Option F) allows the environment to remain "warm" at a lower cost. Options A, C, D, and E are incorrect. Stopping instances moves the architecture into Pilot Light "territory," and may exceed a 15-minute RTO due to "cold boot" times (Option A). Backup & Restore is the cheapest but highest RTO strategy, which contradicts the "under 15 minutes" RTO requirement (Option C). The question specifically asks for ways to reduce the cost of the secondary region (DR Region, referred to as Region 2), which is consuming 60% of the production budget. Optimizing S3 storage in the Primary Region does nothing to lower the bill for the standing infrastructure in Region 2 (Option D). Multi-Site Active-Active will reduce RTO but will increase the cost, which contradicts the requirement (Option E).

4. A, C. Write Forwarding (Option A) is the specific feature of Aurora Global Database that allows secondary regions to accept write requests. When enabled, the secondary cluster transparently sends these writes to the Primary Writer in Region 1. Once Write Forwarding is enabled, the application must connect to the local cluster endpoint in Region 2. Setting the `aurora_replica_read_consistency` parameter (Option C) is critical because it determines how the application waits for those forwarded writes to replicate back to the secondary region, ensuring that the user sees their own updates (read-after-write consistency). Without this configuration, the application would likely block the write attempt before it even reached the database engine. Options B, D, E, and F are incorrect. A Global Database can only ever have one writer globally (Option B). Promoting a node in Region 2 while Region 1 is active would require "detaching" the cluster, which breaks the Global Database topology (Option D). Aurora Multi-Master is a single-region feature and does not support Multi-Region Global Database architectures (Option E). While a switchover is possible, swapping regional roles every hour is operationally complex, causes connection "flapping," and does not solve the underlying need for simultaneous active-active behavior. Replication in a Global Database happens at the Storage Layer, not the individual instance level. There is no such feature as "Instance-level CRR" for Aurora replicas (Option F).

5. A, D. AWS Backup Restore plans (Option A) allow engineers to pre-map the "Destination Metadata" (Subnets, Security Groups, VPCs). This ensures that when a restore is triggered, the instance lands in the correct networking context without manual configuration. Route 53 Application Recovery Controller (ARC) is the premier tool for regional readiness (Option D). It monitors if the DR region is ready (e.g., enough capacity, correct settings) and provides the "Routing Control" to shift traffic away from the failed region. Options B, C, E, and F are incorrect. Manual logging using AWS CloudTrail (Option B) defeats the purpose of a fully automated DR. Snapshots are moved between regions via the AWS Backup Copy Rule, not S3 Transfer Acceleration (Option C). AWS Config (Option E) is for compliance auditing, not for orchestrating the deletion of production resources during a DR restore. Manual AMI creation (Option F) is the opposite of the fully automated requirement.

6. B. The correct answer is B because a backup plan is merely a set of rules (the "when" and "how long") that remains dormant until it is told "what" to back up via a Backup Selection. Option A is incorrect because manual snapshots bypass the centralized management and lifecycle automation provided by AWS Backup. Option C is incorrect because S3 CRR is a feature for objects in user-managed S3 buckets, not for EC2 instance volumes. Option D is incorrect because modifying vault permissions to be "public" is a severe security violation and does not impact the trigger logic of the backup plan. Option E is incorrect because AWS Backup is a service-side orchestrator that does not require an agent to be installed on standard EC2 instances to perform snapshots.

7. A. The correct answer is A because AWS Backup restores only the Aurora shared storage volume; it does not automatically provision the compute nodes (the instances) required to process SQL queries. Option B is incorrect because a single recovery point captures the entire cluster, but the restoration process for Aurora is inherently a two-stage workflow where compute must be added manually after storage is ready. Option C is incorrect because networking visibility does not solve the lack of a compute node and introduces significant security risks. Option D is incorrect because storage auto-scaling handles disk capacity, not the provisioning of DB engine instances. Option E is incorrect because Write Forwarding is a feature of Aurora Global Databases, not a standalone restored cluster, and it requires a healthy primary region, which does not exist in this disaster scenario.

8. D. The correct answer is D because Backup & Restore is the only pattern where you pay almost exclusively for the storage of backups (recovery points) in the DR region, with zero cost for compute or active database storage until the moment of restoration. Option A is incorrect because Multi-Site Active-Active is the most expensive pattern, requiring full-scale production environments in both regions simultaneously. Option B is incorrect because Warm Standby requires a scaled-down but functional version of your infrastructure to be running 24/7. Option C is incorrect because Pilot Light requires a live database storage volume to be continuously active in the DR region to receive replication. Option E is incorrect because Aurora Global Database requires a secondary cluster to be permanently provisioned, which carries a continuous storage cost.

9. C. The correct answer is C because AWS Backup and its underlying S3 storage are regional services, meaning that once a recovery point is created, it is stored redundantly across multiple AZs within that region for high durability. Option A is incorrect because EBS volumes are zonal resources; they exist in only one AZ and cannot be attached to instances in another zone without being converted to a snapshot first. Option B is incorrect because EC2 instances are zonal and tied to the physical hardware of a specific AZ. Option D is incorrect because Security Groups are regional VPC-level resources that can be applied to instances in any AZ within that VPC. Answer E is incorrect because Aurora is a regional service specifically designed to survive the loss of an entire AZ by replicating data across at least three zones.

10. C. The correct answer is C because the backup plan is the central "brain" or orchestrator that contains the rules for when a backup happens (Schedule) and where it should be copied (Copy Actions). Option A is incorrect because a Vault is a passive container for storage and does not have the logic to trigger schedules or copies. Option B is incorrect because a Restore Testing plan is used for validating backups after they exist, not for the initial creation and replication of those backups. Option D is incorrect because the IAM role provides the permissions to do the work, but does not contain the logic or schedule. Option E is incorrect because the Backup Gateway is used specifically for backing up on-premises VMware environments to AWS, not for orchestrating cloud-native EC2 and Aurora backups.

11. B. The correct answer is B because a 404 error indicates that the ALB successfully reached the instance, but the web server could not find a file at the requested path; changing the path to a known valid file like `/index.html` ensures that the ALB receives the expected `200 OK` response. Option A is incorrect because increasing the success threshold only makes the check stricter and does not solve the underlying file-not-found error. Option C is incorrect because health checks require inbound traffic from the ALB to the instances, not outbound traffic from the instances to the ALB. Option D is incorrect because Route 53 routing policies do not affect how an ALB communicates with its backend targets in a Target Group. Option E is incorrect because it is a disruptive architectural change that avoids the misconfiguration rather than fixing the standard HTTP health check logic.

12. B. The correct answer is B because Route 53 cannot detect an application failure on its own; it requires a linked health check to monitor the endpoint and signal when the Primary record should be considered unhealthy to initiate the failover to the Secondary record. Option A is incorrect because regional failover happens at the DNS level and does not require private network connectivity between the two VPCs. Option C is incorrect because a high TTL actually delays failover as resolvers will cache the broken IP address for 24 hours; a low TTL is preferred for DR. Option D is incorrect because Cross-Zone Load Balancing affects traffic

distribution within a region, not DNS failover between regions. Option E is incorrect because the primary benefit of Failover Routing is its ability to perform the shift automatically without human intervention.

13. A. The correct answer is A because Route 53 health checkers are public AWS services located outside of your VPC; they can only monitor public IP addresses or endpoints reachable via the Internet. Option B is incorrect because moving a database to a public subnet is a massive security risk and should never be done to facilitate a health check. Option C is incorrect because the CloudWatch Agent is for metrics and logs, not for enabling DNS-level health checks for private IPs. Option D is incorrect because Route 53 natively supports TCP-based health checks on any port. Option E is incorrect because even with a service tag allowed, the public Route 53 checkers have no physical route to reach a private IP address in a restricted subnet.

14. B. The correct answer is B because decreasing the unhealthy threshold reduces the number of failed checks required to mark a target as sick, and decreasing the "Health check interval" makes those checks happen more frequently (e.g., every 5 seconds instead of 30). Option A is incorrect because the healthy threshold only controls how fast an instance returns to service, not how fast it is removed. Option C is incorrect because increasing the timeout and the unhealthy threshold would actually make the ALB take longer to detect a failure. Option D is incorrect because cross-zone load balancing is a traffic distribution setting and does not affect health check timing. Option E is incorrect because HTTPS checks often take slightly longer due to the SSL/TLS handshake and do not inherently increase the frequency of the probes.

15. B. The correct answer is B because the default EC2 health check only monitors the physical "liveness" of the hardware; changing the type to ELB allows the ASG to listen to the load balancer's health status and replace instances that fail application-level checks. Option A is incorrect because it relies on manual intervention, which defeats the purpose of auto-scaling automation. Option C is incorrect because Route 53 health checks are used for DNS routing and do not directly govern the lifecycle of instances within an auto-scaling group. Option D is incorrect because changing the protocol does not change how the ASG interprets the health signal. Option E is incorrect because SSM is a management tool and not the standard mechanism for triggering ASG instance replacements based on load balancer status.

16. C. The correct answer is C because a "shallow" health check only validates that the specific instance and its local web server are functional; it purposely avoids checking shared dependencies like databases to prevent a single backend issue from causing the load balancer to mark every healthy web server as failed. Options A, B, and D are incorrect because they describe "deep" health checks, which, while thorough, can lead to false positives where healthy web servers are terminated due to external or shared resource issues. Option E is incorrect because health checks are intended to test availability via a specific port/protocol, not to monitor system performance metrics like CPU, which is handled by CloudWatch alarms and scaling policies.

17. D. The correct answer is D because the standard operational workflow for establishing a health check involves defining the specific endpoint path (e.g., `/ready`) on the Target Group and then observing the status in the ALB's "Target Health" dashboard to ensure that the instances transition from the "Initial" state to "Healthy." Option A is incorrect because

cross-zone load balancing is a traffic distribution feature and does not govern the setup or verification of a health check path. Option B is incorrect because a threshold of 1 is too aggressive for most production environments and can lead to "flapping," where instances are marked unhealthy before they have finished their normal initialization. Option C is incorrect because Route 53 configuration is a DNS-level step that occurs after the ALB and its health checks are already functional. Option E is incorrect because the ALB needs inbound access to the instances; instances do not need to fetch scripts from S3 to respond to a standard ALB health check probe.

18. B. The correct answer is B because the Multi-AZ deployment feature is specifically designed to provide high availability with a single, persistent DNS endpoint. When a failure occurs, AWS automatically updates the DNS `CNAME` record to point to the standby instance, allowing the application to reconnect to the same connection string without manual configuration updates. Option A is incorrect because a Read Replica has its own unique endpoint; promoting it requires a manual update to the application's configuration, which violates the requirement. Option C is incorrect because restoring a snapshot creates a new instance with a different endpoint and takes significantly longer than the two-minute RTO. Option D is incorrect because ALBs are designed for HTTP/HTTPS or TCP traffic to application servers, not for managing database failover between independent RDS instances. Option E is incorrect because a zero-day retention period actually disables backups and does not provide a Multi-AZ standby or automated failover capabilities.

19. A. The correct answer is A because a Statically Stable architecture requires that you pre-provision enough capacity in the remaining zones to handle the full load without needing to scale out. In a three-AZ setup, if you place 50% of your required capacity in each of the three zones (total 150%), the loss of any single zone (50%) leaves exactly 100% of the required capacity remaining, ensuring the application stays online without triggering new instance launches. Option B is incorrect because it relies on the ASG's ability to scale out during a failure, which is not statically stable and could fail if the AWS Control Plane is congested. Option C is incorrect because a single-AZ deployment provides no fault tolerance. Answer D is incorrect because if one of the two zones fails, only 50% of the capacity remains, which violates the SLA. Option E is incorrect because it is a reactive scaling strategy, which is the opposite of the "pre-provisioned" static stability pattern.

20. D. The correct answer is D because an Amazon Aurora Cluster with a Reader instance is the definition of a statically stable database architecture. Since the Reader instance is already provisioned, powered on, and "warm" in a different AZ, the failover process is a simple DNS `CNAME` swap. The system does not need to call the AWS Control Plane to create or launch new hardware during the failure. Option A is incorrect because relying on auto-scaling to launch new capacity during a failure is a reactive strategy, not a statically stable one; if the Control Plane is congested, the new instance may fail to launch. Option B is incorrect because Backup & Restore is the most reactive strategy possible and carries a high RTO. Option C is incorrect because manual or scripted promotion of a Cross-Region Replica is a "Control Plane" mutation that is not statically stable for a zonal failure. Option E is incorrect because in a standard RDS Multi-AZ (non-cluster) deployment, the standby is "passive" and does not have an accessible IP address or endpoint to serve traffic; it is for failover only.

Deployment, Provisioning, and Automation

THE AWS CERTIFIED CLOUDOPS ENGINEER ASSOCIATE (SOA-C03) EXAM OBJECTIVES COVERED IN THIS CHAPTER MAY INCLUDE, BUT ARE NOT LIMITED TO THE FOLLOWING:

✓ **Domain 3: Deployment, Provisioning, and Automation**

- 3.1 Provision and maintain cloud resources
- 3.2 Automate the management of existing resources

Modern cloud operations depend on the ability to deploy, provision, and automate infrastructure in a safe, consistent, and repeatable way. As environments grow across multiple regions and accounts, manual provisioning is unsustainable because it becomes a source of risk, drift, and operational inconsistency. This chapter explores how CloudOps engineers use *Infrastructure as Code (IaC)*, automated deployment pipelines, and multi-account provisioning tools to build systems that are reliable and scalable by design, extending the systems operations fundamentals introduced in Chapters 3 and 6. You will apply the operational skills learned earlier—SSM Automation for controlled execution and EC2 Image Builder pipelines for automated AMI and container image creation—to larger, end-to-end automation workflows that build, deploy, and govern infrastructure at scale. These practices directly support the Operational Excellence pillar of the AWS Well-Architected Framework, by aligning with the principles of "Safely automate where possible," "Make frequent, small, reversible changes," and "Refine operations procedures frequently." Automation is not optional at scale—it is the mechanism that allows CloudOps teams to operate predictably and recover quickly.

While this chapter introduces tools such as AWS CloudFormation, AWS CDK, CloudFormation StackSets, and deployment services like CodeDeploy and CodePipeline, the focus is not on turning the reader into a full-time developer. The SOA-C03 exam does not expect candidates to write complex application code or build sophisticated CI/CD systems from scratch. Instead, it expects CloudOps engineers to understand how automation frameworks enable consistent provisioning, how IaC reduces drift and operational risk, and how deployment strategies such as blue/green and canary releases support safe, incremental change. The emphasis is on operational mastery—knowing how to use these tools to enforce governance, improve reliability, and streamline day-to-day operations.

Automation also plays a critical role in multi-account and Multi-Region environments, which are now the norm for enterprise AWS deployments. CloudOps engineers must understand how to provision shared resources across accounts using AWS Resource Access Manager (AWS RAM), how to deploy standardized infrastructure baselines using CloudFormation StackSets, and finally how to integrate third-party tools such as HashiCorp Terraform and Git-based workflows into their operational pipelines. These capabilities allow organizations to scale their CloudOps practices without increasing operational overhead. By the end of this chapter, you will understand how IaC, deployment automation, and multi-account provisioning form the backbone of modern cloud operations—and how these skills map directly to the SOA-C03 exam objectives.

Infrastructure as Code (IaC) Fundamentals

The Performance Efficiency pillar of the AWS Well-Architected Framework identifies Infrastructure as Code (IaC) as a key principle to run efficient high-performing cloud workloads. The idea is that infrastructure, just like applications, should be defined, deployed, and managed through code—not through manual clicks (sometimes informally referred to as "ClickOps") or ad hoc scripts. IaC provides the structure, repeatability, and governance needed to operate reliably at scale. It also forms the foundation for the deployment, provisioning, and automation skills tested in the SOA-C03 exam.

IaC shifts the CloudOps mindset from "configure servers" to "declare desired state." Instead of manually creating VPCs, subnets, IAM roles, or EC2 instances, you define them in templates or code constructs. AWS CloudFormation and the AWS Cloud Development Kit (AWS CDK) are the primary AWS-native IaC tools, and both ultimately produce CloudFormation templates that AWS deploys in a predictable, controlled manner. This declarative model ensures that infrastructure is reproducible, version-controlled, and auditable—qualities that directly support the governance and reliability principles you explored in Chapters 6 and 7.

To understand why IaC is so central to CloudOps, it helps to break down the core operational benefits it provides. The following sections highlight the four capabilities that make IaC indispensable for modern AWS environments and directly relevant to the SOA-C03 exam.

Idempotency

A core benefit of IaC is *idempotency*: the ability to apply the same template repeatedly and always achieve the same deterministic result. Idempotency eliminates configuration drift, reduces human error, and enables automated remediation workflows. When combined with AWS Config and CloudTrail, IaC becomes part of a closed-loop operational model: detect drift, remediate drift, and enforce desired state. This is why IaC is not just a provisioning technique—it is a foundational CloudOps discipline.

Environment Parity

IaC enables *environment parity*, ensuring that development, staging, and production environments are created from the same templates. This consistency reduces deployment risk, simplifies troubleshooting, and supports predictable failover strategies. Environment parity ties directly into the business continuity concepts from Chapter 7, where reliable recovery depends on consistent infrastructure definitions across regions and accounts.

Version Control

IaC templates and CDK code live in Git repositories, enabling peer review, change tracking, and rollback. This aligns infrastructure changes with the same governance model used for application code. Version control also enables Git-based automation workflows, where pull requests trigger CI/CD pipelines that validate, test, and deploy infrastructure changes. These workflows are increasingly common in enterprise CloudOps teams and are explicitly referenced in the SOA-C03 exam objectives.

Automation at All Layers

IaC supports automation at every layer of cloud operations. Whether you are deploying a single VPC or provisioning hundreds of accounts through AWS Organizations, IaC provides the mechanism to scale operational patterns without increasing operational overhead. CloudFormation StackSets, AWS CDK, AWS CodePipeline, and third-party tools like HashiCorp Terraform all build on the same principle: infrastructure should be automated, repeatable, and governed through code. The rest of this chapter builds on these fundamentals, showing how CloudFormation, CDK, Resource sharing, deployment strategies, and automation tools work together to create a mature, scalable CloudOps practice.

AWS CloudFormation

AWS CloudFormation is the foundational Infrastructure as Code (IaC) service in AWS and one of the most important tools for CloudOps engineers preparing for the SOA-C03 exam. CloudFormation enables you to define AWS Resources in declarative templates and deploy them as *stacks* in a predictable, controlled, and repeatable manner. Whether you are provisioning a single VPC or deploying standardized infrastructure across hundreds of accounts, CloudFormation provides the automation, governance, and operational consistency required for modern cloud operations. It also integrates deeply with AWS Organizations, AWS Config, AWS CloudTrail, and deployment services, making it a central component of the CloudOps lifecycle.

CloudFormation is not a developer-centric tool; it is an operational automation engine. You do not need to write application codes to use it effectively. Instead, you define infrastructure in JSON or YAML templates, and CloudFormation orchestrates the creation, update, and deletion of resources on your behalf. This orchestration includes dependency management, rollback on failure, drift detection, and change sets (which let you preview changes before applying them)—all of which directly support the Operational Excellence principles of making frequent, small, reversible changes and safely automating where possible. The following sections break down the core concepts, operational workflows, and best practices you need to master for both real-world CloudOps work and the SOA-C03 exam.

CloudFormation Template Structure

CloudFormation templates can be authored in YAML or JSON, and both formats are fully supported by AWS. In this book, we use YAML because it is more readable, less verbose, and easier for CloudOps engineers to scan—especially when working with nested stacks, intrinsic functions, and multi-section templates.

CloudFormation templates are divided into several top-level sections, each designed to hold a specific type of information. CloudFormation does not enforce a strict ordering for most sections, but using a logical, human-friendly structure makes templates easier to understand and maintain because values in one section often reference values defined earlier.

When authoring templates, you must not declare duplicate major sections (for example, two `Resources` sections or two `Parameters` sections). Although CloudFormation may accept such a template, the behavior is undefined and can lead to incorrect provisioning, partial deployments, or confusing error messages.

A well-structured template contains each major section at most once, with `Resources` being the only section that is mandatory for creating or updating a stack.

The following example shows the structure of a YAML-formatted template with all available sections.

```
AWSTemplateFormatVersion: version date

Description:
  String

Metadata:
  template metadata

Parameters:
  set of parameters

Rules:
  set of rules

Mappings:
  set of mappings

Conditions:
  set of conditions

Transform:
  set of transforms
```

```
Resources:
  set of resources

Outputs:
  set of outputs
```

Let's explore these sections:

Description The `Description` section lets you include a text string that describes the template. This section must always follow the template format version section.

Resources The `Resources` section is the only required part of a CloudFormation template and represents the core of what the stack will create. Each resource is defined with a unique logical ID, a resource type (such as `AWS::EC2::Instance` or `AWS::S3::Bucket`), and the configuration properties needed for CloudFormation to provision it.

Parameters The `Parameters` section is optional, but it's one of the most useful parts of a CloudFormation template because it makes your stacks flexible. Parameters let you inject values at deployment time—such as instance types, environment names, or CIDR blocks—without modifying the template itself. These values can then be referenced throughout the template, especially in the `Resources` and `Outputs` sections, allowing you to reuse the same template across multiple environments or configurations.

Outputs The `Outputs` section is optional, but it's extremely useful because it exposes key information about the resources your template creates. Outputs return values such as ARNs, IDs, or URLs—details you often need for operational tasks, automation pipelines, or for passing into other stacks. By defining outputs, you make it easy to retrieve important resource information without digging through the console or writing custom scripts.

Mappings The `Mappings` section acts like a static lookup table for values that change based on predictable factors such as region, environment, or account type. You define key–value pairs and retrieve them using the `Fn::FindInMap` intrinsic function (explained in the next section) inside your `Resources` or `Outputs` sections. Mappings are ideal when you need different configuration values—like AMI IDs or environment settings—without introducing conditional logic or parameters.

Conditions The `Conditions` section allows you to control whether certain resources are created or whether specific properties are applied. Conditions evaluate to true or false based on parameters, mappings, or built-in pseudo parameters such as `AWS::Region`. This is especially useful for environment-specific deployments—for example, creating NAT Gateways only in production or applying different settings in specific regions. Conditions help reduce template duplication and support cost-optimized architectures.

Rules The `Rules` section validates parameter values before CloudFormation creates or updates a stack. Rules let you enforce constraints such as allowed combinations, required relationships, or organizational standards. For example, you can ensure that a parameter is only set to certain values in specific regions. While not used in every template, rules are valuable in enterprise environments where guardrails and input validation are essential.

Transform The `Transform` section applies macros that preprocess the template before CloudFormation evaluates it. The most common example is the AWS Serverless Application Model (SAM), which lets you write simplified serverless definitions that CloudFormation expands into full resource configurations. You can also use the `AWS::Include` transform to pull in external template snippets, enabling modular design. Transforms are optional but powerful when working with serverless architectures or reusable template components.

Metadata The `Metadata` section lets you attach additional information to your template. This data doesn't affect how CloudFormation creates resources, but it can store helpful context such as team details, deployment notes, or tool-specific configuration. You can also use the `AWS::CloudFormation::Interface` key in this section to define how parameters are grouped and sorted in the CloudFormation console. This is a useful operational feature that you can use to present parameters in a clearer, more guided layout for your CloudOps team, especially when a template exposes many configuration options:

```
Metadata:
  AWS::CloudFormation::Interface:
    ParameterGroups:
      - Label:
          default: Group Label
        Parameters:
          - Parameter1
          - Parameter2
    ParameterLabels:
      Parameter1:
        default: Friendly Name for Parameter1
```

Metadata is often used by automation frameworks, and it's a convenient place to keep user-defined key–value pairs that improve clarity without impacting stack behavior.

With the structure and purpose of each template section now clear, we can shift from how CloudFormation templates are written to how they are actually deployed and managed in practice. The next section walks through the core operational workflows—creating stacks, reviewing changes, and detecting drift—using examples you'll encounter in day-to-day CloudOps work.

Operating CloudFormation Stacks

Now that you understand how CloudFormation templates are structured, you can shift to the operational side—how stacks are created, updated, reviewed, and monitored.

Creating Stacks

To explain how CloudFormation operates in practice, we'll start by deploying a very small, intentionally simple CloudFormation template. This template provisions a single-node ElastiCache Redis OSS cluster. It's not meant to be production-ready; instead, it gives us a clean, easy-to-follow example that we can use throughout the rest of this chapter.

```
AWSTemplateFormatVersion: '2010-09-09'
Description: Simple ElastiCache Redis OSS cluster

Parameters:
  CacheNodeType:
    Type: String
    Default: cache.t3.micro

  NumCacheNodes:
    Type: Number
    Default: 1

Resources:
  RedisCluster:
    Type: AWS::ElastiCache::CacheCluster
    Properties:
      Engine: redis
      CacheNodeType: !Ref CacheNodeType
      NumCacheNodes: !Ref NumCacheNodes
      AutoMinorVersionUpgrade: true
      PreferredMaintenanceWindow: "sun:05:00-sun:09:00"

Outputs:
  RedisEndpoint:
    Value: !GetAtt RedisCluster.RedisEndpoint.Address
```

Before deploying the stack, save this YAML as `redis.yaml` in your working directory. The CLI commands that follow use the `file://redis.yaml` syntax to load this file from your local machine.

This example uses the default VPC, which allows CloudFormation to automatically assign subnets, routing, and a default security group. In a real CI/CD workflow, you would explicitly define the VPC, subnet groups, security groups, engine version, and other networking details. Here, we intentionally skip all of that so we can focus on CloudFormation's operational lifecycle—creating stacks, reviewing changes, updating resources, and detecting drift—without overwhelming the reader with infrastructure design.

```
aws cloudformation create-stack \
  --stack-name redis-demo \
  --template-body file://redis.yaml \
  --parameters ParameterKey=CacheNodeType,ParameterValue=cache.t3.micro
```

In this command:

- `create-stack`: Tells CloudFormation to deploy a new stack.
- `--stack-name redis-demo`: Sets the human-readable name for your stack. You will use this name later to update, delete, or view the stack in the AWS CloudFormation Console.

- `--template-body file://redis.yaml`: Tells the CLI where to find your template file. The `file://` prefix is mandatory when referencing a file on your local machine; without it, the CLI treats the string as the template text itself.
- `--parameters`: This flag allows you to provide input values for the keys defined in your template's `Parameters` section.
  - `ParameterKey=CacheNodeType`: Identifies which parameter in the YAML you are targeting.
  - `ParameterValue=cache.t3.micro`: Provides the specific value to use. If you omit a parameter that has a default value in the YAML (like `NumCacheNodes`), CloudFormation will automatically use that default.

When you run the command, CloudFormation responds immediately with metadata about the stack creation request. The actual provisioning happens asynchronously in the background:

```
{
    "StackId": "arn:aws:cloudformation:us-east-1:123456789012:stack/
redis-demo/1a2b3c4d-5678-90ab-cdef-11111EXAMPLE"
}
```

This output simply confirms that CloudFormation has accepted the request and created a stack record. It does not mean the Redis OSS cluster is ready yet. CloudFormation will now begin creating the resources defined in the template, and you can monitor progress in the AWS Console or with:

```
aws cloudformation describe-stacks \
  --stack-name redis-demo
```

If anything fails—such as insufficient permissions—CloudFormation automatically rolls back the entire deployment, ensuring that you never end up with partially created infrastructure.

For more information, visit: `https://docs.aws.amazon.com/cli/latest/reference/cloudformation/create-stack.html` and `https://docs.aws.amazon.com/cli/latest/reference/cloudformation/describe-stacks.html`.

Reviewing Changes with Change Sets

Once your stack is deployed, the next operational question is: *What happens when we want to change it?* CloudFormation gives you a safe way to preview updates before applying them through a feature called *Change Sets*. This is especially important in production environments where an unintended modification could cause downtime or data loss.

Suppose you want to scale up the Redis OSS cluster node type from `cache.t3.micro` to `cache.t3.small`. You update the template locally by replacing the old instance type with the desired instance type:

```
Parameters:
  CacheNodeType:
    Type: String
    Default: cache.t3.small   # changed
```

Save the file and create a change set with the following command:

```
aws cloudformation create-change-set \
  --stack-name redis-demo \
  --template-body file://redis.yaml \
  --change-set-name scale-redis \
  --description "Scale Redis cluster to t3.small"
```

The command returns an output similar to this:

```
{
    "Id": "arn:aws:cloudformation:us-east-1:123456789012:changeSet/scale-redis/
abcd1234-ef56-7890-abcd-11111EXAMPLE",
    "StackId": "arn:aws:cloudformation:us-east-1:123456789012:stack/
redis-demo/1a2b3c4d-5678-90ab-cdef-11111EXAMPLE"
}
```

This output confirms that CloudFormation has created a Change Set but has not applied it yet. The `"Id"` key in the response denotes the actual `ChangeSetId`. You can preview the change set with the command:

```
aws cloudformation describe-change-set \
  --stack-name redis-demo \
  --change-set-name scale-redis
```

A sample output looks like this:

```
{
    "ChangeSetId": "arn:aws:cloudformation:us-east-1:123456789012:changeSet/
scale-redis/abcd1234-ef56-7890-abcd-11111EXAMPLE",
    "ChangeSetName": "scale-redis",
    "StackId": "arn:aws:cloudformation:us-east-1:123456789012:stack/
redis-demo/1a2b3c4d-5678-90ab-cdef-11111EXAMPLE",
    "StackName": "redis-demo",
    "Description": "Scale Redis cluster to t3.small",
    "Parameters": [
        {
```

```
            "ParameterKey": "CacheNodeType",
            "ParameterValue": "cache.t3.small"
        },
        {
            "ParameterKey": "NumCacheNodes",
            "ParameterValue": "1"
        }
    ],
    "CreationTime": "2023-10-27T14:30:00.000Z",
    "ExecutionStatus": "AVAILABLE",
    "Status": "CREATE_COMPLETE",
    "StatusReason": null,
    "NotificationARNs": [],
    "Capabilities": [],
    "Tags": [],
    "Changes": [
        {
            "Type": "Resource",
            "ResourceChange": {
                "Action": "Modify",
                "LogicalResourceId": "RedisCluster",
                "PhysicalResourceId": "simple-redis-cluster",
                "ResourceType": "AWS::ElastiCache::CacheCluster",
                "Replacement": "False",
                "Scope": [
                    "Properties"
                ],
                "Details": [
                    {
                        "Target": {
                            "Attribute": "Properties",
                            "Name": "CacheNodeType",
                            "RequiresRecreation": "Never"
                        },
                        "Evaluation": "Static",
                        "ChangeSource": "DirectModification"
                    }
                ]
            }
        }
    ]
}
```

The `StackId` is the unique Amazon Resource Name (ARN) assigned to the stack when it is created. Since a Change Set is essentially a proposed update to a specific existing stack, both the `create-change-set` and `describe-change-set` commands will refer back to that same parent `StackId`. If you see a different `StackId`, it means you are looking at a different environment entirely (e.g., a "Staging" stack vs. a "Production" stack).

This Change Set preview shows exactly how CloudFormation intends to update your stack: it lists the parameters that will be used during the update, identifies which resources will change, and highlights the specific property—in this case, `CacheNodeType`—that triggered the modification. It also tells you whether the update requires resource replacement (Replacement: False means an in-place update is possible), and whether the change affects only properties or other aspects of the resource. In short, this output is your safety check before applying any update, ensuring you fully understand the impact of your template changes. With this preview complete, we're ready to apply the update in the next subsection.

For more information, visit: `https://docs.aws.amazon.com/cli/latest/reference/cloudformation/create-change-set.html` and `https://docs.aws.amazon.com/cli/latest/reference/cloudformation/describe-change-set.html`.

Updating Stacks

Executing a Change Set tells CloudFormation to proceed with the modifications it previewed earlier. This is where CloudFormation's orchestration engine takes over—evaluating dependencies, determining whether resources can be updated in place, and rolling back safely if something goes wrong.

```
aws cloudformation execute-change-set \
  --stack-name redis-demo \
  --change-set-name scale-redis
```

A successful execution of this command simply exits with a return code of `0`. This is because the command is asynchronous; it tells CloudFormation to start the update process, but it doesn't wait for the update to finish before returning control to your terminal.

Since the command is silent, CloudOps engineers typically use one of these two methods to confirm the update is actually happening:

Check Stack Status Run `describe-stacks` to see if the status has changed to `UPDATE_IN_PROGRESS`

```
aws cloudformation describe-stacks \
  --stack-name redis-demo \
  --query "Stacks[0].StackStatus"
```

Use a Waiter Use the CLI "waiter" to pause your script until the update is complete. This command will produce no output until the stack reaches a final state.

```
aws cloudformation wait stack-update-complete \
  --stack-name redis-demo
```

Although Change Sets are the safer option, CloudFormation also allows you to update a stack directly:

```
aws cloudformation update-stack \
  --stack-name redis-demo \
  --template-body file://redis.yaml
```

Direct updates begin immediately and are typically used in development or automated pipelines where the update behavior is well understood.

For more information, visit `https://docs.aws.amazon.com/cli/latest/reference/cloudformation/execute-change-set.html`, `https://docs.aws.amazon.com/cli/latest/reference/cloudformation/wait/stack-update-complete.html`, and `https://docs.aws.amazon.com/cli/latest/reference/cloudformation/update-stack.html`.

Protection Mechanisms

As you work with stack updates, it helps to understand how CloudFormation protects resources throughout the update and deletion lifecycle. At the stack level, CloudFormation offers safeguards such as *stack policies*, which are always defined in JSON and attached to a stack to restrict which resources can be modified during an update, and *termination protection*, which you enable as a stack setting to prevent accidental deletion. At the resource level, CloudFormation provides `DeletionPolicy` and `UpdateReplacePolicy`, both specified declaratively within the resource definition in your YAML or JSON template. These attributes control what happens when a resource is deleted or must be replaced during an update—whether CloudFormation should retain it, snapshot it, or remove it. Together, these mechanisms give CloudOps engineers fine-grained control over both update-time behavior and resource-lifecycle outcomes, especially for stateful components where unintended replacement or deletion can have operational impact.

CloudFormation Service Role

While lifecycle policies determine what CloudFormation does to resources during updates and replacements, CloudFormation also needs permission to perform those actions. A CloudFormation *service role* is an IAM role that CloudFormation assumes when executing a stack operation. Instead of relying on the permissions of the user or automation pipeline that initiated the deployment, CloudFormation uses the permissions defined in this role to create, update, or delete resources on your behalf. This supports both least-privilege execution and separation of duties: CloudOps engineers can deploy infrastructure without needing broad IAM permissions, while administrators retain control over what CloudFormation itself is allowed to manage.

You associate a service role with a stack by specifying its ARN when creating or updating the stack. In the CLI, this is done using the `--role-arn` flag, which tells CloudFormation which IAM role to assume for the operation. Once set, CloudFormation continues to use this role for all subsequent updates to the stack. This ensures consistent, centrally governed permissions across deployments—an important safeguard in regulated, multi-account, or production environments where CloudFormation's access must be tightly controlled.

A service role, once attached to a stack, is used for all future operations unless explicitly replaced. A user must have `iam:PassRole` to associate a service role with a stack. If a user has permission to operate on a stack that already has a service role assigned, CloudFormation will assume that role to perform the actions—even if the user lacks `iam:PassRole`—which can lead to privilege escalation if the role grants broader permissions than the user. Always keep the service role strictly least-privilege.

Detecting and Remediating Drift

Even with well-designed CloudFormation workflows, it's common for manual changes to slip into your environment—especially during troubleshooting, emergency fixes, or when multiple teams share the same AWS account. When a resource is modified outside of CloudFormation, the stack becomes *drifted*, meaning the actual configuration no longer matches the template. CloudFormation provides drift detection to help you identify these discrepancies and restore consistency.

Imagine someone updates the Redis OSS cluster's maintenance window directly in the AWS Management Console. This change is now invisible to CloudFormation, and the stack is technically out of sync with the template.

Because scanning live resources can take several minutes depending on the stack size, CloudOps engineers use a multi-step process to detect and remediate drifts:

Step 1: Initiating Drift Detection

Use `detect-stack-drift` to get the `StackDriftDetectionId`.

```
aws cloudformation detect-stack-drift \
  --stack-name redis-demo
```

Sample output:

```
{
    "StackDriftDetectionId": "1a229160-e4d9-xmpl-ab67-0a4f93df83d4"
}
```

Step 2: Monitoring Detection Status

Use the `StackDriftDetectionId` with `describe-stack-drift-detection-status` to see if the scan is finished.

```
aws cloudformation describe-stack-drift-detection-status \
  --stack-drift-detection-id "1a229160-e4d9-xmpl-ab67-0a4f93df83d4"
```

Example output:

```
{
    "StackDriftDetectionId": "1a229160-e4d9-xmpl-ab67-0a4f93df83d4",
    "DetectionStatus": "DETECTION_IN_PROGRESS"
}
```

Wait until the `DetectionStatus` changes to `DETECTION_COMPLETE` before moving to the next step.

Step 3: Viewing Drift Results

Once the status is `DETECTION_COMPLETE`, use `describe-stack-resource-drifts` to see which specific properties (like your maintenance window) have changed.

```
aws cloudformation describe-stack-resource-drifts \
  --stack-name redis-demo
```

A sample output would look like this:

```
{
    "StackResourceDrifts": [
        {
            "StackId": "arn:aws:cloudformation:us-east-1:123456789012:stack/
redis-demo/1a2b3c4d-5678-90ab-cdef-11111EXAMPLE",
            "LogicalResourceId": "RedisCluster",
            "PhysicalResourceId": "simple-redis-cluster",
            "ResourceType": "AWS::ElastiCache::CacheCluster",
            "ExpectedProperties": "{\"PreferredMaintenanceWindow\":\"
sun:05:00-sun:09:00\", ...}",
            "ActualProperties": "{\"PreferredMaintenanceWindow\":\"
wed:02:00-wed:06:00\", ...}",
            "PropertyDifferences": [
                {
                    "PropertyPath": "/PreferredMaintenanceWindow",
                    "ExpectedValue": "sun:05:00-sun:09:00",
                    "ActualValue": "wed:02:00-wed:06:00",
                    "DifferenceType": "NOT_EQUAL"
                }
            ],
            "StackResourceDriftStatus": "MODIFIED",
            "Timestamp": "2023-10-27T15:00:00.000Z"
        }
    ]
}
```

Here are the key elements of the drift report:

- `StackResourceDriftStatus: MODIFIED`: This confirms that the resource still exists but its configuration has been changed outside of CloudFormation.
- `PropertyPath`: Identifies exactly which attribute has drifted—in this case, the `PreferredMaintenanceWindow`.
- `ExpectedValue` vs. `ActualValue`: This is the "Data Diff." It explicitly shows that your template expects Sunday morning, but the live resource is set to Wednesday night.
- `DifferenceType: NOT_EQUAL`: Indicates that a property value was changed. Other types include `ADD` (if a property was added manually) or `REMOVE` (if a property was deleted).

CloudFormation only detects drift for properties explicitly defined in your template. If your YAML didn't specify a `PreferredMaintenanceWindow` and you changed it in the console, CloudFormation would not flag it as drifted because it has no `ExpectedValue` to compare it against. To have CloudFormation track a resource property for purposes of determining drift, explicitly set the property value, even if you are setting it to the default value.

For more information, visit `https://docs.aws.amazon.com/cli/latest/reference/cloudformation/detect-stack-drift.html`, `https://docs.aws.amazon.com/cli/latest/reference/cloudformation/describe-stack-drift-detection-status.html`, and `https://docs.aws.amazon.com/cli/latest/reference/cloudformation/describe-stack-resource-drifts.html`.

Step 4: Remediating Drift with Drift-Aware Change Sets

If the template represents the correct desired state, you can remediate drift directly when creating a change set by using a drift-aware deployment mode. This instructs CloudFormation to update only the properties that differ from the template. For the Redis OSS cluster example—where the maintenance window was manually changed in the console—you can create a change set that restores the expected value:

```
aws cloudformation create-change-set \
  --stack-name redis-demo \
  --template-body file://redis.yaml \
  --change-set-name revert-drift \
  --deployment-mode REVERT_DRIFT
```

The use of the `--deployment-mode REVERT_DRIFT` flag reverts only the drifted properties, such as the `PreferredMaintenanceWindow` in this case, without modifying any other part of the stack, thereby restoring the stack to its defined "source of truth."

After creating the drift-aware change set, you must apply it to perform the remediation:

```
aws cloudformation execute-change-set \
  --stack-name redis-demo \
  --change-set-name revert-drift
```

For more information, visit `https://docs.aws.amazon.com/AWSCloudFormation/latest/UserGuide/drift-aware-change-sets.html#drift-aware-change-sets-cli`.

CloudFormation in Multi-Account Environments

In modern AWS environments, CloudFormation rarely operates within a single account. Organizations increasingly rely on multi-account structures—often built with AWS Organizations or Control Tower—to isolate workloads, enforce governance, and simplify security boundaries. In these setups, CloudFormation becomes the mechanism that ensures every account starts from a consistent, compliant baseline. For CloudOps engineers, the challenge is understanding how CloudFormation behaves when infrastructure must be deployed, updated, and governed across many accounts rather than just one.

StackSets are the centerpiece of this model. They allow you to define infrastructure once and roll it out across multiple accounts and regions, with CloudFormation handling orchestration, retries, and per-account execution. The SOA-C03 exam expects you to understand the difference between self-managed and service-managed StackSets, how administration and execution roles enforce least privilege, and how automatic deployments work when new accounts join an Organizational Unit. These capabilities are essential for rolling out organization-wide guardrails, IAM roles, logging configurations, and network baselines at scale.

Operating CloudFormation across accounts also introduces new operational considerations. Failures may occur in only one target account, drift can appear in unexpected places, and updates must be coordinated without disrupting workloads. CloudOps engineers must know how to monitor StackSet operations, interpret per-account deployment statuses, and remediate drift across a fleet of accounts. In multi-account environments, CloudFormation becomes not just an IaC tool but a governance and consistency engine—an essential skillset for both real-world CloudOps work and the SOA-C03 exam.

AWS Cloud Development Kit (AWS CDK)

The AWS Cloud Development Kit (CDK) builds on the same declarative foundation as CloudFormation but lets you define infrastructure using familiar programming languages such as TypeScript, JavaScript, Python, Java, C#, and Go. Instead of writing YAML or

JSON templates directly, you express infrastructure as reusable, strongly typed constructs that compile down to CloudFormation templates at deployment time. This gives teams the benefits of IaC—repeatability, version control, and predictable deployments—while enabling richer abstraction and code reuse.

CDK's construct model is its core strength. At the lowest level, *L1 constructs* map directly to CloudFormation resources, while L2 and L3 constructs provide higher-level, opinionated building blocks that encapsulate best practices. This allows you to define complex infrastructure patterns—VPCs, ECS services, Lambda functions, or CI/CD pipelines—with far less boilerplate than raw CloudFormation. Because constructs are just code, they can be packaged, shared, and versioned across teams, enabling consistent patterns throughout an organization.

When you deploy a CDK application, the toolkit synthesizes your code into a CloudFormation template and then uses CloudFormation to manage the lifecycle of the resulting stack. This means CDK inherits CloudFormation's strengths—drift detection, change sets, rollback protection, and stack-level governance—while offering a more expressive authoring experience. For the exam, remember that CDK is not a replacement for CloudFormation; it is a higher-level framework that ultimately produces CloudFormation templates and relies on CloudFormation for deployment and state management.

As you move beyond authoring and deploying infrastructure with CloudFormation and CDK, the next challenge is operating securely in multi-account and Multi-Region environments. The following section explores how AWS enables you to share and govern resources within organizational boundaries.

Sharing Resources Across Accounts and Regions

As organizations adopt multi-account architectures, the need to share infrastructure components across accounts and regions becomes unavoidable. AWS Resource Access Manager (RAM) provides the foundation for this model by allowing centrally managed resources—such as subnets, Transit Gateways, and Route 53 Resolver rules—to be shared securely with other accounts or entire Organizational Units (OUs).

AWS Resource Access Manager (AWS RAM)

In a well-structured multi-account landing zone (MALZ), the networking team typically centralizes all VPC infrastructure inside a dedicated Network Account, while application teams deploy workloads in separate accounts grouped under Organizational Units (OUs). This separation of duties is intentional: it keeps network governance centralized while allowing application teams to operate independently.

AWS Resource Access Manager (RAM) is the service that enables this model. RAM allows the Network Account to share subnets with workload accounts so they can deploy resources into centrally managed networks—without gaining permission to modify routing, CIDRs, or security boundaries.

Understanding how RAM distinguishes between the caller (the principal producing the share) and the recipient (the account or OU consuming the share) is essential for both real-world CloudOps and the SOA-C03 exam.

RAM also exposes condition keys that let you precisely control who can create shares and who can receive them, as listed in Table 8.1.

These condition keys are particularly relevant when used in SCPs to constrain who is allowed to create subnet shares and who is allowed to receive them, enforcing strict governance across the organization.

The following example shows how a principal (Network Admin) in the Network Account shares a subnet with a Workloads OU and how SCPs enforce strict governance around who can create and receive subnet shares.

Creating a Subnet Share

Refer to Figure 8.1 as you read through this example—the diagram visually reinforces each step of the following subnet-sharing workflow.

Step 1: Enabling Organization-Wide Resource Sharing

Use a principal (e.g., Org Admin) in the Management Account (`<Management-Account-ID>`) with the required IAM permissions:

- `ram:EnableSharingWithAwsOrganization`
- `iam:CreateServiceLinkedRole`
- `organizations:enableAWSServiceAccess`
- `organizations:DescribeOrganization`

and run the following command:

TABLE 8.1 AWS RAM Condition Keys for Resource Sharing Governance

Condition Key	Meaning
`aws:PrincipalAccount`	The account that owns the principal performing the RAM action
`ram:RequestedResourceType`	The type of resource being shared (e.g., `ec2:Subnet`)
`ram:Principal`	The recipient of the share (account or OU)

FIGURE 8.1 VPC sharing in a multi-account landing zone.

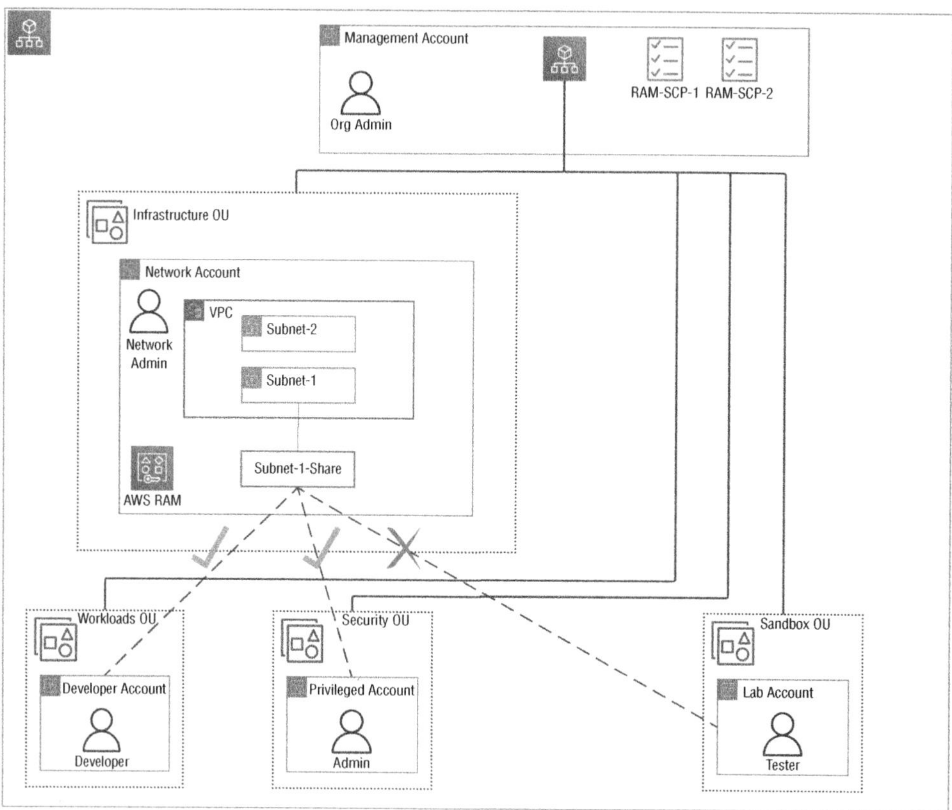


```
aws ram enable-sharing-with-aws-organization
```

The command returns an output similar to this as a confirmation that resource sharing is now enabled in your AWS Organization:

```
{
    "returnValue": true
}
```

Step 2: Creating the Resource Share

Use a principal in the Network Account (`<Network-Account-ID>`) with the required IAM permissions:

- `ram:CreateResourceShare`
- `ram:AssociateResourceShare`
- `ec2:DescribeVpcs`
- `ec2:DescribeSubnets`

and run the following command:

```
aws ram create-resource-share \
    --name Subnet-1-Share \
    --resource-arns arn:aws:ec2:<Region>:<Network-Account-
ID>:subnet/<Subnet-ID> \
    --principals '[
        "arn:aws:organizations::<Management-
Account-ID>:ou/<Organization-ID>/<Workloads-OU-ID>",
        "<AWS-Privileged-Account-ID>"
    ]' \
    --allow-external-principals false
```

In this command:

- `--name`: A friendly name for the *resource share*.
- `--resource-arns`: ARN of the subnet being shared.
- `--principals`: The list of recipients (OU or AWS account).
- `--allow-external-principals false`: Restricts sharing to your AWS Organization only.

The command generates an output similar to this:

```
{
    "resourceShare": {
        "resourceShareArn": "arn:aws:ram:<Region>:<Network-Account-ID>:resource
-share/<Resource-Share-UUID>",
        "name": "Subnet-1-Share",
        "owningAccountId": "<Network-Account-ID>",
        "allowExternalPrincipals": false,
        "status": "ACTIVE",
        "statusMessage": "The resource share is created and available for
use.",
        "creationTime": "2026-04-10T02:38:45.166+00:00",
        "lastUpdatedTime": "2026-04-10T02:38:45.166+00:00",
        "featureSet": "STANDARD"
    },
    "clientToken": "<Unique-Idempotency-Token-UUID>"
}
```

The new resource share `Subnet-1-Share` is illustrated in Figure 8.1. Notice how the resource share is "owned" by the Network Account in the Infrastructure OU.

`<AWS-Privileged-Account-ID>` represents a highly privileged, tightly controlled "break-glass" account. It is intentionally allowed to consume subnet shares for tasks such as emergency troubleshooting, critical recovery, and controlled administrative operations.

For more information, visit https://docs.aws.amazon.com/cli/latest/reference/ram/create-resource-share.html.

Step 3: Launching Resources into the Shared Subnet

Upon successful creation, the authorized recipients of the resource share—limited in our model to principals in accounts belonging to the Workloads OU and the privileged break-glass account—can deploy resources into the shared subnet.

Use a principal in the Privileged Account with these required IAM permissions to launch an EC2 instance in the shared subnet:

- ec2:RunInstances
- ec2:CreateNetworkInterface
- ec2:DescribeSubnets

```
aws ec2 run-instances \
  --subnet-id <Subnet-ID> \
  --image-id <AMI-ID> \
  --instance-type t3.micro
```

Principals in accounts belonging to the Workload OU (e.g., Developer) and principals in the Privileged Account (e.g., Admin) can deploy resources into the shared subnet, but cannot modify the subnet, route tables, NACLs, or VPC configuration.

Since the recipients of the resource share are accounts in the same AWS Organization, access to the resource share is automatic. Had the recipients been accounts outside our AWS Organization (controlled in the CLI command `aws ram create-resource-share` by setting the `--allow-external-principals true`), they would have been required to accept an invitation to access the resource share.

Restricting Access to the Subnet Share

To prevent uncontrolled or accidental consumption of shared network resources, this example applies two Service Control Policies—RAM-SCP-1 and RAM-SCP-2—to tightly govern who can create and who can receive subnet shares. RAM-SCP-1 ensures that only principals operating within the Network Account can initiate subnet-sharing actions, blocking all other accounts from creating or associating subnet shares. RAM-SCP-2 then restricts who may receive those shares, allowing only principals in the Workloads OU and a single privileged break-glass account to accept and use the shared subnet. Together, these SCPs enforce a clear, least-privilege boundary around subnet sharing and prevent arbitrary accounts from consuming centrally managed network resources.

RAM-SCP-1 denies subnet-sharing operations unless the caller's account is the Network Account.

```
{
  "Version": "2012-10-17",
  "Statement": [
    {
      "Sid": "DenySubnetSharingFromNonNetworkAccounts",
      "Effect": "Deny",
      "Action": [
        "ram:CreateResourceShare",
        "ram:AssociateResourceShare"
      ],
      "Resource": "*",
      "Condition": {
        "StringNotEquals": {
          "aws:PrincipalAccount": "<Network-Account-ID>"
        },
        "StringEqualsIfExists": {
          "ram:RequestedResourceType": "ec2:Subnet"
        }
      }
    }
  ]
}
```

RAM-SCP-2 restricts who can be the recipient of subnet shares.

```
{
  "Version": "2012-10-17",
  "Statement": [
    {
      "Sid": "RestrictSubnetShareTargets",
      "Effect": "Deny",
      "Action": [
        "ram:CreateResourceShare",
        "ram:AssociateResourceShare"
      ],
      "Resource": "*",
      "Condition": {
        "ForAnyValue:StringNotEquals": {
          "ram:Principal": [
            "arn:aws:organizations::<Management-
Account-ID>:ou/o-<Organization-ID>/<Workloads-OU-ID>",
            "<AWS-Privileged-Account-ID>"
          ]
        },
        "StringEqualsIfExists": {
          "ram:RequestedResourceType": "ec2:Subnet"
        }
      }
    }
  ]
}
```

In RAM-SCP-2, notice the syntax of the Workloads OU ARN:

`arn:aws:organizations::<Management-Account-ID>:ou/o-<Organization-ID>/<Workloads-OU-ID>`

In a shared VPC (VPC Sharing), costs are split between the VPC owner (`<Network-Account-ID>`) and the participants (`<AWS-Privileged-Account-ID>`, `<Workloads-OU-ID>`). Participants pay for their own application resources (EC2, RDS, Lambda) and data transfer costs for Inter-AZ traffic, Peering, Internet Gateways, and Direct Connect. The VPC owner pays for the VPC infrastructure, including NAT Gateways (hourly and processing), Transit Gateways, VPC endpoints (PrivateLink), and public IPv4 addresses. Data transfer within the same Availability Zone—identified by the AZ-ID (e.g., `use1-az1`) rather than the account-specific AZ name (e.g., `us-east-1a`)—is free, even when the communicating resources belong to different AWS accounts.

Deployment Strategies and Services

In a multi-account AWS environment, CloudOps engineers must understand the common deployment strategies used to roll out application and infrastructure changes safely. At a high level, AWS supports several patterns—such as rolling updates, blue/green deployments, and canary releases—that help minimize downtime and reduce the blast radius of changes. While the SOA-C03 exam does not test these strategies in depth, candidates are expected to recognize when controlled, incremental deployments are preferable to all-at-once updates.

AWS also provides several services that support these deployment approaches, each suited to different workloads and operational models. AWS CodeDeploy enables automated deployments for EC2, ECS, Lambda, and on-premises instances. While it offers built-in support for blue/green patterns across most platforms, canary and linear traffic-shifting configurations are available exclusively for ECS and Lambda; EC2 and on-premises deployments typically rely on in-place or traditional blue/green instance swaps. AWS CodePipeline orchestrates CI/CD workflows, integrating with CodeBuild, CodeDeploy, and third-party tools to automate end-to-end release processes. For containerized workloads, Amazon ECS and Amazon EKS support rolling and blue/green deployments through their respective service-update mechanisms, while Lambda offers traffic-shifting aliases for gradual rollouts.

From a CloudOps perspective, the key takeaway is that deployment services must integrate cleanly with the organization's governance, monitoring, and rollback mechanisms. CloudFormation and CDK continue to manage infrastructure state, while deployment tools handle application-level changes. For the exam, remember that the focus is on operational awareness rather than deep CI/CD expertise: you should understand the purpose of these deployment strategies and services, how they reduce risk, and how they fit into a well-governed multi-account environment.

Third-Party Tools for Deployment Automation

Many organizations complement AWS-native deployment tools with third-party solutions that provide additional flexibility, portability, or workflow standardization. While the SOA-C03 exam does not require deep expertise in these tools, CloudOps engineers should be aware of the broader ecosystem and understand how these tools integrate with AWS environments.

HashiCorp Terraform is one of the most widely adopted third-party Infrastructure-as-Code frameworks. Unlike CloudFormation and CDK, which are AWS-native, Terraform is cloud-agnostic and uses its own declarative language (HCL) to define infrastructure across multiple providers. Terraform maintains state externally—often in an S3 bucket with native state locking—and applies changes through a plan/apply workflow similar to CloudFormation change sets. For CloudOps engineers, the key point is that Terraform can manage AWS Resources reliably at scale, but it operates outside AWS Organizations and requires separate governance, state management, and access controls.

Git-based workflows also play a central role in deployment automation. In many organizations, infrastructure and application code are stored in Git repositories, and changes are deployed through pull requests, branch protections, and automated pipelines. Whether using GitHub, GitLab, Bitbucket, or AWS CodeCommit, the workflow typically centers on version control, peer review, and automated testing before changes reach production. This model aligns well with IaC practices, enabling predictable, auditable deployments across multiple AWS accounts.

For the exam, remember that third-party tools are not tested directly; what matters is understanding how they fit into a well-governed AWS environment. Terraform, Git-based workflows, and similar tools can complement AWS-native services, but CloudOps engineers must ensure that identity, permissions, state management, and deployment automation remain consistent with organizational standards. With this final piece, you now have a complete view of the deployment and provisioning ecosystem relevant to the SOA-C03 exam.

Summary

This chapter opened by reinforcing the value of Infrastructure as Code in modern CloudOps environments, highlighting how declarative, version-controlled infrastructure enables predictable, repeatable operations across multiple AWS accounts. Building on that foundation, the chapter focused on AWS CloudFormation as the primary AWS-native engine for provisioning and managing infrastructure. Key operational capabilities—such as change sets and drift detection—were emphasized as essential tools for maintaining configuration integrity and ensuring that deployed resources remain aligned with their templates over time.

The chapter then introduced the AWS Cloud Development Kit (CDK) as a higher-level, code-centric way to define CloudFormation templates. While CDK was covered only briefly, the core takeaway is that it synthesizes down to CloudFormation and inherits all of CloudFormation's operational behaviors. CDK simply provides a more expressive developer experience, enabling teams to build reusable constructs and reduce template boilerplate without changing the underlying deployment model.

A major focus of the chapter was AWS Resource Access Manager (RAM), which enables centrally managed resources—such as subnets, Transit Gateways, and Resolver rules—to be shared securely across accounts and regions. RAM's invitation workflow and the use of tightly scoped Service Control Policies were highlighted as critical governance mechanisms. These controls ensure that only authorized accounts can create or accept resource shares, preventing accidental or unauthorized consumption of shared infrastructure in multi-account landing zones.

The chapter concluded with a high-level look at deployment strategies and the tools that support them. Rolling, blue/green, and canary deployments were introduced as common patterns for reducing risk during application updates, and AWS services such as CodeDeploy, CodePipeline, ECS, EKS, and Lambda were noted for their support of these approaches. Finally, third-party tools like HashiCorp Terraform and Git-based workflows were acknowledged as common components of real-world CloudOps environments, complementing AWS-native services while requiring their own governance and state-management considerations.

Exam Essentials

Understand the purpose of Infrastructure as Code (IaC). IaC enables predictable, repeatable, and version-controlled infrastructure deployments. Know that AWS CloudFormation is the primary AWS-native IaC engine used to provision, update, and manage resources safely.

Know the key operational features of AWS CloudFormation. Change sets and drift detection are essential exam concepts. Drift detection is especially important: it identifies when deployed resources no longer match the template, helping maintain configuration integrity across accounts and regions.

Recognize what the AWS Cloud Development Kit (CDK) adds. CDK provides a higher-level, code-centric way to define infrastructure, but it ultimately synthesizes into CloudFormation templates. For the exam, remember that CDK does not replace CloudFormation—it builds on it.

Understand how AWS Resource Access Manager (RAM) enables cross-account sharing. RAM allows centrally managed resources—such as subnets, Transit Gateways, and Resolver rules—to be shared securely across accounts and OUs. Know that RAM uses invitations for inter-organization resource sharing, whereas intra-organization resource sharing is automatic when organizational sharing is enabled (by a principal in the management account with proper permissions). Know that Service Control Policies can restrict who can create resource shares and who can use them.

Be familiar with high-level deployment strategies. Rolling, blue/green, and canary deployments reduce risk during application updates. You don't need deep CI/CD expertise, but you should know that services like CodeDeploy, CodePipeline, ECS, EKS, and Lambda support these patterns.

Recognize the role of third-party tools in real-world CloudOps environments. Terraform provides a cloud-agnostic IaC option with its own state-management model, while Git-based workflows offer standardized, auditable deployment pipelines. These tools are not tested directly, but you should understand how they complement AWS-native services.

Review Questions

1. A CloudOps engineer updates a CloudFormation stack, but the update requires replacing an Auto Scaling group. Before approving the change, they want to confirm whether any downstream stacks consuming exported values will be affected. What should they use?
   - **A.** Drift detection
   - **B.** Stack policies
   - **C.** StackSets
   - **D.** Change sets

2. A workload account has accepted a RAM share for a subnet. The account can see the subnet but cannot attach a security group to an ENI created in that subnet. What is the most likely cause?
   - **A.** The security group belongs to a different VPC.
   - **B.** The subnet is private.
   - **C.** The ENI quota is exceeded.
   - **D.** The subnet is shared incorrectly.

3. A CloudOps engineer wants to ensure that a CloudFormation-managed IAM role cannot be modified by administrators during stack updates, but still allows the stack to be deleted if needed. What should they configure?
   - **A.** Termination protection
   - **B.** Stack policies
   - **C.** Drift detection
   - **D.** Permission boundaries

4. A team uses CDK to define infrastructure. During synthesis, they notice that the generated CloudFormation template includes more resources than expected due to high-level constructs. What is the best way to understand what CDK is generating?
   - **A.** Enable termination protection.
   - **B.** Review the synthesized template.
   - **C.** Use drift detection.
   - **D.** Deploy the stack and inspect resources afterward.

5. A CloudOps engineer in a Network Account shares a subnet with a Workloads OU using AWS RAM. The resource share is configured with `--allow-external-principals false` and the organization has RAM sharing enabled. A workload account administrator reports that they never received an invitation to accept. What is the most likely explanation?

   A. The resource share was created incorrectly and must be re-created.

   B. The invitation was sent to the management account instead of the workload account.

   C. Intra-organization shares do not require invitation acceptance when organizational sharing is enabled.

   D. The workload account must enable RAM in its account settings before invitations appear.

6. A company uses AWS Organizations and needs to share a central Transit Gateway (TGW) with 50 accounts across three Organizational Units (OUs). A CloudOps engineer must ensure that any new accounts added to these OUs automatically receive standardized VPC Flow Logs and monitoring IAM roles. What is the most operationally efficient solution?

   A. Share the TGW with the Organization root via RAM. Use a CloudFormation StackSet with Service-Managed Permissions and Automatic Deployment targeting the three OUs for the logging and roles.

   B. Share the TGW with the three OU IDs via RAM. Use a CloudFormation StackSet with Service-Managed Permissions and Automatic Deployment targeting the same OUs for the logging and roles.

   C. Use a CloudFormation StackSet with Self-Managed Permissions to deploy the TGW, Flow Logs, and IAM roles to all 50 accounts using a manual list of Account IDs.

   D. Share the TGW with the three OUs via RAM. Use SSM Automation to manually run a Python script against each account to deploy the logging and IAM roles.

7. A CloudOps engineer wants to deploy a new ECS service version with minimal risk. They want to test the new version with a small percentage of traffic before shifting fully. Which AWS service provides the most controlled traffic-shifting mechanism?

   A. ECS rolling update

   B. Lambda aliases

   C. CodeDeploy blue/green for ECS

   D. CloudFormation update policies

8. A workload account can see a shared Route 53 Resolver rule but cannot apply it to its VPC. The Network Account confirms the share is correct. What is the next step?

   A. Verify that the VPC is in the same region as the rule.

   B. Re-share the rule using a resource-based policy.

   C. Enable termination protection on the rule.

   D. Create a new Resolver endpoint.

9. A company uses AWS Organizations with service-managed CloudFormation StackSets. The security team deploys a StackSet that provisions a standard logging configuration to all accounts in the Production OU. A new account is created and moved into the Production OU. What happens to the StackSet deployment?
   - A. The administrator must manually add the new account to the StackSet target list.
   - B. CloudFormation automatically deploys the stack instance to the new account.
   - C. The new account must accept the StackSet deployment through an invitation.
   - D. The StackSet must be updated and re-deployed to include the new account.

10. A CloudOps engineer updates a CloudFormation stack that manages an RDS instance and a Lambda function. The Lambda function update succeeds, but the RDS parameter group change fails due to an invalid parameter value. What does CloudFormation do by default?
   - A. It keeps the Lambda update and marks the stack as `UPDATE_FAILED`.
   - B. It rolls back all changes, returning both resources to their previous state.
   - C. It pauses the update and waits for the engineer to fix the parameter.
   - D. It deletes the failed resource and completes the update for the remaining resources.

11. A CloudOps engineer updates a CloudFormation stack that manages a VPC. The update requires replacing the VPC, which would cascade into replacing many dependent resources. Before approving the change, the engineer wants to understand the full impact. What should they do?
   - A. Enable termination protection.
   - B. Review the synthesized CDK output.
   - C. Run drift detection.
   - D. Generate a change set.

12. A workload account has access to a shared subnet through AWS RAM. An engineer in the workload account tries to modify the route table associated with the shared subnet but receives an "Access Denied" error. The engineer has full EC2 permissions in the workload account. What is the most likely cause?
   - A. The engineer's IAM policy does not include `ec2:ReplaceRoute`.
   - B. Participants in a shared VPC cannot modify the owner's route tables, subnets, or network configuration.
   - C. The RAM resource share does not include the route table as a shared resource.
   - D. The subnet's NACL is blocking the API call.

13. A CloudOps team has been defining infrastructure using CDK L2 constructs such as `s3.Bucket` and `lambda.Function`. A new requirement forces them to use a CloudFormation resource type that has no L2 construct available, so they must use the L1 `CfnResource` equivalent instead. What additional operational burden should the team expect?

    A. They must explicitly configure all resource properties, including defaults that L2 constructs would have provided automatically.

    B. The L1 construct will not generate a CloudFormation template, so they must write one manually.

    C. The L1 construct cannot be deployed in the same stack as L2 constructs.

    D. They must switch the entire CDK application to a different programming language.

14. A team uses CDK to define infrastructure. They want to ensure that all synthesized CloudFormation templates follow organizational tagging standards before deployment. What is the most effective approach?

    A. Enable termination protection on all stacks.

    B. Use CDK aspects to enforce tagging.

    C. Use drift detection after deployment.

    D. Use StackSets to deploy tags globally.

15. A CloudOps engineer discovers that a CloudFormation-managed security group has been modified directly in the AWS Management Console. The engineer wants to restore the security group to match the CloudFormation template. What is the most effective approach?

    A. Delete the security group and run a stack update.

    B. Manually revert the security group rules in the console to match the template.

    C. Create a standard change set with the original template values.

    D. Create a change set with `--deployment-mode REVERT_DRIFT` to reconcile the drift.

16. A company uses AWS Organizations and wants to deploy a standardized VPC configuration to all accounts in the Production OU using CloudFormation StackSets. They also need to deploy the same configuration to a partner account outside the organization. Which StackSets permission model supports both requirements?

    A. Service-managed permissions, since they work with any AWS account.

    B. Self-managed permissions, since they support both intra-org and external accounts.

    C. Service-managed permissions for the OU, combined with a separate self-managed StackSet for the external account.

    D. A single StackSet with delegated administrator permissions.

17. A CloudOps team manages two CloudFormation stacks: a networking stack that creates a VPC and subnets, and an application stack that deploys EC2 instances into those subnets. The application stack needs the subnet IDs from the networking stack. What is the most operationally maintainable way to pass these values between stacks?
    - **A.** Hard-code the subnet IDs in the application stack's Parameters section.
    - **B.** Use Outputs with Export in the networking stack and `Fn::ImportValue` in the application stack.
    - **C.** Store the subnet IDs in an S3 file and read them during deployment.
    - **D.** Use the same template for both stacks and deploy them together.

18. A workload account can see a shared subnet but cannot attach an ENI to it. The Network Account confirms the share is correct. What should the CloudOps engineer check next?
    - **A.** Whether the subnet is private
    - **B.** Whether the ENI quota is exceeded
    - **C.** Whether the principal has `ec2:CreateNetworkInterface`
    - **D.** Whether the subnet has a route to the Internet

19. A CloudOps engineer wants to ensure that infrastructure changes triggered by Git commits automatically deploy across multiple accounts after testing. Which combination best supports this?
    - **A.** CodeDeploy and CloudFormation
    - **B.** CodePipeline and CodeBuild
    - **C.** CloudFormation and RAM
    - **D.** CodePipeline and StackSets

20. A company uses both Terraform and CloudFormation to manage AWS infrastructure. During a routine audit, the team discovers that a security group managed by CloudFormation has been modified by a Terraform configuration, causing both tools to report drift. What is the best long-term solution to prevent this from recurring?
    - **A.** Run CloudFormation drift detection before every Terraform apply.
    - **B.** Store Terraform state in the same S3 bucket as CloudFormation templates.
    - **C.** Establish clear resource ownership boundaries so each resource is managed by only one tool.
    - **D.** Import all CloudFormation resources into Terraform state.

Answers to Review Questions

1. D. Change sets reveal whether resources in the stack will be modified or replaced, helping the engineer assess the impact before applying the update. Option A detects manual drift, Option B protects resources during updates, and Option C deploys stacks across accounts but does not preview impacts.

2. A. Security groups must belong to the same VPC as the ENI. Option B does not block SG attachment, Option C affects ENI creation but not SG attachment, and Option D would prevent subnet visibility entirely.

3. B. Stack policies prevent updates to specific resources. Option A blocks deletion of the entire stack, Option C only detects changes, and Option D limits IAM permissions but does not protect CloudFormation resources.

4. B. Reviewing the synthesized template shows exactly what CDK will deploy. Option A is unrelated, Option C detects post-deployment drift, and Option D is reactive rather than proactive.

5. C. When sharing within an AWS Organization that has organizational sharing enabled, recipients automatically gain access to shared resources without needing to accept an invitation. Invitations are only generated for inter-organization (cross-organization) or external sharing. The share was created correctly (Option A). Intra-organization resource shares with `--allow-external-principals false` targeting an OU are the standard pattern. RAM sends invitations to the principal specified in the share, not to the management account (Option B). However, in this scenario no invitation is sent at all. There is no account-level RAM enablement setting (Option D) that controls invitation delivery. RAM sharing is controlled at the organization level.

6. B. Sharing via RAM at the OU level is the most secure and efficient method, as it automatically grants access to new accounts within those OUs without over-sharing to the entire organization. Pairing this with a Service-Managed StackSet with Automatic Deployment ensures that any new account joining the OU is instantly and automatically provisioned with the required logging and IAM resources without manual intervention. Sharing with the Organization root (Option A) violates least privilege by exposing the TGW to accounts that don't need it. Self-Managed StackSets (Option C) require manual IAM setup in every account and do not support automatic deployment for new accounts. SSM Automation (Option D) is a procedural tool; it lacks the declarative "desired state" orchestration and automatic scaling for new accounts that StackSets provide.

7. C. CodeDeploy blue/green for ECS supports controlled traffic shifting. Option A updates tasks but does not provide granular traffic control, Option B applies to Lambda only, and Option D manages stack updates, not traffic.

8. A. Resolver rules are region-specific. Option B is impossible (RAM has no resource-based policies), Option C is irrelevant, and Option D is unrelated to rule association.

9. B. Service-managed StackSets with automatic deployment enabled will automatically deploy stack instances to new accounts when they are added to a target OU. This is a key governance capability for multi-account environments. With service-managed permissions and automatic deployment enabled, manual intervention (Option A) is not required when accounts join the target OU. StackSets do not use an invitation model (Option C). Deployment is controlled by the StackSet administrator and the OU targeting configuration. The StackSet does not need to be updated (Option D). Automatic deployment handles new accounts joining the OU without any changes to the StackSet configuration.

10. B. By default, CloudFormation rolls back all changes when any resource update fails. Both the Lambda function and the RDS instance revert to their previous configurations, and the stack status becomes `UPDATE_ROLLBACK_COMPLETE`. CloudFormation does not partially apply updates by default (Option A). When any resource update fails, the entire stack update is rolled back. CloudFormation does not pause updates by default (Option C). The disable-rollback option exists but must be explicitly enabled and is not the default behavior. CloudFormation does not delete failed resources during an update (Option D). It reverts them to their previous state.

11. D. Change sets reveal replacements and cascading impacts before execution. Option A prevents deletion, Option B applies only to CDK workflows, and Option C detects manual drift but not update impacts.

12. B. When a subnet is shared via RAM, participant accounts can launch resources into the subnet but cannot modify the subnet itself, its route tables, NACLs, or any other VPC-level configuration. These remain under the exclusive control of the VPC owner account. The issue is not missing IAM permissions in the workload account (Option A). Even with full EC2 permissions, participants cannot modify resources owned by the sharing account. Route tables are not shared as separate RAM resources (Option C). They are part of the VPC infrastructure controlled by the owner. NACLs filter network traffic, not API calls (Option D). API calls go through the AWS control plane and are governed by IAM, not network ACLs.

13. A. L1 constructs map directly to CloudFormation resources with no additional defaults or helper methods. Properties that L2 constructs set automatically (such as S3-managed encryption for `s3.Bucket`) must be configured explicitly when using the L1 equivalent. The team loses convenience methods like `grantRead()` as well. L1 constructs do generate CloudFormation templates (Option B). All CDK constructs, whether L1 or L2, synthesize into CloudFormation during `cdk synth`. L1 and L2 constructs can coexist in the same stack (Option C). CDK applications commonly mix construct levels depending on resource support. Construct level is independent of programming language (Option D). L1 and L2 constructs are available in all CDK-supported languages.

14. B. CDK aspects enforce tagging at synthesis time. Option A is unrelated, Option C is reactive, and Option D deploys stacks but does not enforce tagging rules.

15. D. Drift-aware change sets, created with `--deployment-mode REVERT_DRIFT`, compare the actual resource state against the template and generate changes to bring drifted resources back in line with their template definitions. This is the recommended CloudFormation-native approach for drift remediation. Deleting a CloudFormation-managed resource outside of CloudFormation (Option A) can cause the stack to enter a failed state.

CloudFormation expects to manage the lifecycle of its resources. Manually reverting changes in the console (Option B) is error-prone and does not leverage CloudFormation's orchestration. It also does not update CloudFormation's knowledge of the resource state. A standard change set (Option C) compares the new template to the previous template. If the template has not changed, a standard change set would show no changes and would not address the drift.

16. C. Service-managed StackSets support OU-level targeting and automatic deployment within the organization, while self-managed StackSets can deploy to external accounts where the execution role has been created. Using both models covers the full requirement without sacrificing governance for internal accounts. Service-managed permissions (Option A) only work with accounts within the same AWS Organization. They cannot deploy to accounts outside the organization. Self-managed permissions (Option B) can deploy to any account where the execution role exists, but they do not support OU-level targeting or automatic deployment to new accounts. Using self-managed for everything sacrifices the governance benefits of service-managed permissions. Delegated administrator (Option D) allows a non-management account to administer StackSets, but it does not change the permission model's scope. A single StackSet cannot target both an OU (service-managed) and an external account (self-managed).

17. B. CloudFormation Outputs with Export allow one stack to expose values that other stacks can consume using `Fn::ImportValue`. This creates a managed cross-stack reference that CloudFormation tracks, preventing the exporting stack from deleting or modifying exported resources while they are in use. Hard-coding resource IDs (Option A) creates a brittle dependency. If the networking stack is redeployed and subnet IDs change, the application stack would break without manual updates. Storing values in S3 (Option C) introduces an external dependency and requires custom logic to read the file during deployment. This bypasses CloudFormation's built-in cross-stack reference tracking. Combining unrelated infrastructure into a single template (Option D) reduces modularity and increases the blast radius of changes. Separate stacks with cross-stack references is the recommended pattern.

18. C. ENI creation requires explicit IAM permissions. Options A and D do not block ENI creation, and Option B is possible but less exam-relevant.

19. D. CodePipeline handles CI/CD automation, and StackSets deploy infrastructure across accounts. Option A deploys applications only, Option B handles CI/CD but not multi-account infrastructure rollout, and Option C is unrelated to CI/CD.

20. C. The fundamental issue is that two tools are managing the same resource. Establishing clear ownership boundaries, where each AWS Resource is managed by exactly one IaC tool, eliminates the conflict entirely. This is the recommended governance practice for mixed-tool environments. Running drift detection before every Terraform apply (Option A) detects conflicts but does not prevent them. It adds operational overhead without solving the root cause. Storing Terraform state alongside CloudFormation templates (Option B) does not prevent resource ownership conflicts. State storage location is unrelated to which tool manages which resources. Importing all CloudFormation resources into Terraform (Option D) would consolidate management into one tool, but it requires migrating all existing CloudFormation stacks and may not be feasible or desirable for an organization that uses both tools for different purposes.

Security and Compliance

THE AWS CERTIFIED CLOUDOPS ENGINEER ASSOCIATE (SOA-C03) EXAM OBJECTIVES COVERED IN THIS CHAPTER MAY INCLUDE, BUT ARE NOT LIMITED TO THE FOLLOWING:

✓ **Domain 4: Security and Compliance**

- 4.1 Implement and manage security and compliance tools and policies
- 4.2 Implement strategies to protect data and infrastructure

Security and compliance are core areas of cloud operations, and in the CloudOps cycle you learned in Chapter 1, this chapter represents a deep dive into the fourth phase: Secure. By the time a workload reaches this phase, it has already been deployed, monitored, and sustained through operational maturity. Now the focus shifts from "Is it running well?" to "Is it protected, controlled, and compliant?" The Secure phase is where CloudOps engineers ensure that every deployed resource is governed by strong identity controls, encrypted appropriately, monitored for threats, and aligned with organizational and regulatory requirements.

This chapter directly addresses the responsibilities that define the Secure phase. You will implement IAM policies, enforce MFA, apply resource-level controls, and troubleshoot access issues using CloudTrail, IAM Access Analyzer, and the Policy Simulator. You will also learn how to protect data through classification schemes, encryption at rest and in transit, and secure secret storage. These are not abstract security concepts—they are operational tasks that CloudOps engineers perform daily to ensure that workloads remain trustworthy and resilient. The Secure phase is where governance becomes real: SCPs restrict what accounts can do, Trusted Advisor highlights misconfigurations, and Security Hub aggregates findings that must be remediated quickly and consistently.

The SOA-C03 exam expects you to think like a CloudOps engineer who fully understands the Secure phase as an ongoing responsibility, not a one-time configuration step. Security is continuous: findings must be triaged, misconfigurations must be corrected, and controls must evolve as workloads change. This chapter gives you the operational patterns, CLI workflows, and mental models needed to execute the Secure phase with confidence. By mastering these tools and practices, you ensure that everything you deploy is not only functional and scalable, but also secure by design, auditable by default, and compliant at every stage of its lifecycle.

Implementing Security and Compliance Tools and Policies

Implementing security and compliance tools and policies begins with controlling the very first entry point of any attack surface: Identity. In the CloudOps cycle, this is where the Secure phase becomes operational—where CloudOps teams use tools and declarative policies to enforce who can access AWS Resources, how they authenticate, and under what conditions. The former includes procedural, step-by-step mechanisms built using the AWS CLI, AWS CDK, and orchestration workflows that apply security controls programmatically. These "imperative" tools (this term originates from imperative programming in computer science) allow CloudOps engineers to configure password policies, enable MFA, create roles, and automate identity-related guardrails with precision and repeatability. The latter—declarative policies such as IAM policies, resource-based policies, and Service Control Policies (SCPs)—represent Policy-as-Code, defining the desired security state rather than the steps to achieve it. These policies express the rules that govern identity, authorization, and compliance across accounts and resources, ensuring that identity boundaries remain enforced regardless of how workloads evolve.

Because identity is the root of all authorization decisions, this section starts by addressing IAM-related vulnerabilities head-on: enforcing strong password hygiene, strengthening authentication with MFA, and—ideally—removing the burden of authentication entirely by federating access through an external Identity Provider integrated with AWS IAM Identity Center (formerly known as AWS Single Sign-On). These capabilities build directly on the IAM foundations you established in Chapter 2, where we introduced IAM principals, policies, trust relationships, and the core mental model of "who can do what on which resource." Now, in the Secure phase, you apply those foundations with operational rigor, using AWS tools and policies to harden identity pathways and ensure that every subsequent security control rests on a trustworthy authentication and authorization layer.

Implementing IAM Features

IAM is the foundation of AWS security, and everything in the Secure phase of the CloudOps cycle begins here. As a CloudOps engineer, you must be able to configure password policies, enforce MFA, create IAM Roles, manage federated identities, and apply resource policies and conditions—but more importantly, you must understand how these security controls collectively harden the very first entry point of the attack surface: identity. This section builds directly on the IAM fundamentals introduced in Chapter 2, where you learned about IAM principals, IAM policies, trust relationships, resource policies, SCPs, and the core authorization model that governs every AWS API call. Now, in the Secure phase, you apply those concepts operationally by addressing IAM-related vulnerabilities in a structured progression: first by enforcing strong password hygiene, then by strengthening authentication with MFA, and finally by reducing the reliance on long-lived IAM Users altogether through federation with an external Identity Provider integrated into AWS IAM Identity Center (formerly known as AWS Single Sign-On). This sequence mirrors CloudOps best practices and provides you—preparing for the SOA-C03 exam—with a natural, intuitive path from basic identity controls to more mature, centralized authentication models.

Password Policies

Password policies are the first and most basic safeguard in the identity layer. Even though modern AWS environments increasingly rely on federation and short-lived credentials, many organizations still maintain IAM Users for legacy systems, automation, or break-glass access.

For this reason, CloudOps engineers must know how to enforce password complexity, rotation, and self-service management.

To update the account password policy, you need the IAM permission `iam:UpdateAccountPasswordPolicy`.

The following command applies a strong password policy to all IAM Users in the AWS account where the command is executed. The policy is account-scoped, meaning it affects every IAM User defined in that account.

```
aws iam update-account-password-policy \
  --minimum-password-length 14 \
  --require-symbols \
  --require-numbers \
  --require-uppercase-characters \
  --require-lowercase-characters \
  --allow-users-to-change-password \
  --max-password-age 90
```

In this command:

- `--minimum-password-length`: Enforces long passwords.
- `--require-symbols`: Requires special characters.
- `--require-numbers`: Requires digits.
- `--require-uppercase-characters`: Requires uppercase letters.
- `--require-lowercase-characters`: Requires lowercase letters.
- `--allow-users-to-change-password`: Enables self-service rotation.
- `--max-password-age`: Forces rotation every 90 days.

The command works in:

- Standalone AWS accounts
- AWS Organizations member accounts
- AWS Control Tower–managed accounts

For more information, visit: `https://docs.aws.amazon.com/cli/latest/reference/iam/update-account-password-policy.html`.

Neither AWS Organizations nor AWS Control Tower provides a built-in feature to centrally manage a single IAM password policy across all member accounts. While AWS Organizations allows for central management of many security aspects—such as Service Control Policies (SCPs) and root credentials—standard IAM password policies (which define rules for complexity, length, and rotation) are still managed at the individual AWS account level.

Multi-Factor Authentication (MFA)

MFA is the second layer of defense after password hygiene and is one of the most effective controls for reducing account takeover risk. Even strong passwords can be phished, reused, or brute-forced. MFA ensures that authentication requires something you know (a password) and something you have (a physical or virtual device). In the Secure phase of the CloudOps cycle, MFA is mandatory for privileged users, break-glass accounts, and any identity with elevated permissions such as `AdministratorAccess`. This section walks through the full lifecycle of MFA: registration and setup, authentication, and programmatic MFA.

Registration and Setup

The registration phase involves two distinct actors:

- The **CloudOps engineer** or **Security Administrator:** Creates and enables the MFA device using the AWS CLI.
- The **IAM User** (e.g., Alice): Scans the QR code and generates the MFA codes used to activate the device.

This separation of duties is intentional and aligns with real-world operational practice: administrators provision MFA devices, while users enroll by scanning the QR code with their authenticator app. To complete activation, the user shares two consecutive one-time codes with the administrator, who runs the `enable-mfa-device` command. These codes are time-limited (30 seconds) and can't be reused, which limits the attack surface window. For environments where this handoff is unacceptable, AWS supports a self-service model where users manage their own MFA devices. For more information, visit: `https://docs.aws.amazon.com/IAM/latest/UserGuide/tutorial_users-self-manage-mfa-and-creds.html`.

The identity performing the CLI operations must have:

- `iam:CreateVirtualMFADevice`
- `iam:EnableMFADevice`
- `iam:ListMFADevices` (optional, for verification)
- `iam:ResyncMFADevice` (optional, for drift correction)

These permissions apply only to the AWS account where the command is executed. No AWS Organizations or Control Tower dependencies exist.

Step 1: Creating a Virtual MFA Device

The following command shows how a CloudOps engineer (or a Security Administrator) creates the virtual MFA device and generates a QR code for the user Alice to scan.

```
aws iam create-virtual-mfa-device \
  --virtual-mfa-device-name AliceMFA \
  --outfile AliceMFA.png \
  --bootstrap-method QRCodePNG
```

In this command:

- `--virtual-mfa-device-name AliceMFA`: Is the logical name for the MFA device in IAM.
- `--outfile AliceMFA.png`: Saves the QR code image to a file for the user to scan.
- `--bootstrap-method QRCodePNG`: Specifies that the bootstrap data should be provided as a PNG QR code.

For more information, visit: `https://docs.aws.amazon.com/cli/latest/reference/iam/create-virtual-mfa-device.html`.

Step 2: Enabling the MFA Device for an IAM User

After the QR code is created, the IAM User (not the admin) scans it with their authenticator app. The app generates two consecutive six-digit codes. The CloudOps engineer then binds the MFA device to the user using those codes.

The user scanning the QR code is *not* the same identity performing the CLI command. This separation ensures security, auditability, and least privilege.

The following command activates the MFA device for IAM User `alice` by validating two consecutive MFA codes generated by Alice's authenticator app.

```
aws iam enable-mfa-device \
  --user-name alice \
  --serial-number arn:aws:iam::111122223333:mfa/AliceMFA \
  --authentication-code1 123456 \
  --authentication-code2 789012
```

In this command:

- `--user-name alice`: The IAM User you (the CloudOps engineer) are assigning the device to.
- `--serial-number arn:aws:iam::111122223333:mfa/AliceMFA`: The unique ARN of the virtual MFA device created in Step 1.
- `--authentication-code1 123456`: First six-digit code generated by the user's authenticator app.
- `--authentication-code2 789012`: Second consecutive six-digit code used to verify time sync.

For more information, visit: `https://docs.aws.amazon.com/cli/latest/reference/iam/enable-mfa-device.html`.

Authentication with MFA

Once MFA is enabled, the authentication experience changes. With the AWS Management Console, the flow follows these steps:

1. User enters username and password.
2. AWS prompts for the six-digit MFA code.
3. Only if both are correct does the session begin.

For programmatic access, MFA becomes part of the STS token generation process (covered in the upcoming section).

MFA Enforcement

Enabling MFA is not enough—you must enforce that certain actions require MFA. This is done using IAM policy conditions that check whether MFA was present when the request was made.

Here is a policy snippet that denies all actions unless MFA is present. This is commonly used for IAM Users who must authenticate with MFA before performing any CLI/API operations.

```
{
  "Version": "2012-10-17",
  "Statement": [
    {
      "Effect": "Deny",
      "Action": "*",
      "Resource": "*",
      "Condition": {
        "BoolIfExists": {
          "aws:MultiFactorAuthPresent": "false"
        }
      }
    }
  ]
}
```

In the JSON document:

- `"Effect": "Deny"` Explicitly denies access if the condition matches.
- `"Action": "*"` Applies to all AWS API actions.
- `"Resource": "*"` Applies to all resources.
- `"aws:MultiFactorAuthPresent"` Evaluates whether MFA was used for the request.
- `"BoolIfExists": "false"` Denies access if MFA is not present.

When you enforce this policy, it's essential to understand which IAM entities it applies to and how you, as a CloudOps engineer, can effectively enforce MFA across different identity types. IAM evaluates MFA conditions differently depending on whether the identity is an IAM User, an IAM Group, or an IAM Role, and the enforcement mechanism changes accordingly.

Enforcing MFA Using IAM Users and IAM Groups

You can attach the policy directly to a specific IAM User to force them to use MFA for any console or CLI action.

```
aws iam put-user-policy \
  --user-name alice \
  --policy-name EnforceMFA \
  --policy-document file://mfa-policy.json
```

You can also attach the policy directly to a specific IAM Group. In fact, this is the recommended best practice. By attaching the policy to a group (e.g., a "Developers" group), every user added to that group automatically inherits the MFA requirement.

Because IAM Users authenticate directly, the condition key `aws:MultiFactorAuthPresent` evaluates correctly. When attached to a user or group, this policy ensures that:

- All CLI/API calls must use MFA-backed STS credentials, and
- Any request made without MFA is explicitly denied, regardless of other permissions.

This is the most common and straightforward MFA enforcement pattern in real CloudOps environments.

```
aws iam put-group-policy \
  --group-name Developers \
  --policy-name EnforceMFA \
  --policy-document file://mfa-policy.json
```

Enforcing MFA Using IAM Roles

As you learned in Chapter 2, IAM Roles do not authenticate with passwords or MFA devices. Instead, roles are assumed by another principal (user, service, or federated identity). Because of this, MFA enforcement for roles works differently.

There are two valid ways to enforce MFA for IAM Roles:

Permissions Policy You can include an MFA condition (such as `aws:MultiFactorAuthPresent`) directly in the role's *permissions policy*. This prevents the *role session* from performing certain actions unless the caller who assumed the role had already authenticated with MFA. This method works only when the caller is an IAM User who authenticated with MFA before assuming the role.

```
aws iam put-role-policy \
  --role-name ReadOnlyRole \
  --policy-name EnforceMFA \
  --policy-document file://mfa-policy.json
```

Trust Policy You can enforce MFA in the role's *trust policy*, which controls who is allowed to assume the role. This prevents the role from being assumed unless the caller has already authenticated with MFA. This is the most reliable and widely used method because it enforces MFA *before* privilege escalation occurs.

```
aws iam update-assume-role-policy \
  --role-name ReadOnlyRole \
  --policy-document file://trust-policy-with-mfa.json
```

Table 9.1 shows the correct attachment points for MFA enforcement across IAM identities.

MFA for Programmatic Access

Programmatic access is often where the most sensitive operations occur, because automation, scripts, and CLI workflows typically interact directly with infrastructure. Long-lived access keys (`AccessKeyId` and `SecretAccessKey`) are one of the most common sources of compromise. They can leak through logs, end up in Git repositories, or be copied across machines without anyone noticing. Once exposed, they allow an attacker to operate without ever touching the console, and without any second factor to stop them.

Requiring MFA for programmatic access changes this dynamic entirely. Instead of relying on long-lived keys, users must authenticate with MFA and then request short-lived session credentials through AWS Security Token Service (STS). These temporary credentials expire quickly and are tied to a recent MFA event, meaning every CLI or API call is backed by strong authentication. This significantly reduces the blast radius of compromised keys and ensures that programmatic access follows the same Zero-Trust principles as console access.

This section explains how MFA integrates into programmatic workflows, how CloudOps engineers enforce MFA-only access for CLI/API calls, and how IAM evaluates MFA conditions during STS operations.

TABLE 9.1 MFA Enforcement Across IAM Identity Types

Identity Type	Can You Attach the MFA-Only Identity Policy?	How MFA Enforcement Works
IAM User	✔ Yes	Identity policy enforces MFA for all CLI/API calls.
IAM Group	✔ Yes	Applies MFA enforcement to all users in the group.
IAM Role (permissions policy)	⚠ Yes, but limited	Enforces MFA only if the caller authenticated with MFA.
IAM Role (trust policy)	✔ Yes (recommended)	Prevents role assumption unless MFA was used.

To obtain MFA-backed session credentials, the IAM User must have the permission `sts:GetSessionToken`, which requires an MFA code to work. If the IAM User is assuming a role that requires MFA, they also need the permission `sts:AssumeRole`. These permissions apply only within the AWS account where the request is made.

Obtaining Temporary Credentials with MFA

The most common pattern is for an IAM User to request temporary credentials using `sts:GetSessionToken`. The user must provide:

- The ARN of their MFA device
- A valid six-digit MFA code
- An optional session duration

The following command exemplifies this request:

```
aws sts get-session-token \
  --serial-number arn:aws:iam::111122223333:mfa/alice \
  --token-code 654321 \
  --duration-seconds 3600
```

In this command, the credentials are defined as follows:

- `--serial-number`: ARN of the user's MFA device. This ties the request to a specific MFA device.
- `--token-code`: The current six-digit MFA code from the authenticator app.
- `--duration-seconds`: Lifetime of the temporary credentials (one hour here).

The response includes the following data: `AccessKeyId`, `SecretAccessKey`, `SessionToken`, and `Expiration`. These credentials must be exported into environment variables or stored in a named AWS CLI profile.

```
export AWS_ACCESS_KEY_ID="ASIA...."
export AWS_SECRET_ACCESS_KEY="abcd...."
export AWS_SESSION_TOKEN="IQoJb3JpZ2luX2VjE..."
```

Once exported, all subsequent CLI/API calls use MFA-backed credentials.

If an IAM Role requires MFA, the IAM User must authenticate with MFA before assuming the role. The trust policy enforces this:

```
"Condition": {
  "Bool": {
    "aws:MultiFactorAuthPresent": "true"
  }
}
```

The following command shows how the user can assume the role programmatically.

```
aws sts assume-role \
  --role-arn arn:aws:iam::111122223333:role/ReadOnlyRole \
  --role-session-name AliceSession \
  --serial-number arn:aws:iam::111122223333:mfa/alice \
  --token-code 654321
```

In this command:

- `--role-arn`: The role being assumed.
- `--role-session-name`: Logical name for the session (appears in CloudTrail).
- `--serial-number`: ARN of the user's MFA device.
- `--token-code`: The current MFA code.

The response contains two top-level objects: `Credentials` and `AssumedRoleUser`. The former includes `AccessKeyId`, `SecretAccessKey`, `SessionToken`, and `Expiration`. The latter includes metadata about the role session.

```
{
    "Credentials": {
        "AccessKeyId": "ASIAIOSFODNN7EXAMPLE",
        "SecretAccessKey": "wJalrXUtnFEMI/K7MDENG/bPxRfiCYEXAMPLEKEY",
        "SessionToken": "IQoJb3JpZ2luX2VjEGoaCXVzLWVhc3QtMSJGMEQCID9v...",
        "Expiration": "2026-03-17T14:35:00Z"
    },
    "AssumedRoleUser": {
        "AssumedRoleId": "AROA123456789EXAMPLE:AliceSession",
        "Arn": "arn:aws:sts::111122223333:assumed-role/ReadOnlyRole/
AliceSession"
    }
}
```

To summarize, the workflow to obtain temporary credentials with MFA programmatically is as follows:

1. The user logs into their authenticator app.
2. The user runs `sts:GetSessionToken` with MFA.
3. The user exports the temporary credentials.
4. The user optionally assumes a role that also requires MFA.
5. All CLI/API calls use MFA-backed session credentials.

This workflow eliminates long-lived access keys, ties every request to a recent MFA event, ensures that any privilege escalation requires MFA, and provides clear MFA context in CloudTrail for auditing.

Federated Identities

Federated identities allow users to access AWS without you having to create or manage IAM Users in your AWS accounts. Instead of storing passwords or MFA devices in IAM, AWS trusts an external identity provider (IdP) to authenticate the user and assert who they are. This model is central to modern CloudOps because it eliminates long-lived IAM credentials, centralizes identity governance, and ensures that authentication policies—such as MFA, password rotation, and conditional access—are enforced consistently across the organization.

In a federated workflow, users authenticate with an external IdP such as Microsoft Entra ID, Okta, Ping Identity, or any SAML 2.0/OIDC-compatible provider. After successful authentication, the IdP issues a token that AWS Security Token Service (STS) exchanges for temporary role credentials. The user never receives an IAM password or access key; instead, they operate entirely through short-lived STS sessions. This dramatically reduces the attack surface and aligns with Zero-Trust principles.

Federated identities always assume an IAM Role, which means authorization is controlled through role permissions and trust policies, not through IAM policies attached to IAM Users. The trust policy defines which IdP can assume the role and under what conditions—such as requiring MFA, restricting specific groups, or enforcing session tags. Because the external IdP handles authentication, MFA enforcement happens before the user reaches AWS, and AWS simply validates the MFA context included in the IdP token. This makes federation the most secure and scalable identity model for Multi-Account environments.

From an operational perspective, federation simplifies onboarding and offboarding, centralizes compliance, and eliminates the need to rotate IAM credentials. AWS CloudTrail logs clearly show the federated user's identity through session tags and role session names, providing strong auditability. For CloudOps engineers, the key takeaway is that federated identities authenticate externally, authorize through IAM Roles, and always operate using temporary STS credentials—making them the preferred identity pattern for enterprise AWS environments.

As a CloudOps engineer, implementing federation is a predictable, repeatable workflow: configure AWS to trust the external IdP, create roles that federated users can assume, and map IdP groups to those roles. The following step-by-step process shows how to implement federation with Okta using the AWS CLI. A similar process applies to other external IdPs.

Step 1: Creating the SAML Provider in AWS

Before AWS can trust Okta, you must register Okta as a SAML identity provider. Okta exposes a SAML metadata XML file that contains its certificates and endpoints. By uploading this metadata to AWS, you establish a trust anchor that AWS will use to validate SAML assertions coming from Okta. This step effectively tells AWS, "I trust this external identity provider to authenticate my users."

The following command shows how to create a SAML provider in AWS. To run this command, a CloudOps engineer needs:

- `iam:CreateSAMLProvider`
- `iam:ListSAMLProviders` (optional but useful for verification)

These permissions are typically granted through an administrative or identity-management role.

```
aws iam create-saml-provider \
  --name OktaProvider \
  --saml-metadata-document file://okta-metadata.xml
```

In this command:

- `--name`: Logical name for the SAML provider inside AWS.
- `--saml-metadata-document`: Path to the Okta metadata XML file downloaded from the Okta admin console.

If the command succeeds, AWS returns the ARN of the new SAML provider: `arn:aws:iam::111122223333:saml-provider/OktaProvider`.

This ARN is required in the trust policy of any IAM Role that Okta users will assume.

To learn more, visit: `https://docs.aws.amazon.com/cli/latest/reference/iam/create-saml-provider.html`.

Step 2: Creating the IAM Role for Federated Users

Federated users never receive IAM credentials. Instead, they authenticate with Okta and assume an IAM Role that defines what they can do in AWS. To enable this, you create a role with a trust policy that explicitly allows Okta (via the SAML provider ARN) to call `sts:AssumeRoleWithSAML`. This step establishes the authorization boundary: Okta authenticates the user and AWS authorizes them through the role.

To create the role and upload the trust policy, the CloudOps engineer needs:

- `iam:CreateRole`
- `iam:PutRolePolicy` or `iam:UpdateAssumeRolePolicy`
- `iam:GetRole` (optional for verification)

These permissions are standard for CloudOps engineers managing identity and access.

As you learned in Chapter 2, to create an IAM Role, you need to create a trust policy first, which tells AWS who is authorized to assume the role.

Step 2.1: Creating the Trust Policy

Save this JSON document as `okta-trust-policy.json`:

```
{
  "Version": "2012-10-17",
  "Statement": [
    {
      "Effect": "Allow",
      "Principal": {
        "Federated": "arn:aws:iam::111122223333:saml-provider/OktaProvider"
      },
      "Action": "sts:AssumeRoleWithSAML",
```

```
        "Condition": {
          "StringEquals": {
            "SAML:aud": "https://signin.aws.amazon.com/saml"
          }
        }
      }
    ]
}
```

Because this is a trust policy, the `Principal` element defines who is allowed to assume the role. In this case, the principal is the SAML provider representing Okta we created in Step 1. This tells AWS: "Only SAML assertions issued by this Okta provider may assume this role."

The `Condition` block further restricts the trust relationship. The key `SAML:aud` ensures that the SAML assertion is intended for AWS sign-in (`https://signin.aws.amazon.com/saml`). This prevents assertions meant for other services or applications from being used to assume AWS roles.

Calling this out explicitly helps you reinforce the difference between *who can assume a role* (trust policy) and *what the role can do* (permissions policy). This distinction appears frequently on the exam.

Step 2.2: Creating the IAM Role

With the trust policy in place, we can now create the IAM Role with the following command:

```
aws iam create-role \
  --role-name OktaReadOnly \
  --assume-role-policy-document file://okta-trust-policy.json
```

In this command:

- `--role-name`: Name of the IAM Role Okta users will assume.
- `--assume-role-policy-document`: The trust policy created in Step 2.1.

After creating the IAM Role, it still has no permissions. A trust policy only defines who may assume the role, not what the role can do. To make the role functional, you must attach a permissions policy, which is exactly what Step 3 covers.

To learn more, visit: `https://docs.aws.amazon.com/cli/latest/reference/iam/create-role.html`.

Step 3: Attaching a Permissions Policy to the Role

The trust policy determines who can assume the role, but the permissions policy determines what the role can do once assumed. Instead of creating a custom policy, we use an AWS-managed policy—`arn:aws:iam::aws:policy/ReadOnlyAccess`—because it is simple, exam-aligned, and demonstrates the principle of least privilege.

This is exactly the right approach for SOA-C03: AWS-managed policies are widely used, easy to reference, and reduce operational overhead.

To attach a permission policy to an IAM Role, the CloudOps engineer needs the following permissions:

- `iam:AttachRolePolicy`
- `iam:ListAttachedRolePolicies` (optional)

```
aws iam attach-role-policy \
  --role-name OktaReadOnly \
  --policy-arn arn:aws:iam::aws:policy/ReadOnlyAccess
```

In this command:

- `--role-name`: The role created in Step 2.
- `--policy-arn`: The AWS-managed policy granting read-only access.

To learn more, visit: `https://docs.aws.amazon.com/cli/latest/reference/iam/attach-role-policy.html`.

Step 4: Configuring Okta to Send SAML Assertions to AWS

Once AWS is prepared to trust the external identity provider (Okta), the next step is configuring that IdP to authenticate users and send SAML assertions to AWS. Although the exact UI varies between providers such as Okta, Microsoft Entra ID, Ping Identity, or ADFS, the underlying process is always the same. The IdP must be told which AWS account it is federating into, which IAM Roles exist in that account, and which users or groups are allowed to assume those roles. The IdP then uses this information to construct a SAML assertion that AWS can validate.

The most important concept for SOA-C03 candidates is understanding *how IdP groups map to AWS IAM Roles*. The IdP does not push groups into AWS. Instead, the IdP embeds role mappings inside the SAML assertion using a special attribute named:

`https://aws.amazon.com/SAML/Attributes/Role`

Each entry in this attribute contains a pair:

`role-arn,provider-arn`

This is the mechanism by which AWS learns which roles the user is allowed to assume. Here is a concrete example based on our scenario:

```
<Attribute Name="https://aws.amazon.com/SAML/Attributes/Role">
    <AttributeValue>
        arn:aws:iam::111122223333:role/OktaReadOnly,
        arn:aws:iam::111122223333:saml-provider/OktaProvider
    </AttributeValue>
</Attribute>
```

This tells AWS:

- Which IAM Role the user may assume
- Which SAML provider issued the assertion

If the user belongs to multiple IdP groups mapped to multiple AWS roles, the IdP simply adds more `<AttributeValue>` entries—one per role.

```
<Attribute Name="https://aws.amazon.com/SAML/Attributes/Role">
    <AttributeValue>
        arn:aws:iam::111122223333:role/OktaReadOnly,
        arn:aws:iam::111122223333:saml-provider/OktaProvider
    </AttributeValue>
    <AttributeValue>
        arn:aws:iam::111122223333:role/OktaPowerUser,
        arn:aws:iam::111122223333:saml-provider/OktaProvider
    </AttributeValue>
</Attribute>
```

AWS will show both roles to the user at sign-in.

Step 5: Testing the Federation Flow and Understanding the STS Exchange

After the IdP is configured to send SAML assertions, the final step is validating that AWS can interpret those assertions and issue temporary credentials. When a user selects the AWS application in the IdP portal, the IdP authenticates them (including MFA), determines their group membership, and returns a SAML assertion containing the AWS role mappings. AWS Security Token Service (STS) receives this assertion and checks three things:

- Does the SAML provider ARN match a registered provider in IAM?
- Does the role ARN exist and is it included in the SAML assertion?
- Does the role's trust policy allow `sts:AssumeRoleWithSAML` from this provider?

If all conditions are met, AWS displays the available roles in the console or allows the CLI to call `AssumeRoleWithSAML`. STS then issues a set of short-lived credentials—an access key, secret key, session token, and expiration time—along with identity metadata such as the `AssumedRoleUser` ARN. These credentials reflect the permissions attached to the IAM Role (in our case, the AWS-managed `ReadOnlyAccess` policy).

This final step confirms that the entire federation chain is working:

1. The IdP authenticated the user.
2. The SAML assertion included the correct role mappings.
3. AWS trusted the assertion.
4. STS produced temporary credentials.
5. The IAM permissions policy applied correctly.

For you, as SOA-C03 candidate, understanding this end-to-end flow—especially the mapping and assertion pieces—is far more important than knowing any IdP-specific configuration details.

Troubleshooting Permissions and Auditing

Implementing IAM features—password policies, MFA, IAM Roles, trust policies, and SAML federation—is only the first half of identity security. Once these controls are in place, CloudOps engineers must ensure that identities behave as intended in real workloads. This is where the AWS Well-Architected Framework's Security Pillar becomes especially relevant. Principles such as "Implement a strong identity foundation," "Apply security at all layers," and the foundational principle of least privilege guide not only how IAM is configured, but how it is monitored, validated, and continuously improved. Troubleshooting IAM is therefore not a reactive task; it is a core part of maintaining a secure and resilient cloud environment.

Another key Security Pillar principle is "Maintain traceability," which is effectively the cloud-era corollary of the security principle of nonrepudiation. In traditional security models, *nonrepudiation* ensures that actions can be tied to a specific identity in a way that cannot later be denied. In AWS, this principle is realized through AWS CloudTrail, IAM logs, STS session metadata, and the consistent use of strong identity primitives. Without traceability, IAM failures become guesswork; with traceability, they become diagnosable, auditable, and ultimately solvable. This is why AWS provides a suite of tools—AWS CloudTrail, IAM Access Analyzer, and the IAM Policy Simulator—that together form a complete identity troubleshooting lifecycle.

Finally, troubleshooting IAM is also about prevention, not just diagnosis. The Security Pillar encourages continuous refinement of permissions, detection of unintended access, and proactive validation of policy behavior. CloudTrail shows *what did happen*, Access Analyzer shows *what could happen*, and the Policy Simulator shows *what would happen*. Used together, these tools help CloudOps engineers close the loop between identity design and identity operations, ensuring that the IAM features implemented earlier in the chapter remain secure, least-privilege, and auditable over time.

AWS CloudTrail

You learned AWS CloudTrail in Chapter 6, where we explored its observability and operational monitoring capabilities; in this section, we shift our focus to CloudTrail's security role. CloudTrail is the cornerstone of AWS's ability to maintain traceability, and therefore the operational embodiment of the security principle of nonrepudiation. Every identity-related action—whether performed by an IAM User, a federated identity, an IAM Role, or an AWS service—is recorded as a CloudTrail event. This makes CloudTrail the first and most authoritative source of truth when troubleshooting IAM issues. If a user encounters an `AccessDenied` error, CloudTrail reveals exactly who made the request, when it occurred, what action was attempted, and why it failed. Without CloudTrail, IAM troubleshooting becomes guesswork; with CloudTrail, it becomes a disciplined forensic process.

CloudTrail also plays a critical role in validating the IAM features implemented earlier in the chapter. When you create a new federated role, update a trust policy, or modify a permissions policy, CloudTrail confirms whether AWS is interpreting these changes correctly. For example, if a SAML assertion is malformed or a trust policy is missing a principal, CloudTrail will surface the failure in a way that is both auditable and actionable. This reinforces the Security Pillar's principle "Implement a strong identity foundation," because identity controls are only as strong as your ability to observe and verify them.

For CloudOps engineers working in Multi-Account environments, CloudTrail becomes even more powerful through the use of an *organization-wide CloudTrail trail*. This is a centrally managed trail created at the AWS Organizations level that automatically records management events from every account in the organization. Member accounts cannot disable it, modify it, or prevent their events from being logged. CloudTrail achieves this by creating a "shadow trail" in each account, ensuring that all API activity—whether from humans or services—is captured and delivered to a central S3 bucket. This gives CloudOps engineers a single, authoritative audit source across the entire environment, which is essential for troubleshooting permissions, validating identity behavior, and meeting compliance requirements. In short, an organization-wide trail ensures that traceability is not optional; it is enforced.

Beyond troubleshooting, CloudTrail is essential for compliance, governance, and continuous improvement. Many organizations rely on CloudTrail logs to detect suspicious activity, validate change-management processes, and support regulatory audits. Logs can be stored in S3, queried with Athena, streamed to CloudWatch Logs, or integrated with SIEM platforms. CloudTrail is therefore not just a logging service—it is the backbone of identity visibility and the foundation of secure, auditable CloudOps operations.

The following command demonstrates how to use the CLI to search for failed role-assumption attempts—one of the most common IAM troubleshooting scenarios.

```
aws cloudtrail lookup-events \
  --lookup-attributes AttributeKey=EventName,AttributeValue=AssumeRole \
  --max-results 5
```

In this command:

- `--lookup-attributes`: Filters events by a specific attribute. Here we filter by `EventName=AssumeRole` to find role-assumption attempts.
- `--max-results`: Limits the number of events returned.

The command returns:

- `Username` or federated identity
- `EventTime`
- `EventSource` (e.g., `sts.amazonaws.com`)
- `ErrorCode` (e.g., `AccessDenied`)
- `CloudTrailEvent` (full JSON event)

To learn more, visit: `https://docs.aws.amazon.com/cli/latest/reference/cloudtrail/lookup-events.html`.

CloudTrail gives you the "what happened" view. Next, we move to IAM Access Analyzer, which helps you understand why a resource is accessible or blocked.

CloudTrail is a regional service that records events in the region where they occur, but it can be configured to log global service events and aggregate logs across all regions, giving it global visibility.

AWS IAM Access Analyzer

AWS IAM Access Analyzer is the AWS service that operationalizes the principle of least privilege. While CloudTrail shows historical activity, Access Analyzer evaluates resource-based policies—such as S3 bucket policies, IAM Role trust policies, KMS key policies, and Lambda permissions—to determine whether they allow unintended access. This makes it invaluable in environments with federated identities, cross-account access, or complex trust relationships. Access Analyzer helps CloudOps engineers identify misconfigurations before they become incidents, reinforcing the principle "Apply security at all layers."

Access Analyzer can operate at two scopes, and understanding the difference is essential for the exam. An *account-level analyzer* evaluates only the resources within a single AWS account and identifies external access to those resources. An *organization-level analyzer*, created in the Management Account, evaluates resources across every account in the organization and can detect cross-account access patterns that would otherwise be invisible when looking at accounts in isolation. Organization-level analyzers are the preferred choice in Multi-Account environments because they provide a unified view of external access and ensure consistent guardrails across all OUs and workload accounts.

Access Analyzer is also essential for validating architectural changes. When onboarding a new SAML provider, Access Analyzer can confirm that the trust policy correctly references the provider ARN and does not unintentionally allow other principals to assume the role. Similarly, when modifying S3 bucket policies or KMS key policies, Access Analyzer can detect whether the changes introduce public access or cross-account exposure, both of which cause an expansion of the attack surface. This proactive analysis helps ensure that the IAM features implemented earlier in the chapter remain aligned with the principle of least privilege.

Beyond analysis, Access Analyzer includes a powerful operational capability: *policy generation*. This feature analyzes CloudTrail logs to determine the minimum set of actions a principal actually used, and then generates a least-privilege policy based on real activity. This is one of the most effective ways to continuously refine permissions and prevent privilege creep. Before exploring policy generation, let's look at how to surface Access Analyzer findings. To identify unintended access paths, you can list active findings with:

```
aws accessanalyzer list-findings \
    --analyzer-arn arn:aws:access-analyzer:us-east-1:111122223333:analyzer/
ConsoleAnalyzer-abcd1234 \
    --filter '{
        "status": {
            "eq": ["ACTIVE"]
        }
    }'
```

In this command:

- `--analyzer-arn`: The ARN of the analyzer.
- `--filter`: Uses the JSON syntax for filtering results. In IAM Access Analyzer, a filter is a map where each key is a finding attribute (like `status`) and the value is a criterion (like `eq`) containing a list of strings.

You may see findings such as: "Role trust policy allows assumption by external principal," "S3 bucket is publicly accessible," or "KMS key allows cross-account access." To learn more, visit: `https://docs.aws.amazon.com/cli/latest/reference/accessanalyzer/list-findings.html`.

Generating Policies with Access Analyzer

Policy generation is where Access Analyzer becomes a proactive least-privilege tool. Instead of guessing which permissions a role needs, Access Analyzer derives them from actual CloudTrail usage. This directly supports the principle of least privilege and helps CloudOps engineers shrink overly permissive roles, validate vendor-provided roles, and prepare for audits.

The recommended way to drive policy generation is by using the `--policy-generation-details` and `--cloud-trail-details` flags. The first identifies the principal (such as an IAM Role or an IAM User), while the second defines the CloudTrail source, time ranges, and the service role used for the analysis. Defining these parameters in a JSON file before running the CLI command ensures a repeatable and error-free workflow. This process is especially useful for refining federated roles, Lambda execution roles, or legacy roles with overly broad permissions.

To begin generating a least-privilege policy, create a JSON file `cloudtrail-config.json` that specifies the CloudTrail source, the required access role, and the time range for analysis:

```
{
  "accessRole": "arn:aws:iam::111122223333:role/service-role/
AccessAnalyzerMonitorServiceRole",
  "trails": [
    {
      "cloudTrailArn": "arn:aws:cloudtrail:us-east-1:111122223333:trail/
OrgTrail",
      "regions": ["us-east-1"],
      "allRegions": false
    }
  ],
  "startTime": "2025-01-01T00:00:00Z",
  "endTime": "2025-01-31T23:59:59Z"
}
```

In the JSON document:

- `accessRole`: The IAM Role that Access Analyzer assumes to read your CloudTrail logs in S3.
- `trails`: A list of CloudTrail trail ARNs to include in the analysis. This allows CloudOps engineers to scope analysis to organization trails, regional trails, or workload-specific trails.

  - `cloudTrailArn`: The ARN of the CloudTrail trail that Access Analyzer should read events from (for example, an organization trail or an account-level trail). This points the analysis at the correct log source.
  - `regions`: A list of AWS Regions whose CloudTrail events should be considered. This is essential for workloads that operate in multiple regions or for isolating analysis to a single region.
  - `allRegions`: A Boolean flag that, when set to true, instructs Access Analyzer to analyze CloudTrail events across all regions, even if not explicitly listed.
- `startTime` / `endTime`: The ISO 8601 timestamp window (up to 90 days) of activity you want to convert into a policy. These allow CloudOps engineers to focus on a specific deployment period, incident window, or operational cycle, ensuring that the generated policy reflects actual usage rather than historical noise.

To run the policy generation, use this command:

```
aws accessanalyzer start-policy-generation \
    --client-token "policy-gen-task-001" \
    --policy-generation-details '{
        "principalArn": "arn:aws:iam::111122223333:role/OktaReadOnly"
    }' \
    --cloud-trail-details file://cloudtrail-config.json
```

In this command:

- `--client-token`: This provides idempotency. It ensures that if you run this exact command again (due to a timeout or a retry), AWS recognizes it as the same request and won't start a duplicate job. Any unique string works.
- `--policy-generation-details`: This flag identifies the principal (the IAM Role or User) that you are analyzing to find its least-privilege permissions.
- `--cloud-trail-details`: This points to our `cloudtrail-config.json` file, which contains the log source, the required `accessRole`, and the time window for the analysis.

This level of control makes policy generation operationally powerful: you're not just generating a policy in the abstract—you're generating a least-privilege policy grounded in precisely scoped, real-world activity. The command returns a JSON object containing a `jobId` similar to:

```
{
  "jobId": "pg-0a1b2c3d4e5f6g7h"
}
```

Which can be used to retrieve the generated policy:

```
aws accessanalyzer get-generated-policy \
  --job-id pg-0a1b2c3d4e5f6g7h
```

The outcome is a clean, least-privilege policy based on actual CloudTrail usage:

```
{
  "Version": "2012-10-17",
  "Statement": [
    {
      "Effect": "Allow",
      "Action": [
        "s3:ListBucket",
        "s3:GetObject"
      ],
      "Resource": "*"
    }
  ]
}
```

Ensure you save this job ID, as it is the only way to retrieve the final generated policy once the asynchronous analysis is finished.

To learn more, visit: `https://docs.aws.amazon.com/cli/latest/reference/accessanalyzer/start-policy-generation.html`.

Why Least Privilege Sometimes Includes *

At first glance the generated IAM policy, including `"Resource": "*"` may not look very "least-privileged." But in practice, it often reflects the inherent design of AWS APIs rather than a lapse in security posture. Some AWS actions—such as `iam:ListRoles`, `ec2:DescribeInstances`, or `sts:GetCallerIdentity`—simply do not support resource-level permissions. These operations are defined by AWS as "resource-agnostic," meaning the only valid resource specification is `"*"`.

Even when an action does support resource-level scoping, CloudTrail may not log the specific ARN involved in the request. Access Analyzer relies entirely on CloudTrail events to infer usage, so if CloudTrail does not include the ARN, the tool cannot safely narrow the resource scope. In these cases, Access Analyzer intentionally leans toward correctness and operational safety by using `"Resource": "*"` rather than generating a policy that might break a workload.

For CloudOps engineers, the key insight is that a generated policy is a starting point, not the final product. `"Resource": "*"` often signals either an inherently global action or a place where human refinement is needed. It is your job as a CloudOps engineer tightening resource ARNs, adding conditions, or restructuring permissions as part of the iterative process of enforcing least privilege. In other words, `"*"` does not always mean "overly broad"—sometimes it simply reflects the granularity of the AWS API and the limits of what CloudTrail can observe.

Access Analyzer helps you validate trust relationships, detect unintended access, and generate least-privilege policies. Next, we move to the IAM Policy Simulator, which lets you test permissions before deployment.

IAM Policy Simulator

The IAM Policy Simulator is the final tool in the troubleshooting lifecycle, which also directly supports the principle of least privilege. While CloudTrail shows what happened and Access Analyzer shows what could happen, the Policy Simulator shows what would happen if a principal attempted a specific action. This makes it invaluable for validating new IAM Roles, testing permission boundaries, verifying SCP effects, and confirming that conditions behave as expected.

Operationally, CloudOps engineers use the Policy Simulator to test IAM changes before deploying them. For example, if a role includes an IP-based condition or requires MFA, the simulator can reveal whether the missing context would cause a denial. This prevents misconfigurations from reaching production. The simulator can also test the combined effect of identity-based policies, resource-based policies, permission boundaries, and service control policies—something that is difficult to reason about manually.

The Policy Simulator is especially useful when working with federated identities. Because STS sessions inherit the permissions of the IAM Role, the simulator can validate whether the role's permissions are sufficient for the federated user's tasks. Before running the CLI command, it's helpful to see how the simulator evaluates a simple S3 permission. The following example demonstrates how to test whether a role can list an S3 bucket.

```
aws iam simulate-principal-policy \
  --policy-source-arn arn:aws:iam::111122223333:role/OktaReadOnly \
  --action-names s3:ListBucket \
  --resource-arns arn:aws:s3:::my-logs-bucket
```

In this command:

- `--policy-source-arn`: The ARN of the IAM Role or User whose permissions you want to simulate.
- `--action-names`: The AWS API actions to test.
- `--resource-arns`: The resource to test against.

The command returns an output similar to the following JSON document:

```
{
  "EvaluationResults": [
    {
      "EvalActionName": "s3:ListBucket",
      "EvalResourceName": "arn:aws:s3:::my-logs-bucket",
      "EvalDecision": "allowed",
      "MatchedStatements": [
        {
          "SourcePolicyId": "PolicyInputList.1",
```

```
          "StartPosition": {
            "Line": 1,
            "Column": 1
          },
          "EndPosition": {
            "Line": 12,
            "Column": 2
          }
        }
      ],
      "MissingContextValues": [],
      "OrganizationsDecisionDetail": {
        "AllowedByOrganizations": true
      },
      "PermissionsBoundaryDecisionDetail": {
        "AllowedByPermissionsBoundary": true
      },
      "EvalDecisionDetails": {
        "s3:ListBucket": "allowed"
      },
      "ResourceSpecificResults": [
        {
          "EvalResourceName": "arn:aws:s3:::my-logs-bucket",
          "EvalResourceDecision": "allowed",
          "MatchedStatements": [
            {
              "SourcePolicyId": "PolicyInputList.1",
              "StartPosition": {
                "Line": 1,
                "Column": 1
              },
              "EndPosition": {
                "Line": 12,
                "Column": 2
              }
            }
          ],
          "MissingContextValues": []
        }
      ]
    }
  ]
}
```

Here's the quick interpretation of the output:

- `EvalDecision: "allowed"`: This is the simulator's final verdict. If it were `"explicitDeny"` or `"implicitDeny"`, you'd know exactly where to look next.
- `MatchedStatements`: Shows which policy statement granted the permission. This is very useful when debugging large or layered policies.

- `MissingContextValues`: If the action requires context keys (e.g., MFA, IP conditions, tags), they appear here. This is one of the most powerful parts of the simulator.
- `OrganizationsDecisionDetail`: Shows whether an SCP allowed or denied the action.
- `PermissionsBoundaryDecisionDetail`: Shows whether a permissions boundary affected the result.
- `ResourceSpecificResults`: Breaks down the evaluation *per resource*, which is essential when testing wildcard policies.

To learn more, visit: `https://docs.aws.amazon.com/cli/latest/reference/iam/simulate-principal-policy.html`.

Understanding Implicit Deny vs. Explicit Deny

AWS IAM evaluates every request using a strict hierarchy, and understanding this order is essential for the SOA-C03 exam. All requests begin as an implicit deny—if no policy explicitly allows an action, AWS denies it by default. This baseline deny is not a security event; it is simply the starting point of the authorization model.

An explicit deny, however, is absolute. If any policy—identity-based, resource-based, permissions boundary, or Service Control Policy—contains a `"Deny"` statement that matches the request, that deny overrides all allows. Even if another policy grants permission, the explicit deny wins. This is why explicit denies are used to enforce guardrails and prevent privilege-escalation paths that must never be permitted.

Here is the "golden rule" for a policy evaluation:

1. Default deny: Every request starts with an implicit deny.
2. Explicit deny always wins: If any applicable policy (SCP, Identity-based, Resource-based, or Boundary) contains a Deny, the request is immediately rejected, regardless of any Allow.
3. The allow requirement: If there is no explicit deny, there must be at least one explicit allow from a relevant policy for the request to succeed.
4. Implicit deny (the fallback): If there is no explicit deny and no explicit allow, the request remains denied by default.

For the exam, remember the evaluation order:

Explicit Deny → Allow → Implicit Deny.

If a deny exists anywhere in the evaluation chain, the request fails. Many IAM questions on SOA-C03 hinge on recognizing whether a failure is due to a missing allow (implicit deny) or a guardrail blocking the action (explicit deny).

With the IAM Policy Simulator completing our identity-troubleshooting toolkit, we can now zoom out from individual permissions and examine how these same security principles apply at the organizational level—specifically, how to implement Multi-Account strategies securely using AWS Organizations.

Implementing Multi-Account Strategies Securely

You were introduced to AWS Organizations, AWS Control Tower, Organizational Units (OUs), and Service Control Policies (SCPs) in Chapter 2, where we focused on their structural and governance roles. In this section, we revisit these constructs through the lens of the AWS Security Pillar. A Multi-Account strategy is not just an operational pattern—it is a governance mechanism that enforces least privilege, defense-in-depth, and separation of duties at a scale that IAM alone cannot achieve.

AWS Organizations provides the governance layer that ties these principles together. Instead of relying solely on IAM boundaries within a single account, you use accounts themselves as isolation units. Governance teams define the organizational structure—roots, OUs, and guardrails—while workload teams operate within the boundaries set for them. This is least privilege expressed at the organizational level: workloads are isolated by account, and accounts are constrained by SCPs that enforce global guardrails.

At this point, it's important to understand how AWS Control Tower extends this model. While SCPs act as permission guardrails—controlling who can perform which actions—Control Tower introduces *preventive controls*, which enforce how resources must be configured *before* they are created. Preventive controls evaluate the intended configuration of a resource and block non-compliant deployments, such as creating an unencrypted S3 bucket or disabling CloudTrail logging. Figure 9.1 illustrates the list of preventive controls specific to Amazon S3.

In other words, SCPs restrict actions at the IAM authorization layer, while preventive controls enforce mandatory configuration standards at the governance layer. Together, they

FIGURE 9.1 Amazon S3 preventive controls.

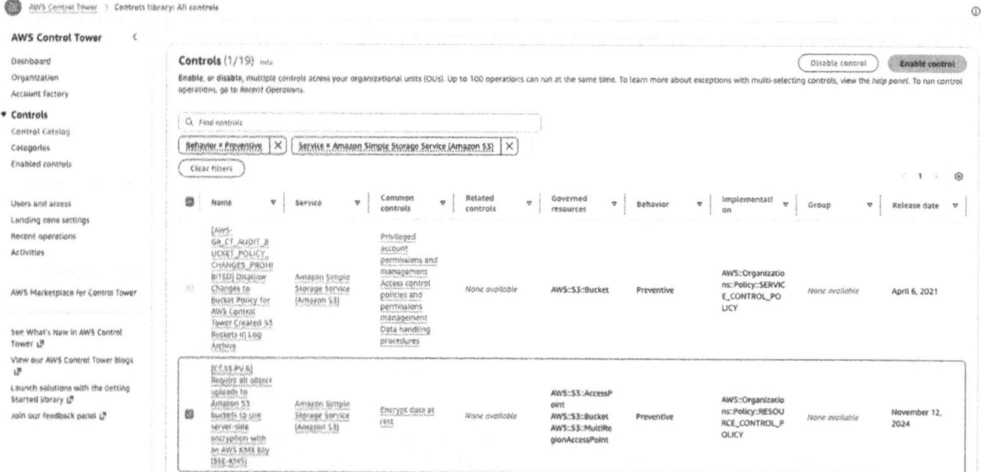

create a layered, non-bypassable enforcement model that keeps every new account and workload aligned with organizational security requirements.

Multi-Account design also strengthens defense-in-depth. Each AWS account becomes a security boundary with its own CloudTrail logs, IAM Roles, VPCs, and resource policies. SCPs add an outer layer of explicit denies that cannot be bypassed by identity-based policies. For example, you can enforce region restrictions or prevent the use of unapproved services across entire OUs. Even if a workload account is compromised, SCPs ensure that the attacker cannot escalate into the management or logging accounts. This layered model is the organizational expression of defense-in-depth.

Finally, Multi-Account strategies operationalize separation of duties. Governance teams manage SCPs, preventive controls, and OU structure in the Management Account, while application teams deploy workloads in their respective accounts. Logging and audit functions live in a dedicated logging account that no workload team can modify. This structural separation ensures that no single role or team has unilateral control over both workloads and the systems that monitor them.

To make this concrete, let's walk through a simple governance example: creating an OU and attaching an SCP that restricts workloads to a specific region. First and foremost, it is essential you understand who is allowed to perform organization-wide operations. The next section provides the details you need to know for the exam.

Understanding Who Can Perform AWS Organizations Operations

AWS Organizations supports Delegated Administration, but only for specific AWS services (such as AWS IAM Identity Center, AWS Security Hub, AWS Config, Amazon GuardDuty, and others). Delegated Administration does not apply to core AWS Organizations governance operations, including:

- Creating OUs
- Creating SCPs
- Attaching or detaching SCPs
- Managing roots
- Managing organization-wide settings

These actions must be performed using an identity with administrative permissions in the Management Account.

This is a critical distinction that often causes confusion. Member accounts cannot modify the organization unless the Management Account has explicitly delegated a specific service—and SCP/OU management is not eligible for delegation.

In practice, this means:

- You authenticate through IAM Identity Center.
- You select the Management Account.
- You assume an administrative role (e.g., `OrganizationAccountAccessRole`, `AWSAdministratorAccess`, or a custom Organizations admin role).
- You run all AWS Organizations CLI commands from that context.

This preserves governance boundaries and enforces separation of duties.

Creating an OU and Attaching an SCP

Before proceeding let's refresh the definition of an OU. An OU is a container for accounts that enables you to organize your accounts to apply policies according to your business requirements. The number of levels deep that you can nest OUs is dependent upon the policy types enabled for that root. For service control policies, the limit is five.

Let's break down this process into three simple steps.

- Step 1: Creating an OU
- Step 2: Creating an SCP
- Step 3: Attaching the SCP to the OU

All commands in this example must be executed using an identity with administrative permissions (e.g., `organizations:CreateOrganizationalUnit`, `organizations:CreatePolicy`, `organizations:AttachPolicy`) in the Management Account. Member-account identities cannot perform these operations.

Step 1: Creating an OU

The following commands create an OU.

```
aws organizations create-organizational-unit \
    --parent-id r-examplerootid \
    --name "Prod-Restricted"
```

In this command:

- `--parent-id`: The ID of the parent container. For top-level OUs, this is the root ID, which always begins with `r-`.
- `--name`: A friendly name for the OU.

For more information, visit: `https://docs.aws.amazon.com/cli/latest/reference/organizations/create-organizational-unit.html`.

Step 2: Creating an SCP

The following commands create an SCP that restricts workloads to a specific region.

```
aws organizations create-policy \
    --content file://deny-nonuseast1.json \
    --name "Deny-Non-USEast1" \
    --type SERVICE_CONTROL_POLICY \
    --description "Denies all actions outside us-east-1"
```

In this command:

- --content: Points to a JSON file containing the SCP.
- --name: A friendly name for the policy.
- --type: Must be SERVICE_CONTROL_POLICY.
- --description: A human-readable summary of the policy.

For more information, visit: https://docs.aws.amazon.com/cli/latest/reference/organizations/create-policy.html.

The following snippet shows the referenced JSON file (deny-nonuseast1.json) containing the SCP:

```
{
  "Version": "2012-10-17",
  "Statement": [
    {
      "Effect": "Deny",
      "Action": "*",
      "Resource": "*",
      "Condition": {
        "StringNotEquals": {
          "aws:RequestedRegion": "us-east-1"
        }
      }
    }
  ]
}
```

This SCP denies all actions outside us-east-1, enforcing a region-compliance requirement. As you learned in Chapter 2, AWS by default attaches the managed FullAWSAccess SCP to every OU and account when Service Control Policies are enabled. Because we have not removed or replaced FullAWSAccess in this example, the effective strategy here is an explicit deny model: FullAWSAccess provides the broad allow, and our custom SCP narrows the permission boundary by explicitly denying actions outside the approved region. This reinforces the idea that SCPs do not grant permissions—they only filter them—and explicit denies always take precedence over inherited allows.

Step 3: Attaching the SCP to the OU

The following commands attach the SCP to the OU.

```
aws organizations attach-policy \
    --policy-id p-abcd1234 \
    --target-id ou-abcd-12345678
```

In this command:

- `--policy-id`: The ID returned when you created the SCP.
- `--target-id`: The ID returned when you created the OU.

For more information, visit: `https://docs.aws.amazon.com/cli/latest/reference/organizations/attach-policy.html`.

Once attached, this SCP applies to all accounts in the OU, enforcing governance at scale.

With these governance guardrails in place, the next step is ensuring that your accounts remain compliant over time—which is where AWS Trusted Advisor's security checks and automated remediation workflows become essential.

Implementing Remediation Based on the Results of AWS Trusted Advisor Security Checks

With your Multi-Account governance structure in place—complete with OUs, SCP guardrails, and clear separation of duties—the next challenge is ensuring that your environment remains compliant over time. Governance is not a one-time configuration; it is a continuous process of assessment, validation, and remediation. This is where AWS Trusted Advisor becomes an essential part of your operational security toolkit.

Trusted Advisor provides automated checks across cost optimization, performance, fault tolerance, service limits, operational excellence, and—most importantly for this chapter—security. These checks help you detect misconfigurations early, before they escalate into incidents. In a Multi-Account environment, Trusted Advisor becomes even more valuable because it surfaces issues that may arise in any member account, regardless of workload or team. This aligns directly with the AWS Security Pillar principles of "Maintain Traceability" and defense-in-depth: you continuously observe, validate, and correct deviations from your intended security posture.

Trusted Advisor's Role in CloudOps

A key nuance that CloudOps engineers must understand is that AWS Trusted Advisor does not perform remediation, nor does it provide immediate, event-driven detection of configuration changes. Instead:

- Use AWS Config for real-time, event-driven detection and for triggering automated remediation. AWS Config evaluates resources the moment they change and can trigger SSM Automation runbooks instantly.
- Use Amazon EventBridge workflows (covered in Chapter 7) for immediate remediation of operational events, such as CloudTrail API activity or resource state changes.
- Use Trusted Advisor for broad environment hygiene, periodic best-practice scanning, and identifying issues that may have slipped through initial deployment controls.

Additionally, Trusted Advisor checks may refresh only every few hours (or weekly, depending on the check), so it is not suitable for real-time enforcement. Instead, it complements AWS Config and Amazon EventBridge by providing periodic, cross-service, cross-account visibility.

If you need to fix something automatically the second it breaks, choose AWS Config. If you need long-term guidance on how to save money or improve architecture, choose Trusted Advisor.

Before diving into the CLI commands, it helps to visualize the remediation workflow at a high level:

- Step 1: Looking up the Trusted Advisor check ID.
- Step 2: Retrieving the Trusted Advisor check results.
- Step 3: Filtering the output (to identify only the resources that failed the check).
- Step 4: Remediating the misconfiguration (Trusted Advisor does not perform remediation).
- Step 5: Refreshing the Trusted Advisor check to confirm that the environment is now compliant.

Step 1: Looking Up the Trusted Advisor Check ID

Trusted Advisor check IDs are predefined identifiers assigned by AWS. They do not appear in the console, and they are not dynamically generated. To retrieve them, make sure you have the `support:DescribeTrustedAdvisorChecks` permission and use:

```
aws support describe-trusted-advisor-checks \
    --language en
```

In this command:

- `--language`: Specifies the language for the returned metadata.

This returns a list of all available checks, including:

- `id`: The check ID
- `name`: The human-readable name
- `category`: Security, cost, performance, and so on
- `metadata`: The meaning of each column in the results

For example, the check ID for "Security Groups—Specific Ports Unrestricted" is: `eW7HH0l7J9`. You will use this ID in the next steps.

You must have a Business, Enterprise On-Ramp, or Enterprise Support plan to use the Amazon Web Services Support API. If you call the Amazon Web Services Support API from an account that doesn't have a Business, Enterprise On-Ramp, or Enterprise Support plan, the `SubscriptionRequiredException` error message appears.

For more information, visit: `https://docs.aws.amazon.com/cli/latest/reference/support/describe-trusted-advisor-checks.html`.

Step 2: Retrieving the Trusted Advisor Check Results

The following command retrieves the results of the "Security Groups—Specific Ports Unrestricted" check. This check identifies security groups that allow inbound access from 0.0.0.0/0 on sensitive ports such as SSH (22) or RDP (3389). You will need the `support:DescribeTrustedAdvisorCheckResult` permission.

```
aws support describe-trusted-advisor-check-result \
    --check-id eW7HH0l7J9 \
    --language en
```

In this command:

- `--check-id`: The unique identifier of the Trusted Advisor check.
- `--language`: Specifies the language for the returned metadata.

This command returns the results of the Trusted Advisor check that has the specified check ID.

For more information, visit: `https://docs.aws.amazon.com/cli/latest/reference/support/describe-trusted-advisor-check-result.html`.

Step 3: Filtering the Output

The following command gives you a clean list of misconfigured security groups that require remediation.

```
aws support describe-trusted-advisor-check-result \
    --check-id eW7HH0l7J9 \
    --language en \
    --query 'result.flaggedResources[*].metadata'
```

In this command:

- `--query`: Filters the output to show only the metadata for flagged resources.

The following is an example of what Trusted Advisor returns when it detects an unrestricted SSH rule on security group `sg-0123456789abcdef0`:

```
[
  [
    "sg-0123456789abcdef0",
    "tcp",
    "22",
    "0.0.0.0/0",
    "i-0abc123def4567890",
    "MySecurityGroup",
    "EC2-VPC",
    "Open port 22 to the world"
  ]
]
```


Step 4: Remediating the Misconfiguration

Trusted Advisor does not perform remediation. It only reports findings. You—as a CloudOps engineer—are responsible for building a mechanism to act on those findings. In our example, to remove an unrestricted SSH rule (0.0.0.0/0 on port 22), we can run, as a one-time fix:

```
aws ec2 revoke-security-group-ingress \
    --group-id sg-0123456789abcdef0 \
    --protocol tcp \
    --port 22 \
    --cidr 0.0.0.0/0
```

To execute the command, you need the `ec2:RevokeSecurityGroupIngress` permission. In this command:

- `--group-id`: The security group to modify.
- `--protocol`: The protocol to revoke (`tcp`).
- `--port`: The port number (`22` for SSH).
- `--cidr`: The CIDR block to remove (`0.0.0.0/0` indicates unrestricted access).

This action removes the insecure rule while leaving all other rules intact.

Following the "Safely automate where possible" Operational Excellence design principle, you may wonder why we remediate this finding manually instead of building automation around it. Wouldn't it make more sense to trigger an EventBridge workflow with an SSM Automation runbook? In many cases, yes—but Trusted Advisor is not an event-driven service and does not detect configuration drift in real time. Its checks refresh only periodically, which makes it unsuitable as a trigger for immediate remediation. For real-time enforcement, AWS Config (Chapter 3) and Amazon EventBridge-based workflows (Chapter 6) are the right tools. Trusted Advisor's role is different: it provides broad, periodic visibility into best-practice gaps across your environment, and manual remediation keeps the example simple and focused on understanding the Trusted Advisor workflow itself.

Step 5: Refreshing the Trusted Advisor Check

To refresh the check and ensure your corrective action is recognized run the command:

```
aws support refresh-trusted-advisor-check \
    --check-id eW7HH0l7J9
```

To execute the command, you need the `support:RefreshTrustedAdvisorCheck` permission. With the corrective action in Step 4, your environment returns to a compliant state. At this point, you've completed the identity- and access-focused portion of the chapter, where the emphasis has been on permissions, governance boundaries, and proactive remediation.

Before we shift into data and infrastructure protection, it's important to understand how CloudOps teams maintain continuous visibility across all these signals. This is where AWS Security Hub enters the picture, acting as the central aggregator that unifies findings from Trusted Advisor, GuardDuty, Inspector, Macie, and other security services. The next section provides a brief overview of how AWS Security Hub strengthens your operational posture and enhances continuous security visibility across your environment.

Understanding AWS Security Hub

AWS Security Hub is the service that brings your entire security posture into one place. Rather than requiring CloudOps engineers to monitor each security service independently, Security Hub aggregates findings from IAM Access Analyzer, AWS Config, Trusted Advisor, GuardDuty, Inspector, and Macie (covered later in the chapter). It normalizes all findings into the AWS Security Finding Format (ASFF), allowing you to analyze issues consistently, automate remediation workflows, and track compliance against frameworks such as CIS, PCI DSS, and the AWS Foundational Security Best Practices standard. For CloudOps teams, this consolidation is essential: it reduces operational blind spots and ensures that high-severity issues surface quickly, regardless of which underlying service detected them.

Security Hub also plays a key role in Multi-Account environments. When delegated administration is enabled, findings from all member accounts flow into a central security account, giving CloudOps engineers a unified, organization-wide view of risk. This aligns directly with the operational principles emphasized throughout this chapter, which result in centralized governance, automated guardrails, and continuous monitoring. With Security Hub in place, the transition from identity-focused controls to data-centric protections becomes seamless, because the same visibility layer continues to track misconfigurations, unencrypted resources, and policy violations as you implement encryption, classification, and secrets-management strategies.

With this foundation established, we now shift from visibility to protection. The next section explores how CloudOps teams classify data, enforce encryption at rest and in transit, and securely manage operational secrets—core capabilities that uphold the AWS Security Pillar and ensure that sensitive information remains safeguarded throughout the CloudOps cycle.

Protecting Data and Infrastructure

With identity and access controls firmly in place, the next responsibility of a CloudOps engineer is ensuring that the data itself—and the infrastructure hosting it—remains protected throughout its lifecycle. This is where the focus shifts from *who* can access resources to *how* those resources are secured. In practice, this means classifying data appropriately, encrypting it at rest and in transit, and storing sensitive operational secrets in a secure, auditable manner. These capabilities form the backbone of the AWS Security Pillar and directly support the principle of "Keeping people away from data" by enforcing automated, control-driven protections rather than relying on human access. Together, they are essential for both operational excellence and exam readiness.

In the following sections, we build on the governance and IAM foundations established earlier in the chapter. You'll see how CloudOps teams use data classification to guide technical controls, how policies and AWS KMS work together to secure data at rest, how ACM and TLS protect data in transit, and how AWS Secrets Manager and Parameter Store safeguard credentials and API keys. Each of these mechanisms reinforces the well-architected mandate to minimize direct human interaction with sensitive data, ensuring that access is mediated through secure services, automation, and least-privilege boundaries.

Implementing a Data Classification Scheme

A strong security posture begins with understanding the sensitivity of the data your workloads handle. Data classification is the process of categorizing information based on its confidentiality, integrity, and availability requirements. While AWS does not enforce a specific classification model, CloudOps engineers typically adopt categories such as Public, Internal, Confidential, and Restricted. These labels guide decisions about encryption, access controls, retention, and monitoring. For example, a public website's static assets may require minimal protection, while customer Personally Identifiable Information (PII) demands strict encryption and access auditing.

In AWS, data classification is not a single service but a framework that informs how you configure services. For instance, if a dataset is classified as Confidential, you might enforce server-side encryption with AWS KMS, restrict IAM access to a narrow set of roles, and enable CloudTrail data events for detailed auditing. Classification also influences network design: highly sensitive workloads may require private subnets, VPC endpoints, strict NACLs, and security group rules. The key is consistency—classification should drive predictable, repeatable security controls across accounts and workloads.

To support classification workflows, CloudOps engineers often use resource tagging. Tags allow you to label resources with their classification level and apply automated policies using AWS Config or Service Control Policies (SCPs). For example, you might enforce that all S3 buckets tagged `Classification=Confidential` must have encryption enabled. The following CLI command shows how to apply such a tag.

You will need the required permission: `s3:PutBucketTagging`.

```
aws s3api put-bucket-tagging \
    --bucket my-confidential-data \
    --tagging 'TagSet=[{Key=Classification,Value=Confidential}]'
```

In this command:

`--bucket`: Specifies the S3 bucket to tag.

`--tagging`: Provides the key–value pairs to apply.

This command returns no output on success, but the tag becomes visible in the S3 console and through subsequent API calls.

For more information, visit: `https://docs.aws.amazon.com/cli/latest/reference/s3api/put-bucket-tagging.html`.

Using Amazon Macie to Validate and Refine Classification

Once you've defined your classification levels and applied tags, the next challenge is ensuring that the data stored across your environment actually matches those classifications. This is where Amazon Macie becomes invaluable. Macie uses machine learning and pattern matching to automatically discover sensitive data—such as PII, financial records, or credentials—inside your S3 buckets. Its findings help you validate or correct your classification tags, ensuring that your tagging strategy reflects the true sensitivity of your data.

For example, if Macie detects PII in a bucket tagged `Classification=Internal`, that's a signal that the classification is incorrect—or that the data was placed in the wrong location. CloudOps teams often integrate Macie findings into automated workflows that update tags, trigger AWS Config rules, or notify security teams. This creates a feedback loop: classification defines the policy, Macie discovers sensitive data, and tagging enforces governance controls.

The following CLI example retrieves all Macie findings. You will need the required permission: `macie2:ListFindings`, `macie2:GetFindings`.

```
aws macie2 list-findings \
    --finding-criteria '{
        "criterion": {
            "severity.score": {
                "gte": 1
            }
        }
    }'
```

In this command:

- `--finding-criteria`: This parameter allows you to filter the results based on specific finding attributes. In this example, we are filtering all findings whose severity score is greater than or equal to 1.

In Amazon Macie, numerical severity scores range from 1 to 3 and map directly to qualitative labels: low (1), medium (2), and high (3). To filter for only "High" severity findings in the CLI, set your `finding-criteria` to `"eq": 3`.

This returns a list of finding IDs.

```
{
  "findingIds": [
    "12345678-aaaa-bbbb-cccc-1234567890ab",
    "98765432-dddd-eeee-ffff-0987654321ff"
  ]
}
```

Macie does not include details in the response. These IDs are then passed to `get-findings`.

```
aws macie2 get-findings \
    --finding-ids 12345678-aaaa-bbbb-cccc-1234567890ab
```

The command returns an output similar to this JSON document:

```
{
  "findings": [
    {
      "accountId": "111122223333",
      "archived": false,
      "category": "CLASSIFICATION",
      "classificationDetails": {
        "jobArn": "arn:aws:macie2:us-east-1:111122223333:classification-job/
abcd1234",
        "result": {
          "mimeType": "text/plain",
          "sensitiveData": [
            {
              "category": "PERSONAL_INFORMATION",
              "detections": [
                {
                  "type": "EMAIL_ADDRESS",
                  "count": 12
                },
                {
                  "type": "NAME",
                  "count": 4
                }
              ],
              "totalCount": 16
            }
```

```
          ],
          "sizeClassified": 20480
        }
      },
      "createdAt": "2024-11-12T14:22:18.123Z",
      "description": "Sensitive data detected in S3 object.",
      "id": "12345678-aaaa-bbbb-cccc-1234567890ab",
      "partition": "aws",
      "region": "us-east-1",
      "resourcesAffected": {
        "s3Object": {
          "bucketName": "my-sensitive-bucket",
          "key": "exports/2024/records.txt",
          "path": "s3://my-sensitive-bucket/exports/2024/records.txt",
          "bucketOwner": "111122223333",
          "etag": "9a8b7c6d5e4f",
          "versionId": "null"
        }
      },
      "schemaVersion": "1.0",
      "severity": {
        "description": "High",
        "score": 3
      },
      "title": "Sensitive data detected",
      "type": "SensitiveData:S3Object/Personal"
    }
  ]
}
```


This output tells you:

- Which bucket contains sensitive data.
- Which object triggered the finding.
- What type of sensitive data was detected (e.g., email addresses).
- How severe the finding is.

From here, you can update the bucket's classification tag accordingly:

```
aws s3api put-bucket-tagging \
    --bucket my-sensitive-bucket \
    --tagging 'TagSet=[{Key=Classification,Value=Confidential}]'
```

Amazon Macie's sensitive-data discovery engine is limited to Amazon S3. It does not scan EBS volumes, RDS databases, DynamoDB tables, EC2 filesystems, Secrets Manager, Parameter Store, or any other storage service. For the SOA-C03 exam, remember: Macie discovers sensitive data in S3 only, making it a natural fit for S3-centric classification and tagging workflows.

For more information, visit: `https://docs.aws.amazon.com/cli/latest/reference/macie2/get-findings.html`.

Encryption at Rest (KMS)

Once data is classified, the next step is to ensure that sensitive information is protected when stored. AWS provides multiple encryption mechanisms, but the most common—and the one emphasized on the SOA-C03 exam—is AWS Key Management Service (KMS). KMS allows you to create and manage cryptographic keys used to encrypt data across services such as S3, EBS, RDS, DynamoDB, and more. Encryption at rest ensures that even if storage media is compromised, the data remains unreadable without the appropriate key.

A CloudOps engineer must understand the difference between AWS-managed keys (AWS-owned or service-managed) and customer-managed keys. Customer-managed keys provide greater control, including rotation schedules, key policies, and cross-account permissions. For workloads classified as Confidential or Restricted, customer-managed keys are often required. This aligns with the Zero-Trust principles discussed earlier: you explicitly define who can use a key, for what purpose, and under what conditions.

A key concept for the exam is that a KMS key is a regional resource—a customer-managed key created in one region cannot be used directly in another. When workloads span multiple regions, AWS KMS multi-region keys provide a seamless solution: they are a set of related keys in different regions that share the same key ID and the same key material, allowing them to be used interchangeably. This means data encrypted with the primary key in one region can be decrypted by a replica key in another region without re-encrypting the data or making a cross-region API call.

The following CLI example creates a customer-managed KMS key.

You will need the required permission: `kms:CreateKey`.

```
aws kms create-key \
    --description "Key for encrypting confidential Aurora data" \
    --key-usage ENCRYPT_DECRYPT \
    --origin AWS_KMS
```

In this command:

- `--description` provides a human-readable purpose for the key.
- `--key-usage` specifies the cryptographic operations allowed.
- `--origin` indicates that AWS KMS generates the key material.

The command returns a JSON structure containing the key ID and ARN—values you will reference when enabling encryption on S3 buckets, EBS volumes, or RDS instances.

```
{
  "KeyMetadata": {
    "AWSAccountId": "123456789012",
    "KeyId": "abcd1234-5678-90ab-cdef-11111EXAMPLE",
    "Arn": "arn:aws:kms:us-east-1:123456789012:key/
abcd1234-5678-90ab-cdef-11111EXAMPLE",
    "CreationDate": 1710800000.0,
    "Enabled": true,
    "KeyUsage": "ENCRYPT_DECRYPT",
    "KeyState": "Enabled",
    "Origin": "AWS_KMS"
  }
}
```


Next, we use the KMS key to encrypt an Aurora cluster.

Keep in mind that Aurora encryption must be enabled at cluster creation time. You cannot encrypt an existing unencrypted cluster directly; instead, you must snapshot → copy with encryption → restore. For new deployments, however, you simply specify the KMS key ARN, as shown in the following example.

```
aws rds create-db-cluster \
    --db-cluster-identifier prod-aurora \
    --engine aurora-mysql \
    --engine-version 8.0.mysql_aurora.3.05.2 \
    --storage-encrypted \
    --kms-key-id arn:aws:kms:us-east-1:123456789012:key/abcd1234-5678-90ab-
cdef-11111EXAMPLE \
    --manage-master-user-password \
    --master-username admin
```

In addition to the `rds:CreateDBCluster` permission, you will need the `kms:DescribeKey` permission to use the newly created KMS key.

In this command:

- `--storage-encrypted`: Enables encryption at rest for the Aurora cluster.
- `--kms-key-id`: Specifies the customer-managed KMS key used for encryption. This is where the ARN from `create-key` is used.
- `--manage-master-user-password`: Instructs RDS to automatically generate a strong password and store it in Secrets Manager.
- `--master-username`: Required even when the password is auto-generated.

The commands return an output similar to:


```
{
  "DBCluster": {
    "DBClusterIdentifier": "prod-aurora",
    "Status": "creating",
```

```
    "StorageEncrypted": true,
    "KmsKeyId": "arn:aws:kms:us-east-1:123456789012:key/
abcd1234-5678-90ab-cdef-11111EXAMPLE",
    "Engine": "aurora-mysql",
    "MasterUsername": "admin",
    "MasterUserSecret": {
      "SecretArn": "arn:aws:secretsmanager:us-east-
1:123456789012:secret:prod-aurora-master-abc123"
    }
  }
}
```

Once the cluster is available, you can create Aurora instances inside it:

```
aws rds create-db-instance \
    --db-instance-identifier prod-aurora-instance-1 \
    --db-cluster-identifier prod-aurora \
    --engine aurora-mysql \
    --db-instance-class db.t3.medium
```

All instances in an encrypted Aurora cluster are automatically encrypted using the same KMS key.

Encryption in Transit

Protecting data at rest is only half the story. CloudOps engineers must also ensure that data remains secure while moving between clients, services, and networks. Encryption in transit is typically achieved using TLS (Transport Layer Security), and AWS Certificate Manager (ACM) plays a central role in provisioning and managing the certificates (X.509) required for HTTPS endpoints. Whether you're securing an Application Load Balancer, CloudFront distribution, or API Gateway endpoint, ACM certificates provide a scalable, automated way to enforce TLS.

The narrative from earlier chapters continues here: just as IAM Roles define *who* can access resources, TLS defines *how securely* that access occurs from "point A" to "point B." Modern CloudOps practices treat TLS as mandatory across the board, not only for sensitive workloads, because unencrypted HTTP is no longer acceptable for any production-grade service. ACM integrates seamlessly with services like Elastic Load Balancing, ensuring that certificates renew automatically—reducing operational overhead and eliminating a common source of outages.

The following CLI example requests a public ACM certificate for a domain. You will need the required permission: `acm:RequestCertificate`.

```
aws acm request-certificate \
    --domain-name api.example.com \
    --validation-method DNS
```

In this command:

- `--domain-name`: Specifies the fully qualified domain name to secure.
- `--validation-method`: Indicates how domain ownership will be verified.

For more information, visit: `https://docs.aws.amazon.com/cli/latest/reference/acm/request-certificate.html`.

The command returns a certificate ARN, which you then attach to an ALB or CloudFront distribution to enforce HTTPS.

Protecting Secrets

The final part of protecting data and infrastructure is securing the operational secrets that power your applications—API keys, database passwords, OAuth tokens, and more. Hard-coding secrets in configuration files or environment variables violates every security principle discussed so far. Instead, AWS provides two primary services for secure secret storage: AWS Secrets Manager and SSM Parameter Store. Both offer encryption at rest using KMS, fine-grained IAM access controls, and auditability through CloudTrail.

AWS Secrets Manager is purpose-built for sensitive credentials and supports automatic rotation for services like Amazon RDS. Parameter Store, part of AWS Systems Manager, is ideal for configuration values and supports both plaintext and encrypted parameters. Unlike AWS Secrets Manager, it does not provide native automatic rotation for stored secrets. The choice depends on your workload, but the principle remains the same: secrets must be stored centrally, encrypted, and accessed only by authorized roles. This ties directly back to the IAM and Zero-Trust concepts introduced earlier in the chapter.

The following CLI example stores database credentials securely. By using a local JSON file, you avoid exposing sensitive data in your terminal history or process logs. You must have the following IAM permission: `secretsmanager:CreateSecret`.

First, create a file named `db-creds.json` with the following structure. Replace the placeholder values with your actual database details:

```
{
    "username": "admin",
    "password": <dba-password>,
    "engine": "mysql",
    "host": "://amazonaws.com",
    "port": 3306
}
```

Next, use the `file://` prefix to reference your JSON file in the following command:

```
aws secretsmanager create-secret \
    --name ProdDBPassword \
    --description "Production MySQL database credentials" \
    --secret-string file://db-creds.json
```

In this command:

- `--name`: Assigns a unique identifier (e.g., `ProdDBPassword`) to the secret within the AWS Region.
- `--description`: Provides context, such as the environment or application owner.
- `--secret-string`: Uses the `file://` notation to load the sensitive JSON object from your local disk. This prevents the sensitive password from being saved in your command history (such as `.bash_history` on Linux/macOS or the PowerShell history on Windows).

Immediately and securely delete the local file to ensure that no plaintext credentials remain on the disk.

For more information, visit: `https://docs.aws.amazon.com/cli/latest/reference/secretsmanager/create-secret.html`.

The command returns a secret ARN, which applications can retrieve securely using IAM Roles—ensuring that sensitive credentials never appear in code repositories, deployment pipelines, or environment variables.

To maximize security, always minimize the number of times a secret is explicitly typed or stored in plaintext. The preferred method is to use native AWS features like `--manage-master-user-password`, which we used for Amazon Aurora in Chapter 4. This allows AWS to generate and manage the secret entirely behind the scenes. If you must use a manual method, provide the secret via a local file (e.g., `--secret-string file://creds.json`) and immediately dispose of that file using a secure overwrite command to ensure no "credential remnants" are left on your disk or in your command history.

Summary

This chapter introduced CloudOps engineers to the idea that securing an AWS environment is an ongoing practice rather than a single configuration step. It began by emphasizing identity as the first boundary of security and showed how every decision—permissions, guardrails, and data protection—fits into a broader operational mindset aligned with AWS's Security Pillar.

The first half of the chapter focused on building strong identity foundations. It walked through the essential IAM features that enforce least privilege, defense-in-depth, and separation of duties. These include password policies, MFA, and federated identities. The chapter then showed how to troubleshoot access issues using CloudTrail, IAM Access Analyzer, and the Policy Simulator. From there, the chapter expanded to Multi-Account governance, explaining how AWS Organizations, OUs, and SCPs help CloudOps engineers manage risk at scale.

The second half of the chapter shifted from who can access resources to how those resources are secured. It began with data classification, showing how resource tagging and Amazon Macie help CloudOps engineers understand the sensitivity of their data and apply consistent controls. This classification model becomes the anchor for the rest of the section.

Next, the chapter explored encryption at rest and the central role of AWS KMS. CloudOps engineers learned how to create customer-managed keys and apply them to real workloads, such as encrypting an Aurora cluster with a newly created key. The chapter then covered encryption in transit, explaining why TLS is now the default expectation for any production-grade service and how ACM simplifies certificate management across AWS.

The chapter concluded with protecting secrets, highlighting why credentials and sensitive configuration values must never be stored in plaintext. AWS Secrets Manager and SSM Parameter Store provide secure, encrypted, auditable storage for operational secrets, completing the journey from identity to data protection. Together, these sections give CloudOps engineers a clear, practical understanding of how to secure AWS workloads end-to-end—both for real-world operations and for the SOA-C03 exam.

Exam Essentials

Know the IAM features to implement a strong identity foundation. A strong identity foundation begins with understanding how IAM policies shape access. Identity-based policies are attached to users, groups, or roles and define what that principal can do across AWS—making them ideal for most permission models and least-privilege enforcement. Resource-based policies, on the other hand, are attached directly to resources such as S3 buckets, KMS keys, or Lambda functions, and are used when you need to grant access to external principals, including cross-account access. MFA strengthens authentication by ensuring that even if credentials are compromised, an attacker cannot gain access without the second factor—making it essential for privileged operations and role assumption. Finally, federated identities are the modern best practice because they eliminate long-lived IAM Users, centralize authentication in an external IdP, and provide short-lived, automatically rotated credentials through IAM Roles. Together, these features form the core of a secure, scalable identity layer that CloudOps engineers must master for both real-world operations and the SOA-C03 exam.

Know the services to troubleshoot permissions and perform auditing. CloudOps engineers must know which AWS tools to reach for when permissions fail or when auditing access is required. AWS CloudTrail is the starting point for understanding what actually happened—it records every API call, who made it, when, and from where, making it essential for auditing and root-cause analysis. When the question is why access was allowed or denied, IAM Access Analyzer helps identify unintended public or cross-account access and evaluates policies to highlight risky permissions. For fine-grained troubleshooting, the IAM Policy

Simulator lets CloudOps engineers test how identity-based and resource-based policies interact, revealing exactly which statements grant or block access. Together, these three services form the core toolkit for diagnosing permission issues and maintaining a secure, auditable AWS environment.

Understand how to implement Multi-Account strategies securely. CloudOps engineers must understand which services enable them to build a secure and scalable multi-account landing zone (MALZ) in AWS. AWS Organizations is the foundation: it lets you group accounts into Organizational Units (OUs) and apply Service Control Policies (SCPs) that set the maximum permissions those accounts can ever receive. SCPs follow the standard evaluation logic—Explicit Deny → Allow → Implicit Deny—making them ideal for enforcing guardrails and compliance such as region restrictions or blocking risky services across entire environments. AWS Control Tower builds on Organizations by providing an automated landing zone with preconfigured OUs, mandatory guardrails, account factory, and continuous governance. Use AWS Organizations when you need flexible, custom governance patterns, and choose AWS Control Tower when you want a turnkey, best-practice Multi-Account setup with built-in compliance controls. Together, these services help CloudOps engineers design and build secure account boundaries, minimize blast radius, and maintain consistent governance across large AWS environments.

Understand the difference between SCPs and preventive controls. SCPs and AWS Control Tower preventive controls both act as guardrails, but they operate at different layers. SCPs restrict who can perform which actions by defining the maximum permissions identities in an account can ever receive—they filter API calls at the IAM authorization layer. Preventive controls, on the other hand, enforce how resources must be configured by blocking non-compliant deployments before they are created, such as unencrypted S3 buckets or disabled CloudTrail logging. In short, SCPs control actions, while preventive controls enforce configuration, and together they provide layered, non-bypassable governance across your AWS environment.

Understand when to use AWS Trusted Advisor and how it fits in the AWS security ecosystem. CloudOps engineers should think of AWS Trusted Advisor as a visibility tool, not a real-time enforcement mechanism. Trusted Advisor periodically scans your environment and highlights misconfigurations—such as open security groups, unencrypted resources, or cost inefficiencies—but it does not react instantly to changes. That role belongs to services like AWS Config, which evaluates resources continuously, and Amazon EventBridge paired with SSM Automation runbooks, which can trigger immediate remediation when a risky change occurs. AWS Trusted Advisor fits earlier in the security workflow: it helps teams spot drift, identify overlooked issues, and maintain broad operational awareness across accounts. For the exam, remember that AWS Trusted Advisor provides insight, while AWS Config and Amazon EventBridge provide real-time guardrails and automated response. Understanding this distinction is key to placing Trusted Advisor correctly within the AWS security ecosystem.

Understand how to classify data and use Amazon Macie with tagging to enforce security controls. CloudOps engineers must know how to classify data in AWS and apply security controls that match its sensitivity. A data classification scheme provides the structure—labels such as Public, Internal, Confidential, or Restricted—while resource tagging turns those labels into actionable metadata that automation, Config rules, and governance tools can evaluate. To validate whether data is stored appropriately, Amazon Macie scans S3 buckets for sensitive information such as PII and financial data, helping teams detect misplaced or unclassified content. Macie's findings can then drive updates to resource tags or trigger remediation workflows, ensuring that the classification model reflects the actual sensitivity of the data. For the exam, remember that classification defines the intent, tagging expresses it across resources, and Macie provides the visibility needed to keep the environment aligned with your security standards.

Know how to protect data with encryption at rest and encryption in transit. CloudOps engineers must understand how AWS protects data both where it is stored and as it moves across networks. Encryption at rest relies on AWS KMS, which provides the keys used by services like S3, EBS, RDS, and Aurora to secure stored data. For the exam, remember that encryption is often enabled at resource creation time and that customer-managed keys offer stronger control through custom key policies, rotation, and cross-account permissions. Encryption in transit is equally essential: TLS is now the default expectation for any production workload, ensuring that data cannot be intercepted or tampered with as it travels between clients and services. AWS Certificate Manager (ACM) simplifies this by issuing and automatically renewing certificates for ALBs, CloudFront, and API Gateway. Together, these mechanisms form the core of AWS's data-protection model, and mastering when and how to apply them is critical for secure, compliant CloudOps operations.

Know how to protect secrets using AWS Secrets Manager. CloudOps engineers must understand how to secure, and store secrets (e.g., database passwords, API keys, etc.) without ever exposing them in code, scripts, or configuration files. AWS Secrets Manager is the primary service for securely handling database passwords, API keys, and other operational secrets. It encrypts every secret with KMS, provides fine-grained access control through IAM, and—most importantly—supports automatic rotation, allowing credentials to be refreshed without downtime or manual intervention. AWS Secrets Manager also integrates directly with services like Amazon RDS and Aurora, making it easy to generate and rotate master passwords securely. While SSM Parameter Store can hold configuration values, AWS Secrets Manager is the preferred choice for high-sensitivity credentials that require lifecycle management, auditing, and rotation. For the exam, remember that protecting secrets is a core part of Zero-Trust operations, and AWS Secrets Manager provides the secure, auditable, and automated workflow needed to keep credentials out of source code and away from long-lived exposure.

Review Questions

1. A CloudOps engineer is reviewing an IAM Role used by an internal automation tool. The role currently has broad permissions, including `s3:*` on all buckets. The engineer wants to restrict access so the tool can only read objects from a specific bucket. What is the most appropriate action?

   A. Replace the policy with an identity-based policy granting only `s3:GetObject` on the required bucket.

   B. Attach a resource-based policy to the bucket granting the tool full access.

   C. Enable MFA for the role to restrict access.

   D. Use an SCP to block all S3 actions except `s3:GetObject`.

2. A CloudOps engineer receives a report that an IAM User deleted an S3 bucket unexpectedly. The engineer checks the CloudTrail event history in `us-east-1` but finds no record of the deletion. The account is part of an AWS Organization with several CloudTrail configurations in place. What is the most likely explanation?

   A. The event was logged only in an organization-level trail configured in a different region.

   B. The event was blocked by an SCP, so CloudTrail did not record it.

   C. The S3 bucket had object-level logging disabled, so the deletion event was not captured.

   D. IAM Access Analyzer suppressed the event because it was not a cross-account action.

3. A company is introducing a new "sandbox" environment for experimentation. Several developer accounts need to be isolated so they cannot launch expensive GPU instance families, while production accounts must remain unaffected. The CloudOps engineer must implement this restriction using AWS Organizations. Which combination of steps should the CloudOps engineer take? (Select TWO.)

   A. Apply an SCP to the sandbox OU denying GPU instance families.

   B. Apply an SCP to the root of the organization denying GPU instances.

   C. Use AWS Config to detect GPU instance launches.

   D. Move the sandbox accounts into a dedicated OU.

   E. Apply a permissions boundary to all IAM Roles in the developer accounts denying GPU instance families.

4. A CloudOps engineer wants to automatically shut down EC2 instances that are publicly exposed. They consider using Trusted Advisor to trigger the automation. Which statement best explains why Trusted Advisor is unsuitable for this purpose?

   A. Trusted Advisor does not support EC2 checks.

   B. Trusted Advisor does not run continuously or trigger real-time remediation.

   C. Trusted Advisor cannot detect public exposure.

   D. Trusted Advisor cannot integrate with EventBridge.

5. A CloudOps engineer wants to ensure that any S3 bucket containing PII is automatically labeled with the correct data-classification tag and evaluated for compliance. Which combination of actions creates a complete solution? (Select TWO.)
   A. Configure Macie to publish findings to EventBridge.
   B. Use IAM Access Analyzer to detect PII.
   C. Use Lambda to update bucket tags when Macie findings appear.
   D. Use S3 Block Public Access.
   E. Use CloudTrail to detect PII uploads.
6. A CloudOps engineer needs an application in Account B to encrypt objects in an S3 bucket in Account A using a customer-managed key in Account A. What must be configured?
   A. A key policy in Account A allowing the IAM Role in Account B to use the key.
   B. A bucket policy in Account A referencing the customer-managed key ARN.
   C. A trust policy in Account B allowing the customer-managed key to assume the role.
   D. A grant in Account B allowing encryption with the customer-managed key.
7. A CloudOps engineer must ensure TLS termination at the ALB while also encrypting traffic between the ALB and backend EC2 instances. Which design meets this requirement?
   A. Terminate TLS at the ALB and send HTTP to instances.
   B. Terminate TLS at the ALB and re-encrypt using TLS on the instances.
   C. Use a Network Load Balancer with TCP passthrough.
   D. Use a resource-based policy to enforce TLS.
8. A CloudOps engineer must rotate a third-party API key stored in Secrets Manager. The API requires a multi-step workflow: create new key, validate it, then activate it. Which TWO components are required? (Select TWO.)
   A. A custom Lambda rotation function implementing all steps.
   B. A Secrets Manager built-in rotation template.
   C. A rotation schedule in Secrets Manager.
   D. A CloudTrail event rule.
   E. A KMS key with automatic rotation.
9. A CloudOps engineer wants to detect IAM Roles across all accounts that can be assumed by principals in external AWS accounts. Which configuration enables this?
   A. An organization-level Access Analyzer
   B. An account-level Access Analyzer in each account
   C. CloudTrail with Athena queries
   D. IAM Policy Simulator

10. A CloudOps engineer must ensure that no account in the "Critical Systems" OU can disable CloudTrail logging. Which governance mechanism enforces this?
   A. An SCP denying `cloudtrail:StopLogging` applied to the OU
   B. A bucket policy on the CloudTrail S3 bucket
   C. A Config rule evaluating CloudTrail status
   D. A resource-based policy on CloudTrail

11. A CloudOps engineer wants to automatically quarantine any S3 bucket where Macie detects PII. Quarantine means applying a restrictive bucket policy and enabling default encryption. Which combination of actions creates a complete solution? (Select TWO.)
   A. Macie publishing findings to EventBridge
   B. IAM Access Analyzer
   C. Lambda applying the restrictive bucket policy
   D. S3 Inventory
   E. Trusted Advisor

12. A CloudOps engineer manages an application that replicates encrypted DynamoDB data from `us-east-1` to `eu-west-1`. The application must decrypt data in both regions without re-encrypting during replication. Which KMS configuration supports this?
   A. Key grants
   B. Imported key material
   C. Asymmetric keys
   D. Multi-Region KMS keys

13. A CloudOps engineer wants federated users to access multiple AWS accounts without assuming roles directly from the IdP. They also want centralized permission management. Which solution meets this requirement?
   A. SAML federation with separate IAM Roles in each account
   B. IAM Users with MFA
   C. IAM Identity Center with permission sets mapped to account roles
   D. Secrets Manager storing temporary credentials

14. A CloudOps engineer is deploying a private API Gateway endpoint inside a VPC. The team requires TLS for all internal traffic. What configuration satisfies this?
   A. Attach an ACM certificate to the private API endpoint.
   B. Use a VPC endpoint policy to enforce TLS.
   C. Use a resource-based policy to enforce TLS.
   D. Use a Network Load Balancer.

15. A CloudOps engineer needs an application in Account B to retrieve a secret stored in Secrets Manager in Account A. What configuration is required?
    - A. A trust policy on the IAM Role in Account B
    - B. A KMS key grant in Account B
    - C. A bucket policy
    - D. A resource-based policy on the secret allowing the IAM Role in Account B

16. A CloudOps engineer must ensure that all accounts in the organization log all management events to a central S3 bucket and that no account can disable logging. Which combination of actions creates a complete solution? (Select TWO.)
    - A. An organization-wide CloudTrail trail
    - B. An SCP denying `cloudtrail:StopLogging`
    - C. A bucket policy allowing only CloudTrail to write logs
    - D. A Config rule evaluating CloudTrail status
    - E. A Macie job scanning logs

17. A CloudOps engineer applies an SCP that denies `kms:DisableKey`. A developer's IAM policy allows disabling the key. What is the outcome?
    - A. The developer cannot disable the key.
    - B. The developer can disable the key.
    - C. The key policy overrides the SCP.
    - D. The SCP is ignored.

18. A CloudOps engineer sees that an IAM Role has `s3:GetObject` allowed in its identity policy, but access to a specific object is still denied. Which tool helps determine whether a bucket policy is blocking access?
    - A. Macie
    - B. CloudTrail
    - C. IAM Policy Simulator
    - D. Trusted Advisor

19. A CloudOps engineer must ensure that all S3 buckets across multiple AWS accounts use server-side encryption with AWS KMS (SSE-KMS) rather than the default SSE-S3. Which solution provides consistent enforcement across the entire Multi-Account environment?
    - A. Use AWS Config rules to evaluate S3 bucket encryption settings across all accounts.
    - B. Use a preventive control in AWS Control Tower that enforces SSE-KMS encryption for all S3 object uploads.
    - C. Use IAM Access Analyzer to detect buckets encrypted with SSE-S3.
    - D. Use a Lambda function triggered by EventBridge to automatically update bucket encryption settings.

20. A CloudOps engineer has configured IAM Access Analyzer at the organization level to detect externally assumable roles. They now need to build automation that remediates findings by updating trust policies and sending security notifications. Which TWO components complete the remediation pipeline? (Select TWO.)

 A. Access Analyzer detecting external access
 B. EventBridge triggering on Access Analyzer findings
 C. Lambda updating the trust policy
 D. Macie scanning the role
 E. Trusted Advisor generating alerts

Answers to Review Questions

1. A. Identity-based policies are the correct way to restrict what a principal can do. A resource-based policy (Option B) is unnecessary because the principal is internal. MFA (Option C) doesn't restrict permissions. SCPs (Option D) are for account-level guardrails, not per-role least privilege.

2. A. CloudTrail is regional by default, and the Event History view only shows events for the region you are currently viewing. If the organization has a Multi-Account, Multi-Region, or organization-level trail configured in a different region (for example, `us-west-2`), the S3 bucket deletion event would appear only in that region's logs. This is the most realistic explanation for why the engineer sees no event in `us-east-1`. Option B is incorrect because SCPs don't suppress CloudTrail logs. Option C is incorrect because object-level logging doesn't affect bucket-deletion management events, and Option D is incorrect because IAM Access Analyzer never filters or hides CloudTrail events.

3. A, D. A targeted SCP (Option A) applied to a dedicated OU (Option D) is the correct governance pattern. Denying at the root (Option B) affects all accounts. Config (Option C) detects but does not prevent. Permissions boundaries (Option E) apply within an account and cannot enforce organization-wide restrictions. They also cannot override broader permissions granted by the account root or other roles.

4. B. Trusted Advisor does publish check-result changes to EventBridge, but its checks refresh only periodically, not in real time. There can be a significant delay between a configuration change and detection, making it unsuitable for real-time remediation. For real-time detection, use AWS Config rules or EventBridge with CloudTrail events. The other options are incorrect. EC2 checks exist (Option A). It can detect public exposure (Option C). Trusted Advisor integrates with EventBridge (Option D).

5. A, C. Macie detects PII (Option A), and Lambda can update tags based on findings (Option C). Access Analyzer (Option B) cannot detect PII. Block Public Access (Option D) does not classify data. CloudTrail (Option E) cannot detect content.

6. A. Cross-account KMS usage requires explicit permission in the key policy. Bucket policies (Option B) do not grant KMS permissions. Trust policies (Option C) are irrelevant. Grants (Option D) are created on the KMS key in Account A, not in Account B. While grants can supplement cross-account access, the key policy in Account A must first allow the cross-account principal, making A the required configuration.

7. B. Dual encryption requires TLS termination at the ALB and re-encryption to the backend. HTTP (Option A) violates requirements. NLB passthrough (Option C) bypasses ALB termination. Policies (Option D) cannot enforce protocol.

8. A, C. Third-party APIs require a custom Lambda function (Option A) and a rotation schedule (Option C). Built-in templates (Option B) only support AWS services. CloudTrail (Option D) is irrelevant. KMS rotation (Option E) does not rotate secrets.

9. A. Only organization-level analyzers detect cross-account access across all accounts. Account-level analyzers (Option B) detect external access to a single account. To cover all accounts, you would need one in every account. An organization-level analyzer (Option A) provides this coverage from a single configuration. CloudTrail (Option C) shows events, not potential access. Policy Simulator (Option D) is manual.

10. A. SCPs enforce maximum permissions across accounts. Bucket policies (Option B) do not prevent API calls. Config (Option C) detects but does not prevent. CloudTrail does not support resource-based policies (Option D).

11. A, C. Macie → EventBridge → Lambda enables automated remediation. Access Analyzer (Option B) cannot detect PII. Inventory (Option D) lists objects, not sensitivity. Trusted Advisor (Option E) is intended for visibility only.

12. D. Multi-Region keys share key material across Regions. Grants (Option A) control permissions, not replication. Imported keys (Option B) are Region-specific. Asymmetric keys (Option C) are irrelevant.

13. C. IAM Identity Center provides centralized authentication and permission sets. While SAML federation (Option A) is a valid federation approach, it does not provide "centralized permission management" because each account's roles must be managed independently. IAM Users (Option B) violate requirements. Secrets Manager (Option D) is not for identity.

14. A. Private API Gateway endpoints still support TLS via ACM. Policies (Options B and C) cannot enforce protocol. NLB (Option D) is irrelevant.

15. D. Secrets Manager supports cross-account access via resource-based policies. If the secret is encrypted with a customer-managed KMS key, the key policy must also grant the cross-account role `kms:Decrypt`. However, the resource-based policy on the secret is the foundational requirement. Trust policies (Option A) do not grant secret access. KMS grants (Option B) are insufficient alone. Bucket policies (Option C) are irrelevant.

16. A, B. Organization trails enforce logging; SCPs prevent disabling. Bucket policies (Option C) protect the bucket but not logging. Config (Option D) detects but does not prevent. Macie (Option E) is irrelevant.

17. A. SCP explicit deny overrides all other permissions, including key policies and IAM policies. SCPs define the maximum permissions for accounts in an OU. Even though the developer's IAM policy allows `kms:DisableKey`, the SCP deny takes precedence. The IAM evaluation order is: explicit deny, then allow, then implicit deny. An explicit deny in any policy (SCP, identity-based, resource-based, or permissions boundary) always wins.

18. C. Policy Simulator evaluates combined identity- and resource-based policies. Macie (Option A) is irrelevant. CloudTrail (Option B) shows events but not evaluation. Trusted Advisor (Option D) is not for troubleshooting.

19. B. AWS Control Tower includes a built-in preventive control that requires all S3 object uploads to use SSE-KMS, enforcing this across all enrolled accounts automatically as part of the landing zone governance model. AWS Config rules (Option A) can detect non-compliant buckets but cannot prevent their creation, making them detective rather than preventive. Access Analyzer (Option C) evaluates access permissions, not encryption configuration. Lambda remediation (Option D) is reactive and introduces drift windows between the non-compliant action and the fix.

20. B, C. EventBridge (Option B) receives Access Analyzer findings and triggers automation workflows, while Lambda (Option C) performs the actual remediation by updating the trust policy and sending notifications. Access Analyzer (Option A) is the source of findings but is not part of the remediation pipeline itself. Macie (Option D) and Trusted Advisor (Option E) do not detect or remediate trust-policy issues.

Networking and Content Delivery

THE AWS CERTIFIED CLOUDOPS ENGINEER ASSOCIATE (SOA-C03) EXAM OBJECTIVES COVERED IN THIS CHAPTER MAY INCLUDE, BUT ARE NOT LIMITED TO THE FOLLOWING:

✓ **Domain 5: Networking and Content Delivery**

- 5.1 Implement and optimize networking features and connectivity
- 5.2 Configure domains, DNS services, and content delivery
- 5.3 Troubleshoot network connectivity issues

Security and networking are inseparable in the cloud, and the previous chapter made that clear. Every control you apply—whether IAM, encryption, or resource policies—ultimately depends on the network paths your workloads use. Now that you've built a strong foundation in security and compliance, this chapter shifts focus to the connective tissue of AWS: the networking layer that determines how your applications communicate, scale, and stay resilient. Understanding these mechanics is essential for CloudOps engineers preparing for the SOA-C03 exam, because secure architectures only work when the underlying network is configured with equal precision.

We begin with configuring VPCs, where you'll learn how AWS isolates, routes, and segments traffic using subnets, route tables, gateways, and endpoints. This section builds directly on the security principles you've already mastered—after all, a VPC is not just a logical routing domain; it's the first line of defense for your workloads. From there, we move into configuring DNS, where Amazon Route 53 becomes your control plane for naming, resolution, and traffic steering. DNS is often overlooked, yet it's one of the most critical components in both availability and security, influencing everything from failover behavior to how clients reach your services.

Finally, we explore configuring CDN and troubleshooting network issues, rounding out the operational skill set expected of a CloudOps engineer. Content delivery through Amazon CloudFront ensures that your applications remain performant and globally accessible, while troubleshooting teaches you how to diagnose real-world issues using tools like VPC Reachability Analyzer, VPC Flow Logs, and Route 53 health checks. By the end of this chapter, you'll see how networking and security form a continuous, interdependent system—and you'll be equipped to configure, optimize, and troubleshoot that system with confidence.

Configuring Amazon Virtual Private Cloud

When you create a Virtual Private Cloud (VPC) in AWS, you're not provisioning a physical network—you're defining a *logical routing domain* that behaves like your own private data center carved out of the AWS global infrastructure. A VPC gives you an isolated IP space, full control over routing behavior, and the ability to shape how resources communicate inside and outside your environment. Figure 10.1 illustrates this idea by showing a VPC with an IP address space of `10.0.0.0/16`, two subnets with two different IP address ranges (`10.0.0.0/24` and `10.0.1.0/24`) placed in different Availability Zones, and a route table with the local route specified.

AWS abstracts away the physical networking layer, so you can focus on intent: which resources should communicate, which should remain private, and which should reach the Internet. This is why the VPC is foundational for SOA-C03 candidates—it's the control plane for traffic flow, connectivity, and security.

To work effectively with a VPC, you need to understand the building blocks that determine how traffic moves and how workloads stay secure. Subnets carve your VPC IP space into segments. Route tables decide where packets go. Internet Gateways and NAT Gateways control how instances reach (or can be reached by) the outside world. Security Groups and Network ACLs enforce who can talk to whom.

Before we lay the first building block of a VPC, it's important to remember that every VPC lives inside an AWS Account. In Figure 10.1, `Account 1` owns the entire VPC and controls everything that happens inside it. While the VPC defines the network logic, the Account is the overarching administrative, billing, and security boundary. It's the primary "blast radius" container—ensuring that identities, permissions, and costs remain isolated from other environments. For you as a CloudOps engineer, the AWS Account is the locked

FIGURE 10.1 A VPC as a logical routing domain.

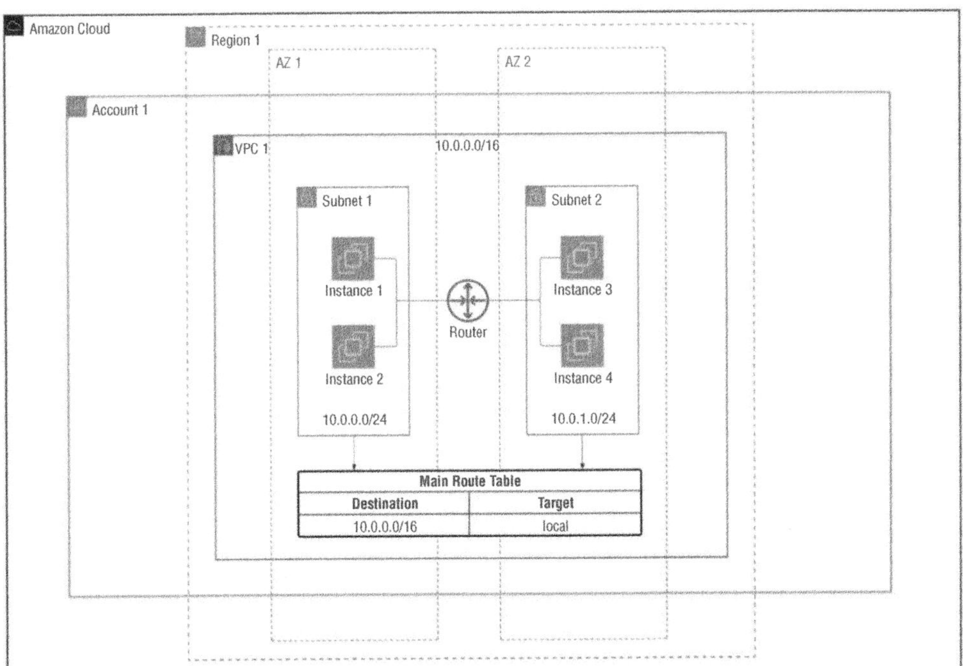

gate at the end of the driveway, and the VPC is the fenced yard inside; you rely on both boundaries to maintain a secure and well-governed cloud environment.

With this mental model in place, the next section gives you a concise, exam-ready tour of each element and how they work together to form the backbone of AWS networking.

VPC Core Components

With the VPC now framed as a logical routing domain, it's time to look at the components that give it structure and behavior. These are the building blocks every CloudOps engineer must master before configuring private connectivity, hybrid networking, or multi-account architectures. Each component plays a specific role in shaping how traffic flows, how workloads stay isolated, and how AWS enforces security boundaries inside the VPC.

Subnet

A subnet is a segment of the VPC's IP address space, carved out from the VPC's CIDR block. Subnets let you organize your network into logical zones—typically separating resources that need Internet access from those that must remain private. Because each subnet lives entirely within a single Availability Zone, subnet design directly affects your application's resilience and failover strategy.

Subnets are AZ-scoped (i.e., a single subnet cannot span zones). VPCs are region-scoped.

Subnets themselves are not inherently "public" or "private." That distinction comes from the route table associated with the subnet. If the route table sends `0.0.0.0/0` to an Internet Gateway, the subnet is considered public. If it sends outbound traffic to a NAT Gateway or keeps it internal, the subnet is private. This separation is foundational for CloudOps engineers who need predictable, secure traffic flows.

To create a subnet use the following command:

```
aws ec2 create-subnet \
  --vpc-id vpc-1234567890abcdef0 \
  --cidr-block 10.0.1.0/24 \
  --availability-zone us-east-1a
```

In this command:

- `--vpc-id`: The ID of the VPC where the subnet will be created. This ties the subnet to the VPC's routing domain and CIDR space.
- `--cidr-block`: The IPv4 CIDR range assigned to the subnet. It must be a non-overlapping segment of the VPC's CIDR block.
- `--availability-zone`: Specifies the AZ where the subnet will physically reside. Subnets are AZ-scoped, so this flag determines placement and redundancy strategy.

For the exam, remember: a subnet CIDR block must not overlap the CIDR block of an existing subnet in the VPC. Also, after you create a subnet, you can't change its CIDR block. To learn more, visit: `https://docs.aws.amazon.com/cli/latest/reference/ec2/create-subnet.html`.

Internet Gateway

An Internet Gateway (IGW) enables bidirectional communication between your VPC and the public Internet. Attaching an IGW to a VPC is required for public IPv4 and IPv6 connectivity, but it does not automatically make any subnet public. Only subnets whose route tables explicitly send traffic to the IGW gain Internet access. This separation of attachment and routing is a common exam pitfall.

The IGW is horizontally scaled and highly available by design, so you don't need to manage redundancy. It also performs one-to-one NAT for public IPv4 addresses, allowing EC2 instances with public IPs to communicate with the Internet. For CloudOps engineers, the IGW is the key to enabling controlled, secure public access while keeping private workloads isolated.

The following example shows how to create and attach an Internet Gateway to a VPC.

```
IGW_ID=$(aws ec2 create-internet-gateway \
  --query 'InternetGateway.InternetGatewayId' \
  --output text)

aws ec2 attach-internet-gateway \
  --internet-gateway-id $IGW_ID \
  --vpc-id vpc-1234567890abcdef0
```

In this command:

- `--query`: Extracts the IGW ID from the JSON output.
- `--output text`: Returns only the ID.
- `--internet-gateway-id`: IGW to attach.
- `--vpc-id`: VPC receiving the IGW.

A common exam scenario involves a "public" subnet that cannot reach the Internet. Often, the fix isn't just adding an Internet Gateway (IGW) to the VPC; it's ensuring the specific route table associated with that subnet has a route (`0.0.0.0/0`) pointing to that IGW.

Route Table

A route table determines where packets go when they leave a subnet. Every subnet must be associated with *exactly* one route table, and every route table includes the implicit *local route* that enables communication between all subnets inside the VPC. This built-in route is what makes the VPC a logical routing domain—subnets can always reach each other unless explicitly restricted by security controls. Route tables are therefore the AWS resource that defines how traffic exits the VPC or moves between network segments.

One critical detail to understand is that the local route cannot be removed, and its destination always matches the VPC CIDR block. However, its target can be replaced to redirect intra-VPC traffic through a middlebox appliance, and more specific routes within the VPC CIDR take precedence via longest prefix match. In other words, the logical routing domain created by the VPC is preserved by design. If you need to restrict communication between subnets, you must use Security Groups or Network ACLs (covered later in this chapter), not routing. This distinction—routing defines reachability, security controls define permission—is a recurring theme on the SOA-C03 exam.

Understanding Route Precedence and Association

Route precedence in AWS is intentionally simple: the most specific route always wins. AWS evaluates routes using longest prefix match, not the order in which routes appear. For example, a route for `10.0.1.0/24` takes precedence over a broader `10.0.0.0/16` route because `/24` is more specific than `/16`. This deterministic behavior ensures that traffic always follows the most precise path available. The base for this behavior is the immutable local route, which covers the VPC's own CIDR block and provides the default path for intra-VPC traffic. However, more specific routes within that CIDR range take precedence via longest prefix match.

Route association determines which subnets use which route table. A route table can be associated with many subnets, but a subnet can only be associated with one route table at a time. This association defines the subnet's routing behavior and is what makes a subnet "public," "private," or part of a specialized routing domain (such as for VPC Peering or Transit Gateway attachments). Mis-associating a subnet is one of the most common causes of unexpected connectivity issues, making route table associations a critical troubleshooting skill for CloudOps engineers.

Public subnets route Internet-bound traffic to an Internet Gateway, while private subnets typically route outbound traffic to a NAT Gateway. You can also add routes to VPC Peering connections, Transit Gateways, or VPC endpoints. Understanding route precedence, association, and the role of the immutable local route is essential for designing predictable network architectures and diagnosing routing problems quickly.

The following sequence of commands demonstrates the full lifecycle of configuring a public route table: creating it, capturing its ID for automation, optionally tagging it for clarity, and finally adding a default route to the Internet Gateway in the newly created route table.

```
RTB_ID=$(aws ec2 create-route-table \
  --vpc-id vpc-1234567890abcdef0 \
  --query 'RouteTable.RouteTableId' \
  --output text)
```

In this command:

- `--vpc-id`: VPC where the route table will be created.
- `--query`: Extracts the `RouteTableId` from the JSON output.
- `--output text`: Returns only the ID, making it easy to store in a variable.

Tagging is not required for functionality, but it is a CloudOps best practice. Tags make it far easier to identify, audit, and automate routing resources—especially in environments with multiple route tables.

```
aws ec2 create-tags \
  --resources $RTB_ID \
  --tags Key=Name,Value=PublicRouteTable
```

In this command:

- `--resources`: Resource ID to tag (the route table).
- `--tags`: Key/value pairs to assign.

The last command adds a default route to the Internet Gateway in the newly created route table:

```
aws ec2 create-route \
  --route-table-id $RTB_ID \
  --destination-cidr-block 0.0.0.0/0 \
  --gateway-id $IGW_ID
```

In this command:

- `--route-table-id`: Route table to modify.
- `--destination-cidr-block`: IP range the route applies to.
- `--gateway-id`: Target for the route (IGW).

To learn more, visit: `https://docs.aws.amazon.com/cli/latest/reference/ec2/create-route-table.html`.

NAT Gateway

While an Internet Gateway (IGW) allows two-way communication for public instances, the NAT Gateway provides one-way outbound egress for private instances. This ensures they can pull security patches or connect to external APIs without being reachable from the public Internet. By performing Source Network Address Translation (SNAT), the gateway replaces a private instance's internal IP with its own public Elastic IP, effectively masking your backend architecture while facilitating essential updates. This one-way flow is a non-negotiable requirement for maintaining a secure, RFC 1918-compliant private environment.

To operationalize this, you—as a CloudOps engineer—must place the NAT Gateway in a public subnet and update the private subnet's route table to point all quad-zero traffic (`0.0.0.0/0`) to the NAT Gateway's ID. While AWS manages the underlying scaling and software, you remain responsible for the logical routing and ensuring that the stateless NACLs on the public subnet allow the return traffic on ephemeral ports. Failure to align these routing and firewall rules is the most common cause of "Connection Timeout" errors in private workloads.

For the exam, you must distinguish between two HA strategies. Traditionally, the NAT Gateway is a zonal resource; to prevent a single AZ outage from impacting Internet access for your entire VPC, you must deploy one NAT Gateway per AZ and point each zone's route table to its local gateway. However, you can now leverage the regional NAT gateway to simplify operations. This newer model provides built-in redundancy across multiple zones automatically, though you should choose the zonal approach if the exam scenario specifically prioritizes minimizing inter-AZ data transfer costs.

To round out the core components of VPC security, we must look at the two layers of defense a CloudOps engineer manages: Security Groups and Network Access Control Lists (NACLs). These tools represent a "Defense in Depth" strategy where the security of your architecture does not rely on a single gatekeeper, but on overlapping layers that protect both the individual resource and the subnet at large.

Security Group

The Security Group (SG) is your first line of defense, acting as a virtual, stateful firewall that operates at the Elastic Network Interface (ENI) level. For a CloudOps engineer, the most vital characteristic to master is its stateful nature: if you allow an inbound request on port 443, the Security Group automatically remembers this *State* and allows the response to exit the instance, regardless of your outbound rules. This significantly simplifies administrative overhead, as you only need to define the rules for the initiation of the traffic. Security Groups are unique in that they only support *Allow* rules; by default, all traffic is denied unless an explicit rule exists, and there is no way to explicitly *Deny* a specific IP address—that task is reserved for the NACL (covered in the next section).

Operationally, the true power of this model lies in Security Group Referencing. Rather than managing a brittle list of static IP addresses, you can create a rule that allows traffic from any ENI associated with a specific "Source" Security Group ID. This creates a dynamic, self-healing network: as your web tier scales in or out with Auto Scaling, each new ENI carries the trusted Security Group identity, allowing it to communicate with the database tier automatically. To modify these protections at scale, a CloudOps engineer uses the AWS CLI `modify-network-interface-attribute` command to update the security profile of a specific ENI.

```
# Example: Attaching a Security Group to a specific ENI ID
# Note: This replaces all existing groups on the ENI with the IDs provided
aws ec2 modify-network-interface-attribute \
    --network-interface-id eni-0123456789abcdef0 \
    --groups sg-0a1b2c3d4e5f6g7h8
```

In this command:

- `--network-interface-id`: This flag targets the specific Elastic Network Interface (ENI) you wish to modify. In a multi-homed EC2 instance, each network interface has a unique ID (e.g., `eni-1a2b3c4d`). This ensures you are applying security rules to the correct "network plug"—for instance, securing the management interface (`eth1`) differently than the public-facing data interface (`eth0`).

- `--groups`: This flag identifies the Security Group ID(s) to be associated with the ENI. A critical operational detail for the exam is that this flag replaces the existing list of Security Groups. If an ENI is currently protected by `sg-AAA` and you run the command with `--groups sg-BBB`, the ENI will no longer be protected by `sg-AAA`. To have both, you must pass them as a space-separated list (e.g., `--groups sg-AAA sg-BBB`).

From a troubleshooting perspective, CloudOps engineers often use VPC Flow Logs to audit Security Group behavior. If an application is failing to connect despite having the correct port open, the engineer must verify that the traffic is not being implicitly denied because it does not match any of the Security Group's allow rules. Since Security Groups are applied at the Network Interface (ENI) level rather than the subnet level, they provide fine-grained control that allows different instances—even within the same subnet—to have completely different access profiles. To implement these rules via the command line, you would use the AWS CLI `authorize-security-group-ingress` command to define your ingress policy.

```
# Allow inbound HTTPS (port 443) from a specific CIDR block
aws ec2 authorize-security-group-ingress \
    --group-id sg-0123456789abcdef0 \
    --protocol tcp \
    --port 443 \
    --cidr 203.0.113.0/24
```

In this command:

- `--group-id`: This flag identifies the specific Security Group you are modifying. In production environments, it is best practice to use the unique ID (e.g., `sg-0123456789abcdef0`) rather than the group name to avoid errors in VPCs where naming conventions might overlap.
- `--protocol`: This specifies the IP protocol to be used for the rule. Common values include `tcp`, `udp`, and `icmp`. If you need to allow all traffic regardless of the protocol, you can use the value `-1`.
- `--port`: This defines the destination port range. For a single port like `HTTPS`, you simply enter `443`. If you were opening a range for an application, you would format it as start-port-end-port (e.g., `8000-8080`).
- `--cidr`: This flag identifies the source of the traffic. It uses Classless Inter-Domain Routing (CIDR) notation to specify a single IP or a range of IPs allowed to connect. In the example provided, `203.0.113.0/24` represents a specific subnet of 256 addresses.

As an alternative to the `--cidr` flag, CloudOps engineers frequently use `--source-group` to implement Security Group referencing. This allows you to permit traffic based on a Security Group ID instead of a static IP, which is the "Gold Standard" for AWS Well-Architected networking because it remains valid even as your backend instances change their private IP addresses during scaling events.

Network ACL

While Security Groups protect individual network interfaces (ENIs), Network Access Control Lists (NACLs) operate as a stateless, subnet-level firewall. Because NACLs apply *uniformly* to every resource within the subnet, CloudOps engineers treat them as a coarse-grained mechanism for broad network control rather than a fine-grained security tool.

Unlike Security Groups, NACLs process rules in a strict numerical order (from lowest to highest), and the first rule that matches the traffic is immediately applied. This allows for the *Explicit Deny* rules that Security Groups lack. If your environment is under a Distributed Denial of Service (DDoS) attack or you identify a malicious IP range, the NACL is where you will place an "Egress/Ingress Deny" rule to block that traffic at the subnet boundary before it even reaches your instances.

The stateless nature of NACLs is the most frequent source of configuration errors and exam pitfalls. Because the NACL has no memory of a connection, it does not automatically allow response traffic. If you allow inbound `HTTPS` traffic on port `443`, you must also create an outbound rule to allow the response to return to the user via ephemeral ports (typically `1024-65535`). A CloudOps engineer who forgets this outbound rule will find that their web servers are technically "up and running" but completely unreachable, as the NACL will drop the return packets. This requirement adds complexity but provides a rigorous level of control necessary for high-compliance environments.

In a well-architected VPC, the NACL serves as the "gate" that defines the subnet's purpose. For instance, a private subnet NACL might be configured to deny all inbound traffic from the Internet while allowing only specific internal CIDR blocks.

A subnet can be associated with only one NACL at a time, though a single NACL can protect multiple subnets.

When making changes, it is a best practice to use the AWS CLI `create-network-acl-entry` command to insert new rules with sufficient "room" between rule numbers (e.g., increments of 100) to allow for future adjustments without renumbering the entire list.

Table 10.1 highlights the key differences between Security Groups and NACLs that you must know for the exam.

VPC Endpoint

As a CloudOps engineer, one of your primary goals is to partner with the Security Operations (SecOps) team to minimize the "blast radius" and reduce the attack surface of your network. VPC Endpoints allow you to connect your VPC to supported AWS services and VPC endpoint services powered by AWS PrivateLink without requiring an Internet Gateway, NAT Gateway, VPN connection, or AWS Direct Connect connection. This ensures that traffic between your

TABLE 10.1 Security Group vs. NACL Comparison

Feature	Security Group	NACL
Scope	Instance (ENI)	Subnet
State	Stateful (returns allowed)	Stateless (returns must be explicit)
Rules	Allow only	Allow and deny
Order	All rules evaluated	Numerical order (first match wins)

VPC and AWS services does not leave the Amazon network, providing both enhanced security and significant cost savings by avoiding NAT Gateway data processing charges.

VPC endpoints come in two "flavors": *interface endpoints* and *gateway endpoints*. A solid understanding of the two is essential to balancing cost optimization with network security and performance.

Interface VPC Endpoints (AWS PrivateLink)

Interface endpoints are the most versatile type of endpoint, functioning as a collection of one or more Elastic Network Interfaces (ENIs) with private IP addresses from your subnet's IP address range. They act as a local entry point for traffic destined for a wide array of AWS services (such as SQS, EventBridge, EC2, etc.) or AWS PrivateLink-enabled services. The former group of services—those natively integrated with PrivateLink—can be reached privately without traversing the public Internet, allowing workloads in private subnets to interact with AWS APIs using only internal IP paths. This eliminates the need for NAT Gateways or Internet Gateways for these calls, reduces exposure to the public Internet, and often simplifies compliance requirements. The latter group—partner or third-party services exposed through PrivateLink—extends the same private-connectivity model to external providers, enabling organizations to consume SaaS (Software as a Service) applications without ever sending traffic over the public Internet.

For a CloudOps engineer, the operational beauty of interface endpoints lies in private DNS. When enabled, the standard public DNS hostname for the service (e.g., `events.us-east-1.amazonaws.com`) resolves to the private IP addresses of the endpoint's ENIs. This allows your applications to keep using the same code and SDKs while the traffic silently shifts from the public Internet to the private AWS backbone.

From a security perspective, interface endpoints are governed by Security Groups. Because the endpoint manifests as an ENI in your subnet, you must configure a Security Group to allow inbound traffic (typically on port 443) from the resources in your VPC that need to reach the service. This provides a granular level of control that gateway endpoints lack. As a CloudOps engineer, you are also responsible for ensuring high availability by deploying the interface endpoint across multiple subnets in different Availability Zones. AWS will provide a unique ENI and private IP for each Availability Zone you select, ensuring that a zonal failure does not break your connection to critical AWS management APIs.

When it comes to cost optimization, interface endpoints carry a different financial profile than their gateway counterparts. Unlike the free gateway endpoints, interface VPC endpoints incur a cost based on two factors: a flat hourly fee for each Availability Zone where the endpoint is provisioned, and a tiered data processing charge per GB of data that passes through the interface. For a CloudOps engineer, this means you must weigh the security benefits of PrivateLink against the budget, ensuring you only enable endpoints in the specific AZs where your workloads reside and monitoring CloudWatch metrics to prevent unexpected billing spikes from high-throughput data transfers.

Protecting Interface Endpoints with Data Perimeters

Protecting interface endpoints often involves verifying their *VPC endpoint policy*—a resource-based policy attached to the endpoint itself. A VPC endpoint policy is commonly used for data perimeter security to prevent data exfiltration for all traffic passing through the endpoint. Even if your Security Groups and NACLs allow the traffic, the endpoint policy can limit certain actions—such as restricting only a specific IAM role to publish events to an Amazon EventBridge Event Bus. Figure 10.2 illustrates this use case.

An application runs on an EC2 instance, hosted in a private subnet of a VPC. The EC2 instance has an IAM role attached to it (`MyEC2ApplicationRole`). The application has business logic to publish events to an Amazon EventBridge custom event bus (`MyCustomEventBus`). The key requirement is that the events must be published privately

FIGURE 10.2 Interface VPC endpoint architecture.

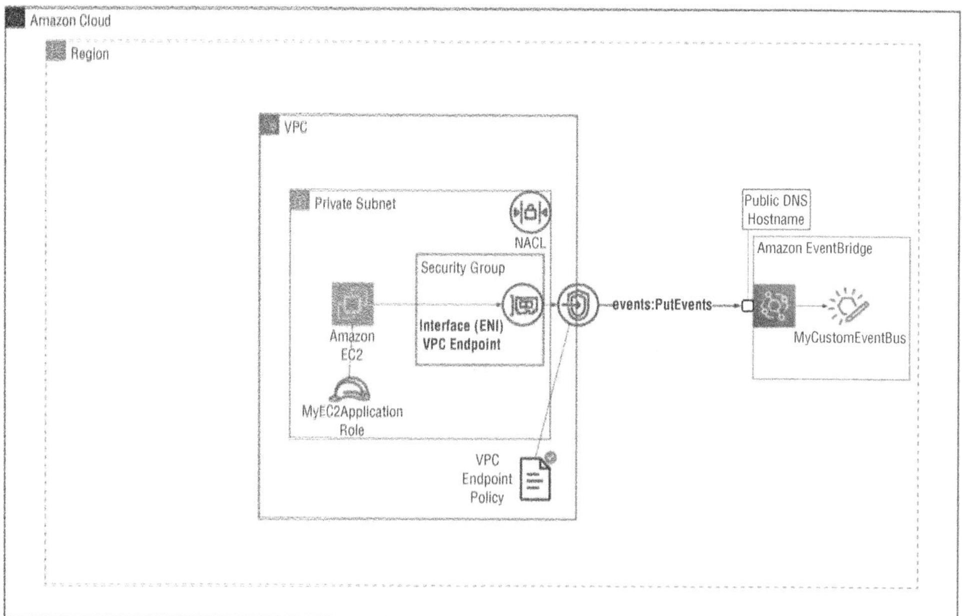

over the AWS network backbone, ensuring that traffic never traverses the public Internet and is strictly limited to a specific destination.

To achieve this, an interface VPC endpoint for EventBridge is deployed within the VPC. The security of this connection is governed by a VPC endpoint policy that explicitly restricts the data flow. Unlike a default "Full Access" policy, this configuration hardcodes the destination to one specific resource: `arn:aws:events:us-east-1:123456789012:event-bus/MyCustomEventBus`. By naming this ARN directly, you create a pinned connection. This ensures that even if the application code were modified—maliciously or accidentally—to point to a different event bus (such as one in a personal or competitor's AWS account), the VPC endpoint would physically block the request at the network layer.

Furthermore, the policy restricts the Principal to the `MyEC2ApplicationRole`. This creates a secondary layer of protection known as Identity Pinning. It ensures that even if other instances or users within the same VPC have the broad IAM permissions to `PutEvents`, they cannot use this specific private tunnel to do so. The endpoint acts as a specialized, identity-aware gate that only opens for a specific worker (the IAM role) delivering a specific package (the Event) to a specific address (the EventBus ARN), providing a robust layered defense against internal lateral movement and external data exfiltration.

Here is the complete JSON policy for the "pinned ARN" use case. This configuration ensures that only your specific EC2 role can use this endpoint, and it can only reach your specific custom EventBridge bus.

```
{
  "Version": "2012-10-17",
  "Statement": [
    {
      "Sid": "RestrictPutEventsToSpecificRoleAndSpecificBus",
      "Effect": "Allow",
      "Principal": {
        "AWS": "arn:aws:iam::123456789012:role/MyEC2ApplicationRole"
      },
      "Action": "events:PutEvents",
      "Resource": "arn:aws:events:us-east-1:123456789012:event-bus/
MyCustomEventBus"
    }
  ]
}
```

The key elements in the JSON policy are:

- **Principal:** Only traffic originated by the principal `MyEC2ApplicationRole` is allowed. If a developer logs into the EC2 instance as a different user, they will be blocked by the endpoint policy.
- **Action:** Only `events:PutEvents` is permitted. This prevents any administrative changes to the bus through this private link.
- **Resource:** Only the specific ARN for `MyCustomEventBus` is reachable. This is your primary defense against data exfiltration to external AWS accounts.

- **Effect:** An explicit `Allow` in a VPC endpoint policy creates a restricted boundary. Because every VPC endpoint starts with a default "Full Access" policy, replacing it with our specific JSON snippet triggers an Implicit Deny for everything not mentioned.

To attach a VPC endpoint policy for a VPC endpoint via the CLI, save the JSON file (e.g., `endpoint-policy.json`) and use the following `aws ec2 modify-vpc-endpoint` command. This allows you to programmatically enforce resource-level security boundaries without manual console intervention.

```
# Example: Applying a custom policy to an existing Interface Endpoint
aws ec2 modify-vpc-endpoint \
    --vpc-endpoint-id vpce-0123456789abcdef0 \
    --policy-document file://endpoint-policy.json
```

For the exam make sure you understand the following flags:

- `--vpc-endpoint-id`: This uniquely identifies the endpoint you wish to secure. Since endpoints are regional, ensure your CLI is configured for the correct AWS Region.
- `--policy-document`: This flag accepts the policy in valid JSON format. Using the `file://` prefix is the "CloudOps standard," as it allows you to version-control your policies in a repository rather than typing long, error-prone strings directly into the terminal.
- `--reset-policy`: If you want to discard a custom policy and return the endpoint to its default "Full Access" state (not recommended), you can use this flag instead of providing a document.

To learn more, visit: `https://docs.aws.amazon.com/cli/latest/reference/ec2/modify-vpc-endpoint.html`.

Table 10.2 highlights the three security layers you need to know for the exam when securing an interface VPC endpoint.

TABLE 10.2 Interface VPC Endpoint Security Layers

Layer	Associated With	Purpose
VPC Endpoint Policy	VPC Endpoint ARN	Controls *who* (IAM principal) can do *what* (action) on *which* resource.
Security Group	ENI	Controls network flow (inbound/outbound port, source CIDRs).
Network ACL	Subnet	Stateless packet filtering for the entire subnet where the ENIs live.

For you, as a CloudOps engineer, balancing these three layers (Security Groups, NACLs, and VPC endpoint policies) is a common exam scenario and a daily operational task. You can quickly describe an endpoint's configuration using the AWS CLI `describe-vpc-endpoints` command to verify its state and DNS entries.

An interface VPC endpoint maps to *exactly* one AWS PrivateLink service name. Remember: One interface endpoint = one service. However, a subnet can have multiple interface endpoints for different AWS services, or even multiple interface endpoints for the same service (allowed but rare). While you can put many interface endpoints in one subnet, many organizations place them in dedicated shared services subnets.

Gateway VPC Endpoints

Gateway endpoints are a specialized type of endpoint available exclusively for Amazon S3 and Amazon DynamoDB. Unlike interface endpoints, they do not use ENIs or private IP addresses. Instead, they function as a routing target in your VPC route table. When you create a gateway endpoint, AWS automatically adds a prefix list—a logical grouping of CIDR blocks for the service—to your selected route tables. You—as a CloudOps engineer—must ensure that the route table for every subnet requiring private access to S3 or DynamoDB is updated to point to the gateway endpoint (e.g., `pl-7ba54012 -> vpce-0a1b2c3d4e`).

Figure 10.3 shows the list of CIDR blocks assigned to the prefix list for Amazon S3 in `us-east-2`. Remember, this list is specific to a region because AWS exposes Amazon S3 using region-specific IP ranges, meaning the addresses used in Ohio (`us-east-2`) differ from those in Northern Virginia (`us-east-1`). Since a gateway endpoint works by injecting these regional S3 routes directly into your VPC's route table, the prefix list must remain

FIGURE 10.3 Prefix list for Amazon S3 in us-east-2.

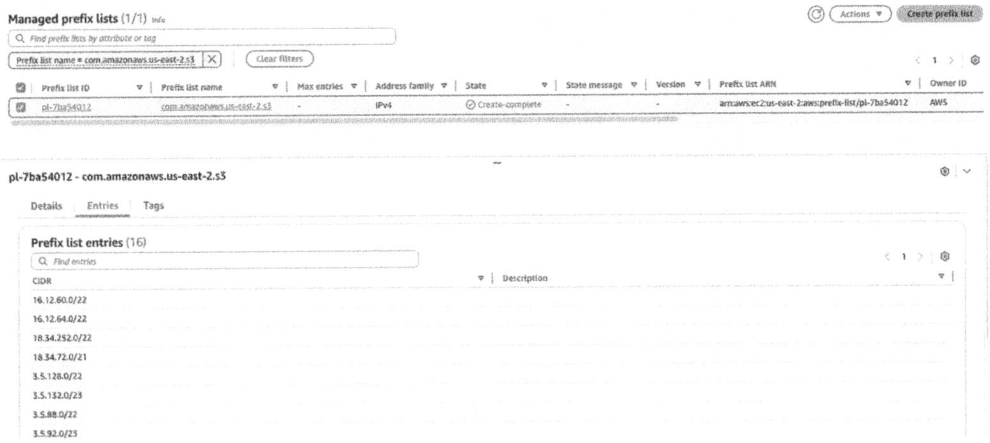

region-bound to ensure that your private traffic is routed to the correct regional service entry point—without ever traversing the public Internet.

The most significant advantage of gateway VPC endpoints for a CloudOps engineer is that they are entirely free of charge. There are no hourly fees or data processing costs associated with them. In a high-traffic environment where instances are constantly reading or writing massive amounts of data to S3 (or DynamoDB), routing that traffic through a NAT Gateway would be a massive architectural failure. By shifting that traffic to a gateway VPC endpoint, you immediately eliminate NAT data charges and improve throughput, as the traffic bypasses the bandwidth limits of a NAT Gateway. This makes them a "must-have" optimization for any production VPC.

Protecting Gateway Endpoints with Organization-Wide Data Perimeters

Despite their simplicity and cost-effectiveness, gateway endpoints require careful policy management. Because they do not use Security Groups, you must rely on Endpoint Policies and IAM roles to control access. A common CloudOps task is to restrict a gateway endpoint so that it only allows traffic to Amazon S3 buckets owned by your organization, preventing data exfiltration where a malicious actor might try to upload sensitive company data to a personal S3 bucket.

Figure 10.4 illustrates a scenario where we want to limit consumption of S3 buckets owned by our organization (`o-xxxxxxxxxxx`) to only principals in the organization. Each EC2 instance is associated to its own IAM role. For this use case we would apply the following JSON policy to the gateway endpoint:

FIGURE 10.4 Gateway VPC endpoint with organizational perimeter.

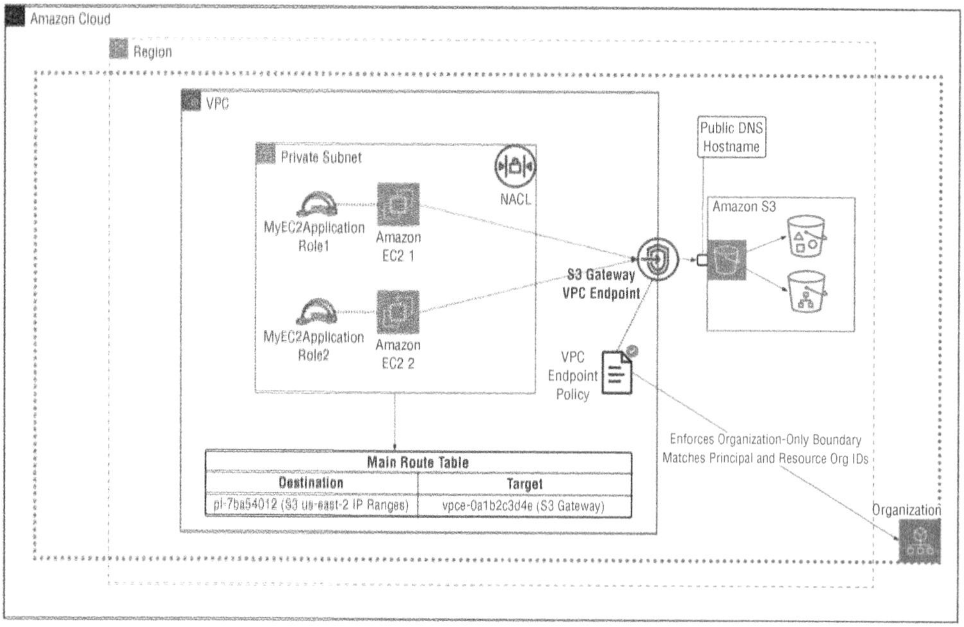

```
{
  "Version": "2012-10-17",
  "Statement": [
    {
      "Sid": "EnforceOrganizationBoundaryForS3",
      "Effect": "Allow",
      "Principal": "*",
      "Action": [
        "s3:GetObject",
        "s3:PutObject",
        "s3:ListBucket"
      ],
      "Resource": [
        "arn:aws:s3:::*",
        "arn:aws:s3:::*/*"
      ],
      "Condition": {
        "StringEquals": {
          "aws:PrincipalOrgID": "o-xxxxxxxxxxx",
          "aws:ResourceOrgID": "o-xxxxxxxxxxx"
        }
      }
    }
  ]
}
```

Here is the breakdown of the JSON endpoint policy:

- **Principal:** In a gateway endpoint policy, using a wildcard for the principal is the standard for operational efficiency. Instead of hardcoding a single IAM Role ARN—which would break connectivity for any new services you add later—you use `*` to indicate any identity. You then use the condition block below to narrow down to only the identities that belong to your trusted organization.
- **Action:** This defines the specific API calls permitted. For S3, a CloudOps engineer usually allows `s3:GetObject`, `s3:PutObject`, and `s3:ListBucket`. By omitting `s3:DeleteBucket`, you are ensuring that even an administrator connected through this private endpoint cannot accidentally (or maliciously) delete a production bucket, as the endpoint policy acts as a final filter.
- **Resource:** While `arn:aws:s3:::*` and `arn:aws:s3:::*/*` look broad, their scope is physically limited by the `ResourceOrgID` condition. It tells the VPC endpoint: "You may carry traffic to any S3 resource, provided it passes the organizational ownership test defined in the condition block."
- **Condition:**
  - `aws:PrincipalOrgID`: This is your identity guardrail. It ensures that only IAM roles or users belonging to your specific AWS Organization (`o-xxxxxxxxxxx`) can utilize this endpoint. It prevents an external actor with their own AWS credentials from using your private network to access their resources.

- `aws:ResourceOrgID`: This is the exfiltration controller. It is arguably the most important flag for a CloudOps engineer. It ensures the endpoint only allows traffic destined for S3 buckets that are owned by our AWS Organization. If an instance attempts to reach a bucket in a personal or third-party account, the endpoint will block the request at the network layer, regardless of how permissive the EC2 instance's IAM role might be.
- **Effect:** This is the fundamental "on/off switch" for the statement. In AWS, the default posture for any new policy is an Implicit Deny—if a permission isn't explicitly granted, it doesn't exist. By setting the `Effect` to `Allow`, you are creating a specific, authorized path through the VPC endpoint. However, you must remember that an Explicit Deny (if added in another statement) always defeats an Allow. This "Deny-overrides-Allow" logic is the cornerstone of AWS security, and fully aligns with the principle of least privilege.

The previous example demonstrated how *global condition keys* can be used to restrict the endpoint so that it only permits traffic where both the identity (the IAM role) and the Resource (the S3 bucket) belong to your organization. This "double-lock" strategy ensures that even if an identity has broad S3 permissions, it cannot physically send data to a bucket outside your corporate boundary. To learn more, visit: `https://docs.aws.amazon.com/IAM/latest/UserGuide/reference_policies_condition-keys.html`.

There are two important takeaways worth highlighting:

- First, for a CloudOps engineer, favoring Principal: `"*"` paired with the `aws:PrincipalOrgID` condition over a hardcoded ARN (as described in Figure 10.2) is a best practice in operational scalability. While hardcoding a specific identity follows the principle of least privilege in a vacuum, it also creates a "rigid" architecture that requires manual intervention every time a new service, logging agent, or IAM role is added to the VPC. By anchoring your security to the Organization ID, you establish a dynamic trust boundary that automatically encompasses any authorized resource within your corporate umbrella. This approach ensures that your VPC endpoint policy functions as a broad regional guardrail—allowing your entire cloud estate to benefit from secure, private connectivity without the administrative burden of micro-managing individual ARNs as your environment grows.

If a question asks for the most operationally efficient way to restrict access to a whole organization, look for the `aws:PrincipalOrgID` condition. If it asks to restrict access to one specific, high-security instance, then hardcoding the IAM Role ARN as the principal is the correct "Least Privilege" answer.

- Second, if you notice in Figure 10.4, you still see a NACL protecting the perimeter of our private subnet. While Security Groups are not applicable as a perimeter defense for gateway VPC endpoints (because gateway endpoints don't use ENIs), you may wonder whether NACLs are an alternative, or a supplemental way to enable layered, defense-in-depth for gateway endpoints. From a CloudOps perspective, however, attempting to use NACLs for this purpose is considered a significant architectural anti-pattern.

Because NACLs do not support AWS Managed Prefix Lists, you cannot simply reference "Amazon S3" as a target; instead, you would be forced to manually maintain dozens of individual public IP CIDR blocks that AWS frequently updates, leading to static configurations and inevitable connectivity outages. Furthermore, as a stateless firewall, a NACL lacks the resource-level intelligence of an endpoint policy; it can only block an IP address, whereas an endpoint policy can distinguish between your corporate S3 bucket and a malicious actor's bucket, providing the identity-aware "Data Perimeter" that a simple network-layer filter cannot achieve.

If the exam asks how to restrict access to specific S3 buckets while using a gateway endpoint, the answer is always endpoint policies or S3 bucket policies, never NACLs.

Interface and Gateway VPC Endpoints Comparison

Table 10.3 highlights the key differences between interface and gateway VPC endpoints you must know for the exam.

By eliminating the need to traverse the public Internet for AWS service traffic, gateway endpoints complete our tour of internal VPC components and set the stage for more complex architectures where your network must reach far beyond its own boundaries.

Configuring Private Connectivity

Building on the private, optimized access provided by VPC endpoints, a CloudOps engineer's responsibility often extends beyond the boundaries of a single VPC. In the networking world, we categorize these movements as *North-South* and *East-West* traffic. While North-South refers to data moving between your VPC and the outside world (the Internet or on-premises), East-West traffic describes the lateral movement of data between your AWS

TABLE 10.3 Interface Endpoint vs. Gateway Endpoint Comparison

Feature	Interface Endpoint	Gateway Endpoint
Technology	ENI (PrivateLink)	Route Table Target
Supported services	Most AWS Services	S3 and DynamoDB only
Cost	Hourly + Data Processing	Free
Security	Security Groups + NACLs + VPC Endpoint Policies	VPC Endpoint Policies only
DNS	Supports Private DNS	Uses Prefix Lists

resources—such as communication between a production VPC and a shared services VPC. As you scale, your primary goal is to ensure this East-West traffic remains entirely within the AWS private backbone, avoiding the latency, cost, and security risks of the public Internet.

This section covers the core exam objectives for extending your RFC 1918 private IP space across multiple accounts, regions, and hybrid environments. For a CloudOps engineer, this isn't just about "making a connection"—it's about architecting for transitivity, scalability, and resilience. Whether you are managing a handful of point-to-point links or a global hub-and-spoke network, the following components represent your toolkit for building a seamless, high-performance private highway.

VPC Peering

VPC Peering is the most direct way to connect two VPCs, allowing them to route traffic using private IPv4 or IPv6 addresses. For the certification, the most critical concept to internalize is that peering is non-transitive. If VPC A is peered with VPC B, and VPC B is peered with VPC C, VPC A cannot communicate with VPC C through the middleman. This limitation means that as your East-West traffic needs grow, you would eventually need a complex "full-mesh" of peering connections, which becomes an administrative nightmare for a CloudOps team to manage.

From a troubleshooting perspective, the two primary points of failure in peering are overlapping CIDR blocks and incomplete routing. You cannot peer VPCs that share any part of the same IP range (e.g., two VPCs both using `10.0.0.0/16`). Once a peering connection is established via the AWS CLI `create-vpc-peering-connection` command, your primary responsibility is to manually update the Route Tables in both VPCs. If an instance in VPC A cannot ping an instance in VPC B, your first step is to verify that the route exists (pointing to `pcx-xxxx`) and that the Security Groups in the destination VPC explicitly allow the private IP range of the source VPC.

Operational mastery also requires understanding the acceptance workflow. A peering request must be accepted by the owner of the peer VPC before traffic can flow. This is a common exam "gotcha" in cross-account scenarios where an engineer might initiate a request from a Dev account but forget to log into the Shared Services account to accept the peering connection. Furthermore, remember that peering does not support "Edge-to-Edge" routing; you cannot use a peering connection to reach a VPN or Direct Connect attached to the peered VPC, as the traffic will simply be dropped.

Transit Gateway (TGW)

As your architecture scales to dozens or hundreds of VPCs, the administrative burden of managing a full mesh of peering connections becomes unsustainable. This is where the AWS Transit Gateway (TGW) becomes instrumental in centralizing connectivity, simplifying routing, and replacing complex peering meshes with a scalable architecture. Acting as a regional network transit hub, the TGW provides a *hub-and-spoke* model that supports transitive routing. This allows you to connect thousands of VPCs and on-premises networks to a single central gateway, drastically reducing "routing sprawl" by centralizing all lateral East-West traffic into a single point of inspection and control.

Operational mastery of the TGW involves managing Transit Gateway Route Tables and Attachments. Unlike standard VPC route tables, TGW route tables allow you to create sophisticated isolation policies—such as allowing "Spoke" VPCs to talk to a "Shared Services" VPC for centralized logging, while strictly preventing those Spokes from communicating with each other. If a new VPC is added to the network but cannot reach the central hub, a CloudOps engineer must verify the Attachment status and ensure the TGW route table has successfully "propagated" the new CIDR block. You can audit these connections using the AWS CLI `describe-transit-gateway-vpc-attachments` command.

Troubleshooting TGW often centers on Availability Zone (AZ) Affinity. When you attach a VPC to a TGW, you must specify which AZs the TGW should use. If you only select `us-east-1a` but your instances reside in `us-east-1b`, the traffic will fail to reach the gateway. As a CloudOps engineer, you must ensure that the Transit Gateway Attachment includes at least one subnet in every AZ where you have resources. This Multi-AZ attachment strategy ensures that your regional hub remains resilient and does not become a single point of failure for your internal East-West traffic.

Figure 10.5 illustrates a reference multi-account architecture where the network account centrally owns the Transit Gateway and shares it across the organization using AWS Resource Access Manager (AWS RAM). The TGW connects to attachments in multiple VPCs, including the Shared Services VPC. This VPC hosts CloudOps tools such as SSM documents and SSM Automation runbooks in dedicated operations subnets (`subnet-ops-a`, `subnet-ops-b`). The Shared Services VPC also hosts AWS Managed AD in identity subnets (`subnet-ad-a`, `subnet-ad-b`). The TGW connects also to attachments in a workload VPC in the Workloads OU, which exposes application resources in subnets across two Availability Zones (`subnet-app-a`, `subnet-app-b`), and data resources in subnets `subnet-data-a`, and `subnet-data-b`. The Network Account also hosts a dedicated Endpoints VPC containing interface endpoints for core AWS services, as well as an Inspection VPC where firewall appliances operate behind their own TGW attachments. Together, these components demonstrate the hub-and-spoke connectivity model that CloudOps engineers must understand for the SOA-C03 exam: the TGW provides centralized, scalable routing; the Network Account owns shared network infrastructure; and each VPC participates through isolated, AZ-distributed attachments that maintain high availability and clear operational boundaries.

Site-to-Site VPN and Direct Connect (DX)

The final piece of private connectivity is reaching back to the on-premises data center, completing the North-South hybrid circuit. An AWS Site-to-Site VPN is the go-to solution for rapid, encrypted connectivity over the public Internet. While it is cost-effective and can be provisioned in minutes, it is architecturally limited to 1.25 Gbps per tunnel. Even with Equal-Cost Multi-Path (ECMP) to aggregate multiple tunnels, the traffic remains subject to Internet conditions—unpredictable congestion and varying BGP hops that cause jitter and inconsistent latency.

For workloads requiring high bandwidth and predictable, sub-millisecond latency, a CloudOps engineer must implement AWS Direct Connect (DX). Direct Connect provides a dedicated physical fiber connection that bypasses the Internet entirely. In terms of high

FIGURE 10.5 Transit Gateway reference architecture.

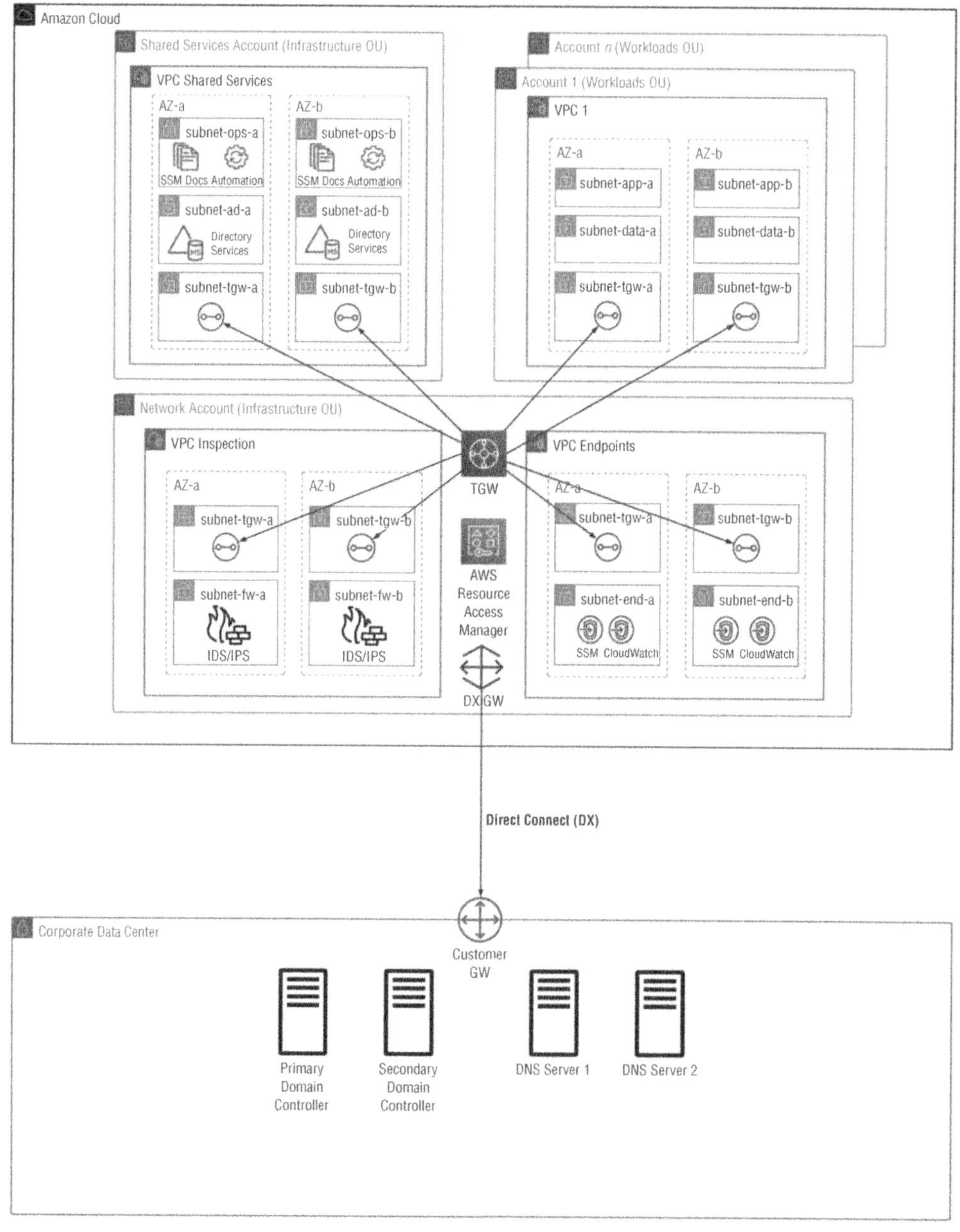

bandwidth, this means dedicated ports at 1 Gbps, 10 Gbps, 100 Gbps, or even 400 Gbps. For smaller requirements, AWS Direct Connect Partners offer hosted connections with granular increments starting at 50 Mbps. This dedicated path ensures a deterministic network experience where latency remains stable, often in the low single-digit milliseconds, regardless of global Internet traffic spikes.

Troubleshooting these hybrid links requires a deep understanding of BGP (Border Gateway Protocol) and MTU (Maximum Transmission Unit). A common CloudOps challenge is the fragmentation of large packets; while a VPN is typically limited to a 1500-byte MTU (often less due to IPsec overhead), Direct Connect supports Jumbo Frames (up to 9001 bytes). This significantly reduces CPU overhead and stabilizes latency for massive data transfers, such as moving 2+ TB of daily database logs. If a tunnel shows as up and running, but data isn't flowing, you should verify BGP peering status or check for MTU mismatches that cause silent packet drops.

Resilience is the hallmark of a senior CloudOps engineer's design. The "Gold Standard" architecture—and a recurring exam theme—is to use Direct Connect as the primary path and a Site-to-Site VPN as a cost-effective failover. By manipulating BGP AS_PATH prepending or BGP Communities, you can ensure that AWS prefers the high-speed DX line during normal operations but automatically re-routes traffic over the encrypted VPN tunnel if the physical fiber is ever severed.

Table 10.4 summarizes the key differences between site-to-site VPNs and DX that you need to know for the exam.

While Direct Connect and VPN provide the physical North-South highways for your hybrid traffic, they only solve half of the connectivity puzzle. For you, as a CloudOps

TABLE 10.4 Site-to-site VPN vs. Direct Connect Comparison

Feature	Site-to-Site VPN	Direct Connect (DX)
Max bandwidth	~1.25 Gbps per tunnel (up to 5 Gbps with large tunnels)	Up to 400 Gbps per port
Latency	Variable	Deterministic (low-ms, jitter-free)
MTU support	1,500 bytes (standard)	Up to 9,001 bytes (Jumbo Frames)
Setup time	Minutes to hours (self-service)	Weeks to months (requires physical fiber)
Cost profile	Low upfront; hourly connection fees + standard Internet Data Transfer Out (DTO)	Higher upfront; hourly port-hour fees + significantly lower DTO rates
Encryption	IPsec encrypted by default (AES-128/256)	Not encrypted by default; requires MACsec for Layer 2 or VPN over DX for Layer 3 security

engineer, establishing a private IP path is only functional if your on-premises servers can resolve the DNS hostnames of your internal AWS Resources, and vice versa. To bridge this gap between routing and resolution, we must move from the physical layer to the naming layer in our next section.

Configuring Domain Name System (DNS) Services

DNS is one of the most foundational components of any cloud environment, yet it often remains invisible until something breaks. Every application endpoint, API gateway, load balancer, and hybrid network path ultimately depends on DNS to translate human-readable names into routable IP addresses. For CloudOps engineers, DNS is not simply a naming mechanism—it is a critical operational control plane that influences availability, failover behavior, hybrid connectivity, and the overall reliability of distributed systems. Understanding how DNS works in AWS is therefore essential for maintaining stable environments and executing effective Business Continuity and Disaster Recovery (BCDR) strategies.

In Chapter 2, we introduced the concept of Fault Isolation Boundaries—the layered fault domains AWS uses to contain failures: Availability Zones isolate data-center-level faults, regions isolate large-scale geographic failures, and global services operate above regional boundaries. Amazon Route 53 is one of the clearest examples of a global control-plane service. Unlike Region-scoped services such as EC2, RDS, or VPC, Route 53's control plane is globally distributed and not tied to any single region. This means that hosted zones, DNS records, routing policies, health checks, and query logging configurations are all managed through a control plane that sits outside the region-level fault domain. Even if an entire region becomes unavailable, Route 53 continues to function, continues to answer DNS queries, and continues to enforce routing policies that direct traffic to healthy endpoints.

This global nature of Route 53 has direct implications across the CloudOps cycle. During the Deploy phase, DNS becomes part of the application's entry point and must be provisioned consistently across environments. In the Monitor phase, DNS health checks and query logs provide early indicators of degraded endpoints or misrouted traffic. During the Sustain phase—the heart of CloudOps work—Route 53's global resilience ensures that service reachability is maintained even when regional workloads degrade or fail. In the Secure phase, DNS query logging and Resolver rules help enforce controlled name-resolution paths and detect anomalous or unauthorized behavior. Finally, during the Optimize phase, routing policies such as weighted or latency-based routing allow CloudOps teams to shape traffic, improve performance, and execute controlled rollouts without disrupting clients.

In operational environments, CloudOps engineers rarely modify DNS manually. Instead, DNS configurations are typically managed through Infrastructure as Code (IaC) tools such as AWS CloudFormation, the AWS Cloud Development Kit (CDK), or HashiCorp Terraform. These tools ensure that DNS changes are version-controlled, peer-reviewed, and deployed consistently across accounts and Regions. While this chapter uses the AWS CLI to illustrate the underlying API interactions—which is essential for exam readiness and conceptual clarity—it is important to recognize that IaC-driven automation is the standard approach for managing DNS in production. This automation supports every phase of the CloudOps cycle: DNS records are created during the Deploy phase, monitored through health checks and logs, sustained through controlled rollouts, secured through policy-driven IaC pipelines, and optimized through safe, repeatable routing-policy updates.

In other words, Route 53 is not just a DNS service—it is a global routing control plane that underpins the reliability, continuity, and operational stability of your cloud workloads. With this conceptual foundation in place, we can now explore how to configure Route 53 and Route 53 Resolver using the AWS CLI, how to implement routing policies that support BCDR strategies, and how to enable DNS query logging for operational visibility. Each section builds on the idea that DNS is a strategic component of the CloudOps toolkit—one that must be understood not only in terms of configuration syntax, but also in terms of its role in sustaining and optimizing cloud workloads.

Configuring Amazon Route 53

Route 53 is AWS's globally distributed authoritative DNS service. It is responsible for answering DNS queries for your domains, integrating with AWS services like load balancers and CloudFront, and supporting advanced routing policies that influence how traffic flows during normal operations and during failover events. For CloudOps engineers, Route 53 is a critical operational tool: it enables controlled rollouts, blue/green deployments, cross-Region failover, and internal service discovery.

Before you can create DNS records, you must create a hosted zone, which acts as the container for all DNS entries associated with a domain. Public hosted zones serve Internet-facing domains, while private hosted zones serve internal names within one or more VPCs. Private hosted zones are especially important in multi-account or hybrid environments, where consistent internal naming conventions reduce operational complexity and improve troubleshooting workflows.

Once hosted zones are created, CloudOps engineers typically automate DNS record creation as part of deployment pipelines. This ensures that DNS changes are version-controlled, repeatable, and auditable—all key operational requirements. The AWS CLI, along with IaC tools such as AWS CloudFormation, the AWS CDK, and HashiCorp Terraform, plays a central role in this automation, allowing DNS changes to be integrated into CI/CD workflows, infrastructure-as-code pipelines, and cross-account provisioning routines.

Creating Hosted Zones

Hosted zones are the foundational building blocks of Route 53. They define the DNS namespace for your domain and store the DNS records that determine how clients reach your workloads. CloudOps engineers often create hosted zones programmatically as part of environment provisioning, ensuring that DNS is consistently configured across development, staging, and production environments.

Public hosted zones are used for Internet-facing domains. When you register a domain or migrate DNS to Route 53, you create a public hosted zone that becomes the authoritative source for DNS queries on the public Internet. Private hosted zones, on the other hand, are used for internal service discovery within VPCs. They allow you to create internal naming conventions such as `db12.aws.example.com`, which are essential for multi-tier architectures and hybrid environments.

Creating a Public Hosted Zone

The following command creates a public hosted zone for the domain `example.com`:

```
aws route53 create-hosted-zone \
  --name example.com \
  --caller-reference "$(date +%s)"
```

In this command:

- `--name`: The domain name for which Route 53 becomes authoritative.
- `--caller-reference`: Ensures the request is unique. You must use a unique string every time you submit a `create-hosted-zone` request. This value can be any unique string, for example, a date/time stamp.

Creating a Private Hosted Zone

To create a private hosted zone you set the `PrivateZone` key to `true` in the value of the `--hosted-zone-config` flag. The following command creates a private hosted zone (PHZ) associated with a specific VPC:

```
aws route53 create-hosted-zone \
  --name aws.example.com \
  --vpc '{
    "VPCRegion": "us-east-1",
    "VPCId": "vpc-1234567890abcdef0"
  }' \
  --hosted-zone-config '{
    "Comment": "Private zone for internal services",
    "PrivateZone": true
  }' \
  --caller-reference "$(date +%s)"
```

In this command:

- `--vpc`: JSON object specifying the VPC to associate with the hosted zone.
  - `VPCRegion`: Region where the VPC resides.
  - `VPCId`: Identifier of the VPC.
- `-- hosted-zone-config`: JSON object defining metadata and marking the zone as private.

- `Comment`: Human-readable description.
- `PrivateZone`: Must be `true` for private hosted zones.

For a complete reference of this command, visit: `https://docs.aws.amazon.com/cli/latest/reference/route53/create-hosted-zone.html`.

Associating a VPC

In multi-account or shared-services architectures, you often need to associate the same private hosted zone with multiple VPCs. To associate an additional VPC to an existing private hosted zone use the following command:

```
aws route53 associate-vpc-with-hosted-zone \
  --hosted-zone-id Z123456ABCDEFG \
  --vpc '{
    "VPCRegion": "us-west-2",
    "VPCId": "vpc-0abc1234def567890"
  }'
```

In this command:

- `--hosted-zone-id`: Identifies the hosted zone to modify.
- `--vpc`: JSON object specifying the additional VPC.
  - `VPCRegion`: Region of the VPC.
  - `VPCId`: VPC identifier.

To learn more, visit: `https://docs.aws.amazon.com/cli/latest/reference/route53/associate-vpc-with-hosted-zone.html`.

Creating DNS Records

Once a hosted zone exists, you populate it with DNS records. DNS records determine how clients reach your workloads, and they play a central role in application availability, performance, and failover behavior. CloudOps engineers frequently automate DNS record creation during deployments, ensuring that DNS changes are consistent and auditable.

Creating an A Record

The following command creates a simple A record pointing to an IPv4 address:

```
aws route53 change-resource-record-sets \
  --hosted-zone-id Z123456ABCDEFG \
  --change-batch '{
    "Changes": [
      {
        "Action": "CREATE",
        "ResourceRecordSet": {
          "Name": "app.example.com",
          "Type": "A",
          "TTL": 60,
          "ResourceRecords": [
            { "Value": "203.0.113.10" }
```

```
          ]
        }
      }
    ]
  }'
```

In this command:

- `--change-batch`: JSON payload describing the DNS change.
  - `Changes`: List of changes to apply.
  - `Action`: `CREATE`, `UPSERT`, or `DELETE`.
  - `ResourceRecordSet`: DNS record definition.
    - `Name`: FQDN of the record.
    - `Type`: DNS record type (A, AAAA, CNAME, etc.).
    - `TTL`: Time-to-live in seconds.
    - `ResourceRecords`: List of IPs or values.

Creating an Alias Record to an ALB

The following command creates an Alias A record pointing to an Application Load Balancer:

```
aws route53 change-resource-record-sets \
  --hosted-zone-id Z123456ABCDEFG \
  --change-batch '{
    "Changes": [
      {
        "Action": "UPSERT",
        "ResourceRecordSet": {
          "Name": "web.example.com",
          "Type": "A",
          "AliasTarget": {
            "HostedZoneId": "Z35SXDOTRQ7X7K",
            "DNSName": "my-alb-123456.us-east-1.elb.amazonaws.com",
            "EvaluateTargetHealth": true
          }
        }
      }
    ]
  }'
```

In this command:

- `AliasTarget`: Defines the AWS-managed endpoint to route traffic to.
  - `HostedZoneId`: Hosted zone ID of the ALB.
  - `DNSName`: DNS name of the ALB.
  - `EvaluateTargetHealth`: Enables health-based routing.

To learn more, visit: `https://docs.aws.amazon.com/cli/latest/reference/route53/change-resource-record-sets.html`.

Configuring Route 53 Resolver (Hybrid DNS)

Hybrid environments introduce a unique set of DNS challenges because name resolution must work consistently across AWS VPCs, on-premises networks, and sometimes multiple cloud providers. Inside a VPC, DNS resolution is handled by the `AmazonProvidedDNS` service, which is always reachable at the `.2` address of the VPC CIDR block (for example, `10.0.0.2` in a `10.0.0.0/16` VPC). This `.2` address is not a real EC2 instance—it is a highly available, distributed service that provides recursive DNS resolution for resources inside the VPC. For CloudOps engineers, understanding the role of this `.2` address is essential because it is the default DNS resolver for EC2 instances, Lambda functions in VPCs, ECS tasks, and any workload that relies on VPC DNS. It is also the foundation upon which Route 53 Resolver builds hybrid DNS capabilities.

However, the `AmazonProvidedDNS` service only resolves names that are either public or defined in private hosted zones associated with the VPC (e.g., `aws.example.com`). It cannot resolve on-premises domains such as `db15.corp.example.com`, Active Directory service records, or legacy internal DNS zones. This is where Route 53 *Resolver* becomes critical. Resolver extends the VPC's DNS capabilities by providing inbound endpoints, outbound endpoints, and Resolver rules that determine how specific domain suffixes should be resolved. Outbound endpoints allow AWS workloads to forward DNS queries to on-premises DNS servers, whereas inbound endpoints allow on-premises systems to resolve private hosted zone records inside AWS. Resolver rules act as the routing table for DNS queries, determining which domains should be forwarded, which should be resolved locally, and which should use the default `AmazonProvidedDNS`.

From an operational perspective, CloudOps engineers are responsible for ensuring that DNS resolution behaves predictably across hybrid networks—especially during migrations, failovers, and BCDR events. This includes designing Resolver rules that correctly route internal domains, ensuring outbound endpoints are deployed across multiple subnets for high availability, and validating that Security Groups and network ACLs allow DNS traffic (UDP/TCP 53) between AWS and on-premises DNS servers. Engineers must also understand how the .2 resolver interacts with Resolver rules: workloads still send queries to the .2 address, but Route 53 Resolver intercepts and evaluates those queries against its rule set before deciding whether to resolve them locally or forward them externally. This layered model is central to hybrid DNS reliability and is a core competency for CloudOps engineers operating in enterprise environments.

Creating Route 53 Resolver Endpoints and Rules

The following sections walk you through the practical workflow for configuring Route 53 Resolver in hybrid environments. Resolver endpoints allow DNS queries to flow between AWS and on-premises networks, enabling unified name resolution across distributed architectures.

Creating an Outbound Resolver Endpoint

The workflow to create an outbound resolver endpoint follows this three-step Resolver pattern:

1. Create the outbound endpoint.
2. Define the forwarding rule.
3. Associate the rule with the VPC.

These steps map cleanly to the network path, routing logic, and scope of application. Workloads continue sending DNS queries to the VPC+2 (.2) resolver, but Resolver intercepts those queries and applies this configuration chain to determine whether to resolve them locally or forward them to on-premises DNS servers.

Step 1: Create the Outbound Endpoint

The following command creates an outbound resolver endpoint, which allows AWS workloads to forward DNS queries to on-premises DNS servers:

```
aws route53resolver create-resolver-endpoint \
  --creator-request-id "$(date +%s)" \
  --name outbound-hybrid-endpoint \
  --direction OUTBOUND \
  --security-group-ids sg-0123456789abcdef0 \
  --ip-addresses '[
    {
      "SubnetId": "subnet-1a",
      "Ip": "10.0.1.5"
    },
    {
      "SubnetId": "subnet-1b",
      "Ip": "10.0.2.5"
    }
  ]'
```

In this command:

- `--creator-request-id`: Unique string for idempotency.
- `--name`: Human-readable name for the endpoint.
- `--direction`: Must be `OUTBOUND` to forward queries externally.
- `--security-group-ids`: Security groups applied to the endpoint ENIs; must allow `UDP/TCP 53`.
- `--ip-addresses`: List of (at least two) ENIs to create:
  - `SubnetId`: Subnet where the ENI is created.
  - `Ip`: Optional static IP; AWS assigns one if omitted.

Upon successful execution, the command returns a JSON object similar to the following output (truncated for clarity):

```
{
  "ResolverEndpoint": {
    "Id": "rslvr-out-1234567890abcdef",
    "CreatorRequestId": "1709481234",
    "Arn": "arn:aws:route53resolver:us-east-1:111122223333:resolver-endpoint/
rslvr-out-1234567890abcdef",
    "Direction": "OUTBOUND",
    "IpAddressCount": 2,
    "Name": "outbound-hybrid-endpoint",
    "Status": "CREATING"
  }
}
```

We will use the value of the `ResolverEndpoint Id` in the next command to define a rule for this outbound resolver endpoint.

Figure 10.6 illustrates the two outbound resolvers endpoints we just created.

To learn more, visit: `https://docs.aws.amazon.com/cli/latest/reference/route53resolver/create-resolver-endpoint.html`.

Step 2: Define the Forwarding Rule

The following command creates a Resolver rule that forwards queries for the `corp.example.com` domain to an on-premises DNS server:

```
aws route53resolver create-resolver-rule \
  --creator-request-id "$(date +%s)" \
  --name forward-onprem \
  --rule-type FORWARD \
  --domain-name corp.example.com \
  --target-ips '[
    {
      "Ip": "192.168.1.10",
      "Port": 53
    }
  ]' \
  --resolver-endpoint-id rslvr-out-1234567890abcdef
```

In this command:

- `--creator-request-id`: Unique string for idempotency.
- `--rule-type FORWARD`: Sends matching queries to external DNS servers.
- `--domain-name`: Domain suffix to match (e.g., `corp.example.com`).
- `--target-ips`: List of DNS servers to forward queries to:
  - `Ip`: On-prem DNS server IP.
  - `Port`: Usually 53.
- `--resolver-endpoint-id`: The ID of the outbound resolver endpoint that you want to use to route DNS queries to the IP addresses that you specify in `--target-ips`.

FIGURE 10.6 Outbound endpoint architecture with two Availability Zones.

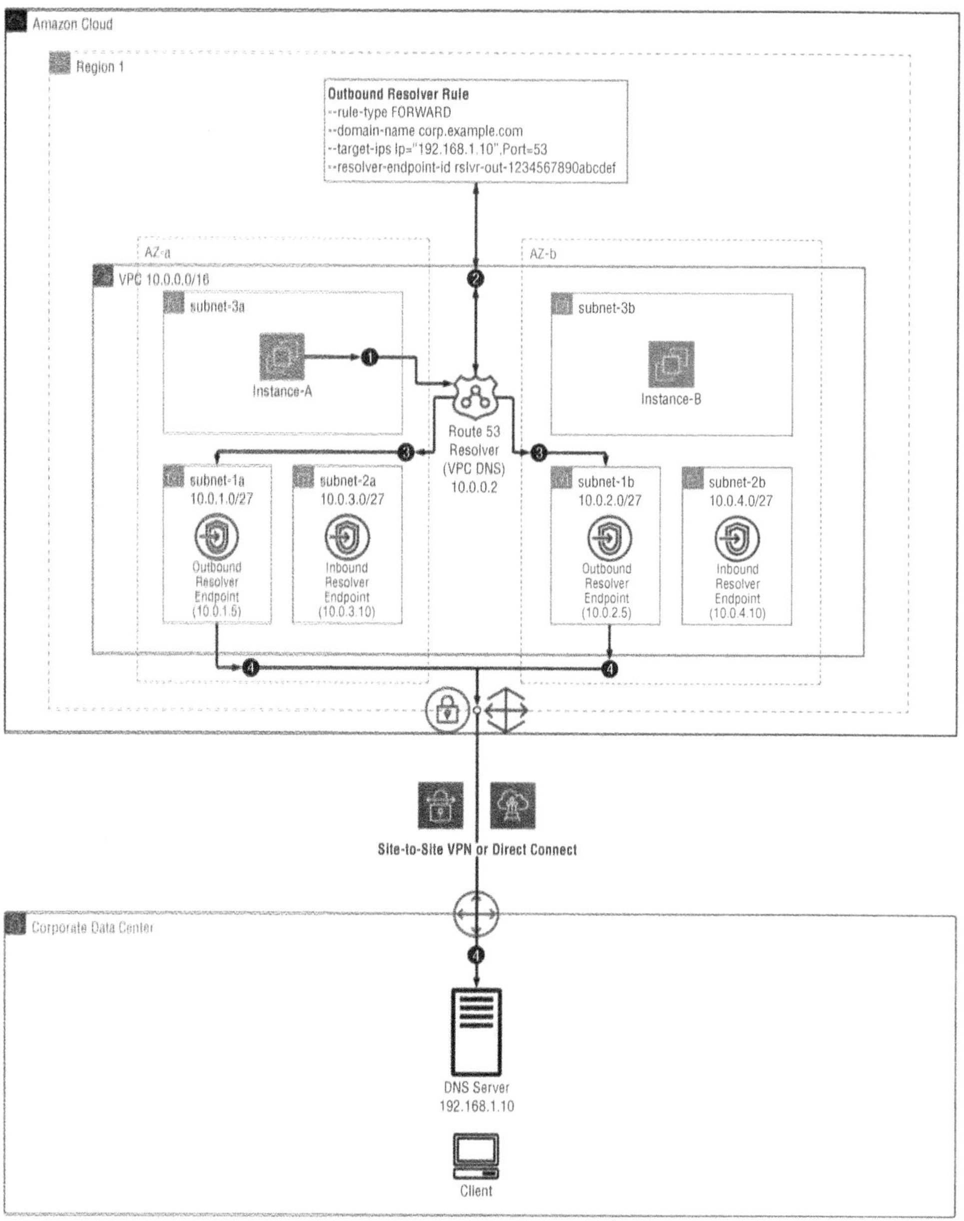

To learn more, visit: `https://docs.aws.amazon.com/cli/latest/reference/route53resolver/create-resolver-rule.html`.

Step 3: Associate the Rule with the VPC

The following command associates the forwarding rule with a VPC so that workloads inside the VPC use it:

```
aws route53resolver associate-resolver-rule \
  --resolver-rule-id rslvr-rr-abcdef123456 \
  --vpc-id vpc-1234567890abcdef0
```

In this command:

- `--resolver-rule-id`: Identifies the rule to associate.
- `--vpc-id`: The VPC that will use the rule for DNS resolution.

To learn more, visit: `https://docs.aws.amazon.com/cli/latest/reference/route53resolver/associate-resolver-rule.html`.

Figure 10.6 shows the outbound resolver pattern in action. When a workload on `Instance-A` attempts to access a resource whose URI (Uniform Resource Identifier) ends with `corp.example.com`, the instance first sends its DNS query to the Route 53 Resolver (Step 1). The Resolver evaluates the outbound forwarding rule for `corp.example.com`—which specifies rule-type `FORWARD`, the on-premises target IP `192.168.1.10:53`, and the associated outbound endpoint ID `rslvr-out-1234567890abcdef`—and selects it as the most specific match (Step 2). The Resolver then forwards the query to the two outbound resolver endpoint ENIs (`10.0.1.5` and `10.0.2.5`), which are deployed in separate subnets and Availability Zones for resilience (Step 3). Finally, each endpoint can forward the DNS query across the hybrid link to the on-premises DNS server at `192.168.1.10`, where the authoritative answer for `corp.example.com` is resolved (Step 4).

Operationally, outbound Route 53 resolver configuration always follows the same three-step workflow: create the outbound endpoint, define a forwarding rule, and associate that rule with one or more VPCs. As illustrated in Figure 10.6, outbound endpoints are zonal resources, so CloudOps engineers deploy at least two IP addresses across different subnets for resilience, and Security Groups must explicitly allow outbound DNS traffic (UDP/TCP 53) to on-premises resolvers. Forwarding rules determine which domains are sent to which external DNS servers, and they are evaluated using DNS suffix matching: a rule applies when the queried domain ends with the rule's domain name. When multiple rules could match a query, Route 53 Resolver selects the one with the longest and most specific suffix, ensuring that narrow, intentional rules override broader ones—for example, a rule for `corp.example.com` takes precedence over a general rule for `example.com` when resolving `db.corp.example.com`. This behavior enables precise hybrid DNS routing and prevents broad forwarding rules from unintentionally capturing traffic meant for more specific domains.

Creating an Inbound Resolver Endpoint

Inbound resolver endpoints allow DNS resolvers in on-premises networks to query private DNS records hosted inside your VPC. This is the inverse of outbound forwarding: instead of AWS sending DNS queries to on-premises, your on-premises DNS servers send queries into AWS. CloudOps engineers typically deploy inbound endpoints in hybrid architectures where workloads span AWS and data centers, and where private Route 53 zones must be resolvable from outside the VPC. Before configuring on-premises resolvers, you must first create the inbound endpoint that exposes AWS DNS to external networks.

```
aws route53resolver create-resolver-endpoint \
  --creator-request-id "$(date +%s)" \
  --name inbound-hybrid-endpoint \
  --direction INBOUND \
  --security-group-ids sg-0123456789abcdef0 \
  --ip-addresses '[
    {
      "SubnetId": "subnet-2a",
      "Ip": "10.0.3.10"
    },
    {
      "SubnetId": "subnet-2b",
      "Ip": "10.0.4.10"
    }
  ]'
```

In this command:

- `--creator-request-id`: Unique string for idempotency.
- `--name`: Human-readable name for the endpoint.
- `--direction`: Must be `INBOUND` to accept DNS queries from external networks into AWS.
- `--security-group-ids`: Security groups applied to the endpoint ENIs; must allow `UDP/TCP 53`.
- `--ip-addresses`: List of (at least two) ENIs to create:
  - `SubnetId`: Subnet where the ENI is created.
  - `Ip`: Optional static IP; AWS assigns one if omitted.

Figure 10.7 illustrates the two inbound resolvers endpoints we just created.

Inbound endpoints do not require forwarding rules; they automatically resolve any private hosted zones associated with the VPC. Because they are zonal resources, CloudOps engineers deploy at least two IP addresses across different subnets to ensure resilience, and Security Groups must explicitly allow inbound DNS traffic (UDP/TCP 53) from on-premises resolver IPs. On-premises DNS servers must be configured to forward AWS-specific queries to the inbound endpoint IPs, ensuring that hybrid workloads can resolve private AWS names consistently. Inbound endpoints are commonly used in split-horizon DNS architectures and form the AWS-side entry point for DNS queries originating outside the cloud environment.

FIGURE 10.7 Inbound endpoint architecture with two Availability Zones.

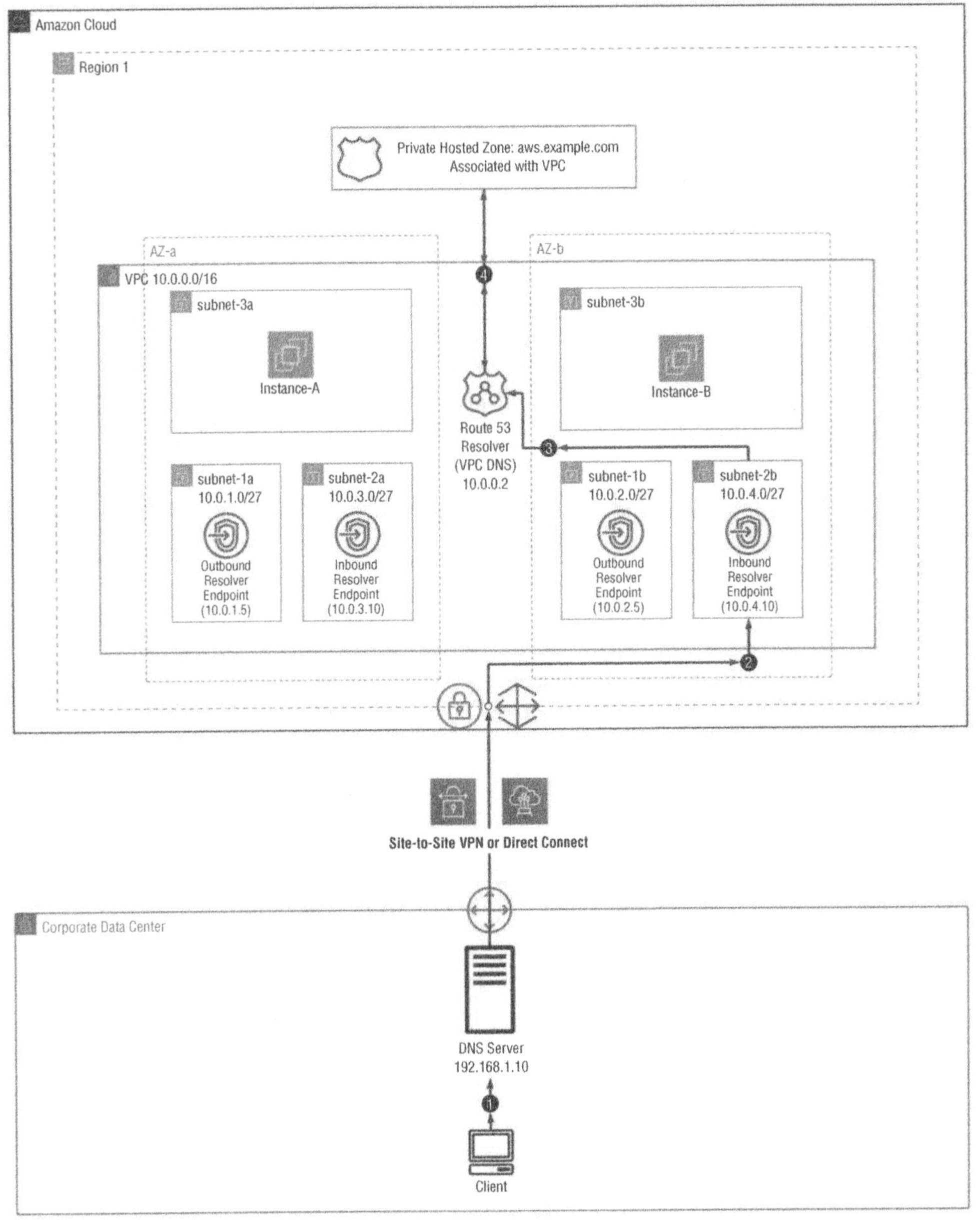

Figure 10.7 illustrates the inbound resolver pattern in action. When a client in the on-premises environment attempts to access a resource whose URI ends with `aws.example.com`, the client first sends its DNS query to the on-premises DNS Server (Step 1). The on-premises DNS Resolver evaluates its forwarding configuration and determines that queries for `aws.example.com` should be sent to the inbound resolver endpoint in AWS at `10.0.4.10` (Step 2). The inbound endpoint receives the query and passes it to the Route 53 Resolver inside the VPC—represented by the VPC DNS address `10.0.0.2`—which now becomes responsible for resolving the name (Step 3). Finally, the Route 53 Resolver identifies that the domain `aws.example.com` is authoritative in the Private Hosted Zone associated with the VPC, and retrieves the corresponding record (Step 4).

For hybrid DNS architectures, deploy inbound and outbound resolver endpoints in different subnets and different Availability Zones. This separation improves resilience, keeps security boundaries clean, and prevents a single subnet or AZ failure from impacting both DNS directions.

Implementing Route 53 Routing Policies and DNS Query Logging

Once hybrid DNS resolution is in place, CloudOps engineers must ensure that traffic entering the environment is routed intelligently and that DNS behavior is observable. Route 53 routing policies and DNS query logging form the operational layer that sits above resolver and authoritative DNS. While resolver governs how names are resolved inside hybrid networks, routing policies determine where clients are directed, and query logging provides the visibility needed to validate, troubleshoot, and optimize DNS behavior. Together, these capabilities allow CloudOps teams to shape traffic, enforce failover strategies, and maintain a clear operational picture of DNS activity across distributed systems.

Routing policies are especially important in Multi-Region and multi-environment architectures. They allow CloudOps engineers to control how clients reach workloads during deployments, migrations, and BCDR events. Weighted routing supports gradual traffic shifting during blue/green rollouts, while failover routing ensures that clients are automatically redirected to healthy endpoints when primary systems degrade. These policies operate at the global Route 53 control plane, meaning they remain functional even if a Region becomes impaired—a critical property for high-availability architectures.

DNS query logging complements routing policies by providing the visibility required to validate routing decisions and detect anomalies. Query logs reveal which clients are resolving which names, how frequently, and from which networks. This is invaluable for troubleshooting hybrid DNS issues, verifying that forwarding rules are working as intended, and identifying misconfigurations such as stale records or unexpected traffic patterns. For CloudOps engineers, DNS logs are not optional—they are a core operational signal that supports monitoring, security, and compliance workflows.

The following sections walk through the key routing policies and logging configurations CloudOps engineers must master for the SOA-C03 exam and for real-world operations.

Weighted Routing

Weighted routing allows CloudOps teams to distribute traffic across multiple endpoints based on assigned weights. This is commonly used for blue/green deployments, A/B testing, and gradual migrations between environments. Because weighted routing is evaluated at the global Route 53 control plane, it provides a reliable mechanism for shifting traffic without modifying application code or redeploying infrastructure.

The following command creates two weighted A records for traffic shifting:

```
aws route53 change-resource-record-sets \
  --hosted-zone-id Z123456ABCDEFG \
  --change-batch '{
    "Changes": [
      {
        "Action": "UPSERT",
        "ResourceRecordSet": {
          "Name": "api.example.com",
          "Type": "A",
          "SetIdentifier": "blue",
          "Weight": 80,
          "TTL": 30,
          "ResourceRecords": [
            { "Value": "203.0.113.20" }
          ]
        }
      },
      {
        "Action": "UPSERT",
        "ResourceRecordSet": {
          "Name": "api.example.com",
          "Type": "A",
          "SetIdentifier": "green",
          "Weight": 20,
          "TTL": 30,
          "ResourceRecords": [
            { "Value": "203.0.113.21" }
          ]
        }
      }
    ]
  }'
```

In this command:

- `--hosted-zone-id`: Hosted zone containing the record.
- `--change-batch`: JSON payload describing the DNS changes.

- `Action`: `UPSERT`: Creates or updates the record.
- `SetIdentifier`: Unique name for each weighted record.
- `Weight`: Determines traffic distribution (higher = more traffic).
- `TTL`: Controls caching behavior.
- `ResourceRecords`: IP addresses for each endpoint.

Weighted routing is a powerful operational tool because it allows CloudOps engineers to shift traffic gradually, observe system behavior, and roll back instantly if needed—all without touching application infrastructure.

Failover Routing

Failover routing supports the active-passive architectures you learned in Chapter 7 by directing traffic to a secondary endpoint when the primary becomes unhealthy. Route 53 evaluates health checks at the global control plane, ensuring that failover decisions remain reliable even during regional outages.

The following command configures primary and secondary failover records:

```
aws route53 change-resource-record-sets \
  --hosted-zone-id Z123456ABCDEFG \
  --change-batch '{
    "Changes": [
      {
        "Action": "UPSERT",
        "ResourceRecordSet": {
          "Name": "app.example.com",
          "Type": "A",
          "SetIdentifier": "primary",
          "Failover": "PRIMARY",
          "TTL": 30,
          "ResourceRecords": [
            { "Value": "203.0.113.50" }
          ],
          "HealthCheckId": "12345678-abcd-ef00-1234-abcdef987654"
        }
      },
      {
        "Action": "UPSERT",
        "ResourceRecordSet": {
          "Name": "app.example.com",
          "Type": "A",
          "SetIdentifier": "secondary",
          "Failover": "SECONDARY",
          "TTL": 30,
          "ResourceRecords": [
            { "Value": "203.0.113.51" }
          ]
        }
      }
    ]
  }'
```

In this command:

- `Failover`: Must be `PRIMARY` or `SECONDARY`.
- `HealthCheckId`: Determines when failover occurs.
- `SetIdentifier`: Distinguishes the two records.
- `TTL`: Short TTLs improve failover responsiveness.

Failover routing is central to BCDR strategies because it provides a globally resilient mechanism for redirecting traffic when primary systems degrade.

Additional Route 53 Routing Policies

To round out the picture of how Route 53 influences traffic flow, it's important to recognize that weighted routing and failover routing represent only two of the mechanisms CloudOps engineers rely on to shape global DNS behavior. Weighted routing enables controlled traffic shifting during deployments, while failover routing ensures continuity during outages—but neither addresses performance optimization, geographic policy requirements, or lightweight load distribution. These additional operational needs are met by other routing policies that Route 53 provides, each designed to solve a different class of traffic-management problem. Understanding these complementary policies helps CloudOps engineers choose the right tool for each scenario, whether the goal is to direct users to the closest Region, comply with jurisdictional constraints, or return multiple healthy endpoints for improved client-side resilience. The following routing policies complete the set of mechanisms CloudOps teams use to deliver predictable, efficient, and policy-aligned global traffic behavior.

Simple Routing

Simple routing is the most straightforward Route 53 policy and is used when a domain should resolve to a single, definitive endpoint. There is no traffic distribution, no health-based decision-making, and no geographic or latency awareness. CloudOps engineers typically use simple routing for foundational services such as internal APIs, static websites, or single-region workloads where DNS complexity is unnecessary. Because it returns exactly one record, it is also the easiest policy to reason about during troubleshooting, making it a reliable default when advanced routing behavior is not required.

Latency-Based Routing

Latency-based routing directs clients to the AWS Region that provides the lowest network latency, improving user experience for globally distributed applications. Route 53 determines latency by continuously measuring performance between AWS Regions and Internet networks. This policy is especially useful for Multi-Region architectures where workloads are deployed in parallel across continents. For CloudOps engineers, latency-based routing reduces the need for manual traffic engineering and helps ensure that users automatically connect to the closest healthy endpoint without requiring application-level logic.

Geolocation Routing

Geolocation routing allows DNS responses to vary based on the geographic location of the requester, such as country or continent. This is particularly valuable for compliance-driven workloads, content localization, and region-specific service behavior. Unlike latency-based routing, which optimizes for performance, geolocation routing optimizes for policy—ensuring that users in specific jurisdictions are directed to the correct infrastructure. CloudOps engineers often use this policy to enforce data residency requirements or to direct traffic to region-specific deployments that comply with local regulations.

Multivalue Answer Routing

Multivalue answer routing returns multiple healthy IP addresses for a single DNS query, functioning as a lightweight form of load balancing. Each record can be associated with a health check, and Route 53 only returns healthy endpoints. While not a replacement for Application Load Balancers or NLBs, multivalue routing is useful for simple, distributed architectures where clients can handle basic load distribution or retry logic. CloudOps engineers often use this policy for microservices, IoT workloads, or edge-deployed systems where simplicity and resilience are more important than advanced load-balancing features.

Routing Policies Comparison

Table 10.5 summarizes all Route 53 routing policies and provides a consolidated view of when each approach is most appropriate.

TABLE 10.5 Route 53 Routing Policies Comparison

Scenario/Goal	Recommended Routing Policy
Simple Mapping: Point one domain to one specific IP or AWS resource.	Simple routing
Canary/A-B Testing: Distribute traffic in specific proportions (e.g., 90/10) to test a new version.	Weighted routing
User Experience: Route users to the AWS Region that provides the lowest round-trip network latency.	Latency routing
Disaster Recovery: Automatically redirect traffic to a Passive DR Site or standby environment when the primary fails.	Failover routing (requires Route 53 health checks)
Compliance/Localization: Route users based on their physical location to meet data residency laws or serve local content.	Geolocation routing
Lightweight Balancing: Return up to eight healthy resource records to provide basic, DNS-level load balancing.	Multivalue Answer routing

Enabling DNS Query Logging

After defining how Route 53 directs client traffic through various routing policies, CloudOps engineers also need visibility into how those DNS decisions play out in practice.

DNS query logging provides visibility into how clients resolve names, which is essential for troubleshooting, auditing, and validating routing behavior. Logs can be sent to Amazon CloudWatch Logs, Amazon S3, or Amazon Data Firehose. CloudOps engineers typically use CloudWatch Logs for real-time analysis and S3 for long-term retention.

The following command enables DNS query logging for a hosted zone:

```
aws route53 create-query-logging-config \
  --hosted-zone-id Z123456ABCDEFG \
  --cloud-watch-logs-log-group-arn
arn:aws:logs:us-east-1:111122223333:log-group:/aws/route53/queries
```

In this command:

- `--hosted-zone-id`: Hosted zone to log.
- `--cloud-watch-logs-log-group-arn`: Destination log group for DNS query logs.

To learn more, visit: `https://docs.aws.amazon.com/cli/latest/reference/route53/create-query-logging-config.html`.

Query logging is invaluable for validating hybrid DNS behavior, confirming that forwarding rules are applied correctly, and detecting anomalies such as unexpected query volumes or unauthorized internal lookups.

Routing policies and query logging form a complementary operational pair. Routing policies shape how traffic flows across Regions, environments, and failover paths, while query logs provide the visibility needed to validate those routing decisions. In hybrid environments, logs also help confirm that Resolver rules are working as intended and that queries are being forwarded to on-premises DNS servers when appropriate. For CloudOps engineers, mastering both capabilities is essential for maintaining predictable, observable, and resilient DNS behavior—and for succeeding on the SOA-C03 exam.

Configuring Content and Service Distribution

After exploring Amazon Route 53 and its globally distributed control plane, it is natural for you, as a CloudOps engineer, to extend your thinking to how AWS delivers content and application traffic across the world. Route 53 demonstrates how AWS uses a global network of edge locations to make DNS decisions close to users, improving resilience and reducing latency. This same design philosophy—global reach, distributed infrastructure, and edge-based decision-making—underpins AWS's content-delivery and traffic-optimization services. Amazon CloudFront and AWS Global Accelerator both operate at the global edge, using AWS's worldwide network to accelerate content, optimize traffic flow, and improve application availability.

Amazon CloudFront and AWS Global Accelerator build on the conceptual foundation introduced with Amazon Route 53: global services provide global consistency. CloudFront is, in fact, a global service—just like Route 53—because its caching layers, edge locations, and request-routing logic operate across AWS's worldwide network rather than within a single Region. Global Accelerator follows the same pattern, using Static Anycast IP addresses and the AWS backbone to route traffic to the optimal AWS endpoint. By transitioning from Route 53's global DNS routing to CloudFront's global content caching and Global Accelerator's global network routing, you experience a smooth conceptual progression: from global name resolution, to global content delivery, to global traffic optimization. This continuity reinforces AWS's edge-centric architecture and prepares you for the operational details that follow.

Amazon CloudFront

Amazon CloudFront is AWS's global Content Delivery Network (CDN), designed to deliver static and dynamic content with low latency and high transfer speeds. You rely on CloudFront to push content closer to users, reduce load on your origins, and enforce security controls at the edge. CloudFront integrates deeply with S3, Application Load Balancers (ALBs), API Gateway, Lambda@Edge, CloudFront Functions, AWS WAF (Web Application Firewall), AWS Shield, and Origin Shield. Understanding these integrations is essential for achieving operational excellence, performance efficiency, reliability, and security in your architectures.

CloudFront operates across AWS's global edge network, routing user requests to the nearest edge location before forwarding them to your origin. This architecture gives you several operational advantages: reduced latency, improved cache hit ratios, lower origin traffic, and the ability to apply security policies at the edge using AWS WAF. CloudFront also supports advanced features such as signed URLs, signed cookies, origin failover, and fine-grained cache policies that allow you to control exactly how content is cached and served.

Amazon CloudFront Integrations

CloudFront rarely operates in isolation. In real-world architectures, it becomes the global entry point that integrates with a variety of AWS services—each serving a different operational purpose. As a CloudOps engineer, understanding these integration patterns is essential because CloudFront's behavior, performance characteristics, and security posture change depending on the origin or service it fronts. Whether CloudFront is delivering static content from Amazon S3, accelerating dynamic applications behind an Application Load Balancer, securing APIs with AWS WAF, or executing logic at the edge with Lambda@Edge, each integration introduces its own configuration model, caching strategy, and operational responsibilities. This section walks through the most common CloudFront integrations you will encounter in production and on the SOA-C03 exam, giving you a clear, structured view of how CloudFront interacts with the broader AWS ecosystem.

With that context in place, the following sections break down each integration individually. Each one explains the operational rationale, the architectural pattern, and the configuration steps you need to understand to deploy CloudFront effectively in that scenario.

Integrating CloudFront with Amazon S3 (Static Content Delivery)

Static content delivery is the most common and operationally efficient CloudFront pattern. When you place CloudFront in front of an S3 bucket, you immediately gain global distribution, reduced latency, and dramatically lower S3 GET costs due to caching at the edge. This pattern is foundational for websites, SPAs (Single Page Applications), media delivery, and any workload where content does not change frequently. Because S3 is inherently durable and CloudFront is globally distributed, this integration gives you a highly reliable, cost-efficient, and secure content delivery pipeline.

From an operational perspective, CloudFront with S3 is also the cleanest way to enforce security best practices. By using Origin Access Control (OAC), you ensure that your S3 bucket is never publicly accessible, and all access flows through CloudFront. This allows you to apply WAF rules, TLS (Transport Layer Security) policies, and caching strategies at the edge. You also gain the ability to use versioned object naming to avoid invalidations, long TTL (Time to Live) intervals for performance efficiency, and fine-grained cache policies to control how CloudFront interacts with your S3 origin.

To create a CloudFront Distribution for S3 Origin you use this command:

```
aws cloudfront create-distribution \
  --distribution-config file://cloudfront-s3-config.json
```

In this command:

- `--distribution-config`: Points to a JSON file containing the full distribution configuration. CloudFront requires a complete configuration document for creation.

The referenced distribution configuration JSON document contains information about the origin(s), the domain and the cache behavior:

```
{
  "CallerReference": "cf-s3-$(date +%s)",
  "Comment": "CloudFront distribution for S3 static assets",
  "Enabled": true,
  "Origins": {
    "Quantity": 1,
    "Items": [
      {
        "Id": "s3-origin",
        "DomainName": "my-static-assets.s3.amazonaws.com",
        "OriginAccessControlId": "E2ABCDEFGHIJKL",
        "S3OriginConfig": {
          "OriginAccessIdentity": ""
        }
      }
    ]
  },
```

```
  "DefaultCacheBehavior": {
    "TargetOriginId": "s3-origin",
    "ViewerProtocolPolicy": "redirect-to-https",
    "AllowedMethods": {
      "Quantity": 2,
      "Items": ["GET", "HEAD"]
    },
    "CachePolicyId": "658327ea-f89d-4fab-a63d-7e88639e58f6"
  }
}
```


In the JSON document:

- Top-Level Fields
  - `CallerReference`: Ensures idempotency.
  - `Comment`: Human-readable description.
  - `Enabled`: Activates the distribution.
- Origins
  - `Id`: Unique origin identifier.
  - `DomainName`: S3 bucket endpoint.
  - `OriginAccessControlId`: Enables OAC.
  - `S3OriginConfig`: Required for S3 origins.
- DefaultCacheBehavior
  - `TargetOriginId`: Links behavior to origin.
  - `ViewerProtocolPolicy`: Redirects HTTP to HTTPS.
  - `AllowedMethods`: GET/HEAD only.
  - `CachePolicyId`: AWS optimized static caching policy.

To learn more, visit: `https://docs.aws.amazon.com/cli/latest/reference/cloudfront/create-distribution.html`.

Integrating CloudFront with Application Load Balancers (Dynamic Content)

When CloudFront sits in front of an ALB, you gain a powerful combination of global acceleration, edge-based security, and reduced load on your backend. This pattern is ideal for dynamic web applications, microservices, and APIs that require low latency and high availability. CloudFront terminates TLS at the edge, reducing the number of TLS handshakes your ALB must handle. It also pools TCP connections, reducing connection churn and improving backend efficiency.

Operationally, CloudFront with ALB is one of the most flexible and secure architectures you can deploy. You can attach AWS WAF to block malicious traffic before it reaches your VPC, use Origin Shield to reduce ALB load, and configure cache policies to cache semi-dynamic content. You also gain the ability to use Lambda@Edge or CloudFront Functions for request normalization, authentication, or routing logic. This integration is essential for high-traffic, globally distributed applications.

To create a CloudFront Distribution for ALB Origin you tell the `aws cloudfront create-distribution` command to use an ALB as origin in the distribution configuration as follows:

```
aws cloudfront create-distribution \
  --distribution-config file://cloudfront-alb-config.json
```

In this command:

- `--distribution-config`: Points to the JSON file defining the ALB origin and cache behavior.

```
{
  "CallerReference": "cf-alb-$(date +%s)",
  "Comment": "CloudFront distribution for ALB dynamic content",
  "Enabled": true,
  "Origins": {
    "Quantity": 1,
    "Items": [
      {
        "Id": "alb-origin",
        "DomainName": "my-app-alb-123456.us-east-1.elb.amazonaws.com",
        "CustomOriginConfig": {
          "OriginProtocolPolicy": "https-only",
          "OriginSSLProtocols": ["TLSv1.2"]
        }
      }
    ]
  },
  "DefaultCacheBehavior": {
    "TargetOriginId": "alb-origin",
    "ViewerProtocolPolicy": "redirect-to-https",
    "AllowedMethods": {
      "Quantity": 7,
      "Items": ["GET", "HEAD", "OPTIONS", "PUT", "POST", "PATCH", "DELETE"]
    },
    "CachePolicyId": "b2884449-e4de-46a7-ac36-70bc7f1ddd6d",
    "OriginRequestPolicyId": "88a5eaf4-2fd4-4709-b370-b4c650ea3fcf"
  }
}
```

In the JSON document:

- Origins
  - `Id`: Unique origin identifier.
  - `DomainName`: ALB DNS name.
  - `CustomOriginConfig`: Required for non-S3 origins.
  - `OriginProtocolPolicy`: Forces HTTPS to ALB.
  - `OriginSSLProtocols`: Enforces TLS 1.2.

- DefaultCacheBehavior
  - `AllowedMethods`: Full HTTP method set for APIs.
  - `CachePolicyId`: AWS optimized dynamic caching policy.
  - `OriginRequestPolicyId`: Controls forwarded headers/cookies/query strings.

Integrating CloudFront with API Gateway (Global API Acceleration)

CloudFront integrates naturally with API Gateway because API Gateway itself uses CloudFront under the hood. When you configure a custom domain name for API Gateway, you gain full control over CloudFront's caching, security, and routing behavior. This allows you to apply WAF rules, configure cache policies, and use Lambda@Edge for request normalization or authentication.

Operationally, CloudFront with API Gateway is ideal for global APIs that require low latency and consistent performance. You can cache GET responses at the edge, reduce throttling at API Gateway, and enforce security policies before traffic reaches your API. This integration is essential for building globally distributed, secure, and scalable API architectures.

To create a Custom Domain for API Gateway (CloudFront-Backed) you use this command:

```
aws apigateway create-domain-name \
  --domain-name api.example.com \
  --certificate-arn arn:aws:acm:us-east-1:123456789012:certificate/abcd1234
```

In this command:

- `--domain-name`: The custom domain for your API.
- `--certificate-arn`: ACM (AWS Certificate Manager) certificate for HTTPS.

To learn more, visit: `https://docs.aws.amazon.com/cli/latest/reference/apigateway/create-domain-name.html`.

Integrating CloudFront with AWS WAF

AWS WAF (Web Application Firewall) is a managed service that protects your applications from common web exploits such as SQL injection, cross-site scripting (XSS), bot attacks, and malicious request patterns. At the heart of WAF is the Web ACL (Web Access Control List), which is simply a collection of rules that inspect incoming HTTP(S) requests and decide whether to allow, block, or count them. A Web ACL can include AWS-managed rule groups, vendor-managed rule groups, or your own custom rules. If you're new to WAF, think of a Web ACL as a programmable security policy that evaluates every request before it reaches your application. Many of the AWS-managed rule groups are designed specifically to mitigate risks from the OWASP Top 10, the industry's most widely recognized list of critical web application vulnerabilities.

CloudFront integrates with AWS WAF by acting as the enforcement point for the Web ACL. When you associate a Web ACL with a CloudFront distribution, every viewer request is evaluated at the edge—before it ever reaches your origin, your VPC, or your compute layer. This is a major operational advantage: malicious traffic is filtered globally, at scale, and as close to the attacker as possible. CloudFront's global edge network becomes the first line of defense, reducing load on your ALB, API Gateway, or S3 origin and improving both security and reliability. Because CloudFront uses the global scope of AWS WAF, the same Web ACL applies consistently across all edge locations worldwide, ensuring uniform protection regardless of where the traffic originates.

From a CloudOps perspective, this integration centralizes your security posture. You define your rules once in the Web ACL, and CloudFront enforces them everywhere. You can block known bad IPs, throttle abusive clients with rate-based rules, inspect headers and query strings, or rely on AWS-managed rule groups to protect against common attack vectors such as injection attacks, cross-site scripting, and other OWASP-aligned threats. WAF logs can be streamed to CloudWatch Logs, S3, or Amazon Data Firehose for real-time analysis, giving you deep visibility into attack patterns. For the SOA-C03 exam, AWS expects you to understand that CloudFront with WAF is the recommended pattern for protecting any Internet-facing application because it combines global scale, low latency, and edge-based security enforcement.

To associate a WAF Web ACL with a CloudFront distribution use the following command:

```
aws cloudfront associate-distribution-web-acl \
    --id EDFDVBD632BHDS5 \
    --web-acl-arn arn:aws:wafv2:us-east-1:123456789012:global/webacl/
ExampleWebACL/a1b2c3d4-5678-90ab-cdef-EXAMPLE11111
```

In this command:

- `--id`: This is the unique Distribution ID of your CloudFront distribution (e.g., `EDFDVBD632BHDS5`).
- `--web-acl-arn`: The ARN of the WAF Web ACL you want to attach.

To learn more, visit: `https://docs.aws.amazon.com/cli/latest/reference/cloudfront/associate-distribution-web-acl.html`.

Integrating CloudFront with AWS Shield

AWS Shield provides managed DDoS protection for applications running on AWS, and CloudFront is one of the services that benefits most directly from this integration. Shield Standard is automatically enabled for all CloudFront distributions at no additional cost, providing protection against common network-layer attacks such as SYN floods, UDP reflection attacks, and volumetric traffic spikes. Because CloudFront operates at the AWS Edge, Shield Standard mitigates these attacks as close to the source as possible, absorbing and filtering malicious traffic before it can impact your origin, your VPC, or your compute layer. This edge-based protection is one of the reasons CloudFront is considered a best-practice front door for any Internet-facing workload.

For mission-critical applications, AWS Shield Advanced adds deeper visibility, enhanced detection, and 24/7 access to the AWS DDoS Response Team (DRT). Shield Advanced also provides cost-protection features that can automatically offset scaling charges incurred during a DDoS event—an important safeguard for workloads that autoscale aggressively under load. When you enable Shield Advanced on a CloudFront distribution, you gain additional protections such as anomaly detection tuned to your traffic patterns, detailed attack diagnostics, and the ability to automatically deploy custom AWS WAF rules in response to detected threats. This creates a layered defense model: CloudFront absorbs and distributes traffic globally, Shield mitigates DDoS attacks at the edge, and WAF enforces application-layer rules.

From a cost perspective, it's important to understand that Shield Advanced is not free. It carries a significant monthly subscription fee, plus additional charges for protected resources. This means Shield Advanced is typically reserved for high-value, high-risk, or compliance-sensitive workloads where the cost of downtime or a DDoS event far exceeds the subscription cost. CloudFront's integration with Shield Advanced helps justify the investment because a single Shield Advanced subscription can protect multiple CloudFront distributions, Route 53 hosted zones, and other supported resources. For CloudOps engineers, the key takeaway is that Shield Standard provides strong baseline protection at no cost, while Shield Advanced offers enterprise-grade DDoS mitigation and cost protection—but requires deliberate budgeting and justification.

Integrating CloudFront with Origin Shield

Origin Shield is an optional CloudFront feature that adds a centralized caching layer between CloudFront edge locations and your origin. Instead of multiple edge locations independently forwarding cache misses to your origin, Origin Shield designates a single regional "shield" location that receives all first-time requests. This dramatically reduces origin load, improves cache hit ratios, and minimizes the number of duplicate requests that reach your backend. For workloads with large objects, expensive compute operations, or high request fan-out, Origin Shield can significantly reduce operational costs and improve performance consistency.

Operationally, Origin Shield is especially valuable when CloudFront fronts an Application Load Balancer, a custom origin, or an S3 bucket serving large volumes of dynamic or semi-static content. By collapsing multiple edge misses into a single request, Origin Shield reduces the risk of origin overload during traffic spikes or cache-busting events. It also improves performance for multi-CDN architectures, media delivery workflows, and workloads that rely heavily on signed URLs or signed cookies. For CloudOps engineers, Origin Shield provides a powerful lever for optimizing backend efficiency, reducing cross-Region data transfer, and improving overall cache effectiveness. When combined with CloudFront's existing caching layers and optional features like Lambda@Edge or WAF, Origin Shield helps create a highly scalable, resilient, and cost-efficient content delivery architecture.

Integrating CloudFront with Lambda@Edge and CloudFront Functions (Programmability at the Edge)

CloudFront Functions and Lambda@Edge extend CloudFront's capabilities by allowing you to run logic directly at AWS Edge locations. As a CloudOps engineer, these tools give you the ability to manipulate requests and responses *before* they ever reach your origin, enabling powerful use cases such as URL rewrites, header normalization, authentication, A/B testing, and custom routing.

CloudFront Functions are designed for lightweight, high-performance JavaScript transformations that run at the viewer request or viewer response stage. They are ideal for simple, latency-sensitive operations that must execute at extremely high scale.

Lambda@Edge, on the other hand, provides a full Node.js runtime and can run at all four CloudFront lifecycle events: viewer request, viewer response, origin request, and origin response. This makes Lambda@Edge suitable for more complex logic such as JWT (JSON Web Token) validation, request signing, dynamic routing, or modifying origin requests based on cookies or headers. Because Lambda@Edge executes globally, you gain the ability to enforce consistent behavior across all CloudFront edge locations without deploying infrastructure in multiple Regions. This combination of global reach, low latency, and programmable logic makes Lambda@Edge a powerful tool for operational excellence, performance efficiency, and security.

The following Lambda@Edge function inspects the incoming request, checks whether the viewer used HTTP, and if so, returns a 301 redirect to the HTTPS version of the same URL. If the request is already using HTTPS, the function simply passes it through unchanged. This is a classic example of enforcing security at the edge without modifying your origin infrastructure.

```
'use strict';

exports.handler = async (event) => {
    const request = event.Records[0].cf.request;

    // If the viewer used HTTP, redirect to HTTPS
    if (request.headers['cloudfront-forwarded-proto'] &&
        request.headers['cloudfront-forwarded-proto'][0].value === 'http') {

        return {
            status: '301',
            statusDescription: 'Moved Permanently',
            headers: {
                location: [{
                    key: 'Location',
                    value:
`https://${request.headers.host[0].value}${request.uri}`
                }]
            }
        };
    }

    // Otherwise, continue normally
    return request;
};
```

Although simple redirects are best implemented using CloudFront functions, the aforementioned example uses Lambda@Edge because it provides a clear, easy-to-follow demonstration of how Lambda@Edge processes viewer-request events.

Save the JavaScript code into a file named `redirect-to-https.js`. Zip the file so Lambda can accept it:

```
zip redirect-to-https.zip redirect-to-https.js
```

Lambda requires ZIP packaging or Container images for deployment. To create the Lambda function in `us-east-1` (required for Lambda@Edge), use this command:

```
aws lambda create-function \
  --function-name my-edge-function \
  --runtime nodejs18.x \
  --handler redirect-to-https.handler \
  --zip-file fileb://redirect-to-https.zip \
  --role arn:aws:iam::123456789012:role/lambda-edge-execution-role \
  --region us-east-1
```

In this command:

- `--function-name`: Name of the Lambda function.
- `--runtime`: Node.js runtime used by Lambda@Edge.
- `--handler`: File and exported handler function.
- `--zip-file`: Uploads the zipped JavaScript file as binary using `fileb://`.
- `--role`: IAM role granting Lambda permission to run.
- `--region`: Must be `us-east-1` for Lambda@Edge.

To learn more, visit: `https://docs.aws.amazon.com/cli/latest/reference/lambda/create-function.html`.

Next, publish a version for your newly created Lambda@Edge function:

```
aws lambda publish-version \
  --function-name my-edge-function \
  --region us-east-1
```

Finally, once the function is published, attach it to your CloudFront distribution:

```
aws cloudfront update-distribution \
  --id E1234567890ABC \
  --distribution-config file://updated-distribution-config.json \
  --if-match $(aws cloudfront get-distribution-config --id E1234567890ABC
--query "ETag" --output text)
```

In this command:

- `--id`: CloudFront distribution ID.
- `--distribution-config`: Updated configuration including the Lambda association.
- `--if-match`: Ensures you update the correct version of the distribution.

The referenced `updated-distribution-config.json` looks like this:

```
{
  "DefaultCacheBehavior": {
    "TargetOriginId": "alb-origin",
    "ViewerProtocolPolicy": "redirect-to-https",
    "LambdaFunctionAssociations": {
      "Quantity": 1,
      "Items": [
        {
          "EventType": "viewer-request",
          "LambdaFunctionARN": "arn:aws:lambda:us-east-
1:123456789012:function:my-edge-function:1",
          "IncludeBody": false
        }
      ]
    }
  }
}
```

From an operational standpoint, Lambda@Edge requires careful planning because functions must be deployed in the `us-east-1` Region and must reference a published version rather than `$LATEST`. Updates take time to propagate across all edge locations, so you should expect a short delay before changes take effect globally. Logging occurs in the Region where the function executes, which means logs may be distributed across multiple Regions depending on where your users are located. CloudFront Functions are generally preferred for lightweight, latency-sensitive tasks due to their lower cost and faster execution, whereas Lambda@Edge is better suited for complex logic such as authentication, request signing, or dynamic routing. As a CloudOps engineer, you should choose the right tool based on performance requirements, complexity, and the operational impact of global propagation.

Remember that Lambda@Edge functions must be created in `us-east-1` and must reference a published version, not `$LATEST`. CloudFront cannot use an unpublished or region-local Lambda function. Also expect questions where the correct answer is to use CloudFront functions for simple viewer-request logic (header rewrites, redirects) and Lambda@Edge for heavier logic (authentication, routing, request signing).

CloudFront and DDoS Protection

CloudFront is not only a global content-delivery service—it is also one of the most effective DDoS mitigation layers available in AWS. When you place CloudFront in front of your application, every request—legitimate or malicious—first terminates at one of AWS's globally distributed edge locations. This means CloudFront absorbs and filters traffic long before it reaches your VPC, your ALB, or your compute layer. As a CloudOps engineer, this gives you a powerful operational advantage: you can protect your backend infrastructure from volumetric attacks, reduce the blast radius of malicious traffic, and maintain application availability even under extreme load. CloudFront's global network is engineered to withstand massive traffic spikes, and it automatically leverages AWS Shield Standard to mitigate common Layer 3 and Layer 4 attacks without requiring any configuration on your part.

From a reliability and security perspective, CloudFront acts as a global protective shield for your application. It terminates TCP connections at the edge, collapses duplicate requests, and uses intelligent routing to ensure that only clean, validated traffic reaches your origin. When combined with AWS WAF, CloudFront also protects against Layer 7 attacks such as SQL injection, cross-site scripting, bot traffic, and credential-stuffing attempts. For workloads requiring even stronger guarantees, CloudFront integrates seamlessly with AWS Shield Advanced, giving you enhanced detection, cost-protection benefits, and access to the AWS DDoS Response Team (DRT). For the SOA-C03 exam, AWS expects you to recognize that CloudFront is not just a performance accelerator—it is a security boundary that improves availability, reduces operational risk, and protects your origin from both intentional and unintentional traffic surges.

Identify and Remediate CloudFront Caching Issues

You learned in Chapter 1 how the CloudOps cycle is defined by five phases: Deploy, Monitor, Sustain, Secure, and Optimize. For a CloudOps engineer, the work does not end once the initial distribution is provisioned. Upon successful deployment, a CloudFront distribution immediately enters the Monitor phase, where real-time telemetry is gathered to ensure health. This leads naturally into the Sustain phase, where you ensure high availability and content freshness, the Secure phase, where you defend the edge against malicious traffic, and finally the Optimize phase, where you fine-tune caching logic to maximize performance and minimize costs.

Caching is a double-edged sword within this cycle: when it functions correctly, it provides lightning-fast global performance and massive cost savings by shielding your origin; when it fails, it can serve *stale* data or drive up your AWS bill through constant "Cache Misses." Mastering this section involves closing the loop between the Monitor and Optimize phases, specifically by understanding the feedback loop between CloudFront metrics and the specific configuration changes required to remediate performance bottlenecks. This requires a deep understanding of how header forwarding, query string parameters, and TTL settings influence the "hit-or-miss" behavior of the global edge network.

Monitoring and Key Performance Metrics

CloudFront integrates deeply with Amazon CloudWatch, providing a real-time pulse of your global delivery. For you, as a CloudOps engineer, interpreting these metrics is the first step in diagnosing why a user in one part of the world might be experiencing higher latency than another. You must monitor the health of your edge traffic using a core set of metrics that reveal the efficiency of your caching strategy and the reliability of your origin backend.

Table 10.6 summarizes the metrics you need to know for the exam.

TABLE 10.6 Amazon CloudFront Key Metrics

Metric Name	Description	Tuning Insight
`CacheHitRate`	The percentage of requests served directly from the edge cache without hitting the origin.	Low? Audit your cache policy. Ensure you aren't "cache-busting" with unnecessary cookies, headers, or unique query strings.
`OriginLatency`	The time (ms) it takes for your origin (S3/ALB) to respond to a request.	High? Check your origin's health. Consider enabling Origin Shield to consolidate regional requests and reduce backend load.
`4xxErrorRate`	The percentage of requests resulting in client-side errors (e.g., 403 Forbidden, 404 Not Found).	Spiking? Check for expired Signed URLs, incorrect S3 bucket paths, or WAF rules blocking legitimate traffic.
`5xxErrorRate`	The percentage of requests resulting in server-side errors (e.g., 504 Gateway Timeout).	Spiking? Investigate origin timeouts or Lambda@Edge execution failures. Check the "Origin Response Timeout" setting.
`TotalErrorRate`	The combined percentage of all 4xx and 5xx HTTP status codes.	High? This is your primary "Alert" metric. Use it to trigger a CloudWatch Alarm to notify the DevOps team of a global outage.

Implementing Logging for Deep Analysis

While CloudWatch provides the high-level "what," CloudFront Logs provide the granular "who, where, and how" of your traffic. As an engineer, you must choose the right tool for your specific operational need between Standard Logs for long-term auditing and Real-time Logs for immediate security response.

Enabling Standard Logging

Implementing Standard Logs (also known as Access Logs) is the most common way to audit your distribution for compliance or historical troubleshooting. When enabled, CloudFront collects raw request data and delivers it to an S3 bucket of your choice roughly every hour. While there is no additional charge from CloudFront for enabling these logs, a CloudOps engineer must account for the standard S3 storage and PUT request fees. To optimize costs, it is a best practice to apply an S3 Lifecycle Policy to these logs, automatically transitioning them to S3 Glacier or deleting them after a defined retention period.

To enable standard logging use the following command:

```
# Enable Standard Logging on an existing distribution
aws cloudfront update-distribution \
    --id E123456789EXAMPLE \
    --if-match E2ABCDEFGHIJKL \
    --logging Bucket=my-log-bucket.s3.amazonaws.com,Prefix=cdn-logs/,Include
Cookies=false
```

In this command:

- `--id`: The unique identifier for your CloudFront distribution (e.g., `EDFDVBD6EXAMPLE`).
- `--if-match`: The `ETag` of the current distribution configuration. This is a crucial concurrency control; it ensures that you are updating the most recent version of the config and prevents overwriting changes made by another engineer.
- `--logging`: A compound parameter that defines the target `Bucket`, a folder `Prefix` within that bucket, and `IncludeCookies` (a Boolean that determines if sensitive cookie data is included in the logs, which can increase storage costs).

To learn more, visit: `https://docs.aws.amazon.com/cli/latest/reference/cloudfront/update-distribution.html`.

Enabling Real-Time Logging

For mission-critical applications where every second counts, Real-time Logs provide a high-granularity alternative by delivering data to Amazon Kinesis Data Streams with a latency of just a few seconds. This tier is preferred for automated remediation, such as triggering a Lambda function to update a WAF IP-set the moment a 4xx error spike is detected in the stream.

To enable real-time logging, use the following command:

```
# Create the Real-time Log Configuration pointing to a Kinesis Stream
aws cloudfront create-realtime-log-config \
    --name HighPriorityLogConfig \
    --sampling-rate 100 \
    --fields "timestamp" "c-ip" "sc-status" "cs-uri-stem" \
    --end-points StreamType=Kinesis,KinesisStreamConfig={RoleArn=arn:aws:iam::1
23:role/CFLogRole,StreamArn=arn:aws:kinesis:us-east-1:123:stream/LogStream}
```

In this command:

- `--name`: A unique string to identify this specific log configuration.
- `--sampling-rate`: An integer from 1 to 100 representing the percentage of viewer requests to log. Higher rates provide more data but increase Kinesis processing costs.
- `--fields`: A list of specific log fields you want to capture (e.g., `c-ip` for client IP, `sc-status` for HTTP status code).

- `--end-points`: Defines where the data goes. It requires the `StreamType` (Kinesis) and the `KinesisStreamConfig`, which must include the `RoleArn` (IAM permission for CloudFront to write to the stream) and the `StreamArn` of the target Kinesis data stream.

To learn more, visit: `https://docs.aws.amazon.com/cli/latest/reference/cloudfront/create-realtime-log-config.html`.

Remediating Common Issues

The most frequent challenge you will face is Stale Content. If you push a critical update to your S3 origin but users still see the old version, you must perform a CloudFront Invalidation. This instructs all global edge locations to purge their cached copy of a file so the next request fetches the fresh version from the origin. However, invalidations are a "brute force" tool and can be costly if overused. A more CloudOps-native approach is Object Versioning (e.g., naming your file `style_v2.css`), which forces a natural cache miss and update without manual intervention or invalidation fees.

If you identify a low `CacheHitRate`, your remediation involves Cache Policy adjustments. A common "gotcha" is forwarding unnecessary metadata; if your application forwards a `Session-ID` cookie to CloudFront, every single user will trigger a unique cache entry, effectively dropping your hit rate to zero. By stripping out unnecessary headers and cookies at the edge, you consolidate requests and ensure that one cached object serves thousands of users. This optimization reduces your `OriginLatency` and protects your backend from being overwhelmed during traffic spikes.

To invalidate a specific directory, use this command:

```
aws cloudfront create-invalidation \
    --distribution-id E123456789EXAMPLE \
    --paths "/images/*"
```

In this command:

- `--distribution-id`: The ID of the distribution where you want to purge the cache.
- `--paths`: The space-separated list of paths to invalidate. Using the `*` wildcard (e.g., `/*`) clears the entire cache. While effective for massive updates, it causes a sudden origin surge where your backend is simultaneously hit by requests from every edge location as the global cache attempts to repopulate all at once.

To learn more, visit: `https://docs.aws.amazon.com/cli/latest/reference/cloudfront/create-invalidation.html`.

AWS Global Accelerator

While CloudFront optimizes content via caching (Layer 7), AWS Global Accelerator optimizes the network path (Layer 4). It provides you with two Static Anycast IP addresses that serve as a fixed entry point for your application. The real benefit of Global Accelerator lies in its ability to minimize the "Last Mile"—the distance your users' traffic travels over the unpredictable public Internet. While a CloudOps engineer cannot control a user's local ISP, Global Accelerator ensures that traffic is onboarded onto the AWS Global Private Network at the edge location physically closest to the user, often just one or two hops away.

Once the traffic hits the AWS Edge, it enters a private "Fast Lane." It leaves the congested public Internet entirely and travels over a dedicated, congestion-free fiber backbone managed by Amazon directly to your regional endpoints. This deterministic routing significantly reduces jitter and latency for non-HTTP workloads—such as Gaming (UDP), VoIP, or IoT—where even a 50ms spike can impact the user experience. Furthermore, because the IP addresses are static, you overcome "DNS Inertia." If a regional endpoint fails, Global Accelerator detects it via health checks and re-routes traffic at the network layer in seconds, bypassing the delays of DNS TTL propagation that often plague traditional failover strategies.

Automation of this high-performance path involves a three-step process in the Deploy phase of the CloudOps cycle: creating the accelerator, defining the listener gates, and associating the regional endpoint groups.

```
# 1. Create the Accelerator (Returns two Static Anycast IPs)
aws globalaccelerator create-accelerator --name EnterpriseApp --enabled

# 2. Add a Listener to bridge the traffic to your regional resources
aws globalaccelerator create-listener \
    --accelerator-arn arn:aws:globalaccelerator::12345:accelerator/abc-123 \
    --port-ranges FromPort=80,ToPort=80 FromPort=443,ToPort=443 \
    --protocol TCP

# 3. Create the Endpoint Group to link the Listener to a specific Region
aws globalaccelerator create-endpoint-group \
    --listener-arn arn:aws:globalaccelerator::12345:listener/abc-456 \
    --endpoint-group-region us-east-1 \
    --endpoint-configurations EndpointId=arn:aws:elb:us-east-
1:123:loadbalancer/app/my-alb/abc,Weight=128 \
    --traffic-dial-percentage 100
```

In these commands:

- `--enabled`: Ensures the accelerator is active and the static IPs are reachable immediately.
- `--port-ranges`: Sets the specific ports (e.g., 80/443) that the accelerator will accept.
- `--protocol`: Determines if the accelerator handles TCP or UDP traffic.
- `--endpoint-group-region`: Defines the physical AWS Region where your resources reside.
- `--endpoint-configurations`: Identifies the specific ALB, NLB, or EIP and its relative Weight for load balancing within the region.
- `--traffic-dial-percentage`: A powerful throttle (0-100) that allows a CloudOps engineer to perform regional evacuations or Canary testing by shifting traffic away from or toward a specific region instantly.

TABLE 10.7 Amazon CloudFront vs. AWS Global Accelerator

Feature	Amazon CloudFront	AWS Global Accelerator
Focus	Caching (reduces Origin load)	Path optimization (reduces jitter/latency)
OSI Layer	Layer 7 (HTTP/S)	Layer 4 (TCP/UDP)
Middle Mile	Public Internet + AWS Backbone	AWS Private Fiber Backbone only
IP Address	Dynamic DNS hostnames	Two static anycast IPs
Best For	Static assets, Video, Web Apps	Gaming, VoIP, Global Failover, IoT

Table 10.7 illustrates the critical architectural differences between the two edge services you just learned, helping you determine which tool to prioritize during the Optimize phase of the CloudOps cycle.

Troubleshooting Network Connectivity

To wrap up the Networking and Content Delivery chapter, we move into the "day two" operations that define a CloudOps engineer's expertise. Building a network is only half the battle; the real test comes when the packets stop flowing. In this section, you will learn how to systematically isolate failures across the VPC stack, interpret the "digital breadcrumbs" left in your logs, and use Amazon CloudWatch to move from reactive firefighting to proactive observability.

In this section, you will learn how to navigate the complex web of AWS networking to identify and resolve connectivity failures. For a CloudOps engineer, troubleshooting is a disciplined process of elimination—moving from the individual Elastic Network Interface (ENI) up to the Transit Gateway, and from the stateless NACL to the stateful Security Group. By mastering these diagnostic patterns, you ensure that your global infrastructure remains as resilient as it is performant.

Troubleshooting VPC Configurations

When an application cannot reach its destination, a CloudOps engineer's first task is to isolate whether the "gate" is closed or the "road" is missing. You begin at the Security Group level; because it is stateful and resides at the ENI, a failure here usually results in a "Connection Timeout." If the Security Group allows the traffic, you must then check the Network ACL (NACL). Unlike Security Groups, NACLs are stateless; a common exam "gotcha" is a configuration where the inbound traffic is allowed, but the outbound rule for return traffic on ephemeral ports (1024-65535) is missing, causing the connection to fail silently at the subnet boundary.

If the firewalls are clear, you must verify the "road" via Route Tables. Every subnet must have a route to its destination, whether that is an Internet Gateway (IGW) for public traffic or a NAT Gateway for private egress. A frequent point of failure for private instances is an incorrectly configured NAT Gateway. Remember that the NAT Gateway itself must live in a public subnet with a route to an IGW. If your internal East-West traffic is failing across VPCs, inspect your Transit Gateway (TGW) route tables. Ensure that the VPC attachments are active and that the TGW route table has successfully propagated the CIDR blocks of all participating spokes.

```
# Example: Verify the route table of a specific subnet to check for a
0.0.0.0/0 route
aws ec2 describe-route-tables \
  --filters "Name=association.subnet-id,Values=subnet-12345"

# Example: Confirm the status of a NAT Gateway
aws ec2 describe-nat-gateways \
  --nat-gateway-ids nat-0a1b2c3d4e5f6g7h8
```

VPC Reachability Analyzer

Before you start analyzing actual traffic logs, you must first verify that your network infrastructure is even capable of carrying that traffic. This is where VPC Reachability Analyzer comes in.

Think of the difference between VPC Reachability Analyzer and tools for analyzing logs such as VPC Flow Logs (discussed next) like this:

- **VPC Reachability Analyzer** (the Pipes): checks if the plumbing is connected correctly.
- **VPC Flow Logs** (the Water): tells you if water is actually flowing through it.

VPC Reachability Analyzer is a configuration-based tool. It performs a static check of your VPC components—Security Groups, NACLs, Route Tables, and Gateways—to see if a path exists between two points. It does not send any actual packets. This allows you to troubleshoot connectivity errors before an application is even turned on.

If you think about it, this makes sense because if your infrastructure "pipes" are broken—for example, a missing route to an Internet Gateway—the "water" (data) never reaches its destination, and VPC Flow Logs may not show you exactly where the break is. VPC Reachability Analyzer, however, will point to the exact faulty "pipe."

Testing a path involves two steps. First, define the source/destination path.

```
aws ec2 create-network-insights-path \
    --source i-0123456789abcdef0 \
    --destination i-0987654321fedcba0 \
    --protocol tcp \
    --destination-port 443
```

In this command:

- `--source`: The ID of the resource where the traffic originates (e.g., an EC2 instance).

- `--destination`: The ID of the target resource you are trying to reach.
- `--protocol`: The network protocol to test; for web traffic, this is almost always TCP.
- `--destination-port`: The specific port you are testing. In this example, we use 443, the standard port for secure HTTPS traffic.

Second, start the actual analysis. Using `NetworkInsightsPathId` from the previous command triggers the configuration check.

```
aws ec2 start-network-insights-analysis \
    --network-insights-path-id nip-0123456789abcdef0
```

In this command:

- `--network-insights-path-id`: The unique ID for the path you just defined.

If the destination is unreachable, AWS provides a "hop-by-hop" breakdown, identifying the specific Security Group rule or route table entry causing the blockage. Once you've confirmed the "pipes" are connected, you are ready to move on to the next section to monitor the "water" with VPC Flow Logs.

For more information, visit: `https://docs.aws.amazon.com/cli/latest/reference/ec2/create-network-insights-path.html` and `https://docs.aws.amazon.com/cli/latest/reference/ec2/start-network-insights-analysis.html`.

VPC Flow Logs

When the "pipes" are connected but the "water" still isn't flowing, logs provide the forensic evidence needed to identify exactly where the blockage is happening. For a CloudOps engineer, VPC Flow Logs are the most critical tool in the kit. They capture information about the IP traffic going to and from network interfaces in your VPC. By analyzing the action field (`ACCEPT` or `REJECT`), you can immediately determine if a Security Group or NACL is blocking a request. If the Flow Log shows `REJECT` on the ingest, the issue is almost certainly an Inbound Rule. If it shows `ACCEPT` on ingest but the application still fails, you are likely looking at a missing outbound rule in a stateless NACL.

To enable VPC Flow Logs via the CLI, you must first ensure you have an IAM role with a trust policy that allows the `vpc-flow-logs.amazonaws.com` service to assume it. Once the role and permissions are in place, you can create the flow log for a specific VPC, subnet, or ENI.

```
# Example: Enabling VPC Flow Logs to CloudWatch Logs
aws ec2 create-flow-logs \
    --resource-type VPC \
    --resource-ids vpc-0a1b2c3d4e5f6g7h8 \
    --traffic-type ALL \
    --log-group-name /aws/vpc/flowlogs \
    --deliver-logs-permission-arn arn:aws:iam::123456789012:role/
VPCFlowLogsRole
```

In this command:

- `--resource-type`: Specifies the type of resource to monitor (`VPC`, `Subnet`, or `NetworkInterface`).
- `--resource-ids`: The unique ID of the target resource.
- `--traffic-type`: Determines if you capture `ACCEPT`, `REJECT`, or `ALL` traffic.
- `--log-group-name`: The destination log group in CloudWatch Logs.
- `--deliver-logs-permission-arn`: The ARN of the IAM role that grants permissions to publish logs to CloudWatch.

To learn more, visit: `https://docs.aws.amazon.com/cli/latest/reference/ec2/create-flow-logs.html`.

Beyond the VPC, you must analyze logs at the application and edge layers. ELB Access Logs provide detailed information about requests sent to your load balancer, helping you identify if 5xx errors originate from the balancer or backend targets. AWS WAF Web ACL Logs are essential for security troubleshooting, showing which web request was blocked by specific rules. Similarly, CloudFront Logs and Container Logs (via CloudWatch Logs) allow you to trace a user's request from the global edge to a specific microservice.

Remediating Hybrid and Private Connectivity

Hybrid connectivity introduces the complexity of the North-South bridge between AWS and your data center. If your Site-to-Site VPN or Direct Connect (DX) fails, your troubleshooting starts with the BGP (Border Gateway Protocol) session. A CloudOps engineer uses the AWS Console or CLI to check the BGP status; if it is "Down," the routers are not exchanging routes, and no traffic will flow. For Direct Connect, you must also verify the physical layer—checking light levels on the fiber and ensuring the Virtual Interface (VIF) is in the available state.

Remediation often involves managing the BGP Best Path Selection. If traffic is taking the slow VPN path instead of the fast DX path, you must use AS_PATH Prepending or BGP Communities to influence the priority. For Private Connectivity issues involving VPC endpoints, the "double-lock" logic is usually the culprit. If an instance cannot reach S3 privately, verify that the VPC endpoint policy hasn't explicitly denied the action and that the instance's Security Group allows outbound traffic to the S3 Prefix List (`pl-xxxxxx`).

DNS Troubleshooting Checklist

When your private IP "highways" are clear but your resources still cannot find one another, use this checklist to isolate the failure. For the SOA-C03 exam, pay close attention to the Split-Horizon and Resolver Endpoint scenarios, as these are common high-stakes troubleshooting tasks.

Verify VPC DNS Attributes Ensure `enableDnsHostnames` and `enableDnsSupport` are set to `True` in your VPC configuration. If these are disabled, the Route 53 Resolver (the .2 address) will not function, and your instances will fail to resolve even standard AWS public hostnames.

Audit Private Hosted Zone (PHZ) Associations If an EC2 instance cannot resolve a name like `db.internal`, verify that the PHZ is explicitly associated with the VPC where the instance resides. Remember, a PHZ is invisible to any VPC not on its association list.

Identify Split-Horizon Conflicts If you are using Split-Horizon DNS (the same name for Public and Private zones), remember that the Route 53 Resolver gives absolute precedence to the private hosted zone. If a record exists in your Public zone but is missing from the Private one, an internal instance will receive an NXDOMAIN error. The resolver will not "fall back" to the public Internet to find the missing record.

Inspect Resolver Endpoint Security Groups Inbound and outbound endpoints are represented by ENIs. If hybrid resolution is failing, check the Security Groups attached to these ENIs. An Inbound Endpoint must allow UDP/TCP Port 53 from your on-premises DNS IPs; an outbound endpoint must allow UDP/TCP Port 53 to your on-premises DNS IPs.

Validate Resolver Rules For outbound failures, verify that a Forwarding Rule exists for the specific on-premises domain (e.g., `corp.example.com`) and that it is associated with the VPC. Without this rule, the VPC will attempt to resolve the internal domain via the public Internet, resulting in a failure.

Check On-Premises Forwarders For Inbound failures, the issue is often on the corporate side. Ensure your on-premises DNS server is configured to forward queries for your AWS subdomain (e.g., `aws.example.com`) specifically to the inbound resolver endpoint IP addresses.

Analyze Query Logs If you are still unable to isolate the failure, use the AWS CLI to analyze your Route 53 Resolver Query Logs.

```
# Example: Filter CloudWatch Logs for a specific 'NXDOMAIN' error
aws logs filter-log-events \
    --log-group-name /aws/route53/resolver-query-logs \
    --filter-pattern "NXDOMAIN" \
    --limit 10
```

In this command:

- `--log-group-name`: This specifies the exact destination in CloudWatch Logs where your Route 53 Resolver Query Logging is being sent. In a production environment, this is usually a centralized group like `/aws/route53/resolver-query-logs`.
- `--filter-pattern`: This is your search criteria. By using `"NXDOMAIN"`, you are telling the CLI to only return log events where the DNS query failed because the domain name does not exist.
- `--limit`: This flag controls the volume of data returned. Setting a limit (e.g., 10) prevents your terminal from being overwhelmed by thousands of log lines, allowing you to focus on the most recent failures during a live troubleshooting session.

Configuring CloudWatch Network Monitoring Services

To move from reactive troubleshooting to proactive observability, a CloudOps engineer must leverage Amazon CloudWatch for comprehensive network observability. Rather than waiting for a user to report a slow application, you should set CloudWatch Alarms on specific metrics like `ErrorPortAllocation`—which indicates that a NAT Gateway has exhausted its available source ports—or `TransitGatewayBytesIn/Out` to detect unusual traffic spikes that may signal a misconfiguration or a security event. By creating centralized CloudWatch Dashboards, you can visualize the health of your Route 53 Health Checks and Global Accelerator endpoints in a single pane of glass, ensuring your global traffic steering is performing as expected.

Furthermore, AWS provides three distinct network monitoring services under the Amazon CloudWatch "umbrella" to ensure end-to-end visibility. First, **Network Flow Monitor** allows you to perform deep VPC-to-VPC and cross-service traffic analysis using specialized agents to map communication patterns. Second, **Internet Monitor** provides a health baseline for your Internet-facing traffic, alerting you to regional ISP outages or health events that impact your global users. Finally, you should implement **Network Synthetic Monitor** (formerly known as CloudWatch Network Monitor) to track the performance of your hybrid network. This service provides continuous visibility into packet loss and round-trip latency between your AWS workloads and your on-premises probes by actively probing the path. By setting specific thresholds on these performance metrics, you can be alerted the moment a failing Direct Connect link or a congested ISP path begins to degrade the user experience. This allows you to trigger automated failover scripts or notify your telecommunications provider before the performance degradation impacts business operations.

The following command serves as a refresher on how to use the CloudWatch CLI to create a metric alarm, building on the foundational monitoring concepts you learned in Chapter 6.

```
# Example: Creating a CloudWatch Alarm for NAT Gateway port exhaustion
aws cloudwatch put-metric-alarm \
    --alarm-name "NAT-Port-Exhaustion" \
    --metric-name ErrorPortAllocation \
    --namespace AWS/NATGateway \
    --statistic Sum \
    --period 60 \
    --threshold 1 \
    --comparison-operator GreaterThanOrEqualToThreshold \
    --evaluation-periods 1 \
    --alarm-actions arn:aws:sns:us-east-1:123456789012:MyNotifyTopic
```

In this command:

- `--alarm-name`: A unique, descriptive name for the alarm (e.g., `NAT-Port-Exhaustion`). This name appears in notification emails and the CloudWatch console.
- `--metric-name`: The specific data point you are monitoring. In this case, `ErrorPortAllocation` tracks the number of times a connection request failed because the NAT Gateway ran out of ephemeral ports.

- `--namespace`: The service category the metric belongs to. `AWS/NATGateway` ensures that CloudWatch looks at the managed NAT service metrics rather than EC2 or ELB metrics.
- `--statistic`: The mathematical transformation applied to the metric. `Sum` is used here to count the total number of errors occurring within the defined period.
- `--period`: The length of time, in seconds, over which the statistic is applied. `60` means CloudWatch evaluates the port errors every minute.
- `--threshold`: The numerical value that, if crossed, triggers the alarm. Setting this to `1` ensures you are alerted as soon as a single port allocation error occurs.
- `--comparison-operator`: The logic used to compare the metric against the threshold. `GreaterThanOrEqualToThreshold` ensures the alarm triggers if the error count is `1` or higher.
- `--evaluation-periods`: The number of consecutive periods the threshold must be breached before the alarm changes to the `ALARM` state. A value of `1` provides the fastest possible alert.
- `--alarm-actions`: The Amazon Resource Name (ARN) of the action to take. Most commonly, this points to an SNS topic that sends a notification to the CloudOps team via email or SMS.

Mastering the connectivity, distribution, and troubleshooting of AWS networking completes one of the most challenging technical domains for the SOA-C03 exam. As a CloudOps engineer, you have evolved from understanding simple routing to architecting global, resilient, and highly secure data perimeters that bridge the gap between cloud-native resources and legacy on-premises environments. With your infrastructure now optimized for performance and visibility, you have established a solid foundation for any high-scale workload. We are now ready to apply the final, business-critical lens to this architecture—ensuring that your high-performance network is as fiscally responsible as it is technically sound—in the final chapter covering cost optimization.

Summary

Networking is one of the most critical elements of a distributed system. In this chapter, you explored how to configure, monitor, secure, and troubleshoot the AWS networking and content delivery services. Every resilient architecture begins with the VPC, a regional logical routing domain that serves as the foundation for your isolated environment. As a CloudOps engineer, you learned to carve this space into zonal subnets, using Route Tables as the "brain" to direct traffic. Whether you're managing North-South flows to the Internet via Internet Gateways and NAT Gateways, or keeping East-West traffic internal, the VPC provides the structure required to ensure that resources are reachable, redundant, and logically organized.

Security within this network is a tiered responsibility that balances the granular, stateful control of Security Groups at the ENI level with the broad, stateless enforcement of NACLs at the subnet boundary. You have mastered the "double-lock" security model by implementing VPC endpoints—both interface (PrivateLink) and gateway types—to keep sensitive service traffic off the public Internet. By applying endpoint policies and leveraging AWS Organizations, you moved beyond simple firewalls to create robust data perimeters that prevent unauthorized access and data exfiltration.

As your infrastructure scales, you learned to bridge isolated environments using VPC Peering for direct links and the Transit Gateway for a scalable, hub-and-spoke regional architecture. For the hybrid-cloud mission, you saw how to balance the rapid, encrypted deployment of Site-to-Site VPNs against the high-bandwidth, deterministic performance of Direct Connect. By mastering the "language" of the network, you now know how to use BGP Communities and AS_PATH prepending to ensure your traffic always takes the most efficient path home, even during a physical fiber failure.

Global service discovery and traffic steering are handled at the naming layer via Amazon Route 53. You learned how to solve the "split-brain" DNS challenge in hybrid environments using inbound and outbound resolver endpoints, ensuring seamless resolution across the cloud and the data center. Furthermore, by implementing advanced routing policies—such as latency, weighted, and failover—you can transform DNS from a simple directory into a powerful tool for automated disaster recovery and global performance optimization.

Finally, you extended your reach to the global edge by deploying Amazon CloudFront to cache content and AWS Global Accelerator to provide a static, low-jitter "fast lane" for TCP/UDP applications. To close the CloudOps cycle, you mastered the art of troubleshooting, using VPC Flow Logs to identify blocked packets and CloudWatch Alarms to proactively monitor for port exhaustion or latency spikes.

Exam Essentials

Understand the core elements of a VPC. To truly understand the core elements of a VPC, a CloudOps engineer must view the Virtual Private Cloud not merely as a boundary, but as a sophisticated, software-defined ecosystem that mirrors a traditional data center. At its foundation, the VPC is a region-scoped container defined by a primary CIDR block, which you then carve into Availability Zone-specific subnets to ensure high availability. Within this environment, the Implicit Router serves as the invisible conductor, using Route Tables to determine the next hop for every packet, whether it is staying local for East-West communication or heading North-South toward an Internet Gateway for public access or a Virtual Private Gateway (VGW) and Transit Gateway (TGW) to bridge the gap to your corporate data center. By mastering these atomic components—the IPs, the subnets, and the routing logic—you establish the baseline required to implement the advanced security and connectivity strategies that follow in the CloudOps cycle.

Know the difference between Security Groups and NACLs. Security Groups operate at the ENI level and are stateful, meaning they intelligently remember a connection; if you allow an inbound request, the return traffic is automatically permitted regardless of outbound rules. Conversely, Network ACLs (NACLs) operate at the subnet level and are stateless, requiring you to explicitly define both inbound and outbound rules, including the return path for ephemeral ports. While Security Groups only support "Allow" rules to provide granular, identity-based security for East-West traffic, NACLs support both "Allow" and "Deny" rules, making them the ideal tool for a CloudOps engineer to implement broad, CIDR-based "North-South" perimeters, such as blocking a malicious range of IP addresses at the very edge of the network. Think of a Security Group as the "shield" protecting the resource (ENI) and a NACL as the "fence" protecting the subnet.

Know the difference between interface VPC endpoints and gateway VPC endpoints. Interface endpoints, powered by AWS PrivateLink, manifest as Elastic Network Interfaces (ENIs) with private IP addresses within your specific subnets. They are the primary tool for securing East-West traffic to the majority of AWS services and are governed by Security Groups, offering granular, interface-level control at a cost of an hourly fee plus data processing. In contrast, gateway endpoints are unique to Amazon S3 and DynamoDB; they do not use ENIs or IPs but instead function as a target in your VPC route table. Because they are a logical routing layer rather than an IP-addressable interface, gateway endpoints are provided at no additional cost and are secured primarily via VPC endpoint policies, making them the most fiscally responsible choice for high-volume data transfers to storage and database layers.

Understand how to prevent data exfiltration from a compute resource hosted in a VPC. To understand how to prevent data exfiltration from a compute resource hosted in a VPC, a CloudOps engineer must shift from a network-centric security model to a zero-trust data perimeter. Because standard Security Groups and NACLs are often too coarse to block an authorized user from uploading data to an unmanaged external account, you must implement a double-lock defense using VPC endpoint policies and IAM Service Roles. By routing your East-West traffic through a gateway or interface VPC endpoint, you gain the ability to attach a resource-based policy that explicitly restricts traffic to only your specific Organization ID or approved S3 buckets. When paired with an EC2 Instance Profile that lacks permissions to reach the public Internet via a NAT Gateway, this architecture ensures that even a compromised compute resource is physically and logically "caged" within your private network, effectively neutralizing the threat of an attacker exfiltrating sensitive company data to an external, unauthorized AWS resource.

Know when to use an outbound resolver endpoint vs. an inbound resolver endpoint. You implement an outbound resolver endpoint when your AWS Resources—such as an EC2 instance in a private subnet—need to "ask" for the IP address of a server residing in your corporate data center (e.g., `srv1.corp.internal`). In this scenario, the query travels North-South out of the VPC to your on-premises DNS servers. Conversely, you utilize an inbound resolver endpoint when your on-premises servers need to resolve names for resources living inside your private hosted zones (e.g., `db.aws.internal`). In this case, your data center's DNS forwards the request into the VPC, where the inbound endpoint acts as a local "receptionist" to provide the answer. By deploying both endpoints across multiple Availability Zones, you ensure that your hybrid naming environment remains highly available and that your East-West service discovery is never interrupted by a single zonal failure.

Understand when to use Amazon CloudFront vs. AWS Global Accelerator. You deploy Amazon CloudFront primarily for Layer 7 HTTP/S workloads where static or dynamic content—such as images, videos, or web pages—can be cached at global Edge Locations to reduce origin load and latency. In contrast, you implement AWS Global Accelerator for Layer 4 TCP/UDP workloads where caching is not applicable, such as Gaming, VoIP, or IoT data ingestion. While CloudFront relies on DNS-based routing that can suffer from "propagation lag," Global Accelerator provides two Static Anycast IP addresses that remain fixed even during a regional failover. This allows you to onboard a user's traffic onto the AWS Global Private Network as close to their physical location as possible, bypassing the congested public Internet and providing a deterministic, low-jitter "fast lane" directly to your regional endpoint groups.

Review Questions

1. A CloudOps engineer has a private subnet containing EC2 instances that need to download security patches from the Internet. The instances must not be reachable from the Internet. Which configuration correctly facilitates this North-South egress?
   - **A.** Attach an IGW to the VPC and add a route in the private subnet's route table pointing `0.0.0.0/0` to the IGW.
   - **B.** Deploy a NAT Gateway in the private subnet and point the default route to it.
   - **C.** Deploy a NAT Gateway in a public subnet and add a route in the private subnet's route table pointing `0.0.0.0/0` to the NAT Gateway.
   - **D.** Create an egress-only Internet Gateway and associate it with the private IPv4 addresses.
   - **E.** Use a VPC Peering connection to a shared services VPC that has an Internet Gateway.
2. You are troubleshooting a "Connection Timeout" error for an application trying to reach an RDS instance in another subnet. You verify the NACL allows the traffic. What is the most likely culprit?
   - **A.** The NACL lacks an outbound rule for ephemeral ports.
   - **B.** The Security Group of the RDS instance does not have an Inbound Rule for the application's CIDR/SG.
   - **C.** The route table is missing a local route for the VPC CIDR.
   - **D.** The RDS instance is in a different Availability Zone.
   - **E.** The VPC Flow Logs are not enabled, preventing the connection.
3. An organization wants to ensure that data uploaded to S3 from an EC2 instance in a private subnet never traverses the public Internet. Which solution is most cost-effective?
   - **A.** Create an Interface VPC Endpoint for S3.
   - **B.** Create a Gateway VPC Endpoint for S3 and update the route tables.
   - **C.** Use a NAT Gateway to route traffic to the S3 public endpoint.
   - **D.** Set up a Site-to-Site VPN to route S3 traffic through an on-premises proxy.
   - **E.** Enable S3 Transfer Acceleration on the bucket.
4. A hybrid environment requires on-premises servers to resolve the DNS name `app.aws.internal` hosted in an AWS Private Hosted Zone. How should this be implemented?
   - **A.** Create an Outbound Resolver Endpoint and a forwarding rule for `aws.internal`.
   - **B.** Establish a VPC Peering connection with the on-premises data center.
   - **C.** Attach an Internet Gateway and allow Port 53 in the NACL.
   - **D.** Use a Public Hosted Zone instead of a Private Hosted Zone.
   - **E.** Create an Inbound Resolver Endpoint and point on-premises DNS forwarders to its IP addresses.

5. You need to distribute 20% of traffic to a new Canary deployment of your application. Which Route 53 routing policy should you use?
   A. Simple Routing
   B. Failover Routing
   C. Latency Routing
   D. Weighted Routing
   E. Multivalue Answer Routing

6. Which metric should a CloudOps engineer monitor to identify if a CloudFront distribution's cache settings are inefficient?
   A. `OriginLatency`
   B. `4xxErrorRate`
   C. `CacheHitRate`
   D. `TotalErrorRate`
   E. `FieldLevelEncryptionErrorCount`

7. A company uses a Transit Gateway (TGW) to connect 50 VPCs. Some "Spoke" VPCs cannot communicate with the "Shared Services" VPC. Which two steps are required to remediate this? (Select TWO.)
   A. Disable Source/Destination checks on all EC2 instances.
   B. Ensure that the Spoke VPC Route Tables have a route for the Shared Services CIDR pointing to the TGW ID.
   C. Create a full mesh of VPC Peering connections between all 50 VPCs.
   D. Verify that the TGW route table has associations and propagations for the involved VPC attachments.
   E. Change the NACL on the Shared Services subnet to "Allow All" for the `0.0.0.0/0` range.
   F. Replace the TGW with an Internet Gateway in each Spoke VPC.

8. Which two characteristics are unique to AWS Global Accelerator compared to Amazon CloudFront? (Select TWO.)
   A. It provides two static anycast IP addresses.
   B. It supports Layer 7 HTTP caching at edge locations.
   C. It is designed to optimize the network path for TCP and UDP traffic.
   D. It requires an S3 bucket as an origin.
   E. It uses DNS-based routing to resolve hostnames to edge locations.
   F. It automatically integrates with AWS WAF for SQL injection protection.

9. A CloudOps engineer is investigating why a private EC2 instance cannot access an S3 bucket via a Gateway VPC Endpoint. Which two areas should be checked? (Select TWO.)
   A. The outbound rules of the instance's Security Group for the S3 Prefix List.
   B. The inbound rules of the Gateway VPC Endpoint's Security Group.
   C. The route table associated with the instance's subnet for an S3 Prefix List target.
   D. The public IP address assigned to the EC2 instance.
   E. The Internet Gateway status for the VPC.
   F. The BGP Community tags on the Direct Connect Virtual Interface.

10. You want to audit all `REJECT` actions at the network level for a specific application. Which two logging/monitoring configurations will provide this data? (Select TWO.)
   A. Enable CloudFront real-time logs with a 100% sampling rate.
   B. Enable VPC Flow Logs and filter for the `REJECT` action.
   C. Use CloudWatch Logs Insights to query the `/aws/vpc/flowlogs` log group.
   D. Review AWS CloudTrail logs for `UnauthorizedOperation` events.
   E. Enable S3 Server Access Logging for the application's data bucket.
   F. Monitor the `EstimatedCharges` metric in CloudWatch.

11. A CloudOps engineer is configuring a new VPC. They create a public subnet and an Internet Gateway (IGW), but instances in the subnet still cannot reach the Internet. What are the most likely missing steps? (Select TWO.)
   A. The instances do not have a public IPv4 address or an elastic IP.
   B. The NACL is stateful and blocking the return traffic.
   C. The route table for the public subnet does not have an entry for `0.0.0.0/0` pointing to the IGW.
   D. The Security Group needs an inbound rule for port 80 from `0.0.0.0/0`.
   E. The VPC does not have a Virtual Private Gateway attached.

12. You notice that a private EC2 instance is successfully sending data to S3 via a Gateway Endpoint, but it cannot ping the S3 service. Why is this occurring?
   A. The Security Group on the EC2 instance is blocking ICMP traffic.
   B. The Gateway Endpoint policy explicitly denies the `icmp:ping` action.
   C. Gateway Endpoints are logical routing targets and do not support ICMP/Ping traffic.
   D. The NACL for the private subnet is missing an outbound rule for S3.
   E. The EC2 instance does not have an IAM role with S3 permissions.

13. A CloudOps engineer needs to ensure that users in Australia are routed to the Sydney Region, while users in the UK are routed to the London Region for a localized web experience. Which Route 53 policy is best?

    A. Latency Routing

    B. Geolocation Routing

    C. Geoproximity Routing

    D. Multivalue Answer Routing

    E. Failover Routing

14. When implementing an Inbound Resolver Endpoint for hybrid DNS, why must a CloudOps engineer select at least two subnets in different Availability Zones?

    A. To increase the total throughput of DNS queries to 20 Gbps.

    B. To allow the Inbound Endpoint to resolve both private and public hosted zones.

    C. To maintain High Availability (HA) and meet the AWS Service Level Agreement (SLA).

    D. To separate inbound traffic from outbound traffic.

    E. To prevent the Split-Horizon DNS conflict.

15. A CloudFront distribution is returning "Access Denied" errors for an S3 origin, even though the files exist. You want to ensure the S3 bucket is NOT public. What should you implement?

    A. S3 bucket policies allowing Principal: *

    B. CloudFront signed cookies

    C. Origin Access Control (OAC) and a corresponding S3 Bucket Policy

    D. A NAT Gateway in the S3 bucket's VPC

    E. Lambda@Edge to rewrite the request headers

16. You need to implement a service discovery mechanism where resources in VPC-A can reach a service in VPC-B without Peering or a Transit Gateway. Which two steps are required to use VPC Endpoint Services (PrivateLink)? (Select TWO.)

    A. Create a Network Load Balancer (NLB) in VPC-B to front the service.

    B. Enable "Acceptance Required" on the VPC endpoint service configuration.

    C. Associate an Internet Gateway with the service provider VPC.

    D. Create an Interface VPC endpoint in VPC-A pointing to the service name from VPC-B.

    E. Add a route to VPC-A's route table pointing to the VPC-B CIDR.

    F. Use a Gateway Load Balancer to inspect the traffic.

17. A CloudOps engineer notices that a private EC2 instance can reach S3 using a Gateway Endpoint but cannot reach an SQS queue via an Interface Endpoint. Which two configurations should be verified? (Select TWO.)
   - A. The Security Group associated with the SQS interface endpoint allows inbound traffic on port 443 from the EC2 instance.
   - B. The route table includes a Prefix List entry for the SQS service.
   - C. The EC2 instance has "private DNS names" enabled for the SQS VPC endpoint.
   - D. The SQS queue has a resource-based policy allowing the `vpc-id`.
   - E. The NAT Gateway is provisioned in a public subnet within the same AZ as the EC2.
   - F. The interface endpoint is associated with an outbound resolver rule.

18. A CloudFront distribution is returning 504 (Gateway Timeout) errors. Which two actions should a CloudOps engineer take to remediate this? (Select TWO.)
   - A. Increase the "Origin Response Timeout" in the CloudFront Origin settings.
   - B. Invalidate the entire cache using the `/*` path.
   - C. Check the performance and resource utilization of the origin server (ALB/EC2).
   - D. Update the CloudFront Cache Policy to forward all cookies.
   - E. Enable "Origin Shield" to reduce the number of concurrent requests to the origin.
   - F. Change the Viewer Protocol Policy to "Redirect HTTP to HTTPS."

19. A CloudOps engineer needs to prevent an EC2 instance from exfiltrating data to an S3 bucket in a personal account. The instance must still be able to access the company's production S3 buckets. Which configuration is most secure?
   - A. Remove the NAT Gateway and use only a Gateway VPC endpoint with a restrictive policy.
   - B. Use a Security Group to block all outbound traffic to the S3 public IP range.
   - C. Apply a Deny rule in the NACL for the personal S3 bucket's IP addresses.
   - D. Use an IAM policy with a condition for `s3:ResourceAccount` set to the personal account ID.
   - E. Enable S3 Block Public Access on the production bucket.

20. An on-premises application needs to resolve `service.production.aws.internal`. You have an Inbound Resolver Endpoint in your VPC. The on-premises DNS forwarder is configured correctly, but queries are timing out. VPC Flow Logs show `ACCEPT` for traffic to the inbound endpoint IPs. What should you check?
   - A. The `$LATEST` version of the resolver endpoint.
   - B. The NACL of the subnet containing the inbound endpoint to ensure that port 53 UDP/TCP is allowed.
   - C. The outbound resolver rule for the on-premises domain.
   - D. The Recursion Desired (RD) flag in the on-premises DNS query.
   - E. The private hosted zone's association with the VPC containing the inbound endpoint.

Answers to Review Questions

1. C. A NAT Gateway must live in a public subnet (with an IGW route) to function. The private subnet then routes traffic to it. Options A, B, D, E are incorrect. Option A (makes instances public), Option B (NAT needs IGW access), Option D (IPv6 only), and Option E (Peering is non-transitive for IGWs).

2. B. A Security Group failure typically results in a "timeout" (silent drop). If it were a NACL issue, it would likely be a "Connection Refused" if stateless rules were mismatched, but SGs are the first line of defense at the ENI. Options A, C, D, E are incorrect. Option A (NACL issues usually show as `REJECT` in logs, not just timeout, and NACL was already verified), Option C (Local routes are implicit), Option D (VPC traffic is regional), and Option E (Logs don't cause failures).

3. B. Gateway endpoints for S3/DynamoDB are free and require no ENIs, making them the most cost-effective way to keep traffic private. Options A, C, D, E are incorrect. Option A (Incurs hourly/data fees), Option C (Traverses internet/incurs NAT fees), Option D (High latency/cost), and Option E (Uses public internet).

4. E. Inbound endpoints allow external (on-prem) queries to enter the VPC to resolve names in Private Hosted Zones. Options A, B, C, D are incorrect. Option A (Used for AWS-to-On-Prem queries), Option B (Peering is for VPC-to-VPC), Option C (Unsafe/not for PHZ), and Option D (Exposes internal names).

5. D. Weighted routing allows you to assign specific percentages to different resource records. Options A, B, C, E are incorrect. Option A (One-to-one), Option B (Primary/Passive), Option C (Speed-based), and Option E (Random healthy records).

6. C. `CacheHitRate` measures how often content is served from the edge. A low rate means requests are constantly hitting the origin, indicating inefficient TTL or cache-key settings. Options A, B, D, E are incorrect. Option A (Origin health), Options B and D (Client/Server errors), and Option E (Security specific).

7. B, D. You must have a route in the VPC route table (the "road" to the TGW) and proper TGW route table logic (the "brain" of the hub). Options A, C, E, F are incorrect. Option A (For NAT instances), Option C (Administrative complexity/unnecessary with TGW), Option E (Unsafe), and Option F (Removes private connectivity).

8. A, C. Global Accelerator uses static anycast IPs and operates at Layer 4 (TCP/UDP) for path optimization. Options B, D, E, F are incorrect. Option B (CloudFront), Option D (CloudFront/Optional), Option E (CloudFront/Route 53), and Option F (CloudFront).

9. A, C. You must have the route in the table and the Security Group must allow the egress to the S3 Prefix List. Options B, D, E, F are incorrect. Option B (Gateway Endpoints don't have SGs), Option D (Private instances don't have public IPs), Option E (Gateway endpoints bypass IGWs), and Option F (Irrelevant to VPC internal endpoints).

10. B, C. VPC Flow Logs capture the `REJECT`s, and Logs Insights is the tool used to query and analyze those logs. Options A, D, E, F are incorrect. Option A (Edge level, not VPC), Option D (IAM/API level, not network packet level), Option E (Storage level), and Option F (Billing).

11. A, C. For the instances to reach the Internet, they must have a Public IPv4 address (an EIP, or an IPv6 address) and be in a subnet with a route table that explicitly points default traffic (`0.0.0.0/0`) to the Internet Gateway. Options B, D, E are incorrect. Option B (NACLs are stateless), Option D (Inbound isn't required for outbound egress), and Option E (For VPNs).

12. C. Gateway Endpoints exist only as entries in a route table. They do not have an IP address or an interface that can respond to an ICMP ping request. Options A, B, D, E are incorrect. Option A (Even if allowed, there is no target to ping), Option B (Policies govern API actions, not ICMP), D (Traffic is already succeeding), and Option E (Affects APIs, not pings).

13. B. Geolocation Routing allows you to route traffic based on the geographic location (continent or country) of your users. Options A, C, D, E are incorrect. Option A (Based on speed, not necessarily political boundaries), Option C (Based on physical distance and "bias"), Option D (Load balancing), and Option E (Disaster recovery).

14. C. AWS requires at least two IP addresses in different Availability Zones for resolver endpoints to ensure DNS resolution continues if one AZ goes down. Options A, B, D, E are incorrect. Option A (Not for throughput), Option B (Resolved by default), Option D (Direction is set at the endpoint level, not per AZ), and Option E (Logical naming issue).

15. C. OAC is the modern standard to ensure S3 content is only accessible via CloudFront, keeping the bucket private from the public Internet. Options A, B, D, E are incorrect. Option A (Makes it public), Option B (For restricted content access, not origin security), Option D (Networking, not permissions), and Option E (Overly complex for this use case).

16. A, D. PrivateLink requires an NLB on the provider side and an Interface Endpoint on the consumer side. Options B, C, E, F are incorrect. Option B (Optional/Not required for discovery), Option C (PrivateLink is private), Option E (No routing needed), and Option F (For third-party security appliances).

17. A, C. Interface Endpoints require Security Groups to allow traffic in, and private DNS is required for the instance to resolve the standard SQS DNS name to the private endpoint IP. Options B, D, E, F are incorrect. Option B (For Gateway endpoints), Option D (Queue policy is IAM-based), Option E (Endpoints bypass NAT), and Option F (Resolver rules are for hybrid DNS).

18. A, C. A 504 error means the origin failed to respond in time. You must either give the origin more time or fix the backend performance bottleneck. Options B, D, E, F are incorrect. Option B (For stale content), Option D (Reduces hit rate), Option E (Consolidates, but doesn't fix a timeout), and Option F (Redirect logic).

19. A. By removing the NAT Gateway, you remove the path to the public Internet/unmanaged buckets. The VPC endpoint policy then provides the "gate" that only allows traffic to trusted resource ARNs or Organization IDs. Options B, C, D, E are incorrect. Option B (IP ranges are too broad), Option C (NACLs don't support DNS names), Option D (Should allow production, not just deny one), and Option E (Doesn't stop exfiltration).

20. E. An inbound resolver endpoint cannot resolve a Private Hosted Zone unless that specific zone is associated with the VPC where the Endpoint lives. Options A, B, C, D are incorrect. Option A (Endpoints don't have versions), Option B (Flow logs showed `ACCEPT`), Option C (For VPC-to-On-Prem), and Option D (Resolver handles recursion).

Cost Optimization

THE AWS CERTIFIED CLOUDOPS ENGINEER ASSOCIATE (SOA-C03) EXAM OBJECTIVES COVERED IN THIS CHAPTER MAY INCLUDE, BUT ARE NOT LIMITED TO THE FOLLOWING:

✔ **Domain 1: Monitoring, Logging, Analysis, Remediation, and Performance Optimization**

- 1.3 Implement performance optimization strategies for compute, storage, and database resources

✔ **Domain 2: Reliability and Business Continuity**

- 2.3 Implement backup and restore strategies

✔ **Domain 5: Networking and Content Delivery**

- 5.1 Implement and optimize networking features and connectivity

Cost optimization is not an isolated discipline in cloud operations—it's the connective tissue that runs through every architectural decision, operational workflow, and monitoring strategy. Throughout this book, we have consistently highlighted how cost considerations influence nearly every domain: compute choices, storage lifecycle policies, networking patterns, observability pipelines, automation strategies, and even resilience design. CloudOps engineers preparing for the SOA-C03 exam must internalize that cost is never a "later" concern. It is a first-class operational metric, just as important as performance, reliability, and security.

For exam candidates familiar with the previous version of the exam (SOA-C02), cost optimization was its own standalone domain (Domain 6, Tasks 6.1 and 6.2), but in SOA-C03 it has been folded into Domain 1, Task 1.3 "Implement performance optimization strategies for compute, storage, and database resources"—an important shift that explains why this book still includes a dedicated cost chapter, even though the current blueprint no longer treats cost as a separate domain.

In this final chapter, we shift from the embedded cost-awareness you've seen across the book to a formal exploration of the AWS services and frameworks that directly support cost governance. While many AWS services indirectly influence cost, there are three cost-specific tools that SOA-C03 candidates must know thoroughly: AWS Cost and Usage Reports (CUR), AWS Cost Explorer, and AWS Savings Plans. These services form the foundation of AWS cost visibility, analysis, and long-term optimization. Understanding how they work—and how CloudOps teams use them in real environments—is essential for both the exam and your day-to-day operational practice.

This chapter also revisits the Cost Optimization pillar of the AWS Well-Architected Framework, expanding on its design principles, best practices, and the frugal engineering mindset that allows teams to build efficient, scalable, and sustainable cloud architectures. Together, these concepts give you a complete, end-to-end understanding of how to manage cost as a disciplined, continuous operational function.

Cost Management Services

AWS provides a suite of cost-management tools that give CloudOps engineers visibility into spending, usage patterns, and optimization opportunities. These tools operate at different levels of granularity and serve different operational needs—from high-level dashboards to raw, queryable datasets. Mastering them allows you to move from reactive cost reviews to proactive, data-driven cost governance.

AWS Cost and Usage Reports

AWS Cost and Usage Reports (CUR) are the most comprehensive and detailed source of cost and usage data available in AWS. If you think of AWS billing as a telemetry stream, CUR is the full-fidelity log—every event, every resource, every hour, captured with precision.

CUR delivers massive datasets to an S3 bucket of your choice. Cost and usage data can be aggregated in hourly, daily, or monthly intervals. These files contain line-item detail for every billable action across your AWS accounts. Because of their size and richness, CUR datasets are often queried using Amazon Athena, loaded into Amazon Redshift for long-term analytics, or visualized through Amazon QuickSight dashboards tailored to engineering, finance, or leadership.

CUR becomes indispensable when you need to:

- Investigate unexpected cost spikes at a granular level
- Attribute costs accurately across teams, applications, or environments
- Build automated cost-monitoring pipelines
- Perform long-term forecasting and trend analysis
- Validate the financial impact of architectural changes

For CloudOps engineers, CUR is the authoritative dataset that supports deep cost governance. On the SOA-C03 exam, expect CUR to appear in scenarios involving detailed cost analysis, chargeback/showback, or advanced reporting.

AWS Cost Explorer

AWS Cost Explorer provides a visual, interactive interface for analyzing AWS spending. Where CUR gives you raw data, Cost Explorer gives you actionable insights. It's designed for day-to-day operational visibility—the tool you open when you need to understand cost trends, identify anomalies, or evaluate the financial impact of recent changes.

Cost Explorer allows you to:

- View historical spending across services, regions, and accounts
- Forecast future costs based on usage patterns
- Filter and group costs by tags, cost categories, or linked accounts
- Analyze usage trends for EC2, RDS, S3, and other services
- Review recommendations for Savings Plans and Reserved Instances
- Integrate with Cost Anomaly Detection for proactive alerts

For CloudOps engineers, Cost Explorer becomes the operational cockpit for cost awareness. It helps you validate whether scaling policies are behaving as expected, whether new workloads are consuming more resources than anticipated, and whether your environment is trending toward or away from budget expectations.

On the SOA-C03 exam, Cost Explorer is often associated with forecasting, anomaly detection, and tag-based cost allocation.

Savings Plans

Savings Plans are AWS's flexible, commitment-based pricing model that provides significant discounts on compute usage. They are the modern evolution of Reserved Instances, offering simpler management and broader applicability.

As of the writing of this book, Savings Plans come in four types:

- **Compute Savings Plans**
  - Apply to any EC2 instance, regardless of region, instance family, OS, or tenancy
  - Also apply to AWS Fargate and AWS Lambda
  - Offer the highest flexibility and broadest coverage
- **Database Savings Plans**
  - Apply to database services including Amazon RDS, Aurora, DynamoDB, ElastiCache, DocumentDB, Timestream, Neptune, Keyspaces, DMS, and OpenSearch Service
  - Cover both instance-based and serverless database consumption (where supported)
  - Provide flexible discounts across database engines without locking you to a specific instance family
  - Ideal for teams standardizing on managed database services but needing engine or instance-type agility
- **EC2 Instance Savings Plans**
  - Apply to a specific instance family within a region
  - Offer deeper discounts than Compute Savings Plans
  - Ideal for predictable, steady-state workloads
- **SageMaker AI Savings Plans**
  - Apply to SageMaker AI training, inference, and notebook usage
  - Designed for ML-heavy environments

Savings Plans require you to commit to a specific *$ per hour* spend for one or three years. Payment options (All Upfront, Partial Upfront, No Upfront) allow you to balance cash flow with discount levels.

For CloudOps engineers, Savings Plans are a strategic lever for reducing compute costs without sacrificing architectural flexibility. They require careful analysis of historical usage, steady-state workloads, and long-term demand patterns.

On the SOA-C03 exam, expect questions that test your ability to choose the right Savings Plan type based on workload characteristics and operational constraints.

For any specific workload, you cannot stack a Database Savings Plan with an existing Amazon RDS Reserved Instance or DynamoDB Reserved Capacity for the same usage. While they can coexist in your account to cover different resources, AWS prioritizes applying Reserved Instances and Reserved Capacity first to eligible usage before applying any remaining Database Savings Plan commitment.

Cost Optimization Pillar

As you learned at the begin of the chapter, cost optimization in AWS is not a one-off "cost cutting exercise"; it's a continuous discipline that lives inside the CloudOps lifecycle. Every phase—Deploy, Monitor, Sustain, Secure, Optimize—has cost-relevant decisions baked into it. The Cost Optimization pillar of the AWS Well-Architected Framework gives you a vocabulary and a structure for those decisions, so you're not just reacting to high bills, but designing and operating with cost in mind from day one.

For SOA-C03 candidates, this pillar is especially important because it connects directly to how you think as a CloudOps engineer: you're not only keeping systems healthy and secure, you're also making sure they're economically sustainable. In this section, we first walk through the design principles of the Cost Optimization pillar, then translate them into practical best practices and frugal architecture patterns that map cleanly onto the CloudOps cycle.

Design Principles

AWS defines several core design principles for cost optimization. We expand each one, show how it plays out in real CloudOps work, and explicitly map it to the phases of the CloudOps cycle. Think of these principles as "lenses" you apply repeatedly as workloads evolve.

Implement Cloud Financial Management

"Cloud financial management" is about treating cost as a first-class operational metric, not just a monthly surprise for finance. It means you have processes, tools, and ownership around understanding, forecasting, and controlling cloud spend. You don't just know what you're spending—you know why, where, and who is responsible.

This principle pushes CloudOps teams to collaborate with finance, product, and leadership. It also encourages building shared dashboards, defining budgets, and making cost visible to the teams that generate it. Over time, this creates a culture where engineers naturally ask, "What's the cost impact?" alongside "What's the latency?" or "What's the error rate?"

How it Maps to the CloudOps Cycle

Deploy During deployment, you define tagging standards (e.g., Environment, Application, Owner, CostCenter) and ensure that infrastructure as code (IaC) templates enforce them.

You also decide which accounts, OU structure, and cost categories will be used for reporting. This is where you "wire in" financial observability from the start.

Monitor You integrate cost metrics and budgets into your monitoring stack. For example, you use AWS Budgets and Cost Explorer to track spend against thresholds, and you surface cost KPIs in the same dashboards as performance and availability metrics. Cost anomalies become operational events, not just billing surprises.

Sustain In day-to-day operations, you review cost reports regularly, participate in cost review meetings, and adjust capacity or configurations based on observed trends. You might refine Auto Scaling policies, adjust retention periods, or decommission unused resources as part of routine operations.

Secure Financial management intersects with security when you consider least privilege and account boundaries. For example, restricting who can launch expensive instance types or create high-cost resources is both a security and cost control measure.

Optimize Here, cloud financial management drives structured optimization cycles: you analyze CUR data, evaluate Savings Plans, and prioritize optimization initiatives based on ROI. This is where you turn insights into concrete savings.

Adopt a Consumption Model

Adopting a consumption model means you pay only for what you actually use, and you actively avoid paying for idle capacity. This is one of the core promises of cloud computing—but it doesn't happen automatically. You must design and operate systems so that capacity scales with demand, and non-essential resources are shut down when not needed.

This principle encourages you to embrace elasticity, serverless, and event-driven patterns. It also pushes you to challenge "always-on" assumptions inherited from on-premises thinking.

How it Maps to the CloudOps Cycle

Deploy You choose services and architectures that support elasticity: Auto Scaling groups, Lambda, Fargate, managed databases with storage autoscaling, and S3 instead of fixed file servers. You design environments (especially dev/test) with the expectation that they can be paused or scaled down.

Monitor You track utilization metrics—CPU, memory, I/O, request rates—and compare them to provisioned capacity. Low utilization is a signal that you're not fully aligned with a consumption model. You also monitor idle resources (e.g., unattached EBS volumes, unused Elastic IPs).

Sustain You implement schedules to stop non-production instances outside business hours, adjust Auto Scaling policies based on observed patterns, and periodically clean up unused resources. CloudOps teams become guardians of "no idle waste."

Secure From a security perspective, reducing idle resources also reduces attack surface. Fewer running instances, open endpoints, and unused services mean fewer things to secure and patch.

Optimize You use utilization data to right-size instances, move to serverless where appropriate, and refine scaling policies. You might also introduce automation (Lambda, Step Functions) to enforce shutdown schedules and cleanup routines.

Measure Overall Efficiency

Measuring overall efficiency means you don't look at cost in isolation—you look at value per dollar. A system that is cheaper but fails frequently or performs poorly is not efficient. Conversely, a system that costs more but delivers significantly more business value may be the better choice.

This principle encourages you to think in terms of cost per transaction, cost per request, or cost per business outcome, rather than just total monthly spend. It also aligns cost optimization with performance and reliability, not against them.

How it Maps to the CloudOps Cycle

Deploy You define SLOs (Service Level Objectives) and understand the expected traffic and business value of the workload. You choose architectures that can meet those SLOs at a reasonable cost, and you document assumptions about expected efficiency (e.g., target cost per 1,000 requests).

Monitor You track both technical metrics (latency, error rate, throughput) and cost metrics (spend per service, per environment). Over time, you derive efficiency metrics like cost per request or cost per user. If cost rises faster than usage, that's a signal to investigate.

Sustain You adjust configurations to maintain efficiency: tuning cache sizes, adjusting concurrency limits, refining database indexes, or changing storage classes. CloudOps teams ensure that performance remains acceptable without over-provisioning.

Secure Security controls (e.g., logging, encryption, WAF) have cost implications. Measuring efficiency helps you balance security requirements with cost, ensuring you're not overspending on unnecessary or redundant controls while still meeting compliance and risk thresholds.

Optimize You run experiments: try different instance families, caching strategies, or data partitioning approaches, and compare efficiency metrics. Optimization becomes a data-driven process, not guesswork.

Stop Spending Money on Undifferentiated Heavy Lifting

"Undifferentiated heavy lifting" refers to all the infrastructure work that doesn't directly contribute to your unique business value: managing databases, patching operating systems, running message brokers, maintaining monitoring stacks, and so on. AWS managed services exist precisely to take this burden off your plate.

This principle encourages you to move from self-managed infrastructure on EC2 to managed services like RDS, DynamoDB, SQS, SNS, EventBridge, and fully managed observability tools. While managed services may sometimes appear more expensive on a raw price basis, they often reduce total cost of ownership by eliminating operational overhead and reducing failure modes.

How it Maps to the CloudOps Cycle

Deploy You choose managed services by default unless there is a strong reason not to. Instead of deploying your own MySQL on EC2, you use RDS. Instead of running Kafka, you consider MSK or SQS/SNS/EventBridge depending on the use case. Your IaC templates reflect this bias toward managed services.

Monitor Managed services come with built-in metrics, logs, and integration with CloudWatch. You monitor them like any other component, but you no longer monitor OS-level details, patch cycles, or cluster health for those layers.

Sustain Operations teams shift from "keeping servers alive" to "configuring and tuning managed services." You spend less time on patching, backups, and failover orchestration, and more time on capacity planning and configuration.

Secure Managed services often provide security features out of the box: encryption at rest, automatic patching, IAM integration, and fine-grained access control. This reduces both security risk and the operational cost of maintaining secure configurations.

Optimize With less time spent on undifferentiated tasks, you can focus optimization efforts on application logic, data models, and usage patterns. You can also more easily experiment with different service configurations (e.g., RDS instance classes, DynamoDB capacity modes) to find cost-efficient setups.

Analyze and Attribute Expenditure

Analyzing and attributing expenditure means you can answer: Who is spending what, on which workloads, and why? This is where tagging, cost categories, consolidated billing, and tools like CUR and Cost Explorer come together.

Without proper attribution, cost optimization becomes guesswork and accountability is blurred. With it, teams can own their costs, product managers can understand the financial impact of features, and leadership can make informed trade-offs.

How it Maps to the CloudOps Cycle

Deploy You define and enforce a tagging strategy from the start. IaC templates ensure that all resources are created with required tags. You also design your AWS Organizations structure and cost categories to reflect your business (e.g., by product, team, environment).

Monitor You use Cost Explorer, CUR, and budgets filtered by tags, accounts, or cost categories. This allows you to see cost per application, per environment, or per team. Anomalies can be traced back to specific owners.

Sustain CloudOps teams regularly review cost reports segmented by tags and categories. When a cost spike occurs, they can quickly identify which workload or team is responsible and investigate further.

Secure Tagging and account structure also support security boundaries. For example, separating production and non-production accounts helps both cost attribution and blast radius control. IAM policies can restrict who can create or modify high-cost resources.

Optimize With clear attribution, you can prioritize optimization efforts where they matter most—high-cost workloads, rapidly growing services, or teams with the largest spend. You can also implement chargeback or showback models to incentivize cost-aware behavior.

Best Practices

The design principles give you the "why" and "how to think." Best practices give you the "what to do" on a recurring basis. These practices are where CloudOps engineers live day-to-day, and they map naturally into the lifecycle phases.

Right-Size Resources

You regularly review utilization metrics and adjust instance types, database sizes, and storage classes. Tools like AWS Compute Optimizer and Trusted Advisor provide recommendations based on historical usage. Right-sizing is not a one-time event; it's a recurring operational task.

- **Deploy:** Start with reasonable sizes, not oversized "just in case."
- **Monitor:** Track utilization and compare against thresholds.
- **Sustain:** Apply right-sizing changes during maintenance windows.
- **Secure:** Ensure that changes don't break security baselines (e.g., AMI hardening).
- **Optimize:** Use recommendations and experiments to converge on efficient configurations.

Use Elasticity

You design systems to scale in and out automatically. Auto Scaling groups, Lambda concurrency, and event-driven architectures allow you to match capacity to demand.

- **Deploy:** Build with Auto Scaling and serverless patterns.
- **Monitor:** Watch scaling events and ensure that they align with traffic patterns.
- **Sustain:** Tune scaling policies based on real behavior.
- **Secure:** Ensure scaling doesn't bypass security controls (e.g., IAM roles, security groups).
- **Optimize:** Refine thresholds and cooldowns to avoid over- or under-scaling.

Choose the Right Pricing Model

You match workloads to pricing models: On-Demand for unpredictable usage, Savings Plans for steady-state, and Spot for fault-tolerant or batch jobs.

- **Deploy:** Classify workloads by predictability and criticality.
- **Monitor:** Track usage patterns to validate assumptions.
- **Sustain:** Adjust commitments (Savings Plans) as workloads evolve.

- **Secure:** Ensure Spot usage doesn't compromise critical security or compliance workloads.
- **Optimize:** Continuously refine the mix of On-Demand, Savings Plans, and Spot.

Optimize Data Transfer

You design architectures that minimize expensive data movement: use VPC endpoints, CloudFront, and thoughtful AZ/region placement.

- **Deploy:** Place resources to minimize cross-AZ/region traffic where possible.
- **Monitor:** Track data transfer costs by service and path.
- **Sustain:** Adjust architectures (e.g., add CloudFront, consolidate NAT Gateways).
- **Secure:** Ensure that private connectivity (VPC endpoints, PrivateLink) also strengthens security.
- **Optimize:** Iterate on caching, peering, and routing strategies.

Use Managed Services

Pick RDS, DynamoDB, SQS, SNS, EventBridge, and other managed services over self-managed equivalents.

- **Deploy:** Default to managed services unless there's a strong reason not to.
- **Monitor:** Use built-in metrics and logs.
- **Sustain:** Focus on configuration and capacity, not patching and backups.
- **Secure:** Leverage built-in encryption, IAM integration, and compliance features.
- **Optimize:** Tune configurations (e.g., RDS instance class, DynamoDB capacity mode) for cost.

Implement Cost Governance

Establish policies, guardrails, and review processes around cost.

- **Deploy:** Enforce tagging, SCPs, and IAM policies that prevent uncontrolled spend.
- **Monitor:** Use budgets, alerts, and anomaly detection.
- **Sustain:** Run regular cost reviews and hygiene tasks.
- **Secure:** Treat financial exposure as a risk to be controlled.
- **Optimize:** Use governance insights to drive targeted optimization efforts.

Frugal Architecture Principles

Frugal architecture is the natural culmination of everything a CloudOps engineer learns about cost optimization. It's not about cutting corners or building "cheap" systems; it's about designing with intention, eliminating waste, and ensuring that every dollar spent contributes to reliability, security, performance, and—most importantly—business value. In practice, frugality begins with the architectural choices you make. Serverless services, event-driven patterns, and managed offerings allow you to avoid the hidden tax of idle capacity and operational overhead. When you choose Lambda over a self-managed EC2 fleet, or SQS over a home-grown queue, you're not just simplifying operations—you're embracing a model where cost naturally aligns with usage. This mindset encourages you to build systems that scale gracefully, shrink automatically, and never consume more resources than they need.

A frugal architecture also embraces the idea that workloads should be resilient enough to take advantage of discounted capacity models. When you design for graceful degradation—using retries, idempotent operations, and distributed patterns—you unlock the ability to run portions of your workload on Spot Instances or other opportunistic compute options. This is where cost optimization and resilience reinforce each other: the more tolerant your system is to interruptions, the more aggressively you can pursue low-cost compute. CloudOps engineers quickly learn that resilience patterns are not just about uptime; they are also about enabling economic efficiency at scale. The SOA-C03 exam reflects this by presenting scenarios where the "right" answer is the one that balances reliability with cost-aware architectural choices.

Storage is another domain where frugality becomes a continuous discipline rather than a one-time decision. Data naturally grows, ages, and shifts in access patterns, and frugal architectures anticipate this evolution. Instead of treating storage as a static choice, you design with lifecycle transitions in mind—moving objects from S3 Standard to Infrequent Access, then to Glacier, and eventually to Deep Archive as they lose relevance. This automated tiering ensures that your storage footprint remains aligned with actual business needs, not historical habits. It also reinforces the CloudOps principle that cost optimization is inseparable from operational hygiene: the more disciplined you are about retention, lifecycle rules, and data placement, the more sustainable your environment becomes over time.

Finally, frugal architectures rely heavily on automation to maintain their efficiency. Even the most carefully designed system will drift toward waste if left unattended. Automated cleanup routines, scheduled shutdowns for non-production environments, snapshot rotation policies, and periodic resource audits ensure that your environment stays lean without requiring constant manual intervention. This is where the CloudOps lifecycle comes full circle: you deploy with cost in mind, monitor usage patterns, operate with discipline, secure your environment against unnecessary exposure, and continuously optimize through automation and refinement. Frugality, in this sense, is not a constraint—it's a philosophy that empowers CloudOps engineers to build systems that are elegant, resilient, and economically responsible. It's the mindset that transforms cost optimization from a task into a habit, and from a habit into a defining characteristic of modern cloud operations.

Frugal Architecture in Action

Frugal architecture becomes most meaningful when you see how it influences real operational decisions. While the principles of frugality guide your mindset, CloudOps engineers ultimately demonstrate cost awareness through the choices they make about compute, databases, storage, data protection (security), and network design. The SOA-C03 exam reflects this by presenting scenarios where cost-efficient thinking must be applied to concrete AWS services you've already studied in earlier chapters. In the following examples, we revisit databases, Amazon EBS, point-in-time recovery, and network architectures—not to re-explain the services themselves, but to show how frugal thinking transforms them into powerful cost-optimization levers. These examples illustrate how the principles of right-sizing, lifecycle awareness, and architectural intentionality translate into measurable savings in real CloudOps environments.

Reducing Cost by Optimizing Database Performance

Cost optimization begins with deep visibility into how your data layer consumes resources. You learned in Chapter 4 how Amazon RDS Performance Insights can help you move beyond surface-level monitoring to identify the specific "expensive" queries driving up your bill. When you pinpoint a query responsible for a massive CPU spike, you can tune the SQL or add missing indexes rather than simply throwing expensive hardware at the problem. Complementing this with CloudWatch alarms for critical metrics like CPU utilization, connection counts, and IOPS ensures you are alerted the moment a workload trends toward inefficiency, allowing for proactive adjustments before costs spiral.

Strategic configuration changes further bridge the gap between high performance and low cost. Instance right-sizing ensures you aren't paying for idle CPU or RAM, while storage autoscaling eliminates the need to over-provision disk space for future growth, charging you only for what you actually use. For read-heavy applications, deploying read replicas is a classic frugal move; it allows you to offload traffic from a high-tier primary instance to smaller, more cost-effective nodes, improving application latency while keeping the primary instance lean and specialized for write operations.

At its core, a Frugal Database design—characterized by efficient indexing, lean schemas, and optimized query patterns—serves as the ultimate cost-saving engine. When a database is architected for efficiency, it requires fewer compute cycles and less I/O to deliver results, directly lowering the baseline requirements for your underlying infrastructure. For a deeper dive into the specific mechanics of these features, refer back to Chapter 4, where we examined each AWS database service through the lenses of performance optimization and scalability and elasticity.

Reducing Cost by Optimizing Amazon EBS Volume Types

Back in Chapter 5, you explored the performance characteristics and use cases of Amazon EBS volume types. Here, we shift the lens to cost efficiency. EBS is one of the most common sources of silent overspending in AWS environments because volumes are often over-provisioned "just in case" or left running long after their associated workloads have changed. Frugal architecture encourages you to treat EBS not as a static choice but as a dynamic resource that should evolve with workload behavior.

For example, `gp3` volumes offer a baseline of 3,000 IOPS and 125 MiB/s throughput at a significantly lower cost than `gp2`, and they allow you to provision additional IOPS and throughput independently. This makes `gp3` the default frugal choice for most general-purpose workloads. Conversely, `io2` and `io2 Block Express` provide high durability and predictable performance, but they come at a premium. A frugal CloudOps engineer uses these only when the workload's performance profile truly demands it—and validates that need through monitoring rather than assumption.

Frugality also means continuously revisiting EBS usage. Snapshots accumulate over time, unattached volumes linger after instance termination, and workloads evolve in ways that may justify switching volume types. Automation plays a key role here: scheduled cleanup routines, snapshot lifecycle policies, and periodic right-sizing reviews ensure that EBS costs remain aligned with actual usage. The SOA-C03 exam often tests this operational intuition—recognizing when a workload is over-provisioned, when `gp3` is the better choice, or when a high-performance volume is justified.

Reducing Cost with Point-in-Time Recovery (PITR)

In Chapter 7, you learned how point-in-time recovery (PITR) supports the Backup & Restore disaster recovery pattern. Here, we focus on the cost implications of PITR and how frugal architecture helps you use it wisely. PITR is a powerful feature—whether in Amazon RDS, DynamoDB, or AWS Backup—but it can also become expensive if retention periods are set too generously or applied uniformly across all environments.

Frugal architecture encourages you to align PITR retention with the actual business value of the data. Production databases may require 7, 14, or even 35 days of PITR depending on compliance needs, but development and test environments rarely need the same level of protection. Reducing retention for non-critical environments—or disabling PITR entirely where appropriate—can significantly lower storage costs without compromising resilience where it matters.

Another frugal practice is using lifecycle policies to transition older backups to lower-cost storage tiers. AWS Backup supports cold storage for long-term retention, and RDS snapshots can be exported to S3 for archival. These transitions reduce cost while preserving recovery options. Finally, frugality means avoiding redundant protection. If a workload already uses versioned S3 buckets, DynamoDB PITR, and AWS Backup vaulting, you may be paying for overlapping layers of protection. The SOA-C03 exam frequently tests your ability to identify when PITR is appropriate, when it's excessive, and how to tune retention for cost-effective resilience.

Reducing Cost by Optimizing Network Architectures

Chapter 10 introduced the fundamentals of AWS networking, including VPC design, routing, connectivity, and content delivery. In this section, we revisit those concepts through the lens of frugal architecture. Network costs are often overlooked because they don't appear as a single line item—they're distributed across services as data transfer charges. Yet for many organizations, data transfer becomes one of the most significant and least understood contributors to monthly spend.

Frugal network design begins with minimizing unnecessary data movement. Cross-Availability Zone traffic, for example, incurs charges that can accumulate quickly in chatty architectures (typically $0.01 per GB in each direction in US regions; pricing varies by region). Placing tightly coupled components in the same AZ, using VPC endpoints to avoid NAT Gateway egress charges, and leveraging PrivateLink for service-to-service communication all reduce transfer costs while improving security. Similarly, CloudFront can dramatically reduce S3 data transfer charges by serving cached content from edge locations rather than repeatedly pulling from the origin.

Another frugal practice is consolidating NAT Gateways. While NAT Gateways are highly available within an AZ, deploying one per subnet is rarely necessary and can multiply costs. A frugal architecture uses a shared NAT Gateway per AZ or, when possible, eliminates NAT entirely by using VPC endpoints or designing workloads that do not require outbound Internet access. The SOA-C03 exam often presents scenarios where the correct answer involves recognizing an inefficient network pattern—such as excessive cross-AZ traffic, unnecessary NAT usage, or missing CloudFront caching—and proposing a more cost-effective alternative.

Optimizing NAT Gateway Architecture

Be aware of the following when optimizing your NAT Gateway architecture:

- **Per-subnet redundancy:** If you have multiple private subnets in the same AZ, they can all share a single NAT Gateway. Deploying per-subnet *multiplies* the fixed hourly charge without adding any functional benefit.
- **Idle hourly charges:** Each NAT Gateway incurs a fixed hourly fee (~$0.045/hour—US East rates, pricing varies by region, see AWS VPC Pricing). In a "chatty" environment with ten unnecessary gateways, you are paying for idle infrastructure 24/7.
- **Data processing fees:** NAT Gateways charge ~$0.045 per GB processed. If you haven't implemented Gateway VPC endpoints for S3 or DynamoDB, you are paying this premium on every byte of data that could otherwise be routed for free.

If a scenario asks for the most cost-effective way to provide Internet access to private instances in a Multi-AZ VPC, look for the answer that suggests one NAT Gateway per AZ (for HA) or one NAT Gateway per VPC (for maximum savings), rather than one per subnet.

Closing Thoughts

As you reach the end of this guide, take a moment to appreciate the breadth of what you've learned. We began with the foundations of cloud operations—AWS's global infrastructure, multi-account governance, and the operational models that shape modern cloud environments. From there, each chapter added a new dimension: compute, containers, databases, storage, observability, resilience, automation, security, networking, and finally cost optimization. Together, these domains form the full operational landscape that the SOA-C03 exam expects you to navigate with confidence.

Across all eleven chapters, a consistent theme emerged: CloudOps is not a collection of isolated skills but a continuous lifecycle. You deploy workloads, monitor their behavior, sustain and secure them, and then optimize based on what you learn. Every service and pattern you studied—whether Auto Scaling, DynamoDB, CloudWatch, IAM, or EventBridge—fits into this cycle. By seeing how these pieces interlock, you've developed the instincts that define a true CloudOps engineer: the ability to balance reliability, security, automation, and cost in every decision you make.

This final chapter brought that mindset into sharp focus by making cost optimization explicit. Cost has been woven into every topic you've studied, but here you learned the dedicated tools and principles—AWS CUR, Cost Explorer, Savings Plans, and the Well-Architected Cost Optimization pillar—that turn cost awareness into a disciplined practice. When you design intentionally, monitor thoughtfully, operate with discipline, and optimize continuously, cost efficiency becomes a natural outcome of operational excellence.

As you close this book, you're not just preparing for an exam—you're stepping into a role that shapes the stability, security, and financial sustainability of the systems your organization depends on. The AWS services and principles will evolve, but the mindset you've built here will remain a steady guide. Approach every workload with clarity, curiosity, and purpose, and you'll not only succeed on the SOA-C03 exam—you'll excel as a CloudOps engineer who elevates every environment you touch.

Summary

This chapter concluded our journey by bringing cost optimization into full focus and showing how deeply it connects to every aspect of cloud operations. You learned that cost is not a constraint but a dimension of good engineering—one that influences how workloads are designed, deployed, monitored, and evolved. AWS provides three essential tools for achieving this visibility and control: AWS Cost and Usage Reports (CUR) for granular analysis, AWS Cost Explorer for interactive trend monitoring and forecasting, and Savings Plans for long-term compute and database cost reduction. Together, these services give CloudOps engineers the financial insight needed to operate AWS environments with confidence and clarity.

Building on that foundation, the chapter explored the Cost Optimization pillar of the AWS Well-Architected Framework. Rather than treating cost as an afterthought, the pillar encourages you to adopt a mindset where financial efficiency is part of every architectural decision. You examined the design principles—such as adopting a consumption model, measuring efficiency, and eliminating undifferentiated heavy lifting—and saw how each principle maps directly to the CloudOps lifecycle. This mapping reinforces that cost optimization is not a separate workflow but a natural extension of deploying, monitoring, operating, securing, and refining workloads.

The chapter then translated these principles into practical best practices that CloudOps engineers apply daily. Right-sizing compute and storage, using elasticity to match capacity with demand, choosing the right pricing model, optimizing data transfer, and enforcing cost governance all become part of the operational rhythm. These practices help ensure that workloads remain efficient as they grow and evolve. You also learned that cost optimization is not just about reducing spend—it's about aligning cost with business value, improving operational efficiency, and designing systems that scale responsibly.

Finally, the chapter brought frugality to life through real-world examples. You revisited familiar services—Amazon EBS, DynamoDB PITR, and AWS networking—but now through the lens of cost-efficient architecture. These scenarios demonstrated how small, intentional decisions can produce meaningful savings without compromising performance or reliability. By the end of this chapter, you have gained not only the tools and techniques for cost optimization but also the operational intuition the SOA-C03 exam expects: the ability to recognize waste, design with purpose, and operate with financial awareness as a core competency of CloudOps engineering.

Exam Essentials

Understand the difference between AWS Cost and Usage Reports and AWS Cost Explorer. For the SOA-C03 exam, it's essential to understand the distinct roles of AWS Cost and Usage Reports (CUR) and AWS Cost Explorer. CUR is the authoritative, granular dataset that captures every billable event across your AWS environment. It's designed for deep analysis, long-term trend modeling, and integration with tools like Athena, Redshift, and QuickSight. Cost Explorer, on the other hand, is your day-to-day operational dashboard—ideal for visualizing spending trends, filtering by tags or accounts, forecasting future costs, and reviewing Savings Plans recommendations. The exam often tests whether you can choose the right tool for the right level of analysis, so remember: CUR is raw telemetry; Cost Explorer is interactive insight.

Know the four types of Savings Plans. Savings Plans are a major topic in SOA-C03 because they represent AWS's most flexible and impactful compute and database discount model. You must know the four types: Compute Savings Plans, which apply broadly across EC2, Fargate, and Lambda; Database Savings Plans, which provide flexible discounts across various database engines and deployment types; EC2 Instance Savings Plans, which are tied to a specific instance family in a region; and SageMaker AI Savings Plans, which reduce costs for machine learning workloads. The exam expects you to recognize which plan fits a given workload pattern—steady-state compute, database-centric, predictable instance families, or ML-focused environments—and to understand how hourly spend commitments and payment options influence long-term savings.

Master the Cost Optimization pillar of the Well-Architected Framework. The Cost Optimization pillar provides the mindset behind efficient cloud operations, and the exam frequently tests your understanding of its design principles. You should be able to explain how adopting a consumption model, measuring overall efficiency, eliminating undifferentiated heavy lifting, and attributing expenditure all map to the CloudOps lifecycle. These principles guide decisions about right-sizing, elasticity, managed services, and governance. SOA-C03 scenarios often require you to identify the most cost-effective operational choice—not just the technically correct one—so internalizing these principles is key to selecting the best answer.

Apply frugal architecture principles to real AWS services. Frugal architecture is where cost optimization becomes practical, and the exam expects you to apply these ideas to real AWS services. You should understand how to choose the right EBS volume type for a workload, how to use DynamoDB Point-in-Time Recovery (PITR) for cost-effective data protection, and how to design network architectures that minimize cross-AZ traffic, NAT Gateway charges, and unnecessary data transfer. These examples reflect the exam's scenario-based style: you're given a workload and asked to identify the most cost-efficient configuration without sacrificing performance or resilience.

Know how to design a cost-effective network architecture in AWS. Network design is one of the most common sources of hidden cost, and SOA-C03 candidates must recognize the patterns that lead to unnecessary spending. You should understand when to use VPC endpoints to avoid NAT Gateway egress charges, how CloudFront reduces S3 data transfer costs, why consolidating NAT Gateways matters, and how cross-AZ traffic can inflate bills in chatty architectures. The exam often presents networking scenarios where the technically functional design is not the financially optimal one, and your ability to spot the frugal alternative is a key differentiator for passing the test.

Review Questions

1. A CloudOps engineer is reviewing the monthly AWS bill and notices that NAT Gateway data processing charges are significantly higher than expected. The VPC Flow Logs indicate that most of the traffic is moving between private EC2 instances and an S3 bucket in the same region. Which action will provide the most cost savings?
   - A. Replace the NAT Gateway with an egress-only Internet Gateway.
   - B. Create a Gateway VPC endpoint for Amazon S3 and update the subnet route tables.
   - C. Move the EC2 instances to a public subnet and use an Internet Gateway.
   - D. Increase the size of the EC2 instances to take advantage of better network throughput.
   - E. Enable S3 Transfer Acceleration for the bucket.
2. A company has a large fleet of EC2 instances with predictable usage patterns over the next three years. However, the engineering team plans to migrate some workloads from x86-based instances to Graviton-based instances in six months. Which pricing model offers the most flexibility to accommodate this change while maximizing savings?
   - A. Standard Reserved Instances
   - B. Convertible Reserved Instances
   - C. EC2 Instance Savings Plans
   - D. Compute Savings Plans
   - E. Spot Instances
3. A CloudOps engineer needs to identify which specific untagged resources are driving up costs and trace them back to their origin. Which tool provides the necessary granularity for this investigation?
   - A. AWS Cost Explorer
   - B. AWS Budgets
   - C. AWS Cost and Usage Reports (CUR) with Resource IDs enabled
   - D. AWS Trusted Advisor
   - E. AWS Pricing Calculator
4. An application uses Amazon EBS `gp2` volumes for its data tier. The performance requirements are consistently 3,000 IOPS, regardless of the volume size. The current volume is 500 GiB. Which two actions would reduce costs without impacting the required performance? (Select TWO.)
   - A. Migrate the volumes from `gp2` to `gp3`.
   - B. Increase the volume size to 1,000 GiB to gain more burst credits.
   - C. Provision exactly 3,000 IOPS on the new `gp3` volume.
   - D. Switch the volume type to `io2` and provision 3,000 IOPS.
   - E. Keep the baseline 3,000 IOPS included with `gp3` and pay only for storage.
   - F. Migrate the volume to Cold HDD (`sc1`).

5. A CloudOps team is establishing a cost optimization program. Which action aligns with the Cloud Financial Management best practice area of the Well-Architected Framework?
   - **A.** Over-provisioning resources to ensure zero downtime.
   - **B.** Implementing a tagging policy to allocate costs to specific business units.
   - **C.** Using On-Demand instances for all production workloads.
   - **D.** Disabling AWS Organizations to keep accounts separate.
   - **E.** Relying solely on Monthly Invoices for cost analysis.
6. A disaster recovery (DR) strategy requires the ability to restore a DynamoDB table to any point in time within the last 30 days. The team is currently taking manual snapshots every day, which is becoming expensive and operationally heavy. What is the most cost-effective and efficient alternative?
   - **A.** Increase the frequency of manual snapshots to every hour.
   - **B.** Enable DynamoDB point-in-time recovery (PITR).
   - **C.** Export the table to S3 Glacier Deep Archive every day.
   - **D.** Use AWS Backup to manage daily snapshots and set a lifecycle policy to 30 days.
   - **E.** Replicate the table to a second region using Global Tables.
7. A "chatty" microservices application is deployed in a VPC across two Availability Zones (AZs). A CloudOps engineer notices high DataTransfer-Regional-Bytes costs. Which architectural change would reduce these costs?
   - **A.** Consolidate the application into a single Availability Zone.
   - **B.** Implement an Application Load Balancer (ALB) with Cross-Zone load balancing enabled.
   - **C.** Deploy instances in each AZ and use AZ-local endpoints to keep traffic within the same zone.
   - **D.** Use a public IP address for all internal communication.
   - **E.** Enable VPC Flow Logs to monitor the traffic.
8. A CloudOps engineer needs to estimate next quarter's spending for a budget planning meeting based on historical usage patterns. Which tool allows they to see a forecast of expected spending for the next three months based on historical data?
   - **A.** AWS Trusted Advisor
   - **B.** AWS Cost Explorer
   - **C.** AWS Compute Optimizer
   - **D.** AWS CloudTrail
   - **E.** AWS Health Dashboard

9. A company has several AWS accounts under one AWS Organization. The company's finance team notices that individual accounts aren't reaching S3 volume pricing tiers and has asked your CloudOps team how Consolidated Billing could help. How does Consolidated Billing help reduce the overall cost of the organization? (Select TWO.)
   - **A.** It automatically applies a 10% discount to all services.
   - **B.** It combines usage from all accounts to reach volume pricing tiers faster (e.g., S3 storage tiers).
   - **C.** It allows Savings Plans and Reserved Instances purchased in one account to be shared across all accounts.
   - **D.** It eliminates the need for IAM policies in member accounts.
   - **E.** It makes all Data Transfer between member accounts free.

10. A CloudOps engineer is using AWS Compute Optimizer to review a fleet of M5 instances. The tool identifies several instances as "Over-provisioned." What is the first step they should take to act on this recommendation safely?
    - **A.** Terminate the instances immediately.
    - **B.** Review the "Resource Efficiency" score in Cost Explorer.
    - **C.** Check the CloudWatch metrics for CPU and Memory to verify the utilization levels over a representative period.
    - **D.** Switch all instances to Spot Instances.
    - **E.** Purchase a Savings Plan for the recommended instance size.

11. A CloudOps engineer is managing a legacy environment using `gp2` EBS volumes. The volumes are 100 GiB in size but require a consistent throughput of 200 MiB/s. The engineer notices that the volumes are frequently hitting throughput limits. What is the most cost-effective way to meet the throughput requirement?
    - **A.** Increase the `gp2` volume size to 1 TiB to increase the throughput baseline.
    - **B.** Change the volume type to `gp3` and provision the required 200 MiB/s throughput.
    - **C.** Change the volume type to `io2` and provision 2,000 IOPS.
    - **D.** Strip two 50 GiB `gp2` volumes together in a RAID 0 configuration.
    - **E.** Enable EBS Optimization on the EC2 instance type.

12. A company has 50 AWS accounts managed under AWS Organizations. The CloudOps team wants to identify which accounts are responsible for the highest unblended costs for data transfer. Which tool or report should be used to provide the most detail across the entire organization?
    - **A.** AWS Trusted Advisor
    - **B.** The individual monthly invoices of the member accounts
    - **C.** AWS Cost Explorer with grouping by "Linked Account" and "Usage Type"
    - **D.** AWS Budgets with a monthly cost filter
    - **E.** Amazon CloudWatch anomaly detection

13. An application's database requires point-in-time recovery (PITR) to protect against accidental deletes. The database is currently running on Amazon RDS for MySQL. What is the most cost-effective way to ensure a CloudOps engineer can recover data from any second within the last 14 days?
   A. Create a manual snapshot every hour.
   B. Set the Backup Retention Period to 14 days in the RDS instance settings.
   C. Use AWS Backup to create a daily backup with a 14-day expiration.
   D. Enable RDS Multi-AZ to replicate data to a standby instance.
   E. Export RDS logs to CloudWatch Logs and use Log Insights to reconstruct data.

14. To follow the Cost Optimization pillar of the Well-Architected Framework, an organization wants to implement "Demand Profiling." Which two actions align with this strategy? (Select TWO.)
   A. Using Auto Scaling to match capacity to changes in demand.
   B. Purchasing three-year Standard Reserved Instances for all resources.
   C. Using Amazon CloudFront to cache content and reduce load on origin servers.
   D. Manually turning off all development instances every Friday evening.
   E. Increasing the threshold of all CloudWatch alarms to reduce notification costs.
   F. Disabling Multi-AZ for all production databases.

15. A CloudOps engineer is tasked with reducing network costs. They find that a web server in `us-east-1a` is frequently communicating with a database in `us-east-1b`. Both are in the same VPC. Which solution reduces the data transfer costs? (Select TWO.)
   A. Move the database to a public subnet.
   B. Place the web server and the database in the same Availability Zone.
   C. Implement an interface VPC endpoint for the communication.
   D. Enable VPC Peering between the two subnets.
   E. Use VPC Flow Logs to compress the data.
   F. Use private IP addresses for communication instead of public IPs.

16. A CloudOps engineer is reviewing the AWS Cost and Usage Reports (CUR) and sees a high volume of DataTransfer-Out-Bytes. They want to identify which specific S3 buckets are responsible for these Internet egress costs. What must be enabled for the CUR to provide this level of detail?
   A. Detailed Monitoring
   B. S3 Server Access Logs
   C. S3 Inventory
   D. Resource IDs
   E. Cost Explorer Forecasting

17. An organization has several "bursty" workloads that run for only a few hours at a time, but they must run to completion without interruption. Which EC2 pricing model is the most cost-effective?
    A. Dedicated Hosts
    B. Compute Savings Plans
    C. On-Demand Instances
    D. Spot Instances
    E. Reserved Instances

18. A CloudOps engineer is using AWS Compute Optimizer and sees a recommendation to change an EC2 instance type from `m5.large` to `t3.medium`. What is a potential risk of following this recommendation without further analysis?
    A. T3 instances do not support EBS optimization.
    B. T3 instances can only be launched in a single Availability Zone.
    C. T3 instances are more expensive than M5 instances.
    D. T3 instances use CPU Credits, which may be exhausted during sustained high loads.
    E. T3 instances do not support IPv6.

19. As part of a routine check, a CloudOps engineer has discovered unassociated elastic IP addresses and is suspecting there are also idle load balancers. Which AWS service provides a cost optimization check that specifically identifies unassociated elastic IP addresses and idle load balancers?
    A. AWS Systems Manager
    B. AWS Trusted Advisor
    C. Amazon Inspector
    D. AWS Health Dashboard
    E. AWS Compute Optimizer

20. An organization wants to implement a Tagging Policy across all accounts to ensure every resource has a Project and CostCenter tag. Which AWS service can enforce this by preventing the creation of resources that do not have these tags?
    A. AWS Organizations Service Control Policies (SCPs)
    B. AWS Cost Explorer
    C. AWS Tag Editor
    D. AWS IAM Group Policies
    E. AWS Budgets

Answers to Review Questions

1. B. Gateway VPC endpoints for S3 are free and eliminate the $0.045/GB data processing charge associated with NAT Gateways. Options A, C, D, and E are incorrect. Egress-Only IGWs are for IPv6 only. Moving to public subnets reduces security. Instance sizing doesn't change NAT processing fees. Transfer Acceleration increases costs.

2. D. Compute Savings Plans provide the most flexibility, covering multiple instance families (e.g., M5 to M6g), regions, and even Fargate or Lambda, regardless of the CPU architecture. Options A, B, C, and E are incorrect. Standard RIs are locked to a specific family. Convertible RIs allow changes but require a manual exchange process. EC2 Instance Savings Plans are locked to a specific family. Spot is for interruptible workloads, not predictable ones.

3. C. The CUR is the most granular cost data source. When "Resource IDs" are enabled, it lists every single resource and its cost, which can be cross-referenced with CloudTrail to find the creator. Options A, B, D, and E are incorrect. Explorer is great for trends but lacks per-resource ID granularity unless configured specifically, and even then, CUR is more detailed. Budgets are for threshold alerts. Trusted Advisor gives high-level checks. The Calculator is for pre-deployment estimates.

4. A, E. `gp3` volumes are ~20% cheaper per GB than `gp2`. Every `gp3` volume includes 3,000 IOPS for free, so you save on the storage price while meeting the performance requirement for free. Options B, C, D, and F are incorrect. Increasing size increases cost. You don't need to pay for the 3,000 IOPS; they are baseline. `io2` is much more expensive, and `sc1` cannot provide 3,000 IOPS.

5. B. Establishing a cost-aware culture includes cost allocation. Tagging allows the business to understand who is spending what, which is a core tenet of the framework. Options A, C, D, and E are incorrect. Over-provisioning is the opposite of optimization. Predictable production should use Savings Plans/RIs. AWS Organizations enables consolidated billing/discounts. Invoices lack the detail needed for true optimization.

6. B. PITR provides continuous backups and allows restoration to any second in the last 35 days. It eliminates the manual effort and "storage gaps" of snapshots. Options A, C, D, and E are incorrect. Increases cost/effort. Glacier is for long-term storage, but the restore time (RTO) would be too high. AWS Backup is great but PITR is more granular for DynamoDB specifically. Global Tables is for HA, not cost-effective DR.

7. C. Data transfer between AZs costs $0.01/GB. Keeping traffic local to the AZ eliminates this charge. Options A, B, D, and E are incorrect. Removes High Availability (HA), which is a risky optimization. Cross-Zone load balancing actually increases cross-AZ traffic. Public IPs incur egress charges and are insecure. Monitoring doesn't reduce the cost.

8. B. Cost Explorer provides visualization of past spend and uses machine learning to provide a forecast for future spend. Options A, C, D, and E are incorrect. Option A advises on security/cost/performance. Option C advises on instance sizing. Option D logs API calls and Option E notifies about service outages.

9. B, C. Volume tiers (S3, CloudFront) are reached sooner when usage is aggregated. Also, unused capacity in one account "floats" to cover eligible usage in other accounts. Options A, D, and E are incorrect. No automatic flat discount exists. IAM is still required, and data transfer between accounts still follows standard AZ/regional rules.

10. C. Before downsizing (right-sizing), they must verify the utilization data. Compute Optimizer is a recommendation engine, but the engineer must ensure the "representative period" includes peak loads. Options A, B, D, and E are incorrect. Option A is too aggressive and causes downtime. In Option B, score is high-level. Spot is for different workloads (Option D). They should right-size before committing to a Savings Plan (Option E).

11. B. `gp3` volumes provide a baseline of 125 MiB/s for free and allow you to pay for additional throughput (up to 2,000 MiB/s) independently of volume size. This is significantly cheaper than over-provisioning a `gp2` volume just to get more speed. Options A, C, D, and E are incorrect. Increasing `gp2` size to 1 TiB is expensive. `io2` is for extreme performance and is much costlier. RAID 0 increases complexity and costs roughly the same as `gp2`. EBS optimization is an instance feature, not a volume throughput increase.

12. C. Cost Explorer allows the CloudOps team to view consolidated data across the organization. By grouping by "Linked Account," they can see the split per account, and "Usage Type" will isolate specific data transfer costs. Options A, B, D, and E are incorrect. Trusted Advisor shows optimizations, not a cost breakdown (Option A). Member accounts in an Organization do not receive individual invoices; the management account receives one consolidated bill (Option B). Budgets are for threshold alerts (Option D). Anomaly detection finds spikes but doesn't provide a multi-account breakdown (Option E).

13. B. In RDS, setting a Backup Retention Period (between 1 and 35 days) automatically enables PITR. This is a built-in feature that is more efficient and cost-effective than manual snapshots. Options A, C, D, and E are incorrect. Manual snapshots are expensive to store and operationally heavy. AWS Backup manages snapshots, but the RDS native backup retention is the standard way to achieve PITR. Multi-AZ is for high availability, not for recovering from accidental data deletion (deletes are replicated). Option E is technically impossible for data reconstruction.

14. A, C. Demand profiling is about understanding and managing the demand on your resources. Auto Scaling adjusts supply to meet demand, and CloudFront reduces the demand reaching your backend servers. Options B, D, E, and F are incorrect. Option B commits to fixed capacity. Option D is a manual process, not "profiling." Options E and F compromise operations and availability for small savings.

15. B, F. In Option B, the data transfer within the same AZ is free, whereas cross-AZ transfer costs $0.01/GB. In Option F, communication via public IPs always incurs data transfer charges, even within the same AZ; private IPs avoid this. Options A, C, D, and E are incorrect. Public subnets increase security risk and costs. VPC endpoints are for AWS services, not EC2-to-EC2 communication. Peering is for different VPCs. Flow logs monitor traffic; they don't compress it.

16. D. Enabling resource IDs in the CUR settings adds a column for the specific resource (like an S3 bucket name or EC2 instance ID), allowing the CloudOps engineer to see exactly which resource generated each line item of cost. Options A, B, C, and E are incorrect. Detailed monitoring is for CloudWatch metrics. Access logs show who accessed the bucket but don't integrate directly into the CUR for cost analysis. S3 Inventory lists objects, not costs. Forecasting predicts future spend.

17. C. For "bursty," short-term workloads that cannot be interrupted, On-Demand is the best choice. You pay only for what you use and the instance won't be reclaimed like a Spot instance. Options A, B, D, and E are incorrect. Option A is for licensing/compliance. Options B and E require a one or three-year commitment, which isn't ideal for "bursty" occasional use. Finally, Spot instances can be interrupted, which violates the "run to completion" requirement (Option D).

18. D. T3 is a burstable instance family. While it is cheaper, it relies on CPU credits. If the workload is sustained rather than bursty, the instance performance will be throttled once credits are spent. Options A, B, C, and E are incorrect. T3 supports EBS optimization. Options B and E are false; T3 is Multi-AZ and supports IPv6. T3 is cheaper.

19. B. Trusted Advisor includes specific cost-optimization checks for idle resources, including unassociated EIPs, idle ELBs, and underutilized EBS volumes. Options A, C, D, and E are incorrect. Option A is for management. Option C is for security scanning. Option D is for service status. Option E focuses on right-sizing EC2, EBS, and Lambda.

20. A. SCPs can be used to deny the `ec2:RunInstances` (and other create actions) if specific tags are not present in the request. This is a common way to enforce governance at the organization level. Options B, C, D, and E are incorrect. Options B and E are for monitoring/reporting. Option C is for bulk tagging existing resources. Option D is a viable solution, but SCPs are more effective for enforcing it across all accounts in an organization.

Index

Note: Page numbers in *italics* and **bold** refers to figures and tables respectively.

A

B

C

D

E

S

T

U

V

W

Online Test Bank

To help you study for your AWS CloudOps Engineer Certification (Associate [SOA-C03] Exam), register to gain one year of FREE access after activation to the online interactive test bank—included with your purchase of this book!

To access our learning environment, simply visit `www.wiley.com/go/sybextestprep`, follow the instructions to register your book, and instantly gain one year of FREE access after activation to:

- Practice test questions, so you can practice in a timed and graded setting
- Flashcards
- A searchable glossary

Printed and bound by CPI Group (UK) Ltd, Croydon, CR0 4YY

12/07/2026

14919294-0002